PENDANT NUMBERS
OF THE
ROYAL NAVY

A Record of the Allocation of Pendant Numbers to Royal Navy Warships and Auxiliaries

Ben Warlow and Steve Bush

Seaforth
PUBLISHING

First published in Great Britain in 2021 by
Seaforth Publishing,
A division of Pen & Sword Books Ltd,
47 Church Street,
Barnsley S70 2AS

www.seaforthpublishing.com

British Library Cataloguing in Publication Data
A catalogue record for this book is available from the British Library

ISBN 978 1 5267 9378 2 (HARDBACK)
ISBN 978 1 5267 9379 9 (EPUB)
ISBN 978 1 5267 9380 5 (KINDLE)

Pen & Sword Books Limited incorporates the imprints of Atlas,
Archaeology, Aviation, Discovery, Family History, Fiction, History, Maritime, Military,
Military Classics, Politics, Select, Transport, True Crime, Air World, Frontline Publishing,
Leo Cooper, Remember When, Seaforth Publishing, The Praetorian Press, Wharncliffe
Local History, Wharncliffe Transport, Wharncliffe True Crime and White Owl.

Typeset and designed by Steve Bush

Printed and bound in Great Britain by TJ Books Ltd, Padstow

Contents

Ben Warlow

Ben Warlow was born and educated in Devonport, entering the Navy through Dartmouth in 1957. After training in the frigate VIGILANT and destroyer CARRON, he served in the cruiser GAMBIA, fast patrol boat BOLD PATHFINDER, cruiser TIGER, frigates TENBY, EASTBOURNE, RHYL and AJAX, and then the Commando carrier BULWARK. After spells in training establishments and on various staffs he returned to sea in Naval Parties, firstly in the RMS QUEEN ELIZABETH 2 for the Falklands War, and then in RFA RELIANT (a trial mercantile helicopter carrier) for operations off the Lebanon. Afterwards he was at the Fleet Headquarters at Northwood for almost eight years as one of the Operations Room Officers. In all he served over 40 years in the Navy, over half at sea. Such a wide-ranging career has furthered his interest in ships and the sea. He has compiled several books about ships and the Navy, and also written the definitive reference books on Royal Naval Battle Honours and on Shore establishments, as well as writing a history of the Supply and Secretariat (Logistic) Branch of the Navy. He was awarded the Oswald Cross for his work on the supply branch examinations. For many years he has also been the Editor of, and written articles for, the magazine *Warship World*.

Steve Bush

Steve Bush was born and educated in Coventry. He entered the Royal Navy, at HMS Raleigh, Torpoint, in 1978. During the next twenty-two years he served in the frigates AJAX, DIDO, EURYALUS, SIRIUS, GALATEA, BRAVE and LONDON. His career saw several operational deployments to the Gulf, including the 1991 Gulf War. On leaving the Royal Navy in 2000 he joined Maritime Books, editing their in-house publications. He took up the position of Editor of *Warship World* and *Warship World Pictorial Review* magazines from 2003-2017. He has compiled several books including *British Warships & Auxiliaries* (Editions 2003-2018); *US Navy Warships & Auxiliaries* (Editions 1-3); *British Warships & Auxiliaries 1952*; *The Trafalgar 2005 Fleet Review* and *The Royal Navy in Focus 1980-89*.

Preface

"There are known knowns. These are things we know that we know. There are known unknowns. That is to say, there are things that we know we don't know. But there are also unknown unknowns. There are things we don't know we don't know".

Donald Rumsfeld
US Secretary of Defence 1975-1977

When Donald Rumsfeld made his 'known knowns' speech, he wasn't talking about pendant numbers - but he might as well have been. Those six short sentences so ably sum up why no-one else has attempted to compile such a work!

A fascination, which has endured over many decades, has led us to this point. A volume which, we hope, will record those "known knowns", shed light on some of those 'known unknowns' and perhaps stimulate debate on the 'unknown unknowns'.

Despite many records, previously thought lost, now emerging, there are still large gaps in our knowledge of pendant numbers, particularly with regard to early dates and implementation - much was left to specific area commands and complete records are hard to find - if they even exist. This effort is further complicated by the many published sources which contain disparities. Without recourse to primary sources, or photographs, it is difficult to confirm, or disprove, such published data. Although this work is far from complete - the 2020 Coronavirus pandemic restrictions have had a massive impact on our ability to confirm new information and new photographs and snippets are being constantly received - it was decided that it was time to draw a line in the sand and publish this - Version 1.0 as it were. There is a limitless knowledge base out there and, it is hoped, that others with a similar fascination for the subject might come forward and try to fill in gaps and tighten up time frames - perhaps even offer clues as to new sources of information.

As time goes on it is hoped that this volume will expand to include the un-named vessels and that, one day, all of the unknowns will eventually become knowns.

Ben Warlow & Steve Bush
2021

Pendant vs Pennant

Flags, that are longer than they are broad, were originally referred to as pendants, due to their tendency to hang down - therefore being pendant (adj: to hang down). It is from the use of such pendants that 'pendant numbers' received their nomenclature. Although the origins of the word stem from the adjective, the noun, describing the flag, has long since been pronounced as pennant and over time the spelling has changed to reflect this. Either spelling is correct.
The traditional pendant has been used throughout this volume.

Introduction

The need to easily identify warships has always been a requirement of warfare at sea. During the Age of Sail, there was no such thing as a standard ship design. Ships were rated by their role and the number of guns they carried and individual ships could be identified by such things as figureheads and ornate woodwork around the bow structures and stern galleries - many such carvings being brightly painted and gilded. The unnecessary cost of such embellishments was an extravagance that was getting out of hand and in the early 18th century an Admiralty directive restricted the amount that could be spent on such adornment, and eventually banned it outright.

With the arrival of steam ships, figureheads were, in the most part, consigned to history and ships badges and mottos were introduced to graphically represent ships. After WW1 The Ships' Badges Committee was established and an Admiralty Advisor on Heraldry was appointed. This was amalgamated in 1983 with the Ships' Names Committee (founded in 1913) to create the Ships' Names and Badges Committee. Although this system of badges would give ships an individual identity, they were of no use in a tactical situation.

In 1903 warships gave up their Victorian colour scheme of black hulls, white superstructure and buff funnels and masts. This was replaced by an overall grey colour scheme. As the major warship classes operated in squadrons, there were occasions when many ships of the same class could be manocuvring together - the need for rapid identification was obvious. In 1909, the use of funnel bands was introduced, initially in the Channel Fleet, so that ships of the same class could be distinguished from one another. There was no standard system until 1911 when a class would have bands of white, red or black displayed on the funnels in various positions and thicknesses. Some were adopted for specific exercises (as were two figure codes painted on turret sides), while others became permanent squadron markings. Each squadron was assigned a single colour and the codes applied alphabetically within each squadron. Changes to assigned markings were introduced by Admiralty Letter (e.g. *Apollo* - 1 white band on foremost funnel; *Brilliant* - one white band on each funnel; *Melpomene* - 1 red band on after funnel). This was a rather cumbersome system and the markings were removed from most ships by 1914.

One of the issues facing the Royal Navy at the time was the wide variety of ships it had. When destroyers (for example) were ordered, they were built to the builder's own design. This could lead to complications in obtaining spare parts for engines, guns etc. as each ship was equipped with different machinery and armament. It also led to inconsistency in performance. The ships could have different turning circles, making fleet manoeuvres difficult - and perhaps interesting and exciting. So standardisation came in. Ships were now built to a specified design which, in turn, brought about a degree of sameness, making it harder to distinguish one ship from another. To resolve that problem, ships were now allocated visual identities. Early photographs suggest that a large number of torpedo boat destroyers (TBD) and destroyers, which were mostly painted black, had an alphabetic character painted on their hulls or forward funnels. This system, however, merely indicated the class of vessel and could not be used to identify an individual ship.

In the Royal Navy specific ship identities were represented by a series of alpha-numeric flags. The flags used for identification are either a set of numerals or a set comprising a single alphabetic flag and two or three numerals. These flags are rectangular, triangular or tapered shapes. The tapered form is known as a pendant and is predominantly used to indicate numbers. If the alphabetic flag in such a combination is hoisted before the numerics it is known as a flag superior and if after the numerics it is a flag inferior. This arrangement, intended for visual signalling, was to make up the pendant number allocated to every British warship and auxiliary for identification purposes, eventually being painted on the ship's side as a further visual identification making. The terminology of flags superior, inferior and pendant is still used when refering to the painted up numbers.

The first numbers were issued locally, and changed frequently. They were published in an Admiralty Fleet Order in 1914, and were for the destroyers *Stag* (P06) and *Mallard* (P08). Initially the numbers were issued for manoeuvres only, and the limit on numbers was just 100, i.e. numbers 00 - 99. The addition of a letter flag superior produced a further 100 combinations for each letter used. Originally the flag flown above (superior) to the pendant numbers indicated the ship base port or unit - 'N' for Nore, 'P' for Portsmouth, 'D' for Devonport and 'G' for Grand Fleet. Later the 'F' series was also allocated to the Grand Fleet. Later still, extra lists were made available by the use of a variety of flags flown superior (above) to the numbers. To further increase the numbers available special code pendants were used, sometimes after the number, i.e. flag inferior, and other times in combination with the flag superior. In these cases the special pendants Answer, Code, Numeral and Oblique - representing the characters 'A', 'C', 'N' and '/' were used. These could further expand the available numbers. In 1917 it was decided to stop using the number 13 - though there were exceptions later. Originally the pendant numbers were only used in home waters and were allocated by the Admiralty Pendant Board. Ships on foreign stations were not assigned numbers unless there was an expectation of them returning to home waters. Admirals in command of foreign stations were expected to assign numbers locally to those vessels in their command. This could result in ships serving on different stations carrying the same number. By mid 1916 destroyers were painting the numbers on their sides and sterns. The actual number allocated to the ships changed frequently - either as a security measure or to reflect squadron re-organisations. There seems to have been an attempt to rationalise the system in 1918 as the list introduced in January of that year matches numerical order of pendants with an alphabetical order of ship names within each flag group (e.g. D00 = *Afridi*; D01 = *Albacore* etc.). Lists were allocated by Admiralty Pendant Boards and were issued quarterly, although this period was extended towards the end of WW1. Changes to individual numbers were issued by Admiralty Fleet Orders.

Battleships, battlecruisers, cruisers, aircraft carriers, fast minelayers and destroyer leaders were assigned pendant numbers for visual signalling purposes, but at first these were not painted on the sides. These numbers were flown by ships on occasions such as entering and leaving harbour - and an early code of naval signals can sometimes assist in reading these.

As warship numbers declined at the end of WW1, particularly destroyer numbers, a reappraisal of the system saw a re-allocation of flag superiors with 'D' and 'H' replacing former destroyer flags. The Tribal class were originally allocated flag 'L' but this was changed to flag 'F' in December 1938. At this period flag 'N' was allocated to survey ships and flag 'T' to river gunboats. Changes were also made in the case of submarines which had a combination of alphabetic flags superior and inferior to numerics but these were gradually standardised and only an alphabetic superior used. Some cruisers were also subject to change and used flag 'I' superior. No changes were introduced for capital ships, which continued to use numeric identities.

In 1939 the flag superior system stood at:

Battleships & Battlecruisers:	Nil
Cruisers/Aircraft Carriers:	I
Submarines:	Nil - a flag inferior indicated the ship's class, e.g: H for H class
Destroyers:	D, H or F
Escort Destroyers/Patrol Vessels:	L (changed to F from December 38)
Corvettes:	M
Patrol Vessels/BDVs:	P
Netlayers/Tenders:	T
Repair Ships:	Nil

By the following year, the numbers of ships entering service, particularly with regard to escort vessels, and the re-roling of others, necessitated a further review of the system. Additional flags superior were introduced and in some categories, numbers were extended from two to three characters to allow for the increase in ship numbers. Flag 'L' was now used for Hunt class escort destroyers under construction and converted V and W class destroyers. Flags 'D' and 'F' were changed to 'I' and 'G', with war construction being assigned the latter until the 'T' class, which adopted flag 'R'. An exception to this was the R class which, together with destroyers taken over from overseas customers, or Allied ships serving as HM Ships, were assigned flag 'H' numbers. A reversion to flag 'G' was made with the Weapon and cancelled G classes. Subsequent war construction conformed to the new system and frigates, as they came into service, were allocated 'K' flag superior. Exceptions were the ex-US Coast Guard cutters which were given flag 'Y' and the Kil class escorts received flag '5' superior. Unlike US Navy warships, whose numbers are sequential throughout each ship type (e.g. the first battleship was BB-1, the second BB-2 etc. - with the number remaining with the ship throughout its life) the Royal Navy allocated numbers as available, with gaps in sequences, created by decommissioned or lost ships, being filled by newer vessels. Therefore later build ships, such as the later Battle class destroyers and Daring class were allocated earlier flag 'I' numbers. As with all wars at sea, there was a huge demand for auxiliary warships - those taken up from trade and pressed into service for a variety of roles. Many of these vessels were initially assigned flag '4', but as the war moved forward, ships were quickly retasked and given new roles, sometimes operating in several roles within a very short period of time. In some, but not all, cases this involved the allocation of a new number. Tracking these has proved to be very difficult as not all records exist and many ships changed roles so often that paperwork assigning new numbers could not keep up.

The 1940 changes resulted in the following:

Battleships & Battlecruisers:	Nil
Cruisers/Aircraft Carriers:	D
Submarines:	N or P
Destroyers:	H, I (ex D), G (ex F) or R
Escort Destroyers:	I
Escort Vessels:	U
Patrol Vessels/Corvettes/Frigates:	K
Ex-USCG Cutters/Store Carriers:	Y
Motor Launches:	Q
Coastal Motor Boats/MASBs/MGBs/SGBs:	S
Motor Torpedo Boats:	V
Minesweepers/Survey Vessels:	J
Minelayers:	M
Auxiliary Patrol Vessels/Auxiliary Minesweepers/River Gunboats/Trawlers:	T or FY
Monitors:	F
Cable vessels/Boom Defence Vessels/ Netlayers/Drifters:	Z
Tugs/Salvage Vessels/RFAs:	X
Armed Merchant Cruisers:	F
Convoy Escorts/Auxiliary AA Ships/ Armed Yachts:	4
Coastal Escorts:	5
Wreck Dispersal Vessels:	DV

Auxiliary AA Vessels/Special Service Vessels:	D or F
Landing Ships:	F
Air Rescue Boats:	B

A special set of pendant numbers was issued for ships operating in the British Pacific Fleet, with a separate list for those ships operating as part of the Fleet Train. The former was along the lines of the 1948 system of 'C' for cruisers, 'D' for destroyers etc, whilst the latter was simply with a flag superior of 'B'. There was also a system with an 'A' flag superior, but, no official record of this has been found, though there are the odd puzzling photographs of escort carriers, sloops and minesweepers wearing these numbers.

The actual flag superior letter allocated to types of ships changed during the war years - although ships usually retained the same number - and the present system of 'D' for destroyers, 'F' for frigates etc, was only introduced in a rationalisation in 1948. This involved a certain amount of re-numbering amongst existing vessels but was largely limited to adding, or subtracting, 100, 200, etc from their original numbers.

The 1948 changes remain in effect:

Auxiliaries:	A
Cruisers:	C
Destroyers:	D
Frigates:	F
Hydrographic Vessels:	H (from 1998)
Miscellaneous:	K
Amphibious Warfare Vessels:	L
Mine Countermeasures Vessels:	M
Minelayers:	N
Patrol Vessels:	P
Aircraft Carriers:	R
Submarines:	S
Yard Vessels:	Y

The 1948 system was used as the basis for the numbering system subsequently applied to NATO warships. With the exception of the US Navy and the Canadian Navy, which used a system based on hull numbers, the NATO system provided for the allocation of number blocks within each category to prevent repetition of numbers within NATO. Although this system is still in use, in reality individual nations seem to be selecting their own number series as duplications are slowly appearing (e.g. minehunters of the Spanish Navy Segura class and the Royal Navy Hunt class share numbers M31 - M36). Although some types of RN ship carried consecutive numbers, such sequences have not been assigned to destroyers and frigates until the first of the Type 45 destroyers and the Type 22 frigates entered service.

Post WW2 not all ships displayed their numbers. It wasn't until the late 1950s that aircraft carriers and cruisers had numbers painted up and ships of the Royal Fleet Auxiliary did not display their pendant numbers until 1963, bringing them in line with HM Ships. Moving in the opposite direction was the submarine service. They displayed numbers until 1966 when, due to the covert nature of their trade, it was determined that, externally, submarines would remain anonymous.

With the occasional introduction of a new flag superior ('H' for survey vessels in 1998) the pendant number system has not changed since the end of WW2. However, the external appearance of RN warships has. Post war, RN warships displayed bright paintwork, with black boot-topping and mast tops, with numbers displayed on sides and stern. Funnels had black funnel caps and, in the case of leaders or half leaders, a funnel band or stripe. Ship's boats were also brightly coloured with white superstructure and coloured hulls. Liferafts were white and the ship's name was displayed in red on both quarters. During the Falklands Conflict of 1982, warships deployed to the South Atlantic having adopted a low visibility colour scheme. Ships had their pendant numbers painted over and all other paintwork covered in grey. While this provided some form of anonymity, it is said that the main reason for this change was less strategic and more tactical. TV guided missiles, known to be in the Argentine inventory, were said to operate on a monochrome image with large contrast shifts between white and black aiding their targetting - thus painting everything a uniform grey helped to counter this. The one drawback was that both sides operated Type 42 destroyers and, to prevent blue-on-blue engagements, RN Type 42s received a broad vertical black stripe from funnel top to waterline! However, since 1982, the RN and RFA maintained the low visibility grey appearance. Pendant numbers, boot tops and masts have returned to their original colours as have names on the quarters, but boats, life rafts and funnel bands have not.

Today, Navy Command Information Warfare (IW) Division is responsible for the allocation of pendant numbers and flight deck letters. These are allocated when the build project team contact IW Division for pendant numbers/flight deck letter assignments. Pendant number assignments are taken from the UK block of allocations for each class of vessel and published in Allied Communications Procedures. The latest numbers issued have been for the three Type 26 frigates on order (*Glasgow* - F88/GW; *Cardiff* - F89/CR and *Belfast* - F90/BF).

Style of Pendant Numbers

When pendant numbers first appeared on the side of a ship, there seemed to be little direction as to the form these numbers should take. Colours, style, size and even placement, appeared to be at the whim of those tasked with applying them - they varied from black to white, some with block shadows, some without.

During WW2, when many ships carried camouflage schemes the numbers were directed to be of a contrasting colour, so as to be easily visible.

Post war pendant number colours were still varied, with red, white and black letters all being used. Today, pendants comprise black letters with a white outline for surface ships with a grey hull. Those with differing colour hulls have a contrasting colourway - the ice patrol ship *Protector*, with its red hull, displays white characters.

Application of pendant numbers became less random, with Admiralty Fleet Orders directing dimensions, spacing and placement of numbers for each type of ship, with 'Painting on Instructions'.

In 1949 CAFO 263/49 included the following instructions with regard to landing ships:

The visual call sign allocated to landing ships and craft is to be painted on the hull as follows:-

   (a) Each ship and craft is to have her visual call sign painted at the stern and on each side of the bow. In cases where the kedge anchor or fittings preclude painting at the stern, e.g. L.S.T. (3), the visual call sign is to be painted on each quarter.

   (b) The fore and aft position of the visual call sign is to be such that:-
      (i) The fore end of the number on the bow is 2ft abaft the hawse pipe, where fitted.
      (ii) The fore end of the number on the quarter is in line with the after end of the superstructure.
   (c) The letters and numbers are to be of the following dimensions:-

   Landing Ships on the bow and quarter:-

      6ft Deep; 4ft wide; 8 in block; Figures spaced 2ft apart

   Major Landing Craft on the bow and quarter:-

      3ft deep; 2ft wide; 5 in block; Figures spaced 1ft apart

   Minor Landing Craft on the bow and at the stern:-

      9 in deep; 7 in wide; 2½ in block; Figures spaced 2½ in apart

It is to be noticed that there is no specific typeface so it is not uncommon to find representations of some of the characters more rounded than others as the dimension blocks allow for some degree of interpretation by the painters.

Funnel Markings

It was mentioned earlier that funnel markings were used as a means of identification prior to the introduction of pendant numbers. By the start of WW2 a system of funnel banding was in use to identify the flotilla to which a destroyer belonged. In two funnel ships destroyer leaders carried a 4ft black band around the top of the forward funnel. Divisional commanders carried a two foot band 3ft from the top of the fore funnel. In the Home fleet this band was to be white; in the Mediterranean, red and in the China Fleet, black. Single funnel destroyer leaders carried a 3ft black band around the top of their funnel. Divisional commanders were marked with a 2ft bar on both sides and parallel to the axis of the funnel, running from the underside of the upper flotilla band downwards for six feet. This bar was to be the same colour as the upper band of the flotilla marking. The flotilla marking was to be on the after, or only, funnel, marked with two foot bands, two feet apart, the upper band being 3ft from the top of the funnel. The markings in 1944 were:

1st Flotilla:	One red	15th Flotilla:	One red over two black
2nd Flotilla:	Two red	16th Flotilla:	One red over one white
3rd Flotilla:	No marking	17th Flotilla:	One red over two white
4th Flotilla:	No marking	18th Flotilla:	One white over one black
5th Flotilla:	No marking	19th Flotilla:	One white over two black
6th Flotilla:	One white	20th Flotilla:	Two white over one black
7th Flotilla:	Two white	21st Flotilla:	Two white over one red
8th Flotilla:	Three white	22nd Flotilla:	No marking
9th Flotilla:	One black over two white	23rd Flotilla:	Unknown
10th Flotilla:	No marking	24th Flotilla:	One black over one red
11th Flotilla:	One black over two red	25th Flotilla:	Three black
12th Flotilla:	One white over one red	26th Flotilla:	Two black bars forming a V
13th Flotilla:	One white over two red	27th Flotilla:	One black band with black bar
14th Flotilla:	One red over one black		on funnel line

Post war, the funnel bands were replaced by squadron numbers displayed on the funnel of both destroyers and frigates. The leader and half leader markings remained until 1982. In February 2002 individual destroyer and frigate squadrons were disbanded and replaced with the Devonport, Faslane and Portsmouth Flotillas bringing to an end squadron markings on funnels.

Although some classes of ship had displayed individual emblems on funnels or superstructure, in the past, it has now become standard practice for ships to carry motifs, taken from their ship's badge, on the funnel. In some cases, the destroyer *Dragon* and the patrol vessel *Tamar*, these motifs are even larger and carried on the hull.

SCOPE OF THE BOOK

This record of pendant numbers is the result of many years' research, of both primary and secondary sources, in an effort to try and produce a definitive record, while at the same time recognising that there remain many gaps in both records and knowledge. For the sake of brevity, this volume concentrates on named vessels, with the exception of submarines which are included in their entirety.

Information is displayed in four columns, below each pendant number, comprising ship name, date, type and period. *Date* is, in the main, the launch date. Where this is unknown, a completion date or commissioning date is included. This, it is felt, should be sufficient, in combination with the type, for the reader to be able to identify a specific ship, where more than one of the same name applies. In some instances it has not yet been possible to provide a definitive identity for a ship. In this case the date is represented by (....).

Period refers to the time that a specific number was assigned to a particular vessel. In many cases it has not been possible to identify both start and end dates due to gaps in records. It should also be remembered that a start date did not necessarily mean that the ship displayed the number for that exact period - if at all. Application of new numbers may have occurred during maintenance periods or during subsequent alongside time. In times of war, such paperwork as pendant lists lagged behind actual events, so it was not unusual for numbers to be issued in new lists long after the recipient vessel had been lost. In these instances the entry in the period column will include the word *sunk* to indicate that the issue date post dates the loss. A date followed by a dash indicates that the vessel remains in service.

ACKNOWLEDGEMENTS

Grateful thanks are due to the staff of the Admiralty Library and the Naval Historical Branch, Ministry of Defence, Alicia Henneberry and Onaona Guay of the National Archives and Records Administration at College Park, Maryland, Rob Garratt of the Naval History Section, Sea Power Centre - Australia, John Smith of the Naval Historical Society of Australia, Commander Leon Steyn of the South African Naval Museum and Navy Command Secretariat - FOI Section. Thanks must also go to Graham Naylor of the Plymouth Naval History Library, who, despite Covid-19 restrictions, still found a secure way of sharing much needed information. Also thanks to the many correspondents, over many years, who have helped with research along the way - including Ross Gillett, Brian Hargreaves, David Hobbs MBE, Geoffrey Hudson, Samuel Loring Morison and Dave Wright.

REFERENCES

Admiralty Pendant Lists - 1915 Onwards.

ADM1/18609 - Memorandum Record of Understanding reached in conference 17-19 December 1944 concerning the employment of the BPF.

ADM1/19133 - BPF Turnover to American Tactical Doctrine and Signalling Methods.

BR 619 (2) 1944 - Distinguishing Pendants and Signal Letters of HM Ships, RFAs, MFAs etc.

Confidential Admiralty Fleet Orders - Various dates

DNC 4(A) 1944 - US Navy Visual Call Sign Book.

ACP 113 - Allied Communications Publication - Call Sign Book for Ships (Various dates)

A Blue Water Navy: Operational History of the RCN 43-45 (Douglas et al)

Afridi to Nizam (English)

Allied Escort Ships of World War II (Elliott)

Amazon to Ivanhoe (English)

Australian and New Zealand Warships 1914-1945 (Gillett)

British Aircraft Carriers (Hobbs)

British and Empire Warships of the Second World War (Lenton)

British Battleships 1919-1945 (Burt)

British Battleships (Parkes)

British Cruisers (Friedman)

British Destroyers 1892-1953 (March)

British Warships 1914-1919 (Dittmar & Colledge)

Canada's Flower Class Corvettes (Lynch)

Combat Fleets of the World (Various dates)

Fifty Years of Naval Tugs (Hannan)

Flush Deck Destroyers in World War Two (Arnold)

Flush Decks and Four Pipes (Alden)

Frigates of the RCN 1943-1974 (MacPherson)

Jane's Fighting Ships (Various dates)

Kamikaze: The British Pacific Fleet (Eadon)

Minesweepers of the RCN 1938-45 (MacPherson)

'N' Class (Payne & Lind)

New Zealand Naval Vessels (McDougall)

No Higher Purpose: Operational History of the RCN 39-43 (Douglas et al)

Obdurate to Daring (English)
River Class Destroyers of the RCN (MacPherson)
Sloops 1926-1946 (Hague)
The British Destroyer (Manning)
The British Pacific Fleet (Hobbs)
The Design & Construction of British Warships Vol 1-3 (Brown)
The Hunts (English)
The Kellys (Langtree)
The Royal Australian Navy 1939-1942 (Hermon Gill)
The Royal Australian Navy 1942-1945 (Hermon Gill)
The Royal Fleet Auxiliary: A Century of Service (Adams & Smith)
The Royal New Zealand Navy (Burgess)
The Towns (Hague)
V & W Class Destroyers (Preston)
Very Special Ships: Abdiel Class Fast Minelayers (Nicholson)
Warships of World War II (Lenton & Colledge)

ABBREVIATIONS USED

ABS	Armed Boarding Ship	CMS	Coastal Minesweeper
ABV	Armed Boarding Vessel	Ctl	Control
Ac	Aircraft		
AMC	Armed Merchant Cruiser	DS	Depot Ship
AMD	Auxiliary Mine Destructor Vessel		
AOR	Auxiliary Replenishment Oiler	Esc	Escort
AS	Anti-Submarine	Exam	Examination
Aux AA	Auxiliary Anti-Aircraft Vessel		
Aux MS	Auxiliary Minesweeper	FAC	Fast Attack Craft
Aux PV	Auxiliary Patrol Vessel	FFN	Free French Navy
		FPV	Fishery Protection Vessel
BBV	Boom Barrage Vessel	FR	French Navy
BDV	Boom Defence Vessel	FTB	Fast Training Boat
BGV	Boom Gate Vessel		
BPF	British Pacific Fleet	Gb	Gunboat
		HDML	Harbour Defence Motor Launch
Car	Carrier		
CDS	Coastal Defence Ship	IMH	Inshore Minehunter
Cg	Coastguard	IMS	Inshore Minesweeper

Iss	Issuing	RAN	Royal Australian Navy
IT	Italian Navy	RCL	Ramped Craft Logistic
LCT	Landing Craft Tank	RCN	Royal Canadian Navy
LCT	Landing Craft Logistic	RFA	Royal Fleet Auxiliary
LPD	Landing Platform Dock	RHN	Royal Hellenic Navy
LPH	Landing Platform Helicopter	RIN	Royal Indian Navy
LSC	Landing Ship Carrier	RML	Rescue Motor Launch
LSD	Landing Ship Dock	RNLN	Royal Netherlands Navy
LSD(A)	Landing Ship Dock (Auxiliary)	RNoN	Royal Norwegian Navy
LSF(D)	Landing Ship Fighter Direction	RNR	Royal Naval Reserve
LSH	Landing Ship Headquarters	RNZN	Royal New Zealand Navy
LSH(L)	Landing Ship Headquarters (Large)	RPN	Royal Pakistan Navy
LSHQ	Landing Ship Headquarters		
LSI	Landing Ship Infantry	SAN	South African Navy
LSI(L)	Landing Ship Infantry (Large)	SDB	Seaward Defence Boat
LSI(M)	Landing Ship Infantry (Medium)	SGB	Steam Gunboat
LSL	Landing Ship Logistic	SML	Survey Motor Launch
LST	Landing Ship Tank	Sp	Ship
LST(Q)	Landing Ship Tank (Headquarters)	SSV	Special Service Vessel
MAC	Motor Attendant Craft	TCV	Tank Cleaning Vessel
MCM	Mine Countermeasures	TBD	Torpedo Boat Destroyer
MFV	Motor Fishing Vessel	Trg	Training
MMS	Motor Minesweeper	TRV	Torpedo Recovery Vessel
MS	Minesweeper/Minesweeping	TS	Training Ship
	Sloop		
MTB	Motor Torpedo Boat	USN	United States Navy
OBV	Ocean Boarding Vessel	Vsl	Vessel
OPV	Offshore Patrol Vessel		
Pax	Passenger	WDV	Wreck Dispersal Vessel
PCE	Patrol Craft, Escort		
POR	Portugal		

Chapter 1
Surface Fleet Pendant Numbers

No Flag Superior

Pre 1940: Battleships; Battlecruisers; Cruisers; Aircraft Carriers; Repair Ships. (Various pendants superior and inferior were used to increase number range)

1940-48: Battleships; Battlecruisers; Cruisers; Aircraft Carriers; Depot Ships; Base and Accommodation Ships.

1948: None.

00

Dreadnought	1906	Battleship	9.15 - 4.16
Achilles	1905	Cruiser	1.18 - 4.18
Queen Elizabeth	1913	Battleship	4.18 - ....

01

Agamemnon	1906	Battleship	9.15 - 4.16
Active	1911	Cruiser	1.18 - 4.18
Canada	1913	Battleship	4.18 - ....
Malaya	1915	Battleship	1940 - 1948

02

Neptune	1909	Battleship	9.15 - 4.16
Africa	1905	Battleship	1.18 - 4.18
Comus	1914	Cruiser	4.18 - ....
Collingwood	1908	Battleship	4.18 - 1922
Valiant	1914	Battleship	1940 - 1945

03

Weymouth	1910	Cruiser	9.15 - 4.16
Agamemnon	1906	Battleship	1.18 - 4.18
Warspite	1913	Battleship	1940 - 1948

04

Lord Nelson	1906	Battleship	9.15 - 4.16
Agincourt	1913	Battleship	1.18 - 4.18
Cassandra	1916	Cruiser	4.18 - 12.18
Barham	1914	Battleship	1940 - 11.41
Venerable	1943	Ac Carrier	1943 - 1948

05

Defence	1907	Cruiser	9.15 - 5.16
Ajax	1912	Battleship	1.18 - 4.18
Indomitable	1907	Battlecruiser	4.18 - 1921

Royal Sovereign	1915	Battleship	1940 - 1944
Gloire FR	1933	Cruiser	BR619(2)[1]

06

Conqueror	1911	Battleship	9.15 - 4.16
Albemarle	1901	Battleship	1.18 - 4.18
Malaya	1915	Battleship	4.18 - ....
Revenge	1915	Battleship	1940 - 1948

07

Albemarle	1901	Battleship	9.15 - 4.16
Antrim	1903	Cruiser	1.18 - 4.18
Birkenhead	1915	Cruiser	4.18 - ....
Ramillies	1916	Battleship	1940 - 1948

08

New Zealand	1911	Battlecruiser	9.15 - 4.16
Aurora	1913	Cruiser	1.18 - 4.18
Royal Oak	1914	Battleship	1940 - Sunk
Swiftsure	1943	Cruiser	1944 - 1948

09

Antrim	1903	Cruiser	9.15 - 4.16
Australia RAN	1911	Battlecruiser	1.18 - 4.18
Agincourt	1913	Battleship	4.18 - 1921
Resolution	1915	Battleship	1940 - 1948

10

Queen Elizabeth	1913	Battleship	9.15 - 4.16
Barham	1914	Battleship	1.18 - 4.18
Centaur	1916	Cruiser	4.18 - ....
Indefatigable	1942	Ac Carrier	1942 - 1948

[1] BR619(2) - Annotation indicates numbers listed in BR619(2) dated 1944. A specific time period for these pendants has not been determined as no other reference to these numbers has yet been found.

11

Emperor of India	1913	Battleship	9.15 - 4.16
Bellerophon	1907	Battleship	1.18 - 4.18
Boadicea	1908	Cruiser	4.18 - ....
Liverpool	1937	Cruiser	1937 - 1948

12

Exmouth	1901	Battleship	9.15 - 4.16
Bellona	1909	Cruiser	1.18 - 4.18
Warspite	1913	Battleship	4.18 - ....
Aurora	1936	Cruiser	1936 - 1948

13

Indefatigable	1909	Battlecruiser	9.15 - 5.16

14

Queen Mary	1912	Battlecruiser	9.15 - 5.16
Benbow	1913	Battleship	1.18 - 4.18
Iron Duke	1912	Battleship	4.18 - ....
Kenya	1939	Cruiser	1939 - 1948

15

Duke of Edinburgh	1904	Cruiser	9.15 - 4.16
Birkenhead	1915	Cruiser	1.18 - 4.18
Concord	1916	Cruiser	4.18 - ....
Manchester	1937	Cruiser	1937 - 8.42
Colossus	1943	Ac Carrier	1944 - 1948

16

St Vincent	1908	Battleship	9.15 - 4.16
Birmingham	1913	Cruiser	1.18 - 4.18
Emperor of India	1913	Battleship	4.18 - ....
Edinburgh	1938	Cruiser	1938 - 5.42
Triumph	1944	Ac Carrier	1945 - 1948

17

Lowestoft	1913	Cruiser	9.15 - 4.16
Blanche	1909	Cruiser	1.18 - 4.18
Penelope	1914	Cruiser	4.18 - ....
Duke of York	1940	Battleship	1940 - 1948

18

Warrior	1905	Cruiser	9.15 - 6.16
Blonde	1910	Cruiser	1.18 - 4.18
Chatham	1911	Cruiser	4.18 - 1920
Iron Duke	1912	Battleship	1940 - 1946

19

Cochrane	1905	Cruiser	9.15 - 4.16
Boadicea	1908	Cruiser	1.18 - 4.18
Zealandia	1904	Battleship	4.18 - 6.18
Dragon	1917	Cruiser	9.18 - ....
Birmingham	1936	Cruiser	1936 - 1948

20

Suffolk	1903	Cruiser	1914 - 9.15
Bristol	1910	Cruiser	1.18 - 4.18
Castor	1915	Cruiser	4.18 - ....
Neptune	1933	Cruiser	1933 - 12.41
Bellerophon	1945	Cruiser	1944
Tiger (ex Bellerophon)	1945	Cruiser	1944 - 1948

21

Centurion	1911	Battleship	9.15 - 4.16
Britannia	1904	Battleship	1.18 - 4.18
Ramillies	1916	Battleship	4.18 - ....
Glasgow	1936	Cruiser	1936 - 1948
Magnificent RCN	1944	Ac Carrier	1948 - 1957

22

Lion	1910	Battlecruiser	9.15 - 4.16
Caledon	1916	Cruiser	1.18 - 4.18
Carysfort	1914	Cruiser	4.18 - ....
Ajax	1934	Cruiser	1934 - 1948

23

Russell	1901	Battleship	9.15 - 4.16
Calliope	1914	Cruiser	1.18 - 4.18
Renown	1916	Battlecruiser	4.18 - ....
Vanguard	1944	Battleship	1944 - 1948

24

Achilles	1905	Cruiser	9.15 - 4.16
Calypso	1917	Cruiser	1.18 - 4.18
Colossus	1910	Battleship	4.18 - ....
Sheffield	1936	Cruiser	1936 - 1948

25

Africa	1905	Battleship	9.15 - 4.16
Cambrian	1916	Cruiser	1.18 - 4.18
Champion	1915	Cruiser	4.18 - ....
Medway	1928	Depot Ship	1939 - 1940
Superb	1943	Cruiser	1943 - 1948

26

Collingwood	1908	Battleship	9.15 - 4.16
Canada	1913	Battleship	1.18 - 4.18
Repulse	1916	Battlecruiser	4.18 - ....
Arethusa	1934	Cruiser	1934 - 1948

27

Britannia	1904	Battleship	9.15 - 4.16
Canterbury	1915	Cruiser	1.18 - 4.18
Fearless	1912	Cruiser	4.18 - ....
Lion	Canc	Battleship	Canc 1945
Hawke	Canc	Cruiser	Canc 1945

28

Canada	1913	Battleship	9.15 - 4.16
Caradoc	1916	Cruiser	1.18 - 4.18
Birmingham	1913	Cruiser	4.18 - ....
Nelson	1925	Battleship	1940 - 1948

29

Princess Royal	1911	Battlecruiser	9.15 - 4.16
Cardiff	1917	Cruiser	1.18 - 4.18
Revenge	1915	Battleship	4.18 - ....
Rodney	1925	Battleship	1940 - 1948

30

Carnarvon	1903	Cruiser	1914 - 1.18
Caroline	1914	Cruiser	1.18 - 4.18
Cambrian	1916	Cruiser	4.18 - ....
Despatch	1919	Cruiser	6.22 - ....
Ceylon	1942	Cruiser	1942 - 1948

31

Commonwealth	1903	Battleship	9.15 - 4.16
Carysfort	1914	Cruiser	1.18 - 4.18
Commonwealth	1903	Battleship	4.18 - 6.18
Vindictive	1918	Ac Carrier	10.18 - ....
Bonaventure	1939	Cruiser	1939 - 3.41
Warrior	1944	Ac Carrier	1944 - 1948

32

Thunderer	1911	Battleship	9.15 - 4.16
Cassandra	1916	Cruiser	1.18 - 4.18
Diamond	1904	Cruiser	4.18 - 6.18
Danae	1918	Cruiser	7.18 - ....
Howe	1940	Battleship	1940 - 1948

33

Cornwallis	1901	Battleship	19.15 - 4.16
Castor	1915	Cruiser	1.18 - 4.18
Galatea	1914	Cruiser	4.18 - ....
Cleopatra	1940	Cruiser	1940 - 1948

34

Valiant	1914	Battleship	9.15 - 4.16
Centaur	1916	Cruiser	1.18 - 4.18
Barham	1914	Battleship	4.18 - ....
Repulse	1916	Battlecruiser	1940 - 12.41
Defence	1944	Cruiser	1944 - 1948

35

Nottingham	1913	Cruiser	9.15 - 8.16
Centurion	1911	Battleship	1.18 - 4.18
Southampton	1912	Cruiser	4.18 - ....
Belfast	1938	Cruiser	1938 - 1948

36

Berwick	1902	Cruiser	1914 - 9.15
Centaur	1916	Cruiser	9.15 - 4.16
Ceres	1917	Cruiser	1.18 - 4.18
Thunderer	1911	Battleship	4.18 - 1921
Temeraire	Canc	Battleship	Canc 1944

37

Chatham	1911	Cruiser	9.15 - 4.16
Champion	1915	Cruiser	1.18 - 4.18
Conquest	1915	Cruiser	4.18 - ....
Dido	1939	Cruiser	1939 - 1948

38

Devonshire	1904	Cruiser	9.15 - 4.16
Chatham	1911	Cruiser	1.18 - 4.18
Royal Oak	1914	Battleship	4.18 - ....
Victorious	1939	Ac Carrier	1940 - 1948

39

Vanguard	1909	Battleship	9.15 - 7.17
Chester	1915	Cruiser	1.18 - 4.18
Cardiff	1917	Cruiser	4.18 - ....
Devonshire	1927	Cruiser	1927 - 1948

40

Ajax	1912	Battleship	9.15 - 4.16
Cleopatra	1915	Cruiser	1.18 - 4.18
Furious	1916	Ac Carrier	4.18 - ....
Dorsetshire	1927	Cruiser	1929 - 4.42
Sumatra RNLN	1920	Cruiser	BR619(2)

41

Dominion	1903	Battleship	9.15 - 4.16
Cochrane	1905	Cruiser	1.18 - 4.18
Dominion	1903	Battleship	4.18 - 6.18
Carlisle	1918	Cruiser	11.18 - ....
King George V	1939	Battleship	1940 - 1948

42

Tiger	1915	Battlecruiser	9.15 - 4.16
Collingwood	1908	Battleship	1.18 - 4.18
Dublin	1912	Cruiser	4.18 - ....
Euryalus	1939	Cruiser	1939 - 1948

43

Duncan	1901	Battleship	9.15 - 4.16
Colossus	1910	Battleship	1.18 - 4.18
Valiant	1914	Battleship	4.18 - ....
Phoebe	1939	Cruiser	1939 - 1948

44

Liverpool	1909	Cruiser	9.15 - 4.16
Commonwealth	1903	Battleship	1.18 - 4.18
Caroline	1914	Cruiser	4.18 - ....
Jamaica	1940	Cruiser	1940 - 1948

45

Birmingham	1913	Cruiser	9.15 - 4.16
Comus	1914	Cruiser	1.18 - 4.18
Phaeton	1914	Cruiser	4.18 - ....
Conqueror	Canc	Battleship	Canc 1945
Emile Bertin FR	1933	Cruiser	BR619(2)

46

Fearless	1912	Cruiser	9.15 - 4.16
Concord	1916	Cruiser	1.18 - 4.18
Ajax	1912	Battleship	4.18 - ....
Trinidad	1940	Cruiser	1940 - 5.42

47

Hercules	1910	Battleship	9.15 - 4.16
Conqueror	1911	Battleship	1.18 - 4.18
Inflexible	1907	Battlecruiser	4.18 - 1921
Furious	1916	Ac Carrier	1940 - 1948

48

Temeraire	1907	Battleship	9.15 - 4.16
Conquest	1915	Cruiser	1.18 - 4.18
Curlew	1917	Cruiser	4.18 - ....
Vindictive	1918	Ac Carrier	9.19 - ....
Gambia	1940	Cruiser	1940 - 1948

49

Superb	1907	Battleship	9.15 - 4.16
Constance	1915	Cruiser	1.18 - 4.18
Superb	1907	Battleship	4.18 - 1922
Argus	1917	Ac Carrier	9.19 - ....
Thunderer	Canc	Battleship	Canc 1944
Hercules	1945	Ac Carrier	1945 - 1948

50

Formidable	1898	Battleship	1914 - 1.15
Hampshire	1903	Cruiser	2.15 - 6.16
Cordelia	1914	Cruiser	1.18 - 4.18
Chester	1915	Cruiser	4.18 - ....
Tiger	Canc	Cruiser	Canc 1946
Courageous	1916	Ac Carrier	1940 - Sunk

51

Essex	1901	Cruiser	9.15 - 4.16
Courageous	1916	Battlecruiser	1.18 - 4.18
Benbow	1913	Battleship	4.18 - ....
Hood	1918	Battlecruiser	3.20 - ....
Perseus	1944	Ac Carrier	1944 - 1948

52

Orion	1910	Battleship	9.15 - 4.16
Dartmouth	1910	Cruiser	1.18 - 4.18
Sydney RAN	1912	Cruiser	4.18 - ....
Enterprise	1919	Cruiser	4.20 - ....
Bermuda	1941	Cruiser	1941 - 1948

53

Agincourt	1913	Battleship	9.15 - 4.16
Devonshire	1904	Cruiser	1.18 - 4.18
New Zealand	1911	Battlecruiser	4.18 - ....
Prince of Wales	1939	Battleship	1940 - 12.41
Minotaur	1943	Cruiser	1943 - 1944
Ontario RCN (ex *Minotaur*)	1943	Cruiser	1944 - 1945

54

Audacious	1912	Battleship	1914 - 10.14
Repulse	1916	Battlecruiser	9.15 - 4.16
Dominion	1903	Battleship	1.18 - 4.18
Hercules	1910	Battleship	4.18 - 1921
Kent	1926	Cruiser	1926 - 1945

55

Monarch	1911	Battleship	9.15 - 4.16
Donegal	1902	Cruiser	1.18 - 4.18
Caradoc	1916	Cruiser	4.18 - ....
Suffolk	1926	Cruiser	1926 - 1945

56

Erin	1913	Battleship	9.15 - 4.16
Dreadnought	1906	Battleship	1.18 - 4.18
Glorious	1916	Battlecruiser	4.18 - ....
Cornwall	1926	Cruiser	1926 - 4.42
Montcalm FR	1935	Cruiser	BR619(2)

57

Warspite	1913	Battleship	9.15 - 4.16
Dublin	1912	Cruiser	1.18 - 4.18
Resolution	1915	Battleship	4.18 - ....
Cumberland	1926	Cruiser	1926 - 1948

58

Gloucester	1909	Cruiser	9.15 - 4.16
Duke of Edinburgh	1904	Cruiser	1.18 - 4.18
Ceres	1917	Cruiser	4.18 - ....
Fiji	1939	Cruiser	1939 - 5.41
Richelieu FR	1939	Battleship	BR619(2)

59

Royal Sovereign	1915	Battleship	9.15 - 4.16
Duncan	1901	Battleship	1.18 - 4.18
Canterbury	1915	Cruiser	4.18 - ....
Newfoundland	1941	Cruiser	1941 - 1948

60

Hibernia	1905	Battleship	9.15 - 4.16
Emperor of India	1913	Battleship	1.18 - 4.18
Monarch	1911	Battleship	4.18 - 1922
Nigeria	1939	Cruiser	1939 - 1948

61

King George V	1911	Battleship	9.15 - 4.16
Erin	1913	Battleship	1.18 - 4.18
Coventry	1917	Cruiser	4.18 - ....
Argonaut	1941	Cruiser	1941 - 1948

62

Hindustan	1903	Battleship	9.15 - 4.16
Essex	1901	Cruiser	1.18 - 4.18
Curacoa	1917	Cruiser	4.18 - ....
Gloucester	1937	Cruiser	1937 - 5.41
Glory	1943	Ac Carrier	1943 - 1948

63

Implacable	1899	Battleship	9.15 - 4.16
Exmouth	1901	Battleship	1.18 - 4.18
Bellerophon	1907	Battleship	4.18 - 1921
Bellona	1942	Cruiser	1942 - 1948

64

Irresistible	1898	Battleship	1914 - 3.15
Renown	1916	Battlecruiser	9.15 - 4.16
Fearless	1912	Cruiser	1.18 - 4.18
Blonde	1910	Cruiser	4.18 - 1920
Theseus	1944	Ac Carrier	1944 - 1948

65

Black Prince	1904	Cruiser	9.15 - 5.16
Furious	1916	Battlecruiser	1.18 - 4.18
Caledon	1916	Cruiser	4.18 - ....
Berwick	1926	Cruiser	1926 - 1945

66

King Edward VII	1903	Battleship	9.15 - 1.16
Ceres	1917	Cruiser	6.17 - 1.18
Galatea	1914	Cruiser	1.18 - 4.18
Marlborough	1912	Battleship	4.18 - ....
Emerald	1920	Cruiser	1.26 - ....
Uganda	1941	Cruiser	1940 - 1943
Quebec RCN	1941	Cruiser	1944 - 1948
(ex Uganda)			

67

Royal Oak	1914	Battleship	9.15 - 4.16
Glorious	1916	Battlecruiser	1.18 - 4.18
Lion	1910	Battlecruiser	4.18 - ....
Formidable	1939	Ac Carrier	1940 - 1948

68

Dublin	1912	Cruiser	9.15 - 4.16
Gloucester	1909	Cruiser	1.18 - 4.18
Princess Royal	1911	Battlecruiser	4.18 - ....
Exeter	1929	Cruiser	1929 - 3.42
Ocean	1944	Ac Carrier	1945 - 1948

69

Natal	1905	Cruiser	9.15 - 12.15
Caledon	1916	Cruiser	4.17 - 1.18
Hercules	1910	Battleship	1.18 - 4.18
Cordelia	1914	Cruiser	4.18 - ....
London	1927	Cruiser	1927 - 1948

70

London	1899	Battleship	9.15 - 4.16
Hibernia	1905	Battleship	1.18 - 4.18
King George V	1911	Battleship	4.18 - ....
Achilles	1932	Cruiser	1932 -1948

71

Lancaster	1902	Cruiser	9.15 - 4.16
Hindustan	1903	Battleship	1.18 - 4.18
Minotaur	1906	Cruiser	4.18 - 6.18
Dauntless	1918	Cruiser	11.18
Galatea	1934	Cruiser	1934 - 12.41
Vengeance	1944	Ac Carrier	1944 - 1948

72

Bellerophon	1907	Battleship	9.15 - 4.16
Implacable	1899	Battleship	1.18 - 4.18
Yarmouth	1911	Cruiser	4.18 - ....
Renown	1916	Battlecruiser	1940 - 1948

73

Zealandia	1904	Battleship	9.15 - 4.16
Inconstant	1914	Cruiser	1.18 - 4.18
Dreadnought	1906	Battleship	4.18 - 1921
Shropshire	1928	Cruiser	1928 - 1945

74

Ramillies	1916	Battleship	9.15 - 4.16
Indomitable	1907	Battlecruiser	1.18 - 4.18
Shannon	1906	Cruiser	4.18 - 6.18
Calcutta	1918	Cruiser	8.19 - ....
Hermione	1939	Cruiser	1939 - 6.42

75

Benbow	1913	Battleship	9.15 - 4.16
Inflexible	1907	Battlecruiser	1.18 - 4.18
Royalist	1915	Cruiser	4.18 - ....
Leander	1931	Cruiser	1931 - 1948

76

Calliope	1914	Cruiser	9.15 - 4.16
Iron Duke	1912	Battleship	1.18 - 4.18
Erin	1913	Battleship	4.18 - 1922
Newcastle	1936	Cruiser	1936 - 1948

77

| Indomitable | 1907 | Battlecruiser | 9.15 - 4.16 |

King George V	1911	Battleship	1.18 - 4.18
Inconstant	1914	Cruiser	4.18 - ....
Glorious	1916	Ac Carrier	1940 - 6.40
Majestic	1945	Ac Carrier	1945 - 1948

78

Cordelia	1914	Cruiser	9.15 - 4.16
Lancaster	1902	Cruiser	1.18 - 1920
Calliope	1914	Cruiser	4.18 - ....
Norfolk	1928	Cruiser	1928 - 1948

79

Marlborough	1912	Battleship	9.15 - 4.16
Lion	1910	Battlecruiser	1.18 - 4.18
Neptune	1909	Battleship	4.18 - 1922
Anson	1940	Battleship	1940 - 1948

80

Argyll	1904	Cruiser	9.15 - 10.15
Curlew	1917	Cruiser	8.17 - 1.18
Liverpool	1909	Cruiser	1.18 - 4.18
Undaunted	1914	Cruiser	4.18 - ....
Mauritius	1939	Cruiser	1939 - 1948

81

Prince of Wales	1902	Battleship	9.15 - 4.16
London	1899	Battleship	1.18 - 4.18
Australia RAN	1911	Battlecruiser	4.18 - ....
Frobisher	1920	Cruiser	9.24 - ....
Black Prince	1942	Cruiser	1942 - 1948

82

Queen	1902	Battleship	9.15 - 4.16
Lord Nelson	1906	Battleship	1.18 - 4.18
Calypso	1917	Cruiser	4.18 - ....
Sirius	1940	Cruiser	1940 - 1948

83

Inflexible	1907	Battlecruiser	9.15 - 4.16
Lowestoft	1913	Cruiser	1.18 - 4.18
Centurion	1911	Battleship	4.18 - ....
Southampton	1936	Cruiser	1936 - 1.41

84

Resolution	1915	Battleship	9.15 - 4.16
Malaya	1915	Battleship	1.18 - 4.18
Blanche	1909	Cruiser	4.18 - ....
Diadem	1942	Cruiser	1942 - 1948

85

Invincible	1907	Battlecruiser	9.15 - 5.16
Marlborough	1912	Battleship	1.18 - 4.18
St Vincent	1908	Battleship	4.18 - 1921
Orion	1932	Cruiser	1932 - 1948

86

Roxburgh	1904	Cruiser	9.15 - 4.16
Melbourne RAN	1912	Cruiser	1.18 - 4.18
Orion	1910	Battleship	4.18 - 1922
Implacable	1939	Ac Carrier	1940 - 1948

87

Caroline	1914	Cruiser	9.15 - 4.16
Minotaur	1906	Cruiser	1.18 - 4.18
Bellona	1909	Cruiser	4.18 - ....
Illustrious	1939	Ac Carrier	1940 - 1948

88

Carysfort	1914	Cruiser	9.15 - 4.16
Monarch	1911	Battleship	1.18 - 4.18
Cleopatra	1915	Cruiser	4.18 - ....
Capetown	1919	Cruiser	11.19 - ....
Charybdis	1940	Cruiser	1940 - 10.43
Jeanne d'Arc FR	1930	Cruiser	BR619(2)

89

Southampton	1912	Cruiser	9.15 - 4.16
Neptune	1909	Battleship	1.18 - 4.18
Royal Sovereign	1915	Battleship	4.18 - ....
Royalist	1942	Cruiser	1942 - 1948

90

Falmouth	1910	Cruiser	9.15 - 8.16
New Zealand	1911	Battlecruiser	1.18 - 4.18
Constance	1915	Cruiser	4.18 - ....
York	1927	Cruiser	1927 - 3.41
Georges Leygues FR	1936	Cruiser	BR619(2)

91

Minotaur	1906	Cruiser	2.15 - 4.16
Orion	1910	Battleship	1.18 - 4.18
Tiger	1915	Battlecruiser	4.18 - ....

92

Shannon	1906	Cruiser	9.15 - 4.16
Penelope	1914	Cruiser	1.18 - 4.18
Temeraire	1907	Battleship	4.18 - 1921
Diomede	1919	Cruiser	4.22 - ....
Indomitable	1940	Ac Carrier	1940 - 1948

93

Colossus	1910	Battleship	9.15 - 4.16
Phaeton	1914	Cruiser	1.18 - 4.18
Melbourne RAN	1912	Cruiser	4.18 - ....
Naiad	1939	Cruiser	1939 - 3.42
Terrible	1944	Ac Carrier	1944 - 1948

94

Iron Duke	1912	Battleship	9.15 - 4.16
Prince of Wales	1902	Battleship	1.18 - 4.18

Courageous	1916	Battlecruiser	4.18 - ....
Eagle	1918	Ac Carrier	1920 - 8.42

95

Bulwark	1905	Battleship	1914 - 11.14
Yarmouth	1911	Cruiser	2.15 - 4.16
Princess Royal	1911	Battlecruiser	1.18 - 4.18
Conqueror	1911	Battleship	4.18 - ....
Hermes	1919	Ac Carrier	6.20 - ....
Spartan	1942	Cruiser	1942 - 1.44
Powerful	1945	Ac Carrier	1945 - 1948

96

Venerable	1899	Battleship	9.15 - 4.16
Queen	1902	Battleship	1.18 - 9.18
New York USN	1912	Battleship	9.18 - ....
Dunedin	1918	Cruiser	8.19 - ....
Raleigh	1919	Cruiser	9.20 - 8.22
Sussex	1928	Cruiser	1928 - 1948

97

Barham	1914	Battleship	9.15 - 4.16
Queen Elizabeth	1913	Battleship	1.18 - 4.18
Wyoming USN	1911	Battleship	9.18 - ....
Cairo	1919	Cruiser	9.19 - ....
Penelope	1935	Cruiser	1935 - 2.44
Leviathan	1945	Ac Carrier	Incomplete

98

Revenge	1915	Battleship	9.15 - 4.16
Ramillies	1916	Battleship	1.18 - 4.18
Delaware USN	1909	Battleship	9.18 - ....
Effingham	1921	Cruiser	7.25 - ....
Scylla	1940	Cruiser	1940 - 1948

99

Bristol	1910	Cruiser	9.15 - 4.16
Renown	1916	Battlecruiser	1.18 - 4.18
Florida USN	1910	Battleship	9.18 - ....
Durban	1919	Cruiser	9.21 - ....
Blake	1945	Cruiser	1945 - 1948

0A

Canterbury	1915	Cruiser	9.15 - 4.16
Repulse	1916	Battlecruiser	1.18 - 4.18
Texas USN	1912	Battleship	9.18 - ....

1A

Cleopatra	1915	Cruiser	9.15 - 4.16
Resolution	1915	Battleship	1.18 - 4.18
Arkansas USN	1911	Battleship	9.18 - ....

2A

Theseus	1892	Cruiser	1914 - 9.15
Concord	1916	Cruiser	9.15 - 4.16

Revenge	1915	Battleship	1.18 - 4.18
Nevada USN	1914	Battleship	9.18 - ....

3A

Malaya	1915	Battleship	9.15 - 4.16
Roxburgh	1904	Cruiser	1.18 - 4.18
Utah USN	1909	Battleship	9.18 - ....

4A

Royalist	1915	Cruiser	9.15 - 4.16
Royal Oak	1914	Battleship	1.18 - 4.18
Oklahoma USN	1914	Battleship	9.18 - ....

5A

Inconstant	1914	Cruiser	9.15 - 4.16
Royal Sovereign	1915	Battleship	1.18 - 4.18

6A

Phaeton	1914	Cruiser	9.15 - 4.16
Royalist	1915	Cruiser	1.18 - 4.18
Delhi	1918	Cruiser	11.18 - ....

7A

Vindictive	1899	Cruiser	1914 - ....
Hecla	1878	Depot Ship	9.15 - 4.16
St Vincent	1908	Battleship	1.18 - 4.18
Colombo	1918	Cruiser	6.19 - ....

8A

Resolution	1915	Battleship	1914 - ....
Penelope	1914	Cruiser	9.15 - 4.16
Shannon	1906	Cruiser	1.18 - 4.18
Hawkins	1917	Cruiser	7.19 - ....

9A

Birkenhead	1915	Cruiser	9.15 - 4.16
Southampton	1912	Cruiser	1.18 - 4.18

A0

Royal Arthur	1891	Cruiser	1914 - 9.15
Caradoc	1916	Cruiser	6.17 - ....
Superb	1907	Battleship	1.18 - 4.18

A1

Cyclops	1905	Depot Ship	9.15 - 4.16
Sydney RAN	1912	Cruiser	1.18 - 4.18

A2

Active	1911	Cruiser	9.15 - 4.16
Temeraire	1907	Battleship	1.18 - 4.18

A3

Cambrian	1916	Cruiser	9.15 - 4.16
Thunderer	1911	Battleship	1.18 - 4.18

A4

Crescent	1892	Cruiser	1914 - 9.15
Sandhurst	1905	Depot Ship	1.16 - 4.16
Tiger	1915	Battlecruiser	1.18 - 4.18

A5

Edgar	1890	Cruiser	1914 - 9.15
Undaunted	1914	Cruiser	1.18 - 4.18

A6

Endymion	1891	Cruiser	1914 - 9.15
Valiant	1914	Battleship	1.18 - 4.18

A7

Gibraltar	1892	Cruiser	1914 - 9.15
Comus	1914	Cruiser	3.16 - 1.18
Curacoa	1917	Cruiser	1.18 - 4.18

A8

Grafton	1892	Cruiser	1914 - 9.15
Venerable	1899	Battleship	1.18 - 4.18

A9

Hawke	1891	Cruiser	1914 - 10.14
Dartmouth	1910	Cruiser	2.15 - 4.16
Warspite	1913	Battleship	1.18 - 4.18

0C

Galatea	1914	Cruiser	9.15 - 4.16
Weymouth	1910	Cruiser	1.18

1C

Bellona	1909	Cruiser	9.15 - 4.16
Yarmouth	1911	Cruiser	1.18 - 4.18

2C

Undaunted	1914	Cruiser	9.15 - 4.16
Zealandia	1904	Battleship	1.18 - 4.18

3C

Arethusa	1913	Cruiser	9.15 - 2.16
Cassandra	1916	Cruiser	6.17 - 1.18
Curlew	1917	Cruiser	1.18 - 4.18

4C

Boadicea	1908	SCruiser	9.15 - 4.16
Coventry	1917	Cruiser	1.18 - 4.18

5C

Comus	1914	Cruiser	9.15 - 3.16

6C

Blanche	1909	Cruiser	9.15 - 4.16

7C

Vindictive	1899	Cruiser	1914 - 9.15
Titania	1915	Depot Ship	1.16 - 4.16

8C

Assistance	1900	Depot Ship	9.15 - 4.16

9C

Donegal	1902	Cruiser	9.15 - 4.16

C0

Conquest	1915	Cruiser	9.15 - 4.16

C1

Aurora	1913	Cruiser	9.15 - 4.16
Ambrose	1903	Depot Ship	1.18 - ....

C2

Blenheim	1890	Depot Ship	9.15 - 4.16
Assistance	1900	Depot Ship	1.18 - ....

C3

Blake	1889	Depot Ship	9.15 - 1.18

C4

Castor	1915	Cruiser	9.15 - 4.16
Blenheim	1890	Depot Ship	1.18 - ....

C5

Constance	1915	Cruiser	9.15 - 4.16
Cyclops	1905	Depot Ship	1.18 - ....

C6

Australia RAN	1911	Battlecruiser	2.15 - 4.16
Greenwich	1915	Depot Ship	1.18 - ....

C7

Blonde	1910	Cruiser	9.15 - 4.16
Hecla	1878	Depot Ship	1.18 - ....

C8

Champion	1915	Cruiser	9.15 - 4.16
Platypus RAN	1916	Depot Ship	1.18 - ....

C9

Chester	1915	Cruiser	9.15 - 4.16
Sandhurst	1905	Depot Ship	1.18 - ....

AC

Woolwich	1912	Depot Ship	9.15 - 4.16
Titania	1915	Depot Ship	1.18 - ....

CA

Greenwich	1915	Depot Ship	1.16 - 4.16
Woolwich	1912	Depot Ship	1.18 - ....

Flag 'A' Superior

Pre 1940: None

1940–48: British Pacific Fleet

1948: Survey Vessels (to 1998); RFAs; Depot Ships; Tugs and Auxiliaries

A00			
Britannia	1953	Royal Yacht	1954 - 1997
A70			
Echo	1957	Survey Ship	1957 - 1985
A71			
Enterprise	1958	Survey Ship	1958 - 1985
A72			
Egeria	1958	Survey Ship	1958 - 1985
Cameron	1991	Mooring Vsl	1991 -
A75			
Tidespring	1962	Tanker	1963 - 1992
A76			
Tidepool	1962	Tanker	1963 - 1982
A77			
Pearleaf	1959	Tanker	1959 - 1986
A78			
Plumleaf	1960	Tanker	1960 - 1986
A79			
Bayleaf	1954	Tanker	1959 - 1973
Appleleaf	1975	Tanker	1979 - 1989
A80			
Orangeleaf	1955	Tanker	1959 - 1978
A81			
Brambleleaf	1953	Tanker	1959 - 1972
Brambleleaf	1976	Tanker	1980 - 2009
A82			
Cherryleaf	1953	Tanker	1959 - 1966
Cherryleaf	1962	Tanker	1973 - 1980
A83			
Appleleaf	1955	Tanker	1959 - 1970
Melton	1981	Tender	1981 - 2008
A84			
Reliant	1953	Store Ship	1957 - 1976
Menai	1981	Tender	1981 - 2008
A85			
Faithful	1957	Tug	1957 - 1981

A86			
Forceful	1957	Tug	1957 - 1981
Gleaner	1983	Survey Ship	1983 - 2018
A87			
Favourite	1958	Tug	1958 - 1979
Meon	1982	Tender	1981 - 2008
A88			
Agile	1958	Tug	1958 - 1985
A89			
Advice	1958	Tug	1958 - 1984
A90			
Accord	1957	Tug	1957 - 1985
A91			
Griper	1958	Tug	1958 - 1979
Milford	1982	Tender	1982 - 2001
A92			
Grinder	1958	Tug	1958 - 1979
Manly	1981	Tender	1981 - 1991
A93			
Dexterous	1956	Tug	1956 - 1981
A94			
Director	1956	Tug	1956 - 1979
Mentor	1981	Tender	1981 - 1991
A95			
Typhoon	1958	Tug	1960 - 1989
A96			
Tidereach	1954	Tanker	1954 - 1979
Sea Crusader	1996	RoRo	1996 - 2003
A97			
Tiderace	1954	Tanker	1956 - 1958
Tideflow	1954	Tanker	1958 - 1975
Milbrook	1981	Tender	1981 - 1992
Sea Chieftain	1998	RoRo	Canc 1998

Tiderace was renamed *Tideflow* on 28 June 1958 in order to avoid confusion with her sister *Tiderange*. The order for *Sea Chieftain* was cancelled in 1998 when the builder went bankrupt. She never entered RFA service.

A98

Tiderange	1954	Tanker	1954 - 1958
Tidesurge	1954	Tanker	1958 - 1976
Sea Centurion	1997	RoRo	1998 - 2002

Tiderange was renamed *Tidesurge* on 28 June 1958.

A99

Tide Austral	1954	Tanker	1955 - 1962
Beaulieu	1963	Tender	1963 - 1986

A100

Wave Emperor	1944	Tanker	1948 - 1958
Beddgelert	1963	Tender	1963 - 1994

A101

Freebooter	1940	Tug	1948 - 1959
Bembridge	1964	Tender	1964 - 1991

A102

C633	1945	Lighter	1948 - 1956
Airedale	1961	Tug	1961 - 1985

A103

Bacchus	1936	Distilling Sp	1948 - 1962
Bibury	1964	Tender	1964 - 1986
Sultan Venturer	1964	Tender	1986 - 1992

Bibury renamed *Sultan Venturer* in 1986 as tender to HMS *Sultan*

A104

Eaglesdale	1940	Tanker	1948 - 1958
Blakeney	1964	Tender	1964 - 1986

A105

Easedale	1941	Tanker	1948 - 1959
Brodick	1964	Tender	1964 - 1984

A106

Belgol	1917	Tanker	1948 - 1958
Alsation	1961	Tug	1961 - 1993

A107

Boxol	1917	Tanker	1948 - 1948
Eddybay	1951	Tanker	1951 - 1962
Messina	1982	Tender	1982 - 1995

A108

Wave Monarch	1944	Tanker	1948 - 1960
Triumph	1944	Repair Ship	1965 - 1981

A109

Abbeydale	1936	Tanker	1948 - 1959
Bayleaf	1981	Tanker	1982 - 2011

A110

Hengist (ex *Decision*)	1941	Tug	1948 - 1965
Orangeleaf	1975	Tanker	1984 - 2015

A111

Frisky	1941	Tug	1948 - Sold
Cyclone	1942	Tug	1963 - 1982
Oakleaf	1981	Tanker	1986 - 2007

A112

Impetus	1940	Tug	1948 - 1967
Felicity	1969	Tug	1969 - 1997

A113

C614	1943	Lighter	1948 - 1956
Alice	1961	Tug	1961 - 1982

A114

Derwentdale	1941	Tanker	1948 - 1959
Magnet	1979	DG Vessel	1979 - 1997

A115

Airsprite	1942	Spirit Carrier	1948 - 1963
Lodestone	1979	DG Vessel	1979 - 1995

A116

Celerol	1917	Tanker	1948 - 1958
Agatha	1961	Tug	1961 - 1982

A117

Alaunia	1925	Repair Ship	1948 - 1957
Audrey	1961	Tug	1961 - 1982

A118

Artifex	1924	Repair Ship	1948 - 1955

A119

Wave Laird	1946	Tanker	1948 - 1970

A120

Limol	1917	Tanker	1948 - 1953

A121

Bulawayo	1937	Tanker	1948 - 1950
Agnes	1961	Tug	1961 - 1983

A122

Roc	1945	Store Ship	1948 - 1959
Olynthus	1964	Tanker	1965 - 1967
Olwen	1964	Tanker	1967 - 1969

Olynthus was renamed *Olwen* in 1967 to avoid confusion

with the submarine *Olympus*.

A123

Elmol	1917	Tanker	1948 - 1955
Olna	1965	Tanker	1966 - 2000

A124

C85	1940	Lighter	1948 - 1956
Oleander	1964	Tanker	1965 - 1967
Olmeda	1964	Tanker	1967 - 1994

Oleander was renamed *Olmeda* on 16 October 1967 to avoid confusion with the frigate *Leander*

A125

Mediator	1944	Tug	1948 - 1964

A126

Fortol	1917	Tanker	1948 - 1958
Cairn	1965	Tug	1965 - 2000

A127

Birchol	1946	Tanker	1948 - 1965
Torrent	1971	TRV	1971 - 2001

A128

Bishopdale	1937	Tanker	1948 - 1959
Torrid	1971	TRV	1971 - 1991

A129

Wave Premier	1946	Tanker	1948 - 1959
Dalmation	1965	Tug	1965 - 2003

A130

Gold Ranger	1941	Tanker	1948 - 1973
Roebuck	1985	Survey	1985 - 1998

A131

Flamer	1940	Tug	1948 - 1965
Reliant	1976	Store Ship	1983 - 1986
Scott	1996	Survey Ship	1996 - 1998

A132

Titania	1915	Depot Ship	1948 - 1949
Eddybeach	1951	Tanker	1951 - 1962
Diligence	1980	Repair Ship	1984 - 2016

A133

Arndale	1937	Tanker	1948 - 1960
Hecla	1964	Survey Ship	1964 - 1997

A134

Rame Head	1944	Repair Ship	1948 - 2007

A135

Nordenfelt	1945	Arm Carrier	1948 - 1971
Argus	1980	PCRS	1988 -

A136

Bullhead	1944	Cable Ship	1948 - Sold
Tidespring	2015	Tanker	2015 -

A137

Larchol	1917	Tanker	1948 - 1954
Hecate	1965	Survey Ship	1965 - 1991
Tiderace	2015	Tanker	2015 -

A138

Rockmount	1945	Tug	1948 - Sold
Herald	1973	Survey Ship	1973 - 1998
Tidesurge	2016	Tanker	2016 -

A139

Bonaventure	1942	Depot Ship	1948 - 12.48
Cracker	1899	Tug	1949 - 1956
Tideforce	2017	Tanker	2017 -

A140

Jaunty	1941	Tug	1948 - 1965
Tornado	1979	TRV	1979 - 2008

A141

Antic	1943	Tug	1948 - 1969
Torch	1979	TRV	1979 - 1999

A142

Assidious	1943	Tug	1948 - 1958
Tormentor	1979	TRV	1979 - 2007

A143

Mixol	1916	Tanker	1948 - 1948
Toreador	1980	TRV	1980 - 1997

A144

Dingledale	1941	Tanker	1948 - 1959
Hydra	1965	Survey Ship	1965 - 1986

A145

Guardian	1932	Netlayer	1948 - 1962
Daisy	1968	Tug	1968 - 1989

A146

Protector	1936	Netlayer	1948 - 1970
Waterman	1977	Water Carrier	1977 - 2008

Protector was refitted as an ice patrol ship in 1955.

A147

Empire Edward	1942	Tug	1948 - 1955

Energetic	1942	Tug	1955 - 1965
Frances	1979	Tug	1979 - ....

A148
Emphatic	1943	Tug	1948 - 1958
Fiona	1973	Tug	1973 - 2007

A149
Reserve	1942	Tug	1948 - Ret'd
Florence	1980	Tug	1980 - 2008

A150
Allegiance	1943	Tug	1948 - 1962
Genevieve	1980	Tug	1980 - 2008

A151
Dewdale	1941	Tanker	1948 - 1959

A152
Green Ranger	1941	Tanker	1948 - 1962
Georgina	1973	Tug	1973 - 1996

A153
Ausonia	1921	Depot Ship	1948 - 1965
Example	1985	Patrol Craft	1985 - 1994

A154
Elderol	1917	Tanker	1948 - 1954
Explorer	1986	Patrol Craft	1986 - 1994

A155
Prestol	1917	Tanker	1948 - 1952
Deerhound	1966	Tug	1966 - 1996

A156
Deepwater	1939	Trials Ship	1948 - 1960
Daphne	1968	Tug	1968 - 1996

A157
Blue Ranger	1941	Tanker	1948 - 1972
Loyal Helper	1977	Tender	1977 - 1996

A158
Duncansby Head	1944	Repair Ship	1948 - 1969
Supporter	1977	Tender	1977 - 1996
(ex *Loyal Supporter*)			

A159
Empire Salvage	1940	Tanker	1948 - Ret'd
Loyal Watcher	1978	Tender	1978 - 1996

A160
Bullfrog	1944	Cable Ship	1948 - Sold
Fort Dunvegan	1944	Store Ship	1948 - 1968
Loyal Volunteer	1978	Tender	1978 - 1994

A161
Scotol	1916	Tanker	1948 - Sold
Loyal Mediator	1978	Tender	1978 - 2001

A162
Serbol	1917	Tanker	1948 - 1953
Elkhound	1966	Tug	1966 - 1996

A163
Black Ranger	1940	Tanker	1948 - 1973
Express	1988	Patrol Craft	1988 - 1994

A164
Adamant	1940	Depot Ship	1948 - 1966
Goosander	1973	Mooring Vsl	1973 - ....

A165
Envoy	1944	Tug	1948 - 1965
Pochard	1973	Mooring Vsl	1973 - 1991

A166
Rockforest	1945	Tug	1948 - Sold
Kathleen	1972	Tug	1972 - 1996

A167
Teakol	1946	Tanker	1948 - 1969
Exploit	1988	Patrol Craft	1988 - 1994

Example (A153), *Exploit* (A167), *Explorer* (A154) and *Express* (A163) were originally ordered for the RNXS as *Loyal Example, Loyal Exploit, Loyal Explorer* and *Loyal Express*, but following a protracted construction period, the *Loyal* prefix was dropped prior to the vessels entering service.

A168
Broomdale	1937	Tanker	1948 - 1959
Labrador	1966	Tug	1966 - 1996

A169
Brown Ranger	1940	Tanker	1948 - 1975

A170
Echodale	1940	Tanker	1948 - 1959
Kitty	1972	Tug	1972 - 2010

A171
Energetic	1902	Tug	1948 - 1953
Endurance	1956	Ice Patrol Sp	1967 - 1991
Endurance	1990	Ice Patrol Sp	1992 - 2008

A172
Expert	1945	Tug	1948 - 1968
Lesley	1973	Tug	1973 - 2010

A173

Ennerdale	1941	Tanker	1948 - 1958
Dorothy	1968	Tug	1968 - 1991
Protector	2001	Ice Patrol Sp	2011 -

A174

Emulous	1942	Tug	1948 - 1961
Lilah	1973	Tug	1973 - 2002

A175

Enigma	1944	Tug	1948 - 1962
Mary	1973	Tug	1973 - 1997

A176

Bullfinch	1940	Cable Ship	1948 - Sold
Polar Circle	1990	Ice Patrol Sp	1991 - 1992

A177

Enforcer	1944	Tug	1948 - 1963
Edith	1968	Tug	1969 - 1995

A178

Empire Imp	1942	Tug	1948 - 1959
Appleleaf	1916	Tanker	1948 - Sold
Husky	1969	Tug	1969 - 2011

A179

Resource	1928	Repair Ship	1948 - 1953
Whimbrel	1944	Trials Vsl	.... - ....

A180

Woolwich	1934	Depot Ship	1948 - 1962
Mastiff	1966	Tug	1966 - 2001

A181

Hickorol	1917	Tanker	1948 - Sold
Irene	1972	Tug	1972 - 1996

A182

Wave King	1944	Tanker	1948 - 1956
Saluki	1969	Tug	1969 - 2010

A183

Expeller	1942	Tug	1948 - 1967
Isabel	1972	Tug	1972 - 1996

A184

Maine	1924	Hospital Ship	1948 - 1954

A185

Maidstone	1937	Depot Ship	1948 - 1978
Salmoor	1985	Salvage Vsl	1985 - 2008

A186

Fort Rosalie	1944	Store Ship	1948 - 1972

Salmaster	1985	Salvage Vsl	1985 - 2001

A187

Forth	1938	Depot Ship	1948 - 1979
Salmaid	1986	Salvage Vsl	1986 - 2008

A188

Montclare	1921	Depot Ship	1948 - 1954
Pointer	1967	Tug	1967 - 1993

A189

Holm Sound	1944	Repair Ship	1948 - Sold
Setter	1969	Tug	1969 - 2005

A190

Wolfe	1920	Depot Ship	1948 - 1952
Eddycliff	1952	Tanker	1952 - 1964
Joan	1972	Tug	1972 - 2004

A191

Berry Head	1944	Repair Ship	1948 - 1987
Bovisand	1997	Pax Ferry	1997 - 2008

A192

Spa	1941	Water Carrier	1948 - 1970
Cawsand	1997	Pax Ferry	1997 - 2008

A193

Wave Master	1944	Tanker	1948 - 1962
Joyce	1972	Tug	1972 - 1996

A194

Tyne	1940	Depot Ship	1948 - 1972

A195

Unicorn	1941	Maint Ship	1948 - 1959

A196

Briton (ex-Bandit)	1938	Tug	1948 - 1960
Gwendoline	1973	Tug	1973 - 1996

A197

Perseus	1944	Maint Ship	1952 - 1958
Sealyham	1967	Tug	1967 - 1996

A198

Pioneer	1944	Maint Ship	1953 - 1954
Eddyrock	1952	Tanker	1953 - 1967
Helen	1974	Tug	1974 - ....

A199

Driver	1942	Tug	1948 - 1964
Myrtle	1973	Tug	1973 - 2011

A200

Rollicker	1918	Tug	1948 - 1952

Vidal	1951	Survey Ship	1951 - 1976

A201

C642	1946	Lighter	1948 - 1956
Spaniel	1967	Tug	1967 - 2010

A202

Cape Wrath	1945	Repair Ship	1948 - 1951
Eddyreef	1952	Tanker	1951 - 1958
Nancy	1973	Tug	1973 - 1996

A203

Sprightly	1942	Tug	1948 - Sold

A204

Robert Dundas	1938	Store Ship	1948 - 1971

A205

Portland Bill	1945	Repair Ship	1948 - 1951
Eddycove	Canc	Tanker	Canc 1952
Norah	1973	Tug	1973 - 2004

A206

Ripon	1945	Ac Transport	1948 - 1959
Celia	1965	Tug	1966 - 1971

A207

Wave Prince	1945	Tanker	1948 - 1966
Llandovery	1973	Tender	1973 - 1996

A208

Egerton	1943	Tug	1948 - 1958
Lamlash	1973	Tender	1973 - 2001

Egerton (A208) (ex *Empire Darby*). Renamed and transferred to the Admiralty in 1948.

A209

Earner	1943	Tug	1948 - 1964

A210

Wave Regent	1945	Tanker	1948 - 1959
Charlotte	1966	Tug	1966 - 1989

A211

Wave Sovereign	1945	Tanker	1948 - 1966
Lechlade	1972	Tender	1972 - 2001

A212

Wave Ruler	1946	Tanker	1948 - 1975

A213

Freshbrook	1941	Water Carrier	1948 - 1963
Ennerdale	1962	Tanker	1968 - 1970
Endeavour	1966	TRV	1975 - 1998

A214

Seafox	1946	Store Ship	1948 - 1958

A215

Wave Protector	1944	Tanker	1948 - 1958

A216

Olna	1944	Tanker	1948 - 1967
Bee	1970	Arm Carrier	1969 - 2002

A217

Walrus	1945	Ac Transport	1948 - 1953
Skua (ex *Walrus*)	1945	Ac Transport	1953 - 1962
Christine	1967	Tug	1967 - 1989

A218

Samsonia	1942	Tug	1948 - 1974
Clare	1967	Tug	1967 - 1985

A219

Dodman Point	1945	Repair Ship	1948 - 1963
Dewdale	1965	Tanker	1967 - 1974

A220

Wave Victor	1943	Tanker	1948 - 1971
Loyal Moderator	1973	Tender	1973 - 1994

A221

Perseverance	1931	Tug	1948 - 1958
Derwentdale	1964	Tanker	1967 - 1974
Forceful	1985	Tug	1985 - 2008

A222

Spapool	1946	Water Carrier	1948 - 1976
Nimble	1985	Tug	1985 - 2008

A223

Nimble	1941	Tug	1948 - 1970
Powerful	1985	Tug	1985 - 2008

A224

Spabrook	1944	Water Carrier	1948 - 1976
Adept	1980	Tug	1980 - 2008

A225

Mull of Kintyre	1945	Repair Ship	1948 - ....
Bustler	1980	Tug	1980 - 2008

A226

Mull of Galloway	1944	Repair Ship	1948 - ....
Capable	1981	Tug	1981 - 2008

A227

Spabeck	1943	Water Carrier	1948 - 1966
Careful	1982	Tug	1982 - 2008

A228

Robust	1907	Tug	1948 - 1957
Faithful	1985	Tug	1985 - 2008

A229

Fort Duquesne	1944	Store Ship	1948 - 1967
Cricket	1973	Arm Carrier	1969 - 1995
Colonel Templer	1966	Trials Ship	2001 - 2008

A230

Fort Langley	1944	Store Ship	1948 - 1970
Cockchafer	1973	Arm Carrier	1973 - 2001

A231

Reclaim	1948	Salvage Ship	1948 - 1979
Dexterous	1986	Tug	1986 - 2008

A232

Rockcliffe	1945	Tug	1948 - Sold
Kingarth	1944	Salvage Ship	1948 - 1986
Adamant	1992	Pax Ferry	1992 - 2008

A233

Rockwing	1945	Tug	1948 - Sold

A234

Salvage Duke	1943	Salvage Ship	1948 - Sold

A235

Prompt	1943	Tug	1951 - 1975

A236

Fort Charlotte	1944	Store Ship	1948 - 1967
Wakeful	1965	Tug	1974 - 1987

A237

Fort Constantine	1944	Store Ship	1948 - 1969

A238

Reliant	1922	Store Ship	1948 - Sold
Amherst	1935	Store Ship	1952 - 1964

A239

Ranpura	1924	Repair Ship	1948 - 1963
Gnat	1969	Arm Carrier	1969 - 1995

A240

Bustler	1941	Tug	1948 - 1973

A241

Robert Middleton	1938	Store Ship	1948 - 1975

A242

Wave Baron	1946	Tanker	1948 - 1969

A243

Tryphon	1942	Tug	1948 - 1958

A244

Wave Commander	1944	Tanker	1948 - 1958

A245

Wave Conqueror	1943	Tanker	1948 - 1958

A246

Wave Duke	1944	Tanker	1948 - 1960

A247

Wave Governor	1944	Tanker	1948 - 1960

A248

Wave Liberator	1944	Tanker	1948 - 1959

A249

Wave Knight	1945	Tanker	1948 - 1964

A250

Petrobus	1917	Spirit Carrier	1948 - 1959
Sheepdog	1969	Tug	1969 - 2008

A251

Blackburn	1946	Ac Transport	1948 - 1949
Lydford	1969	Tender	1986 - 1996

Lydford (A251) recommissioned and renamed 1986 after service as *Alert* (P252) as RN patrol vessel off Ulster. Originally named *Loyal Governor* (A510) when first commissioned.

A252

Nasprite	1940	Spirit Carrier	1948 - 1954
Doris	1968	Tug	1968 - 1990

A253

Philol	1916	Tanker	1948 - 1967
Ladybird	1970	Arm Carrier	1970 - 2006

A254

Prosperous	1942	Tug	1948 - 1965
Meavy	1970	Tender	1986 - 1992
Sultan Venturer	1970	Tender	1992 - 2001

Meavy recommissioned and renamed 25.10.1986 after service as *Vigilant* (P254) as RN patrol vessel off Ulster. Originally named *Loyal Factor* (A382) when first commissioned.

A255

St Day	1918	Tug	1948 - Sold

A256

Adherent	1940	Tug	1948 - 1960

A257

Spaburn	1946	Water Carrier	1948 - 1976

A258

Rapidol	1917	Tanker	1948 - Sold
Eddycreek	1953	Tanker	1953 - 1963

A259
St Margarets	1943	Cable Ship	1948 - 1985

A260
Spalake	1946	Water Carrier	1948 - 1976

A261
Thornol	1935	Tanker	1948 - Sold
Eddyfirth	1953	Tanker	1953 - 1981

A262
Hartland Point	1944	Repair Ship	1948 - 1979
Dispenser	1943	Salvage Vsl	1973 - 1976

A263
Tampeon	1938	Tug	1948 - 1964
Cicala	1970	Arm Carrier	1970 - 1996

A264
Reward	1944	Tug	1948 - 1976

A265
Wave Chief	1946	Tanker	1948 - 1974

A266
Vagrant	1943	Tug	1948 - 1968

A267
Moorburn	1942	Mooring Vsl	1948 - 1962

A268
Moormyrtle	1945	Mooring Vsl	1948 - ....
Green Rover	1968	Tanker	1969 - 1992

A269
Moorcock	1942	Mooring Vsl	1948 - ....
Grey Rover	1969	Tanker	1970 - 2006

A270
Moorside	1945	Mooring Vsl	1948 - ....
Blue Rover	1969	Tanker	1970 - 1993

A271
Mooress	1943	Mooring Vsl	1948 - ....
Gold Rover	1973	Tanker	1974 - 2017

A272
Moorfire	1941	Mooring Vsl	1948 - ....
Scarab	1971	Arm Carrier	1971 - 1996

A273
Moorfowl	1919	Mooring Vsl	1948 - ....
Black Rover	1973	Tanker	1974 - 2015

A274
Moorgrieve	1944	Mooring Vsl	1948 - ....
Ettrick	1970	Tender	1970 - 1995

A275
Viscol	1916	Tanker	1948 - 1950

A276
Lasso	1938	Cable Ship	1948 - 1959

A277
Elsing	1970	Tender	1970 - 1995

A278
Atlas	1909	Tug	1948 - 1958

A279
Rockland	1945	Tug	1948 - Sold

A280
Rambler	1908	Tug	1948 - 1951
Resurgent	1950	Store Ship	1951 - 1979
Newhaven	2000	Pax Ferry	2000 - 2008

A281
Kinbrace	1944	Salvage Ship	1948 - 1990
Nutbourne	2000	Pax Ferry	2000 - 2008

A282
Irwell	(....)	....	1948 - ....
Netley	2000	Pax Ferry	2000 - 2008

A283
Grapeshot	1945	Tug	1948 - 1974
Oban	2000	Pax Ferry	2000 - 2008

A284
Rowanol	1946	Tanker	1948 - 1971
Oronsay	2000	Pax Ferry	2000 - 2008

A285
Fort Beauharnois	1944	Store Ship	1948 - 1962
Auricula	1979	Trials Ship	1979 - 1995
Omagh	2000	Pax Ferry	2000 - 2008

A286
Restive	1940	Tug	1948 - 1964
Padstow	2000	Pax Ferry	2000 - 2008

A287
War Hindoo	1919	Tanker	1948 - 1958
Eddymull	Canc	Tanker	Canc 1952

A288
War Brahmin	1919	Tanker	1948 - 1959
Sea Giant	1954	Tug	1950 - 1980

A289
War Bharata	1919	Tanker	1948 - Sold
Confiance	1955	Tug	1956 - 1984

A290
War Afridi	1919	Tanker	1948 - 1950

Confident	1956	Tug	1956 - 1984

A291
King Salvor	1942	Salvage Ship	1948 - 1953
Kingfisher	1942	Dive Ship	1953 - 1958
(ex *King Salvor)*			

A292
Prince Salvor	1943	Salvage Ship	1948 - 1966

A293
Careful	1945	Tug	1948 - 1973

A294
War Pindari	1919	Tanker	1948 - Sold

A295
War Sudra	1920	Tanker	1948 - 1951
Eddyness	1953	Tanker	1954 - 1963

A296
Rockglen	1945	Tug	1948 - 1954

A297
Impudence	(....)	....	1948 - ....

A298
Iva	(....)	....	1948 - ....

A299
Exhorter	1937	Tug	1948 - 1962

A300
Oakol	1946	Tanker	1948 - 1965

A301
Challenger	1931	Survey Ship	1948 - 1954
Natal SAN	1944	Survey Ship	1957 - 1972

A302
Dalrymple	1945	Survey Ship	1948 - 1966

A303
Dampier	1945	Survey Ship	1948 - 1968

A304
Franklin	1937	Survey Ship	1948 - 1956

A305
Industrious	1902	Tug	1948 - 1959

A306
Integrity	1942	Tug	1948 - 1964

A307
Cook	1945	Survey Ship	1948 - 1964

A308
Scott	1938	Survey Ship	1948 - 1964
Ilchester	1974	Dive Ship	1974 - 2003

A309
Seagull	1937	Survey Ship	1948 - 1951
Warden	1945	Tug	1951 - 1965
Instow	1974	Dive Ship	1974 - 2003

A310
Shackleton	1936	Survey Ship	1953 - 1965
Ironbridge	1974	Dive Ship	1978 - 2002
(ex *Invergordon*)			

A311
Owen	1945	Survey Ship	1948 - 1965
Invergordon	1974	Dive Ship	1974 - 1978

A312
Warrego RAN	1940	Survey Ship	1948 - 1963

A313
Chainshot	1946	Tug	1948 - 1973

A314
Platypus RAN	1916	Depot Ship	1948 - 1958

A315
Buchan Ness	1945	Repair Ship	1948 - 1959

A316
Fort Sandusky	1944	Store Ship	1948 - 1972

A317
Masterful	1942	Tug	1948 - 1958
Bulldog	1967	Survey Ship	1968 - 1998

A318
Pert	1916	Tug	1948 - 1961
Ixworth	1974	Dive Ship	1974 - 2004

A319
Recovery	1908	Tug	1948 - 1958
Beagle	1967	Survey Ship	1968 - 1998

A320
Retort	1918	Tug	1948 - 1958
Fox	1967	Survey Ship	1967 - 1989

A321
Protea SAN	1941	Survey Ship	1948 - 1962

A322
SML322	1941	Survey Ship	1949 - 1959
Bridget	1963	Tug	1963 - 1983

A323
SML 323	1941	Survey Ship	1949 - ....
Betty	1962	Tug	1962 - 1983

A324
SML 324	1941	Survey Ship	1949 - 1959
Barbara	1963	Tug	1963 - 1982

A325
SML 325	1942	Survey Ship	1949 - 1958
Brenda	1963	Tug	1963 - 1983

17

A326

SML 326	1943	Survey Ship	1949 - 1959
Boxer	1962	Tug	1962 - 1977
Foxhound (ex *Boxer*)	1962	Tug	1977 - 1995

RMAS *Boxer* was renamed *Foxhound* in 1977 when the former name was allocated to a new Type 22 frigate.

A327

SML 327	1944	Survey Ship	1949 - 1953
Beagle	1963	Tug	1963 - 1967
Basset (ex *Beagle*)	1963	Tug	1967 - 1995

A328

Annet	1943	WDV	1948 - 1958
Collie	1964	Tug	1964 - 2001

A329

Ranpura	1924	Repair Ship	1948 - 1960
Retainer	1950	Store Ship	1954 - 1978

A330

Bardsey	1942	TCV	1950 - 1959
Corgi	1964	Tug	1964 - 1995

A331

Surf Pilot	1938	Oiler	1951
Bern	1942	TCV	1956 - 1978

Surf Pilot was the former *Yung Hao*, an impounded Chinese tanker. In 1951 she was to have been assigned to the RFA but was never commissioned and instead served as a tender to HMS *Terror*, Singapore.

A332

Caldy	1943	TCV	1951 - 1983

A333

Coll	1941	TCV	1950 - 1975

A334

Damsay	1942	TCV	1956 - 1959

A335

Earraid	1941	WDV	1948 - 1951
Fawn	1968	Survey Ship	1968 - 1991

A336

Fetlar	1941	WDV	1950- 1960
Lundy	1942	TCV	1956 - 1982

A337

Flatholm	1943	WDV	1948 - 1960

A338

Graemsay	1942	TCV	1957 - 1978

A339

Lindisfarne	1943	Trawler	1948 - 1958
Lyness	1966	Store Ship	1966 - 1980

A340

Lundy	1942	Trawler	1948 - 1950

A341

Fotherby	1969	Tender	1969 - 1993

A342

Neave	1942	WDV	1948 - 1951

A343

Scalpay	1942	WDV	1948 - Sold

A344

Skomer	1943	TCV	1948 - 1979
Stromness	1966	Store Ship	1967 - 1983
Impulse	1993	Tug	1993 - 2008

A345

Tarbatness	1967	Store Ship	1967 - 1980
Impetus	1993	Tug	1993 - 2008

A346

Switha	1942	TCV	1950 - 1981

A348

Trondra	1941	WDV	.... - 1957
Felsted	1970	Tender	1970 - 1997

A349

Freshwater	1940	Waca	1948 - 1968

A350

Cartmel	1967	Tender	1967 - 1993

A351

Cawsand	1968	Tender	1968 - 1984

A352

Meda (ex *SML352*)	1943	Survey Ship	1949 - 1966

Renamed in 1949, *Meda* (A352) was the former *HDML 1301* which in turn was renamed *SML352* in 1948. Confidential Admiralty Fleet Order 263/49 (dated 19.8.49) which assigned pendant A352 lists the vessel as *SML 1301*.

A353

Elkstone	1970	Tender	1970 - 1999

A354

Froxfield	1970	Tender	1970 - 1994

A355

Epworth	1970	Tender	1969 - 1999

A356

C668 (ex *VIC 96*)	1945	Oil Lighter	1949 - 1972
Fulbeck	1969	Tender	1969 - 1997

A357

Surf Patrol	1951	Tanker	1951 - 1961
Datchet	1968	Dive Ship	1968 - 1994

A358

C112	(....)	Oil Lighter	1948 - ....

A360

Loyalty	(....)	Tender	.... - ....

A361

Roysterer	1972	Tug	1972 - 1996
Endeavour	1966	TRV	1966 - ....

A362

Dispenser	1943	Mooring Vsl	1954 - 1973
Dolwen	1976	Tender	1976 - 1990

A363

Denmead	1969	Tender	1969 - 1996

A364

St Clears	1919	Tug	1948 - Sold
Whitehead	1970	Trials Ship	1970 - 1994

A365

Surf Pioneer	1951	Tanker	1951 - 1960

A366

West Cocker	1919	Tug	Sunk 1942
Robust	1971	Tug	1971 - 1997

A367

Newton	1975	Trials Ship	1975 - 2008

A368

Warden	1989	Trials Ship	1989 -

A369

Empire Demon	1942	Tug	1948 - 1965

A370

C648	1946	Oil Lighter	1948 - 1958

A371

C677	(....)	Oil Lighter	1948 - ....

A372

Empire Fred	1942	Tug	1948 - 1973

A373

West Bay	1918	Tug	1948 - 1953

A374

Ancient	1915	Tug	1948 - 1953

A375

Snider	1945	Arm Carrier	1948 - 1964

A376

Gatling	1945	Arm Carrier	1948 - 1970

A377

Maxim	1945	Arm Carrier	1948 - 1977

A378

Kinterbury	1980	Arm Carrier	1980 - 2006

A379

Encore	1944	Tug	1948 - 1967
Throsk	1977	Arm Carrier	1977 - 1992

A380

Cedardale	1939	Tanker	1948 - 1959

A381

Dwarf	1936	Tender	1948 - ....
Cricklade	1970	Tender	1970 - 1996

A382

Empire Netta	1945	Tug	1948 - 1967
Loyal Factor	1970	Tender	1974 - 1975
St George	1981	Arm Carrier	1981 - 1989
Arrochar	1981	Arm Carrier	1989 - 2006

Loyal Factor was renamed *Vigilant* (P254) in 1975 for operations in Northern Ireland. *St George* was operated by the Army Royal Corps of Transport (1981 - 1989) before being transferred to the Royal Maritime Auxiliary Service in 1989 and renamed RMAS *Arrochar*.

A383

Brigand	1937	Tug	1948 - 1960
Appleby	1965	Tender	1965 - 1999

A384

Crocodile	1940	Tug	1948 - Sold
Salventure	1942	Salvage Vsl	1948 - 1950

A385

Cautious	1940	Tug	1948 - 1964
Fort Grange	1976	Store Ship	1978 - 2000
Fort Rosalie	1976	Store Ship	2000 -

Fort Grange (A385) was renamed *Fort Rosalie* on 1 June 2000 to prevent confusion with the newly commissioned *Fort George* (A388).

A386

Saucy	1942	Tug	1948 - 1960
Fort Austin	1978	Store Ship	1979 -

A387

Girdle Ness	1945	Trials Ship	1948 - 1970
Fort Victoria	1990	AOR	1994 -

A388

Rockpigeon	1945	Tug	1948 - Sold
Fort George	1991	AOR	1993 - 2011

A389

Buckie Burn	1919	Tug	1948 - 1958
Clovelly	1972	Tender	1970 - 1994

Wave Knight	2000	Tanker	2003 -

A390

Samson	1953	Tug	1953 - 1977
Wave Ruler	2001	Tanker	2003 -

A391

Alligator	1940	Tug	1948 - 1958
(ex Charon)			
Criccieth	1970	Tender	1970 - 1992

A392

Glencoe	1971	Tender	1971 - 2000

A393

Empire Plane	1941	Tug	1948 - 1957
Dunster	1969	Tender	1969 - 2000

A394

Boxer	1942	LST	1948 - 1958
Fintry	1970	Tender	1970 - 1997

A395

Enfield	1945	Arm Carrier	1948 - 1969

A396

Empire Rita	1945	Tug	1948 - 1959
Frisky	1945	Tug	1959 - 1970
(ex Empire Rita)			

A397

Derby Haven	1944	Depot Ship	1948 - Sold
Empire Rosa	1945	Tug	1948 - 1970

A398

Marauder	1938	Tug	1948 - 1958

A399

Empire Zona	1945	Tug	1948 - 1958
Resolve	1945	Tug	1958 - 1973
(ex Empire Zona)			

In 1942 twenty-four RN trawlers were sent to the US East Coast and loaned/assigned to the US Navy to help in the battle against the U-Boats operating in US coastal waters. While they retained Royal Navy crews, the ships were assigned US visual call signs. These numbers comprised A401-A421. Three of the trawlers, *Northern Princess* (lost 7.3.42), *St Cathan* (lost 11.4.42) and *Senateur Duhamel* (lost 6.5.42) were not assigned numbers, possibly due to their early loss. Further RN vessels, including destroyers and corvettes which operated on convoy escort duties off the US coast, were also assigned numbers with A, D or P flag superiors. They were listed in the 1942 edition of DNC(4) Part 2. It is not known if these identities were actually applied to ship hulls.

A401

Arctic Explorer	1936	AS Trawler	1942 - ....

A402

Bedfordshire	1935	AS Trawler	1942 - 5.42
Grasmere	1970	Tender	1970 - ....

A403

Buttermere	1939	AS Trawler	1942 - ....

A404

Cape Warwick	1937	AS Trawler	1942 - ....
Bacchus	1962	Store Ship	1962 - 1981

A405

Coventry City	1937	AS Trawler	1942 - ....

A406

Hertfordshire	1936	AS Trawler	1942 - ....
Hebe	1962	Store Ship	1962 - 1978

A407

Kingston Ceylonite	1935	AS Trawler	1942 - 6.42

A408

Lady Elsa	1937	AS Trawler	1942 - ....

A409

Lady Rosemary	1937	AS Trawler	1942 - ....

A410

Le Tigre	1937	AS Trawler	1942 - ....

A411

Northern Chief	1936	AS Trawler	1942 - ....

A412

Northern Dawn	1936	AS Trawler	1942 - ....

A413

Northern Duke	1936	AS Trawler	1942 - ....

A414

Northern Isles	1936	AS Trawler	1942 - ....

A415

Norwich City	1937	AS Trawler	1942 - ....

A416

Pentland Firth	1934	AS Trawler	1942 - 9.42

A417

Stella Polaris	1936	AS Trawler	1942 - ....

A418

St Loman	1936	AS Trawler	1942 - ....

A419

St Zeno	1940	AS Trawler	1942 - ....

A420

Wastwater	1939	AS Trawler	1942 - ....

A421

Wellard	1937	AS Trawler	1942 - ....

A422			
Queen Wilhelmina RNLN	1942	Escort Ship	BPF 45/46
A423			
King Haakon VII RNoN	1942	Escort Ship	BPF 45/46
A424			
Jan van Brakel RNLN	1936	Minelayer	BPF 45/46
A425			
Van Kingbergen RNLN	1939	Sloop	BPF 45/46
A426			
Clarkia	1940	Corvette	1942 - ....
Bearn FR	1920	Ac Carrier	BPF 45/46
A427			
Athene	1940	Ac Transport	1942 - ....
Swan RAN	1936	Sloop	BPF 45/46
A428			
Engadine	1941	Depot Ship	11.42 - 7.43
Warrego RAN	1940	Sloop	BPF 45/46
A430			
Cap des Palmes FR	1935	AMC	BPF 45/46
A431			
La Grandiere FR	1939	Sloop	BPF 45/46
A432			
Chasseur 6 FR	1943	Sub Chaser	BPF 45/46
A433			
Chasseur 5 FR	1943	Sub Chaser	BPF 45/46
A434			
Dragueur 301 FR	1943	MS	BPF 45/46
A435			
Mameli IT	(....)	....	BPF 45/46
A452			
Slinger	1942	Esc Carrrier	BPF 45/46
A460			
Striker	1942	Esc Carrrier	BPF 45/46
A468			
Woodcock	1942	Sloop	BPF 45/46
A480			
Resource	1966	Arm Carrier	1967 - 1997
A482			
Kinloss	1945	Mooring Ship	1948 - 1989
A486			
Regent	1966	Arm Carrier	1977 - 1992
A488			
Cromarty	1970	Tender	1970 - 1994
A490			
Dornoch	1970	Tender	1970 - 1997
A492			
Ocean Salvor	1943	Salvage Vsl	1948 - 1958

A494			
Salvalour	1944	Salvage Vsl	1948 - 1955
A495			
RML 495	1942	RML	1949 - 1957
A496			
RML 496	1942	RML	1949 - 1959
A497			
Salveda	1943	Salvage Vsl	1943 - 1960
A498			
RML 498	1942	RML	1949 - 1955
A499			
Salvestor	1942	Salvage Vsl	1948 - 1970
A500			
Salvictor	1944	Salvage Vsl	1948 - 1966
A501			
Salvigil	1945	Salvage Vsl	1948 - 1962
A502			
Salviola	1945	Salvage Vsl	1948 - 1959
Rollicker	1971	Tug	1971 - 1997
A503			
Sea Salvor	1943	Salvage Vsl	1948 - 1971
A504			
Sparkler	1940	Tug	1948 - 1957
A505			
Succour	1943	Salvage Vsl	1948 - 1973
A506			
Swin	1944	Salvage Vsl	1948 - 1967
A507			
Uplifter	1943	Salvage Vsl	1948 - 1977
A508			
Capable	1945	Tug	1948 - 1972
A510			
Loyal Governor	1969	Tender	1969 - 1975
A512			
RML 512	1942	RML	1949 - 1958
A515			
RML 515	1942	RML	1949 - 1958
A529			
RML 529	1942	RML	1949 - 1957
A731			
Ruler	1943	Esc Carrrier	BPF 45/46
A771			
Yunnan RAN	1934	Arma	BPF 45/46
A772			
Bishopdale RAN	1937	Tanker	BPF 45/46
A773			
Brajara RAN	1934	Tanker	BPF 45/46
A774			
Kurumba RAN	1916	Tanker	BPF 45/46
A775			
Reserve RAN	1942	Tug	BPF 45/46

A776			
Sprightly RAN	1942	Tug	BPF 45/46
A1766			
Headcorn	1971	Tender	1971 - 2001
A1767			
Hever	1971	Tender	1971 - 2002
A1768			
Harlech	1972	Tender	1972 - 2001
A1769			
Hambledon	1972	Tender	1972 - 2001

A1770			
Loyal Chancellor	1971	Tender	1972 - 1998
A1771			
Loyal Proctor	1972	Tender	1972 - 1994
A1772			
Holmwood	1972	Tender	1972 - 1999
A1773			
Horning	1972	Tender	1972 - 2001
A2780			
Woodlark	1958	Survey Ship	1964 - 1985

Flag 'B' Superior

Pre 1940:   None

1940-48:   Air Rescue Boats (not listed); British Pacific Fleet (Battleships & Fleet Train)

1948:   Battleships and Monitors

B1			
Anson	1940	Battleship	BPF 45/46
B2			
Duke of York	1940	Battleship	BPF 45/46
B3			
Howe	1940	Battleship	BPF 45/46
B4			
King George V	1939	Battleship	BPF 45/46
B5			
Nelson	1925	Battleship	BPF 45/46
B6			
Queen Elizabeth	1913	Battleship	BPF 45/46
B7			
Renown	1916	Battlecruiser	BPF 45/46
B8			
Richelieu FR	1939	Battleship	BPF 45/46
B9			
Rodney	1925	Battleship	BPF 45/46
B01			
Malaya	1915	Battleship	1948 - 1948
B02			
Valiant	1914	Battleship	1948 - 1948
B06			
Revenge	1915	Battleship	1948 - 1948
B07			
Ramillies	1916	Battleship	1948 - 1948
B09			
Resolution	1915	Battleship	1948 - 1948
B10			
Queen Elizabeth	1913	Battleship	1948 - 1948
B16			
Fratton	1925	ABV	1940 - 1945
B17			
Duke of York	1940	Battleship	1948 - 1951
B23			
Vanguard	1944	Battleship	1948 - 1960
B28			
Nelson	1925	Battleship	1948 - 1948
B29			
Rodney	1925	Battleship	1948 - 1948
B32			
Howe	1940	Battleship	1948 - 1950
B41			
King George V	1939	Battleship	1948 - 1950

B50			
Caio Duilio IT	1913	Battleship	1948 - ....
B51			
Andrea Doria IT	1916	Battleship	1948 - ....
B61			
Jean Bart FR	1940	Battleship	1948 - ....
B62			
Richelieu FR	1939	Battleship	1948 - ....
B70			
Yavuz Turk	1911	Battleship	1948 - ....
B72			
Renown	1916	Battlecruiser	1948 - 1948
B79			
Anson	1940	Battleship	1948 - 1951
B98			
Abercrombie	1942	Monitor	1948 - 1954
B99			
Roberts	1941	Monitor	1948 - 1965
B201			
Lothian	1938	LSH	BPF 45/46
B206			
Empire Arquebus	1943	LSI(L)	BPF 45/46
B207			
Empire Battleaxe	1943	LSI(L)	BPF 45/46
B208			
Empire Mace	1943	LSI(L)	BPF 45/46
B209			
Empire Spearhead	1943	LSI(L)	BPF 45/46
B210			
Glen Earn	1938	LSI(L)	BPF 45/46
B211			
Lamont	1939	LSI(L)	BPF 45/46
B221			
Avon Vale	1940	Destroyer	BPF 45/46
B222			
Beaufort	1941	Destroyer	BPF 45/46
B223			
Bicester	1941	Destroyer	BPF 45/46
B224			
Melbreak	1942	Destroyer	BPF 45/46
B225			
Talybont	1943	Destroyer	BPF 45/46
B226			
Bleasdale	1941	Destroyer	BPF 45/46

Pendant	Name	Year	Type	Notes
B227	Brissenden	1942	Destroyer	BPF 45/46
B228	Cowdray	1941	Destroyer	BPF 45/46
B229	Easton	1942	Destroyer	BPF 45/46
B230	Stevenstone	1942	Destroyer	BPF 45/46
B231	Haydon	1942	Destroyer	BPF 45/46
B236	Ballarat RAN	1940	MSF	BPF 45/46
B237	Bendigo RAN	1940	MSF	BPF 45/46
B238	Burnie RAN	1940	MSF	BPF 45/46
B239	Cairns RAN	1941	MSF	BPF 45/46
B240	Cessnock RAN	1941	MSF	BPF 45/46
B241	Gawler RAN	1941	MSF	BPF 45/46
B242	Geraldton RAN	1941	MSF	BPF 45/46
B243	Goulburn RAN	1940	MSF	BPF 45/46
B244	Ipswich RAN	1941	MSF	BPF 45/46
B245	Kalgoorlie RAN	1941	MSF	BPF 45/46
B246	Launceston RAN	1941	MSF	BPF 45/46
B247	Lismore RAN	1940	MSF	BPF 45/46
B248	Maryborough RAN	1940	MSF	BPF 45/46
B249	Pirie RAN	1941	MSF	BPF 45/46
B250	Tamworth RAN	1942	MSF	BPF 45/46
B251	Toowoomba RAN	1941	MSF	BPF 45/46
B252	Whyalla RAN	1941	MSF	BPF 45/46
B253	Wollongong RAN	1941	MSF	BPF 45/46
B254	Courier	1943	MSF	BPF 45/46
B255	Felicity	1944	MSF	BPF 45/46
B256	Hare	1944	MSF	BPF 45/46
B257	Liberty	1944	MSF	BPF 45/46
B258	Michael	1944	MSF	BPF 45/46
B259	Minstrel	1944	MSF	BPF 45/46
B260	Wave	1944	MSF	BPF 45/46
B261	Welcome	1944	MSF	BPF 45/46
B262	Coquette	1943	MSF	BPF 45/46
B263	Mary Rose	1943	MSF	BPF 45/46
B264	Moon	1943	MSF	BPF 45/46
B265	Providence	1943	MSF	BPF 45/46
B266	Avon	1943	Frigate	BPF 45/46
B267	Barle	1942	Frigate	BPF 45/46
B268	Crane	1942	Sloop	BPF 45/46
B269	Derg	1943	Frigate	BPF 45/46
B270	Findhorn	1942	Frigate	BPF 45/46
B271	Helford	1943	Frigate	BPF 45/46
B272	Odzani	1943	Frigate	BPF 45/46
B273	Parrett	1943	Frigate	BPF 45/46
B274	Pheasant	1942	Sloop	BPF 45/46
B275	Plym	1943	Frigate	BPF 45/46
B276	Redpole	1943	Sloop	BPF 45/46
B277	Usk	1943	Frigate	BPF 45/46
B278	Whimbrel	1942	Sloop	BPF 45/46
B279	Woodcock	1942	Sloop	BPF 45/46
B280	Amethyst	1943	Sloop	BPF 45/46
B281	Arbutus	1944	Corvette	BPF 45/46
B282	Black Swan	1939	Sloop	BPF 45/46
B283	Enchantress	1934	Sloop	BPF 45/46
B284	Erne	1940	Sloop	BPF 45/46

B285			
Hart	1943	Sloop	BPF 45/46
B286			
Magpie	1943	Sloop	BPF 45/46
B287			
Mermaid	1943	Sloop	BPF 45/46
B288			
Hind	1943	Sloop	BPF 45/46
B289			
Aire	1943	Frigate	BPF 45/46
B290			
Widemouth Bay	1944	Frigate	BPF 45/46
B291			
Alacrity	1944	Sloop	BPF 45/46
B292			
Opossum	1944	Sloop	BPF 45/46
B293			
Peacock	1943	Sloop	BPF 45/46
B294			
Pelican	1938	Sloop	BPF 45/46
B295			
Starling	1942	Sloop	BPF 45/46
B296			
Helvig	1937	Base Ship	BPF 45/46
B297			
Stork	1936	Sloop	BPF 45/46
B301			
Artifex	1924	Repair Ship	BPF 45/46
B302			
Assistance	1944	Repair Ship	BPF 45/46
B303			
Diligence	1944	Repair Ship	BPF 45/46
B304			
Resource	1928	Repair Ship	BPF 45/46
B311			
Flamborough Head	1944	Repair Ship	BPF 45/46
B312			
Unicorn	1941	Maint Ship	BPF 45/46
B316			
Cuillin Sound	1944	Repair Ship	BPF 45/46
B317			
Deer Sound	1939	Repair Ship	BPF 45/46
B319			
Holm Sound	1944	Repair Ship	BPF 45/46
B326			
Beauly Firth	1944	Repair Ship	BPF 45/46
B327			
Moray Firth	1944	Repair Ship	BPF 45/46
B328			
Solway Firth	1944	Repair Ship	BPF 45/46
B332			
Empire Pitcairn	1944	Repair Ship	BPF 45/46
(See *Moray Firth* B327)			
B336			
Alaunia	1925	Repair Ship	BPF 45/46
B337			
Ranpura	1924	Repair Ship	BPF 45/46
B341			
Empire Penang	1944	Repair Ship	BPF 45/46
(See *Mullion Cove* B342)			
B342			
Mullion Cove	1944	Repair Ship	BPF 45/46
B343			
Dullisk Cove	1944	Repair Ship	BPF 45/46
B346			
Perseus	1944	Maint Ship	BPF 45/46
B347			
Pioneer	1944	Maint Ship	BPF 45/46
B351			
Portland Bill	1945	Repair Ship	BPF 45/46
B352			
Selsey Bill	1945	Repair Ship	BPF 45/46
B356			
Beachy Head	1944	Repair Ship	BPF 45/46
B357			
Berry Head	1944	Repair Ship	BPF 45/46
B358			
Rattray Head	1945	Repair Ship	BPF 45/46
B359			
Rame Head	1944	Repair Ship	BPF 45/46
B361			
Kelantan	1921	Depot Ship	BPF 45/46
B366			
Mull of Kintyre	1945	Repair Ship	BPF 45/46
B371			
Bonaventure	1942	Depot Ship	BPF 45/46
B376			
Adamant	1940	Depot Ship	BPF 45/46
B377			
Aorangi	1924	Depot Ship	BPF 45/46
B381			
Montclare	1921	Depot Ship	BPF 45/46
B382			
Tyne	1940	Depot Ship	BPF 45/46
B386			
Maidstone	1937	Depot Ship	BPF 45/46
B391			
Gryfevale	1929	Distilling Sp	BPF 45/46
B392			
Stag Pool	1930	Distilling Sp	BPF 45/46
B394			
Empire Clyde	1924	Hospital Ship	BPF 45/46
B395			
Gerusalemme	1919	Hospital Ship	BPF 45/46
B396			
Maunganui RNZN	1911	Hospital Ship	BPF 45/46
B397			
Ophir	1928	Hospital Ship	BPF 45/46
B398			
Oxfordshire	1912	Hospital Ship	BPF 45/46

B399			
Tjitjalengka	1938	Hospital Ship	BPF 45/46
B400			
Vasna	1917	Hospital Ship	BPF 45/46
B401			
City of Paris	1920	Accom Ship	BPF 45/46
B402			
Lancashire	1917	Accom Ship	BPF 45/46
B403			
Southern Prince	1940	Accom Ship	BPF 45/46
B406			
Menestheus	1929	Amenities Sp	BPF 45/46
B411			
Leonian	1936	Battlecruiser	BPF 45/46
B412			
Fernmoor	1936	Battlecruiser	BPF 45/46
B416			
Barbain	1940	BDV	BPF 45/46
B417			
Barnwell	1940	BDV	BPF 45/46
B418			
Barthorpe	1940	BDV	BPF 45/46
B419			
Bartizan	1943	BDV	BPF 45/46
B421			
Atlas	1909	Collier	BPF 45/46
B422			
Empire Wolfe	1941	Collier	BPF 45/46
B423			
Empire Boswell	1942	Collier	BPF 45/46
B424			
Edna	(....)	Collier	BPF 45/46
B426			
Springdale	1937	Repair Ship	BPF 45/46
B431			
Gurna	1919	Mine Iss Sp	BPF 45/46
B432			
Prome	1937	Mine Iss Sp	BPF 45/46
B433			
Empire Cheer	1943	Mine Iss Sp	BPF 45/46
B436			
Guardian	1932	Netlayer	BPF 45/46
B437			
Protector	1936	Netlayer	BPF 45/46
B441			
King Salvor	1942	Salvage Vsl	BPF 45/46
B442			
Salvestor	1942	Salvage Vsl	BPF 45/46
B443			
Salvictor	1944	Salvage Vsl	BPF 45/46
B446			
Advantage	1942	Tug	BPF 45/46
B447			
Aimwell	1942	Tug	BPF 45/46
B448			
Cheerly	1943	Tug	BPF 45/46
B449			
Destiny	1942	Tug	BPF 45/46
B450			
Eminent	1942	Tug	BPF 45/46
B451			
Empire Josephine	1944	Tug	BPF 45/46
B452			
Empire Sam	1942	Tug	BPF 45/46
B453			
Integrity	1942	Tug	BPF 45/46
B454			
Lariat	1942	Tug	BPF 45/46
B455			
St Giles	1919	Tug	BPF 45/46
B456			
Weasel	1943	Tug	BPF 45/46
B457			
Rockcliffe	1945	Tug	BPF 45/46
B458			
Rockglen	1945	Tug	BPF 45/46
B459			
Rockwing	1945	Tug	BPF 45/46
B460			
Rockforest	1945	Tug	BPF 45/46
B461			
Rockland	1945	Tug	BPF 45/46
B462			
Rockmount	1945	Tug	BPF 45/46
B463			
Rockpigeon	1945	Tug	BPF 45/46
B464			
Rockport	1945	Tug	BPF 45/46
B466			
HDML 1183 RNZN	1942	HDML	BPF 45/46
B467			
HDML 1184 RNZN	1942	HDML	BPF 45/46
B468			
HDML 1185 RNZN	1942	HDML	BPF 45/46
B469			
HDML 1186 RNZN	1942	HDML	BPF 45/46
B470			
HDML 1187 RNZN	1943	HDML	BPF 45/46
B471			
HDML 1188 RNZN	1943	HDML	BPF 45/46
B472			
HDML 1189 RNZN	1943	HDML	BPF 45/46
B473			
HDML 1190 RNZN	1943	HDML	BPF 45/46
B474			
HDML 1191 RNZN	1943	HDML	BPF 45/46
B475			
HDML 1192 RNZN	1943	HDML	BPF 45/46

B476			
HDML 1193 RNZN	1943	HDML	BPF 45/46
B477			
HDML 1194 RNZN	1943	HDML	BPF 45/46
B478			
HDML 1400	1944	HDML	BPF 45/46
B479			
HDML 1459	1944	HDML	BPF 45/46
B480			
HDML 1481	Canc	HDML	BPF 45/46
B481			
HDML 1482	Canc	HDML	BPF 45/46
B482			
HDML 1483	1944	HDML	BPF 45/46
B483			
HDML 1489	1944	HDML	BPF 45/46
B484			
HDML 1494	Canc	HDML	BPF 45/46
B496			
Lewes	1918	Target Ship	BPF 45/46
B501			
Carelia	1938	Tanker	BPF 45/46
B502			
Darst Creek	1943	Tanker	BPF 45/46
B503			
Empire Silver	1940	Tanker	BPF 45/46
B504			
Lomo Novio	1943	Tanker	BPF 45/46
B505			
Empire Crest	1944	Tanker	BPF 45/46
B506			
Aase Maersk	1930	Tanker	BPF 45/46
B507			
Arndale	1937	Tanker	BPF 45/46
B508			
Broomdale	1937	Tanker	BPF 45/46
B509			
Brown Ranger	1940	Tanker	BPF 45/46
B510			
Cedardale	1939	Tanker	BPF 45/46
B511			
Dingledale	1941	Tanker	BPF 45/46
B512			
Eaglesdale	1940	Tanker	BPF 45/46
B513			
Empire Herald	1945	Tanker	BPF 45/46
(ren *Wave Prince* 1946)			
B514			
Empire Neptune	1945	Tanker	BPF 45/46
B515			
Green Ranger	1941	Tanker	BPF 45/46
B516			
Olna	1944	Tanker	BPF 45/46
B517			
Rapidol	1917	Tanker	BPF 45/46
B518			
San Adolfo	1935	Tanker	BPF 45/46
B519			
San Amado	1934	Tanker	BPF 45/46
B520			
San Ambrosio	1935	Tanker	BPF 45/46
B521			
Serbol	1917	Tanker	BPF 45/46
B522			
Wave Regent	1945	Tanker	BPF 45/46
B523			
Wave Emperor	1944	Tanker	BPF 45/46
B524			
Wave Governor	1944	Tanker	BPF 45/46
B525			
Wave King	1944	Tanker	BPF 45/46
B526			
Wave Monarch	1944	Tanker	BPF 45/46
B527			
Golden Meadow	1943	Tender	BPF 45/46
B528			
Iere	1928	Tender	BPF 45/46
B529			
Seven Sisters	(....)	Tender	BPF 45/46
B530			
Echodale	1940	Tanker	BPF 45/46
B531			
Fort Colville	1943	Store Ship	BPF 45/46
B532			
Fort Langley	1944	Store Ship	BPF 45/46
B533			
Vacport	1939	Tanker	BPF 45/46
B536			
Corinda	1937	Store Ship	BPF 45/46
B537			
Darvel	1924	Store Ship	BPF 45/46
B538			
Gudrun Maersk	1936	Store Ship	BPF 45/46
B539			
Hermelin	1940	Store Ship	BPF 45/46
B540			
Heron	1937	Store Ship	BPF 45/46
B541			
Kheti	1927	Store Ship	BPF 45/46
B542			
Kistna	1923	Store Ship	BPF 45/46
B543			
Kola	1924	Store Ship	BPF 45/46
B544			
Pacheco	1927	Store Ship	BPF 45/46
B545			
Prince De Liege	1926	Store Ship	BPF 45/46
B546			
Prinses Maria Pia	1938	Store Ship	BPF 45/46

B547				
Robert Maersk	1937	Store Ship	BPF 45/46	
B548				
Thyra S	1936	Store Ship	BPF 45/46	
B556				
Bacchus	1936	Distilling Sp	BPF 45/46	
B557				
Bosphorus	1934	Store Ship	BPF 45/46	
B558				
City of Dieppe	1929	Store Ship	BPF 45/46	
B559				
Fort Rosalie	1944	Store Ship	BPF 45/46	
B560				
Fort Sandusky	1944	Store Ship	BPF 45/46	
B561				
Fort Wayne	1944	Store Ship	BPF 45/46	
B562				
Jaarstroom	1922	Store Ship	BPF 45/46	
B563				
Maruda	(....)	Store Ship	BPF 45/46	
B564				
San Andres	1921	Store Ship	BPF 45/46	
B565				
Slesvig	1938	Store Ship	BPF 45/46	
B566				
Talune	1929	Store Ship	BPF 45/46	
B576				
Denbighshire	1938	Store Ship	BPF 45/46	
B577				
Fort Alabama	1944	Stores Ship	BPF 45/46	
B578				
Fort Constantine	1944	Store Ship	BPF 45/46	
B579				
Fort Dunvegan	1944	Store Ship	BPF 45/46	
B580				
Fort Edmondton	1944	Store Ship	BPF 45/46	
B581				
Fort Kilmar	1944	Store Ship	BPF 45/46	
B582				
Fort Providence	1944	Store Ship	BPF 45/46	
B583				
Fort Wrangell	1944	Store Ship	BPF 45/46	
B584				
Glenartney	1939	Store Ship	BPF 45/46	
B585				
Buffalo Park	1944	Store Ship	BPF 45/46	
B586				
Fort Beauharnois	1944	Store Ship	BPF 45/46	
B587				
Fort Charlotte	1944	Store Ship	BPF 45/46	
B588				
Fort Duquesne	1944	Store Ship	BPF 45/46	
B595				
Bentley	1943	Frigate	BPF 45/46	
B596				
Bigbury Bay	1944	Frigate	BPF 45/46	
B597				
Braithwaite	1943	Frigate	BPF 45/46	
B598				
Buckingham RCN	1944	Frigate	BPF 45/46	
B599				
Cardigan Bay	1944	Frigate	BPF 45/46	
B600				
Carlplace RCN	1944	Frigate	BPF 45/46	
B601				
Carnarvon Bay	1945	Frigate	BPF 45/46	
B602				
Cygnet	1942	Frigate	BPF 45/46	
B603				
Fort Erie RCN	1944	Frigate	BPF 45/46	
B604				
Grou RCN	1943	Frigate	BPF 45/46	
B605				
Inch Arran RCN	1944	Frigate	BPF 45/46	
B606				
Modeste	1944	Sloop	BPF 45/46	
B607				
Montreal RCN	1943	Frigate	BPF 45/46	
B608				
Port Colborne RCN	1943	Frigate	BPF 45/46	
B609				
Poundmaker RCN	1944	Frigate	BPF 45/46	
B610				
Prestonian RCN	1944	Frigate	BPF 45/46	
B611				
Prince Robert RCN	1930	AA Vsl	BPF 45/46	
B612				
Start Bay	1945	Frigate	BPF 45/46	
B613				
St Austell Bay	1944	Frigate	BPF 45/46	
B614				
St Brides Bay	1945	Frigate	BPF 45/46	
B615				
St Pierre RCN	1943	Frigate	BPF 45/46	
B616				
Strathadam RCN	1944	Frigate	BPF 45/46	
B617				
Sussexvale RCN	1944	Frigate	BPF 45/46	
B618				
Swansea RCN	1942	Frigate	BPF 45/46	
B619				
Veryan Bay	1944	Frigate	BPF 45/46	
B620				
Victoriaville RCN	1944	Frigate	BPF 45/46	
B621				
Wentworth RCN	1943	Frigate	BPF 45/46	
B622				
Whitesand Bay	1944	Frigate	BPF 45/46	

Pendant	Name	Year	Type	Fleet
B623				
Antigonish RCN		1944	Frigate	BPF 45/46
B624				
Beacon Hill RCN		1943	Frigate	BPF 45/46
B625				
Bentinck		1943	Frigate	BPF 45/46
B626				
Cape Breton RCN		1942	Frigate	BPF 45/46
B627				
Cap de la Madeleine RCN		1944	Frigate	BPF 45/46
B628				
Capilano RCN		1944	Frigate	BPF 45/46
B629				
Charlottetown RCN		1941	Frigate	BPF 45/46
B630				
Cotton		1943	Frigate	BPF 45/46
B631				
Dunver RCN		1942	Frigate	BPF 45/46
B632				
Fitzroy		1943	Frigate	BPF 45/46
B633				
Flamingo		1939	Sloop	BPF 45/46
B634				
Kirkland Lake RCN		1944	Frigate	BPF 45/46
B635				
La Hulloise RCN		1943	Frigate	BPF 45/46
B636				
Levis RCN		1943	Frigate	BPF 45/46
B637				
New Waterford RCN		1943	Frigate	BPF 45/46
B638				
Orkney RCN		1943	Frigate	BPF 45/46
B639				
Outremont RCN		1943	Frigate	BPF 45/46
B640				
Prince Rupert RCN		1943	Frigate	BPF 45/46
B641				
Royal Mount RCN		1944	Frigate	BPF 45/46
B642				
Springhill RCN		1943	Frigate	BPF 45/46
B643				
St Catherines RCN		1942	Frigate	BPF 45/46
B644				
St John RCN		1943	Frigate	BPF 45/46
B645				
Stormont RCN		1943	Frigate	BPF 45/46
B646				
St Stephen RCN		1944	Frigate	BPF 45/46
B647				
Waskesin RCN		1942	Frigate	BPF 45/46
B648				
Wild Goose		1942	Sloop	BPF 45/46
B649				
Wren		1942	Sloop	BPF 45/46
B650				
Cauvery		1943	Sloop	BPF 45/46
B651				
Godavari		1940	Sloop	BPF 45/46
B652				
Hotham		1943	Frigate	BPF 45/46
B653				
Spragge		1943	Frigate	BPF 45/46
B701				
Bulan		1924	Cable Ship	BPF 45/46
B702				
St Margarets		1943	Cable Ship	BPF 45/46
B711				
Erin		1932	Store Ship	BPF 45/46
B712				
Eros		1936	Store Ship	BPF 45/46
B731				
Shillay		1944	Danlayer	BPF 45/46
B732				
Trodday		1945	Danlayer	BPF 45/46
B741				
Enticer		1944	Tug	BPF 45/46
B742				
Envoy		1944	Tug	BPF 45/46
B743				
Growler		1942	Tug	BPF 45/46
B744				
Mediator		1944	Tug	BPF 45/46
B745				
Reward		1944	Tug	BPF 45/46
B746				
Samson		1942	Tug	BPF 45/46
B801				
Rowena		1944	MSF	BPF 45/46
B802				
Seabear		1943	MSF	BPF 45/46
B803				
Thisbe		1943	MSF	BPF 45/46

Flag 'C' Superior

Pre 1940:   Coast Guard/Fishery Protection Vessels, Torpedo Gunboat, USN ships operating with RN
1940-48:   British Pacific Fleet
1948:   Cruisers

C1
Achilles   1932   Cruiser   BPF 45/46
C2
Leander RNZN   1931   Cruiser   BPF 45/46
C3
Hobart RAN   1934   Cruiser   BPF 45/46
C4
Bushnell USN   1915   Depot Ship   6.18 - ....
C11
Liverpool   1937   Cruiser   1948 - 1958
C12
Aurora   1936   Cruiser   1948 - Sold
C14
Kenya   1939   Cruiser   1948 - 1962
C19
Birmingham   1936   Cruiser   1948 - 1960
C20
Tiger   1945   Cruiser   1948 - 1986
C21
Glasgow   1936   Cruiser   1948 - 1958
C24
Sheffield   1936   Cruiser   1948 - 1967
C25
Superb   1943   Cruiser   1948 - 1957
C26
Arethusa   1934   Cruiser   1948 - 1949

C30
Ceylon   1942   Cruiser   1948 - 1959
Australia RAN   1927   Cruiser   BPF 45/46

C33
Cleopatra   1940   Cruiser   1948 - 1958

C34
Lion   1944   Cruiser   1948 - 1975
Shropshire RAN   1928   Cruiser   BPF 45/46

C35
Belfast   1938   Cruiser   1948 - 1971
C37
Dido   1939   Cruiser   1948 - 1958

C39
Devonshire   1927   Cruiser   1948 - 1954

Tromp RNLN   1937   Cruiser   BPF 45/46
C42
Euryalus   1939   Cruiser   1948 - 1959
C43
Phoebe   1939   Cruiser   1948 - 1956

C44
Jamaica   1940   Cruiser   1948 - 1960
Adelaide RAN   1918   Cruiser   BPF 45/46

C48
Gambia   1940   Cruiser   1948 - 1968
C52
Bermuda   1941   Cruiser   1948 - 1965
C53
Ontario RCN   1943   Cruiser   1948 - 1949
C55
Suffolk   1926   Cruiser   1948 - ....
C57
Cumberland   1926   Cruiser   1948 - 1959

C59
Newfoundland   1941   Cruiser   1948 - 1959
J. v. Heemskerk RNLN 1939   Cruiser   BPF 45/46

C60
Nigeria   1939   Cruiser   1948 - 1957

C61
Argonaut   1941   Cruiser   1948 - 1955
Westralia RAN   1929   AMC   BPF 45/46

C63
Bellona   1942   Cruiser   1948 - 1956
C69
London   1927   Cruiser   1948 - 1950
C70
Achilles   1932   Cruiser   1948 - ....
C73
Shropshire   1928   Cruiser   1948 - ....

C74
Delhi RIN   1932   Cruiser   1948 - 1978
  (ex Achilles)

30

C75

Argus	1904	Cg/FPV	9.15 - 1.17
Argon (ex *Argus*)	1904	Cg/FPV	1.17 - ....
Leander	1931	Cruiser	1948 - 1949

C76

Thrush	1889	Cg/FPV	9.15 - 3.16
Halcyon	1894	Torpedo Gb	1.18 - 11.19
Kanimbla RAN	1935	LSI(L)	BPF 45/46
Newcastle	1936	Cruiser	1948 - 1959

C77

Watchful	1911	Cg/FPV	9.15 - 1.18
Julia	1897	Cg/FPV	1.18 - ....
Manoora RAN	1934	AMC	BPF 45/46

C78

Safeguard	1914	Cg/FPV	9.15 - 1.18
Ringdove	1889	Cg/FPV	1.18 - ....
Norfolk	1928	Cruiser	1948 - 1950

C80

Julia	1897	Cg/FPV	9.15 - 1.18
Safeguard	1914	Cg/FPV	1.18 - 9.18
Mauritius	1939	Cruiser	1948 - 1965

C81

Squirrel	1904	Cg/FPV	9.15 - 1.18
Seagull	1889	Torpedo Gb	1.18 - 9.18
Safeguard	1914	Cg/FPV	9.18 - ....
Black Prince RNZN	1942	Cruiser	1948 - 1966

C82

Halcyon	1894	Torpedo Gb	9.15 - 1.18
Spanker	1889	Torpedo Gb	1.18 - 9.18
Seagull	1889	Torpedo Gb	9.18 - ....
Sirius	1940	Cruiser	1948 - 1956

C83

Squirrel	1904	Cg/FPV	1.18 - 9.18
Spanker	1889	Torpedo Gb	9.18 - ....
Southampton	1936	Cruiser	Sunk 1941

C84

Ringdove	1889	Cg/FPV	9.15 - 12.15
Watchful	1911	Cg/FPV	1.18 - 9.18
Diadem	1942	Cruiser	1948 - 1956

C85

Seagull	1889	Torpedo Gb	9.15 - 1.18
Squirrel	1904	Cg/FPV	9.18 - ....

C86

Spanker	1889	Torpedo Gb	9.15 - 1.18
Watchful	1911	Cg/FPV	9.18 - ....

C89

Royalist	1942	Cruiser	1948 - 1956

C96

Sussex	1928	Cruiser	1948 - 1950

C98

Scylla	1940	Cruiser	1948 - 1950

C99

Blake	1945	Cruiser	1948 - 1979

C161

Argonaut	1941	Cruiser	BPF 45/46

C162

Belfast	1938	Cruiser	BPF 45/46

C163

Bermuda	1941	Cruiser	BPF 45/46

C164

Black Prince RNZN	1942	Cruiser	BPF 45/46

C165

Ceylon	1942	Cruiser	BPF 45/46

C166

Cleopatra	1940	Cruiser	BPF 45/46

C167

Euryalus	1939	Cruiser	BPF 45/46

C168

Gambia	1940	Cruiser	BPF 45/46

C169

Glasgow	1936	Cruiser	BPF 45/46

C170

Jamaica	1940	Cruiser	BPF 45/46

C171

Liverpool	1937	Cruiser	BPF 45/46

C172

Newfoundland	1941	Cruiser	BPF 45/46

C173

Phoebe	1939	Cruiser	BPF 45/46

C174

Sussex	1928	Cruiser	BPF 45/46

C175

Uganda	1941	Cruiser	BPF 45/46

C176

Royalist	1942	Cruiser	BPF 45/46

C177

Cumberland	1926	Cruiser	BPF 45/46

C178

London	1927	Cruiser	BPF 45/46

C179

Newcastle	1936	Cruiser	BPF 45/46

C180

Nigeria	1939	Cruiser	BPF 45/46

C181

Suffolk	1926	Cruiser	BPF 45/46

C182

Swiftsure	1943	Cruiser	BPF 45/46

C183

Mauritius	1939	Cruiser	BPF 45/46

C184

Ontario HMCS	1943	Cruiser	BPF 45/46

C185

Superb	1943	Cruiser	BPF 45/46

C186

Devonshire	1927	Cruiser	BPF 45/46

Flag 'D' Superior

Pre 1940:   Cruisers, Destroyers, Torpedo Gunboats (Pendant A inferior used to increase destroyer numbers)

1940-48:   Cruisers; Aircraft Carriers; Escort Carriers; Large Aircraft Transports; Transports for Crashed Aircraft; Special Service Vessels; Aux AA Ships; British Pacific Fleet Destroyers

1948:   Destroyers

D4

Stuart RAN	1918	Destroyer	BPF 45/46

D5

Arunta RAN	1940	Destroyer	BPF 45/46

D6

Vendetta RAN	1917	Destroyer	BPF 45/46

D7

Van Galen RNLN	1941	Destroyer	BPF 45/46

D8

Tjerk Hiddes RNLN	1941	Destroyer	BPF 45/46

D9

Bataan RAN	1944	Destroyer	BPF 45/46

D00

Afridi	1907	Destroyer	9.15 - 12.19
Princess Margaret	1914	Minelayer	9.18 - 11.19
Stuart RAN	1918	Destroyer	1.22 - 1940
Paris FR	1912	Battleship	1940 - 1945

D01

Arab	1901	Destroyer	12.14 - 9.15
Amazon	1908	Destroyer	9.15 - 1.18
Albacore	1906	Destroyer	1.18 - 8.19
Angora	1911	Minelayer	9.18 - 11.19
Montrose	1918	Destroyer	1922 - 1940
Ameer	1942	Esc Carrrier	1942 - 1946
Caprice	1943	Destroyer	1948 - 1973

D02

Avon	1896	Destroyer	12.14 - 9.15
Cossack	1907	Destroyer	9.15 - 1.18
Albatross	1898	Destroyer	1.18 - 9.18
Wahine	1913	Minelayer	9.18 - 11.19
Senator	1918	Destroyer	1922- 1936
Inglefield	1936	Destroyer	1936 - 4.40
Attacker	1941	Esc Carrrier	1941 - 1946
Zest	1943	Destroyer	1948 - 1954
Devonshire	1960	Destroyer	1960 - 1978

D03

Bittern	1897	Destroyer	12.14 - 9.15
Crusader	1909	Destroyer	9.15 - 1.18
Amazon	1908	Destroyer	1.18 - 9.18
Amphitrite	1898	Cruiser	9.18 - 11.19

Sepoy	1918	Destroyer	1923 - 1932
Icarus	1936	Destroyer	1936 - 4.40
Ranee	1943	Esc Carrrier	1943 - 1946
Concord	1945	Destroyer	1948 - 1962

D04

Ghurka	1907	Destroyer	9.15 - 1.18
Angler	1897	Destroyer	1.18 - 5.20
Majestic	1895	Battleship	12.14 - 5.15
Euryalus	1901	Cruiser	9.18 - 11.19
Seraph	1918	Destroyer	1923 - 1934
Onslaught	1941	Destroyer	1944 - 1950
Savoia IT	1935	Cruiser	BR619(2)
Voyager RAN	1952	Destroyer	1952 - 1969

D05

Earnest	1896	Destroyer	12.14 - 9.15
Mohawk	1907	Destroyer	9.15 - 1.18
Arab	1901	Destroyer	1.18 - 4.18
Zulu	1909	Destroyer	1.18 - 9.18
London	1899	Battleship	9.18 - 11.19
Shark	1912	Destroyer	10.21 - 1.25
Nairana	1943	Esc Carrrier	1943 - 1946
Daring	1949	Destroyer	1948 - 1971

D06

Forth	1886	Depot Ship	12.14 - 4.15
Nubian	1909	Destroyer	9.15 - 10.16
Arno	1914	Destroyer	1.18 - 3.18
Oriole	1916	Destroyer	3.18 - 9.18
Perdita	1910	Minelayer	9.18 - 11.19
Sikh	1918	Destroyer	10.21 - 1.25
Keith	1930	Destroyer	1.25 - 4.40
Myngs	1943	Destroyer	1948 - 1954
Africa	Canc	Ac Carrier	Canc 1945
Hampshire	1961	Destroyer	1961 - 1976

D07

Onyx	1892	Depot Ship	12.14- 4.15
Saracen	1908	Destroyer	9.15 - 1.18
Arun	1903	Destroyer	1.18 - 9.18
Anzac	1917	Destroyer	9.19 - 12.20
Somme	1918	Destroyer	10.21 - ....
Patroller	1943	Esc Carrrier	1943 - 1946

Caesar	1944	Destroyer	1948 - 1965

D08

Pactolus	1896	Depot Ship	12.14 - 4.15
Tartar	1907	Destroyer	9.15 - 1.18
Avon	1896	Destroyer	1.18 - 9.18
Success	1918	Destroyer	9.19 - 12.20
Sparrowhawk	1918	Destroyer	1.22 - ....
Albion	1945	Ac Carrier	1945 - 1948
Vendetta RAN	1954	Destroyer	1954 - 1969

D09

Violet	1897	Destroyer	12.14 - 9.15
Viking	1909	Destroyer	9.15 - 1.18
Bat	1896	Destroyer	1.18 - 9.18
Douglas	1918	Destroyer	9.18 - 11.18
Seymour	1916	Destroyer	11.18 - 1.19
Tattoo	1918	Destroyer	1.19 - 4.19
Spear	1918	Destroyer	10.21 - ....
Imperial	1936	Destroyer	1936 - 4.40
Trumpeter	1942	Esc Carrrier	1942 - 1946
Dunkirk	1945	Destroyer	1948 - 1964

D10

Adventure	1904	Cruiser	12.14 - 4.15
Zulu	1909	Destroyer	9.15 - 11.16
Bittern	1897	Destroyer	1.18 - 4.18
Broke	1914	Destroyer	9.18 - 1.19
Swordsman	1918	Destroyer	11.19 - 12.20
Speedy	1918	Destroyer	1.22 - ....
Tourmaline	1919	Destroyer	1925 - ....
Intrepid	1936	Destroyer	1936 - 4.40
Audacity	1939	Esc Carrrier	1941 - 12.41
Rajah	1943	Esc Carrrier	1943 - 1946
Warramunga RAN	1942	Destroyer	BPF 45/46
Cassandra	1943	Destroyer	1948 - 1965

D11

Arun	1903	Destroyer	9.15 - 1.18
Bonetta	1907	Destroyer	1.18 - 6.20
Stalwart	1918	Destroyer	9.19 - 12.20
Splendid	1918	Destroyer	10.21 - ....
Impulsive	1937	Destroyer	1937 - 4.40
Courbet FR	1911	Battleship	1940 - 1944
Grenville	1942	Destroyer	BPF 45/46
Quadrant RAN	1942	Destroyer	1948 - 1954
Vampire RAN	1956	Destroyer	1959 - 1969

D12

Opossum	1895	Destroyer	12.14 - 9.15
Boyne	1904	Destroyer	9.15 - 9.18
Milne	1914	Destroyer	9.18 - 9.19
Tasmania	1918	Destroyer	9.19 - 12.20
Sportive	1918	Destroyer	10.21 - ....
Striker	1942	Esc Carrrier	1942 - 1946

Kempenfelt	1943	Destroyer	BPF 45/46
Saumarez	1942	Destroyer	1948 - ....
Kent	1961	Destroyer	1961 - 1997

D13

Magnificent	1894	Battleship	12.14 - 4.15
Cherwell	1903	Destroyer	9.15 - 1.18
Napier RAN	1940	Destroyer	BPF 45/46

D14

Dee	1903	Destroyer	9.15 - 1.18
Brazen	1896	Destroyer	1.18 - 11.19
Swallow	1918	Destroyer	10.21 - ....
Avenger	1940	Esc Carrrier	1940 - 11.42
Nepal	1941	Destroyer	BPF 45/46
Arrogant	Canc	Ac Carrier	Canc 1945
Armada	1943	Destroyer	1948 - 1960

D15

Bonetta	1907	Destroyer	12.14 - 9.15
Derwent	1903	Destroyer	9.15 - 5.17
Brilliant	1891	Cruiser	12.17 - 1.18
Bullfinch	1898	Destroyer	1.18 - 4.18
Swordfish	1916	Patrol Vessel	6.18 - 9.18
Torch	1918	Destroyer	10.21 - ....
Nizam RAN	1940	Destroyer	BPF 45/46
Vindex	1943	Esc Carrrier	1943 - 1948
Cavendish	1944	Destroyer	1948 - 1966

D16

Doon	1903	Destroyer	9.15 - 1.18
Boxer	1894	Destroyer	1.18 - 2.18
Faulknor	1914	Destroyer	9.18 - 5.20
Tribune	1918	Destroyer	1.22 - ....
Skate	1917	Destroyer	1931 - 1937
Ivanhoe	1937	Destroyer	1937 - 4.40
Norman RAN	1940	Destroyer	BPF 45/46
Venture RCN	1925	Depot Ship	1943 - 1946
Crescent	1944	Destroyer	To Canada
London	1961	Destroyer	1961 - 1981

Crescent was transferred to Canada on completion in 1945 prior to D16 being assigned (1948) and the number was, therefore, never applied.

D17

Bullfinch	1898	Destroyer	12.14 - 9.15
Eden	1903	Destroyer	9.15 - 6.16
Cherwell	1903	Destroyer	1.18 - 9.18
Trinidad	1918	Destroyer	1.22 - ....
Stuart Prince	1940	LSF	1940 - ....
Quadrant RAN	1942	Destroyer	BPF 45/46
Alamein	1945	Destroyer	1948 - 1964

D18

Diana	1895	Cruiser	12.14 - 4.15
Ettrick	1903	Destroyer	9.15 - 1.18
Conflict	1894	Destroyer	1.18 - 9.18
Marksman	1915	Destroyer	1.19 - 11.19
Tumult	1918	Destroyer	10.21 - 1.25
Kempenfelt	1931	Destroyer	1.25 - 10.39
Assiniboine RCN (ex *Kempenfelt*)	1931	Destroyer	10.39 - 4.40
Battler	1942	Esc Carrrier	1942 - 1946
Quality RAN	1942	Destroyer	BPF 45/46
St Kitts	1944	Destroyer	1948 - 1962
Antrim	1967	Destroyer	1967 - 1984

D19

Charm	1902	Tug	2.15 - 4.15
Exe	1903	Destroyer	9.15 - 1.18
Cossack	1907	Destroyer	1.18 - 9.18
Ithuriel	1916	Destroyer	9.18 - 11.19
Malcolm	1919	Destroyer	11.19 - 1940
Queenborough RAN	1942	Destroyer	BPF 45/46
Zephyr	1943	Destroyer	1948 - 1953
Queen	1943	Esc Carrrier	1943 - 1946
Glamorgan	1964	Destroyer	1964 - 1986

D20

Foyle	1903	Destroyer	9.15 - 3.17
Zubian	1917	Destroyer	8.17 - 1.18
Crane	1896	Destroyer	1.18 - 6.18
Manly	1914	Destroyer	9.18 - 1.19
Wallace	1918	Destroyer	1.19 - 1938
Quiberon RAN	1942	Destroyer	BPF 45/46
Jacob van Heemskerk RNLN	1939	Cruiser	1940 - 1946
Comus	1945	Destroyer	1948 - 1958
Fife	1964	Destroyer	1964 - 1987

D21

Joanetta	1911	Tug	4.15 - 9.15
Garry	1905	Destroyer	9.15 - 1.18
Crusader	1909	Destroyer	1.18 - 9.18
Wryneck	1918	Destroyer	1.19 - 1939
Quickmatch RAN	1941	Destroyer	BPF 45/46
Shah	1943	Esc Carrrier	1943 - 1945
Chivalrous	1945	Destroyer	1948 - 1954
Norfolk	1967	Destroyer	1967 - 1981

D22

Highflyer	1898	Cruiser	12.14 - 4.15
Itchen	1903	Destroyer	9.15 - 1.18
Cygnet	1898	Destroyer	1.18 - 1.19
Waterhen	1918	Destroyer	1.19 - 1940
Albatross RAN	1928	Seaplane Car	1940 - 1946
Quilliam RAN	1941	Destroyer	BPF 45/46
Aisne	1945	Destroyer	1948 - 1968

D23

Sylvia	1897	Destroyer	12.14 - 9.15
Kale	1904	Destroyer	9.15 - 1.18
Cynthia	1898	Destroyer	1.18 - 1.19
Walker	1917	Destroyer	1.19 - 11.19
Vimiera	1917	Destroyer	1.25 - 1940
Premier	1943	Esc Carrrier	1943 - 1946
Ulster	1942	Destroyer	BPF 45/46
Teazer	1943	Destroyer	1948 - 1954
Bristol	1969	Destroyer	1969 -

D24

Success	1901	Destroyer	12.14 - 12.14
Liffey	1904	Destroyer	9.15 - 1.18
Dee	1903	Destroyer	1.18 - 9.18
Miranda	1914	Destroyer	9.18 - 1.19
Walrus	1917	Destroyer	1.19 - 1938
Tracker	1942	Esc Carrrier	1942 - 1945
Ulysses	1943	Destroyer	BPF 45/46
Gravelines	1944	Destroyer	1948 - 1961

D25

Antelope	1893	Torpedo Gb	12.14 - 4.15
Moy	1904	Destroyer	9.15 - 1.18
Nymphe	1911	Destroyer	1.18 - 6.18
Whirlwind	1917	Destroyer	9.18 - 11.18
Warwick	1917	Destroyer	1.19 - 1940
Athene	1940	Ac Transport	1940 - 1945
Undaunted	1943	Destroyer	BPF 45/46
Carysfort	1944	Destroyer	1948 - 1969

D26

Mallard	1896	Destroyer	12.14 - 9.15
Ness	1905	Destroyer	9.15 - 1.18
Desperate	1896	Destroyer	1.18 - 1.19
Watchman	1917	Destroyer	1.19 - 1940
Slinger	1942	Esc Carrrier	1942 - 1946
Undine	1943	Destroyer	BPF 45/46
Comet	1944	Destroyer	1948 - 1961

D27

Caesar	1896	Battleship	12.14 - 4.15
Nith	1905	Destroyer	1.16 - 1.18
Doon	1903	Destroyer	1.18 - 9.18
Moorsom	1914	Destroyer	9.18 - 1.19
Whirlwind	1917	Destroyer	1.19 - 11.19
Viceroy	1917	Destroyer	11.19 -1921
Walker	1917	Destroyer	1.21 - 1940
Charger	1941	Esc Carrrier	Canc 1941
Urania	1943	Destroyer	BPF 45/46
Savage	1942	Destroyer	1948 -1962

D28

Monmouth	1901	Cruiser	12.14 - 4.15
Ouse	1905	Destroyer	9.15 - 1.18

Dove	1898	Destroyer	1.18 - 1.19
Vanity	1916	Destroyer	1.19 - 1940
Tromp RNLN	1937	Destroyer	1940 - 1946
Urchin	1943	Destroyer	BPF 45/46
Verulam	1943	Destroyer	1948 -1951

D29

Locust	1896	Destroyer	12.14 - 9.15
Rother	1904	Destroyer	9.15 - 1.18
Earnest	1896	Destroyer	1.18 - 1.19
Vanessa	1918	Destroyer	1.19 - 1940
Perth	1934	Cruiser	1940 - 3.42
Ursa	1943	Destroyer	BPF 45/46
Audacious	1946	Ac Carrier	1946
Eagle (ex-*Audacious*)	1946	Ac Carrier	1946 - 1948
Charity	1944	Destroyer	1948 - 1958

D30

Stour	1905	Destroyer	9.15 - 1.18
Orcadia	1916	Destroyer	1.18 - 1.19
Valorous	1917	Destroyer	1.19 - 11.19
Woolston	1918	Destroyer	11.19 - 12.20
Whirlwind	1917	Destroyer	12.20 - 1940
Despatch	1919	Cruiser	1940 - 1945
Wager	1943	Destroyer	BPF 45/46
Carron	1944	Destroyer	1948 - 1967

D31

Cornwall	1902	Cruiser	2.15 - 4.15
Swale	1905	Destroyer	9.15 - 1.18
Electra	1896	Destroyer	1.18 - 1.19
Voyager	1918	Destroyer	1.19 - 1940
Arbiter	1943	Esc Carrrier	1943 - 1946
Wakeful	1943	Destroyer	BPF 45/46
Broadsword	1946	Destroyer	1948 - 1968

D32

Albatross	1898	Destroyer	12.14 - 9.15
Test	1905	Destroyer	9.15 - 1.18
Ettrick	1903	Destroyer	1.18 - 1.19
Vivien	1918	Destroyer	1.19 - 11.19
Viscount	1917	Destroyer	11.19 - 12.20
Versatile	1917	Destroyer	1.21 - 1940
Chaser	1942	Esc Carrrier	1942 - 1946
Wessex	1943	Destroyer	BPF 45/46
Camperdown	1944	Destroyer	1948 - 1970
Daring	2006	Destroyer	2006 -

D33

Challenger	1902	Cruiser	12.14 - 4.15
Teviot	1903	Destroyer	9.15 - 1.18
Exe	1903	Destroyer	1.18 - 9.18
Murray	1914	Destroyer	9.18 - 1.19
Vancouver	1917	Destroyer	1.19 - 4.28

Vimy (ex *Vancouver*)	1917	Destroyer	4.28 - 1940
Canberra RAN	1927	Cruiser	1940 - 8.42
Whelp	1943	Destroyer	BPF 45/46
Terpsichore	1943	Destroyer	1948 -1954
Dauntless	2007	Destroyer	2007 -

D34

Dove	1898	Destroyer	12.14 - 9.15
Ure	1904	Destroyer	9.15 - 1.18
Express	1897	Destroyer	1.18 - 1.19
Velox	1917	Destroyer	1.19 - 1940
Whirlwind	1943	Destroyer	BPF 45/46
Bulwark	1945	Ac Carrier	1945 - 1948
Cockade	1944	Destroyer	1948 - 1964
Diamond	2007	Destroyer	2007 -

D35

Waveney	1903	Destroyer	9.15 - 1.18
Fairy	1897	Destroyer	1.18 - 9.18
Morris	1914	Destroyer	9.18 - 1.19
Versatile	1917	Destroyer	1.19 - 11.19
Wolsey	1918	Destroyer	11.19 - 12.20
Wrestler	1918	Destroyer	12.20 - ....
Pegasus	1917	Seaplane Car	1940 - 1948
Wizard	1943	Destroyer	BPF 45/46
Diamond	1950	Destroyer	1952 - 1981
Dragon	2008	Destroyer	2008 -

D36

Hannibal	1896	Battleship	12.14 - 4.15
Angler	1897	Destroyer	9.15 - 1.18
Falcon	1899	Destroyer	1.18 - 9.18
Termagant	1915	Destroyer	9.18 - 9.19
Vivacious	1917	Destroyer	11.19 - 1940
Vindictive	1918	Cruiser	1940 - 1945
Wrangler	1943	Destroyer	BPF 45/46
Chieftain	1945	Destroyer	1948 - 1961
Defender	2009	Destroyer	2009 -

D37

Cumberland	1902	Cruiser	12.14 - 4.15
Coquette	1897	Destroyer	9.15 - 1.18
Fame	1896	Destroyer	1.18 - 9.18
Mansfield	1914	Destroyer	9.18 - 9.19
Vortigern	1917	Destroyer	11.19 - 1940
Dasher	1941	Esc Carrrier	1941- 3.43
Racehorse	1942	Destroyer	BPF 45/46
Tobruk RAN	1947	Destroyer	1950 - 1969
Duncan	2010	Destroyer	2013 -

D38

Foresight	1904	Cruiser	12.14 - 4.15
Cygnet	1898	Destroyer	9.15 - 1.18
Fawn	1897	Destroyer	1.18 - 9.18
Trident	1915	Destroyer	9.18 - 5.21

Ambuscade	1926	Destroyer	8.25 - 4.40	*Albatross*	1898	Destroyer	9.15 - 1.18
Begum	1942	Esc Carrrier	1942 - 1946	*Greyhound*	1900	Destroyer	1.18 - 9.18
Raider	1942	Destroyer	BPF 45/46	*Senator*	1918	Destroyer	9.18 - 1.19
Nizam	1940	Destroyer	1948 -	*Wolfhound*	1918	Destroyer	11.19 - 1.21
				Valhalla	1917	Destroyer	1.21 - 1931
D39				*Imogen*	1936	Destroyer	1936 - 4.40
Griffon	1896	Destroyer	12.14 - 9.15	*Danae*	1918	Cruiser	1940 - 1944
Cynthia	1898	Destroyer	9.15 - 1.18	*Conrad* ORP	1918	Cruiser	1944 - 1946
Fervent	1895	Destroyer	1.18 - 9.18	(ex *Danae*)			
Amazon	1926	Destroyer	8.25 - 4.40	*Rotherham*	1942	Destroyer	BPF 45/46
Rapid	1942	Destroyer	BPF 45/46	*Lagos*	1944	Destroyer	1948 - 1960
Centaur	1945	Ac Carrier	1945 - 1948				
Zealous	1944	Destroyer	1948 -1955	**D45**			
				Hearty	1885	Survey	12.14 - 9.15
D40				*Avon*	1896	Destroyer	9.15 - 1.18
Illustrious	1896	Battleship	12.14 - 4.15	*Griffon*	1896	Destroyer	1.18 - 1.19
Desperate	1896	Destroyer	9.15 - 1.18	*Westminster*	1918	Destroyer	1.19 - 1939
Flying Fish	1897	Destroyer	1.18 - 9.18	*Dauntless*	1918	Cruiser	1940 - 1945
Velox	1917	Destroyer	9.18 - 11.18	*Teazer*	1943	Destroyer	BPF 45/46
Spenser	1917	Destroyer	1.19 - 1936	*Tenacious*	1943	Destroyer	1948 - 1951
Redoubt	1942	Destroyer	BPF 45/46				
Searcher	1942	Esc Carrrier	1942 - 1945	**D46**			
Troubridge	1942	Destroyer	1948 - 1955	*Prince George*	1895	Battleship	12.14 - 4.15
				Bat	1896	Destroyer	9.15 - 1.18
D41				*Oracle*	1915	Destroyer	1.18 - 1.19
Leander	1882	Depot Ship	12.14 - 4.15	*Winchelsea*	1917	Destroyer	1.19 - 1940
Fame	1896	Destroyer	9.15 - 1.18	*Dragon*	1917	Cruiser	1940 - 7.44
Garry	1905	Destroyer	1.18 - 9.18	*Tenacious*	1943	Destroyer	BPF 45/46
Myngs	1914	Destroyer	9.18 - 1.19				
Walpole	1918	Destroyer	1.19 - 1940	**D47**			
Curacao	1917	Cruiser	1940 - 10.42	*Sunfish*	1895	Destroyer	12.14 - 9.15
Relentless	1942	Destroyer	BPF 45/46	*Brazen*	1896	Destroyer	9.15 - 1.18
Volage	1943	Destroyer	1948 - 1952	*Kale*	1904	Destroyer	1.18 - 6.18
				Matchless	1914	Destroyer	9.18 - 1.19
D42				*Westcott*	1918	Destroyer	1.19 - 1940
Mars	1896	Battleship	12.14 - 4.15	*Adelaide* RAN	1928	Cruiser	1940 - 1946
Mallard	1896	Destroyer	9.15 - 1.18	*Termagant*	1943	Destroyer	BPF 45/46
Pasley	1916	Destroyer	1.18 - 1.19	*Gabbard*	1945	Destroyer	1948 - 1953
Windsor	1918	Destroyer	1.19 - 1940				
Curlew	1917	Cruiser	1940 - 5.40	**D48**			
Empress	1942	Esc Carrrier	1942 - 1946	*Victorious*	1895	Battleship	12.14 - 4.15
Rocket	1942	Destroyer	BPF 45/46	*Bullfinch*	1898	Destroyer	9.15 - 1.18
				Kangaroo	1900	Destroyer	1.18 - 1.19
D43				*Vidette*	1918	Destroyer	1.19 - 1940
Vigilant	1900	Destroyer	12.14 - 9.15	*Sydney* RAN	1934	Cruiser	1940 - 11.41
Stag	1899	Destroyer	9.15 - 1.18	*Campania*	1943	Esc Carrrier	1943 - 1948
Gipsy	1897	Destroyer	1.18 - 1.19	*Terpsichore*	1943	Destroyer	BPF 45/46
Wessex	1918	Destroyer	1.19 - 1940	*Contest*	1944	Destroyer	1948 - 1960
Coventry	1917	Cruiser	1940 - 9.42				
Roebuck	1942	Destroyer	BPF 45/46	**D49**			
New Zealand	Canc	Ac Carrier	Canc 1946	*Orwell*	1898	Destroyer	12.14 - 9.15
Matapan	1945	Destroyer	1948 - 1979	*Cheerful*	1897	Destroyer	9.15 - 1.18
				Kestrel	1898	Destroyer	1.18 - 1.19
D44				*Valentine*	1917	Destroyer	1.19 - 1940
Vixen	1900	Destroyer	12.14 - 9.15	*Argus*	1917	Ac Carrier	1940 - 1945

Troubridge	1942	Destroyer	BPF 45/46
Onslow	1941	Destroyer	1948 - 1949

D50

Jupiter	1895	Battleship	12.14 - 4.15
Crane	1896	Destroyer	9.15 - 1.18
Leopard	1897	Destroyer	1.18 - 4.18
Melpomene	1915	Destroyer	9.18 - 1.19
Shakespeare	1917	Destroyer	1.19 - 1936
Tumult	1942	Destroyer	BPF 45/46
Venus	1943	Destroyer	1948 - 1951

D51

Dove	1898	Destroyer	9.15 - 1.18
Leven	1898	Destroyer	1.18 - 1.19
Vectis	1917	Destroyer	1.19 - 1936
Atheling	1942	Esc Carrrier	1942 - 1946
Tuscan	1942	Destroyer	BPF 45/46
Chevron	1944	Destroyer	1948 - 1969

D52

Amphitrite	1898	Cruiser	12.14 - 9.15
Electra	1896	Destroyer	9.15 - 1.18
Liffey	1904	Destroyer	1.18 - 1.19
Vega	1917	Destroyer	1.19 - 1938
Enterprise	1919	Cruiser	1940 - 1945
Tyrian	1942	Destroyer	BPF 45/46
Chaplet	1944	Destroyer	1948 - 1965

D53

Roebuck	1901	Destroyer	12.14 - 9.15
Fairy	1897	Destroyer	9.15 - 1.18
Lively	1899	Destroyer	1.18 - 1.19
Venetia	1917	Destroyer	1.19 - 1940
Caledon	1916	Cruiser	1940 - 1945
Avon Vale	1940	Destroyer	BPF 45/46
Undaunted	1943	Destroyer	1948 - 1953

D54

Falcon	1899	Destroyer	9.15 - 1.18
Locust	1896	Destroyer	1.18 - 6.18
Mentor	1914	Destroyer	9.18 - 1.19
Verulam	1917	Destroyer	1.19 - 11.19
Vanquisher	1917	Destroyer	11.19 - 1940
Giorgios Averoff RHN	1910	Cruiser	1940 - 1945
Blackmore	1941	Destroyer	BPF 45/46
Zodiac	1944	Destroyer	1948 - 1954

D55

Skirmisher	1904	Cruiser	12.14 - 4.15
Fawn	1897	Destroyer	9.15 - 1.18
Mallard	1896	Destroyer	1.18 - 1.19
Vesper	1917	Destroyer	1.19 - 1940
Brecon	1942	Destroyer	BPF 45/46
Smiter	1943	Esc Carrrier	1943 - 1946

Finisterre	1944	Destroyer	1948 - 1965

D56

Charybdis	1893	Cruiser	12.14 - 4.15
Flirt	1897	Destroyer	9.15 - 1.18
Mermaid	1898	Destroyer	1.18 - 9.18
Orestes	1916	Destroyer	11.18 - 1.19
Vimiera	1917	Destroyer	1.19 - 1.21
Wolfhound	1918	Destroyer	1.21 - 1940
Penguin	1916	Depot Ship	1940 - 1941
Calpe	1941	Destroyer	BPF 45/46
Petard	1941	Destroyer	1948 -1953

D57

Thorn	1900	Destroyer	12.14 - 9.15
Flying Fish	1897	Destroyer	9.15 - 1.18
Mohawk	1907	Destroyer	1.18 - 1.19
Violent	1917	Destroyer	1.19 - 1936
Fidelity	1920	SSV	1940 - 12.42
Croome	1941	Destroyer	BPF 45/46
Polyphemus	Canc	Ac Carrier	Canc 1945
Cossack	1944	Destroyer	1948 - 1961

D58

Eclipse	1894	Cruiser	12.14 - 9.15
Gipsy	1897	Destroyer	9.15 - 1.18
Moy	1904	Destroyer	1.18 - 9.18
Nugent	1917	Destroyer	9.18 - 1.19
Serapis	1918	Destroyer	1.22 - ....
Cardiff	1917	Cruiser	1940 - 1945
Eggesford	1942	Destroyer	BPF 45/46
Milne	1941	Destroyer	1948 - 1959

D59

Doris	1896	Cruiser	12.14 - 4.15
Greyhound	1900	Destroyer	9.15 - 1.18
Ness	1905	Destroyer	1.18 - 9.18
Phoebe	1916	Destroyer	9.18 - 11.21
Sirdar	1918	Destroyer	1.22 - ....
Skeena RCN	1930	Destroyer	1930 - 4.40
Ceres	1917	Cruiser	1940 - 1945
Farndale	1940	Destroyer	BPF 45/46
Anzac RAN	1948	Destroyer	1951 - 1969

D60

Isis	1896	Cruiser	12.14 - 4.15
Kestrel	1898	Destroyer	9.15 - 1.18
Nith	1905	Destroyer	1.18 - 9.18
Swift	1907	Destroyer	9.18 - 1.19
Campbell	1918	Destroyer	1.19 - 1940
Caradoc	1916	Cruiser	1940 - 1945
Cockade	1944	Destroyer	BPF 45/46
Sluys	1945	Destroyer	1948 - 1953

D61

Talbot	1895	Cruiser	12.14 - 4.15
Leopard	1897	Destroyer	9.15 - 1.18
Nubian	1909	Destroyer	1.18 - 1.19
Whitley	1918	Destroyer	1.19 - 1.21
Valkyrie	1917	Destroyer	1.21 - 1936
Ilex	1937	Destroyer	1937 - 4.40
Calypso	1917	Cruiser	1940 - 6.40
Barfleur	1943	Destroyer	BPF 45/46
Elephant	1953	Ac Carrier	1945
Hermes	1953	Ac Carrier	1945 - 1948
(ex *Elephant*)			
Chequers	1944	Destroyer	1948 - 1954

D62

Sprightly	1900	Destroyer	12.14 - 9.15
Arno	1914	Destroyer	9.15 - ....
Leven	1898	Destroyer	9.15 - 1.18
Opossum	1895	Destroyer	1.18 - 1.19
Wrestler	1918	Destroyer	1.19 - 11.19
Wild Swan	1919	Destroyer	11.19 - 1940
Khedive	1943	Esc Carrrier	1943 - 1946
Camperdown	1944	Destroyer	BPF 45/46
Jutland	1946	Destroyer	1948 - 1961

D63

Mermaid	1898	Destroyer	9.15 - 1.18
Orwell	1898	Destroyer	1.18 - 9.18
Termagant	1915	Destroyer	9.18 - 1.19
Woolston	1918	Destroyer	1.19 - 11.19
Verity	1919	Destroyer	11.19 - 1940
Hobart	1934	Cruiser	1940 - 1948
Caesar	1944	Destroyer	BPF 45/46
Haida RCN	1942	Destroyer	1948

D63 assigned to *Haida* but not used in Canadian service.

D64

Osprey	1897	Destroyer	9.15 - 1.19
Wolsey	1918	Destroyer	1.19 - 11.19
Vansittart	1919	Destroyer	11.19 - 1940
Fencer	1942	Esc Carrrier	1942 - 1946
Cambrian	1943	Destroyer	BPF 45/46
Scorpion	1946	Destroyer	1948 - 1963

D65

Ostrich	1900	Destroyer	9.15 - 1.19
Wakeful	1917	Destroyer	1.19 - 11.19
Codrington	1929	Destroyer	1.25 - 11.39
Sir Walter Raleigh	1908	Min. Tender	1942 - 1946
Caprice	1943	Destroyer	BPF 45/46
St James	1945	Destroyer	1948 - 1958

D66

Racehorse	1900	Destroyer	9.15 - 1.18

Ouse	1905	Destroyer	1.18 - 9.18
Mastiff	1914	Destroyer	9.18 - 1.19
Winchester	1918	Destroyer	1.19 - 11.19
Wivern	1919	Destroyer	11.19 - 1940
Emerald	1920	Cruiser	1940 - 1945
Zambesi	1943	Destroyer	1948 - 1959

D67

Roebuck	1901	Destroyer	9.15 - 1.18
Panther	1897	Destroyer	1.18 - 1.19
Valkyrie	1917	Destroyer	1.19 - 11.19
Wishart	1919	Destroyer	11.19 - 1940
Carlisle	1918	Cruiser	1940 - 1945
Carron	1944	Destroyer	BPF 45/46
Tyrian	1942	Destroyer	1948 - 1951

D68

Gossamer	1890	Gunboat	12.14 - 9.15
Star	1896	Destroyer	9.15 - 1.18
Peterel	1899	Destroyer	1.18 - 9.18
Sikh	1918	Destroyer	11.18 - 1.19
Valhalla	1917	Destroyer	1.19 - 11.19
Vampire RAN	1917	Destroyer	11.19 - 1940
Gibraltar	Canc	Ac Carrier	Canc 1945
Carysfort	1944	Destroyer	BPF 45/46
Barrosa	1945	Destroyer	1948 - 1968

D69

Panther	1897	Destroyer	12.14 - 9.15
Sylvia	1897	Destroyer	9.15 - 1.18
Porcupine	1895	Destroyer	1.18 - 1.19
Vendetta	1917	Destroyer	1.19 - 1940
Tynwald	1936	AA Ship	1940 - 11.42
Cavalier	1944	Destroyer	BPF 45/46
Paladin	1941	Destroyer	1948 - 1954

D70

Severn	1913	Monitor	12.14 - 4.15
Thorn	1900	Destroyer	9.15 - 1.18
Quail	1895	Destroyer	1.18 - 9.18
Orford	1916	Destroyer	11.18 - 1.19
Vampire	1917	Destroyer	1.19 - 11.19
Mackay	1918	Destroyer	11.19 - 1940
Ravager	1942	Esc Carrrier	1942 - 1946
Penn	1941	Destroyer	BPF 45/46
Solebay	1944	Destroyer	1948 - 1962

D71

Velox	1902	Destroyer	9.15 - 10.15
Racehorse	1900	Destroyer	1.18 - 1.19
Verdun	1917	Destroyer	1.19 - 11.19
Volunteer	1919	Destroyer	11.19 - 1940
Engadine	1941	Depot Ship	1941 - 1946
Cassandra	1943	Destroyer	BPF 45/46
Constance	1944	Destroyer	1948 - 1955

D72

Vigilant	1900	Destroyer	9.15 - 1.18
Roebuck	1901	Destroyer	1.18 - 1.19
Viceroy	1917	Destroyer	1.19 - 11.19
Veteran	1919	Destroyer	11.19 - 1940
Ruler	1943	Esc Carrrier	1943 - 1946
Cavendish	1944	Destroyer	BPF 45/46
Wizard	1943	Destroyer	1948 - 1952

D73

Violet	1897	Destroyer	9.15 - 1.18
Rother	1904	Destroyer	1.18 - 1.19
Viscount	1917	Destroyer	1.19 - 11.19
Vivien	1918	Destroyer	11.19 - 1938
Pursuer	1942	Esc Carrrier	1942 - 1946
Armada	1943	Destroyer	BPF 45/46
Cavalier	1944	Destroyer	1948 -

D74

Vixen	1900	Destroyer	9.15 - 1.18
Saracen	1908	Destroyer	1.18 - 1.19
Tactician	1918	Destroyer	1.19 - 9.19
Wanderer	1919	Destroyer	9.19 - 1940
Delhi	1918	Cruiser	1940 - 1945
Hogue	1944	Destroyer	1948 - 1962

D75

Leopard	1897	Destroyer	12.14 - 9.15
Vulture	1898	Destroyer	9.15 - 1.18
Seal	1897	Destroyer	1.18 - 1.19
Tintagel	1918	Destroyer	1.19 - 11.19
Venomous	1918	Destroyer	11.19 - 1940
Cresence	1936	Ac Transport	1940 - 1945
Trafalgar	1944	Destroyer	BPF 45/46
Virago	1944	Destroyer	1948 - 1951

D76

Albacore	1906	Destroyer	9.15 - 1.18
Spiteful	1899	Destroyer	1.18 - 1.19
Trojan	1918	Destroyer	1.19 - 11.19
Witherington	1919	Destroyer	11.19 - 1940
Pioneer	1944	Ac Carrier	1944 - 1948
Algonquin RCN	1943	Destroyer	BPF 45/46
Consort	1944	Destroyer	1948 - 1961

D77

Seal	1897	Destroyer	12.14 - 9.15
Arab	1901	Destroyer	9.15 - 1.18
Sprightly	1900	Destroyer	1.18 - 1.19
Tara	1918	Destroyer	1.19 - 11.19
Whitshed	1919	Destroyer	11.19 - 1940
Nabob	1943	Esc Carrrier	1943 - 8.44
Haida RCN	1942	Destroyer	BPF 45/46
Trafalgar	1944	Destroyer	1948 - 1963

D78

Bonetta	1907	Destroyer	9.15 - 1.18
Stag	1899	Destroyer	1.18 - 1.19
Wolverine	1919	Destroyer	12.20 - 1940
Archer	1939	Esc Carrrier	1939 - 1946
Huron RCN	1942	Destroyer	BPF 45/46
Wessex	1943	Destroyer	1948 -1950

D79

Thrasher	1895	Destroyer	12.14 - 9.15
Earnest	1896	Destroyer	9.15 - 1.18
Star	1896	Destroyer	1.18 - 6.18
Stour	1905	Destroyer	6.18 - 9.18
Observer	1916	Destroyer	11.18 - ....
Tomahawk	1918	Destroyer	1.22 - 6.25
Saguenay RCN	1930	Destroyer	1932 - 1940
Iroquois RCN	1941	Destroyer	BPF 45/46
Puncher	1943	Esc Carrrier	1943 - 1946
Cadiz	1944	Destroyer	1948 - 1955

D80

Express	1897	Destroyer	9.15 - 1.18
Stour	1905	Destroyer	1.18 - 9.18
Botha	1914	Destroyer	9.18 - 1920
Tuscan	1919	Destroyer	1.22 - ....
Micmac RCN	1943	Destroyer	BPF 45/46
Trailer	1942	Esc Carrrier	1942 - 1943
Hunter (ex Trailer)	1942	Esc Carrrier	1943 - 1945
Barfleur	1943	Destroyer	1948 - 1966
Sheffield	1971	Destroyer	1971 - 1982

D81

Circe	1892	Torpedo Gb	12.14 - 9.15
Griffon	1896	Destroyer	9.15 - 1.18
Sunfish	1895	Destroyer	1.18 - 1.19
Tempest	1917	Destroyer	1.19 - 11.19
Bruce	1918	Destroyer	11.19 - 1938
Frobisher	1920	Cruiser	1940 - 1945
Sioux RCN	1943	Destroyer	BPF 45/46
Zebra	1944	Destroyer	1948 - 1958

D82

Kangaroo	1900	Destroyer	9.15 - 1.18
Surly	1894	Destroyer	1.18 - 1.19
Taurus	1917	Destroyer	1.19 - 11.19
Torbay	1919	Destroyer	11.19 - 12.20
Valorous	1917	Destroyer	12.20 - 1938
Calcutta	1918	Cruiser	1940 - 6.41
Reaper	1943	Esc Carrrier	1943 - 1946
Hogue	1944	Destroyer	BPF 45/46
Creole	1945	Destroyer	1948 - 1956

D83

Lively	1899	Destroyer	9.15 - 1.18
Swale	1905	Destroyer	1.18 - 1.19

Teazer	1917	Destroyer	1.19 - 11.19
Tourmaline	1919	Destroyer	12.19 - 1.22
Broke (ex *Rooke*)	1920	Destroyer	1.22 - 1940
Thane	1943	Esc Carrrier	1943 - 1946
Ulster	1942	Destroyer	1948 - 1953

D84

Express	1897	Destroyer	12.14 - 9.15
Locust	1896	Destroyer	9.15 - 1.18
Sylvia	1897	Destroyer	1.18 - 3.18
Meteor	1914	Destroyer	9.18 - 1.19
Rowena	1916	Destroyer	1.19 - 11.19
Tyrian	1919	Destroyer	12.19 - 1.22
Keppel	1920	Destroyer	4.25 - 1940
Australia RAN	1927	Cruiser	1940 - 1945
Comet	1944	Destroyer	BPF 45/46
Saintes	1944	Destroyer	1948 - 1962

D85

Quail	1895	Destroyer	12.14 - 9.15
Myrmidon	1900	Destroyer	9.15 - 1.18
Syren	1900	Destroyer	1.18 - 1.19
Restless	1916	Destroyer	1.19 - 11.19
Turquoise	1918	Destroyer	11.19 - 1.22
Shikari	1919	Destroyer	1924 - 1943
Trouncer	1943	Esc Carrrier	1943 - 1946
Comus	1945	Destroyer	BPF 45/46
Cambrian	1943	Destroyer	1948 - 1971

D86

Orwell	1898	Destroyer	9.15 - 1.18
Tartar	1907	Destroyer	1.18 - 1.19
Rigorous	1916	Destroyer	1.19 - 11.19
Strenuous	1905	Destroyer	11.19 - 1.22
Thracian	1920	Destroyer	1.22 - 6.40
Hawkins	1917	Cruiser	1940 - 1945
Consort	1944	Destroyer	BPF 45/46
Agincourt	1945	Destroyer	1948 - 1972
Birmingham	1973	Destroyer	1973 - 1999

D87

Pincher	1910	Destroyer	2.15 - 9.15
Panther	1897	Destroyer	9.15 - 1.18
Test	1905	Destroyer	1.18 - 9.18
Medina	1916	Destroyer	11.18 - 1.19
Rosalind	1916	Destroyer	1.19 - 11.19
Sturdy	1919	Destroyer	11.19 - 12.20
Venturous	1917	Destroyer	12.20 - ....
Isis	1936	Destroyer	1936 - 4.40
Cairo	1919	Cruiser	1940 - 8.42
Constance	1944	Destroyer	BPF 45/46
Newcastle	1975	Destroyer	1975 - 2004

D88

Harpy	1909	Destroyer	2.15 - 9.15
Peterel	1899	Destroyer	9.15 - 1.18
Teviot	1903	Destroyer	1.18 - 6.18
Radiant	1916	Destroyer	9.18 - 1.19
Sterling	1918	Destroyer	1.19 - 12.20
Tenedos	1918	Destroyer	12.20 - 1.22
Wren	1919	Destroyer	2.23 - 1940
Capetown	1919	Cruiser	1940 - 1945
Contest	1944	Destroyer	BPF 45/46
Glasgow	1976	Destroyer	1976 - 2004

D89

Basilisk	1910	Destroyer	2.15 - 9.15
Quail	1895	Destroyer	9.15 - 1.18
Thorn	1900	Destroyer	1.18 - 9.18
Retriever	1917	Destroyer	9.18 - 11.19
Stormcloud	1919	Destroyer	1.20 - 12.20
Witch	1919	Destroyer	12.20 - 1940
Colombo	1918	Cruiser	1940 - 1945
Concord	1945	Destroyer	BPF 45/46
Iroquois RCN	1941	Destroyer	1948
Exeter	1978	Destroyer	1978 - 2008

D89 assigned to *Iroquois* but not used in Canadian service.

D90

Scorpion	1910	Destroyer	2.15 - 3.18
Seal	1897	Destroyer	9.15 - 1.18
Thrasher	1895	Destroyer	1.18 - 1.19
Grenville	1916	Destroyer	1.19 - 12.20
Douglas	1918	Destroyer	12.20 - 1940
Speaker	1943	Esc Carrrier	1943 - 1946
Cossack	1944	Destroyer	BPF 45/46
Cheviot	1944	Destroyer	1948 - 1962
Southampton	1979	Destroyer	1979 - 2009

D91

Lively	1899	Destroyer	12.14 - 9.15
Spiteful	1899	Destroyer	9.15 - 1.18
Ure	1904	Destroyer	1.18 - 1.19
Redoubt	1916	Destroyer	1.19 - 11.19
Thanet	1918	Destroyer	11.19 - 12.20
Viceroy	1917	Destroyer	1.21 - 1940
Stalker	1942	Esc Carrrier	1942 - 1945
Finisterre	1944	Destroyer	BPF 45/46
Childers	1945	Destroyer	1948 - 1963
Nottingham	1980	Destroyer	1980 - 2008

D92

Savage	1910	Destroyer	2.15 - 9.15
Sprightly	1900	Destroyer	9.15 - 1.18
Vigilant	1900	Destroyer	1.18 - 9.18
Sorceress	1916	Destroyer	9.18 - 11.19
Turbulent	1916	Destroyer	11.19 - 12.20
Viscount	1917	Destroyer	12.20 - 1940
Diomede	1919	Cruiser	1940 - 1945

Gravelines	1944	Destroyer	BPF 45/46
Liverpool	1980	Destroyer	1980 - 2012

D93

Tara	1918	Destroyer	12.14 - 9.15
Syren	1900	Destroyer	9.15 - 1.18
Viking	1909	Destroyer	1.18 - 9.18
Sylph	1916	Destroyer	9.18 - 11.19
Stonehenge	1919	Destroyer	11.19 - 12.20
Verdun	1917	Destroyer	1.21 - 1940
Dunedin	1918	Cruiser	1940 - 11.41
Lagos	1944	Destroyer	BPF 45/46
Malta	Canc	Ac Carrier	Canc 1946
Vigilant	1942	Destroyer	1948 - 1951

D94

Rattlesnake	1910	Destroyer	2.15 - 9.15
Thrasher	1895	Destroyer	9.15 - 1.18
Violet	1897	Destroyer	1.18 - 9.18
Radstock	1916	Destroyer	9.18 - 11.19
Shamrock	1919	Destroyer	11.19 - 1.22
Whitehall	1919	Destroyer	7.24 - 1940
Activity	1942	Esc Carrrier	1942 - 1945

D95

Maine II	1906	Hospital Ship	12.14 - 9.15
Wolf	1897	Destroyer	9.15 - 1.18
Vixen	1900	Destroyer	1.18 - 9.18
Raider	1916	Destroyer	9.18 - 11.19
Sardonyx	1919	Destroyer	11.19 - 12.20
Woolston	1918	Destroyer	1.21 - 1940
Hermes	1919	Ac Carrier	1940 - 4.42
Zenith	1944	Destroyer	1948 - 1955
Manchester	1980	Destroyer	1980 - 2011

D96

Scourge	1910	Destroyer	2.15 - 9.15
Conflict	1894	Destroyer	9.15 - 4.17
Waveney	1903	Destroyer	1.18 - 9.18
Offa	1916	Destroyer	11.18 - ....
Seawolf	1918	Destroyer	11.19 - 12.20
Worcester	1919	Destroyer	9.22 - 1940
Monmouth	Canc	Ac Carrier	Canc 1945
Crossbow	1945	Destroyer	1948 - 1970
Gloucester	1982	Destroyer	1982 - 2011

D97

Reliance	1910	Store Carrier	12.14 - 4.15
Fervent	1895	Destroyer	9.15 - 1.18
Wolf	1897	Destroyer	1.18 - 1.19
Ready	1916	Destroyer	1.19 - 11.19
Serene	1918	Destroyer	11.19 - 12.20
Whitley	1918	Destroyer	12.20 - 1938
Biter	1940	Esc Carrrier	1940 - 1945
Corunna	1945	Destroyer	1948 - 1967

Edinburgh	1982	Destroyer	1982 - 2013

D98

Wolf	1897	Destroyer	12.14 - 9.15
Lightning	1895	Destroyer	9.15 - Sunk
Zephyr	1895	Destroyer	1.18 - 1.19
Sesame	1918	Destroyer	11.19 - 12.20
Wolsey	1918	Destroyer	1.21 - 1938
Effingham	1921	Cruiser	1940 - 5.40
Emperor	1942	Esc Carrrier.	1942 - 1946
York	1982	Destroyer	1982 - 2012

D99

Petroleum	1902	Oiler	1914 - 9.15
Opossum	1895	Destroyer	9.15 - 1.18
Zubian	1917	Destroyer	1.18 - 1.19
Duncan	1932	Destroyer	1932 - 4.40
Durban	1919	Cruiser	1940 - 6.44

Zubian was constructed from the forward end of *Zulu* and the rear and mid sections of *Nubian*. *Nubian*'s bow had been destroyed by a torpedo from a German destroyer on 27.10.1916 off Folkestone. *Zulu* had her stern blown off by a mine near Dunkirk on 8.11.1916. Both wrecks were then towed to Chatham where *Zubian* was constructed by joining the foreparts of *Zulu* with the stern of *Nubian*. She was commissioned on 7.6.1917.

D100

Jervis	1938	Destroyer	1948 - Sold

D101

Hotspur	1936	Destroyer	1948 - Sold

D103

Kempenfelt	1943	Destroyer	1948 - 1957

D104

Cayuga RCN	1945	Destroyer	1948 - 1949

D105

Urania	1943	Destroyer	1948 - 1953

D106

Decoy	1949	Destroyer	1949 - 1969

D107

Nonsuch (ex *Z.38*)	1941	Destroyer	1948 - 1949

D108

Dainty	1950	Destroyer	1950 - 1971
Cardiff	1974	Destroyer	1974 - 2005

D110

Micmac RCN	1943	Destroyer	1948 - 1949

D114

Defender	1950	Destroyer	1950 - 1972

D115

Raider	1942	Destroyer	1948 - Sold

D117

Algonquin RCN	1943	Destroyer	1948 - 1949

D118					**D177**			
Battleaxe	1945	Destroyer	1948 - 1964		*Penn*	1941	Destroyer	1948 - 1950
Coventry	1974	Destroyer	1974 - 1982		**D178**			
					Fame	1934	Destroyer	1948 - 1949
D119					**D180**			
Delight	1950	Destroyer	1950 - 1970		*Opportune*	1942	Destroyer	1948 - 1955
D120					**D185**			
Crusader RCN	1944	Destroyer	1948 - 1949		*Relentless*	1942	Destroyer	1948 - 1951
D121					**D186**			
Tumult	1942	Destroyer	1948 - 1953		*Musketeer*	1941	Destroyer	1948 - 1955
D123					**D187**			
Warramunga RAN	1942	Destroyer	1948 - 1959		*Whirlwind*	1943	Destroyer	1948 - 1953
D125					**D189**			
Nepal	1941	Destroyer	1948 - 1956		*Termagant*	1943	Destroyer	1948 - 1952
D126					**D191**			
Diana	1952	Destroyer	1952 - 1969		*Bataan* RAN	1944	Destroyer	1948 - 1954
D129					**D192**			
Offa	1941	Destroyer	1948 - 1949		*Rocket*	1942	Destroyer	1948 - 1949
D130					**D195**			
Arunta RAN	1940	Destroyer	1948 - 1957		*Roebuck*	1942	Destroyer	1948 - 1952
D135					**D196**			
Marne	1940	Destroyer	1948 - 1958		*Nootka* RCN	1944	Destroyer	1948 - 1949
D136					**D197**			
Nubian	1937	Destroyer	1948 - 1949		*Grenville*	1942	Destroyer	1948 - 1953
D137					**D198**			
Kelvin	1939	Destroyer	1948 - 1949		*Orwell*	1942	Destroyer	1948 - 1952
D138					**D199**			
Rapid	1942	Destroyer	1948 - 1953		*Urchin*	1943	Destroyer	1948 - 1954
D139					**D200**			
Obdurate	1942	Destroyer	1948 - 1959		*Stuart* RAN	1918	Destroyer	1948 - 10.48
D141					**D204**			
Redoubt	1942	Destroyer	1948 - 1949		*Onslaught*	1941	Destroyer	1948 - 1950
D142					**D209**			
Undine	1943	Destroyer	1948 - 1953		*Rotherham*	1942	Destroyer	1948 - 1949
D149					**D211**			
Norman RAN	1940	Destroyer	1948 - 1958		*Racehorse*	1942	Destroyer	1948 - 1949
D151					**D222**			
Ashanti	1937	Destroyer	1948 - Sold		*Ursa*	1943	Destroyer	1948 - 1954
D154					**D224**			
Duchess RAN	1951	Destroyer	1952 - 1964		*Huron* RCN	1942	Destroyer	1948 - 1949
D156					**D231**			
Tuscan	1942	Destroyer	1948 - 1950		*Vigo*	1946	Destroyer	1948 - 1959
D158					**D232**			
Wrangler	1943	Destroyer	1948 - 1956		*Lookout*	1950	Destroyer	1948 - Sold
D159					**D237**			
Wakeful	1943	Destroyer	1948 - 1953		*Whelp*	1943	Destroyer	1948 - 1953
D164					**D243**			
Sioux RCN	1943	Destroyer	1948 - 1949		*Tartar*	1937	Destroyer	1948 - Sold
D165					**D248**			
Noble	1941	Destroyer	1948 - 1955		*Obedient*	1942	Destroyer	1948- 1962
D168					**D250**			
Crispin	1945	Destroyer	1948 - 1958		*Kimberley*	1939	Destroyer	1948 - 1949
D169					**D252**			
Ulysses	1943	Destroyer	1948 - 1953		*Matchless*	1941	Destroyer	1948 - 1957

D261

Javelin	1938	Destroyer	1948 - Sold

D262

Quality RAN	1942	Destroyer	1948 - 1958

D270

Queenborough RAN	1942	Destroyer	1948 - 1954

D273

Meteor	1941	Destroyer	1948 - 1958

D275

Eskimo	1937	Destroyer	1948 - 1949

D278

Wessex	1943	Destroyer	1948 - 1955

D281

Quiberon RAN	1942	Destroyer	1948 - 1957

D292

Quickmatch RAN	1941	Destroyer	1948 - 1955

D297

Napier RAN	1940	Destroyer	1948 - 1956

D298

Wager	1943	Destroyer	1948 - 1957

D0A

Porcupine	1895	Destroyer	9.15 - 1.18

Zulu	1909	Destroyer	1.18 - 3.18
Nonpareil	1916	Destroyer	9.18 - ....

D1A

Ranger	1895	Destroyer	9.15 - 4.17
Oriole	1916	Destroyer	1.18 - 3.18
Paladin	1916	Destroyer	11.18 - ....

D2A

Sunfish	1895	Destroyer	9.15 - 1.18
Plucky	1916	Destroyer	11.18 - ....

D3A

Surly	1894	Destroyer	9.15 - 1.18
Wallace	1918	Destroyer	2.19 - 11.19

D4A

Zephyr	1895	Destroyer	9.15 - 1.18

D5A

Bittern	1897	Destroyer	9.15 - 1.18

D6A

Arno	1914	Destroyer	9.15 - 1.18

Flag 'F' Superior

Pre 1940: Destroyers (Various pendants superior and inferior were used to increase number range)

1940-48: Monitors; Aircraft Maintenance Carriers; Small Aircraft Transports; Armed Merchant Cruisers; Ocean and Armed Boarding Vessels; Special Service Vessels; Aux AA Ships; Coastal or Controlled Minelayers; Depot Ships; Repair and Maintenance Ships; Base and Accomodation Ships; Landing Ships.

1948: Frigates

F00
Gabriel	1915	Destroyer	1.17 - 6.18
Saumerez	1916	Destroyer	1.19 - 1.22
Jervis	1938	Destroyer	1939 - 1940
Minerva (ex M33)	1915	Monitor	1940 - 1946

F01
Medway	1916	Destroyer	1.17 - 3.18
Ursula	1917	Destroyer	3.18 - 1.19
Ulster	1917	Destroyer	1.19 - 1.22
Kelly	1938	Destroyer	1939 - 1940
Marshal Soult	1915	Monitor	1940 - 1946
Quadrant RAN	1942	Frigate	1953 - 1957

F02
Moresby	1915	Destroyer	1.17 - 1.18
Narborough	1916	Destroyer	1.18 - 3.18
Westminster	1918	Destroyer	3.18 - 1.19
Umpire	1917	Destroyer	1.19 - 1.22
Erebus	1916	Monitor	1940 - 1944
Beachy Head	1944	Repair Ship	1944 - 1946
Liddesdale	1940	Frigate	1948 - 1948
Queenborough RAN	1942	Frigate	12.54 -1969

F03
Nepean	1916	Destroyer	1.17 - 3.18
Wescott	1918	Destroyer	3.18 - 1.19
Undine	1917	Destroyer	1.19 - 1.22
Cossack	1937	Destroyer	1939 - 5.40
Terror	1916	Monitor	1940 - 1941
Quiberon RAN	1942	Frigate	1957 - 1964

F04
Nerissa	1916	Destroyer	1.17 - 1.18
Urchin	1917	Destroyer	1.18 - 1.22
Menelaus (ex M31)	1915	Monitor	1940 - 1945
Girdle Ness	1945	Depot Ship	1945 - 1948
Quickmatch RAN	1941	Frigate	1955 - 1963

F05
Nicator	1916	Destroyer	1.17 - 1.18

Nerissa	1916	Destroyer	1.18 - 6.18
Valkyrie	1917	Destroyer	9.18 - 1.19
Ursa	1917	Destroyer	1.19 - 1.22
Cathay	1925	AMC	1940 - 1942
Portland Bill	1945	Repair Ship	1945 - 1948
Atherstone	1939	Frigate	1948 - 1957

F06
Obdurate	1916	Destroyer	1.17 - 1.18
Norseman	1916	Destroyer	1.18 - 3.18
Vectis	1917	Destroyer	3.18 - 1.19
Ursula	1917	Destroyer	1.19 - 1.22
Medusa (ex M29)	1919	Depot Ship	1940 - 1941
Talbot (ex Medusa)	1919	Depot Ship	1941 - 1944
Bigbury Bay	1944	Frigate	1948 - 1959

F07
Octavia	1916	Destroyer	1.17 - 1.18
Obdurate	1916	Destroyer	1.18 - 6.18
Vidette	1918	Destroyer	6.18 - 1.19
Tirade	1917	Destroyer	1.19 - 1.22
Afridi	1937	Destroyer	1939 - 1940
Forth	1938	Depot Ship	1940 - 1948
Actaeon	1945	Frigate	1948 - 1958

F08
Oracle	1915	Destroyer	1.17 - 1.18
Vanquisher	1917	Destroyer	1.18 - 6.18
Woolston	1918	Destroyer	6.18 - 11.19
Tower	1917	Destroyer	1.19 - 1.22
Cochrane	1903	Depot Ship	1940 - 1946
Exmoor	1941	Frigate	1948 - 1953
Urania	1943	Frigate	1955 - 1971

F09
Onslow	1916	Destroyer	1.17 - 1.18
Octavia	1916	Destroyer	1.18 - 3.18
Vega	1917	Destroyer	3.18 - 1.19
Trenchant	1916	Destroyer	1.19 - 1.22
Easton	1942	Frigate	1948 - 1953
Troubridge	1942	Frigate	1957 - 1970

F10

Pelican	1916	Destroyer	1.17 - 1.18
Ursa	1917	Destroyer	1.18 - 1.19
Parker	1916	Destroyer	1.19 - 1922
Greenwich	1915	Depot Ship	1940 - 1946
Natal SAN	1944	Frigate	1948 - ....
Aurora	1962	Frigate	1962 - 1987

F11

Narborough	1916	Destroyer	1.17 - 1.18
Oriana	1916	Destroyer	1.18 - 3.18
Paladin	1916	Destroyer	9.18 - 1.19
Tristram	1917	Destroyer	1.19 - 1.22
Moreton Bay	1921	AMC	1940 - 1941
Jumna RIN	1940	Frigate	1948 - 1950

F12

Nereus	1916	Destroyer	1.17 - 1.18
Vehement	1917	Destroyer	1.18 - 6.18
Windsor	1918	Destroyer	9.18 - 1.19
Truculent	1917	Destroyer	1.19 - 12.20
Tancred	1917	Destroyer	12.20 - 1.22
Kashmir	1939	Destroyer	1939 - 1940
Arawa	1939	AMC	1940 - 1941
Bamborough Castle	1944	Frigate	1948 - 1959
Achilles	1968	Frigate	1968 - 1990

F13

Norseman	1916	Destroyer	1.17 - 1.18

F14

Oriana	1916	Destroyer	1.17 - 1.18
Paladin	1916	Destroyer	1.18 - 3.18
Venetia	1917	Destroyer	3.18 - 1.19
Tyrant	1917	Destroyer	1.19 - 11.19
Keppel	1920	Destroyer	12.20 - 1925
Victoria & Albert	1899	Royal Yacht	1940 - 1948
Beaufort	1941	Frigate	1948 - 1954
Leopard	1955	Frigate	1955 - 1975

F15

Patrician	1916	Destroyer	1.18 - 9.18
Walpole	1918	Destroyer	9.18 - 1.19
Sabrina	1916	Destroyer	1.19 - 11.19
Sarpedon	1916	Destroyer	11.19 - 1.21
Loyal	1941	Destroyer	Pre-build
Ranchi	1925	AMC	1940 - 1943
Eggesford	1942	Frigate	1948 - 1958
Euryalus	1963	Frigate	1963 - 1989

F16

Oriole	1916	Destroyer	1.17 - 1.18
Penn	1916	Destroyer	1.18 - 3.18
Verdun	1917	Destroyer	9.18 - 1.19
Sybille	1917	Destroyer	1.19 - 11.19

Redgauntlet	1916	Destroyer	11.19 - 1.22
Letitia	1925	AMC	1940 - 1941
Stevenstone	1940	Frigate	1948 - 1959
Diomede	1969	Frigate	1969 - 1988

F17

Orpheus	1916	Destroyer	1.17 - 1.18
Ulster	1917	Destroyer	1.18 - 1.19
Relentless	1916	Destroyer	1.19 - 11.19
Sceptre	1917	Destroyer	11.19 - 1.22
Alaunia	1925	AMC	1940 - 1944
Ulysses	1943	Frigate	1955 - 1963

F18

Paladin	1916	Destroyer	1.17 - 1.18
Pigeon	1916	Destroyer	1.18 - 3.18
Wolfhound	1918	Destroyer	3.18 - 1.19
Rival	1916	Destroyer	1.19 - 11.19
Salmon	1916	Destroyer	11.19 - 1.22
Zulu	1937	Destroyer	1939 - 5.40
Cheshire	1927	AMC	1939 - 1943
Berry Head	1944	Repair Ship	1944 - 1948
Flamingo	1939	Frigate	1948 - 1957
Galatea	1963	Frigate	1963 - 1987

F19

Penn	1916	Destroyer	1.17 - 1.18
Pylades	1916	Destroyer	1.18 - 3.18
Verulam	1917	Destroyer	3.18 - 1.19
Seymour	1916	Destroyer	11.19 - 1.22
Hampton	1919	Minelayer	1940 - ....
Dodman Point	1945	Depot Ship	1945 - 1948
Terpsichore	1943	Frigate	1953 - 1966

F20

Petard	1916	Destroyer	1.17 - 1.18
Rival	1916	Destroyer	1.18 - 6.18
Whitley	1918	Destroyer	11.18 - 1.19
Stuart RAN	1918	Destroyer	1.19 - 1.22
Gurkha	1937	Destroyer	1939 - 4.40
Hecla	1940	Depot Ship	1940 - 11.42
Snipe	1945	Frigate	1948 - 1960

F21

Vanquisher	1917	Destroyer	1917 - ....
Pigeon	1916	Destroyer	1.17 - 1.18
Venturous	1917	Destroyer	1.18 - 9.18
Serapis	1918	Destroyer	9.18 - 1.19
Sportive	1918	Destroyer	1.19 - 1.22
Punjabi	1937	Destroyer	1939 - 5.40
Antenor	1925	AMC	1940 - 1942
Dart	1942	Frigate	1948 - 1957
Jumna RIN	1940	Sloop	1948 - 1950
Jamuna RIN	1940	Sloop	1950 - 1980
(ex Jumna)			

F22

Pasley	1916	Destroyer	1.17 - 1.18
Tarpon	1917	Destroyer	1.18 - 9.18
Swallow	1918	Destroyer	1.19 - 1.22
Jackal	1938	Destroyer	1939 - 1940
Patroclus	1923	AMC	1940 - 11.40
Hilary	1931	LSHQ	1940 - 1946
Wheatland	1941	Frigate	1948 - 1955

F23

Patrician	1916	Destroyer	9.15 - 1.18
Telemachus	1917	Destroyer	1.18 - 9.18
Spear	1918	Destroyer	1.19 - 1.22
Kanimbla RAN	1935	AMC	1940 - 1943
Teazer	1943	Frigate	1952 - 1965

F24

Rival	1916	Destroyer	1.17 - 1.18
Tower	1917	Destroyer	1.18 - 11.19
Steadfast	1918	Destroyer	11.19 - 12.20
Splendid	1918	Destroyer	12.20 - 1.22
Maori	1937	Destroyer	1939 - 5.40
Tyne	1940	Depot Ship	1940 - 1948
Blencathra	1940	Frigate	1948 - 1957

F25

Tristram	1917	Destroyer	1.18 - 1.19
Seraph	1918	Destroyer	1.19 - 1.22
Medway	1928	Depot Ship	1940 - 6.42
Carnarvon Castle	1926	AMC	1942 - 1944
Hartland Point	1944	Repair Ship	1944 - 1948
Southdown	1940	Frigate	1948 - 1956

F26

Osiris	1916	Destroyer	1.17 - 1.18
Umpire	1917	Destroyer	1.18 - 1.19
Tumult	1918	Destroyer	1.19 - 1.22
Matabele	1937	Destroyer	1939 - 5.40
Maloja	1923	AMC	1940 - 1941
Mull of Galloway	1944	Repair Ship	1944 - 1948
Petard	1941	Frigate	1956 - 1965

F27

Oberon	1916	Destroyer	1.17 - 1.18
Vanoc	1917	Destroyer	1.18 - 6.18
Speedy	1918	Destroyer	1.19 - 1.22
Lucia	1907	Depot Ship	1940 - 1948
Lynx	1955	Frigate	1955 - 1974

F28

Pylades	1916	Destroyer	1.17 - 10.17
Vesper	1917	Destroyer	10.17 - 1.18
Vimiera	1917	Destroyer	1.18 - 1.19
Tobago	1918	Destroyer	1.19 - 1.22
Kandahar	1939	Destroyer	1939 - 1940
Aurania	1924	AMC	1940 - 1942
Artifex (ex *Aurania*)	1924	Repair Ship	1942 - 1948
Wren	1942	Frigate	1948 - 1956
Cleopatra	1964	Frigate	1964 - 1992

F29

Versatile	1917	Destroyer	10.17 - 1.18
Vendetta	1917	Destroyer	1.18 - 1.19
Tilbury	1918	Destroyer	1.19 - 11.19
Sparrowhawk	1918	Destroyer	11.19 - 1.22
Worcestershire	1931	AMC	1940 - 1943
Fife Ness	1945	Repair Ship	1945 - 1948
Whimbrel	1942	Frigate	1948 - 1949
Verulam	1943	Frigate	1952 - 1970

F30

Venturous	1917	Destroyer	10.17 - 1.18
Valentine	1917	Destroyer	1.18 - 1.19
Forfar (ex *Montrose*)	1920	AMC	1939 - 12.40
Wuchang	1914	Depot Ship	1941 - 1946
Mermaid	1943	Frigate	1948 - 1958

F31

Vittoria	1917	Destroyer	10.17 - 1.18
Osiris	1916	Destroyer	1.18 - 3.18
Violent	1917	Destroyer	3.18 - 1.19
Tomahawk	1918	Destroyer	1.19 - 1.22
Mohawk	1937	Destroyer	1939 - 4.41
Cyclops	1905	Depot Ship	1940 - 1948
Portage RCN	1942	Frigate	1948 - ....

F32

Vivacious	1917	Destroyer	1917 - 1.18
Vancouver	1917	Destroyer	10.17 - 1.18
Petard	1916	Destroyer	1.18 - 3.18
Nessus	1915	Destroyer	3.18 - 6.18
Wessex	1918	Destroyer	6.18 - 1.19
Tryphon	1918	Destroyer	1.19 - 12.20
Lookout	1940	Destroyer	1940 - ....
Titania	1915	Depot Ship	1940 - 1948
Salisbury	1953	Frigate	1953 - 1985

F33

Nereus	1916	Destroyer	1.18 - 3.18
Tribune	1918	Destroyer	1.19 - 12.20
Tryphon	1918	Destroyer	12.20 - 1.22
Somali	1937	Destroyer	1939 - 5.40
Cavina	1924	OBV	1940 - 1942
Conqueror	1911	Aux AA	1940 - 1945
Opossum	1944	Frigate	1948 - 1960

F34

Velox	1917	Destroyer	10.17 - 1.18
Onslow	1916	Destroyer	1.18 - 3.18
Sardonyx	1919	Destroyer	6.19 - 1.19

Sikh	1918	Destroyer	1.19 - 1.22
Falmouth	1932	Sloop/TS	1948 - 1968
Jaguar	1938	Destroyer	1939 - 1940
Dunottar Castle	1936	AMC	1940 - 1942
Rame Head	1944	Repair Ship	1944 - 1948
Sault Sainte Marie RCN	1942	Frigate	1948 - 1949
Puma	1954	Frigate	1954 - 1972

F35

Vortigern	1917	Destroyer	10.17 - 1.18
Orpheus	1916	Destroyer	1.18 - 3.18
Torbay	1919	Destroyer	6.19 - ....
Senator	1918	Destroyer	1.19 - 1.22
Rajputana	1925	AMC	1940 - 4.41
Queen Mary	1935	Troop	1941 - 1946
Enard Bay	1944	Frigate	1948 - 1956

F36

Oberon	1916	Destroyer	1.18 - 3.18
Verity	1919	Destroyer	3.18 - 1.19
Shark	1912	Destroyer	1.19 - 1.22
Nubian	1937	Destroyer	1939 - 5.40
Buchan Ness	1945	Repair Ship	1945 - 1948
Whitby	1954	Frigate	1954 - 1974

F37

Wakeful	1917	Destroyer	1.18 - 1.19
Torch	1918	Destroyer	1.19 - 1.22
Kelvin	1939	Destroyer	1939 - 1940
Wolfe	1920	AMC	1940 - 1948
New Liskeard RCN	1944	Frigate	1948 - 1949
Jaguar	1957	Frigate	1957 - 1979

F38

Viceroy	1917	Destroyer	3.18 - 1.19
Tempest	1917	Destroyer	11.19 - 1.22
Cygnet	1942	Frigate	1948 - 1956
Arethusa	1963	Frigate	1963 - 1989

F39

Vesper	1917	Destroyer	3.18 - 1.19
Taurus	1917	Destroyer	11.19 - 1.22
Ranpura	1924	AMC	1940 - 1942
Ranpura	1924	Repair Ship	1942 - 1948
Hind	1943	Frigate	1948 - 1958
Naiad	1963	Frigate	1963 - 1987

F40

Winchelsea	1917	Destroyer	3.18 - 1.19
Bruce	1918	Destroyer	1.19 - 11.19
Teazer	1917	Destroyer	11.19 - 1.22
Jervis Bay	1922	AMC	1939 - 11.40
Lively	1941	Destroyer	1941 - Sunk
Roberts	1941	Monitor	1941 - 1948

Narbada RIN	1942	Sloop	1948 - 1948
Jhelum RPN (ex Narbada)	1942	Sloop	1948 - 1959
Sirius	1964	Frigate	1964 - 1963

F41

Lassoo	1915	Destroyer	9.15 - 1.18
Sabre	1919	Destroyer	1.19 - 1.22
Aorangi	1924	AMC	1944 - 1946
Volage	1943	Frigate	1951 - 1972

F42

Lochinvar	1915	Destroyer	1916 - 1.18
Seafire	1918	Destroyer	1.19 - 1.22
Laconia	1922	AMC	1940 - 9.42
Spurn Point	1945	Repair Ship	1945 - 1948
Modeste	1944	Frigate	1948 - 1961
Phoebe	1964	Frigate	1964 - 1991

Between 1973-77 a British TV series *"Warship"* was produced in the UK. It centred around the operations of a fictional frigate, *HMS Hero*. *Phoebe* played the role of *Hero* but, on occasion, over the 45 episodes, she was not available for filming, so the role was taken up by six other frigates, who, for continuity, were painted up with the pendant number F42. The other ships were *Danae*, *Dido*, *Diomede*, *Hermione*, *Juno* and *Jupiter*.

F43

Abdiel	1915	Destroyer	1.17 - 1.18
Searcher	1919	Destroyer	1.19 - 1.22
Tartar	1937	Destroyer	1939 - 5.40
Largs	1938	LSH(L)	1940 - 1945
Torquay	1954	Frigate	1954 - 1985

F44

Talisman	1915	Destroyer	1.17 - 1.18
Somme	1918	Destroyer	1.19 - 1.22
Maidstone	1937	Depot Ship	1940 - 1948
Tenacious	1943	Frigate	1952 - 1965

F45

North Star	1916	Destroyer	1.17 - 1.18
Splendid	1918	Destroyer	1.19 - 11.19
Rowena	1916	Destroyer	11.19 - 1.22
Montrose	1918	Destroyer	9.18 - 1.19
Khartoum	1939	Destroyer	1939 - 6.40
Hector	1924	AMC	1940 - 1942
Wild Goose	1942	Frigate	1948 - 1956
Minerva	1964	Frigate	1964 - 1992

F46

Nugent	1917	Destroyer	1.17 - 1.18
Skate	1917	Destroyer	3.18 - 1.19
Scimitar	1918	Destroyer	1.19 - 1.22

Juno	1938	Destroyer	1939 - 1940
Dungeness	1945	Repair Ship	1945 - 1948
Kistna RIN	1943	Sloop	1948 - 1981

F47

Termagant	1915	Destroyer	1.17 - 1.18
Sturgeon	1917	Destroyer	3.18 - 1.19
Scythe	1918	Destroyer	1.19 - 1.22
Voltaire	1923	AMC	1940 - 4.41
Fleetwood	1936	Frigate	1948 - 1959
Danae	1965	Frigate	1965 - 1990

F48

Sharpshooter	1917	Destroyer	9.15 - 4.16
Bruce	1918	Destroyer	6.18 - 1.19
Seabear	1918	Destroyer	1.19 - 1.22
Manoora RAN	1934	LSI	1940 - 1942
Dundas	1953	Frigate	1953 - 1979

F49

Sturgeon	1917	Destroyer	9.15 - 4.16
Abdiel	1915	Destroyer	1.18 - 10.19
Sepoy	1918	Destroyer	1.19 - 1.22
Cormorin	1924	AMC	1940 - 4.41
Cape Wrath	1945	Repair Ship	1945 - 1948
Pheasant	1942	Frigate	1948 - 1961

F50

Trident	1915	Destroyer	1.17 - 1.18
Botha	1914	Destroyer	1.18 - 9.18
Shamrock	1918	Destroyer	8.19 - ....
Douglas	1918	Destroyer	1.19 - 12.20
Torbay	1919	Destroyer	12.20 - 1.22
Kimberley	1939	Destroyer	1939 - 5.40
Springbank	1926	Aux AA	1940 - 9.41
Centurion	1911	Battleship	1940 - 1944
Queen Elizabeth	1938	Troop	1940 - 1945
Rochester	1931	Sloop	1948 - 1951
Venus	1943	Frigate	1952 - 1972

F51

Satyr	1916	Destroyer	9.15 - 4.16
Redgauntlet	1916	Destroyer	7.17 - 8.17
Frobisher	1920	Destroyer	1.18 - 1.19
Sirdar	1918	Destroyer	1.19 - 11.19
Venturous	1917	Destroyer	11.19 - 12.20
Serene	1918	Destroyer	12.20 - 1.22
Ashanti	1937	Destroyer	1939 - 1940
Laurentic	1927	AMC	1939 - 11.40
Aquitania	1913	Troop	1940 - 1948
Grafton	1954	Frigate	1954 - 1971

F52

Lochinvar	1915	Destroyer	1.18 - 1.19
Sparrowhawk	1918	Destroyer	1.19 - 11.19

Verdun	1917	Destroyer	1.19 - 12.20
Wolfhound	1918	Destroyer	12.20 - 1.22
Andes	1939	Troop	1940 - 1948
Godavari RIN	1940	Sloop	1948 - 1948
Sind RPN	1940	Frigate	1948 - 1959
(ex *Godavari*)			
Juno	1965	Frigate	1965 - 1992

F53

Phoebe	1916	Destroyer	1.17 - 10.17
North Star	1916	Destroyer	1.18 - 9.18
Volunteer	1919	Destroyer	9.18 - 1.19
Serapis	1918	Destroyer	1.19 - 11.19
Valorous	1917	Destroyer	11.19 - 12.20
Sardonyx	1919	Destroyer	12.20 - 1.22
Janus	1938	Destroyer	1939 - 1940
Ausonia	1921	Repair Ship	1940 - 1948
Undaunted	1943	Frigate	1954 - 1974

F54

Sylph	1916	Destroyer	9.15 - 4.16
Nugent	1917	Destroyer	1.18 - 9.18
Trinidad	1918	Destroyer	1.19 - 11.19
Versatile	1917	Destroyer	1.19 - 12.20
Grenville	1916	Destroyer	12.20 - 1.22
Cilicia	1938	AMC	1940 - 1944
Selsey Bill	1945	Repair Ship	1945 - 1946
Hardy	1953	Frigate	1953 - 1979

F55

Setter	1916	Destroyer	9.15 - 4.16
Phoebe	1916	Destroyer	1.18 - 9.18
Turbulent	1916	Destroyer	10.19 - 11.19
Scout	1918	Destroyer	1.19 - 11.19
Walker	1917	Destroyer	11.19 - 12.20
Sturdy	1919	Destroyer	12.20 - 1.22
Lightning	1940	Destroyer	Pre-build
California	1923	AMC	1940 - 1942
Empress of Scotland	1930	Troop	1942 - 1948
Silverton	1940	Frigate	1948 - 1958
Waikato RNZN	1964	Frigate	1964 - 1998

F56

Redoubt	1916	Destroyer	1.17 - 1.18
Radiant	1916	Destroyer	1.18 - 1.19
Scotsman	1918	Destroyer	1.19 - 11.19
Whirlwind	1917	Destroyer	11.19 - 12.20
Sterling	1918	Destroyer	12.20 - 1.22
Prince Robert RCN	1930	AMC	1940 - 1948
Test	1942	Frigate	1948 - 1955
Argonaut	1966	Frigate	1966 - 1993

F57

Simoom	1916	Destroyer	9.15 - 1.18
Redoubt	1916	Destroyer	1.18 - 1.19

Simoom	1916	Destroyer	1.19 - 11.19
Wrestler	1918	Destroyer	11.19 - 12.20
Thanet	1918	Destroyer	12.20 - 1.22
Chitral	1925	AMC	1940 - 1944
Black Swan	1939	Frigate	1948 - 1956
Queenborough RAN	1942	Frigate	1960 - 1969
Andromeda	1967	Frigate	1967 - 1993

F58

Redgauntlet	1916	Destroyer	1916 - 1.17
Retriever	1917	Destroyer	1.18 - 1.19
Valkyrie	1917	Destroyer	11.19 - 12.20
Stonehenge	1919	Destroyer	12.20 - 1.22
Manela	1920	Ac Tran	1940 - 1941
Duncansby Head	1944	Repair Ship	1944 - 1948
Hart	1943	Frigate	1948 - 1958
Hermione	1967	Frigate	1967 - 1992

F59

Radiant	1916	Destroyer	1917 - 1.18
Satyr	1916	Destroyer	1.18 - 1.19
Wakeful	1917	Destroyer	12.20 - 1.22
Mashona	1937	Destroyer	1939 - 5.40
Monowai RNZN	1924	AMC	1940 - 1944
Zetland	1942	Frigate	1948 - 1954
Chichester	1955	Frigate	1955 - 1978

F60

Starfish	1916	Destroyer	9.15 - 4.16
Sceptre	1917	Destroyer	1.18 - 1.19
Abdiel	1915	Destroyer	11.19 - 1922
Sea Belle	1928	AMC	1940 - 1946
Alacrity	1944	Frigate	1948 - 1956
Jupiter	1967	Frigate	1967 - 1992

F61

Anzac	1917	Destroyer	2.17 - 4.17
Botha	1914	Destroyer	4.17 - 1.18
Sharpshooter	1917	Destroyer	1.18 - 1.19
Vanoc	1917	Destroyer	1.19 - 1922
Javelin	1938	Destroyer	1939 - 1940
Pretoria Castle	1938	AMC	1938 - 1943
Pretoria Castle	1938	Esc Carrrier	1943 - 1945
Antigonish RCN	1944	Frigate	1948 - 1956
Llandaff	1955	Frigate	1955 - 1976

F62

Skate	1917	Destroyer	9.15 - 1.18
Skilful	1917	Destroyer	1.18 - 1.19
Vanquisher	1917	Destroyer	1.19 - 11.19
Turbulent	1916	Destroyer	12.20 - 1.22
Moray Firth	1944	Repair Ship	1944 - 1948
Pellew	1954	Frigate	1954 - 1971

F63

Recruit	1916	Destroyer	1.17 - 1.18
Springbok	1917	Destroyer	1.18 - 1.19
Venturous	1917	Destroyer	1.19 - 11.19
Sesame	1918	Destroyer	12.20 - 1.22
Royal Ulsterman	1936	LSI	1941 - 1942
Larne	1940	Destroyer	1940
Gurkha (ex Larne)	1941	Destroyer	1941 - Sunk
Scarborough	1955	Frigate	1955 - 1972

F64

Retriever	1917	Destroyer	9.15 - 4.16
Starfish	1916	Destroyer	1.18 - 1.19
Vittoria	1917	Destroyer	1.19 - 11.19
Broke	1920	Destroyer	12.20 - 1.22
Kingston	1939	Destroyer	1939 - 5.40
Adamant	1940	Depot Ship	1940 - 1948
Nereide	1944	Frigate	1948 - 1958

F65

Springbok	1917	Destroyer	9.15 - 4.16
Stork	1916	Destroyer	1.18 - 1.19
Tarpon	1917	Destroyer	1.19 - 11.22
Transylvania	1925	AMC	1940 - 8.40
Mauretania	1906	Troopship	1940 - 1946
Tenby	1955	Frigate	1965 - 1972

F66

Stork	1916	Destroyer	9.15 - 4.16
Surprise	1916	Destroyer	1.18 - 6.18
Marksman	1915	Destroyer	9.18 - 1.19
Telemachus	1917	Destroyer	1.19 - 1.22
Flores RNLN	1925	Gunboat	1941 - 1946
Starling	1942	Frigate	1948 - 1965

F67

Torrent	1916	Destroyer	9.15 - 4.16
Sybille	1917	Destroyer	1.18 - 1.19
Gabriel	1915	Destroyer	1.19 - 1.22
Bedouin	1937	Destroyer	1939 - 5.40
Esperance Bay	1922	AMC	1940 - 1941
Orford Ness	1945	Repair Ship	1945 - 1946
Tyrian	1942	Frigate	1952 - 1965

F68

Tormentor	1917	Destroyer	9.15 - 4.16
Sylph	1916	Destroyer	1.18 - 1.19
Restless	1916	Destroyer	11.19 - 1.22
Ascania	1939	AMC	1940 - 1942

F69

Surprise	1916	Destroyer	9.15 - 1.17
Talisman	1915	Destroyer	1.18 - 6.18
Moon	1915	Destroyer	6.18 - 1.19
Rigorous	1916	Destroyer	11.19 - 1.22

Ulster Monarch	1939	AMC	1942 - 1945
Redpole	1943	Frigate	1948 - 1960
Bacchante	1968	Frigate	1967 - 1982
Wellington RNZN	1968	Frigate	1982 - 1999
(ex *Bacchante*)			

F70

Truculent	1917	Destroyer	1.17 -1.18
Taurus	1917	Destroyer	1.18 - 1.19
Medina	1916	Destroyer	1.19 - 12.20
Prince Henry RCN	1930	AMC	1940 - 1946
Farndale	1940	Frigate	1948 - 1962
Apollo	1970	Frigate	1970 - 1988

F71

Taurus	1917	Destroyer	9.15 - 4.16
Teazer	1917	Destroyer	1.18 - 1.19
Nonpareil	1916	Destroyer	1.19 - 12.20
Asturias	1939	AMC	1940 - 4.44
Sparrow	1946	Frigate	1948 - 1958
Scylla	1968	Frigate	1968 - 1993

F72

Tarpon	1917	Destroyer	9.15 - 4.16
Tempest	1917	Destroyer	1.18 - 1.19
Observer	1916	Destroyer	1.19 - 1.22
Jersey	1938	Destroyer	1939 - 1940
Unicorn	1942	Maint Ship	1940 - 1948
Wizard	1943	Frigate	1956 - 1966
Ariadne	1971	Frigate	1971 - 1992

F73

Termagant	1915	Destroyer	1.18 - 9.18
Swallow	1918	Destroyer	1.18 - 1.19
Offa	1916	Destroyer	1.19 - 12.20
Queen of Bermuda	1932	AMC	1940 - 1943
Rattray Head	1945	Repair Ship	1945 - 1946
Eastbourne	1955	Frigate	1955 - 1984

F74

Thruster	1917	Destroyer	9.15 - 4.16
Tetrarch	1917	Destroyer	1.18 - 1.19
Plucky	1916	Destroyer	1.19 - 12.20
Legion	1940	Destroyer	Pre-build
Aberdonian	1909	Depot Ship	1940 - 1945
Swan RAN	1936	Frigate	1948 - 1962

F75

Torrid	1917	Destroyer	9.15 - 4.16
Thisbe	1917	Destroyer	1.18 - 1.19
Oriana	1916	Destroyer	1.19 - 1.22
Eskimo	1937	Destroyer	1939 - 5.40
Mooltan	1923	AMC	1940 - 1941
Haydon	1942	Frigate	1948 - 1958
Charybdis	1968	Frigate	1968 - 1991

F76

Tempest	1917	Destroyer	9.15 - 4.16
Thruster	1917	Destroyer	1.18 - 1.19
Oracle	1916	Destroyer	1.19 - 12.20
Western Isles	1902	Command Sp	1941 - 1946
Virago	1943	Frigate	1952 - 1963
Mermaid	1966	Frigate	1966 - 1977

F77

Sybille	1917	Destroyer	1.17 - 1.18
Martial	1915	Destroyer	1.18 - 1.19
Pelican	1916	Destroyer	1.19 - 12.20
Camito	1915	OBV	1940 - 5.41
Nieuw Amsterdam	1937	Troopship	1940 - 1946
Blackpool	1957	Frigate	1957 - 1971

F78

Skilful	1917	Destroyer	9.15 - 1.18
Tornado	1917	Destroyer	1.18 - 3.18
Lightfoot	1915	Destroyer	9.18 - 1.19
Steadfast	1918	Destroyer	1.19 - 12.20
Derbyshire	1935	AMC	1940 - 1942
Ile de France	1926	Troop	1942 - 1945
Cottesmore	1940	Frigate	1948 - 1950
Blackwood	1955	Frigate	1955 - 1976
Kent	1998	Frigate	1998 -

F79

Sceptre	1917	Destroyer	1.17 - 1.18
Torrent	1916	Destroyer	1.18 - 9.18
Tarpon	1917	Destroyer	9.18 - 1.19
Tilbury	1918	Destroyer	11.19 - 1.22
Resource	1928	Repair Ship	1940 - 1948
Brissenden	1942	Frigate	1948 - 1961
Portland	1999	Frigate	1999 -

F80

Ulysses	1917	Destroyer	1.17 - 1.18
Torrid	1917	Destroyer	1.18 - 1.19
Nereus	1916	Destroyer	1.19 - 1.22
Woolwich	1934	Depot Ship	1940 - 1948
Hindustan RIN	1930	Sloop	1948 - 1948
Karzad RPN	1930	Frigate	1948 - 1951
(ex *Hindustan* RIN)			
Duncan	1957	Frigate	1957 - 1984
Grafton	1994	Frigate	1994 - 2006

F81

Tirade	1917	Destroyer	9.15 - 4.16
Trident	1915	Destroyer	1.18 - 9.18
Telemachus	1917	Destroyer	9.18 - 1.19
Nizam	1916	Destroyer	1.19 - 12.20
Gruno RNLN	1912	Gunboat	1940 - 1945
Stork	1936	Frigate	1948 - 1958
Sutherland	1996	Frigate	1996 -

F82

Thisbe	1917	Destroyer	9.15 - 4.16
Truculent	1917	Destroyer	1.18 - 1.19
Norseman	1916	Destroyer	1.19 - 1.22
Sikh	1937	Destroyer	1939 - 5.40
Bulolo	1938	LSH(L)	1940 - 1946
Magpie	1943	Frigate	1948 - 1959
Somerset	1994	Frigate	1994 -

F83

Valkyrie	1917	Destroyer	6.17 - 1.18
Ulleswater	1917	Destroyer	1.18 - 1.19
Obdurate	1916	Destroyer	1.19 - 1.22
Edinburgh Castle	1910	Base Ship	1940 - 1945
Ulster	1942	Frigate	1956 - 1977
St Albans	2000	Frigate	2000 -

F84

Vanquisher	1917	Destroyer	9.15- 4.16
Ursula	1917	Destroyer	1.18 - 3.18
Vanoc	1917	Destroyer	9.18 - 1.19
Oberon	1916	Destroyer	1.19 - 12.20
Patrician	1916	Destroyer	12.20 - 1.22
Alynbank	1925	Aux AA	1940 - 1944
Tarbatness	1945	Repair Ship	1945 - 1946
Exmouth	1955	Frigate	1955 - 1979

F85

Tancred	1917	Destroyer	9.15 - 4.16
Marksman	1915	Destroyer	1.18 - 4.18
Vanquisher	1917	Destroyer	9.18 - 1.19
Onslow	1916	Destroyer	1.19 - 12.20
Patriot	1916	Destroyer	12.20 - 1.22
Jupiter	1938	Destroyer	1939 - 1940
Montclare	1921	AMC	1940 - 1948
Arabis	1943	Frigate	1948 - 1957
Keppel	1954	Frigate	1954 - 1977
Cumberland	1986	Frigate	1986 - 2011

F86

Telemachus	1917	Destroyer	9.15 - 4.16
Valkyrie	1917	Destroyer	1.18 - 6.18
Vehement	1917	Destroyer	9.18 - 1.19
Oriole	1916	Destroyer	1.19 - 12.20
Corfu	1931	AMC	1940 - 1944
Mull of Kintyre	1945	Repair Ship	1945 - 1948
Pelican	1938	Frigate	1948 - 1958
Campbeltown	1987	Frigate	1987 - 2011

F87

Tetrarch	1917	Destroyer	9.15 - 4.16
Kempenfelt	1915	Destroyer	1.18 - 3.18
Venturous	1917	Destroyer	9.18 - 1.19
Orpheus	1916	Destroyer	1.19 - 12.20
Lance	1940	Destroyer	1940 - Sunk

Maron	1930	OBV	1940 - 1942
Westernland	1918	Repair Ship	1942 - 1948
Eglinton	1939	Frigate	1948 - 1956
Chatham	1988	Frigate	1988 - 2011

F88

Ursula	1917	Destroyer	9.15 - 4.16
Ithuriel	1916	Destroyer	1.18 - 1.19
Osiris	1916	Destroyer	1.19 - 12.20
Alcantara	1939	AMC	1940 - 1943
Flamborough Head	1944	Repair Ship	1944 - 1948
Lamerton	1940	Frigate	1948 - 1953
Malcolm	1955	Frigate	1955 - 1976
Broadsword	1976	Frigate	1976 - 1995
Grafton	1994	Frigate	2004
Glasgow	Bldg	Frigate	2019 -

Grafton (F80) portrayed the fictional *HMS Suffolk* for the unsuccessful television drama *'Making Waves'* filmed in 2004. During filming she wore the fictional pendant number F88.

F89

Tristram	1917	Destroyer	9.15 - 4.16
Shakespeare	1917	Destroyer	1.18 - 1.19
Pigeon	1916	Destroyer	1.19 - 12.20
Prince David RCN	1930	AMC	1940 - 1948
Allington Castle	1944	Frigate	1948 - 1958
Battleaxe	1977	Frigate	1977 - 1997
Cardiff	Bldg	Frigate	2019 -

F90

Tyrant	1917	Destroyer	4.17 - 1.18
Spenser	1917	Destroyer	1.18 - 1.19
Minion	1915	Destroyer	1.19 - 12.20
Princess Iris	1917	LSC	1941 - 1946
Woodcock	1942	Frigate	1948 - 1955
Brilliant	1978	Frigate	1978 - 1996
Belfast	Bldg	Frigate	2019 -

F91

Ulster	1917	Destroyer	9.15 - 4.16
Verdun	1917	Destroyer	1.18 - 9.18
Gabriel	1915	Destroyer	9.18 - 1.19
Narwhal	1915	Destroyer	1.19 - 12.20
Kipling	1939	Destroyer	1939 - 5.40
Circassia	1937	AMC	1940 - 1942
Murray	1955	Frigate	1955 - 1966
Brazen	1980	Frigate	1980 - 1994

F92

Valorous	1917	Destroyer	9.15 - 4.16
Vega	1917	Destroyer	1.18 - 3.18
Ariel	1911	Destroyer	6.18 - 9.18
Prince	1916	Destroyer	9.18 - 1.19

Portia	1916	Destroyer	1.19 - 12.20
Sandhurst	1905	Depot Ship	1940 - 1946
Exe	1942	Frigate	1948 - 1956
Boxer	1981	Frigate	1981 - 1999

F93

Teazer	1917	Destroyer	9.15 - 4.16
Venetia	1917	Destroyer	1.18 - 3.18
Ferret	1911	Destroyer	9.18 - 1.19
Ossory	1915	Destroyer	1.19 - 1.22
Vigilant	1942	Frigate	1953 - 1963
Beaver	1982	Frigate	1982 - 1999

F94

Umpire	1917	Destroyer	9.15 - 4.16
Vectis	1917	Destroyer	1.18 - 3.18
Legion	1914	Destroyer	9.18 - 1.19
Pylades	1916	Destroyer	1.19 - 12.20
Salopian	1926	AMC	1940 - 5.41
Palliser	1956	Frigate	1956 - 1973
Brave	1983	Frigate	1983 - 1999

F95

Urchin	1917	Destroyer	9.15 - 4.16
Violent	1917	Destroyer	1.18 - 3.18
Sandfly	1911	Destroyer	9.18 - 1.19
Mindful	1915	Destroyer	1.19 - 12.20
Westralia RAN	1929	AMC	1940 - 1943
Sutlej RIN	1940	Sloop	1948 - 1955
London	1984	Frigate	1984 - 1999

F96

Tenacious	1917	Destroyer	9.15 - 4.16
Verulam	1917	Destroyer	1.18 - 3.18
Vittoria	1917	Destroyer	10.18 - 9.19
Sturdy	1919	Destroyer	9.18 - 1.19
Rattlesnake	1910	Destroyer	1.19 - 12.20
Mull of Oa	1945	Repair Ship	1945 - 1946
Peacock	1943	Frigate	1948 - 1956
Sheffield	1986	Frigate	1984 - 2002

F97

Tornado	1917	Destroyer	9.15 - 4.16
Redgauntlet	1916	Destroyer	1.18 - 1.19
Savage	1910	Destroyer	1.19 - 12.20
Canton	1938	AMC	1940 - 1944
Russell	1954	Frigate	1954 - 1985

F98

Tower	1917	Destroyer	9.15 - 4.16
Scott	1917	Destroyer	1.18 - 7.18
Scourge	1910	Destroyer	1.19 - 12.20
Palomares	1939	LSF(D)	1940 - 1946
Orwell	1942	Frigate	1952 - 1965
Coventry	1986	Frigate	1985 - 2001

F99

Valentine	1917	Destroyer	1917 - 1.18
Viceroy	1917	Destroyer	1.18 - 3.18
Steadfast	1918	Destroyer	3.19 - 11.19
Winchester	1918	Destroyer	11.19 - 12.20
Viscount	1917	Destroyer	1.22 - 8.25
Laforey	1941	Destroyer	Pre-build
Carthage	1931	AMC	1940 - 1943
Deer Sound	1939	Repair Ship	1944 - 1946
Lincoln	1959	Frigate	1959 - 1979
Cornwall	1985	Frigate	1985 - 2011

F100

Marsdale	1940	OBV	1940 - 1942

F101

Daffodil	1917	LSC	1941 - 1945
Yarmouth	1959	Frigate	1959 - 1986

F102

Malvernian	1937	OBV	1940 - 7.41
Ying Chow	1905	Training Ship	1942 - 1945
Zest	1943	Frigate	1957 - 1968

F103

Corinthian	1938	OBV	1940 - 1945
Arbutus	1944	Frigate	1948 - 1957
Lowestoft	1960	Frigate	1960 - 1985

F104

Manistee	1920	OBV	1940 - 2.41
Bhadravati RIN	1932	AP Vsl	1939 - 1945
Dido	1961	Frigate	1961 - 1983
Southland RNZN (ex Dido)	1961	Frigate	1983 - 1995

F105

Ariguani	1926	OBV	1940 - 1941
Alnwick Castle	1944	Frigate	1948 - 1958

F106

Registan	1930	OBV	1940 - 1941
Ripon	1945	Ac Transport	1945 - 1948
Assam RIN	1943	Frigate	1948
Brighton	1959	Frigate	1957 - 1981

F107

Maplin	1932	OBV	1940 - 1942
Rothesay	1957	Frigate	1957 - 1988

F108

Llanstephan Castle	1914	Troop Ship	1940 - 1945
Londonderry	1958	Frigate	1958 - 1984

F109

Lady Somers	1929	OBV	1940 - 7.41
Abercrombie	1942	Monitor	1942 - 1948
Leander	1961	Frigate	1961 - 1987

F110

Bachaquero	1937	LST	1941 - 1945
Cauvery RIN	1943	Sloop	1948 - 1977

(renamed *Kaveri* following Indian partition)

F111

Baldur	1937	Base Ship	1940 - 1943
Fernie	1940	Frigate	1948 - 1956
Otago RNZN	1958	Frigate	1960 - 1983

F112

Cape Sable	1936	AMC	1941 - 1946
Albrighton	1941	Frigate	1948 - 1957

F113

Botlea	1917	Q-Ship	1939 - 1941
Blackburn	1946	Ac Transport	1946 - 1948
Falmouth	1959	Frigate	1959 - 1984

F114

City of Durban	1920	AMC	1941 - 1942
Seafox	1946	Ac Tran	1946 - 1948
Ajax	1962	Frigate	1962 - 1985

F115

Royal Scotsman	1936	LSI	1940 - 1942
Berwick	1959	Frigate	1959 - 1985

F116

King Gruffyd	1919	Decoy	3.41 - 9.41
Walrus	1945	Ac Transport	1945 - 1948
Amethyst	1943	Frigate	1948 - 1957

F117

Misoa	1937	LST	1941 - 1945
Ashanti	1959	Frigate	1959 - 1990

F118

Ulster Queen	1929	LSF(D)	1940 - 1946
Talybont	1943	Frigate	1948 - 1961

F119

Bushwood	1930	MS	1940 - 1942
Eskimo	1961	Frigate	1961 - 1980

F120

El Hind	1938	LSI	1940 - 1944
Garth	1940	Frigate	1948 - 1958

F121

Boxer	1942	LST	1942 - 1948
Tumult	1942	Frigate	1957 - 1965

F122

Roc	1945	Ac Transport	1945 - 1948
Gurkha	1960	Frigate	1960 - 1984

F123

Sefton	1943	LSI	1944 - ....
Andelle	1922	AuxMD	1944 - 1945
Crane	1942	Frigate	1948 - 1962

F124

Jamaica Producer	1934	OBV	8.41 - 10.41
Zulu	1962	Frigate	1962 - 1984

F125

Tasajera	1938	LST	1941 - 1945
Mohawk	1962	Frigate	1962 - 1980

F126

Empire Chivalry	1937	Store Ship	1940 - 1946
Bedale	1941	Frigate	1948 - 1952
Plymouth	1959	Frigate	1959 - 1988

F127

Bruiser	1942	LST	1942 - 1944
Penelope	1962	Frigate	1962 - 1991

F128

Karanja	1930	LSI	1940 - 1942
Wilton	1941	Frigate	1948 - 1959

F129

Rhyl	1959	Frigate	1959 - 1983

F130

Burlington	1921	MS	1940 - 1941
Fairfax	1921	Repair Ship	1941 - 1945
(ex-Burlington)			
Eastway	1943	LSD	1945 - 1948
Blankney	1940	Frigate	1948 - 1959

F131

Thruster	1942	LST	1942 - 1944
Chiddingfold	1941	Frigate	1948 - 1954
Nubian	1960	Frigate	1960 - 1981

F132

Keren	1930	LSI	1941 - 1948
Belvoir	1941	Frigate	1948 - 1957

F133

Haitan	1909	Base Ship	1941 - 1946

Tartar		1960	Frigate	1960 - 1984	*Kuthar* RIN	1958	Frigate	1958 - 1977

F134

Philoctetes		1922	Repair Ship	1940 - 1945	**F147**			
Bicester		1941	Frigate	1948 - 1956	*President Steyn* SAN	1961	Frigate	1961 - 1980

F135

F148

Cattistock	1940	Frigate	1948 - 1957	*Holderness*	1940	Frigate	1948 - 1956
				Taranaki RNZN	1959	Frigate	1961 - 1982

F136

Cap des Palmes FR	1935	AMC	1940 - 1945	**F149**			
				Khukri RIN	1956	Frigate	1956 - 1971

F137

Wayland	1921	Repair Ship	1940 - 1945	**F150**			
Hambledon	1939	Frigate	1948 - 1955	*Bleasdale*	1941	Frigate	1948 - 1956
Beas RIN	1958	Frigate	1958 - 1988	*President Kruger* SAN	1960	Frigate	1960 - 1982

F138

F152

Vienna	1929	Depot Ship	1941 - 1945	*Cowdray*	1941	Frigate	1948 - 1959
Rapid	1942	Frigate	1952 - 1974	**F154**			
				Cotswold	1940	Frigate	1948 - 1958

F139

F155

Bonaventure	1942	Depot Ship	1942 - 1948	*Ballinderry*	1942	Frigate	1948 - 1961
Betwa RIN	1958	Frigate	1958 - 1991	**F156**			
				Tuscan	1942	Frigate	1953 - 1963

F140

F157

Highway	1943	LSD	1943 - 1946	*Wrangler*	1943	Frigate	1953 - 1956
Barracuda RIN	1940	Depot Ship	1940 - 1946	**F158**			
Talwar RIN	1958	Frigate	1958 - 1992	*Quantock*	1940	Frigate	1948 - 1954
				F159			

F141

Adria IT	1914	Base Ship	1941 - 1943	*Wakeful*	1943	Frigate	1952 - 1971
Undine	1943	Frigate	1954 - 1960				

F160

F142

Northway	1943	LSD	1943 - 1948	*Empire Halberd*	1943	LSI(L)	1943 - 1944
Brocklesby	1940	Frigate	1948 - 1963	*Silvio*	1943	LSI	1944 - 1946
				(ex *Empire Halberd*)			

F143

F161

Oceanway	1943	LSD	1943 - 1948	*Empire Battleaxe*	1943	LSI	1943 - 1944
Blackmore	1941	Frigate	1948 - 1953	*Donovan*	1943	LSI	1944 - 1946
Trishul	1958	Frigate	1958 - 1992				

F162

F144

Portway	1944	LSD	To US Navy	*Empire Cutlass*	1943	LSI(L)	1943 - 1944
Kirpan RIN	1958	Frigate	1958 - 1977	*Sansovino*	1943	LSI	1944 - 1946
				(ex *Empire Cutlass*)			
				Croome	1941	Frigate	1948 - 1957

F145

F163

Swashway	1944	LSD	To US Navy	*Empire Broadsword*	1943	LSI	1944 - 1944
Whaddon	1940	Frigate	1948 - 1959	**F164**			
President Pretorius SAN	1962	Frigate	1962 - 1985	*Barracuda* RIN	1940	Depot Ship	BR619(2)
				F165			
				Blinjoe RNLN	1940	Depot Ship	BR619(2)

F146

F166

Waterway	1944	LSD	To US Navy	*Kelantan*	1921	Depot Ship	1943 - 1948
Cleveland	1940	Frigate	1948 - 1957				

F167

Pangkor	1929	Depot Ship	1944 - 1946

F168

Lothian	1938	LSH(L)	1944 - 1946

F169

Ambitious	1913	Depot Ship	1940 - 1948
Paladin	1941	Frigate	1956 - 1962
Amazon	1971	Frigate	1971 - 1993

F170

Empire Arquebus	1943	LSI(L)	1943 - 1945
Cicero	1943	LSI(L)	1945
(ex Empire Arquebus)			
Antelope	1972	Frigate	1972 - 1982

F171

Empire Mace	1943	LSI(L)	1943 - 1.45
Galteemore	1943	LSI(L)	1.45 - 10.45
(ex Empire Mace)			
Calpe	1941	Frigate	1948 - 1952
Active	1972	Frigate	1972 - 1994

F172

Empire Spearhead	1943	LSI(L)	1943 - 1945
Ormonde	1943	LSI(L)	1945 - 1946
(ex Empire Spearhead)			
Ambuscade	1973	Frigate	1973 - 1993

F173

Assistance	1944	Repair Ship	1944 - 1946
Melbreak	1942	Frigate	1948 - 1956
Arrow	1974	Frigate	1974 - 1994

F174

Diligence	1944	Repair Ship	1944 - 1946
Middleton	1941	Frigate	1948 - 1957
Alacrity	1974	Frigate	1974 - 1994

F175

Hecla	1944	Repair Ship	1944 - 1948
Barcoo RAN	1943	Frigate	1948 - 1969

F176

Reliance	1944	Repair Ship	US Navy
Dutiful	1944	Repair Ship	1944 - 1948
Brecon	1942	Frigate	1948 - 1962

F177

Faithful	1944	Repair Ship	1944 - 1948

F178

Ionia RHN	(....)	....	BR619(2)

F181

Persimmon	1943	LSI(L)	1944 - 1946
Sackville RCN	1941	Corvette	1948 - 1949

F182

Meynell	1940	Frigate	1948 - 1954

F183

Empire Crossbow	1943	LSI(L)	1943 - 1944
Sainfoin	1943	LSI	1944 - 1946
(ex Empire Crossbow)			

F184

Empire Anvil	1943	LSI(L)	1943 - 1944
Rocksand	1943	LSI	1944 - 1946
(ex Empire Anvil)			
Ardent	1975	Frigate	1975 - 1982

F185

Dullisk Cove	1944	Repair Ship	1944 - 1948
Relentless	1942	Frigate	1951 - 1965
Avenger	1975	Frigate	1975 - 1994

F186

Mullion Cove	1944	Repair Ship	1944 - 1948

F187

Beauly Firth	1944	Repair Ship	1944 - 1948
Whirlwind	1943	Frigate	1953 - 1974

F188

Cuillin Sound	1944	Repair Ship	1944 - 1948

F189

Holm Sound	1944	Repair Ship	1944 - 1948
Termagant	1943	Frigate	1953 - 1959

F190

Solway Firth	1944	Repair Ship	1944 - 1948
Ledbury	1941	Frigate	1948 - 1958

F191

Queen	1942	Patrol Craft	1942 - 1945
Wilhelmina RNLN			

F192

Pytchley	1940	Frigate	1948 - 1956

F193

Rocket	1942	Frigate	1951 - 1964

F195

Roebuck	1942	Frigate	1953 - 1962

F196

Cowslip	1941	Corvette	1948 - 1949
Urchin	1943	Frigate	1954 - 1964

F197

Grenville	1942	Frigate	1954 - 1974

F198

Oakley	1942	Frigate	1948 - 1957

F199			
Tetcott	1941	Frigate	1948 - 1956
F200			
Ursa	1943	Frigate	1953 - 1966
F204			
Tughril RPN	1941	Frigate	1951 - 1963
(ex Onslaught)			
F205			
Mayu Burma *(ex Fal)*	1942	Frigate	1948 - ....
F206			
Avon Vale	1940	Frigate	1948 - 1958
F216			
Karangi RAN	1941	BDV	.... - ....
F217			
Swale	1942	Frigate	1948 - 1955
F219			
Ness	1942	Frigate	1948 - 1956
F221			
Blenheim	1919	Depot Ship	1940 - 1948
Chelmer	1943	Frigate	1948 - 1957
F222			
Teviot	1942	Frigate	1948 - 1955
F224			
Rother	1941	Frigate	1948 - 1955
F229			
Lancaster	1990	Frigate	1990 -
F230			
Wear	1942	Frigate	1948 - 1957
Norfolk	1987	Frigate	1987 - 2005
F231			
Argyll	1989	Frigate	1989 -
F232			
Tay	1942	Frigate	1948 - 1957
Lancaster	1990	Frigate	1987

Lancaster was originally assigned F232, and indeed during build, the appropriate hull section was painted with this number. However, it was noted that F232 was the form used to report collisions and groundings in the Royal Navy and therefore the number is considered unlucky. In 1989 the decision was taken to change the number to F229 and in 1990 she was launched as such.

F233			
Marlborough	1989	Frigate	1989 - 2005
F234			
Iron Duke	1991	Frigate	1991 -

F235			
Jed	1942	Frigate	1948 - 1957
Monmouth	1991	Frigate	1991 -

Monmouth is affectionately known as 'The Black Duke' and is the only ship in service with the Royal Navy that has its name painted in black (rather than red), its gold crown on the funnel is blacked out and she flies a black flag from the mainmast. Additionally, her ceremonial life rings and gangway dodgers are also black. The officers of the ship wear black handkerchiefs in their uniform jacket pocket rather than the more traditional white. All of this reflects the shame associated with the dissolution of the title and the blacking out of the Coat of Arms of the Duke of Monmouth in 1685 following the Monmouth Rebellion against James II of England.

F236			
Montrose	1992	Frigate	1992 -
F237			
Westminster	1992	Frigate	1992 -
F238			
Woodstock RCN	1941	Corvette	1948 - 1949
Northumberland	1992	Frigate	1992 -
F239			
Richmond	1993	Frigate	1993 -
F241			
Kale	1942	Frigate	1948 - 1957
F243			
Kukri RIN	1942	Frigate	1948 - 1951
F246			
Spey	1941	Frigate	1948 - Sold
F248			
Waveney	1942	Frigate	1948 - 1957
F249			
Tippu Sultan RPN	1941	Frigate	1959 - 1963
(ex Onslow)			
F252			
Helford	1943	Frigate	1948 - 1956
F253			
Helmsdale	1943	Frigate	1948 - 1957
F254			
Ettrick	1943	Frigate	1948 - 1953
F256			
Tir (ex Bann) RIN	1942	Frigate	1948 - Sold
F257			
Derg	1943	Frigate	1948 - 1960
F265			
Zulfiquar RPN	1942	Frigate	1948 - 1963
F269			
Meon	1943	Frigate	1948 - 1958
F270			
Nene	1942	Frigate	1948 - 1955

F271
Plym	1943	Frigate	1948 - 1952

F272
Tavy	1943	Frigate	1948 - 1955

F286
Amberley Castle	1943	Frigate	1948 - 1960

F293
Tees	1943	Frigate	1948 - 1955

F294
Towy	1943	Frigate	1948 - 1956

F295
Usk	1943	Frigate	1948 - Sold

F321
New Waterford RCN	1943	Frigate	1948 - 1949

F326
Kapuskasing RCN	1943	Frigate	1948 - 1949

F328
Swansea RCN	1942	Frigate	1948 - 1949

F330
Oshawa RCN	1943	Frigate	1948 - 1949

F336
Wallaceburg RCN	1942	Frigate	1948 - 1949

F337
Winnipeg RCN	1942	Frigate	1948 - 1949

F354
Gascoyne RAN	1943	Frigate	1948 - 1972

F355
Hadleigh Castle	1943	Frigate	1948 - 1959

F356
Odzani	1943	Frigate	1948 - 1957

F362
Portchester Castle	1943	Frigate	1948 - 1957

F363
Hawkesbury RAN	1943	Frigate	1948 - 1962

F364
Lachlan RAN	1944	Frigate	1948 - 1949
Lachlan RNZN	1944	Frigate	1949 - 1974

F365
Lochy	1943	Frigate	1948 - 1956

F367
Taff	1943	Frigate	1948 - 1957

F371
Wye	1943	Frigate	1948 - 1954

F372
Rushen Castle	1943	Frigate	1948 - 1960

F376
Burdekin RAN	1943	Frigate	1948 - 1962

F377
Diamantina RAN	1944	Frigate	1948 - 1972

F379
Carisbrooke Castle	1943	Frigate	1948 - 1958

F383
Flint Castle	1943	Frigate	1948 - 1956

F384
Leeds Castle	1943	Frigate	1948 - 1956

F386
Hedingham Castle	1944	Frigate	1948 - 1957

F387
Berkeley Castle	1943	Frigate	1948 - 1955

F388
Dumbarton Castle	1943	Frigate	1948 - 1960

F389
Knaresborough Castle	1943	Frigate	1948 - 1956

F390
Loch Fada	1943	Frigate	1948 - 1970

F391
Loch Killin	1943	Frigate	1948 - 1960

F392
Shamsher RPN	1943	Frigate	1948 - 1959

F396
Fort Francis RCN	1943	Frigate	1948 -1949

F397
Launceston Castle	1943	Frigate	1948 - 1959

F399
Tintagel Castle	1943	Frigate	1948 - 1958

F406
Barwon RAN	1944	Frigate	1948 - 1962

F407
Beacon Hill RCN	1943	Frigate	1948 - 1949

F408
Culgoa RAN	1944	Frigate	1948 - 1972

F413
Farnham Castle	1944	Frigate	1948 - 1960

F417
Halladale	1944	Frigate	1948 - 1949

F420
Kenilworth Castle	1943	Frigate	1948 - 1956

F421
Taupo RNZN	1944	Frigate	1948 - 1961
Canterbury RNZN	1969	Frigate	1969 - 2005

F422
Hawea RNZN	1944	Frigate	1948 - 1965

F423
Largo Bay	1944	Frigate	1948 - 1958

F424
Pukaki RNZN	1944	Frigate	1948 - 1965

F425
Loch Dunvegan	1944	Frigate	1948 - 1960

F426
Kaniere RNZN	1944	Frigate	1948 - 1966

F428
Loch Alvie	1944	Frigate	1948 - 1965

F429
Loch Fyne	1944	Frigate	1948 - 1970

F430			
Natal SAN (ex-Loch Cree)	1944	Frigate	1945 - 1956
F431			
Loch Tarbert	1944	Frigate	1948 - 1959
F432			
Good Hope SAN	1944	Frigate	1948 - 1965
F433			
Loch Insh	1944	Frigate	1948 - 1962
F434			
Loch Quoich	1944	Frigate	1948 - 1957
F436			
Surprise	1945	Despatch Vsl	1948 - 1965
F437			
Loch Lomond	1944	Frigate	1948 - 1964
F442			
Murchison RAN	1944	Frigate	1948 - 1967
F449			
Pevensey Castle	1944	Frigate	1948 - 1960
F454			
St Stephen RCN	1944	Frigate	1948 - 1949
F517			
Tuturi RNZN	1944	Frigate	1948 - 1961
F523			
Dovey	1943	Frigate	1948 - 1955
F525			
Ribble	1943	Frigate	1948 - 1957
F530			
Oakham Castle	1944	Frigate	1948 - 1958
F532			
Macquarie RAN	1945	Frigate	1948 - 1962
F535			
Shoalhaven RAN	1944	Frigate	1948 - 1962
F583			
Hotham	1943	Frigate	1948 - 1956
F600			
St Brides Bay	1945	Frigate	1948 - 1962
F602			
Transvaal SAN	1944	Frigate	1948 - 1964
F603			
Loch Arkaig	1945	Frigate	1948 - 1960
F604			
Start Bay	1945	Frigate	1948 - 1958
F605			
Tremadoc Bay	1945	Frigate	1948 - 1956
F608			
Padstow Bay	1945	Frigate	1948 - 1959
F609			
Loch Craggie	1944	Frigate	1948 - 1963
F615			
Widemouth Bay	1944	Frigate	1948 - 1957
F616			
Wigtown Bay	1945	Frigate	1948 - 1959
F619			
Loch Glendhu	1944	Frigate	1948 - 1957
F620			
Loch Gorm	1944	Frigate	1948 - 1961
F622			
Burghead Bay	1945	Frigate	1948 - 1959
F624			
Morecambe Bay	1944	Frigate	1948 - 1961
F625			
Loch Katrine	1944	Frigate	1948 - 1949
Rotoiti RNZN	1944	Frigate	1949 - 1965
F627			
Mounts Bay	1945	Frigate	1948 - 1961
F628			
Loch Killisport	1944	Frigate	1948 - 1970
F630			
Cardigan Bay	1944	Frigate	1948 - 1962
F633			
Whitesand Bay	1944	Frigate	1948 - 1956
F634			
St Austell Bay	1944	Frigate	1948 - 1959
F636			
Carnarvon Bay	1945	Frigate	1948 - 1959
F639			
Loch More	1944	Frigate	1948 - 1961
F644			
Cawsand Bay	1945	Frigate	1948 - 1959
F645			
Loch Ruthven	1944	Frigate	1948 - 1967
F647			
Alert	1945	Desp	1948 - 1971
F648			
Loch Scavaig	1944	Frigate	1948 - 1959
F650			
Porlock Bay	1945	Frigate	1948 - 1962
F651			
Veryan Bay	1944	Frigate	1948 - 1959
F655			
Loch Tralaig	1945	Frigate	1948 - 1963
F658			
Loch Veyatie	1944	Frigate	1948 - 1965
F668			
La Hulloise RCN	1940	Frigate	1948 - 1949
F690			
Caistor Castle	1944	Frigate	1948 - 1956
F691			
Lancaster Castle	1944	Frigate	1948 - 1960
F692			
Oxford Castle	1943	Frigate	1948 - 1960
F693			
Morpeth Castle	1943	Frigate	1948 - 1960
F698			
Condamine RAN	1944	Frigate	1948 - 1955

59

FA0

Vectis	1917	Destroyer	8.17 - 1.18
Tilbury	1918	Destroyer	9.18 - 1.19

FA1

Violent	1917	Destroyer	8.17 - 1.18
Shark	1912	Destroyer	1.19 - ....

FA2

Verulam	1917	Destroyer	8.17 - 1.18
Trusty	1918	Destroyer	5.19 - ....

FA3

Vendetta	1917	Destroyer	8.17 - 1.18
Sterling	1918	Destroyer	3.19 - ....

FA4

Redgauntlet	1916	Destroyer	8.17 - 1.18
Tenedos	1918	Destroyer	6.19 - 1.22

FA5

Tuscan	1919	Destroyer	6.19 - ....

FA6

Mackay	1918	Destroyer	6.19 - 11.19

FA7

Whitshed	1919	Destroyer	9.18 - 11.19

FA8

Stronghold	1919	Destroyer	6.19 - 1.22

F0A

Spenser	1917	Destroyer	7.17 - 8.17
Vampire	1917	Destroyer	1917- 1.18
Saladin	1919	Destroyer	4.19 - 11.19

F1A

Vehement	1917	Destroyer	8.17 - 1.18

Vanoc	1917	Destroyer	1.18 - 3.18
Success	1918	Destroyer	4.19 - 1920

F2A

Verdun	1917	Destroyer	8.17 - 1.18
Tattoo	1918	Destroyer	4.19 - 6.19

F3A

Vanquisher	1917	Destroyer	8.17 - 1.18
Swordsman	1918	Destroyer	3.19 - ....

F4A

Vega	1917	Destroyer	8.17 - 1.18
Stalwart	1918	Destroyer	4.19 - 1920

F5A

Vehement	1917	Destroyer	8.17 - 1.18
Sesame	1918	Destroyer	4.19 - ....

F6A

Toreador	1918	Destroyer	4.19 - ....

F7A

Serene	1918	Destroyer	5.19 - ....

F8A

Vanoc	1917	Destroyer	8.17 - 1.18
Sheldrake	1911	Destroyer	9.18 - 1.19

F9A

Valhalla	1917	Destroyer	6.17 - 8.17
Venetia	1917	Destroyer	8.17 - 12.17
Tribune	1918	Destroyer	1.19 - ....

Flag 'G' Superior

Pre 1940: Destroyers (Various pendants superior and inferior were used to increase number range)

1940-48: Destroyers

1948: None

G00

Nessus	1915	Destroyer	9.15 - 1.17
Seymour	1916	Destroyer	3.17 - 9.17
Valorous	1917	Destroyer	1.18 - 3.18
Seymour	1916	Destroyer	3.18 - 9.18
Douglas	1918	Destroyer	9.18 - 1.19
Medway	1916	Destroyer	1.19 - 12.20
Jervis	1938	Destroyer	1940 - 1949

G01

Lassoo	1915	Destroyer	9.15 - 1.18
Magic	1915	Destroyer	1.18 - 3.18
Vivacious	1917	Destroyer	3.18 - 1.19
Nicator	1916	Destroyer	1.19 - 12.20
Kelly	1938	Destroyer	1940 - 5.41
Scourge	1942	Destroyer	1942 - 1945

G02

Opal	1915	Destroyer	9.15 - 1.17
Mandate	1915	Destroyer	1.17 - 1.18
Tenacious	1917	Destroyer	1.18 - 4.18
Mameluke	1915	Destroyer	9.18 - 1.19
Martial	1915	Destroyer	1.19 - 12.20
Nestor RAN	1940	Destroyer	1940 - 1942
Dirk	Canc	Destroyer	Canc 1945

G03

Ophelia	1915	Destroyer	9.15 - 1.17
Manners	1915	Destroyer	1.18 - 3.18
Vortigern	1917	Destroyer	3.18 - 1.19
Mons	1915	Destroyer	1.19 - 12.20
Cossack	1937	Destroyer	5.40 - 1941
Shark	1943	Destroyer	1943 - 1944
Svenner RNoN (ex *Shark*)	1943	Destroyer	1944 - 6.44
Gallant	Canc	Destroyer	Canc 1945

G04

Mindful	1915	Destroyer	9.15 - 1.17
Marmion	1915	Destroyer	1.17 - 3.18
Vancouver	1917	Destroyer	3.18 - 1.19
Obedient	1915	Destroyer	1.19 - 1921
Onslaught	1941	Destroyer	1941 - 1948

G05

Opportune	1915	Destroyer	9.15 - 1.17
Marne	1915	Destroyer	1.17 - 1.18
Skate	1917	Destroyer	1.18 - 3.18
Vittoria	1917	Destroyer	3.18 - 10.18
Wryneck	1918	Destroyer	10.18 - 1.19
Pasley	1916	Destroyer	1.19 - 12.20
Lancaster	1918	Destroyer	1940 - 1948

G06

Lochinvar	1915	Destroyer	9.15 - 1916
Martial	1915	Destroyer	1.17 - 1.18
Tormentor	1917	Destroyer	1.18 - 3.18
Musketeer	1915	Destroyer	11.19 - 1921
Pakenham	1941	Destroyer	1941 - 1943
Poniard	Canc	Destroyer	Canc 1945

G07

Abdiel	1915	Destroyer	9.15 - 1.17
Michael	1915	Destroyer	1.17 - 1.18
Tyrant	1917	Destroyer	1.18 - 3.18
Tancred	1917	Destroyer	3.18 - 1.19
Mounsey	1915	Destroyer	1.19 - 12.20
Afridi	1937	Destroyer	1940- 3.40
Athabaskan RCN	1941	Destroyer	1941 - 4.44
Gael	Canc	Destroyer	Canc 1945

G08

Talisman	1915	Destroyer	9.15 - 1.17
Milbrook	1915	Destroyer	1.17 - 1.18
Tancred	1917	Destroyer	1.18 - 3.18
Walker	1917	Destroyer	3.18 - 1.19
Morning Star	1915	Destroyer	1.19 - 1921
Newark	1918	Destroyer	1940 - 1948

G09

Noble	1915	Destroyer	9.15 - 1.17
Minion	1915	Destroyer	1.18 - 3.18
Watchman	1917	Destroyer	3.18 - 1.19
Minos	1914	Destroyer	1.19 - 12.20
Quilliam	1941	Destroyer	1941 - 1945

G10

Mischief	1915	Destroyer	9.15 - 1.17
Kempenfelt	1915	Destroyer	3.17 - 9.17

Mons	1915	Destroyer	1.18 - 3.18
Versatile	1917	Destroyer	3.18 - 1.19
Miranda	1914	Destroyer	1.19 - 1921
Pathfinder	1941	Destroyer	1941 - 1945

G11

Mameluke	1915	Destroyer	9.15 - 1.17
Mons	1915	Destroyer	1.17 - 1.18
Moon	1915	Destroyer	1.18 - 6.18
Tormentor	1917	Destroyer	3.18 - 1.19
Manly	1914	Destroyer	1.19 - 12.20
Quadrant RAN	1942	Destroyer	1942 - 1948

G12

Nonsuch	1915	Destroyer	9.15 - 1.17
Moon	1915	Destroyer	1.17 - 1.18
Morning Star	1915	Destroyer	1.18 - 3.18
Kempenfelt	1915	Destroyer	3.18 - 1.19
Nerissa	1916	Destroyer	1.19 - 1921
Kashmir	1939	Destroyer	1940 - 5.41
Saumarez	1942	Destroyer	1942 - 1948

G13

Negro	1916	Destroyer	9.15 - 4.16
Morning Star	1915	Destroyer	1.17 - 1.18

G14

Norman	1916	Destroyer	9.15 - 1.17
Mounsey	1915	Destroyer	1.17 - 3.18
Minion	1915	Destroyer	3.18 - 6.18
Sarpedon	1916	Destroyer	9.18 - 1.19
Patrician	1916	Destroyer	1.19 - 12.20
Milne	1941	Destroyer	1941 - 1948

G15

Northesk	1916	Destroyer	9.15 - 1.17
Musketeer	1915	Destroyer	1.17 - 3.18
Romola	1916	Destroyer	3.18 - 1.19
Patriot	1916	Destroyer	1.19 - 12.20
Loyal	1941	Destroyer	1941 - 1946

G16

North Star	1916	Destroyer	9.15 - 1.17
Mystic	1915	Destroyer	1.17 - 3.18
Moon	1915	Destroyer	3.18 - 6.18
Voyager	1918	Destroyer	9.18 - 1.19
Mastiff	1914	Destroyer	1.19 - 12.20
Nonpareil	1941	Destroyer	1941 - 1942
Tjerk Hiddes RNLN (ex Nonpareil)	1941	Destroyer	1942 - 1946

G17

Nugent	1917	Destroyer	9.15 - 1.17
Ossory	1915	Destroyer	1.17 - 1.18
Sturgeon	1917	Destroyer	1.18 - 3.18

Walrus	1917	Destroyer	3.18 - 1.19
Parthian	1916	Destroyer	1.19 - 12.20
Onslow	1941	Destroyer	1941 - 1948

G18

Nepean	1916	Destroyer	9.15 - 1.17
Romola	1916	Destroyer	1.18 - 3.18
Morning Star	1915	Destroyer	3.18 - 6.18
Vanessa	1918	Destroyer	6.18 - 1.19
Napier	1915	Destroyer	1.19 - 12.20
Zulu	1937	Destroyer	5.40 - 9.42
Battleaxe	1945	Destroyer	1945 - 1948

G19

Nereus	1916	Destroyer	9.15 - 1.17
Sarpedon	1916	Destroyer	1.17 - 3.18
Musketeer	1915	Destroyer	3.18 - 6.18
Marksman	1915	Destroyer	6.18 - 9.18
Vanity	1919	Destroyer	9.18 - 9.19
Nonsuch	1915	Destroyer	1.19 - 12.20
Leamington	1918	Destroyer	1940 - 1942
Guernsey	Canc	Destroyer	Canc 1945

G20

Marvel	1915	Destroyer	9.15 - 1.17
Seymour	1916	Destroyer	1.18 - 3.18
Valorous	1917	Destroyer	3.18 - 1.19
Mischief	1915	Destroyer	1.19 - 1921
Gurkha	1937	Destroyer	1940 - 4.40
Savage	1942	Destroyer	1942 - 1948

G21

Gabriel	1915	Destroyer	9.15 - 1.17
Vortigern	1917	Destroyer	1.18 - 3.18
Sarpedon	1916	Destroyer	3.18 - 9.18
Spindrift	1918	Destroyer	9.18 - 1.19
Marvel	1915	Destroyer	1.19 - 12.20
Punjabi	1937	Destroyer	5.40 - 5.42
Rifle	Canc	Destroyer	Canc 1945

G22

Onslaught	1915	Destroyer	9.15 - 1.17
Walker	1917	Destroyer	1.18 - 3.18
Lightfoot	1915	Destroyer	3.18 - 9.18
Turquoise	1918	Destroyer	9.18 - 1.19
Mameluke	1915	Destroyer	1.19 - 12.20
Jackal	1938	Destroyer	1940 - 5.42
Vimiera	Canc	Destroyer	Canc 1945

G23

Ossory	1915	Destroyer	9.15 - 1.17
Watchman	1917	Destroyer	1.18 - 3.18
Marksman	1915	Destroyer	3.18 - 6.18
Truant	1918	Destroyer	9.18 - 1.19
Maenad	1915	Destroyer	1.19 - 12.20

Marksman	1942	Destroyer	1942
Mahratta	1942	Destroyer	1942 - 2.44
(ex Marksman)			
Dagger	Canc	Destroyer	Canc 1945

G24

Termagant	1915	Destroyer	9.15 - 1.17
Viscount	1917	Destroyer	3.18 - 6.18
Milbrook	1915	Destroyer	1.19 - 18.19
Thanet	1918	Destroyer	8.19 - 11.19
Maori	1937	Destroyer	1940 - 2.42
Huron RCN	1942	Destroyer	1942 - 1948

G25

Obedient	1915	Destroyer	9.15 - 1.17
Saumerez	1916	Destroyer	3.17 - 1.18
Valhalla	1917	Destroyer	1.18 - 3.18
Saumerez	1916	Destroyer	3.18 - 1.19
Penn	1916	Destroyer	1.19 - 12.20
Norseman	1941	Destroyer	1941 - 1942
Nepal	1941	Destroyer	1942 - 1948
(ex Norseman)			

G26

Obdurate	1916	Destroyer	9.15 - 1.17
Maenad	1915	Destroyer	1.17 - 1.18
Mameluke	1915	Destroyer	1.18 - 4.18
Sepoy	1918	Destroyer	9.18 - 1.19
Norman	1916	Destroyer	1.19 - 12.20
Matabele	1937	Destroyer	5.40 - 1.42
Success	1943	Destroyer	1943
Stord RNoN	1943	Destroyer	1943 - 1948
(ex Success)			

G27

Oracle	1915	Destroyer	9.15 - 1.17
Mameluke	1915	Destroyer	1.17 - 1.18
Maenad	1915	Destroyer	1.18 - 9.18
Sirdar	1918	Destroyer	11.18 - 1.19
Opportune	1915	Destroyer	1.19 - 12.20
Leeds	1917	Destroyer	1940 - 1948

G28

Nizam	1916	Destroyer	9.15 - 1.17
Marvel	1915	Destroyer	1.18 - 9.18
Waterhen	1918	Destroyer	9.18 - 1.19
Octavia	1916	Destroyer	1.19 - 12.20
Kandahar	1939	Destroyer	1940 - 12.41
Culverin	Canc	Destroyer	Canc 1945

G29

Onslow	1916	Destroyer	9.15 - 1.17
Mary Rose	1915	Destroyer	1.17 - 10.17
Petard	1916	Destroyer	3.18 - 11.18
Seabear	1918	Destroyer	11.18 - 1.19

Plover	1916	Destroyer	1.19 - 12.20
Offa	1941	Destroyer	1941 - 1948

G30

Nestor	1915	Destroyer	9.15 - 1.17
Menace	1915	Destroyer	1.18 - 4.18
Scotsman	1918	Destroyer	6.18 - 1.19
Paladin	1916	Destroyer	1.19 - 12.20
Partridge	1941	Destroyer	1941 - 12.42
Spear	Canc	Destroyer	Canc 1945

G31

Nomad	1916	Destroyer	9.15 - 1.18
Mindful	1915	Destroyer	1.18 - 6.18
Wrestler	1918	Destroyer	6.18 - 1.19
Petard	1916	Destroyer	1.19 - 12.20
Mohawk	1937	Destroyer	1940 - 4.41
Broadsword	1946	Destroyer	1946 - 1948

G32

Ithuriel	1916	Destroyer	9.15 - 3.17
Mischief	1915	Destroyer	1.18 - 9.18
Scythe	1918	Destroyer	9.18 - 1.19
Onslaught	1915	Destroyer	1.19 - 1921
Lookout	1940	Destroyer	1940 - 1948

G33

Orestes	1916	Destroyer	9.15 - 1.17
Munster	1915	Destroyer	1.17 - 6.18
Torch	1918	Destroyer	6.18 - 1.19
Ophelia	1915	Destroyer	1.19 - 12.20
Somali	1937	Destroyer	5.40 - 9.42

G34

Napier	1915	Destroyer	9.15 - 9.18
Tomahawk	1918	Destroyer	9.18 - 1.19
Menace	1915	Destroyer	1.19 - 12.20
Jaguar	1938	Destroyer	1940 - 3.42
Claymore	Canc	Destroyer	Canc 1945

G35

Nerissa	1916	Destroyer	9.15 - 1.17
Marksman	1915	Destroyer	3.17 - 1.18
Narwhal	1915	Destroyer	1.18 - 6.18
Scout	1918	Destroyer	6.18 - 9.18
Stuart	1918	Destroyer	9.18 - 1.19
Munster	1915	Destroyer	1.19 - 1921
Marne	1940	Destroyer	1940 - 1948

G36

Trident	1915	Destroyer	9.15 - 1.17
Narwhal	1915	Destroyer	1.17 - 1.18
Nessus	1915	Destroyer	1.18 - 6.18
Senator	1918	Destroyer	6.18 - 9.18
Voyager	1918	Destroyer	6.18 - 9.18

Speedy	1918	Destroyer	9.18 - 1.19
Northesk	1916	Destroyer	1.19 - 12.20
Nubian	1937	Destroyer	5.40 - 1948

G37

Nonpareil	1916	Destroyer	9.15 - 1.17
Nessus	1915	Destroyer	1.17 - 1.18
Noble	1915	Destroyer	1.18 - 6.18
Vanity	1918	Destroyer	6.18 - 9.18
Tilbury	1918	Destroyer	9.18 - 1.19
Phoebe	1916	Destroyer	1.19 - 1921
Kelvin	1939	Destroyer	1940 - 1948

G38

Orford	1916	Destroyer	9.15 - 1.17
Noble	1915	Destroyer	1.17 - 1.18
Nonsuch	1915	Destroyer	1.18 - 9.18
Trinidad	1918	Destroyer	9.18 - 1.19
Peregrine	1916	Destroyer	1.19 - 12.20
Nizam	1940	Destroyer	1940 - 1948

G39

Narborough	1916	Destroyer	9.15 - 1.17
Nonsuch	1915	Destroyer	1.17 - 1.18
Obedient	1915	Destroyer	1.18 - 6.18
Vivien	1918	Destroyer	6.18 - 1.19
Orcadia	1916	Destroyer	1.19 - 12.20
Obdurate	1942	Destroyer	1942 - 1948

G40

Paladin	1916	Destroyer	9.15 - 1.17
Obedient	1915	Destroyer	1.17 - 1.18
Onslaught	1915	Destroyer	1.18 - 6.18
Wolsey	1918	Destroyer	6.18 - 1.19
Acasta	1912	Destroyer	1.19 - 1921
Lively	1941	Destroyer	1941 - 5.42
Guinevere	Canc	Destroyer	Canc 1945

G41

Observer	1916	Destroyer	9.15 - 1.17
Onslaught	1915	Destroyer	1.17 - 1.18
Opal	1915	Destroyer	1.18 - 3.18
Scimitar	1918	Destroyer	3.18 - 1.19
Rob Roy	1916	Destroyer	1.19 - 11.19
Raider	1916	Destroyer	11.19 - 8.25
Panther	1941	Destroyer	1941 - 10.43

G42

Turbulent	1916	Destroyer	9.15 - 1.17
Opal	1915	Destroyer	1.17 - 1.18
Prince	1916	Destroyer	1.18 - 9.18
Tryphon	1918	Destroyer	11.18 - 1.19
Skate	1917	Destroyer	1.19 - 8.25
Lincoln	1918	Destroyer	1940 - 1941
Lincoln RNoN	1918	Destroyer	1941 - 1943

G42 *Lincoln* transferred to Norway 1941 - 1943 and Russia as *Druzni* 1944 - 1952

G43

Orpheus	1916	Destroyer	9.15 - 1.17
Prince	1916	Destroyer	1.17 - 1.18
Winchester	1918	Destroyer	3.18 - 1.19
Rocket	1916	Destroyer	1.19 - 8.25
Tartar	1937	Destroyer	5.40 - 1948

G44

Oriole	1916	Destroyer	9.15 - 1.17
Strongbow	1916	Destroyer	1.17 - 1.18
Simoom	1916	Destroyer	3.18 - 1.19
Sable	1916	Destroyer	1.19 - 8.25
Martin	1942	Destroyer	1942 - 11.42
Howitzer	Canc	Destroyer	Canc 1945

G45

Offa	1916	Destroyer	9.15 - 1.17
Saumerez	1916	Destroyer	1.18 - 3.18
Valhalla	1917	Destroyer	3.18 - 1.19
Meteor	1914	Destroyer	1.19 - 12.20
Khartoum	1939	Destroyer	1940 - 6.40
Quail	1942	Destroyer	1942 - 6.44
Glowworm	Canc	Destroyer	Canc 1945

G46

Partridge	1916	Destroyer	9.15 - 1.17
Stuart	1918	Destroyer	9.18 - 1.19
Brazen	1896	Destroyer	1.19 - 11.19
Rapid	1916	Destroyer	11.19 - 8.25
Juno	1938	Destroyer	1940 - 5.41
Swift	1943	Destroyer	1943 - 6.44

G47

Narwhal	1915	Destroyer	9.15 - 1.17
Seawolf	1918	Destroyer	9.18 - 1.19
Nugent	1917	Destroyer	1.19 - 12.20
Newmarket	1918	Destroyer	1940 - 1945

G48

Patrician	1916	Destroyer	9.15 - 1.17
Sportive	1918	Destroyer	9.18 - 1.19
Lydiard	1914	Destroyer	1.19 - 12.20
Obedient	1942	Destroyer	1942 - 1948

G49

Frobisher	1916	Destroyer	9.15 - ....
Parker	1916	Destroyer	1.16 - 4.16
Tyrant	1917	Destroyer	6.18 - 1.19
Springbok	1917	Destroyer	1.19 - 8.25
Norman RAN	1940	Destroyer	1940 - 1948

G49 *Parker* was listed in the Pendant List dated 31 July

1915 as *Frobisher*, but was renamed *Parker* prior to launch.

G50

Penn	1916	Destroyer	9.15 - 1.17
Ithuriel	1916	Destroyer	3.17 - 9.17
Anzac	1917	Destroyer	1.18 - 3.18
Vampire	1917	Destroyer	3.18 - 1.19
Starfish	1916	Destroyer	1.19 - 8.25
Kimberley	1939	Destroyer	5.40 - 1948

G51

Octavia	1916	Destroyer	9.15 - 1.17
Medina	1916	Destroyer	1.17 - 1.18
Ithuriel	1916	Destroyer	9.17 - 1.18
Observer	1916	Destroyer	1.18 - 3.18
Norseman	1916	Destroyer	3.18 - 11.18
Tintagel	1918	Destroyer	11.18 - 1.19
Skilful	1917	Destroyer	1.19 - 8.25
Ashanti	1937	Destroyer	1940 - 1948

G52

Parthian	1916	Destroyer	9.15 - 1.17
Nizam	1916	Destroyer	1.17 - 1.18
Medina	1916	Destroyer	1.18 - 11.18
Somme	1918	Destroyer	11.18 - 1.19
Satyr	1916	Destroyer	1.19 - 8.25
Matchless	1941	Destroyer	1941 - 1948

G53

Orcadia	1916	Destroyer	9.15 - 1.17
Nonpareil	1916	Destroyer	1.17 - 1.18
Nizam	1916	Destroyer	1.18 - 11.18
Sparrowhawk	1918	Destroyer	11.18 - 1.19
Romola	1916	Destroyer	1.19 - 8.25
Janus	1938	Destroyer	1940 - 1.44
Grenade	Canc	Destroyer	Canc 1945

G54

Pasley	1916	Destroyer	9.15 - 1.17
Norman	1916	Destroyer	1.17 - 1.18
Nonpareil	1916	Destroyer	1.18 - 6.18
Tactician	1918	Destroyer	11.18 - 1.19
Tetrarch	1917	Destroyer	1.19 - 11.19
Tormentor	1917	Destroyer	11.19 - 8.25
Newport	1917	Destroyer	1940 - 1947

G55

Nicator	1916	Destroyer	9.15 - 1.17
Observer	1916	Destroyer	1.17 - 1.18
Norman	1916	Destroyer	1.18 - 3.18
Spear	1918	Destroyer	9.18 - ....
Tetrarch	1917	Destroyer	11.19 - 8.25
Lightning	1940	Destroyer	1940 - 3.43
Longbow	Canc	Destroyer	Canc 1945

G56

Patriot	1916	Destroyer	9.15 - 1.17
Offa	1916	Destroyer	1.17 - 1.18
Observer	1916	Destroyer	1.18 - 11.18
Sabre	1919	Destroyer	11.18 - 1.19
Sturgeon	1917	Destroyer	1.19 - 8.25
Petard	1941	Destroyer	1941 - 1948

G57

Relentless	1916	Destroyer	9.15 - 1.17
Ophelia	1915	Destroyer	1.17 - 1.18
Offa	1916	Destroyer	1.18 - 3.18
Splendid	1918	Destroyer	11.18 - 1.19
Cockatrice	1912	Destroyer	1.19 - 12.20
Ludlow	1917	Destroyer	1940 - 1945

G58

Pelican	1916	Destroyer	9.15 - 1.17
Opportune	1915	Destroyer	1.17 - 1.18
Ophelia	1915	Destroyer	1.18 - 11.18
Tumult	1918	Destroyer	11.18 - 1.19
Christopher	1912	Destroyer	1.19 - 12.20
Rockingham	1919	Destroyer	1940 - 9.44

G59

Pigeon	1916	Destroyer	9.15 - 1.17
Orford	1916	Destroyer	1.17 - 1.18
Opportune	1915	Destroyer	1.18 - 1.19
Sharpshooter	1917	Destroyer	1.19 - 8.25
Mashona	1937	Destroyer	5.40 - 5.41
Gauntlet	Canc	Destroyer	Canc 1945

G60

Peregrine	1916	Destroyer	9.15 - 1.17
Botha	1914	Destroyer	2.17 - 4.17
Anzac	1917	Destroyer	4.17 - 1.18
Orestes	1916	Destroyer	1.18 - 11.18
Seraph	1918	Destroyer	11.18 - 1.19
Stork	1916	Destroyer	1.19 - 8.25
Ramsey	1919	Destroyer	1940 - 1947

G61

Grenville	1916	Destroyer	9.15 - 3.17
Orestes	1916	Destroyer	1.17 - 1.18
Orford	1916	Destroyer	1.18 - 11.18
Tobago	1918	Destroyer	11.18 - 11.19
Tenacious	1917	Destroyer	11.19 - 8.25
Javelin	1938	Destroyer	1940 - 1948

G62

Rival	1916	Destroyer	9.15 - 1.17
Partridge	1916	Destroyer	1.17 - 3.18
Pylades	1916	Destroyer	3.18 - 1.19
Tara	1918	Destroyer	11.18 - 1.19
Marksman	1915	Destroyer	1.19 - 1922

Quality RAN	1942	Destroyer	1941 - 1948

G63

Rapid	1916	Destroyer	9.15 - 1.17
Patriot	1916	Destroyer	1.17 - 9.18
Ithuriel	1916	Destroyer	1.19 - 1921
Gurkha	1941	Destroyer	1941 - 1.42
Haida RCN	1942	Destroyer	1942 - 1948

G64

Pellew	1916	Destroyer	9.15 - 1.19
Strenuous	1918	Destroyer	1.19 - ....
Rosalind	1916	Destroyer	1.19 - 8.25
Kingston	1939	Destroyer	5.40 - 4.42
Scorpion	1946	Destroyer	1946 - 1947

G65

Plover	1916	Destroyer	9.15 - 1.17
Peregrine	1916	Destroyer	1.17 - 9.18
Velox	1917	Destroyer	11.18 -1.19
Radiant	1916	Destroyer	1.19 - 8.25
Nerissa	1940	Destroyer	1940
Piorun ORP	1940	Destroyer	1940 - 1946
(ex *Nerissa*)			
Noble (ex *Piorun*)	1940	Destroyer	1946 - 1947

G65 *Nerissa* was transferred to Poland as *Piorun* in 1940. She was returned to the Royal Navy in 1946 and renamed *Noble*. She was sold for scrap in 1955.

G66

Petard	1916	Destroyer	9.15 - 1.17
Peyton	1916	Destroyer	1.17 - 11.18
Trojan	1918	Destroyer	11.18 - 1.19
Retriever	1917	Destroyer	1.19 - 8.25
Oribi	1941	Destroyer	1941 - 1946

G67

Plucky	1916	Destroyer	9.15 - 1.17
Plover	1916	Destroyer	1.17 - 1.19
Redoubt	1916	Destroyer	1.19 - 11.19
Bedouin	1937	Destroyer	5.40 - 5.42
Gift	Canc	Destroyer	Canc 1945

G68

Osiris	1916	Destroyer	9.15 - 1.17
Plucky	1916	Destroyer	1.17 - 11.18
Seafire	1918	Destroyer	11.18 - 1.19
Sorceress	1916	Destroyer	1.19 - 11.19
Lewes	1918	Destroyer	1940 - 1946

G69

Oriana	1916	Destroyer	9.15 - 1.17
Relentless	1916	Destroyer	1.17 - 1.19
Sylph	1916	Destroyer	1.19 - 11.19

Paladin	1941	Destroyer	1941 - 1948

G70

Norseman	1916	Destroyer	9.15 - 1.17
Vampire	1917	Destroyer	1.18 - 3.18
Anzac	1917	Destroyer	3.18 - 1.19
Seymour	1916	Destroyer	1.19 - 11.19
Queenborough	1942	Destroyer	1942 - 1948

G71

Ready	1916	Destroyer	9.15 - 1.17
Parker	1916	Destroyer	1.17 - 1.18
Vivacious	1917	Destroyer	1.18 - 3.18
Octavia	1916	Destroyer	3.18 - 1.19
Nimrod	1915	Destroyer	1.19 - 11.19
Reading	1919	Destroyer	1940 - 1945

G72

Peyton	1916	Destroyer	9.15 - 1.17
Osiris	1916	Destroyer	3.18 - 11.18
Searcher	1919	Destroyer	11.18 - 1.19
Kempenfelt	1915	Destroyer	1.19 - 1922
Jersey	1938	Destroyer	1940 - 5.41
Scorpion	1942	Destroyer	1942 - 1945

G73

Portia	1916	Destroyer	9.15 - 1.17
Paladin	1916	Destroyer	3.18 - 9.18
Whirlwind	1917	Destroyer	11.18 - 1.19
Faulknor	1914	Destroyer	1.19 - 11.19
Meteor	1941	Destroyer	1941- 1948

G74

Pheasant	1916	Destroyer	9.15 - 1.17
Penn	1916	Destroyer	3.18 - 1.19
Broke	1914	Destroyer	1.19 - 11.19
Legion	1940	Destroyer	1940 - 3.42
Cutlass	Canc	Destroyer	Canc 1945

G75

Redmill	1916	Destroyer	7.15
Medina	1916	Destroyer	9.15 - 1.17
Parker	1916	Destroyer	1.17 - 1.18
Grenville	1916	Destroyer	1.18 - 3.18
Parker	1916	Destroyer	3.18 - 1.19
Swift	1907	Destroyer	1.19 - 11.19
Eskimo	1937	Destroyer	5.40 - 1948

G75 *Medina* listed in Pendant List dated 31 July 1915 as *Redmill* but renamed *Medina* prior to launch.

G76

Redwing	1916	Destroyer	7.15
Medora	1916	Destroyer	9.15
(ex *Redwing*)			

Medway	1916	Destroyer	9.15 - 1.17
(ex *Medora*)			
Radstock	1916	Destroyer	1.17 - 1.18
Campbell	1918	Destroyer	9.18 - 1.19
Lightfoot	1915	Destroyer	1.19 - 1922
Mansfield	1918	Destroyer	1940 - 1944
Grafton	Canc	Destroyer	Canc 1945

G76 *Medway* listed in Pendant List dated 31 July 1915 as *Redwing* but renamed *Medora* (1915) and *Medway* (1916) prior to entering service. G76 *Mansfield* to Norway 1940 - 1942 then Canada 1942 - 1943.

G77

Prince	1916	Destroyer	9.15 - 1.17
Parthian	1916	Destroyer	1.17 - 1.18
Ulysses	1917	Destroyer	3.18 - 1.19
Botha	1914	Destroyer	1.19 - 11.19
Penn	1941	Destroyer	1941 - 1948

G78

Pylades	1916	Destroyer	9.15 - 1.17
Rapid	1916	Destroyer	1.17 - 1.18
Trenchant	1916	Destroyer	1.18 - 1.19
Redgauntlet	1916	Destroyer	1.19 - 11.19
Quentin	1941	Destroyer	1941 - 12.42
Musket	Canc	Destroyer	Canc 1945

G79

Radstock	1916	Destroyer	9.15 - 1.17
Sabrina	1916	Destroyer	1.17 - 1.18
Undine	1917	Destroyer	3.18 - 1.19
Tancred	1917	Destroyer	1.19 - 11.19
Ripley	1918	Destroyer	1940 - 1945

G80

Oberon	1916	Destroyer	9.15 - 1.17
Orcadia	1916	Destroyer	1.17 - 1.18
Tirade	1917	Destroyer	1.18 - 1.19
Thisbe	1917	Destroyer	1.19 - 11.19
Opportune	1942	Destroyer	1942 - 1948

G81

Raider	1916	Destroyer	9.15 - 1.17
Rowena	1916	Destroyer	1.17 - 1.18
Radstock	1916	Destroyer	1.18 - 1.19
Thruster	1917	Destroyer	1.19 - 11.19
Quiberon	1942	Destroyer	1942 - 1948

G82

Phoebe	1916	Destroyer	9.15 - 1.17
Rocket	1916	Destroyer	1.17 - 1.18
Raider	1916	Destroyer	1.18 - 1.19
Sarpedon	1916	Destroyer	1.19 - 11.19
Sikh	1937	Destroyer	5.40 - 9.43

Carronade	Canc	Destroyer	Canc 1945

G83

Romola	1916	Destroyer	9.15 - 1.17
Northesk	1916	Destroyer	1.17 - 1.18
Rapid	1916	Destroyer	1.18 - 1.19
Nepean	1916	Destroyer	1.19 - 11.19
Isaac Sweers RNLN	1940	Destroyer	1940 - 11.42
Ypres	Canc	Destroyer	Canc 1945

The Battle class destroyer G83 *Ypres* was cancelled but completed as the Daring class destroyer *Delight* (D119) ex *Disdain*.

G84

Portia	1916	Destroyer	1.17 - 1.18
Ready	1916	Destroyer	1.18 - 1.19
Manners	1915	Destroyer	1.19 - 11.19
Noble	1941	Destroyer	1941 - 1942
Van Galen RNLN	1941	Destroyer	1942 - 1946
(ex *Noble*)			

G85

Grenville	1916	Destroyer	3.17 - 1.18
Restless	1916	Destroyer	1.18 - 1.19
Moresby	1915	Destroyer	1.19 - 11.19
Jupiter	1938	Destroyer	1940 - 2.42
Sword (ex *Celt*)	Canc	Destroyer	Canc 1945

G86

Raider	1916	Destroyer	1.17 - 1.18
Rigorous	1916	Destroyer	1.18 - 1.19
Melpomene	1915	Destroyer	1.19 - 11.19
Musketeer	1941	Destroyer	1941 - 1948

G87

Ready	1916	Destroyer	1.17 - 1.18
Rob Roy	1916	Destroyer	1.18 - 1.19
Mansfield	1914	Destroyer	1.19 - 11.19
Lance	1940	Destroyer	1940 - 10.42

G88

Restless	1916	Destroyer	1.17 - 1.18
Rocket	1916	Destroyer	1.18 - 1.19
Myngs	1914	Destroyer	1.19 - 11.19
Richmond	1917	Destroyer	1940 - 1943
Greyhound	Canc	Destroyer	Canc 1945

Richmond (G88) operated by RCN 1942 - 1943 and Russia 1944 - 1949 as *Zhivuchy*.

G89

Pheasant	1916	Destroyer	1.17 - 1.18
Rosalind	1916	Destroyer	1.18 - 1.19
Milne	1914	Destroyer	1.19 - 11.19

Iroquois RCN	1941	Destroyer	1942 - 1944

G90

Hoste	1916	Destroyer	11.16 - 12.16
Rigorous	1916	Destroyer	1.17 - 1.18
Rowena	1916	Destroyer	1.18 - 1.19
Matchless	1914	Destroyer	1.19 - 11.19
Myrmidon	1942	Destroyer	1942
Orkan ORP	1942	Destroyer	1942 - 10.43
(ex *Myrmidon*)			

G91

Sable	1916	Destroyer	1.18 - 1.19
Talisman	1915	Destroyer	1.19 - 11.19
Kipling	1939	Destroyer	5.40 - 5.42

G92

Rob Roy	1916	Destroyer	1.17 - 1.18
Sabrina	1916	Destroyer	1.18 - 1.19
Trident	1915	Destroyer	1.19 - 11.19
Quickmatch	1941	Destroyer	1942 - 1948

G93

Sorceress	1916	Destroyer	1.17 - 1.18
Salmon	1916	Destroyer	1.18 - 1.19
Laverock	1913	Destroyer	1.19 - 11.19
Porcupine	1941	Destroyer	1941 - 12.42

G94

Salmon	1916	Destroyer	1.17 - 1.18
Sorceress	1916	Destroyer	1.18 - 1.19
Lawford	1913	Destroyer	1.19 - 11.19
Serapis	1943	Destroyer	1943 - 1945

G95

Rosalind	1916	Destroyer	1.17 - 1.18
Parker	1916	Destroyer	1.18 - 3.18
Grenville	1916	Destroyer	3.18 - 1.19
Legion	1914	Destroyer	1.19 - 11.19
Montgomery	1918	Destroyer	1940 - 1945

G96

Trenchant	1916	Destroyer	1.17 - 1.18
Ulysses	1917	Destroyer	1.18 - 3.18
Warwick	1917	Destroyer	9.18 - 1.19
Lance	1914	Destroyer	1.19 - 11.19
Crossbow	1945	Destroyer	1945 - 1948

G97

Undine	1917	Destroyer	1.17 - 1.18
Tasmania	1918	Destroyer	9.18 - 1.19
Lookout	1914	Destroyer	1.19 - 11.19
Napier RAN	1940	Destroyer	1940 - 1948

G98

Setter	1916	Destroyer	1916 - 1.17
Venomous	1918	Destroyer	6.19 - 10.19
Laurel	1913	Destroyer	1.19 - 11.19
Orwell	1942	Destroyer	1942 - 1948

G99

Stonehenge	1919	Destroyer	9.18 - 1.19
Liberty	1913	Destroyer	1.19 - 8.19
Laforey	1941	Destroyer	1941 - 3.44
Halberd	Canc	Destroyer	Canc 1945

G0A

Magic	1915	Destroyer	1.18 - 1.19

G1A

Mons	1915	Destroyer	3.18 - 6.18
Mounsey	1915	Destroyer	6.18 - 1.19

G2A

Medway	1916	Destroyer	3.18 - 1.19

G3A

Saumerez	1916	Destroyer	12.16 - 3.17
Mystic	1915	Destroyer	3.18 - 1.19

G4A

Talisman	1915	Destroyer	6.18 - 1.19
Tyrant	1917	Destroyer	9.22 - ....

G5A

Nessus	1915	Destroyer	6.18 - 1.19

G6A

Menace	1915	Destroyer	6.18 - 1.19

G7A

Munster	1915	Destroyer	6.18 - 1.19

G8A

Onslaught	1915	Destroyer	6.18 - 1.19

G9A

Noble	1915	Destroyer	6.18 - 1.19
Valhalla	1917	Destroyer	1.19 - 1.21

GA0

Napier	1915	Destroyer	6.18 - 1.19

GA1

Patrician	1916	Destroyer	9.18 - 1.19
Tuscan	1919	Destroyer	1.21 - ....

GA2

Mameluke	1915	Destroyer	9.18 - 1.19

GA3

Marvel	1915	Destroyer	9.18 - 1.19

GA4

Surprise	1916	Destroyer	1.17 - 1.18
Mischief	1915	Destroyer	9.18 - 1.19
Thracian	1920	Destroyer	1920 - 1.22

GA5

Nonsuch	1915	Destroyer	9.18 - 1.19
Wren	1919	Destroyer	9.21 - ....

GA6

Plucky	1916	Destroyer	9.18 - 1.19
Witch	1919	Destroyer	1.21 - 1922

GA7

Whitehall	1919	Destroyer	2.18 - ....

Petard	1916	Destroyer	11.18 - ....

GA8

Maenad	1915	Destroyer	9.18 - ....
Worcester	1919	Destroyer	11.18 - ....

GA9

Ophelia	1915	Destroyer	11.18 - ....

GC0

Magic	1915	Destroyer	1914 - ....

Flag 'H' Superior

Pre 1940:   Destroyers (Various pendants superior and inferior were used to increase number range)

1940-48:   Destroyers

1998:   Hydrographic Ships

H00

Acheron	1911	Destroyer	12.14 - 1.18
Acasta	1912	Destroyer	1.18 - 1.19
Lark	1913	Destroyer	1.19 - 12.20
Tourmaline	1919	Destroyer	1.22 - 8.25
Comet	1931	Destroyer	1931 - 1938
Restigouche RCN	1931	Destroyer	1938 - 1945
(ex *Comet*)			

H01

Lurcher	1912	Destroyer	12.14 - 1.18
Achates	1912	Destroyer	1.18 - 1.19
Lennox	1914	Destroyer	1.19 - 12.20
Tyrian	1919	Destroyer	1.22 - 1929
Saguenay RCN	1930	Destroyer	1929 - ....
Hotspur	1936	Destroyer	1936 - 1948

H02

Acorn	1910	Destroyer	12.14 - 1.18
Acheron	1911	Destroyer	1.18 - 4.18
Locust	1896	Destroyer	4.18 - 1.19
Achates	1912	Destroyer	1.19 - 12.20
Success RAN	1918	Destroyer	1920 - ....
Turquoise	1918	Destroyer	1.22 - 1932
Exmouth	1934	Destroyer	1934 - 1.40
Le Triomphant FR	1934	Destroyer	BR619(2)

H03

Laforey	1913	Destroyer	12.14 - 1.18
Acorn	1910	Destroyer	1.18 - 4.18
Sylvia	1897	Destroyer	4.18 - 1.19
Midge	1913	Destroyer	1.19 - 12.20
Strenuous	1918	Destroyer	1.22 - 1932
Grenville	1935	Destroyer	1936 - 1.40
Mistral FR	1925	Destroyer	5.40 - 6.44

H04

Shark	1912	Destroyer	12.14 - 1.18
Alarm	1910	Destroyer	1.18 - 4.18
Bullfinch	1898	Destroyer	9.18 - 1.19
Victor	1913	Destroyer	1.19 - 12.20
Tenedos	1918	Destroyer	1923 - 4.42

H05

Alarm	1910	Destroyer	12.14 - 1.18

Bullfinch	1898	Destroyer	4.18 - 9.18
Ambuscade	1913	Destroyer	9.18 - 1.19
Acheron	1911	Destroyer	1.19 - 12.20
Stormcloud	1919	Destroyer	1.22 - 1933
Greyhound	1935	Destroyer	1935 - 5.41
Ithuriel	1941	Destroyer	1942 - 11.42

H06

Lawford	1913	Destroyer	12.14 - 1.18
Archer	1911	Destroyer	1.18 - 4.18
Leopard	1897	Destroyer	4.18 - 1.19
Archer	1911	Destroyer	1.19 - 12.20
Shamrock	1918	Destroyer	1.22 - 1932
Hurricane	1939	Destroyer	1940 - 12.43

H07

Louis	1913	Destroyer	12.14 - 10.15
Grampus	1910	Destroyer	1916 - 1.18
Ariel	1911	Destroyer	1.18 - 9.18
Star	1896	Destroyer	9.18 - 1.19
Beaver	1911	Destroyer	1.19 - 12.20
Seawolf	1918	Destroyer	1.22 - 1930
Defender	1932	Destroyer	1932 - 7.41
Kondouriotis RHN	1931	Destroyer	BR619(2)

H08

Lydiard	1914	Destroyer	12.14 - 1.18
Attack	1911	Destroyer	1.18 - 3.18
Arab	1901	Destroyer	3.18 - 1.19
Hornet	1911	Destroyer	1.19 - 12.20
Saumarez	1916	Destroyer	1.22 - 1930
Eclipse	1934	Destroyer	1934 - 10.43

H09

Cossack	1907	Destroyer	12.14 - 9.15
Melpomene	1915	Destroyer	9.15 - 1.18
Badger	1911	Destroyer	1.18 - 6.18
Nerissa	1916	Destroyer	6.18 - 1.19
Lapwing	1911	Destroyer	1.19 - 12.20
Ulster	1917	Destroyer	1.22 - 1930
Acasta	1929	Destroyer	1930 - 6.40
Rotherham	1942	Destroyer	1942 - 1948

H10

Archer	1911	Destroyer	12.14 - 9.15

Umpire	1917	Destroyer	1.22 - 1929		**H20**			
Encounter	1934	Destroyer	1934 - 3.42		*Leonidas*	1913	Destroyer	12.14 - 1.18
					Beaver	1911	Destroyer	1.18 - 3.18
H11					*Searcher*	1919	Destroyer	1.22 - 1936
Ariel	1911	Destroyer	12.14 - 9.15		*La Bouclier* FR	1937	Destroyer	7.40 - 1945
Swordsman RAN	1918	Destroyer	.... -					
Ursula	1917	Destroyer	1.22 - 1929		**H21**			
Basilisk	1930	Destroyer	1930 - 6.40		*Cameleon*	1910	Destroyer	12.14 - 1.18
Racehorse	1942	Destroyer	1942 - 1948		*Northesk*	1916	Destroyer	1.18 - 3.18
					Nereus	1916	Destroyer	3.18 - 9.18
H12					*Martin*	1910	Destroyer	1.19 - ....
Oak	1912	Destroyer	12.14 - 9.15		*Scimitar*	1918	Destroyer	1.22 - 1948
Tower	1917	Destroyer	1.22 - 1929					
Achates	1929	Destroyer	1929 - 12.42		**H22**			
					Lucifer	1913	Destroyer	12.14 - 1.18
H13					*Brisk*	1910	Destroyer	1.18 - 9.18
Midge	1913	Destroyer	12.14 - 9.15		*Norseman*	1916	Destroyer	11.18 - 1.19
					Ruby	1910	Destroyer	1.19 - 12.20
H14					*Scythe*	1918	Destroyer	1.22 - 1931
Attack	1911	Destroyer	12.14 - 9.15		*Diamond*	1932	Destroyer	1932 - 1936
Stalwart RAN	1918	Destroyer	.... -		*Le Malin* FR	1933	Destroyer	BR619(2)
Redgauntlet	1916	Destroyer	1.22 - 1929					
Active	1929	Destroyer	1929 - 1948		**H23**			
					Lance	1914	Destroyer	12.14 - 1.18
H15					*Broke*	1914	Destroyer	1.18 - 9.18
Badger	1911	Destroyer	12.14 - 9.15		*Boyne*	1904	Destroyer	9.18 - 1.19
Seymour	1916	Destroyer	1.22 - 1929		*Sheldrake*	1911	Destroyer	1.19 - 12.20
Esk	1934	Destroyer	1934 - 8.40		*Seabear*	1918	Destroyer	1.22 - 1931
Raider	1942	Destroyer	1942 - 1948		*Echo*	1934	Destroyer	1934 - 1944
					Navarinon RHN	1934	Destroyer	1944 - 1956
H16					(ex *Echo*)			
Maori	1909	Destroyer	12.14 - 9.15					
Foxhound	1909	Destroyer	1.18 - 6.18		**H24**			
Vimiera	1917	Destroyer	1.22 - 8.25		*Lookout*	1914	Destroyer	12.14 - 1.18
Daring	1932	Destroyer	1932 - 2.40		*Cameleon*	1910	Destroyer	1.18 - 4.18
Ouragan FR	1926	Destroyer	7.40 - 1945		*Onslow*	1916	Destroyer	3.18 - 1.19
					Beagle	1909	Destroyer	1.19 - 12.20
H17					*Torbay*	1919	Destroyer	1.22 - 1928
Beaver	1911	Destroyer	12.14 - 9.15		*Champlain* RCN	1919	Destroyer	1928 - 1932
Grasshopper	1909	Destroyer	1.18 - 6.18		*Hasty*	1936	Destroyer	1936 - 6.42
Teazer	1917	Destroyer	1.22 - 1931					
Escapade	1934	Destroyer	1940 - 1948		**H25**			
					Comet	1910	Destroyer	12.14 - 1916
H18					*Christopher*	1912	Destroyer	1.18 - 1.19
Brisk	1910	Destroyer	12.14 - 9.15		*Bulldog*	1909	Destroyer	1.19 - 12.20
Wolverine	1910	Destroyer	1917 - 3.18		*Tasmania* RAN	1918	Destroyer	1920 - 1925
Pigeon	1916	Destroyer	3.18 - 6.18		*Serene*	1918	Destroyer	1.22 - 1936
Sabre	1919	Destroyer	1.22 - 1945		*La Cordeliere* FR	1937	Destroyer	7.40 - 1944
H19					**H26**			
Mohawk	1907	Destroyer	12.14 - 9.15		*Paragon*	1913	Destroyer	12.14 - 1.18
Harpy	1909	Destroyer	1.18 - 6.18		*Cockatrice*	1912	Destroyer	1.18 - 1.19
Seafire	1918	Destroyer	1.22 - 1933		*Foxhound*	1909	Destroyer	1.19 - 12.20
Harvester	1939	Destroyer	1939 - 3.43		*Sardonyx*	1919	Destroyer	1.22 - 1936
					Tattoo RAN	1918	Destroyer	1920 - 1925

71

H27

Porpoise	1913	Destroyer	12.14 - 1.18
Moresby	1915	Destroyer	1.18 - 1.19
Renard	1909	Destroyer	1.19 - 12.20
Grenville	1916	Destroyer	1.22 - 1933
Electra	1934	Destroyer	1934 - 2.42
Le Terrible FR	1933	Destroyer	BR619(2)

H28

Defender	1911	Destroyer	12.14 - 1.18
Contest	1913	Destroyer	1.18 - 3.18
Orpheus	1916	Destroyer	3.18 - 11.18
Grasshopper	1909	Destroyer	1.19 - 12.20
Sturdy	1919	Destroyer	1.22 - 10.40
Draug RNoN	1908	Destroyer	1940 - 1944

H29

Tartar	1907	Destroyer	12.14 - 9.15
Archer	1911	Destroyer	9.15 - 1.18
Defender	1911	Destroyer	1.18 - 9.18
Narwhal	1915	Destroyer	6.18 - 1.19
Mosquito	1910	Destroyer	1.19 - 12.20
Thanet	1918	Destroyer	1.22 - 1.42
Ierax RHN	1911	Destroyer	BR619(2)

H30

Fortune	1913	Destroyer	12.14 - 1.18
Druid	1911	Destroyer	1.18 - 1.19
Osiris	1916	Destroyer	11.18 - 1.19
Scorpion	1910	Destroyer	1.19 - 12.20
Taurus	1917	Destroyer	1.22 - 1929
Beagle	1930	Destroyer	1930 - 1945

H31

Owl	1913	Destroyer	12.14 - 1.18
Faulknor	1914	Destroyer	1.18 - 9.18
Dee	1903	Destroyer	9.18 - 1.19
Grampus	1910	Destroyer	1.19 - 12.20
Sterling	1918	Destroyer	1.22 - 1933
Griffin	1935	Destroyer	1935 - 4.43
Ottawa II RCN	1935	Destroyer	4.43 - 1945
(ex *Griffin*)			

H32

Garland	1913	Destroyer	12.14 - 1.18
Ferret	1911	Destroyer	1.18 - 9.18
Quail	1895	Destroyer	9.18 - 1.19
Harpy	1909	Destroyer	1.19 - 12.20
Abdiel	1915	Destroyer	1.22 - 1933
Havant	1939	Destroyer	1939 - 6.40
Rapid	1942	Destroyer	1942 - 1948

H33

Druid	1911	Destroyer	12.14 - 1.18
Firedrake	1912	Destroyer	1.18 - 1.19
Basilisk	1910	Destroyer	1.19 - 12.20
Vanoc	1917	Destroyer	1.22 - 1936

H34

Lark	1913	Destroyer	12.14 - 1.18
Forester	1911	Destroyer	1.18 - 3.18
Oriana	1916	Destroyer	6.18 - 1.19
Sceptre	1917	Destroyer	1.19 - 11.19
Rival	1916	Destroyer	11.19 - 12.20
Turbulent	1916	Destroyer	1.22 - 1936
Blyskawica ORP	1936	Destroyer	BR619(2)

H35

Ferret	1911	Destroyer	12.14 - 1.18
Fury	1911	Destroyer	1.18 - 4.18
Oberon	1916	Destroyer	3.18 - 1.19
Torrid	1917	Destroyer	1.19 - 1.22
Sesame	1918	Destroyer	1.22 - 1933
Hunter	1936	Destroyer	1936 - 4.40
G13 RNLN	1913	TBD	1940 - 1942

H36

Victor	1913	Destroyer	12.14 - 9.15
Garland	1913	Destroyer	9.15 - 1.19
Salmon	1916	Destroyer	1.19 - 11.19
Moon	1915	Destroyer	11.19 - 12.20
Telemachus	1917	Destroyer	1.22 - 1929
Antelope	1929	Destroyer	1930 - 1944

H37

Amazon	1908	Destroyer	12.14 - 9.15
Ariel	1911	Destroyer	9.15 - 1.18
Goshawk	1911	Destroyer	1.18 - 11.18
Nereus	1916	Destroyer	11.18
Prince	1916	Destroyer	1.19 - 12.20
Steadfast	1918	Destroyer	1.22 - 1933
Garland	1935	Destroyer	1935 - 1946

H38

Saracen	1908	Destroyer	12.14 - 9.15
Oak	1912	Destroyer	9.15 - 1.18
Grampus	1910	Destroyer	1.18 - 3.18
Warwick	1917	Destroyer	3.18 - 9.18
Fawn	1897	Destroyer	9.18 - 1.19
Marne	1915	Destroyer	1.19 - 12.20
Tilbury	1918	Destroyer	1.22 - 1932
Delight	1932	Destroyer	1932 - 7.40
Spetsai RHN	1932	Destroyer	BR619(2)

H39

Forester	1911	Destroyer	12.14 - 1.18
Hardy	1912	Destroyer	1.18 - 1.19
Mandate	1915	Destroyer	1.19 - 12.20
Skate	1917	Destroyer	1.22 - 1936

H40

Afridi	1907	Destroyer	12.14 - 9.15
Midge	1913	Destroyer	9.15 - 1.18
Hind	1911	Destroyer	1.18 - 6.18
Rival	1916	Destroyer	6.18 - 1.19
Magic	1915	Destroyer	1.19 - 1.22
Springbok	1917	Destroyer	1.22 - 1929
Anthony	1929	Destroyer	1929 - 1948

H41

Spitfire	1912	Destroyer	12.14 - 1.18
Hope	1910	Destroyer	1.18 - 4.18
Whirlwind	1917	Destroyer	4.18 - 9.18
Doon	1903	Destroyer	9.18 - 1.19
Michael	1915	Destroyer	1.19 - 1.22
Skilful	1917	Destroyer	1.22 - 1929
Ardent	1929	Destroyer	1930 - 6.40
Redoubt	1942	Destroyer	1942 - 1948

H42

Fury	1911	Destroyer	12.14 - 1.18
Hornet	1911	Destroyer	1.18 - 6.18
Musketeer	1915	Destroyer	6.18 - 1.19
Mystic	1915	Destroyer	1.19 - 12.20
Retriever	1917	Destroyer	1.22 - 1928
Arrow	1929	Destroyer	1929 - 8.43

H43

Linnet	1913	Destroyer	12.14 - 1.18
Hydra	1912	Destroyer	1.18 - 4.18
Velox	1917	Destroyer	4.18 - 9.18
Greyhound	1900	Destroyer	9.18 - 1.19
Melampus	1914	Destroyer	1.19 - 12.20
Nimrod	1915	Destroyer	1.22 - 1924
Skeena RCN	1930	Destroyer	.... - ....
Havock	1936	Destroyer	1936 - 4.42

H44

Goldfinch	1910	Destroyer	12.14 - 4.15
Melampus	1914	Destroyer	9.15 - 1.17
Jackal	1911	Destroyer	1.18 - 4.18
Nepean	1916	Destroyer	6.18 - 1.19
Medea	1915	Destroyer	1.19 - 12.20
Trojan	1918	Destroyer	1.22 - 1933
Highlander	1939	Destroyer	1939 - 1946

H45

Goshawk	1911	Destroyer	12.14 - 1.18
Laertes	1913	Destroyer	1.18 - 1.19
Mentor	1914	Destroyer	1.19 - 12.20
Truculent	1917	Destroyer	1.22 - 1926
Acheron	1930	Destroyer	1930 - 12.40

H46

Achates	1912	Destroyer	12.14 - 1.18

Lance	1914	Destroyer	1.18 - 1.19
Moorsom	1914	Destroyer	1.19 - 12.20
Tyrant	1917	Destroyer	1.22 - 1936
Belmont	1918	Destroyer	1940 - 1.42

H47

Hind	1911	Destroyer	12.14 - 1.18
Landrail	1914	Destroyer	1.18 - 1.19
Morris	1914	Destroyer	1.19 - 1.22
Sabrina	1916	Destroyer	1.22 - ....
Blanche	1930	Destroyer	1930 - 12.39
L'Incomprise FR	1937	Destroyer	1940 - 1945

H48

Hope	1910	Destroyer	12.14 - 1.18
Lapwing	1911	Destroyer	1.18 - 4.18
Morning Star	1915	Destroyer	6.18 - 1.19
Noble	1915	Destroyer	1.19 - 12.20
Sybille	1917	Destroyer	1.22 - 1926
Crescent	1931	Destroyer	1931 - 1936
Fraser RCN (ex *Crescent*)	1931	Destroyer	1936 - 6.40
Sleipner RNoN	1936	Destroyer	1940 - 1945

H49

Hornet	1911	Destroyer	12.14 - 1.18
Lark	1913	Destroyer	1.18 - 1.19
Lochinvar	1915	Destroyer	1.19 - 12.20
Relentless	1916	Destroyer	1.22 - 1926
Diana	1932	Destroyer	1932 - 9.40
Margaree RCN (ex *Diana*)	1932	Destroyer	9.40 - 10.40
Inconstant	1941	Destroyer	1939 - 1946

H50

Hydra	1912	Destroyer	12.14 - 1.18
Larne	1910	Destroyer	1.18 - 4.18
Obdurate	1916	Destroyer	6.18 - 1.19
Loyal	1913	Destroyer	1.19 - 12.20
Stronghold	1919	Destroyer	1.22 - 3.42
Themistoklis RHN	1942	Destroyer	BR619(2)

H51

Christopher	1912	Destroyer	12.14 - 1.18
Laurel	1913	Destroyer	1.18 - 1.19
Leonidas	1913	Destroyer	1.19 - 12.20
Scout	1918	Destroyer	1.22 - 1946

H52

Ghurka	1907	Destroyer	12.14 - 9.15
Badger	1911	Destroyer	9.15 - 1.18
Laverock	1913	Destroyer	1.18 - 1.19
Lucifer	1913	Destroyer	1.19 - 12.20
Scotsman	1918	Destroyer	1.22 - 1933
Le Fantasque FR	1934	Destroyer	BR619(2)

H53

Laverock	1913	Destroyer	12.14 - 1.18
Lawford	1913	Destroyer	1.18 - 1.19
Linnet	1913	Destroyer	1.19 - 12.20
Simoom	1918	Destroyer	1.22 - 1930
Dainty	1932	Destroyer	1932 - 2.41

H54

Landrail	1914	Destroyer	12.14 - 1.18
Legion	1914	Destroyer	1.18 - 9.18
Peterel	1899	Destroyer	9.18 - 1.19
Ambuscade	1913	Destroyer	1.19 - 12.20
Saladin	1919	Destroyer	1.22 - 1948

H55

Jackal	1911	Destroyer	12.14 - 1.18
Lennox	1914	Destroyer	1.18 - 1.19
Garland	1913	Destroyer	1.19 - 12.20
Toreador	1918	Destroyer	1.22 - 1927
Vancouver	1917	Destroyer	1929 - 1933
Hostile	1936	Destroyer	1936 - 8.40
Z6 RNLN	1915	TBD	1940 - 10.40

H56

Lapwing	1911	Destroyer	12.14 - 1.18
Leonidas	1913	Destroyer	1.18 - 1.19
Oak	1912	Destroyer	1.19 - 12.20
Stalwart RAN	1918	Destroyer	.... - ....
Trusty	1918	Destroyer	1.22 - 1934
La Melpoméne FR	1935	Destroyer	7.40 - 1945

H57

Larne	1910	Destroyer	12.14 - 1.18
Liberty	1913	Destroyer	1.18 - 1.19
Defender	1911	Destroyer	1.19 - 12.20
Spindrift	1918	Destroyer	1.22 - 1934
Hearty	1939	Destroyer	1939 - 2.40
Hesperus (ex Hearty)	1939	Destroyer	2.40 - 1948

H58

Lizard	1911	Destroyer	12.14 - 1.18
Lightfoot	1915	Destroyer	1.18 - 3.18
Foxhound	1909	Destroyer	4.18 - 1.19
Forester	1911	Destroyer	1.19 - 12.20
Salmon	1916	Destroyer	1.22 - 1933
Sable (ex Salmon)	1916	Destroyer	1933 - 1937

H59

Acasta	1912	Destroyer	12.14 - 1.18
Linnet	1913	Destroyer	1.18 - 1.19
Goshawk	1911	Destroyer	1.19 - 12.20
Tetrarch	1917	Destroyer	1.22 - 1934
Gallant	1935	Destroyer	1935 - 9.43
Velite IT	1941	Destroyer	1943 - 1948

H60

Lyra	1910	Destroyer	12.14 - 1.18
Lizard	1911	Destroyer	1.18 - 4.18
Grasshopper	1909	Destroyer	6.18 - 1.19
Hind	1911	Destroyer	1.19 - 12.20
Trenchant	1916	Destroyer	1.22 - 1926
Crusader	1931	Destroyer	1931 - 6.38
Ottawa RCN (ex Crusader)	1931	Destroyer	6.38 - 9.42

H61

Sparrowhawk	1912	Destroyer	12.14 - 1.18
Llewellyn	1913	Destroyer	1.18 - 1.19
Tigress	1911	Destroyer	1.19 - 12.20
Undine	1917	Destroyer	1.22 - 1927
Express	1934	Destroyer	1934 - 6.43
Gatineau RCN (ex Express)	1934	Destroyer	6.43 - 1946

H62

Ambuscade	1913	Destroyer	12.14 - 1.18
Lookout	1914	Destroyer	1.18 - 1.19
Lizard	1911	Destroyer	1.19 - 12.20
Urchin	1917	Destroyer	1.22 - 1930
Faulknor	1934	Destroyer	1934 - 1945

H63

Contest	1913	Destroyer	12.14 - 1.18
Loyal	1913	Destroyer	1.18 - 1.19
Sandfly	1911	Destroyer	1.19 - 12.20
Ursa	1917	Destroyer	1.22 - 1926
Gipsy	1935	Destroyer	1935 - 11.39
La Flore FR	1935	Destroyer	7.40 - 1944

H64

Swift	1907	Destroyer	12.14 - 1.18
Lucifer	1913	Destroyer	1.18 - 1.19
Acorn	1910	Destroyer	1.19 - 12.20
Radstock	1916	Destroyer	1.22 - 1927
Duchess	1932	Destroyer	1931 - 12.39
Beverley	1919	Destroyer	1940 - 4.43

H65

Martin	1910	Destroyer	12.14 - 1.18
Lurcher	1912	Destroyer	1.18 - 1.19
Brisk	1910	Destroyer	1.19 - 12.20
Raider	1916	Destroyer	1.22 - 1928
Boadicea	1930	Destroyer	1930 - 6.44

H66

Crusader	1909	Destroyer	12.14 - 9.15
Beaver	1911	Destroyer	9.15 - 1.18
Lydiard	1914	Destroyer	1.18 - 1.19
Cameleon	1910	Destroyer	1.19 - 12.20
Sorceress	1916	Destroyer	1.22 - 1927

Escort	1934	Destroyer	1934 - 7.40	*Thisbe*	1917	Destroyer	1.22 - 1934
G15 RNLN	1914	TBD	7.40 - 1942	*Bradford*	1918	Destroyer	1940 - 1943

H67
Hardy	1912	Destroyer	12.14 - 9.15
Lyra	1910	Destroyer	1.18 - 4.18
Pigeon	1916	Destroyer	6.18 - 1.19
Fury	1911	Destroyer	1.19 - 12.20
Tancred	1917	Destroyer	1.22 - 1927
Fearless	1934	Destroyer	1934 - 7.41
Panthir RHN	1911	Destroyer	9.40 - 1944

H73
Cockatrice	1912	Destroyer	12.14 - 1.18
Matchless	1914	Destroyer	1.18 - 9.18
Garry	1905	Destroyer	9.18 - 1.19
Nemesis	1910	Destroyer	1.19 - 12.20
Thruster	1917	Destroyer	1.22 - 1934
Burza ORP	1929	Destroyer	BR619(2)

H68
Unity	1913	Destroyer	12.14 - 1.18
Lysander	1913	Destroyer	1.18 - 1.19
Hope	1910	Destroyer	1.19 - 12.20
Redoubt	1916	Destroyer	1.22 - 1927
Foresight	1934	Destroyer	1934 - 8.42

H74
Nereide	1910	Destroyer	12.14 - 1.18
Medea	1915	Destroyer	1.18 - 1.19
Orestes	1916	Destroyer	1.19 - 12.20
Ready	1916	Destroyer	1.22 - 1927
Forester	1934	Destroyer	1934 - 1946

H69
Minstrel	1911	Destroyer	12.14 - 1.18
Manly	1914	Destroyer	1.18 - 9.18
Flying Fish	1897	Destroyer	9.18 - 1.19
Larne	1910	Destroyer	1.19 - 12.20
Sarpedon	1916	Destroyer	1.22 - 1926
Foxhound	1934	Destroyer	1934 - 2.44
Qu'appelle RCN (ex *Foxhound*)	1934	Destroyer	2.44 - 1948

H75
Phoenix	1911	Destroyer	12.14 - 1.18
Melampus	1914	Destroyer	1.18 - 1.19
Pellew	1916	Destroyer	1.19 - 12.20
Rob Roy	1916	Destroyer	1.22 - 1927
Decoy	1932	Destroyer	1932 - 4.43
Kootenay RCN (ex *Decoy*)	1932	Destroyer	4.43 - 1945

H70
Nubian	1909	Destroyer	12.14 - 9.15
Brisk	1910	Destroyer	9.15 - 1.18
Mansfield	1914	Destroyer	1.18 - 9.18
Exe	1903	Destroyer	9.18 - 1.19
Nereide	1910	Destroyer	1.19 - 12.20
Starfish	1916	Destroyer	1.22 - 1930
Fortune	1940	Destroyer	1934 - 5.43
Saskatchewan RCN (ex *Fortune*)	1940	Destroyer	5.43 - 1946

H76
Lightfoot	1915	Destroyer	9.15 - 3.17
Melpomene	1915	Destroyer	1.18 - 9.18
Moy	1904	Destroyer	9.18 - 1.19
Orford	1916	Destroyer	1.19 - 12.20
Rocket	1916	Destroyer	1.22 - 1927
Fury	1934	Destroyer	1934 - 6.44

H71
Lynx	1913	Destroyer	12.14 - 4.16
Parker	1916	Destroyer	4.16 - 3.17
Martin	1910	Destroyer	1.18 - 4.18
Harpy	1909	Destroyer	6.18 - 1.19
Redpole	1910	Destroyer	1.19 - 12.20
Tempest	1917	Destroyer	1.22 - 1934
Grom ORP	1936	Destroyer	1939 - 5.40
Z8 RNLN	1915	TBD	1942 - 1944

H77
Beaver	1911	Destroyer	2.15 - 9.15
Redpole	1910	Destroyer	9.15 - 1.18
Mentor	1914	Destroyer	1.18 - 9.18
Ness	1905	Destroyer	9.18 - 1.19
Peyton	1916	Destroyer	1.19 - 12.20
Rosalind	1916	Destroyer	1.22 - 1927
Boreas	1930	Destroyer	1930 - 2.44
Salamis RHN (ex *Boreas*)	1930	Destroyer	2.44 - 1951

H72
Nemesis	1910	Destroyer	12.14 - 1.18
Mastiff	1914	Destroyer	1.18 - 9.18
Crane	1896	Destroyer	9.18 - 1.19
Minstrel	1911	Destroyer	1.19 - 12.20

H78
Ardent	1913	Destroyer	12.14 - 1.18
Meteor	1914	Destroyer	1.18 - 9.18
Nith	1905	Destroyer	9.18 - 1.19
Murray	1914	Destroyer	1.19 - 12.20
Satyr	1916	Destroyer	1.22 - 1927
Fame	1934	Destroyer	1934 - 1948

H79

Legion	1914	Destroyer	12.14 - 1.18
Midge	1913	Destroyer	1.18 - 1.19
Termagant	1915	Destroyer	1.19 - 1.22
Sceptre	1917	Destroyer	1.22 - 1927
Firedrake	1934	Destroyer	1934 - 12.42

H80

Loyal	1913	Destroyer	12.14 - 1.18
Milne	1914	Destroyer	1.18 - 9.18
Ouse	1905	Destroyer	9.18 - 1.19
Laertes	1913	Destroyer	1.19 - 12.20
Tormentor	1917	Destroyer	1.22 - 1930
Brazen	1930	Destroyer	1930 - 7.40
Demirhisar ᴛᴋ	1941	Destroyer	1941 - 1942

H81

Liberty	1913	Destroyer	12.14 - 1.18
Minos	1914	Destroyer	1.18 - 1.19
Lysander	1913	Destroyer	1.19 - 12.20
Torrid	1917	Destroyer	1.22 - 1934
Broadwater	1919	Destroyer	1940 - 10.41

H82

Rifleman	1910	Destroyer	12.14 - 1.18
Minstrel	1911	Destroyer	1.18 - 4.18
Minion	1915	Destroyer	6.18 - 1.19
Landrail	1914	Destroyer	1.19 - 12.20
Restless	1916	Destroyer	1.22 - 1934
Burnham	1919	Destroyer	1940 - 1944

H83

Nymphe	1911	Destroyer	12.14 - 1.18
Miranda	1914	Destroyer	1.18 - 9.18
Stour	1905	Destroyer	9.18 - 1.19
Llewellyn	1913	Destroyer	1.19 - 12.20
Rigorous	1916	Destroyer	1.22 - 1927
Cygnet	1930	Destroyer	1930 - 9.36
St Laurent ʀᴄɴ	1930	Destroyer	2.37 - 1945
(ex *Cygnet*)			

H84

Faulknor	1914	Destroyer	8.15 - 1.18
Moorsom	1914	Destroyer	1.18 - 9.18
Test	1905	Destroyer	9.18 - 1.19
Owl	1913	Destroyer	1.19 - 12.20
Romola	1916	Destroyer	1.22 - 1930
Brilliant	1930	Destroyer	1930 - 1948

H85

Ruby	1910	Destroyer	12.14 - 1.18
Morris	1914	Destroyer	1.18 - 9.18
Mermaid	1898	Destroyer	9.18 - 1.19
Spitfire	1912	Destroyer	1.19 - 12.20
Rowena	1916	Destroyer	1.22 - 1931

Relentless	1942	Destroyer	1942 - 1948

H86

Zulu	1909	Destroyer	12.14 - 9.15
Attack	1911	Destroyer	1.16 - 1.18
Murray	1914	Destroyer	1.18 - 9.18
Waveney	1903	Destroyer	9.18 - 1.19
Porpoise	1913	Destroyer	1.19 - 12.20
Patrician	1916	Destroyer	1.22 - 1930
Grenade	1935	Destroyer	1935 - 5.40
Vasilissa Olga ʀʜɴ	1938	Destroyer	1941 - 9.43
Gleaner	1983	Survey	1998 - 2018

H87

Sandfly	1911	Destroyer	12.14 - 1.18
Myngs	1914	Destroyer	1.18 - 9.18
Bat	1896	Destroyer	9.18 - 1.19
Unity	1913	Destroyer	1.19 - 12.20
Patriot	1916	Destroyer	1.22 - 1931
Hardy	1936	Destroyer	1936 - 4.40
Sultanhisar ᴛᴋ	1940	Destroyer	1942 - ....
Echo	2002	Survey	2003 -

H88

Sheldrake	1911	Destroyer	12.14 - 1.18
Nemesis	1910	Destroyer	1.18 - 4.18
Obedient	1915	Destroyer	6.18 - 1.19
Hardy	1912	Destroyer	1.19 - 12.20
Wakeful	1917	Destroyer	1.22 - 5.40
Havelock	1939	Destroyer	1939 - 1946
Enterprise	2002	Survey	2003 -

H89

Basilisk	1910	Destroyer	2.15 - 9.15
Staunch	1910	Destroyer	9.15 - 1.18
Nereide	1910	Destroyer	1.18 - 4.18
Mons	1915	Destroyer	6.18 - 1.19
Firedrake	1912	Destroyer	1.19 - 12.20
Tintagel	1918	Destroyer	1.22 - 1930
Grafton	1935	Destroyer	1935 - 5.40
Aetos ʀʜɴ	1911	Destroyer	7.40 - 1944

H90

Viking	1909	Destroyer	12.14 - 9.15
Medusa	1915	Destroyer	9.15 - 1.18
Nimrod	1915	Destroyer	1.18 - 1.19
Lurcher	1912	Destroyer	1.19 - 12.20
Stork	1916	Destroyer	1.22 - 1927
Broadway	1920	Destroyer	1940 - 1948

H91

Laurel	1913	Destroyer	12.14 - 1.18
Parthian	1916	Destroyer	1.18 - 3.18
Mindful	1915	Destroyer	6.18 - 1.19
Badger	1911	Destroyer	1.19 - 12.20

Sharpshooter	1917	Destroyer	1.22 - 1927
Bulldog	1930	Destroyer	1930 - 1945

H92

Tigress	1911	Destroyer	12.14 - 1.18
Oak	1912	Destroyer	1.18 - 1.19
Druid	1911	Destroyer	1.19 - 12.20
Tara	1918	Destroyer	1.22 - 1931
Glowworm	1935	Destroyer	1935 - 4.40
Rocket	1942	Destroyer	1942 - 1948

H93

Lysander	1913	Destroyer	12.14 - 1.18
Owl	1913	Destroyer	1.18 - 1.19
Ferret	1911	Destroyer	1.19 - 12.20
Sable	1916	Destroyer	1.22 - 1926
Hereward	1936	Destroyer	1936 - 5.41
Z7 RNLN	1915	TBD	1942 - 1944

H94

Laertes	1913	Destroyer	12.14 - 1.18
Phoenix	1911	Destroyer	1.18 - 4.18
Sikh	1918	Destroyer	6.18 - 9.18
Peregrine	1916	Destroyer	9.18 - 1.19
Hydra	1912	Destroyer	1.19 - 12.20
Rapid	1916	Destroyer	1.22 - 1926
Burwell	1918	Destroyer	1940 - 1948

H95

Lennox	1914	Destroyer	12.14 - 1.18
Porpoise	1913	Destroyer	1.18 - 1.19
Jackal	1911	Destroyer	1.19 - 12.20
Winchester	1918	Destroyer	1.22 - 1930
Roebuck	1942	Destroyer	1942 - 1948

H96

Marksman	1915	Destroyer	8.15 - 3.17
Redpole	1910	Destroyer	1.18 - 4.18
Pylades	1916	Destroyer	6.18- 9.18
Peyton	1916	Destroyer	9.18 - 1.19
Alarm	1910	Destroyer	1.19 - 12.20
Tarpon	1917	Destroyer	1.22 - 1926
Buxton	1918	Destroyer	1940 - 1945

H97

Firedrake	1912	Destroyer	12.14 - 1.18
Rifleman	1910	Destroyer	1.18 - 4.18
Pylades	1916	Destroyer	11.18 - 1.19
Lyra	1910	Destroyer	1.19 - 12.20
Rival	1916	Destroyer	1.22 - 1926
Hyperion	1936	Destroyer	1936 - 12.40
Blade RNLN (ex *Z5*)	1915	TBD	1941- 1944

H98

Broke	1914	Destroyer	8.15 - 1.18

Ruby	1910	Destroyer	1.18 - 4.18
Pellew	1916	Destroyer	11.18 - 1.19
Nymphe	1911	Destroyer	1.19 - 12.20
Truant	1918	Destroyer	1.22 - 1931
Leopard FR	1924	Destroyer	BR619(2)

H99

Llewellyn	1913	Destroyer	12.14 - 1.18
Sandfly	1911	Destroyer	1.18 - 11.18
Renard	1909	Destroyer	11.18 - 1.19
Rifleman	1910	Destroyer	1.19 - 12.20
Tactician	1918	Destroyer	1.22 - 1930
Hero	1936	Destroyer	1936 - 11.43
Chaudiere RCN (ex *Hero*)	1936	Destroyer	11.43 - 1945

H130

Roebuck	1985	Survey	1998 - 2010
Magpie	2018	Survey	2018 -

H131

Scott	1996	Survey	1998 -

H138

Herald	1973	Survey	1998 - 2001

H209

Kingston Olivine	1930	Trawler	1939 - ....

H317

Bulldog	1967	Survey	1998 - 2001

H319

Beagle	1967	Survey	1998 - 2002

H0A

Manly	1914	Destroyer	8.15 - 1.18
Sheldrake	1911	Destroyer	1.18 - 4.18
Vanquisher	1917	Destroyer	6.18 - 9.18
Norman	1916	Destroyer	9.18 - ....
Rob Roy	1916	Destroyer	11.19 - 1.22
Sylph	1916	Destroyer	1.22 - 8.25

H1A

Mansfield	1914	Destroyer	8.15 - 1.18
Spitfire	1912	Destroyer	1.18 - 1.19
Sirdar	1918	Destroyer	11.19 - 1.22
Tenacious	1917	Destroyer	1.22 - 8.25

H2A

Mons	1915	Destroyer	8.15 - 1.17
Staunch	1910	Destroyer	1917 - 1.18
Vehement	1917	Destroyer	6.18 - 9.18
Serapis	1918	Destroyer	11.19 - 1.22
Sturgeon	1917	Destroyer	1.22 - 8.25

H3A

Mastiff	1914	Destroyer	8.15 - 1.18
Swift	1907	Destroyer	1.18 - 3.18

Ithuriel	1916	Destroyer	1.22 - 8.25		**H5C**			
Anzac RAN	1917	Destroyer	8.25 -		*Botha*	1914	Destroyer	8.15 - 1.18
					H6C			
H4A					*Tipperary*	1915	Destroyer	8.15 - 1.18
Matchless	1914	Destroyer	12.14 - 1.18		**H7C**			
Tigress	1911	Destroyer	1.18 - 4.18		*Menace*	1915	Destroyer	8.15 - 1.17
Vanoc	1917	Destroyer	6.18 - 9.18		**H8C**			
Trinidad	1918	Destroyer	11.19 - 1.22		*Munster*	1915	Destroyer	8.15 - 1.17
Marksman	1915	Destroyer	1.22 - 8.25		**H9C**			
Stalwart RAN	1918	Destroyer	8.25 -		*Medea*	1915	Destroyer	9.15 - 1.17
H5A					**HA0**			
Nimrod	1915	Destroyer	8.15 - 1.18		*Miranda*	1914	Destroyer	8.15 - 3.18
Unity	1913	Destroyer	1.18 - 1.19		*Marne*	1915	Destroyer	3.18 - 1.19
Mischief	1915	Destroyer	1.22 - 8.25		*Rob Roy*	1916	Destroyer	11.19 - 1.22
Success RAN	1918	Destroyer	8.25 -		*Nereus*	1916	Destroyer	1.22 - 8.25
					Parramatta RAN	1910	Destroyer	8.25 - ....
H6A								
Mentor	1914	Destroyer	8.15 - 1.18		**HA1**			
Victor	1913	Destroyer	1.18 - 1.19		*Kempenfelt*	1915	Destroyer	8.15 - 3.17
Scout	1918	Destroyer	11.19 - 1.22		*Michael*	1915	Destroyer	1.18 - 1.19
Morning Star	1915	Destroyer	1.22 - 8.25		*Saladin*	1919	Destroyer	11.19 - 1.22
Tattoo RAN	1918	Destroyer	8.25 - 1933		*Nerissa*	1916	Destroyer	1.22 - 8.25
					Swan RAN	1915	Destroyer	8.25 - ....
H7A								
Meteor	1914	Destroyer	8.15 - 1.18		**HA2**			
Wizard	1895	Destroyer	1.18 - 1.19		*Moorsom*	1914	Destroyer	8.15 - 1.18
Scotsman	1918	Destroyer	11.19 - 1.22		*Milbrook*	1915	Destroyer	1.18 - 1.19
Munster	1915	Destroyer	1.22 - 8.25		*Obdurate*	1916	Destroyer	1.22 - 8.25
Tasmania RAN	1918	Destroyer	8.25 - 1928		*Warrego* RAN	1911	Destroyer	8.25 - ....
H8A					**HA3**			
Milne	1914	Destroyer	8.15 - 10.17		*Morris*	1914	Destroyer	8.15 - 1.18
Scourge	1910	Destroyer	10.17 - 1.19		*Mosquito*	1910	Destroyer	1.18 - 1.19
Simoom	1916	Destroyer	1.19 - 1.22		*Toreador*	1918	Destroyer	11.19 - 1.22
Musketeer	1915	Destroyer	1.22 - 8.25		*Obedient*	1915	Destroyer	1.22 - 8.25
Swordsman RAN	1918	Destroyer	8.25 -		*Torrens* RAN	1915	Destroyer	8.25 - ....
H9A					**HA4**			
Minos	1914	Destroyer	8.15 - 1.18		*Murray*	1914	Destroyer	8.15 - 1.18
Mandate	1915	Destroyer	1.18 - 1.19		*Nicator*	1916	Destroyer	1.18 - 1.19
Nepean	1916	Destroyer	1.22 - 8.25		*Ossory*	1915	Destroyer	1.22 - 8.25
Huon RAN	1914	Destroyer	8.25 -		*Yarra* RAN	1910	Destroyer	8.25 - ....
H0C					**HA5**			
Mounsey	1915	Destroyer	2.15 - 1.17		*Myngs*	1914	Destroyer	8.15 - 1.18
H1C					*Ossory*	1915	Destroyer	1.18 - 1.19
Musketeer	1915	Destroyer	2.15 - 1.17		*Trusty*	1918	Destroyer	11.19 - 1.22
H2C					*Parker*	1916	Destroyer	1.22 - 8.25
Mystic	1915	Destroyer	8.15 - 1.17		*Nepean*	1916	Destroyer	.... - ....
H3C								
Wizard	1895	Destroyer	12.14 - 4.17		**HA6**			
H4C					*Marne*	1915	Destroyer	8.15 - 1.17
Boxer	1894	Destroyer	12.14 - 4.17		*Portia*	1916	Destroyer	1.18 - 1.19

Phoebe	1916	Destroyer	1.22 - 8.25

HA7

Maenad	1915	Destroyer	8.15 - 1.18
Racoon	1910	Destroyer	1.18 - 3.18
Grampus	1910	Destroyer	6.18 - 1.19
Spindrift	1918	Destroyer	11.19 - 1.22
Tirade	1917	Destroyer	1.22 - 8.25

HA8

Mandate	1915	Destroyer	8.15 - 1.18
Pelican	1916	Destroyer	1.18 - 1.19
Tobago	1918	Destroyer	1.22 - 8.25

HA9

Manners	1915	Destroyer	8.15 - 1.17
Savage	1910	Destroyer	1.18 - 1.19
Truant	1918	Destroyer	11.19 - 1.22

HC0

Marigold	1915	Destroyer	12.14 - 9.15
Magic	1915	Destroyer	9.15 - 1.18
Mounsey	1915	Destroyer	6.18 - 9.18

HC1

Moresby	1915	Destroyer	8.15 - 1.17
Manners	1915	Destroyer	6.18 - 1.19

HC2

Marmion	1915	Destroyer	8.15 - 1.17
Pincher	1910	Destroyer	4.18 - 9.18

HC3

Martial	1915	Destroyer	8.15 - 1.17
Scorpion	1910	Destroyer	9.18 - 1.19

HC4

Mary Rose	1915	Destroyer	8.15 - 1.17
Bulldog	1909	Destroyer	9.18 - ....

HC5

Michael	1915	Destroyer	8.15 - 1.17
Beagle	1909	Destroyer	11.19 - 12.20

HC6

Milbrook	1915	Destroyer	8.15 - 1.17
Nizam	1916	Destroyer	9.18 - ....

HC7

Minion	1915	Destroyer	8.15 - 1.18
Bulldog	1909	Destroyer	1.18 - 9.18
Rattlesnake	1910	Destroyer	9.18 - 1.19

HC8

Moon	1915	Destroyer	2.15 - 1.17
Basilisk	1910	Destroyer	9.18 - ....

HC9

Morning Star	1915	Destroyer	2.15 - 1.17

Flag 'H (Int)' Superior

US Navy warships serving with the Royal Navy in 1918 were assigned flag superiors from the International code, as opposed to the Naval code. International flag 'H' was a square flag vertically halved with white and red sections. These numbers were assigned for visual signalling and were not applied to the hull.

H(I)00
Allen USN	1916	Destroyer	1.18 - 6.18
Nicholson USN	1914	Destroyer	6.18 - ....

H(I)01
Ammen USN	1910	Destroyer	1.18 - 6.18
Winslow USN	1915	Destroyer	6.18 - ....

H(I)02
Balch USN	1913	Destroyer	1.18 - ....

H(I)03
Benham USN	1913	Destroyer	1.18 - 6.18
Paulding USN	1910	Destroyer	6.18

H(I)04
Burrows USN	1910	Destroyer	1.18 - 6.18
Trippe USN	1910	Destroyer	6.18 - ....

H(I)05
Caldwell USN	1917	Destroyer	6.18 - ....

H(I)06
Cassin USN	1913	Destroyer	1.18 - 6.18
Cummings USN	1913	Destroyer	6.18 - ....

H(I)07
Conyngham USN	1915	Destroyer	1.18 - 6.18
Sampson USN	1916	Destroyer	6.18 - ....

H(I)08
Cummings USN	1913	Destroyer	1.18 - 6.18
Walke USN	1911	Destroyer	6.18 - ....

H(I)09
Cushing USN	1912	Destroyer	1.18 - ....

H(I)10
Allen USN	1916	Destroyer	6.18 - ....

H(I)11
Downes USN	1913	Destroyer	1.18 - 6.18
Duncan USN	1913	Destroyer	6.18 - ....

H(I)12
Davis USN	1916	Destroyer	1.18 - 6.18

Sterett USN	1910	Destroyer	6.18 - ....

H(I)14
Dixie USN	1893	Depot Ship	1.18 - 6.18
Porter USN	1915	Destroyer	6.18 - ....

H(I)15
Drayton USN	1910	Destroyer	1.18 - 6.18
Jarvis USN	1912	Destroyer	6.18 - ....

H(I)16
Duncan USN	1913	Destroyer	1.18 - 6.18
Melville USN	1915	Depot Ship	6.18 - ....

H(I)17
Ericsson USN	1914	Destroyer	1.18 - 6.18
Wilkes USN	1916	Destroyer	6.18 - ....

H(I)18
Aylwin USN	1912	Destroyer	6.18 - ....

H(I)19
Fanning USN	1912	Destroyer	1.18 - 6.18
Jenkins USN	1912	Destroyer	6.18 - ....

H(I)20
Jacob Jones USN	1918	Destroyer	1.18 - 6.18
Patterson USN	1911	Destroyer	6.18 - ....

H(I)21
Jarvis USN	1912	Destroyer	1.18 - 6.18
Downes USN	1913	Destroyer	6.18 - ....

H(I)22
Jenkins USN	1912	Destroyer	1.18 - 6.18
McDougal USN	1914	Destroyer	6.18 - ....

H(I)23
Manly USN	1917	Destroyer	1.18 - 6.18
Burrows USN	1910	Destroyer	6.18 - ....

H(I)24
McDougal USN	1914	Destroyer	1.18 - 6.18
Wainwright USN	1915	Destroyer	6.18 - ....

H(I)25			
Melville USN	1915	Depot Ship	1.18 - 6.18
Cassin USN	1913	Destroyer	6.18 - ....

H(I)26			
Perkins USN	1910	Destroyer	6.18 - 6.18
Shaw USN	1916	Destroyer	6.18 - ....

H(I)27			
Nicholson USN	1914	Destroyer	1.18 - ....

H(I)28			
O'Brien USN	1915	Destroyer	1.18 - ....

H(I)29			
Fanning USN	1912	Destroyer	6.18 - ....

H(I)30			
Parker USN	1913	Destroyer	1.18 - 6.18
Manly USN	1917	Destroyer	6.18 - ....

H(I)31			
Patterson USN	1911	Destroyer	1.18 - 6.18
Benham USN	1913	Destroyer	6.18 - ....

H(I)32			
Paulding USN	1910	Destroyer	1.18 - 6.18
Warrington USN	1910	Destroyer	6.18 - ....

H(I)33			
Perkins USN	1910	Destroyer	1.18 - 6.18
Conyngham USN	1915	Destroyer	6.18 - ....

H(I)34			
Porter USN	1915	Destroyer	1.18 - 6.18
Wadsworth USN	1915	Destroyer	6.18 - ....

H(I)35			
Davis USN	1916	Destroyer	6.18 - ....

H(I)36			
Rowan USN	1916	Destroyer	1.18 - 6.18
Tucker USN	1915	Destroyer	6.18 - ....

H(I)37			
Sampson USN	1916	Destroyer	1.18 - 6.18
Drayton USN	1910	Destroyer	6.18 - ....

H(I)38			
Shaw USN	1916	Destroyer	1.18 - 6.18
Parker USN	1913	Destroyer	6.18 - ....

H(I)39			
Sterett USN	1910	Destroyer	1.18 - 6.18
Ericsson USN	1914	Destroyer	6.18 - ....

H(I)40			
Trippe USN	1910	Destroyer	1.18 - 6.18
Stockton USN	1917	Destroyer	6.18 - ....

H(I)41			
Tucker USN	1915	Destroyer	1.18 - 6.18
Ammen USN	1910	Destroyer	6.18 - ....

H(I)42			
Beale USN	1912	Destroyer	6.18 - ....

H(I)43			
Terry USN	1909	Destroyer	6.18 - ....

H(I)44			
Wadsworth USN	1915	Destroyer	1.18 - 6.18
Lamson USN	1915	Destroyer	6.18 - ....

H(I)45			
Wainwright USN	1915	Destroyer	1.18 - 6.18
Monaghan USN	1911	Destroyer	6.18 - ....

H(I)46			
Walke USN	1911	Destroyer	1.18 - 6.18
Roe USN	1909	Destroyer	6.18 - ....

H(I)47			
Warrington USN	1910	Destroyer	1.18 - 6.18
Preston USN	1909	Destroyer	6.18 - ....

H(I)48			
Wilkes USN	1916	Destroyer	1.18 - 6.18
Stewart USN	1902	Destroyer	6.18 - ....

H(I)49			
Winslow USN	1915	Destroyer	1.18 - 6.18
Flusser USN	1909	Destroyer	6.18 - ....

H(I)50			
Macdonough USN	1900	Destroyer	6.18 - ....

H(I)51			
Reid USN	1909	Destroyer	6.18 - ....

H(I)52			
Truxtun USN	1902	Destroyer	6.18 - ....

H(I)53			
Smith USN	1909	Destroyer	6.18 - ....

H(I)54			
Whipple USN	1901	Destroyer	6.18 - ....

H(I)55			
Worden USN	1903	Destroyer	6.18 - ....

H(I)56			
McCall USN	1910	Destroyer	6.18 - ....

H(I)57			
Kimberly USN	1917	Destroyer	6.18 - ....

H(I)58			
Sigourney USN	1917	Destroyer	6.18 - ....

H(I)59
Little USN   1917 Destroyer   6.18 - ....

H(I)60
Conner USN   1917 Destroyer   6.18 - ....

H(I)61
Rowan USN   1916 Destroyer   6.18 - ....

H(I)62
Stevens USN   1918 Destroyer   6.18 - ....

Flag 'I' Superior

Pre 1940: *Centurion*; Monitors; Cruisers; Aircraft Carriers; Armed Merchant Cruisers; Ocean and Armed Merchant Vessels; Coastal and Controlled Minelayers; Depot Ships

1940-48: Destroyers

1948: None

I00			
Minerva	1915	Monitor	6.39 - 1940
Stuart RAN	1918	Destroyer	1940 - 1948

I01			
Marshal Soult	1915	Monitor	6.39 - 1940
Montrose	1918	Destroyer	1940 - 1948

I02			
Erebus	1916	Monitor	6.39 - 1940
Inglefield	1936	Destroyer	4.40 - 2.44
Oudenarde	1945	Destroyer	Incomplete

I03			
Terror	1915	Monitor	6.39 - 1940
Icarus	1936	Destroyer	4.40 - 1946

I04			
Melpomene	1915	Training Vsl	6.39 - 1940
Annapolis RCN	1918	Destroyer	1940 - 1945

I05			
Cameron	1919	Destroyer	1940 - 1943
Danae (ex *Vimiera*)	Canc	Destroyer	Canc 1945

I06			
Medusa	1915	Monitor	6.39 - 1940
Keith	1930	Destroyer	4.40 - 6.40
Agincourt	1945	Destroyer	1945 - 1948

I07			
Forth	1938	Depot Ship	6.39 - 1940
Roxborough	1918	Destroyer	1940 - 1944
Waterloo	Canc	Destroyer	Canc 1945

I08			
Cochrane	1905	Depot Ship	6.39 - 1940
Brighton	1918	Destroyer	1940 - 1944
Delight	1950	Destroyer	1946 - 1948

I09			
Dolphin	1902	Depot Ship	6.39 - Sunk
Imperial	1936	Destroyer	4.40 - 5.41
Dunkirk	1945	Destroyer	1945 - 1948

I10			
Greenwich	1915	Depot Ship	6.39 - 1940
Intrepid	1936	Destroyer	4.40 - 9.43
Poictiers	1946	Destroyer	Incomplete

I11			
Impulsive	1937	Destroyer	4.40 - 1945

I12			
St Marys	1918	Destroyer	1940 - 1944

I14			
Victoria & Albert	1899	Royal Yacht	6.39 - 1940
Clare	1920	Destroyer	1940 - 1945

I15			
St Albans	1918	Destroyer	1940 - 1944
Daring	1949	Destroyer	1945 - 1948

I16			
Ivanhoe	1937	Destroyer	4.40 - 9.40
Savage	1942	Destroyer	1942 - 1948
Malplaquet	1946	Destroyer	Incomplete

I17			
Bath	1918	Destroyer	1940 - 1941
Alamein	1945	Destroyer	1945 - 1948

I18			
Assiniboine RCN	1931	Destroyer	10.39 - 1945

I19			
Hampton	1919	Minelayer	6.39 - 1940
Malcolm	1919	Destroyer	1940 - 1945
Desire	Canc	Destroyer	Canc 1945

I20			
Hecla	1940	Depot Ship	6.39 - 1940
Caldwell	1919	Destroyer	1940 - 1944

I21			
Charlestown	1918	Destroyer	1940 - 1944

I22			
Albatross	1928	Repair Ship	6.39 - 1940

Waterhen	1918	Destroyer	1940 - 6.41
Aisne	1945	Destroyer	1945 - 1948
I23			
Castleton	1919	Destroyer	1940 - 1945
I24			
Tyne	1940	Depot Ship	6.39 - 1940
Hamilton	1918	Destroyer	1940 - 1941
Hamilton RCN	1918	Destroyer	1941 - 1945
I25			
Warwick	1917	Destroyer	1940 - 1944
I26			
Plover	1937	Minelayer	6.39 - 1940
Watchman	1917	Destroyer	1940 - 1945
Druid	1952	Destroyer	1945
Diana (ex *Druid*)	1952	Destroyer	1945 - 1948
I27			
Lucia	1907	Depot Ship	6.39 - 1940
Walker	1917	Destroyer	1940 - 1945
Lion	Canc	Battleship	Canc 1945
I28			
Chesterfield	1920	Destroyer	1940 - 1945
I29			
Amphion	1934	Cruiser	1934
Perth RAN (ex *Amphion*)	1934	Cruiser	1934 - 1940
Vanessa	1918	Destroyer	1940 - 1948
I30			
Despatch	1919	Cruiser	6.39 - 1940
Whirlwind	1917	Destroyer	1940 - 7.40
Arunta RAN	1940	Destroyer	1941 - 1948
I31			
Cyclops	1905	Depot Ship	6.39 - 1940
Voyager	1918	Destroyer	1940 - 1942
Somme	Canc	Destroyer	Canc 1945
I32			
Titania	1915	Depot Ship	6.39 - 1940
Versatile	1917	Destroyer	1940 - 1948
I33			
Canberra RAN	1927	Cruiser	1927 - 1940
Vimy (ex *Vancouver*)	1917	Destroyer	1940 - 1948
I34			
Velox	1917	Destroyer	1940 - 1948
I35			
Pegasus	1917	Seaplane Car	6.39 - 1940
Chelsea	1919	Destroyer	1940 - 1944
Demon	Canc	Destroyer	Canc 1945
I36			
Vindictive	1918	Cruiser	1918 - 1940
Vivacious	1917	Destroyer	1940 - 1948
Temeraire	Canc	Battleship	Canc 1944
I37			
Vortigern	1917	Destroyer	1940 - 1942
San Domingo	Canc	Destroyer	Canc 1945
I38			
Philomel	1890	Training Vsl	6.39 - 1940
Ambuscade	1926	Destroyer	4.40 - 1948
I39			
Abdiel	1940	Minelayer	6.39 - 1940
Amazon	1926	Destroyer	4.40 - 1948
I40			
Georgetown	1918	Destroyer	1940 - 1944
Decoy	Canc	Destroyer	Canc 1945
I41			
Curacoa	1917	Cruiser	1917 - 1940
Walpole	1918	Destroyer	1940 - 1945
I42			
Curlew	1917	Cruiser	1917 - 1940
Campbeltown	1919	Destroyer	1940 - 3.42
St Lucia	Canc	Destroyer	Canc 1945
I43			
Coventry	1917	Cruiser	1918 - 1940
Wessex	1918	Destroyer	1940 - 5.40
Sentinel (ren *Scorpion*)	1942	Destroyer	1942
Matapan	1945	Destroyer	1945 - 1948
I44			
Danae	1918	Cruiser	1918 - 1940
Imogen	1936	Destroyer	4.40 - 7.40
Warramunga RAN	1942	Destroyer	1941 - 1948
I45			
Dauntless	1918	Cruiser	1918 - 1940
Churchill	1919	Destroyer	1940 - 1944
Conqueror	Canc	Battleship	Canc 1945
Delight	Canc	Destroyer	Canc 1945
I46			
Dragon	1917	Cruiser	1918 - 1940

Winchelsea	1917	Destroyer	1940 - 1945	*Skeena* RCN	1930	Destroyer	4.40 - 10.44
				Trincomalee	1945	Destroyer	Incomplete
I47							
Adelaide RAN	1918	Cruiser	1922 - 1940	**I60**			
Westcott	1918	Destroyer	1940 - 1945	*Caradoc*	1916	Cruiser	1917 - 1940
Defender	1950	Destroyer	1945 - 1948	*Campbell*	1918	Destroyer	1940 - 1948
I48				**I61**			
Phaeton	1934	Cruiser	1934	*Calypso*	1917	Cruiser	1917 - 1940
Sydney RAN	1934	Cruiser	1934 - 1940	*Ilex*	1937	Destroyer	4.40 - 1945
(ex *Phaeton*)							
Vidette	1918	Destroyer	1940 - 1948	**I62**			
				Redstart	1938	Minelayer	6.39 - 1940
I49				*Wild Swan*	1919	Destroyer	1940 - 1942
Argus	1917	Ac Carrier	6.39 - 1940	*Jutland*	1946	Destroyer	1946 - 1948
Columbia RCN	1918	Destroyer	1940 - 1945				
Thunderer	Canc	Battleship	Canc 1944	**I63**			
				Apollo	1934	Cruiser	1934
I50				*Hobart* RAN	1934	Cruiser	1934 - 1940
Centurion	1911	Battleship	1939 - 1940	(ex *Apollo*)			
Wrestler	1918	Destroyer	1940 - 6.44	*Verity*	1919	Destroyer	1940 - 1948
I51				**I64**			
Albuera	Canc	Destroyer	Canc 1945	*Adamant*	1940	Depot Ship	1940
				Vansittart	1919	Destroyer	1940 - 1946
I52							
Enterprise	1919	Cruiser	1926 - 1940	**I65**			
Salisbury RCN	1919	Destroyer	1940 - 1944	*Codrington*	1929	Destroyer	1940 - 7.40
Dainty	1950	Destroyer	1945 - 1948	*St Clair* RCN	1918	Destroyer	10.40 - 1944
I53				**I66**			
Caledon	1916	Cruiser	1917 - 1940	*Emerald*	1920	Cruiser	1926 - 1940
Venetia	1917	Destroyer	1940 - 10.40	*Wivern*	1919	Destroyer	1940 - 1948
Mons	Canc	Destroyer	Canc 1945				
				I67			
I54				*Carlisle*	1918	Cruiser	1918 - 1940
Vanquisher	1917	Destroyer	1940 - 1948	*Wishart*	1919	Destroyer	1940 - 1945
I55				**I68**			
Vesper	1917	Destroyer	1940 - 1948	*Linnet*	1938	Minelayer	1938 - 1940
				Vampire RAN	1917	Destroyer	1940 - 4.42
I56				*Barrosa*	1945	Destroyer	1945 - 1948
Platypus RAN	1916	Depot Ship	6.39 - 1940				
Wolfhound	1918	Destroyer	1940 - 1948	**I69**			
Decoy	1949	Destroyer	1946 - 1948	*Vendetta*	1917	Destroyer	1940 - 1948
I57				**I70**			
Niagara RCN	1918	Destroyer	1940 - 1945	*Manxman*	1940	Minelayer	6.39 - 1940
				Mackay	1918	Destroyer	1940 - 1948
I58							
Cardiff	1917	Cruiser	1917 - 1940	**I71**			
Namur	1945	Destroyer	Incomplete	*Volunteer*	1919	Destroyer	1940 - 1948
I59				**I72**			
Ceres	1917	Cruiser	1917 - 1940	*Unicorn*	1941	Ac Carrier	See F72

Veteran	1919	Destroyer	1940 - 9.42		**I86**			
Talavera	1945	Destroyer	Incomplete		*Hawkins*	1917	Cruiser	1919 - 1940
					Thracian	1920	Destroyer	6.40 - 12.41
I73					*Trincomalee*	Canc	Destroyer	Canc 1945
Stanley	1919	Destroyer	1940 - 12.41					
Dervish	Canc	Destroyer	Canc 1945		**I87**			
					Cairo	1919	Cruiser	1919 - 1940
I74					*Isis*	1936	Destroyer	4.40 - 7.44
Delhi	1918	Cruiser	1919 - 1940		*Desperate*	Canc	Destroyer	Canc 1945
Wanderer	1919	Destroyer	1940 - 1948					
					I88			
I75					*Capetown*	1919	Cruiser	1922 - 1940
Venomous	1917	Destroyer	1940 - 1948		*Wren*	1919	Destroyer	1940 - 7.40
					Belleisle	Canc	Destroyer	Canc 1945
I76								
Latona	1940	Minelayer	6.39 - 1940		**I89**			
Witherington	1919	Destroyer	1940 - 1948		*Colombo*	1918	Cruiser	1919 - 1940
					Witch	1919	Destroyer	1940 - 1946
I77								
Ringdove	1938	Minelayer	6.39 - 1940		**I90**			
Whitshed	1919	Destroyer	1940 - 1948		*Douglas*	1918	Destroyer	1940 - 1945
Diana	Canc	Destroyer	Canc 1945		**I91**			
					Bataan RAN	1944	Destroyer	1944 - 1948
I78								
Wolverine	1919	Destroyer	1940 - 1946		**I92**			
					Diomede	1919	Cruiser	1922 - 1940
I79					*Viscount*	1917	Destroyer	1940 - 1948
Resource	1928	Depot Ship	6.39 - 1940					
Saguenay RCN	1930	Destroyer	1940 - 1945		**I93**			
					Dunedin	1918	Cruiser	1919 - 1940
I80					*St Francis* RCN	1919	Destroyer	1940 - 1945
Woolwich	1934	Depot Ship	6.39 - 1940					
Sherwood	1919	Destroyer	1940 - 1943		**I94**			
					Whitehall	1919	Destroyer	1940 - 1945
I81					*Duchess*	1951	Destroyer	1945 - 1948
Frobisher	1920	Cruiser	1920 - 1940					
St Croix RCN	1919	Destroyer	1940 - 9.43		**I95**			
Diamond	1950	Destroyer	1945 - 1948		*Hermes*	1919	Ac Carrier	6.39 - 1940
					Wells	1919	Destroyer	1940 - 1945
I82								
Calcutta	1918	Cruiser	1918 - 1940		**I96**			
Navarino	Canc	Destroyer	Canc 1945		*Worcester*	1919	Destroyer	1940 - 1945
I83					**I97**			
Broke	1920	Destroyer	1940 - 1942		*Corunna*	1945	Destroyer	1945 - 1948
River Plate	Canc	Destroyer	Canc 1945					
					I98			
I84					*Effingham*	1921	Cruiser	1925 - 1940
Australia RAN	1927	Cruiser	1928 - 1940		*Omdurman*	Canc	Destroyer	Canc 1945
Keppel	1920	Destroyer	1940 - 1945					
					I99			
I85					*Durban*	1919	Cruiser	1921 - 1940
Canberra RAN	1927	Cruiser	1928 - 1940		*Duncan*	1932	Destroyer	4.40 - 1945
Shikari	1919	Destroyer	6.40 - 1945					

Flag 'J' Superior

Pre 1940:	Survey Vessels
1940–48:	Minesweepers; Paddle Minesweepers, Survey Vessels; Depot Ships; RN Danlayers; RAN/RCN Minesweeping Trawlers; RNoN MS Whalers; Motor Attendant Craft; RCN MMSs.
1948:	None

J00			
Bangor	1940	MS	1940 - 1946
J01			
Doomba RAN	1919	MS	1940 - 1946
J02			
Hazard	1937	MS	1940 - 1949
J03			
Fitzroy	1919	MS	1940 - 1943
J04			
Flinders	1919	MS	1940 - 1946
J05			
Kellett	1919	MS	1940 - 1945
J06			
Alresford	1919	MS	1940 - 1947
J07			
Beaumaris	1940	MS	1940 - 1947
J08			
Bayfield	1941	MS	1940 - 1945

Tranferred to the RCN in 1942 and returned to the RN in 1945

J09			
Cromarty	1941	MS	1941 - 1943
Deepwater	1939	Trials Ship	1945 - 1948
J10			
Alecto	1911	Depot Ship	1940 - 1947
J11			
Bramble	1938	MS	1940 - 1946
J12			
Thames Queen	1898	MS	1940 - 1942
Catherine	1942	MS	1942 - 1947
J14			
Boston	1940	MS	1940 - 1948
J15			
Blyth	1940	MS	1940 - 1947
J16			
Glen Gower	1922	Aux MS	1940 - 1941
Glen More	1922	Aux MS	1941 - 1942

(ex *Glen Gower*)			
Cato	1942	MS	1942 - 7.44
J17			
Speedy	1938	MS	1940 - 1946
J18			
Selkirk	1918	MS	1940 - 1947
J19			
Rothesay	1941	MS	1941 - 1947
J20			
Sandown	1934	Aux AA	1940 - 1942
J21			
Canso RCN	1941	MS	1941 - 1945
J22			
Britomart	1938	MS	1940 - 8.44
J23			
Abingdon	1918	MS	1940 - 4.42
Pique	1942	MS	1943 - 1947
J24			
Hebe	1936	MS	1940 - 11.43
J25			
Coolebar RAN	1939	Aux MS	1940 - 1945
J26			
Glen Usk	1914	Aux AA	1940 - 1942
J27			
Blackpool	1940	MS	1940 - 1946
J28			
Brighton Queen	1905	Aux MS	1940 - 6.40
Chamois	1942	MS	1942 - 1944
J29			
Armentieres RCN	1917	Trawler	1940 - 1946
J30			
Queen of Thanet	1916	Aux MS	1940 - 1944
White Bear	1908	Yacht	1944 - 1947
J31			
Stornoway	1941	MS	1940 - 1946
J32			
Tedworth	1917	MS	1940 - 1946

J33					**J54**			
Stoke	1918	MS		1940 - 5.41	*Moresby* RAN	1918	MS	1938 - 1948
J34								
Tenby	1941	MS		1941 - 1947	**J55**			
					Widnes	1918	MS	1940 - 1941
J35					*Malwa* RIN	1944	MS	1944 - 1948
Nootka RCN	1938	Trawler		1940 - 1943	*Peshawar*	1944	MS	1948 - 1959
Nanoose RCN	1938	Trawler		1943 - 1949	(ex *Malwa*)			
(ex-*Nootka*)								
					J56			
J36					*Huntley*	1919	MS	1940 - 1.41
Rhyl	1940	MS		1940 - 1947				
J37					**J57**			
Pangbourne	1918	MS		1940 - 1947	*Bagshot*	1918	MS	1940 - 1945
					Medway II	1918	MS	1945 - 1947
J38					(ex *Bagshot*)			
Skipjack	1934	MS		1940 - 6.40				
Caraquet RCN	1941	MS		1941 - 1945	**J58**			
					Saltburn	1918	MS	1940 - 1947
J39					**J59**			
Elgin	1919	MS		1940 - 1949	*Peterhead*	1940	MS	1940 - 1944
J40								
Fermoy	1919	MS		1940 - 1941	**J60**			
J41					*Dundalk*	1919	MS	1940 - 10.40
Albury	1918	MS		1940 - 1947	*Jan van Gelder* RNLN	1937	MS	1943 - 1945
J42								
Halcyon	1933	MS		1940 - 1947	**J61**			
J43					*Harrow*	1918	MS	1940 - 1949
Westward Ho	1894	Aux AA		1940 - 1942	**J62**			
J44					*Saltash*	1918	MS	1940 - 1948
Lydd	1918	MS		1940 - 1947	**J63**			
J45					*Gossamer*	1937	MS	1940 - 6.42
Ross	1919	MS		1940 - 1947	**J64**			
J46					*Comox* RCN	1938	Trawler	1940 - 1945
Festubert RCN	1917	Trawler		1940 - 1946	**J65**			
J47					*Bridlington*	1940	MS	1940 - 1946
Sidmouth	1941	MS		1940 - 1947	**J66**			
J48					*Plinlimmon*	1895	Aux MS	1940 - 1942
Medway Queen	1924	Aux MS		1940 - 1944	**J67**			
J49					*Llandudno*	1941	MS	1941 - 1947
Aberdare	1918	MS		1940 - 1947	**J68**			
J50					*Sharpshooter*	1936	MS	1940 - 1947
Bridport	1940	MS		1940 - 1946				
					J69			
J51					*Sphinx*	1939	MS	1940 - 2.40
Waverley	1899	Aux MS		1940 - 4.40	*Ingonish* RCN	1941	MS	1941 - 1945
Squall	1935	MS/ Dlayer		1942 - 1945				
					J70			
J52					*Ypres* RCN	1917	Trawler	1940 - 5.40
Dunoon	1919	MS		1940 - 4.40	**J71**			
Guysborough RCN	1941	MS		1941 - 1945	*Harrier*	1934	MS	1940 - 1947
					J72			
J53					*Worthing*	1941	MS	1941 - 1947
Dunbar	1941	MS		1940 - 1947	**J73**			
					Niger	1936	Sloop	1940 - 7.42

J74			
Queen of Kent	1916	Aux MS	1940 - 1944
J75			
Duchess of Cornwall	1896	Aux MS	1940 - Lost
J76			
Rye	1940	MS	1940 - 1947
J77			
Romney	1940	MS	1940 - 1947
J78			
Sutton	1918	MS	1940 - 1947
J79			
Scott	1938	MS	1940 - 1948
J80			
Skiddaw	1896	Aux MS	1940 - 1942
Packice	1917	Whaler	1941 - 1944
J81			
Investigator RIN	1925	Sloop	1940 - 1947
J82			
Hussar	1934	MS	1940 - 8.44
J83			
Gleaner	1937	MS	1940 - 1948
J84			
Franklin	1937	MS	1940 - 1948
J85			
Seagull	1937	MS	1940 - 1948
J86			
Salamander	1936	MS	1940 - 1944
J87			
Speedwell	1935	MS	1940 - 1946
J88			
Fundy RCN	1938	Trawler	1940 - 1945
J89			
Fareham	1918	MS	1940 - 1944
J90			
Derby	1918	MS	1940 - 1945
J91			
Endeavour	1912	Survey Vsl	1940 - 1945
J92			
City of Rochester	1904	Aux AA	1940 - 5.41
J93			
Leda	1937	MS	1940 - 9.42
J94			
Gaspe RCN	1938	Trawler	1940 - 1948
J95			
Ilfracombe	1941	MS	1941 - 1947
J96			
Research	1939	Survey	1939 - 1948

Research was a composite built brigantine rigged vessel built entirely of non-magnetic material. She languished, incomplete, on the River Dart until being scrapped in 1952.

J97			
Polruan	1940	MS	1940 - 1947
J98			
Challenger	1931	Survey	.... - 1948
J99			
Jason	1937	MS	1940 - 1946
J100			
Gracie Fields	1936	Aux MS	1940 - 5.40
Lockeport RCN	1941	MS	5.40 - 1945
J101			
Essex Queen	1897	Aux MS	1940 - ....
Albacore	1942	MS	1942 - 1948
J102			
Mercury	1934	Aux MS	1940 - 12.40
J103			
Scawfell	1937	Aux MS	1940 - 1941
J104			
Glen Avon	1912	Aux MS	1940 - 1942
Nebula	1929	Aux MS	1941 - 1946
J105			
Brixham	1940	MS	1941 - 1947
J106			
Emperor of India	1906	Aux MS	1939 - 1940
Acute (ex *Alert*)	1942	MS	1942 - 1948
J107			
Duchess of Rothesay	1894	Aux MS	1940 - 1942
J108			
Jeanie Deans	1931	Aux MS	1940 - 1941
J109			
Ambassador	1911	Aux MS	1940 - 1944
J110			
Oriole	1910	Aux MS	1940 - 1944
J111			
Princess Elizabeth	1927	Aux MS	1940 - 1942
J112			
Laguna Belle	1896	Aux MS	1940 - 1942
Hinnoy RNoN	1935	Trawler	1941 - 1946
J113			
Devonia	1905	Aux MS	1940 - 5.40
Southsea	1930	Aux MS	1940 - 2.41
J114			
Marmion I	1906	Aux MS	1940 - 4.41
J115			
Duchess of Fife	1903	Aux MS	1940 - 1945

J116				**J139**			
Bude	1940	MS	1940 - 1946	*Wedgeport*	1941	MS	1941 - 1946
				J140			
J117				*Alarm*	1942	MS	1942 - 1944
Brighton Belle	1900	Aux MS	1940 - 5.40	**J141**			
Parrsboro	1941	MS	1941 - 1948	*Tambar* RAN	1939	Aux MS	1940 - 1943
				J142			
J118				*MAC 1 (MTB 1)*	1936	MAC	1940 - 1942
Snaefell	1907	Aux MS	1940 - 7.41	**J143**			
J119				*Bootle*	1941	MS	1941 - 1947
Fort York	1941	MS	1941 - 1947	**J144**			
J120				*Georgian* RCN	1941	MS	1941 - 1945
Helvellyn	1937	Aux MS	1940 - 1941	**J145**			
J121				*Lismore* RAN	1940	AS/MS	1940 - 1946
Whitehaven	1941	MS	1941 - 1947	**J146**			
J122				*Cowichan* RCN	1940	MS	1940 - 1945
William Scoresby	1925	Survey Vsl	1949 - 1953	**J147**			
J123				*Poole*	1941	MS	1941 - 1947
Seaham	1941	MS	1941 - 1946	**J148**			
J124				*Malpeque* RCN	1940	MS	1940 - 1945
Fraserburgh	1941	MS	1941 - 1947	**J149**			
J125				*Ungava* RCN	1940	MS	1940 - 1946
Goatfell	1934	Aux MS	1940 - 1942	**J150**			
J126				*MAC 2 (MTB 2)*	1936	MAC	1940 - 1942
Felixstowe	1941	MS	1941 - 1943	**J151**			
J127				*Clacton*	1941	MS	1941 - 1943
Eastbourne	1940	MS	1940 - 1947	**J152**			
				Quatsino RCN	1941	MS	1941 - 1945
J128				**J153**			
Cromer	1940	MS	1940 - 1942	*Whyalla* RAN	1941	AS/MS	1941 - 1948
Queen Empress	1912	Aux MS	1942 - 1944	**J154**			
				Nipigon RCN	1940	MS	1940 - 1945
J129							
Deccan RIN	1944	MS	1944 - 1948	**J155**			
J130				*Hartlepool*	1942	MS	1942
Orara RAN	1939	MS	1940 - 1945	*Kathiawar* RIN	1942	MS	1942 - 1948
J131				*Chittagong*	1942	MS	1948 - 1949
Ardrossan	1941	MS	1941 - 1947	(ex *Kathiawar*, ex *Hartlepool*)			
J132							
Ryde	1937	Aux MS	1940 - 1942	**J156**			
J133				*Thunder* RCN	1941	MS	1941 - 1945
Nimbus	1929	Whaler	1941 - 1946	**J157**			
J134				*Toowoomba* RAN	1941	AS/MS	1941 - 1946
Gulnare	1900	Survey	1940 - 1948	**J158**			
J135				*Bathurst* RAN	1940	AS/MS	1940 - 1948
Lorna Doone	1891	Aux MS	1940 - 1942	**J159**			
				Mahone RCN	1940	MS	1940 - 1945
J136				**J160**			
Whippingham	1930	Aux MS	1940 - 1942	*Chignecto* RCN	1940	MS	1940 - 1945
Maaloy RNoN	1935	Trawler	1940 - 1944	**J161**			
				Outarde RCN	1941	MS	1941 - 1945
J137				**J162**			
Tongkol RAN	1939	Trawler	1940 - 1945	*Wasaga* RCN	1941	MS	1941 - 1945
J138				**J163**			
Qualicum	1941	MS	1941 - 1948	*MAC 3 (MTB 3)*	1936	MAC	1940 - 1942

J164			
Middlesbrough	1942	MS	1942 - 1942
Kumaon RIN	1942	MS	1942 - 1949
Kumaon (ex Middlesborough)			
J165			
Minas RCN	1941	MS	1941 - 1945
J166			
Quinte RCN	1941	MS	1941 - 1946
J167			
Goulburn RAN	1940	AS/MS	1940 - 1948
J168			
Chedabucto	1941	MS	1941 - 1943
J169			
Miramichi RCN	1941	MS	1941 - 1945
J170			
Bellechasse RCN	1941	MS	1941 - 1945
J171			
MAC 4 (MTB 4)	1936	MAC	1940 - 1942
J172			
Wollongong RAN	1941	AS/MS	1941 - 1946
J173			
Dornoch	1942	MS	1942 - 1947
J174			
Clayoquot RCN	1940	MS	1940 - 1944
J175			
Cessnock RAN	1941	AS/MS	1941 - 1949
J176			
St Ann RCN	(....)	....	.... - ....
J177			
MAC 7 (MTB 40)	1937	MAC	1940
J178			
Geraldton RAN	1941	AS/MS	1941 - 1946
J179			
Launceston RAN	1941	AS/MS	1941 - 1946
J180			
Padstow	1942	MS	1942 - 1943
Rohilkhand RIN	1942	MS	1943 - 1948
(ex Padstow)			
J181			
Tamworth RAN	1942	AS/MS	1942 - 1946
J182			
Greenock	1942	MS	1942
Baluchistan RIN	1942	MS	1942 - 1948
(ex-Greenock)			
J183			
Cairns RAN	1941	AS/MS	1941 - 1946
J184			
Ballarat RAN	1940	AS/MS	1940 - 1948
J185			
MAC 5 (MTB 5)	1937	MAC	1940 - 12.40

J186			
Ipswich RAN	1941	AS/MS	1941 - 1946
J187			
Bendigo RAN	1940	AS/MS	1941 - 1948
J188			
Gawler RAN	1941	AS/MS	1941 - 1946
J189			
Pirie RAN	1941	AS/MS	1941 - 1946
J190			
Harwich	1942	MS	1942
Khyber RIN	1942	MS	1942 - 1948
(ex Harwich)			
J191			
Broome RAN	1941	AS/MS	1941 - 1946
J192			
Kalgoorlie	1941	AS/MS	1941 - 1946
J193			
Lyme Regis (II)	1942	MS	1942 - 1948
(ex Sunderland)			
J194			
Hythe (ex Banff)	1941	MS	1941 - 1943
J195			
Maryborough	1940	AS/MS	1940 - 1948
J196			
MAC 6 (MTB 19)	1936	MAC	1940 - 1942
J197			
Lyme Regis (I)	1941	MS	1941 - 1942
Rajputana RIN	1941	MS	1942 - 1948
(ex Lyme Regis (I))			
J198			
Burnie RAN	1940	AS/MS	1940 - 1946
J199			
Newhaven	1942	MS	1942 - 1942
Carnatic RIN	1942	MS	1942 - 1948
(ex Newhaven)			
J200			
Clydebank	1941	MS	1941 - 1942
Orissa RIN	1941	MS	1942 - 1948
(ex Clydebank)			
J201			
Geelong RAN	1941	AS/MS	1941 - 1944
J202			
Warrnambool RAN	1941	MS	1941 - 1948
J203			
Rockhampton RAN	1941	AS/MS	1941 - 1948

J204			
Katoomba RAN	1941	AS/MS	1941 - 1948
J205			
Townsville RAN	1941	AS/MS	1941 - 1948
J206			
Lithgow RAN	1940	AS/MS	1941 - 1948
J207			
Mildura RAN	1941	AS/MS	1941 - 1948
J208			
Lantan	1943	MS	1941 - 1942
J209			
Lyemun	1942	MS	Incomplete
J210			
Taitam	1943	MS	Incomplete
J211			
Waglan	1943	MS	Incomplete
J212			
Shippigan RCN	1941	MS	1941 - 1948
J213			
Algerine	1941	MS	1941 - 11.42
J214			
Circe	1942	MS	1942 - 1948
J215			
Vestal	1943	MS	1943 - 1945
J216			
Espiegle	1942	MS	1942 - 1948
J217			
Rattler	1942	MS	1942 - 1943
Loyalty (ex *Rattler*)	1942	MS	1943 - 1944
J218			
Kapunda RAN	1942	AS/MS	1942 - 1948
J219			
Rosario	1943	MS	1943 - 1948
J220			
Tadoussac	1941	MS	1941 - 1946
J221			
Onyx	1942	MS	1942 - 1948
J222			
Wallaroo RAN	1942	MS	1942 - 1943
J223			
Ready	1943	MS	1943 - 1948
J224			
Fantome	1942	MS	1943 - 1948
J225			
Rinaldo	1943	MS	1943 - 1948
J226			
Spanker	1943	MS	1943 - 1948
J227			
Mutine	1942	MS	1942 - 1948
J228			
Tilbury	1942	MS	1942

Konkan RIN	1942	MS	1942 - 1949
(ex *Tilbury*)			
J229			
Cockatrice	1942	MS	1942 - 1948
J230			
Cadmus	1942	MS	1942 - 1948
J231			
Bundaberg RAN	1941	AS/MS	1941 - 1948
J232			
Deloraine RAN	1941	AS/MS	1941 - 1948
J233			
Inverell RAN	1942	AS/MS	1942 - 1948
J234			
Latrobe RAN	1942	AS/MS	1942 - 1948
J235			
Horsham RAN	1942	AS/MS	1942 - 1948
J236			
Glenelg RAN	1942	AS/MS	1942 - 1948
J237			
Madras RIN	1942	AS/MS	1942 - 1948
J238			
Gympie RAN	1942	AS/MS	1942 - 1948
J239			
Punjab RIN	1941	AS/MS	1941 - 1948
J240			
Armidale RAN	1942	AS/MS	1942 - 12.42
J241			
Bunbury RAN	1942	AS/MS	1942 - 1948
J242			
Colac RAN	1941	AS/MS	1941 - 1948
J243			
Bengal RIN	1942	AS/MS	1942 - 1948
J244			
Castlemaine RAN	1941	AS/MS	1941 - 1948
J245			
Oudh RIN	1942	MS	1942 - 1948
J246			
Fremantle RAN	1942	AS/MS	1942 - 1948
J247			
Bihar RIN	1942	MS	1942 - 1949
J248			
Shepparton RAN	1942	AS/MS	1942 - 1948
J249			
Bombay RIN	1941	AS/MS	1941 - 1948
J250			
Burlington RCN	1940	MS	1940 - 1946
J251			
Dubbo RAN	1942	AS/MS	1942 - 1948
J252			
Echuca RAN	1942	AS/MS	1942 - 1948
J253			
Drummondville RCN	1941	MS	1941 - 1945

J254				**J281**			
Swift Current RCN	1941	MS	1942 - 1945	*Kenora* RCN	1941	MS	1941 - 1945
J255				**J282**			
Red Deer RCN	1941	MS	1942 - 1945	*Antares*	1942	MS	1942 - 1946
J256				**J283**			
Medicine Hat RCN	1941	MS	1941 - 1945	*Arcturus*	1942	MS	1942 - 1948
J257				**J284**			
Vegreville RCN	1941	MS	1941 - 1946	*Aries*	1942	MS	1942 - 1948
J258				**J285**			
Grandmere RCN	1941	MS	1941 - 1945	*Bowen* RAN	1942	AS/MS	1942 - 1948
J259				**J286**			
Gananoque RCN	1941	MS	1941 - 1945	*Clinton*	1942	MS	1942 - 1948
J260							
Goderich RCN	1941	MS	1941 - 1945	**J287**			
J261				*Gozo*	1943	MS	1943 - 1948
Kelowna RCN	1941	MS	1941 - 1945	*Berar* RIN	1942	Trawler	1942 - 1948
J262							
Courtenay RCN	1941	MS	1941 - 1945	**J288**			
J263				*Lightfoot*	1942	MS	1942 - 1948
Melville RCN	1941	MS	1941 - 1945	**J289**			
J264				*Melita*	1942	MS	1942 - 1948
Granby RCN	1941	MS	1941 - 1945	**J290**			
J265				*Octavia*	1942	MS	1942 - 1948
Noranda RCN	1941	MS	1941 - 1945	**J291**			
J266				*Pelorus*	1943	MS	1943 - 1948
Lachine RCN	1941	MS	1941 - 1945	**J293**			
J267				*Pickle*	1943	MS	1943 - 1948
Digby RCN	1942	MS	1942 - 1945	**J294**			
J268				*Pincher*	1943	MS	1943 - 1948
Truro RCN	1942	MS	1942 - 1945	**J295**			
J269				*Plucky*	1943	MS	1943 - 1948
Trois Rivieres RCN	1941	MS	1941 - 1945	**J296**			
J270				*Postillion*	1943	MS	1943 - 1948
Brockville RCN	1941	MS	1941 - 1945	**J297**			
J271				*Rattlesnake*	1943	MS	1943 - 1948
Transcona RCN	1941	MS	1941 - 1945	**J298**			
J272				*Recruit*	1943	MS	1943 - 1948
Esquimalt RCN	1941	MS	1941 - 1945	**J299**			
J273				*Rifleman*	1943	MS	1943 - 1948
Bramble (ii)	1945	MS	1945 - 1948	**J300**			
J274				*Skipjack*	1943	MS	1943 - 1948
Larne (ii)	1943	MS	1943 - 1946	**J301**			
J275				*Squirrel*	1944	MS	1944 - 1948
Hydra	1942	MS	1942 - 1948	**J302**			
J276				*Thisbe*	1943	MS	1943 - 1948
Lennox (ii)	1943	MS	1943 - 1948	**J303**			
J277				*Truelove*	1943	MS	1943 - 1948
Orestes	1942	MS	1941 - 1948	**J304**			
J278				*Waterwitch*	1943	MS	1943 - 1948
Llewellyn RCN	1941	MS	1941 - 1948	**J305**			
J279				*Brave*	1943	MS	1943 - 1948
Lloyd George RCN	1941	MS	1941 - 1948	**J306**			
J280				*Fly*	1942	MS	1942 - 1948
Port Hope RCN	1941	MS	1941 - 1945	**J307**			
				Hound	1942	MS	1942 - 1948

J308			
Fancy	1943	MS	1943 - 1948
J309			
Sarnia RCN	1942	MS	1942 - 1945
J310			
Stratford RCN	1942	MS	1942 - 1946
J311			
Fort William RCN	1941	MS	1941 - 1945
J312			
Kentville RCN	1942	MS	1942 - 1945
J313			
Mulgrave RCN	1942	MS	1942 - 1945
J314			
Blairmore RCN	1942	MS	1942 - 1945
J315			
Wagga RAN	1942	AS/MS	1942 - 1948
J316			
Cootamundra RAN	1942	AS/MS	1942 - 1948
J317			
Milltown RCN	1942	MS	1942 - 1945
J318			
Westmount RCN	1942	MS	1942 - 1945
J320			
Sind RIN	Canc	AS/MS	Canc 1945
J321			
Gondwana RIN	Canc	AS/MS	Canc 1945
J322			
Assam RIN	Canc	AS/MS	Canc 1945
J323			
Benalla RAN	1942	AS/MS	1942 - 1948
J324			
Gladstone RAN	1942	AS/MS	1942 - 1948
J325			
Providence	1943	MS	1943 - 1948
J326			
Kapuskasing	1943	MS	1943 - 1948
J327			
Regulus	1943	MS	1943 - 1.45
J328			
Middlesex RCN	1943	MS	1943 - 1946
J329			
Moon (II)	1943	MS	1943 - 1948
J330			
Oshawa RCN	1943	MS	1943 - 1948
J331			
Portage RCN	1942	MS	1942 - 1948
J332			
St Boniface RCN	1942	MS	1942 - 1948
J333			
Seabear	1943	MS	1943 - 1948
J334			
Sault Sainte Marie RCN	1942	MS	1943 - 1948
J335			
Rockcliffe RCN	1943	MS	1944 - 1945
J336			
Wallaceburg	1942	MS	1942 - 1948
J337			
Winnipeg RCN	1942	MS	1942 - 1948
J338			
Strenuous	1942	MS	1942 - 1948
J339			
Tourmaline	1942	MS	1942 - 1948
J340			
Chance	1942	MS	1942 - 1948
J341			
Combatant	1942	MS	1942 - 1946
J342			
Gazelle	1943	MS	1943 - 1946
J343			
Sepoy	1943	MS	US Navy
J344			
Border Cities RCN	1944	MS	1944 - 1948
J345			
Cynthia	1943	MS	1942 - 1946
J346			
Gorgon	1943	MS	1943 - 1946
J347			
Persian	1943	MS	1943 - 1946
J348			
Stawell RAN	1943	AS/MS	1943 - 1948
J349			
Courier	1943	MS	1943 - 1948
J350			
Coquette	1943	MS	1943 - 1948
J351			
Cowra RAN	1943	AS/MS	1943 - 1948
J352			
Grecian	1943	MS	1943 - 1948
J353			
Kiama RAN	1942	AS/MS	1943 - 1948
J354			
Serene	1943	MS	1943 - 1948
J355			
Rockcliffe RCN	1943	MS	1943 - 1948
J356			
Welfare RCN	1943	MS	1943 - 1948
J357			
Daerwood RCN	1943	MS	1943 - 1945
J358			
Rossland RCN	1943	MS	1943 - 1945
J359			
St Joseph RCN	1943	MS	1943 - 1945
J360			
Mary Rose	1943	MS	1943 - 1948
J361			
Parkes RAN	1943	AS/MS	1943 - 1948
J362			
Junee RAN	1943	AS/MS	1943 - 1948

J363				**J393**				
Strahan RAN	1943	AS/MS	1943 - 1948	*Hval V* RNoN	1929	Aux MS	1940 - 1946
J364				**J394**				
Coquitlam RCN	1944	MS	1944 - 1945	*Bortind* RNoN	1912	Trawler	1940 - 1946
J367				**J395**				
Stormcloud	1943	MS	1943 - 1948	*Kalamalka* RCN	1944	MS	1944 - 1945
J369				**J396**				
Felicity	1944	MS	1944 - 1948	*Fort Francis* RCN	1943	MS	1943 - 1948
J370				**J397**				
Flying Fish	1944	MS	1944 - 1948	*New Liskeard* RCN	1944	MS	1944 - 1948
J371				**J398**				
La Vallee RCN	1943	MS	1943 - 1945	*Friendship*	1942	MS	1942 - 1948
J372				**J399**				
Cranbrook RCN	1943	MS	1943 - 1945	*Cybele*	1944	AMD	1944 - 1946
J373				**J400**				
Revelstoke RCN	1943	MS	1943 - 1945	*Magic*	1943	MS	1943 - 1944
J374				**J401**				
Tattoo	1943	MS	1943 - 1948	*Pylades*	1943	MS	1943 - 7.44
J375				**J402**				
Steadfast	1943	MS	1943 - 1946	*Elfreda*	1943	MS	1943 - 1948
J376				**J403**				
Golden Fleece	1944	MS	1944 - 1948	*Fairy*	1943	MS	1943 - 1946
J377				**J404**				
Lioness	1944	MS	1944 - 1948	*Florizel*	1943	MS	1943 - 1948
J378				**J405**				
Prompt	1944	MS	1944 - 1945	*Foam*	1943	MS	1943 - 1946
J379				**J406**				
Lysander	1943	MS	1943 - 1948	*Frolic*	1943	MS	1943 - 1948
J380				**J407**				
Mariner	1944	MS	1944 - 1948	*Jasper*	1943	MS	1943 - 1946
J381				**J421**				
Marmion (II)	1944	MS	1944 - 1948	*Cyrus*	1944	AMD	1944 - 12.44
J382				**J422**				
Sylvia	1944	MS	1944 - 1948	*Imersay*	1944	Trawler	1944 - 1948
J383				**J423**				
Tanganyika	1944	MS	1944 - 1948	*Lingay*	1944	Trawler	1944 - 1948
J384				**J424**				
Rowena	1944	MS	1944 - 1948	*Sandray*	1944	Trawler	1944 - 1948
J385				**J425**				
Wave	1944	MS	1944 - 1948	*Scaravay*	1944	Trawler	1944 - 1948
J386				**J426**				
Welcome	1944	MS	1944 - 1948	*Shillay*	1944	Trawler	1944 - 1948
J387				**J427**				
Chameleon	1944	MS	1944 - 1948	*Sursay*	1944	Trawler	1944 - 1948
J388				**J428**				
Cheerful	1944	MS	1944 - 1948	*Jaseur*	1944	MS	1944 - 1948
J389				**J429**				
Hare	1944	MS	1944 - 1948	*Ronay*	1945	Trawler	1945 - 1948
J390				**J431**				
Jewel	1944	MS	1944 - 1948	*Trodday*	1945	Trawler	1945 - 1948
J391				**J432**				
Liberty	1944	MS	1944 - 1948	*Vaceasay*	1945	Trawler	1945 - 1948
J392				**J433**				
Hydrograaf RNLN	1910	Survey	1940 - 1944	*Laertes*	1944	MS	1944 - 1948

J434				**J460**				
Vallay	1945	Trawler	1945 - 1948	*Nox*	Canc	MS		Canc 1944
J435				**J461**				
Maenad	1944	MS	1944 - 1948	*Odin*	Canc	MS		Canc 1944
J436				**J462**				
Magicienne	1944	MS	1944 - 1948	*Orcadia*	1944	MS		1944 - 1948
J437				**J463**				
Mameluke	1944	MS	1944 - 1948	*Ossory*	1944	MS		1944 - 1948
J438				**J464**				
Mandate	1944	MS	1944 - 1948	*Fireball*	Canc	MS		Canc 1944
J439				**J465**				
Rosamund	1944	MS	1944 - 1948	*Gabriel*	Canc	MS		Canc 1944
J440				**J466**				
Styx	Canc	MS	Canc 1944	*Happy Return*	Canc	MS		Canc 1944
J441				**J467**				
Wiay	1945	Trawler	1944 - 1948	*Balmain* RAN	Canc	Frigate		Canc 1944
J442				**J468**				
Disdain	1945	MS	1945 - 1948	*Nepean* RAN	Canc	Frigate		Canc 1944
J443				**J480**				
Marvel	1944	MS	1944 - 1948	*Alder Lake* RCN	1944	MS		To USSR
J444				**J481**				
Michael	1944	MS	1944 - 1948	*Ash Lake* RCN	Canc	MS		Canc 1944
J445				**J482**				
Minstrel	1944	MS	1944 - 1948	*Beech Lake* RCN	1945	MS		To USSR
J446				**J483**				
Pluto	1944	MS	1944 - 1948	*Birch Lake* RCN	Canc	MS		Canc 1944
J447				**J484**				
Polaris	1944	MS	1945 - 1948	*Cedar Lake* RCN	1945	MS		To USSR
J448				**J485**				
Pyrrhus	1945	MS	1945 - 1948	*Cherry Lake*	Canc	MS		Canc 1944
J449				**J486**				
Romola	1944	MS	1945 - 1948	*Elm Lake* RCN	1945	MS		To USSR
J450				**J487**				
Orsay	1945	Trawler	1945 - 1948	*Fir Lake* RCN	Canc	MS		Canc 1944
J451				**J488**				
Tocogay	1945	Trawler	1945 - 1948	*Hickory Lake*	1944	MS		To USSR
J452				**J489**				
Tahay	1944	Trawler	1944 - 1948	*Larch Lake* RCN	1945	MS		To USSR
J453				**J490**				
Fierce	1945	MS	1945 - 1948	*Maple Lake* RCN	Canc	MS		Canc 1944
J454				**J491**				
Myrmidon	1944	MS	1944 - 1948	*Oak Lake* RCN	Canc	MS		Canc 1944
J455				**J492**				
Mystic	1944	MS	1944 - 1948	*Pine Lake* RCN	1944	MS		To USSR
J456				**J493**				
Nerissa	1944	MS	1944 - 1948	*Poplar Lake*	1945	MS		To USSR
J457				**J494**				
Nicator	Canc	MS	Canc 1944	*Spruce Lake*	1945	MS		To USSR
J459				**J495**				
Nonpariel	Canc	MS	Canc 1944	*Willow Lake*	1945	MS		To USSR

Flag 'K' Superior

Pre 1940:   None

1940-48:   Patrol Vessels; Corvettes; Frigates; RN AS Whalers

1948:   Miscellaneous Vessels (Aviation Training Ships, Seabed Operations Vessel)

K00

Carnation	1940	Corvette	1940 - 1943
Frisio RNLN	1940	Corvette	1943 - 1944
(ex *Carnation*)			

K01

Acanthus	1941	Corvette	1941 - 1946

K02

Shearwater	1939	Sloop	1940 - 1945

K03

Heliotrope	1940	Corvette	1940 - 1945
Dunver RCN	1942	Frigate	1944 - 19487

Heliotrope was transferred to the US Navy in 1942 and renamed USS *Surprise* (PG-63). She was returned to the RN in 1945.

K04

Saxifrage	1941	Corvette	1941 - 1948

K05

Lobelia FR	1941	Corvette	1941 - 1948

K06

Sheldrake	1937	Sloop	1940 - 1945

K07

Dianella	1940	Corvette	1940 - 1948
Lofoten	1945	Aviation Trg	1964 - 1967
Challenger	1981	Diving Ship	1981 - 1990

Some publications suggest that, on conversion to a helicopter training ship, *Lofoten* was initially assigned A07. This has not been confirmed through primary sources.

K08

Spiraea	1940	Corvette	1940 - 1945
Engadine	1966	Aviation Trg	1966 - 1989

K09

Candytuft	1940	Corvette	1940 - 1942
Bogam RAN	Canc	Frigate	Canc 1944

Candytuft was transferred to the US Navy in 1942 and renamed USS *Tenacity* (PG-71). She was returned to the RN in 1945.

K10

Snapdragon	1940	Corvette	1940 - 12.42

K11

Mimosa FR	1941	Corvette	1941 - 6.42

K12

Auricula	1940	Corvette	1940 - 5.42

K14

Primula	1940	Corvette	1940 - 1945

K15

Pansy	1940	Corvette	1940
Heartsease	1940	Corvette	1940 - 1945
(ex-*Pansy*)			
Atholl RCN	1943	Corvette	1943 - 1945

Hearsease was transferred to the US Navy in 1942 and renamed USS *Courage* (PG-70). She was returned to the RN in 1945.

K16

Geranium	1940	Corvette	1940 - 1945

K17

Amaranthus	1940	Corvette	1940 - 1946

K18

Campanula	1940	Corvette	1940 - 1945

K19

Nigella	1940	Corvette	1940 - 1948

K20

Starwort	1941	Corvette	1941 - 1945

K21

Pintail	1939	Sloop	1940 - 6.41
Dart	1942	Frigate	1942 - 1948

K22

Gloxinia	1940	Corvette	1940 - 1945

K23

Jasmine	1941	Corvette	1941 - 1948

K24

Hibiscus	1940	Corvette	1940 - 1945
Campaspe RAN	Canc	Frigate	Canc 1944

Hibiscus was transferred to the US Navy in 1942 and renamed USS *Spry* (PG-64). She was returned in 1945.

K25

Azalea	1940	Corvette	1940 - 1946

K26

Pathan RIN	1918	Sloop	1940 - 6.40

K27

Honeysuckle	1940	Corvette	1940 - 1948

K28

Calendula	1940	Corvette	1940 - 1945

Calendula was transferred to the US Navy in 1942 and renamed USS *Ready* (PG-67). She was returned to the RN in 1945.

K29

Tulip	1940	Corvette	1940 - 1948

K30

Kittiwake	1936	Sloop	1940 - 1945

K31

Camellia	1940	Corvette	1940 - 1946

K32

Coreopsis	1940	Corvette	1940 - 1943
Kriezis RHN	1940	Corvette	1943 - 1952
(ex *Coreopsis*)			

K33

Kingcup	1940	Corvette	1940 - 1946

K34

Gladiolus	1940	Corvette	1940 - 10.41
Ararat RAN	1943	AS/MS	1943 - 1948

K35

Violet	1940	Corvette	1940 - 1948

K36

Clematis	1940	Corvette	1940 - 1945

K37

Veronica	1940	Corvette	1940 - 1945

Veronica was transferred to the US Navy in 1942 and re-named USS *Temptress* (PG-62). She was returned to the RN in 1945.

K38

Mignonette	1941	Corvette	1941 - 1946

K39

Hydrangea	1940	Corvette	1940 - 1945

K40

Peony	1940	Corvette	1940 - 1943
Sachtouris RHN	1940	Corvette	1943 - 1951
(ex *Peony*)			

K41

Sunflower	1940	Corvette	1940 - ....

K42

Mallard	1936	Sloop	1940 - 1945

K43

Freesia	1940	Corvette	1940 - 1946

K44

Wallflower	1940	Corvette	1940 - 1945

K45

Convolvulus	1940	Corvette	1940 - 1945

K46

La Malouine	1940	Corvette	1940 - 1948

K47

Polyanthus	1940	Corvette	1940 - 9.43

K48

Anemone	1940	Corvette	1940 - 1945

K49

Crocus	1940	Corvette	1940 - 1945

K50

Erica	1940	Corvette	1940 - 2.43

K51

Rockrose	1941	Corvette	1941 - 1948

K52

Puffin	1936	Sloop	1940 - 1945

K53

Woodruff	1941	Corvette	1941 - 1945

K54

Marguerite	1940	Corvette	1940 - 1948

K55

Periwinkle	1940	Corvette	1942 - 1945
Naomi RAN	Canc	Frigate	Canc 1944

Periwinkle was transferred to the US Navy in 1942 and renamed USS *Restless* (PG-66). She was returned to the RN in 1945.

K56

Asphodel	1940	Corvette	1940 - 3.44

K57

Sundew	1941	Corvette	1941
Roselys FR	1941	Corvette	1941 - 1948
(ex *Sundew*)			

K58

Aconite	1941	Corvette	1941
L'Aconit FR	1941	Corvette	1941 - 1948
(ex *Aconite*)			

K59

Dahlia	1940	Corvette	1940 - 1945

K60

Lavender	1940	Corvette	1940 - 1946

K61

Pentstemon	1941	Corvette	1941 - 1946

K62

Widgeon	1938	Sloop	1940 - 1948

K63

Picotee	1940	Corvette	1940 - 8.41

K64

Hollyhock	1940	Corvette	1940 - 4.42

K65

Myosotis	1941	Corvette	1941 - 1946

K66

Begonia	1940	Corvette	1940 - 1945
Williamstown	Canc	Frigate	Canc 1944

Begonia was transferred to the US Navy in 1942 and re-named USS *Impulse* (PG-68). She was returned to the RN in 1945.

K67

Snowdrop	1941	Corvette	1941 - 1945

K68

Jonquil	1940	Corvette	1940 - 1945

K69

Heather	1940	Corvette	1940 - 1948

K70

Kingfisher	1935	Sloop	1940 - 1948

K71

Pimpernel	1940	Corvette	1940 - 1945

K72

Godetia	1940	Corvette	1940 - 9.40
Balsam	1942	Corvette	1942 - 1945

K73

Arabis	1940	Corvette	1940 - 1942
Snapdragon	1940	Corvette	1945 - 1946

Initially commissioned into the RN as *Arabis*. She was transferred to the US Navy in 1942 and renamed USS *Saucy* (PG-65). She was returned to the RN in 1945, and recommissioned as *Snapdragon*.

K74

Narcissus	1941	Corvette	1941 - 1945

K75

Celandine	1940	Corvette	1940 - 1945

K76

Orchis	1940	Corvette	1940 - 8.44

K77

Delphinium	1940	Corvette	1940 - 1945

K78

Rhododendron	1940	Corvette	1940 - 1945

K79

Petunia	1940	Corvette	1940 - 1946

K80

Bluebell	1940	Corvette	1940 - 2.45

K81

Mallow	1940	Corvette	1940 - 1944
Nada RYN	1940	Corvette	1944 - 1948
(ex *Mallow*)			

K82

Larkspur	1940	Corvette	1940 - 1945

Larkspur was transferred to the US Navy in 1942 and re-named USS *Fury* (PG-66). She was returned in 1945.

K83

Cyclamen	1940	Corvette	1940 - 1945

K84

Hyacinth	1940	Corvette	1940 - 1943
Apostolis FR	1940	Corvette	1943 - 1952
(ex *Hyacinth*)			

K85

Verbena	1940	Corvette	1940 - 1948

K86

Arbutus (i)	1940	Corvette	1940 - 2.42
Wimmera RAN	Canc	Frigate	Canc 1944

K87

Marigold	1940	Corvette	1940 - 12.42

K88

Clarkia	1940	Corvette	1940 - 1945

K89

Guillemot	1939	Corvette	1940 - 1945

K90

Gentian	1940	Corvette	1940 - 1948

K91

Primrose	1940	Corvette	1940 - 1946

K92

Exe	1942	Frigate	1942 - 1948

K93

Lotus	1942	Corvette	1942
Commandant	1942	Corvette	1942 - 1948
d'Estienne d'Orves FR (ex *Lotus*)			

K94

Columbine	1940	Corvette	1940 - 1948

K95

Dianthus	1940	Corvette	1940 - 1948

K96

Aubretia	1940	Corvette	1940 - 1948

K97

Salvia	1940	Corvette	1940 - 12.41

Avon	1943	Frigate	1943 - 1948		**K118**			
					Napanee RCN	1940	Corvette	1940 - 1946
K98					**K119**			
Zinnia	1940	Corvette	1940 - 8.41		*Orillia* RCN	1940	Corvette	1940 - 1946
Wollondilly RAN	Canc	Frigate	Canc 1944		**K120**			
					Borage	1941	Corvette	1941 - 1946
K99					**K121**			
Gardenia	1940	Corvette	1940 - 11.42		*Rimouski* RCN	1940	Corvette	1940 - 1945
					K122			
K100					*Fleur de Lys*	1940	Corvette	1940 - 10.41
Alyssum	1941	Corvette	1940 - 1941		**K123**			
Alysse FR	1941	Corvette	1941 - 2.42		*Oxlip*	1941	Corvette	1941 - 1946
(ex *Alyssum*)					**K124**			
					Cobalt RCN	1940	Corvette	1940 - 1945
K101					**K125**			
Nanaimo RCN	1940	Corvette	1940 - 1945		*Kenogami* RCN	1940	Corvette	1940 - 1948
K102					**K126**			
Rose RNoN	1941	Corvette	1941 - 10.44		*Burdock*	1940	Corvette	1940 - 1946
K103					**K127**			
Alberni RCN	1940	Corvette	1940 - 8.44		*Algoma* RCN	1940	Corvette	1940 - 1946
K104					**K128**			
Dawson RCN	1941	Corvette	1941 - 3.46		*Samphire*	1941	Corvette	1941 - 1.43
K105					**K129**			
Loosestrife	1941	Corvette	1941 - 1945		*Agassiz* RCN	1940	Corvette	1940 - 1945
K106								
Edmundston RCN	1941	Corvette	1941 - 1945		**K130**			
K107					*Phlox*	1942	Corvette	1942
Nasturtium	1940	Corvette	1940 - 1948		*Lotus* (ii) (ex *Phlox*)	1942	Corvette	1942 - 1948
K108								
Campion	1941	Corvette	1941 - 1948		**K131**			
					Chilliwack RCN	1940	Corvette	1940 - 1945
K109					**K132**			
President	1930	Trawler	1943 - 1945		*Vetch*	1941	Corvette	1941 - 1945
Houduce FR					**K133**			
					Quesnel RCN	1940	Corvette	1940 - 1945
K110					**K134**			
Shediac RCN	1941	Corvette	1941 - 1945		*Clover*	1941	Corvette	1941 - 1948
K111					**K135**			
Pennywort	1941	Corvette	1941 - 1948		*Savorgnan*	1937	Sloop	1940 - 1945
K112					*de Brassa* FR			
Matapedia RCN	1940	Corvette	1940 - 1948		**K136**			
K113					*Shawinigan* RCN	1941	Corvette	1941 - 11.44
Arvida RCN	1940	Corvette	1940 - 1945		**K137**			
K114					*Pink*	1942	Corvette	1942 - 6.44
Bellwort	1941	Corvette	1941 - 1946		**K138**			
K115					*Barrie* RCN	1940	Corvette	1940 - 1948
Levis (i) RCN	1940	Corvette	1940 - 9.41		**K139**			
K116					*Moncton* RCN	1941	Corvette	1941 - 1948
Chambly RCN	1940	Corvette	1940 - 1945		**K140**			
					Coltsfoot	1941	Corvette	1941 - 1945
K117					**K141**			
Ranunculus	1941	Corvette	1941		*Summerside* RCN	1941	Corvette	1941 - 1946
Ranoncule FR	1941	Corvette	1941 - 1948		**K142**			
(ex *Ranunculus*)					*Stonecrop*	1941	Corvette	1941 - 1948

K143			
Louisburg (i) RCN	1941	Corvette	1941 - 2.43
K144			
Meadowsweet	1942	Corvette	1942 - 1948
K145			
Arrowhead	1940	Corvette	1940 - 1945
K146			
Pictou RCN	1940	Corvette	1940 - 1948
K147			
Baddeck RCN	1940	Corvette	1940 - 1948
K148			
Amherst RCN	1940	Corvette	1940 - 1946
K149			
Brandon RCN	1941	Corvette	1941 - 1945
K150			
Eyebright RCN	1940	Corvette	1940 - 1945
K151			
Lunenburg RCN	1941	Corvette	1941 - 1946
K152			
Sherbrooke RCN	1940	Corvette	1940 - 1945
K153			
Sorrel RCN	1940	Corvette	1940 - 1945
K154			
Camrose RCN	1940	Corvette	1940 - 1948
K155			
Windflower RCN	1940	Corvette	1940 - 12.41
K156			
Chicoutimi RCN	1940	Corvette	1940 - 1945
K157			
Dauphin RCN	1940	Corvette	1940 - 1948
K158			
Saskatoon RCN	1940	Corvette	1940 - 1948
K159			
Hepatica RCN	1940	Corvette	1940 - 1945
K160			
Lethbridge RCN	1940	Corvette	1940 - 1948
K161			
Prescott RCN	1941	Corvette	1941 - 1945
K162			
Sudbury RCN	1941	Corvette	1941 - 1946
K163			
Galt RCN	1940	Corvette	1940 - 1945
K164			
Moose Jaw RCN	1941	Corvette	1941 - 1948
K165			
Battleford RCN	1941	Corvette	1941 - 1946
K166			
Snowberry RCN	1940	Corvette	1940 - 1946
K167			
Drumheller RCN	1941	Corvette	1941 - 1946
K168			
The Pas RCN	1941	Corvette	1941 - 1945
K169			
Rosthern RCN	1940	Corvette	1940 - 1946
K170			

Morden RCN	1941	Corvette	1941 - 1945
K171			
Kamsack RCN	1941	Corvette	1941 - 1945
K172			
Trillium RCN	1940	Corvette	1940 - 1945
K173			
Weyburn RCN	1941	Corvette	1941 - 2.43
K174			
Trail RCN	1940	Corvette	1940 - 1945
K175			
Wetaskiwin RCN	1940	Corvette	1940 - 1946
K176			
Kamloops RCN	1940	Corvette	1940 - 1945
K177			
Dunvegan RCN	1940	Corvette	1940 - 1946
K178			
Oakville RCN	1941	Corvette	1941 - 1946
K179			
Buctouche RCN	1940	Corvette	1940 - 1945
K180			
Collingwood	1940	Corvette	1940 - 1945
K181			
Sackville RCN	1941	Corvette	1941 -
K182			
Bittersweet RCN	1940	Corvette	1940 - 1945
K183			
Coriander (ex *Iris*)	1941	Corvette	1941 - 1942
Commandant	1941	Corvette	1942 - 1948
Detroyat (ex *Coriander*) FR			
K184			
Abelia	1940	Corvette	1940 - 1948
K185			
Alisma	1940	Corvette	1940 - 1948
K186			
Anchusa	1941	Corvette	1941 - 1948
K187			
Armeria	1941	Corvette	1941 - 1945
K188			
Aster	1941	Corvette	1941 - 1946
K189			
Bergamot	1941	Corvette	1941 - 1946
K190			
Vervain	1941	Corvette	1941 - 2.45
K191			
Mayflower RCN	1940	Corvette	1940 - 1948
K192			
Bryony	1941	Corvette	1941 - 1948
K193			
Buttercup	1941	Corvette	1941 - 1944
Buttercup RNoN	1941	Corvette	1944 - 1946

Buttercup served as part of the Free Belgian forces from

1941- 44. She was then lent to the Norwegian Navy in 1944 to replace the lost HNoMS *Tunsberg Castle*. She was acquired outright in 1946 and renamed HNoMS *Nordkyn*. In 1950 she was reclassified as a frigate and assigned the number F309.

K194

Fennel RCN	1940	Corvette	1940 - 1945

K195

Chrysanthemum	1941	Corvette	1941- 1942
Commandant	1941	Corvette	1942 - 1948
Drogou (ex *Chrysanthemum*) FR			

K196

Cowslip	1941	Corvette	1941 - 1948

K197

Eglantine RNoN	1941	Corvette	1941 - 1946

K198

Spikenard	1940	Corvette	1940 - 1941
Spikenard RCN	1940	Corvette	1941 - 2.42

K199

Fritillary	1941	Corvette	1941 - 1946

K200

Genista	1941	Corvette	1941 - 1948

K201

Gloriosa	Canc	Corvette	Canc 1941

K202

Harebell	Canc	Corvette	Canc 1941

K203

Hemlock	Canc	Corvette	Canc 1941

K204

Ivy	Canc	Corvette	Canc 1941

K205

Ling	Canc	Corvette	Canc 1941

K206

Marjoram	Canc	Corvette	Canc 1941

K207

Monkshood	1941	Corvette	1941 - 1948

K208

Montbretia RNoN	1941	Corvette	1941 - 11.42

K209

Sweetbriar	1941	Corvette	1941 - 1946

K210

Thyme	1941	Corvette	1941 - 1948

K211

Snowflake	1941	Corvette	1941 - 1948

K212

Nettle	1941	Corvette	1941
Hyderabad RIN	1941	Corvette	1941 - 1948

K213

Poppy	1941	Corvette	1941 - 1946

K214

Potentilla	1941	Corvette	1941 - 1946

Potentilla was commissioned into the RNoN in January 1942 and returned to the RN in March 1944

K215

Nith	1942	Frigate	1942 - 1948

K216

Tamarisk	1941	Corvette	1941 - 1943
Tompazis RHN (ex *Tamarisk*)	1941	Corvette	1943 - 1952

K217

Swale	1942	Frigate	1942 - 1948

K218

Brantford RCN	1941	Corvette	1941 - 1948

K219

Ness	1942	Frigate	1942 - 1948

K220

Midland RCN	1941	Corvette	1941 - 1945

K221

Chelmer	1943	Frigate	1943 - 1948

K222

Teviot	1942	Frigate	1942 - 1948

K223

Timmins RCN	1941	Corvette	1941 - 1945

K224

Rother	1941	Frigate	1941 - 1948

K225

Kitchener RCN	1941	Corvette	1941 - 1945

K226

Godetia	1941	Corvette	1941 - 1945

Godetia served as part of the Free Belgian forces from 1942- 44 before being returned to the RN.

K227

Itchen	1942	Frigate	1942 - 9.43

K228

New Westminster RCN	1941	Corvette	1941 - 1945

K229

Dundas RCN	1941	Corvette	1941 - 1945

K230

Wear	1942	Frigate	1942 - 1948

K231

Calgary RCN	1941	Corvette	1941 - 1945

K232

Tay	1942	Frigate	1942 - 1948

K233

Port Arthur	1941	Corvette	1941 - 1945

K234

Regina RCN	1941	Corvette	1941 - 8.44

K235

Jed	1942	Frigate	1942 - 1948

K236

Fort William RCN	1941	Corvette	1941

HMCS *Fort William* was renamed HMCS *La Malbaie* before commissioning (see K273)

K237

Halifax RCN	1941	Corvette	1941 - 1945

K238

Woodstock RCN	1941	Corvette	1941 - 1945

K239

Test	1942	Frigate	1942 - 1946
Neza RIN (ex Test)	1942	Frigate	1946 - 1948

K240

Vancouver RCN	1941	Corvette	1941 - 1946

K241

Kale	1942	Frigate	1942 - 1948

K242

Ville de Quebec RCN	1941	Corvette	1941 - 1945

K243

Trent	1942	Frigate	1942 - 1946
Kukri RIN (ex Trent)	1942	Frigate	1946 - 1952

K244

Charlottetown RCN	1941	Frigate	1941 - 9.42

K245

Fredericton RCN	1941	Corvette	1941 - 1945

K246

Spey	1941	Frigate	1941 - 1948

K247

Southern Gem	1937	Whaler	1940 - 1945

K248

Waveney	1942	Frigate	1942 - 1948

K249

Southern Pride	1936	Whaler	1940 - 6.44

K250

Tweed	1942	Frigate	1942 - 1.44

K251

Ribble (i)	1943	Frigate	1943
Johan Maurits van Nassau (ex Ribble) RNLN	1943	Frigate	1943

Ribble was transferred prior to completion to the Netherlands where, her number was initially J01 then F802.

K252

Helford	1943	Frigate	1943 - 1948

K253

Helmsdale	1943	Frigate	1943 - 1948

K254

Ettrick	1943	Frigate	1943 - 1944
Ettrick RCN	1943	Frigate	1944 - 1945

K255

Ballinderry	1942	Frigate	1942 - 1948

K256

Bann	1942	Frigate	1942 - 1945
Tir RIN (ex Bann)	1942	Frigate	1945

K257

Derg	1943	Frigate	1943 - 1945

In 1951 *Derg* was renamed *Wessex* when used as an RNVR drill ship and later *Cambria*, before being scrapped in 1960.

K258

Glenarm	1943	Frigate	1943
Strule (ex Glenarm)	1943	Frigate	1943 - 1944

trule transferred to the FFN in 1944 and renamed *Croix de Lorraine* which retained P/no K258 until 1945.

K259

Lagan	1942	Frigate	1942 - 9.43

K260

Moyola	1942	Frigate	1942 - 1944

Moyola transfered to the FFN in 1944 and renamed *Tonkinois* which retained P/no K260 until 1945.

K261

Mourne	1942	Frigate	1942 - 6.44

K262

Aire	1943	Frigate	1943 - 12.46

In March 1946 *Aire* became the Depot Ship at Hong Kong and, for eight months, carried the name *Tamar,* before reverting back to *Aire,* prior to her loss in December the same year.

K263

Braid	1943	Frigate	1943 - 1944

Braid transferred to FFN in 1944 and renamed *L'Aventure* which retained P/no K263 until 1945.

K264
Cam	1943	Frigate	1943 - 1945

K265
Deveron	1942	Frigate	1942 - 1945
Dhanush RIN	1942	Frigate	1945
(ex Devron)			

K266
Fal	1942	Frigate	1942 - 1948
Mayu Burma	1942	Frigate	1948

K267
Frome	1943	Frigate	1943 - 1944

Frome transferred to the FFN in 1944 and renamed *L'Escarmouche* which retained P/no K267 until 1945.

K268
Lambourne	1943	Frigate	1942

Renamed *Dovey* in 1942 prior to being laid down. See K523.

K269
Meon	1943	Frigate	1943 - 1944
Meon RCN	1943	Frigate	1944 - 1945

K270
Nene	1942	Frigate	1942 - 1944
Nene RCN	1942	Frigate	1944 - 1945

K271
Plym	1943	Frigate	1943 - 1948

K272
Tavy	1943	Frigate	1943 - 1948

K273
La Malbaie RCN	1941	Corvette	1941 - 1945
(ex Fort William - K236)			

K274
Betony	1943	Corvette	1943 - 1945
Sind RIN (ex Betony)	1943	Corvette	1945 - 1946

K275
Buddleia	1943	Corvette	1942 - 1943

On completion in 1943 *Buddleia* was transferred to Canada and renamed *HMCS Giffard* (K402).

K276
Amaryllis	Canc	Corvette	Canc 1943

K277
Comfrey	1942	Corvette	1942

Comfrey was transferred to the US Navy in 1942 and renamed USS *Action* (PG-86).

K278
Cornel	1942	Corvette	1942

Cornel was transferred to the US Navy in 1942 and renamed USS *Alacrity* (PG-87).

K279
Dittany	1942	Corvette	1942 - 1946

Dittany was transferred to the US Navy in 1943 and renamed USS *Beacon* (PG-88). She was reassigned to the RN in 1943 and returned to the USN in 1946.

K280
Smilax	1942	Corvette	1943 - 1946

Launched as the US Navy Patrol Gunboat, USS *Tact* (PG 98) she was transferred to the RN under Lend-Lease in 1943 and renamed *Smilax*.

K281
Statice	1943	Corvette	1943 - 1946

Launched as the US Navy Patrol Gunboat, USS *Vim* (PG 99) she was transferred to the RN under Lend-Lease in 1943 and renamed *Statice*.

K282
Linaria	1942	Corvette	1943 - 1946

Launched as the US Navy Patrol Gunboat, USS *Clash* (PG 91) she was transferred to the RN under the Lend-Lease Program in 1943 and renamed *Linaria*.

K283
Willowherb	1943	Corvette	1943 - 1946

Launched as the US Navy Patrol Gunboat, USS *Vitality* (PG 100) she was transferred to the RN under Lend-Lease in 1943 and renamed *Willowherb*.

K284
Flax	1942	Corvette	1942

Flax was transferred to the US Navy in 1942 and renamed USS *Brisk* (PG-89).

K285
Honesty	1942	Corvette	1943 - 1946

Launched as the US Navy Patrol Gunboat, USS *Caprice* (PG 90) she was transferred to the RN under Lend-Lease in 1943 and renamed *Honesty*.

K286

Rosebay	1943	Corvette	1943 - 1946

Launched as the US Navy Patrol Gunboat, USS *Splendor* (PG 97) she was transferred to the RN under Lend-Lease in 1943 and renamed *Rosebay*.

K287

Mandrake	1942	Corvette	1942 - 1943

Mandrake was transferred to the US Navy in 1943 and renamed USS *Haste* (PG-92).

K288

Milfoil	1942	Corvette	1942 - 1943

Milfoil was transferred to the US Navy in 1943 and renamed USS *Intensity* (PG-93).

K289

Musk	1942	Corvette	1942 - 1943

Musk was transferred to the US Navy in 1943 and renamed USS *Might* (PG-94).

K290

Nepeta	1942	Corvette	1942 - 1943

Nepeta was transferred to the US Navy in 1943 and renamed USS *Pert* (PG-95).

K291

Privet	1942	Corvette	1942

Privet was transferred to the US Navy in 1943 and renamed USS *Prudent* (PG-96).

K292

Torridge	1943	Frigate	1943 - 1944

Torridge transferred to FFN in 1944 and renamed *La Surprise* which retained P/no K292 until 1945.

K293

Tees	1943	Frigate	1943 - 1948

K294

Towy	1943	Frigate	1943 - 1948

K295

Usk	1943	Frigate	1943 - 1948

K296

Adur	1942	Frigate	1942
Nadur RCN	1942	Frigate	1942

Ordered as *Adur* and laid down as HMCS *Nadur*, on completion in 1942 was commissioned as USS *Asheville* (PG-101).

K297

Annan (i)	1942	Frigate	1942

Ordered and laid down as *Annan*, and renamed HMCS *Annan* before transfer to the USN before launch in 1942 and renamed USS *Natchez* (PG-102).

K298

Barle	1942	Frigate	1943 - 1946

Launched as the US Navy Patrol Gunboat, *PG-103* she was transferred to the RN under Lend-Lease in 1943 and renamed *Barle*.

K299

Cuckmere	1942	Frigate	1943 - 1946

Launched as the US Navy Patrol Gunboat, *PG-104* she was transferred to the RN under Lend-Lease in 1943 and renamed *Cuckmere*.

K300

Evenlode	1942	Frigate	1943 - 1946

Launched as the US Navy Patrol Gunboat, *Danville* (PG 105) she was transferred to the RN under Lend-Lease in 1943 and renamed *Evenlode*.

K301

Findhorn	1942	Frigate	1943 - 1946

Launched as the US Navy Patrol Gunboat, *PG-106* she was transferred to the RN under Lend-Lease in 1943 and renamed *Findhorn*.

K302

Inver	1942	Frigate	1943 - 1946

Launched as the US Navy Patrol Gunboat, *PG-107* she was transferred to the RN under Lend-Lease in 1943 and renamed *Inver*.

K303

Lossie	1943	Frigate	1943 - 1946

Launched as the US Navy Patrol Gunboat, *PG-108* she was transferred to the RN under Lend-Lease in 1943 and renamed HMS *Lossie*.

K304

Parret	1943	Frigate	1943 - 1946

Launched as the US Navy Patrol Gunboat, *PG-109* she was transferred to the RN under Lend-Lease in 1943 and renamed *Parret*.

K305

Shiel	1943	Frigate	1943 - 1946

Launched as the US Navy Patrol Gunboat, *PG-110* she was transferred to the RN under Lend-Lease in 1943 and renamed *Shiel*.

K306

Bugloss	1943	Corvette	1943 - 1945
Assam RIN	1943	Corvette	1945
(ex *Bugloss*)			

K307

Bulrush	1943	Corvette	1943 - 1944

Laid down as *Bulrush* but commissioned in 1944 as HMCS *Mimico* (see K485)

K308

Friendship	1942	MS	1943 only

K310

Bayntun	1942	Frigate	1942 - 1945

K311

Bazely	1942	Frigate	1942 - 1945

K312

Berry	1942	Frigate	1942 - 1946

K313

Blackwood	1942	Frigate	1942 - 1944

K314

Bentinck	1943	Frigate	1943 - 1946

K315

Byard	1943	Frigate	1943 - 1945

K316

Drury	1943	Frigate	1943 - 1945

K317

Chebogue RCN	1943	Frigate	1943 - 10.44

K318

Jonquiere RCN	1943	Frigate	1943 - 1945

K319

Montreal RCN	1943	Frigate	1943 - 1945

K320

New Glasgow RCN	1943	Frigate	1943 - 1945

K321

New Waterford RCN	1943	Frigate	1943 - 1946

K322

Outremont RCN	1943	Frigate	1943 - 1945

K323

Springhill RCN	1943	Frigate	1943 - 1945

K324

Prince Rupert RCN	1943	Frigate	1943 - 1946

K325

St Catherines RCN	1942	Frigate	1942 - 1945

K326

Port Colborne RCN	1943	Frigate	1943 - 1945

K327

Stormont RCN	1943	Frigate	1943 - 1945

K328

Swansea RCN	1942	Frigate	1942 - 1945

K329

Valleyfield RCN	1943	Frigate	1943 - 5.44

K330

Waskesiu RCN	1942	Frigate	1942 - 1946

K331

Wentworth RCN	1943	Frigate	1943 - 1945

K332

Belleville RCN	1944	Corvette	1944 - 1945

K333

Cobourg RCN	1943	Corvette	1943 - 1945

K335

Frontenac RCN	1943	Corvette	1943 - 1945

K336

Ingersoll RCN	Canc	Corvette	Canc 1943

K337

Kirkland Lake RCN	1944	Frigate	1944 - 1945

K338

Lindsay RCN	1943	Corvette	1943 - 1945

K339

North Bay RCN	1943	Corvette	1943 - 1945

K340

Owen Sound RCN	1943	Corvette	1943 - 1945

K341

Parry Sound RCN	1943	Corvette	1943 - 1945

K342

Peterborough RCN	1944	Corvette	1944 - 1945

K343

St Lambert RCN	1943	Corvette	1943 - 1945

K344

Sea Cliff RCN	1944	Frigate	1944 - 1945

K345

Smiths Falls RCN	1944	Corvette	1944 - 1945

K346

Whitby RCN	1943	Corvette	1943 - 1945

K347

Burges	1943	Frigate	1943 - 1946

K348

Burnet	1943	Corvette	1943 - 1945
Gondwana RIN	1943	Corvette	1945 - 1946
(ex *Burnet*)			

K349

Calder	1943	Frigate	1943 - 1946

K350

Cape Breton	1942	Frigate	1942 - 1946

K351

Duckworth	1943	Frigate	1943 - 1945

K352

Duff	1943	Frigate	1943 - 1945

K353

Essington	1943	Frigate	1943 - 1945

K354

Gascoyne RAN	1943	Frigate	1943 - 1946

K355

Hadleigh Castle	1943	Corvette	1943 - 1946

K356

Odzani	1943	Frigate	1943 - 1948

K357

Riviere du Loup RCN	1943	Corvette	1943 - 1945

K358

Asbestos RCN	1943	Corvette	1943 - 1945

K360

Ceanothus	1943	Corvette	1943
Forest Hill RCN	1943	Corvette	1943 - 1945

(ex *Ceanothus*)

K362

Porchester Castle	1943	Frigate	1943 - 1948

K363

Hawkesbury RAN	1943	Frigate	1943 - 1948

K364

Lachlan RAN	1944	Frigate	1944 - 1948

K365

Lochy	1943	Frigate	1943 - 1948

K366

Ste. Thérèse RCN	1943	Frigate	1943 - 1945

K367

Taff	1943	Frigate	1943 - 1948

K368

Trentonian RCN	1943	Corvette	1943 - 2.45

K369

West York RCN	1944	Corvette	1944 - 1945

K370

Windrush	1943	Frigate	1943 - 1944

Windrush transferred to the FFN in 1944 and renamed *La Decouverte* which retained P/no K370 until 1945.

K371

Wye	1943	Frigate	1943 - 1948

K372

Rushen Castle	1943	Frigate	1943 - 1948

K373

Sandgate Castle	1943	Corvette	1943
St Thomas RCN	1943	Corvette	1943

(ex *Sandgate Castle* - see K488)

K374

Shrewsbury Castle	1944	Corvette	1944
Tunsberg Castle	1944	Corvette	1944 - 12.44

(ex *Shrewsbury Castle*)

K375

Barcoo RAN	1943	Frigate	1943 - 1948

K376

Burdekin RAN	1943	Frigate	1943 - 1948

K377

Diamantina RAN	1944	Frigate	1944 - 1948

K378

Guildford Castle	1943	Corvette	1943
Hespeler RCN	1943	Corvette	1943

(ex *Guildford Castle* - see K489)

K379

Carisbrooke Castle	1943	Corvette	1943 - 1948

K382

Candytuft (ii)	1943	Corvette	1943 - 1944

Candytuft was transferred to the RCN before completion and renamed HMCS *Long Branch* (see K487).

K383

Flint Castle	1943	Corvette	1943 - 1948

K384

Leeds Castle	1943	Corvette	1943 - 1948

K385

Arabis (ii) RNZN	1943	Corvette	1943 - 1948

K386

Amberley Castle	1943	Corvette	1943 - 1948

K387

Berkeley Castle	1943	Corvette	1943 - 1948

K388

Dumbarton Castle	1943	Corvette	1943 - 1948

K389

Knaresborough Castle	1943	Corvette	1943 - 1948

K390

Loch Fada	1943	Frigate	1943 - 1948

K391

Loch Killin	1943	Frigate	1943 - 1948

K392

Nadder	1943	Frigate	1943 - 1945
Shamsher RIN	1943	Frigate	1945 - 1948

(ex *Nadder*)

K393

Tamworth Castle	1944	Corvette	1944
Kincardine RCN	1944	Corvette	1944
(ex *Tamworth Castle* - see K490)			

K394

Thorlock RCN	1944	Corvette	1944 - 1945

K395

Charlock RCN	1943	Corvette	1943 - 1946
Mahratta RIN	1943	Corvette	1946 - 1948
(ex *Charlock*)			

K396

Hedingham Castle	1944	Corvette	1944
Orangeville RCN	1944	Corvette	1944
(ex *Hedingham Castle* - see K491)			

K397

Launceston Castle	1943	Corvette	1943 - 1948

K398

Rising Castle	1944	Corvette	1944
Arnprior RCN	1944	Corvette	1944
(ex *Rising Castle* - see K494)			

K399

Tintagel Castle	1943	Corvette	1943 - 1948

K400

Levis (ii) RCN	1943	Frigate	1943 - 1946

K401

Louisburg (ii) RCN	1943	Corvette	1943 - 1945

K402

Giffard RCN	1943	Corvette	1943 - 1945
(ex *Buddleia* - K275)			

K403

Arbutus (ii) RNZN	1944	Corvette	1940 - 1948

K404

Annan (ii) RCN	1943	Frigate	1943 - 1945

K405

Alnwick Castle	1944	Corvette	1944 - 1948

K406

Barwon RAN	1944	Frigate	1944 - 1948

K407

Beacon Hill	1943	Frigate	1943 - 1946

K408

Culgoa RAN	1945	Frigate	1945 - 1948

K409

Capilano RCN	1944	Frigate	1944 - 1945

K410

Coaticook RCN	1943	Frigate	1943 - 1945

K411

Ribble (ii) RCN	1943	Frigate	1943 - 1944
(ex *Duddon*)			

K412

Bamborough Castle	1944	Corvette	1944 - 1948

K413

Farnham Castle	1944	Frigate	1944 - 1948

K414

Glace Bay RCN	1944	Frigate	1944 - 1945

K415

Hawkesbury RCN	1943	Corvette	1943 - 1945

K416

Hurst Castle	1944	Corvette	1944 - 9.44

K417

Halladale	1944	Frigate	1944 - 1948

K418

Joliette RCN	1943	Frigate	1943 - 1945

K419

Kokanee RCN	1943	Frigate	1943 - 1945

K420

Kenilworth Castle	1943	Corvette	1943 - 1948

K421

Loch Shin	1944	Frigate	1944 - 1946

K422

Loch Eck	1944	Frigate	1944 - 1948

K423

Largo Bay	1944	Frigate	1944 - 1948

K424

Loch Achanalt	1944	Frigate	1944 - 1948

K425

Loch Dunvegan	1944	Frigate	1944 - 1948

K426

Loch Achray	1943	Frigate	1943 - 1946

K427

Luce Bay	1945	Frigate	1945
(*Completed as Dalrymple* - see A302)			

K428

Loch Alvie RCN	1944	Frigate	1944 - 1948

K429

Loch Fyne	1944	Frigate	1944 - 1948

K430

Loch Cree	1944	Frigate	1944
Natal SAN	1944	Frigate	1944 - 1945
(ex-*Loch Cree*)			

K431

Loch Tarbert	1944	Frigate	1944 - 1948

K432

Loch Boisdale	1944	Frigate	1944
Good Hope SAN	1944	Frigate	1944 - 1948
(ex-*Loch Boisdale*)			

K433

Loch Insh	1944	Frigate	1944 - 1948

K434

Loch Quoich	1944	Frigate	1944 - 1948

K435			
Ernard Bay	1944	Frigate	1944 - 1948
K436			
Surprise	1945	Despatch Vsl	1945 - 1948
K437			
Loch Lomond	1944	Frigate	1944 - 1948
K438			
Loch Assynt	1944	Frigate	1944
Derby Haven	1944	Depot Ship	1944 - 1948
(ex *Loch Assynt)*			
K439			
Listowel RCN	Canc	Corvette	Canc 1943
K440			
Lachute RCN	1944	Corvette	1944 - 1948
K441			
Monnow RCN	1943	Frigate	1943 - 1945
K442			
Murchison RAN	1944	Frigate	1944 - 1948
K443			
Maiden Castle	1944	Corvette	1944

Completed as convoy rescue ship *Empire Lifeguard.*

K444			
Matane RCN	1943	Frigate	1943 - 1946
K445			
Meaford RCN	Canc	Corvette	Canc 1943
K446			
Nunnery Castle	1944	Corvette	1944
Bowmanville	1944	Corvette	1944
(ex *Nunnery Castle* - see K493)			
K447			
Northam Castle	1944	Corvette	1944
Humberstone RCN	1944	Corvette	1944
(ex *Northam Castle* - see K497)			
K448			
Orkney RCN	1943	Frigate	1943 - 1946
K449			
Pevensey Castle	1944	Corvette	1944 - 1946
K450			
Pembroke Castle	1944	Corvette	1944
Tillsonburg RCN	1944	Corvette	1944
(ex *Pembroke Castle* - see K496)			
K451			
Riverside RCN	Canc	Corvette	Canc 1943
K452			
Renfrew RCN	Canc	Corvette	Canc 1943

K453			
Sherborne Castle	1944	Corvette	1944
Petrolia RCN	1944	Corvette	1944
(ex *Sherborne Castle* - see K498)			
K454			
St Stephen RCN	1944	Frigate	1944 - 1946
K455			
Strathroy RCN	1944	Corvette	1944 - 1945
K456			
St John RCN	1943	Frigate	1943 - 1945
K457			
Stellarton RCN	1944	Corvette	1944 - 1945
K458			
Teme	1943	Frigate	1943 - 1944
Teme RCN	1943	Frigate	1944 - 3.45
K459			
Thetford Mines RCN	1943	Frigate	1943 - 1945
K460			
Walmer Castle	1944	Corvette	1944
Leaside RCN	1944	Corvette	1944
(ex *Walmer Castle* - see K492)			
K461			
Wolvesey Castle	1944	Corvette	1944
Huntsville RCN	1944	Corvette	1944
(ex *Wolvesey Castle* - see K499)			
K462			
Affleck	1943	Frigate	1943 - 1944
K463			
Aylmer	1943	Frigate	1943 - 1945
K464			
Balfour	1943	Frigate	1943 - 1945
K465			
Bentley	1943	Frigate	1943 - 1945
K466			
Bickerton	1943	Frigate	1943 - 1944
K467			
Bligh	1943	Frigate	1943 - 1945
K468			
Braithwaite	1943	Frigate	1943 - 1945
K469			
Bullen	1943	Frigate	1943 - 1944
K470			
Capel	1943	Frigate	1943 - 12.44
K471			
Cooke	1943	Frigate	1943 - 1946
K472			
Dacres	1943	Frigate	1943 - 1946
K473			
Domett	1943	Frigate	1943 - 1946

K474			
Foley	1943	Frigate	1943 - 1945
K475			
Garlies	1943	Frigate	1943 - 1945
K476			
Gould	1943	Frigate	1943 - 1944
K477			
Grindall	1943	Frigate	1943 - 1945
K478			
Gardiner	1943	Frigate	1943 - 1946
K479			
Goodall	1943	Frigate	1943 - 1945
K480			
Goodson	1943	Frigate	1943 - 1944
K481			
Gore	1943	Frigate	1943 - 1946
K482			
Keats	1943	Frigate	1943 - 1946
K483			
Kempthorne	1943	Frigate	1943 - 1945
K484			
Kingsmill	1943	Frigate	1943 - 1945
K485			
Mimico RCN	1943	Corvette	1943 - 1945
K486			
Forest Hill RCN (ex *Ceanothus*)	1943	Corvette	1944 - 1945
K487			
Long Branch RCN (ex *Candytuft*)	1943	Corvette	1944 - 1945
K488			
St Thomas RCN	1943	Corvette	1943 - 1946
K489			
Hespeler RCN	1943	Corvette	1944 - 1945
K490			
Kincardine RCN	1944	Corvette	1944 - 1946
K491			
Orangeville RCN	1944	Corvette	1944 - 1946
K492			
Leaside RCN	1944	Corvette	1944 - 1946
K493			
Bowmanville RCN	1944	Corvette	1944 - 1946
K494			
Arnprior RCN	1944	Corvette	1944 - 1946
K495			
Coppercliff RCN	1944	Corvette	1944 - 1945
K496			
Tillsonburg RCN	1944	Corvette	1944 - 1946
K497			
Humberstone RCN	1944	Corvette	1944 - 1945
K498			
Petrolia RCN	1944	Corvette	1944 - 1946
K499			
Huntsville RCN	1944	Corvette	1944 - 1946
K500			
Anguilla	1943	Frigate	1943 - 1946
K501			
Antigua	1943	Frigate	1943 - 1946
K502			
Ascension	1943	Frigate	1943 - 1946
K503			
Bahamas	1943	Frigate	1943 - 1946
K504			
Barbados	1943	Frigate	1943 - 1946
K505			
Caicos	1943	Frigate	1943 - 1948
K506			
Cayman	1943	Frigate	1943 - 1946
K507			
Dominica	1943	Frigate	1943 - 1946
K508			
Byron	1943	Frigate	1943 - 1945
K509			
Conn	1943	Frigate	1943 - 1945
K510			
Cotton	1943	Frigate	1943 - 1945
K511			
Cranstoun	1943	Frigate	1943 - 1945
K512			
Cubitt	1943	Frigate	1943 - 1946
K513			
Curzon	1943	Frigate	1943 - 1945
K514			
Lawford	1943	Frigate	1943 - 1944
K515			
Louis	1943	Frigate	1943 - 1946
K516			
Lawson	1943	Frigate	1943 - 1945
K517			
Loch Morlich	1944	Frigate	1944 - 1946
K518			
Grou RCN	1943	Frigate	1943 - 1946
K519			
La Salle RCN	1943	Frigate	1943 - 1945
K520			
Norsyd RCN	1943	Corvette	1943 - 1946
K521			
Hever Castle	1944	Corvette	1944
Coppercliff RCN (ex *Hever Castle* - see K495)	1944	Corvette	1944
K523			
Dovey	1943	Frigate	1943 - 1948
K524			
Sunflower	1940	Corvette	.... - 1948

K525			
Ribble (ii) RCN	1943	Frigate	1944 - 1945
K526			
Awe	1943	Frigate	1943 - 1948
K527			
Corfe Castle	Canc	Corvette	Canc 1943
K528			
Cornet Castle	Canc	Corvette	Canc 1943
K529			
Hedingham Castle	1944	Corvette	1944 - 1948
K530			
Oakham Castle	1944	Corvette	1944 - 1948
K531			
Stone Town RCN	1944	Frigate	1944 - 1945
K532			
Macquarie RAN	1945	Frigate	1944 - 1948
K533			
Warburton RAN	Canc	Frigate	Canc 1944
K534			
Murrumbidgee RAN	Canc	Frigate	Canc 1944
K535			
Shoalhaven RAN	1944	Frigate	1944 - 1948
K536			
Scarborough Castle	1944	Corvette	1944 - 1945

Scarborough Castle completed in 1945 as Convoy Rescue Ship *Empire Peacemaker*.

K537			
York Castle	1944	Corvette	1944
Riviere du Loup RCN	1943	Corvette	1943 - 1948

York Castle completed in 1945 as Convoy Rescue Ship *Empire Comfort*.

K538			
Toronto RCN	1943	Frigate	1943 - 1945
(ex-*Giffard*)			
K540			
Beauharnois	1944	Corvette	1944 - 1945
K550			
Dakins	1943	Frigate	1943 - 1944
K551			
Deane	1943	Frigate	1943 - 1945
K552			
Ekins	1943	Frigate	1943 - 1945
K553			
Fitzroy	1943	Frigate	1943 - 1946
K554			
Redmill	1943	Frigate	1943 - 1945
K555			
Retalick	1943	Frigate	1943 - 1945
K556			
Halstead	1943	Frigate	1943 - 1944

K557			
Riou	1943	Frigate	1943 - 1946
K558			
Rutherford	1943	Frigate	1943 - 1945
K559			
Cosby	1943	Frigate	1943 - 1946
K560			
Rowley	1943	Frigate	1943 - 1945
K561			
Rupert	1943	Frigate	1943 - 1946
K562			
Stockham	1943	Frigate	1943 - 1946
K563			
Seymour	1943	Frigate	1943 - 1946
K564			
Pasley	1943	Frigate	1943 - 1945
K565			
Loring	1943	Frigate	1943 - 1948
K566			
Hoste	1943	Frigate	1943 - 1945
K567			
Moorsom	1943	Frigate	1943 - 1945
K568			
Manners	1943	Frigate	1943 - 1945
K569			
Mounsey	1943	Frigate	1943 - 1946
K570			
Inglis	1943	Frigate	1943 - 1946
K571			
Inman	1943	Frigate	1943 - 1946
K572			
Spragge	1943	Frigate	1943 - 1946
K573			
Stayner	1943	Frigate	1943 - 1945
K574			
Thornborough	1943	Frigate	1943 - 1948
K575			
Trollope	1943	Frigate	1943 - 1944
K576			
Tyler	1943	Frigate	1943 - 1945
K577			
Torrington	1943	Frigate	1943 - 1946
K578			
Narborough	1943	Frigate	1943 - 1946
K579			
Waldegrave	1943	Frigate	1943 - 1945
K580			
Whittaker	1943	Frigate	1943 - 1944
K581			
Holmes	1943	Frigate	1943 - 1945
K582			
Hargood	1943	Frigate	1943 - 1946
K583			
Hotham	1943	Frigate	1943 - 1948

K584					**K612**			
Labuan	1943	Frigate	1943 - 1946		*Loch Ericht*	Canc	Frigate	Canc 1945
K585					**K613**			
Tobago	1943	Frigate	1943 - 1946		*Loch Erisort*	Canc	Frigate	Canc 1945
K586					**K614**			
Montserrat	1943	Frigate	1943 - 1946		*Hollesley Bay*	Canc	Frigate	Canc 1945
K587					**K615**			
Nyasaland	1943	Frigate	1943 - 1946		*Widemouth Bay*	1944	Frigate	1944 - 1948
K588					**K616**			
Papua	1943	Frigate	1943 - 1946		*Wigtown Bay*	1945	Frigate	1945 - 1948
K589					**K617**			
Pitcairn	1943	Frigate	1943 - 1946		*Loch Garve*	Canc	Frigate	Canc 1945
K590					**K618**			
St Helena	1943	Frigate	1943 - 1946		*Loch Glashan*	Canc	Frigate	Canc 1945
K591					**K619**			
Sarawak	1943	Frigate	1943 - 1946		*Loch Glendhu*	1944	Frigate	1944 - 1948
K592					**K620**			
Seychelles	1943	Frigate	1943 - 1946		*Loch Gorm*	1944	Frigate	1944 - 1948
K593					**K621**			
Perim	1943	Frigate	1943 - 1946		*Loch Griam*	Canc	Frigate	Canc 1945
K594					**K622**			
Somaliland	1943	Frigate	1943 - 1946		*Burghead Bay*	1945	Frigate	1945 - 1948
K595					**K623**			
Tortola	1943	Frigate	1943 - 1946		*Loch Harray*	Canc	Frigate	Canc 1945
K596					**K624**			
Zanzibar	1943	Frigate	1943 - 1946		*Morecambe Bay*	1944	Frigate	1944 - 1948
K600					**K625**			
St Brides Bay	1945	Frigate	1945 - 1948		*Loch Katrine*	1944	Frigate	1944 - 1948
K601					**K626**			
Loch Affric	Canc	Frigate	Canc 1945		*Loch Ken*	Canc	Frigate	Canc 1945
					K627			
K602					*Mounts Bay*	1945	Frigate	1945 - 1948
Loch Ard	1944	Frigate	1944		**K628**			
Transvaal san	1944	Frigate	1944 - 1948		*Loch Killisport*	1944	Frigate	1944 - 1948
(ex-*Loch Ard*)					**K629**			
					Loch Kirbister	Canc	Frigate	Canc 1945
K603					**K630**			
Loch Arkaig	1945	Frigate	1945 - 1948		*Cardigan Bay*	1944	Frigate	1944 - 1948
K604					**K631**			
Start Bay	1945	Frigate	1945 - 1948		*Loch Linfern*	Canc	Frigate	Canc 1945
K605					**K632**			
Tremadoc Bay	1945	Frigate	1945 - 1948		*Loch Linnhe*	Canc	Frigate	Canc 1945
K606					**K633**			
Bigbury Bay	1944	Frigate	1944 - 1948		*Whitesand Bay*	1944	Frigate	1944 - 1948
K607					**K634**			
Loch Clunie	Canc	Frigate	Canc 1945		*St Austell Bay*	1944	Frigate	1944 - 1948
K608					**K635**			
Padstow Bay	1945	Frigate	1945 - 1948		*Loch Lyon*	Canc	Frigate	Canc 1945
K609					**K636**			
Loch Craggie	1944	Frigate	1944 - 1948		*Carnarvon Bay*	1945	Frigate	1945 - 1948
					K637			
K611					*Loch Minnick*	Canc	Frigate	Canc 1945
Herne Bay	1945	Frigate	1945		**K638**			
(*Herne Bay* completed as *Dampier* - see A303)					*Pegwell Bay*	1945	Frigate	1945
					(*Pegwell Bay* completed as *Cook* - see A307)			

K639

Loch More	1944	Frigate	1944 - 1948

K640

Thurso Bay	1945	Frigate	1945
(Thurso Bay completed as Owen - see A311)			

K641

Loch Nell	Canc	Frigate	Canc 1945

K642

Loch Odairn	Canc	Frigate	Canc 1945

K643

Loch Ossain	Canc	Frigate	Canc 1945

K644

Cawsand Bay	1945	Frigate	1945 - 1948

K645

Loch Ruthven	1944	Frigate	1944 - 1948

K646

Loch Ryan	Canc	Frigate	Canc 1945

K647

Alert	1945	Despatch Vsl	1945 - 1948

K648

Loch Scavaig	1944	Frigate	1944 - 1948

K649

Loch Scridain	Canc	Frigate	Canc 1945

K650

Porlock Bay	1945	Frigate	1945 - 1948

K651

Veryan Bay	1944	Frigate	1944 - 1948

K652

Loch Tanna	Canc	Frigate	Canc 1945

K653

Loch Tilt	Canc	Frigate	Canc 1945

K654

Loch Torridon	1945	Frigate	1945
Woodbridge Haven	1945	Depot Ship	1945 - 1948
(ex Loch Torridon)			

K655

Loch Tralaig	1945	Frigate	1945 - 1948

K656

Loch Urigill	Canc	Frigate	Canc 1945

K657

Loch Vennacher	Canc	Frigate	Canc 1945

K658

Loch Veyatie	1945	Frigate	1945 - 1948

K659

Loch Watten	Canc	Frigate	Canc 1945

K661

Antigonish RCN	1944	Frigate	1944 - 1948

K662

Prestonian RCN	1944	Frigate	1944 - 1945

K663

Cap de la Madeleine RCN	1944	Frigate	1944 - 1945

K664

Carlplace RCN	1944	Frigate	1944 - 1945

K665

Eastview RCN	1943	Frigate	1943 - 1946

K666

Hallowell RCN	1944	Frigate	1944 - 1945

K667

Incharran RCN	1944	Frigate	1944 - 1945

K668

La Hulloise RCN	1943	Frigate	1943 - 1948

K669

Lanark RCN	1943	Frigate	1943 - 1945

K670

Fort Erie RCN	1944	Frigate	1944 - 1948

K671

Lauzon RCN	1944	Frigate	1944 - 1945

K672

Longueuil RCN	1943	Frigate	1943 - 1946

K673

Magog RCN	1943	Frigate	1943 - 10.44

K675

Poundmaker RCN	1944	Frigate	1944 - 1945

K676

Penetang RCN	1944	Frigate	1944 - 1945

K677

Royal Mount RCN	1944	Frigate	1944 - 1945

K678

Runnymede RCN	1943	Frigate	1943 - 1946

K680

St Pierre RCN	1943	Frigate	1943 - 1945

K681

Stettler RCN	1943	Frigate	1943 - 1945

K682

Strathadam RCN	1944	Frigate	1944 - 1945

K683

Sussexvale RCN	1944	Frigate	1944 - 1948

K684

Victoriaville RCN	1944	Frigate	1944 - 1945

K685

Buckingham RCN	1944	Frigate	1944 - 1945

K686

Fergus RCN	1944	Corvette	1944 - 1945

K687

Guelph RCN	1943	Corvette	1943 - 1945

K688

Merrittonia	1944	Corvette	1944 - 1945

K689

Allington Castle	1944	Corvette	1944 - 1948

K690

Caistor Castle	1944	Corvette	1944 - 1948

K691

Lancaster Castle	1944	Corvette	1944 - 1948

K692

Oxford Castle	1943	Corvette	1943 - 1948

K693

Morpeth Castle	1943	Corvette	1943 - 1948

K694

Barnard Castle	1944	Corvette	1944

Barnard Castle completed in 1945 as Convoy Rescue Ship *Empire Shelter.*

K695

Rayleigh Castle	1944	Corvette	1944

Rayleigh Castle completed in 1945 as Convoy Rescue Ship *Empire Rest.*

K696

Denbigh Castle	1944	Corvette	1944 - 2.45

K698

Condamine RAN	1944	Frigate	1944 - 1948

Flag 'L' Superior

Pre 1940:	Tribal Class destroyers (to Dec 1938); Escort Vessels; Patrol Vessels
1940-48:	Escort Destroyers
1948:	Amphibious Ships

L00

Valorous	1917	Destroyer	1939 - 1948

L01

Bridgewater	1928	Sloop	1939 - 1940

L02

Wolsey	1918	Destroyer	1939 - 1945

L03

Cossack	1937	Destroyer	1937 - 1938
Badsworth	1941	Destroyer	1941 - 1944
Arendal RNoN	1941	Destroyer	1944
(ex *Badsworth*)			

L04

Wryneck	1918	Destroyer	1939 - 1941

L05

Atherstone	1939	Destroyer	1939 - 1948

L06

Sheldrake	1937	Sloop	1939
Avon Vale	1940	Destroyer	1940 - 1948

L07

Afridi	1937	Destroyer	1937 - 1938
Bittern	1937	Sloop	1939 - 4.40
Airedale	1941	Destroyer	1941 - 6.42

L08

Burton	1941	Destroyer	1940 - 1941
Exmoor (ii)	1941	Destroyer	1941 - 1948
(ex *Burton*)			

L09

Cornwallis RIN	1917	Sloop	1939 - 1940
Easton	1942	Destroyer	1942 - 1948

L10

Wrestler	1918	Destroyer	1936 - 1940
Southwold	1941	Destroyer	1941 - 3.42
Fearless	1963	LPD	1963 - 2002

L11

Fernie	1940	Destroyer	1940 - 1948
Intrepid	1964	LPD	1964 - 1999

L12

Sandwich	1928	Sloop	1939 - 1940
Albrighton	1941	Destroyer	1941 - 1948
Ocean	1995	LPH	1996 - 2018

L14

Rosemary	1915	Sloop	1939 - 1940
Beaufort	1941	Destroyer	1941 - 1948
Albion	2001	LPD	2003 -

L15

Fowey	1930	Sloop	1939 - 1940
Eggesford	1942	Destroyer	1942 - 1948
Bulwark	2001	LPD	2004 -

L16

Grimsby	1933	Sloop	1939 - 1940
Stevenstone	1942	Destroyer	1942 - 1948

L17

Berkeley	1940	Destroyer	1940 - 8.42

L18

Zulu	1937	Destroyer	1937 - 1938
Flamingo	1939	Sloop	1939 - 1940
Talybont	1943	Destroyer	1943 - 1948

L19

Lupin	1916	Sloop	1939 - 1940
Haldon	1942	Destroyer	1942
La Combattante FR	1942	Destroyer	1942 - 2.45
(ex *Haldon*)			

L20

Gurkha	1937	Destroyer	1937 - 1938
Garth	1940	Destroyer	1940 - 1948

L21

Pintail	1939	Sloop	1939
Viceroy	1917	Destroyer	1940 - 1945

L22

Folkestone	1930	Sloop	1930 - 1940
Aldenham	1941	Destroyer	1941 - 12.44

L23

Whitley	1918	Destroyer	1938 - 5.40
Niki RHN	1906	Destroyer	1941 - 1945

L24

Maori	1937	Destroyer	1937 - 1938
Blencathra	1940	Destroyer	1940 - 1948

L25

Scarborough	1930	Sloop	1930 - 1940
Southdown	1940	Destroyer	1940 - 1948

L26

Matabele	1937	Destroyer	1937 - 1938
Foxglove	1915	Sloop	1939 - 7.40
Bedale	1941	Destroyer	1941 - 1942
Slazak ORP	1941	Destroyer	1942 - 1946
(ex *Bedale*)			
Bedale (ex Slazak)	1941	Destroyer	1946 - 1948

L27

Hastings	1930	Sloop	1939 - 1940
Goathland	1942	Destroyer	1942 - 7.44

L28

Penzance	1930	Sloop	1939 - 1940
Hurworth	1941	Destroyer	1941 - 10.43

L29

Vimiera	1917	Destroyer	1940 - 1.42

L30

Kittiwake	1936	Sloop	1939
Blankney	1940	Destroyer	1940 - 1948

L31

Mohawk	1937	Destroyer	1937 - 1938
Chrysanthemum	1917	Sloop	1939 - 1941
Chiddingfold	1941	Destroyer	1941 - 1948

L32

Shoreham	1930	Sloop	1939 - 1940
Belvoir	1941	Destroyer	1941 - 1948

L33

Somali	1937	Destroyer	1937 - 1938
Vivien	1918	Destroyer	1940 - 1948

L34

Falmouth	1932	Sloop	1939 - 1940
Bicester	1941	Destroyer	1941 - 1948

L35

Cattistock	1940	Destroyer	1940 - 1948

L36

Nubian	1937	Destroyer	1937- 1938
Leith	1933	Sloop	1939 - 1940
Eskdale RNoN	1942	Destroyer	1942 - 4.43

L37

Hambledon	1939	Destroyer	1939 - 1948

L38

Vanity	1916	Destroyer	1940 - 1948

L39

Shearwater	1939	Sloop	1939
Rockwood	1942	Destroyer	1942- 5.44

L40

Westminster	1918	Destroyer	1939 - 1948

L41

Vega	1917	Destroyer	1940 - 1948

L42

Mallard	1936	Sloop	1939
Brocklesby	1940	Destroyer	1940 - 1948

L43

Tartar	1937	Destroyer	1937 - 1938
Bideford	1931	Sloop	1939 - 1940
Blackmore	1941	Destroyer	1941 - 1948

L44

Parramatta RAN	1939	Sloop	1939 - 1940
Glaisdale	1942	Destroyer	1942 - 1946
Narvik RNoN	1942	Destroyer	1946 - 1948
(ex *Glaisdale*)			

L45

Whaddon	1940	Destroyer	1940 - 1948

L46

Cleveland	1940	Destroyer	1940 - 1948

L47

Fleetwood	1936	Sloop	1939 - 1940
Blean	1942	Destroyer	1942 - 12.42

L48

Holderness	1940	Destroyer	1940 - 1948

L49

Woolston	1918	Destroyer	1940 - 1948

L50

Rochester	1931	Sloop	1939 - 1940
Bleasdale	1941	Destroyer	1941 - 1948

L51

Ashanti	1937	Destroyer	1937 - 1938
Milford	1932	Sloop	1939 - 1940

Bramham	1942	Destroyer	1942 - 1943
Themistoklis RHN (ex *Bramham*)	1942	Destroyer	1943
L52			
Puffin	1936	Sloop	1939
Cowdray	1941	Destroyer	1941 - 1948
L53			
Deptford	1935	Sloop	1939 - 1940
Hatherleigh	1941	Destroyer	1941 - 1942
Kanaris RHN (ex *Hatherleigh*)	1941	Destroyer	1942
L54			
Moresby RAN	1918	Sloop	1939 - 1940
Cotswold	1940	Destroyer	1940 - 1948
L55			
Winchester	1918	Destroyer	1939 - 1946
L56			
Enchantress	1934	Sloop	1939 - 1940
Holcombe	1942	Destroyer	1942 - 12.43
L57			
Black Swan	1939	Sloop	1939 - 1940
Limbourne	1942	Destroyer	1942 - 10.43
L58			
Quantock	1940	Destroyer	1940 - 1948
L59			
Mashona	1937	Destroyer	1937 - 1938
Lowestoft	1934	Sloop	1939 - 1940
Zetland	1942	Destroyer	1942 - 1948
L60			
Mendip	1940	Destroyer	1940 - 1948
L61			
Auckland	1938	Sloop	1939 - 1940
Exmoor (i)	1940	Destroyer	1940 - 2.41
L62			
Widgeon	1938	Sloop	1939
Croome	1941	Destroyer	1941 - 1948
L63			
Dulverton	1941	Destroyer	1941 - 11.43
L64			
Wallace	1918	Destroyer	1939 - 1945
L65			
Wellington	1934	Sloop	1934 - 1940
Bolebroke	1941	Destroyer	1941 - 1942
Pindos RHN (ex *Bolebroke*)	1941	Destroyer	1942
L66			
Quorn	1940	Destroyer	1940 - 8.44
L67			
Bedouin	1937	Destroyer	1937 - 1938
Indus RIN	1934	Sloop	1939 - 1940
Border	1942	Destroyer	1942
Adrias (i) RHN (ex *Border*)	1942	Destroyer	1942 - 10.43
L68			
Eridge	1940	Destroyer	1940 - 8.42
L69			
Valentine	1917	Destroyer	1939 - 1940
Tanatside	1942	Destroyer	1942 - 1946
Adrias (ii) RHN (ex *Tanatside*)	1942	Destroyer	1946
L70			
Kingfisher	1935	Sloop	1939
Farndale	1940	Destroyer	1940 - 1948
L71			
Pathan	1918	Sloop	1939 - 1940
Calpe	1941	Destroyer	1941 - 1948
L72			
Weston	1932	Sloop	1932 - 1940
Oakley (i)	1940	Destroyer	1941 - 1942
Kujawiak ORP (ex *Oakley*)	1940	Destroyer	1942 - 6.42
L73			
Warrego RAN	1940	Sloop	1939 - 1940
Melbreak	1942	Destroyer	1942 - 1948
L74			
Swan RAN	1936	Sloop	1939 - 1940
Middleton	1941	Destroyer	1941 - 1948
L75			
Eskimo	1937	Destroyer	1937 - 1939
Egret	1938	Sloop	1939 - 1940
Haydon	1942	Destroyer	1942 - 1948
L76			
Londonderry	1935	Sloop	1939 - 1940
Brecon	1942	Destroyer	1942 - 1948

L77
Yarra RAN	1935	Sloop	1939 - 1940
Grove	1941	Destroyer	1941 - 6.42
Aspis RHN	1907	Destroyer	1941 - 1945

L78
Cottesmore	1940	Destroyer	1940 - 1948

L79
Clive RIN	1919	Sloop	1939 - 1940
Brissenden	1942	Destroyer	1942 - 1948

L80
Hindustan RIN	1930	Sloop	1939 - 1940

L81
Stork	1936	Sloop	1939 - 1940
Catterick	1941	Destroyer	1941 - 1946

L82
Sikh	1937	Destroyer	1937 - 1938
Meynell	1940	Destroyer	1940 - 1948

L83
Lawrence RIN	1919	Sloop	1939 - 1940
Derwent	1941	Destroyer	1941 - 1948

L84
Dundee	1932	Sloop	1939 - 1940
Hursley	1941	Destroyer	1941 - 1943
Kriti RHN (ex *Hursley*)	1941	Destroyer	1943 - 1948

L85
Heythrop	1940	Destroyer	1940 - 3.42

L86
Pelican	1938	Sloop	1939 - 1940
Wensleydale	1942	Destroyer	1942 - 1948

L87
Eglinton	1939	Destroyer	1939 - 1948

L88
Lamerton	1940	Destroyer	1940 - 1948

L89
Guillemot	1939	Corvette	1939
Penylan	1942	Destroyer	1942 - 12.42

L90
Ledbury	1941	Destroyer	1941 - 1948

L91
Wakeful	1917	Destroyer	1940 - 5.40
Modbury	1942	Destroyer	1942

Miaoulis RHN (ex *Modbury*)	1942	Destroyer	1942

L92
Pytchley	1940	Destroyer	1940 - 1948

L93
Verdun	1917	Destroyer	1940 - 1946

L94
Windsor	1918	Destroyer	1940 - 1948

L95
Lauderdale	1941	Destroyer	1941 - 1946

L96
Tynedale	1940	Destroyer	1940 - 12.43

L97
Aberdeen	1936	Sloop	1936 - 1940

L98
Tickham	1942	Destroyer	1941 - 1942
Oakley (ex *Tickham*)	1942	Destroyer	1942 - 1948

L99
Ibis	1940	Sloop	1940
Tetcott	1941	Destroyer	1941 - 1948

L100
Liddesdale	1940	Destroyer	1940 - 1948

L101
Anzio	1945	LST	1948 - 1949

L102
Attacker	1944	LST	1948 - 1949

L103
Avenger	1945	LST	1948 - 1949

L104
Ben Nevis	1945	LST(Q)	1948 - 1949

L105
Ben Lomond	1945	LST(Q)	1948 - 1949
Arromanches	1981	RCL	1981 - 2015

L106
Buchan Ness	1945	Maint Ship	1948 - 1949
Antwerp	1981	RCL	1981 - 1994

L107
Charger	1944	LST	1948 - 1949
Andalsnes	1981	RCL	1984 - 2012

L108
Puckeridge	1941	Destroyer	1941 - 9.43
Dieppe	1944	LST	1948 - 1949
Abbeville	1984	RCL	1984 - 1994

L109
Fighter	1945	LST	1948 - 1949
Akyab	1984	RCL	1984 - 2014

L110			
Keren	1930	LSI	1948 - 1951
Aachen	1986	RCL	1987 - ....
L111			
Lofoten	1945	LST	1948 - 1949
Arezzo	1986	RCL	1987 - 2014
L112			
Messina	1945	LST	1948 - 1949
Agheila	1987	RCL	1987 - ....
L113			
Audemer	1987	RCL	1987 - 2013
L114			
Narvik	1945	LST	1948 - 1949
L115			
Silverton	1940	Destroyer	1940 - 1941
Krakowiak ORP	1940	Destroyer	1941 - 1946
(ex *Silverton*)			
Puncher	1944	LST	1948 - 1949
L116			
Pursuer	1944	LST	1948 - 1949
L117			
Ravager	1944	LST	1948 - 1949
L118			
Battler	1945	LST	1948 - 1949
L119			
Reggio	1944	LST	1948 - 1949
L120			
Zeebrugge	1945	LST	1948 - 1949
L121			
Salerno	1945	LST	1948 - 1949
L122			
Wheatland	1941	Destroyer	1941 - 1948
Searcher	1944	LST	1948 - 1949
L123			
Slinger	1944	LST	1948 - 1949
L124			
Smiter	1944	LST	1948 - 1949
L125			
St Nazaire	1945	LST	1948 - 1949
L126			
Stalker	1944	LST	1948 - 1949
L127			
Bruiser	1945	LST	1948 - 1949
L128			
Wilton	1941	Destroyer	1941 - 1948
Striker	1945	LST	1948 - 1949

L129			
Suvla	1945	LST	1948 - 1949
L130			
Tracker	1945	LST	1948 - 1949
L131			
Thruster	1945	LST	1948 - 1949
L132			
Chaser	1945	LST	1948 - 1949
L133			
Trouncer	1945	LST	1948 - 1949
L134			
Trumpeter	1945	LST	1948 - 1949
L135			
Walcheren	1945	LST	1948 - 1949
L180			
Hunter	1945	LST	1948 - 1949

The three figure LST(3) numbers (L101 - L180) appear to have been short lived and there is no evidence that they were ever applied to ship hulls. Confidential Admiralty Fleet Order 263/49 was issued in August 1949 and published revised visual callsigns for, among others, Landing Ships. All previous landing ship and craft letter combinations were replaced by the single letter "L" and, in the case of the LST(3)s, reversion to the previous four figure identity.

L369			
Meon	1943	Frigate	1958 - 1965
L3001			
Frederick Clover	1945	LST	1949 - 1966
(ex *LST(3) 3001*)			
L3003			
Anzio	1945	LST	1949 - 1970
(ex *LST(3) 3003*)			
L3004			
Fearless	1963	LPD	1963
Sir Bedivere	1966	LSL	1970 - 2008
L3005			
Intrepid	1964	LPD	1964
Sir Galahad	1966	LSL	1966 - 6.82
Sir Galahad	1986	LSL	1987 - 2007

When under construction MoD publications listed *Fearless* and *Intrepid* with numbers L3004 and L3005 respectively.

L3006			
Tromso	1944	LST	1949 - 1956
(ex *LST(3) 3006*)			

Empire Gannet (ex *Tromso*)	1944	LST	1956 - 1968		*Sir Geraint*	1967	LSL	1970 - 2003
Largs Bay	2003	LSD(A)	2006 - 2011		**L3028**			
					Snowden Smith (ex *LST(3) 3028*)	1944	LST	1949 - 1964
L3007								
Lyme Bay	2005	LSD(A)	2005 -		**L3029**			
L3008					*Chaser*	1945	LST	1949 - 1962
Mounts Bay	2004	LSD(A)	2006 -		*Sir Lancelot*	1963	LSL	1964 - 1989
L3009					**L3031**			
Reginald Kerr (ex *LST(3) 3009*)	1944	LST	1949 - 1966		*LST(3) 3031*	1944	LST	1949 - 1959
Cardigan Bay	2005	LSD(A)	2005 -		*Sultan* (ex *3031*)	1944	LST	1959 - 1970
L3010					**L3033**			
Attacker (ex *LST(3) 3010*)	1944	LST	1949 - 1954		*LST(3) 3033*	1945	LST	1949 - 1956
Empire Cymric (ex *Attacker*)	1944	LST	1954 - 1963		*Empire Shearwater* (ex *3033*)	1945	LST	1956 - 1958
L3012					**L3036**			
L3012	1945	LST(Q)	1945-1949		*Puncher*	1944	LST	1949 - 1961
(Ren *Ben Nevis*. See *L3101*)					*Sir Percivale*	1967	LSL	1970 - 2004
L3013					**L3037**			
L3013	1945	LST(Q)	1945-1949		*Evan Gibb*	1945	LST	1949 - 1963
(Ren *Ben Lomond*. See *L3102*)					**L3038**			
					Fighter	1945	LST	1949 - 1956
L3015					*Empire Grebe* (ex *Fighter*)	1945	LST	1956 - 1968
Battler (ex *LST(3) 3015*)	1945	LST	1949 - 1956					
Empire Puffin (ex *Battler*)	1945	LST	1956 - 1960		**L3041**			
					Empire Doric	1944	LST	1949 - 1954
L3016					**L3042**			
Dieppe (ex *LST(3) 3016*)	1944	LST	1949 - 1980		*Hunter*	1945	LST	1949 - 1956
L3019					*Empire Curlew* (ex *Hunter*)	1945	LST	1956 - 1962
Vaagso (ex *LST(3) 3019*)	1944	LST	1949 - 1959		**L3043**			
L3021					*Messina*	1945	LST	1949 - 1980
Charles Mcleod (ex *LST(3) 3021*)	1944	LST	1949 - 1968		**L3044**			
L3024					*Narvik*	1945	LST	1949 - 1971
Maxwell Brander	1944	LST	1949 - 1968		**L3101**			
L3025					*Ben Nevis*	1945	LST(Q)	1949 - 1965
Bruiser	1945	LST	1949 - 1954		**L3102**			
					Ben Lomond	1945	LST(Q)	1949 - 1960
L3026					**L3504**			
Charger	1944	LST	1949 - 1955		*Pursuer*	1944	LST	1949 - 1956
Empire Nordic (ex *Charger*)	1944	LST	1955 - 1967		*Empire Tern* (ex *Pursuer*)	1944	LST	1956 - 1968
L3027					**L3505**			
Lofoten	1945	LST	1949 - 1964		*Ravager*	1944	LST	1949 - 1961

Sir Tristram	1966 LSL	1970 - 2005	

L3507
Empire Gaelic	1944 LST	1949 - 1954	
(ex *LST(3) 3507*)			

L3508
Searcher	1944 LST	1949	

L3509
Humphrey Gale	1944 LST	1949 - 1961	
(ex *LST(3) 3509*)			

L3510
Slinger	1944 LST	1949 - 1956	
Empire Kittiwake	1944 LST	1956 - 1969	
(ex *Slinger*)			

L3511
Reggio	1944 LST	1949 - 1960	

L3512
Empire Celtic	1945 LST	1949 - 1954	
(ex *LST(3) 3512*)			

L3513
Salerno	1945 LST	1949 - 1961	
Empire Gull	1945 LST	1956 - 1980	
(ex *Salerno*)			

L3515
Stalker	1944 LST	1949 - 2002	

L3516
Striker	1945 LST	1949 - 1970	

L3517
St Nazaire	1945 LST	1949 - 1956	
Empire Skua	1945 LST	1956 - 1968	
(ex *St Nazaire*)			

L3518
Suvla	1945 LST	1949 - 1960	

L3519
Empire Baltic	1945 LST	1949 - 1962	
(ex *LST(3) 3519*)			

L3520
Thruster	1945 LST	1949 - 1956	
Empire Petrel	1945 LST	1956 - 1968	
(ex *Thruster*)			

L3522
Tracker	1945 LST	1949 - 1970	
Sir Caradoc	1972 RoRo	1983 - 1988	

L3523
Trouncer	1945 LST	1949 - 1961	

L3524
Trumpeter	1945 LST	1949 - 1956	
Empire Fulmar	1945 LST	1956 - 1968	
(ex *Trumpeter*)			

L3525
Walcheren	1945 LST	1949 - 1956	
Empire Guillemot	1945 LST	1956 - 1968	
(ex *Walcheren*)			

L3532
Zeebrugge	1945 LST	1949 - 1974	
Sir Lamorak	1972 RoRo	1983 - 1986	

L3534
Empire Cedric	1945 LST	1949 - 1960	
(ex *LST(3) 3534*)			

L4001
LCT(8) 4001	1945 LCT	1949 - 1956	
Redoubt (ex-4001)	1945 LCT	1956 - 1966	
Ardennes	1976 LCL	1976 - 1998	

L4002
LCT(8) 4002	1945 LCT	1949 - 1967	
Agheila (ex 4002)	1945 LCT	1967 - 1979	

L4003
Arakan	1977 LCL	1977 - 1998	

L4025
LCT(8) 4025	1945 LCT	1949 - 1960	

L4037
LCT(8) 4037	1945 LCT	1949 - 1956	
Rampart (ex 4037)	1945 LCT	1956 - 1965	
Akyab (ex Rampart)	1945 LCT	1965 - 1971	

L4038
LCT(8) 4038	1945 LCT	1949 - 1956	
Citadel (ex 4038)	1945 LCT	1956 - 1971	

L4039
LCT(8) 4039	1945 LCT	1949 - 1956	
Parapet (ex 4039)	1945 LCT	1956 - 1966	

L4040
LCT(8) 4040	1945 LCT	1949 - 1956	
Bastion (ex 4040)	1945 LCT	1956 - 1966	

L4041
LCT(8) 4041	1945 LCT	1949 - 1965	
Abbeville (ex 4041)	1945 LCT	1965 -	

L4042

LCT(8) 4042	1945	LCT	1949 - 1958

L4043

LCT(8) 4043	1945	LCT	1949 - 1956
Counterguard (ex 4043)	1945	LCT	1956 - 1965

L4044

LCT(8) 4044	1945	LCT	1949 - 1956
Portcullis (ex 4044)	1945	LCT	1956 - 1973

L4045

LCT(8) 4045	1945	LCT	1949 - 1958

L4049

LCT(8) 4049	1945	LCT	1949 - 1960

L4050

LCT(8) 4050	1945	LCT	1949 - 1960

L4061

LCT(8) 4061	1945	LCT	1949 - 1956
Audemer (ex 4061)	1945	LCT	1956 - 1978

L4062

LCT(8) 4062	1945	LCT	1949 - 1956
Aachen (ex 4062)	1945	LCT	1956 - 1976

L4063

LCT(8) 4063	1945	LCT	1949 - 1956
Jawada (ex 4063)	1945	LCT	1956 - 1960

L4064

LCT(8) 4064	1945	LCT	1949 - 1956
Sallyport (ex 4064)	1945	LCT	1956 - 1966

L4073

LCT(8) 4073	1945	LCT	1949 - 1965
Ardennes (ex 4073)	1945	LCT	1965 - 1970

L4074

LCT(8) 4074	1945	LCT	1949 - 1956
Antwerp (ex 4074)	1945	LCT	1956 - 1970

L4085

LCT(8) 4085	1945	LCT	1949 - 1965
Agedabia (ex 4085)	1945	LCT	1965 - ....

L4086

LCT(8) 4086	1945	LCT	1949 - 1965
Arromanches (ex 4086)	1945	LCT	1965 - 1970

L4097

LCT(8) 4097	1945	LCT	1949 - 1965
Andalnes (ex 4097)	1945	LCT	1965 - ....

L4098

LCT(8) 4098	1945	LCT	1949 - 1960

L4099

LCT(8) 4099	1945	LCT	1949 - 1956
Buttress (ex 4099)	1945	LCT	1956 - 1965

L4128

LCT(8) 4128	1945	LCT	1949 - 1965
Arezzo (ex 4128)	1945	LCT	1965

L4148

LCT(8) 4148	1945	LCT	1949 - 1958

L4156

LCT(8) 4156	1945	LCT	1949 - 1958

L4164

LCT(8) 4164	1945	LCT	1949 - 1965
Arakan (ex 4164)	1945	LCT	1965 - ....

L4165

LCT(8) 4165	1945	LCT	1949 - ....

Flag 'M' Superior

Pre 1940: Armed Boarding Steamers, Armed Merchant Cruisers, Corvettes (under construction), Patrol Sloops, Minesweeping Sloops, Monitors (Answering pendant inferior was used to increase number range)

1940-48: Coastal and Controlled Minelayers; British Pacific Fleet

1948: Mine Warfare Ships

M1

Ariadne	1943	Minelayer	BPF 45/46

M2

Apollo	1943	Minelayer	BPF 45/46

M3

Manxman	1940	Minelayer	BPF 45/46

M00

Hazel	1907	ABS	11.14 - 4.15
Humber	1913	Monitor	4.15 - 1.18
Abercrombie	1915	Monitor	1.18 - ....
Carnation	1940	Corvette	1939 - 1940

M01

Rowan	1909	ABS	11.14 - 4.15
Abercrombie	1915	Monitor	9.15 - 1.18
Earl of Peterborough	1915	Monitor	1.18 - *1921*
Apollo	1943	Minelayer	1943 - 1948
Albacore	1942	MS	1948 - 1962

M02

Woodnut	1906	ABS	11.14 - 4.15
Havelock	1915	Monitor	9.15 - 1.18
Erebus	1916	Monitor	1.18

M03

Partridge	1906	ABS	11.14 - 4.15
Lord Clive	1915	Monitor	4.15 - 9.15
Raglan	1915	Monitor	9.15 - 1.18
General Craufurd	1915	Monitor	1.18 - ....
Heliotrope	1940	Corvette	1939 - 1940
Princess Victoria	1939	Minelayer	1940 - 5.40
Whitethroat RCN	1944	Minelayer	1944 - 1948

M04

Sarnia	1910	ABS	11.14 - 4.15
Earl of Peterborough	1915	Monitor	4.15 - 9.15
Roberts	1915	Monitor	9.15 - 1.18
General Wolfe	1915	Monitor	1.18 - 1921
Teviotbank	1938	Minelayer	1940 - 1944

M05

Heroic	1906	ABS	11.14 - 4.15
General Craufurd	1915	Monitor	4.15 - 9.15
Havelock	1915	Monitor	1.18 - ....
Lobelia	1941	Corvette	1939 - 1940
Colac RAN	1941	AS/MS	1948 - 1953

M06

Snaefell	1910	ABS	11.14 - 4.15
Sir Thomas Picton	1915	Monitor	4.15 - 9.15
Humber	1913	Monitor	1.18 - 1920
Sheldrake	1937	Sloop	1940
Sandmartin (ex Jay)	1926	Trawler	1940 - 1946

M07

Louvain	1897	ABS	10.14 - 4.15
Prince Rupert	1915	Monitor	4.15 - 9.15
Lord Clive	1915	Monitor	1.18 - ....
Daffodil	1940	Corvette	1939 - 1940
St David	1973	MCM	1978 - 1984

M08

Amsterdam	1894	ABS	10.14 - 4.15
Roberts	1915	Monitor	4.15 - 9.15
Lord Clive	1915	Monitor	9.15 - 1.18
Marshal Ney	1915	Monitor	1.18 - ....
Willem van der Zaan RNLN	1938	Minelayer	1940 - 1945
Venturer	1972	MCM	1978 - 1983

M09

Duchess of Devonshire	1897	ABS	11.14 - 4.15
Raglan	1915	Monitor	4.15 - 9.15
Earl of Peterborough	1915	Monitor	9.15 - 1.18
Marshal Soult	1915	Monitor	1.18 - ....
Candytuft	1940	Corvette	1939 - 1940

M10

Duke of Cornwall	1898	ABS	10.14 - 4.15
Prince Eugene	1915	Monitor	4.15 - 1.18
Mersey	1913	Monitor	1.18 - ....
Snapdragon	1940	Corvette	1939 - 1940

Agamemnon	1929	Minelayer	1940 - 1944

M11

Duke of Albany	1907	ABS	10.14 - 4.15
Sir John Moore	1915	Monitor	4.15 - 9.15
Prince Eugene	1915	Monitor	1.18 - ....
Mimosa	1941	Corvette	1939 - 1940
Bramble	1945	MS	1948 - 1961

M12

Caeserea	1910	ABS	10.14 - 4.15
Marshal Ney	1915	Monitor	4.15 - 9.15
Prince Rupert	1915	Monitor	1.18 - ....
Auricula	1940	Corvette	1939 - 1940
Nautilus RNLN	1929	Minelayer	1940 - 1941

M13

Peel Castle	1894	ABS	10.14 - 4.15
Marshal Soult	1915	Monitor	4.15 - 9.15

M14

The Ramsey	1895	ABS	10.14 - 4.15
General Wolfe	1915	Monitor	4.15 - 9.15
Raglan	1915	Monitor	1.18 - Sunk
Primula	1940	Corvette	1939 - 1940

M15

City of Belfast	1893	ABS	11.14 - 4.15
Monitor M15	1915	Monitor	4.15 - 11.17
Blackbird	1943	Minelayer	1943 - 1948
Blyth	1940	MS	1948 - 1948

M16

Royal Scot	1910	ABS	11.14 - 4.15
Monitor M16	1915	Monitor	4.15 - 1920
Geranium	1940	Corvette	1939 - 1940

M17

Fiona	1905	ABS	10.14 - 4.15
Monitor M17	1915	Monitor	4.15 - 1920
Manchester City	1937	Base Ship	1940 - 1946
Skipjack	1943	MS	1948 - 1959

M18

King Orry	1913	ABS	10.14 - 4.15
Monitor M18	1915	Monitor	4.15 - 1920
Campanula	1940	Corvette	1939 - 1940

M19

Carron	1909	ABS	11.14 - 4.15
Monitor M19	1915	Monitor	4.15 - 1920
Hampton	1919	Minelayer	1939 - 1940
M1	1939	Minelayer	1940 - 1943
Miner I (ex *M1*)	1939	Minelayer	1943 - 1948

M20

York	1907	ABS	1.15 - 4.15
Monitor M20	1915	Monitor	4.15 - 1920

M21

Richard Welford	1908	ABS	1.15 - 4.15
Monitor M21	1915	Monitor	4.15 - 10.18
Pintail	1939	Sloop	1939 - 1940
Canso	1941	MS	1948 - Sold

M22

Grangemouth	1908	ABS	1.15 - 4.15
Monitor M22	1915	Monitor	4.15
Dabchick	1942	Minelayer	1942 - 1948

M23

Monitor M23	1915	Monitor	4.15
Jasmine	1941	Corvette	1939 - 1940
Adventure	1924	Minelayer	1940 - 1944

M24

Monitor M24	1915	Monitor	4.15 - 1920

M25

Monitor M25	1915	Monitor	4.15 - 9.19
Azalea	1940	Corvette	1939 - 1940
Stonechat RCN	1944	Minelayer	1944 - 1946

M26

Acacia	1915	Sloop	2.15 - 4.15
Monitor M26	1915	Monitor	4.15 - 1920
Plover	1937	Minelayer	1940 - 1948

M27

Anenome	1915	Sloop	2.15 - 4.15
Monitor M27	1915	Monitor	4.15 - 9.19
Honeysuckle	1940	Corvette	1939 - 1940

M28

Aster	1915	Sloop	2.15 - 4.15
Monitor M28	1915	Monitor	4.15 - 1.18

M29

Bluebell	1915	Sloop	2.15 - 4.15
Monitor M29	1915	Monitor	4.15
Tulip	1940	Corvette	1939 - 1940
Bungaree RAN	1937	Minelayer	1940 - 1946
Cockatrice	1942	MS	1948 - 1963
Brecon	1978	MCM	1978 - 2005

M30

Clacton	1904	Screw MS	1914
Monitor M30	1915	Monitor	4.15 - 5.16
Kittiwake	1936	Sloop	1940
Ledbury	1979	MCM	1979 -

M31			
Daffodil	1915	Sloop	2.15 - 4.15
Monitor M31	1915	Monitor	4.15
Redshank (ex *Turbot)*	1942	Ctl Minelayer	1942 - 1948
Cattistock	1981	MCM	1981 -

M32			
Newmarket	1907	Screw MS	1914 - 4.15
Monitor M32	1915	Monitor	4.15 - 1920
Coreopsis	1940	Corvette	1939 - 1940
Cottesmore	1982	MCM	1982 - 2005

M33			
Folkestone	1903	Screw MS	1914 - 9.15
Monitor M33	1915	Monitor	4.15
Brocklesby	1982	MCM	1982 -

M34			
Reindeer	1897	Screw MS	1914 - 9.15
Gladiolus	1940	Corvette	1939 - 1940
M2	1939	Minelayer	1940 - 1942
Miner II (ex *M2*)	1939	Minelayer	1943 - 1948
Ararat RAN	1943	AS/MS	1948 - 1961
Middleton	1983	MCM	1983 -

M35			
Roedean	1897	Screw MS	1914 - 1.15
Whitby Abbey	1908	Screw MS	2.15 - 9.15
Dulverton	1982	MCM	1982 - 2005

M36			
Hythe	1905	Screw MS	1914 - 9.15
Clematis	1940	Corvette	1939 - 1940
Van Meerlandt RNLN	1920	Minelayer	4.41 - 6.41
Rhyl	1940	MS	1948 - 1948
Bicester	1983	MCM	1983 - 2000

M37			
Dahlia	1915	Sloop	2.15 - 4.15
Veronica	1940	Corvette	1939 - 1940
Chiddingfold	1983	MCM	1983 -

M38			
Daphne	1915	Sloop	2.15 - 4.15
Mignonette	1941	Corvette	1939 - 1940
Abdiel	1940	Minelayer	1940 - 9.43
Atherstone	1986	MCM	1984 - 2017

M39			
Lynn	1889	Screw MS	1914 - 9.15
Hydrangea	1940	Corvette	1939 - 1940
Shearwater	1939	Sloop	1940
Abdiel	1940	Minelayer	1940 - 1948
Hurworth	1984	MCM	1984 -

M40			
Gazelle	1889	Screw MS	1914 - 9.15
Sunflower	1940	Corvette	1939 - 1940
Berkeley	1986	MCM	1986 - 2001

M41			
Foxglove	1915	Sloop	2.15 - 4.15
Loch Nevis	1934	Minelayer	1940 - 1944
Quorn	1988	MCM	1988 - 2017

M42			
Hollyhock	1915	Sloop	2.15 - 4.15
Mallard	1936	Sloop	1940

M43			
Honeysuckle	1915	Sloop	2.15 - 4.15

M44			
Iris	1915	Sloop	2.15 - 4.15
Wallflower	1940	Corvette	1939 - 1940
Atreus	1911	Base Ship	1940 - 1946

M45			
Marigold	1915	Sloop	2.15 - 4.15
Convolvulus	1940	Corvette	1939 - 1940

M46			
Jonquil	1915	Sloop	2.15 - 4.15
Pluto	1944	MS	1948 - 1972

M47			
Laburnum	1915	Sloop	2.15 - 4.15
Polyanthus	1940	Corvette	1939 - 1940
Southern Prince	1929	Minelayer	1940 - 1946

M48			
Larkspur	1915	Sloop	2.15 - 4.15
Anenome	1940	Corvette	1939 - 1940

M49			
Lavender	1915	Sloop	2.15 - 4.15
Crocus	1940	Corvette	1939 - 1940
Helvig	1937	Base Ship	1940 - 1946
Courier	1943	MS	1948 - 1949

M50			
Alsation	1913	AMC	8.14 - 3.16

M51			
Mantua	1908	AMC	8.14 - 9.15
Alsey	1932	Minelayer	1940 - 1946

M52			
Teutonic	1889	AMC	9.14 - 4.15
Puffin	1936	Sloop	1940

M53

Caronia	1905	AMC	8.14 - 9.15
M3	1939	Minelayer	1940 - 1943
Miner III (ex *M3*)	1939	Minelayer	1943 - 1948
Fierce	1945	MS	1948 - 1959

M54

Calgarian	1914	AMC	9.14 - 9.15
Marguerite	1940	Corvette	1939 - 1940

M55

Carmania	1905	AMC	8.14 - 9.15
Corncrake	1942	Trawler	1942 - 1.43
Peshawar RIN	1944	MS	1948 - 1949

M56

Victorian	1904	AMC	8.14 - 4.15
Asphodel	1940	Corvette	1939 - 1940

M57

Empress of Britain	1906	AMC	8.14 - 5.15

M58

Marmora	1903	AMC	8.14 - 9.15

M59

Macedonia	1904	AMC	8.14 - 9.15
Dahlia	1940	Corvette	1939 - 1940
Port Quebec	1939	Minelayer	1940-1943

M60

Otranto	1909	AMC	8.14 - 4.15
Lavender	1940	Corvette	1939 - 1940

M61

Orama	1911	AMC	9.14 - 9.15
Pentstemon	1941	Corvette	1939 - 1940

M62

Edinburgh Castle	1910	AMC	9.14 - 9.15
Widgeon	1938	Sloop	1940
Redstart	1938	Minelayer	1940 - 1941

M63

Armadale Castle	1903	AMC	8.14 - 9.15

M64

Kinfauns Castle	1899	AMC	8.14 - 9.15
Hollyhock	1940	Corvette	1939 - 1940

M65

Empress of Asia	1913	AMC	8.14 - 9.15
Lilac	1915	Sloop	2.15 - 4.15
Myosotis	1941	Corvette	1939 - 1940
Ariadne	1943	Minelayer	1943 - 1948

M66

Empress of Japan	1891	AMC	8.14 - 9.15
Lily	1915	Sloop	2.15 - 4.15
Begonia	1940	Corvette	1939 - 1940

M67

Magnolia	1915	Sloop	2.15 - 4.15
Snowdrop	1941	Corvette	1939 - 1940

M68

Empress of Russia	1913	AMC	8.14 - 9.15
Mallow	1915	Sloop	2.15 - 4.15
Jonquil	1940	Corvette	1939 - 1940
M4	1940	Minelayer	1940 - 1943
Miner IV (ex *M4*)	1940	Minelayer	1943 - 1948

M69

Celtic	1901	AMC	10.14 - 9.15
Linnet	1938	Minelayer	1940 - 1948
Ingonish	1941	MS	1948

M70

Laconia	1912	AMC	10.14 - 9.15
Kingfisher	1935	Sloop	1940
Manxman	1940	Minelayer	1940 - 1948

M71

Laurentic	1908	AMC	1914 - 9.15

M72

Virginian	1905	AMC	11.14 - 4.15
Godetia (i)	1940	Corvette	1940 - 9.40
Alca	1927	Base Ship	1940 - 1946

M73

Otway	1909	AMC	11.14 - 4.15

M74

Cedric	1903	AMC	11.14 - 9.15
Narcissus	1941	Corvette	1939 - 1940
M5	1940	Minelayer	1940 - 1943
Miner V (ex *M5*)	1940	Minelayer	1943 - 1948

M75

Eskimo	1910	AMC	11.14 - 7.15
Avenger	1908	AMC	12.15 - 9.15
Celandine	1940	Corvette	1939 - 1940

M76

Patia	1913	AMC	11.14 - 4.15
Latona	1940	Minelayer	1940 - 10.41

M77

Patuca	1913	AMC	11.14 - 9.15
Delphinium	1940	Corvette	1939 - 1940

Ringdove	1938	Minelayer	1940 - 1948
M78			
Bayano	1913	AMC	11.14 - 3.15
Ebro	1915	AMC	3.15 - 9.15
M79			
Caribbean	1890	Accom Ship	8.14 - 9.15
Petunia	1940	Corvette	1939 - 1940
M80			
Orotava	1889	AMC	11.14 - 9.15
Bluebell	1940	Corvette	1939 - 1940
Jan Van Brakel RNLN	1936	Minelayer	1940 - 1945
M81			
Clan Macnaughton	1911	AMC	11.14 - 2.15
Tocogay	1945	Trawler	1948 - 1958
M82			
Viknor	1888	AMC	11.14 - 1.15
Andes	1913	AMC	3.15 - 9.15
Corncrake (ex *Mackerel*)	1942	Trawler	1940 - 1942
Larkspur	1940	Corvette	1939 - 1940
Kamloops RCN	1940	Corvette	1948 - Sold
M83			
Digby	1913	AMC	11.14 - 9.15
Cyclamen	1940	Corvette	1939 - 1940
Shepperton	1935	Minelayer	1940 - 1948
M84			
Motagua	1912	AMC	11.14 - 9.15
Welshman	1940	Minelayer	1940 - 2.43
M85			
Changuinola	1912	AMC	11.14 - 9.15
Verbena	1940	Corvette	1939 - 1940
M86			
Calyx	1904	AMC	11.14 - 7.16
Arbutus (i)	1940	Corvette	1939 - 1940
M87			
Ambrose	1903	AMC	11.14 - 9.15
Marigold	1940	Corvette	1939 - 1940
M88			
Oropesa	1895	AMC	11.14 - 4.15
M7	1944	Minelayer	1944
Miner VII (ex *M7*)	1944	Minelayer	1944 - 1948
Cheerful	1944	MS	1948 - 1963
M89			
Columbella	1902	AMC	11.14 - 9.15
Guillemot	1939	Sloop	1940
M90			
Hilary	1908	AMC	11.14 - 9.15
M91			
Hildebrand	1911	AMC	11.14 - 9.15
Primrose	1940	Corvette	1939 - 1940
M92			
Ophir	1891	AMC	2.15 - 9.15
M93			
Arlanza	1912	AMC	3.15 - 9.15
Menestheus	1929	Minelayer	1940 - 1944
M94			
Alcantara	1914	AMC	1914 - 3.15
Columbine	1940	Corvette	1939 - 1940
M6	1942	Minelayer	1940 - 1943
MinerVI (ex *M6*)	1942	Minelayer	1943 - 1948
M95			
Mimosa	1915	Sloop	2.15 - 4.15
Dianthus	1940	Corvette	1939 - 1940
M96			
Primrose	1915	Sloop	2.15 - 4.15
Aubretia	1940	Corvette	1939 - 1940
M97			
Sunflower	1915	Sloop	2.15 - 4.15
Salvia	1940	Corvette	1939 - 1940
Polruan	1940	MS	1948 - 1950
M98			
Veronica	1915	Sloop	2.15 - 4.15
Zinnia	1940	Corvette	1939 - 1940
M8	1943	Minelayer	1940 - 1943
Miner VIII (ex *M8*)	1943	Minelayer	1943 - 1948
M99			
Gardenia	1940	Corvette	1939 - 1940
Deccan RIN	1944	MS	1948 - 1949
M100			
Lockeport	1941	MS	1948 - 1.48
M101			
Sandown	1988	MCM	1988 - 2004
M102			
Inverness	1990	MCM	1990 - 2006

M103				**M184**				
Cromer	1990	MCM	1990 - 2001	Ballarat RAN	1940	MS		1948 - Sold
				M186				
M104				Cootamundra RAN	1942	Training Ship		1948 - 1961
Walney	1991	MCM	1991 - 2010	**M187**				
				Bendigo RAN	1941	MS		1948 - Sold
M105				**M190**				
Brixham	1940	MS	1948	Khyber RIN	1942	MS		1948 - 1949
Bridport	1992	MCM	1992 - 2004	**M195**				
				Maryborough RAN	1940	AS/MS		1948 - 1953
M106				**M197**				
Edmundston	1941	Corvette	1940 - 1945	Rajputana RIN	1941	MS		1948 - 1961
Acute	1942	MS	1948 - 1964	**M199**				
Penzance	1997	MCM	1997 -	Carnactic RIN	1942	MS		1948 - 1949
				M200				
M107				Orissa RIN	1941	MS		1948 - 1949
Pembroke	1997	MCM	1997 -	**M203**				
				Rockhampton RAN	1941	AS/MS		1948 - 1949
M108				**M204**				
Bayfield	1941	MS	1948 - 1948	Katoomba RAN	1941	AS/MS		1948 - 1957
Grimsby	1998	MCM	1998 -	**M205**				
				Townsville RAN	1941	AS/MS		1948 - 1949
M109				**M206**				
Bangor	1999	MCM	1999 -	Lithgow RAN	1940	AS/MS		1948 - 1949
M110				**M207**				
Ramsey	1999	MCM	1999 -	Mildura RAN	1941	AS/MS		1948 - 1949
M111				**M214**				
Blyth	2000	MCM	2000 -	Circe	1942	MS		1948 - 1955
M112				**M216**				
Shoreham	2001	MCM	2001 -	Espiegle	1942	MS		1948 - 1966
M131				**M218**				
Ghazi RPN	1942	MS	1948 -	Kapunda RAN	1942	AS/MS		1948 - 1962
M133				**M219**				
Barq RPN	1942	MS	1948 - 1956	Rosario	1943	MS		1948 - 1953
M150				**M221**				
Moresby RAN	1918	MS	1948 - Sold	Onyx	1942	MS		1948 - 1966
M155				**M223**				
Chittagong RPN	1942	MS	1948 - 1956	Ready	1943	MS		1948 - 1951
M158				**M224**				
Bathurst RAN	1940	MS	1948 - Sold	Fraserburgh	1941	MS		1948 - Sold
M163				**M225**				
Skye	1942	Trawler	1948 - 1958	Rinaldo	1943	MS		1948 - 1961
M164				**M226**				
Kumaon RIN	1942	MS	1948 - 1949	Spanker	1943	MS		1948 - 1953
M175				**M227**				
Cessnock RAN	1941	MS	1948 - Sold	Mutine	1942	MS		1948 - 1967
M180				**M228**				
Granby RCN	1941	MS	1948 - Sold	Konkan RIN	1942	MS		1948 - 1951
Rohilkhand RIN	1942	MS	1948 - 1951	(ex Tilbury)				
				M230				
M182				Cadmus	1942	MS		1948 - 1950
Baluchistan RPN	1942	MS	1948 -	**M231**				
M183				Bundaberg RAN	1941	AS/MS		1948 - 1962
Wagga RAN	1942	AS/MS	1948 - 1962	**M232**				
				Deloraine RAN	1941	AS/MS		1948 - 1956

M233			
Inverell RNZN	1942	AS/MS	1948 - 1978
M234			
Latrobe RAN	1942	AS/MS	1948 - 1956
M235			
Horsham RAN	1942	AS/MS	1948 - 1956
M236			
Glenelg RAN	1942	AS/MS	1948 - 1949
M237			
Madras RIN	1942	AS/MS	1948 - 1951
M238			
Gympie RAN	1942	AS/MS	1948 - 1962
M239			
Punjab RIN	1941	MS	1948 - 1949
M241			
Bunbury RAN	1942	AS/MS	1948 - 1962
M243			
Bengal RIN	1942	AS/MS	1948 - 1951
M244			
Castlemaine RAN	1941	AS/MS	1948 - 1949
M245			
Dacca RPN (ex *Oudh* RIN)	1942	MS	1948 - 1959
M246			
Fremantle RAN	1942	AS/MS	1948 - 1962
M247			
Bihar RIN	1942	MS	1948 - 1949
M248			
Shepparton RAN	1942	AS/MS	1948 - 1948
M249			
Bombay RIN	1941	AS/MS	1948 - 1951
M251			
Dubbo RAN	1942	AS/MS	1948 - 1958
M252			
Echuca RNZN	1942	AS/MS	1948 - 1968
M275			
Hydra	1942	MS	1948
M276			
Lennox	1943	MS	1948 - 1961
M277			
Orestes	1942	MS	1948 - 1963
M278			
Llewellyn RCN	1942	MMS	1948 - 1959
M279			
Lloyd George RCN	1943	MMS	1948 - 1959
M285			
Bowen RAN	1942	AS/MS	1948 - 1956
M289			
Melita	1942	MS	1948 - 1959
M290			
Octavia	1942	MS	1948 - 1950
M291			
Pietermaritzburg SAN	1943	MS	1948 - 1991
M293			
Pickle	1943	MS	1948 - 1958
M294			
Pincher	1943	MS	1948 - 1962
M295			
Plucky	1943	MS	1948 - 1962
M297			
Rattlesnake	1943	MS	1948 - 1959
M298			
Recruit	1943	MS	1948 - 1965
M299			
Rifleman	1943	MS	1948 - 1972
M302			
Thisbe	1943	MS	1948 - 1957
M303			
Truelove	1943	MS	1948 - 1957
M304			
Waterwitch	1943	MS	1948 - 1970
M305			
Brave	1943	MS	1948 - 1951
Satellite (ex Brave)	1943	Drill Ship	1951 - 1958
M306			
Fly	1942	MS	1948 - 1949
M307			
Hound	1942	MS	1948 - 1962
M308			
Fancy	1943	MS	1948 - 1957
M323			
Benalla RAN	1942	AS/MS	1948 - 1958
M324			
Gladstone RAN	1942	AS/MS	1948 - 1956
M325			
Providence	1943	MS	1948 - 1958
M329			
Moon	1943	MS	1948 - 1957
M333			
Seabear	1943	MS	1948 - 1958
M341			
Wiay	1945	Trawler	1948 - 1961
M348			
Stawell RNZN	1943	AS/MS	1948 - 1959
M350			
Coquette	1943	MS	1948 - 1958
M351			
Cowra RAN	1943	AS/MS	1948 - 1962
M353			
Kiama RNZN	1943	AS/MS	1948 - 1974
M354			
Serene	1943	MS	1948 - 1959
M356			
Welfare	1943	MS	1948 - 1957
M360			
Mary Rose	1943	MS	1948 - 1957
M361			
Parkes RAN	1943	AS/MS	1948 - 1949

M362			
Junee RAN	1943	AS/MS	1948 - 1962
M363			
Strahan RAN	1943	AS/MS	1948 - 1962
M367			
Stormcloud	1943	MS	1948 - 1959
M373			
Revelstoke RCN	1943	MS	1948 - 1953
M376			
Golden Fleece	1944	MS	1948 - 1960
M377			
Lioness	1944	MS	1948 - 1956
M379			
Lysander	1943	MS	1948 - 1957

Lysander renamed *Cornflower* 3.50-1951, then reverted to original name.

M380			
Mariner	1944	MS	1948 - 1958
M381			
Marmion	1944	MS	1948 - 1959
M382			
Sylvia	1944	MS	1948 - 1958
M383			
Tanganyika	1944	MS	1948 - 1963
M384			
Rowena	1944	MS	1948 - 1958
M385			
Wave	1944	MS	1948 - 1962
M386			
Welcome	1944	MS	1948 - 1962
M387			
Chameleon	1944	MS	1948 - 1966
M389			
Hare	1944	MS	1948 - 1962
M390			
Jewel	1944	MS	1948 - 1966
M391			
Liberty	1944	MS	1948 - 1949
M422			
Imersay	1944	Trawler	1948 - 1959
M424			
Sandray	1944	Trawler	1948 - 1961
M426			
Shillay	1944	Trawler	1948 - 1958
M427			
Sursay	1944	Trawler	1948 - 1967
M428			
Jaseur	1944	MS	1948 - 1956
M429			
Ronay	1945	Trawler	1948 - 1967
M431			
Trodday	1945	Trawler	1948 - 1960

M432			
Vaceasay	1945	Trawler	1948 - 1967
M433			
Laertes	1944	MS	1948 - 1949
M434			
Vallay	1944	Trawler	1948 - 1959
M435			
Maenad	1944	MS	1948 - 1957
M436			
Magicienne	1944	MS	1948 - 1956
M437			
Marmeluke	1944	MS	1948 - 1950
M438			
Mandate	1944	MS	1948 - 1957
M439			
Bloemfontein SAN	1944	MS	1948 - Sold
M443			
Marvel	1944	MS	1948 - 1958
M444			
Michael	1944	MS	1948 - 1956
M445			
Minstrel	1944	MS	1948 - Sold
M447			
Polaris	1944	MS	1948 - 1956
M448			
Pyrrhus	1945	MS	1948 - 1956
M449			
Romola	1944	MS	1948 - 1957
M450			
Orsay	1945	Trawler	1948 - 1957
M452			
Tahay	1944	Trawler	1948 - 1963
M454			
Myrmidon	1944	MS	1948 - 1958
M455			
Mystic	1944	MS	1948 - 1958
M456			
Nerissa	1944	MS	1948 - 1960
M462			
Orcadia	1944	MS	1948 - 1958
M463			
Ossory	1944	MS	1948 - 1959
M1101			
Coniston	1952	CMS	1953 - 1960
M1102			
Alcaston	1953	CMS	1953 - 1957
M1103			
Alfriston	1953	CMS	1954 - 1986
Warsash	1953	CMS	5.54 - 1958
Kilmorey	1953	CMS	1960 - 1975

Alfriston was renamed *Warash* (5.54-58) when attached to Solent Division RNR and *Kilmorey* (1960-75) when attached to Ulster Division RNR.

M1104

Alverton	1952	CMS	1954 - 1962
Thames	1952	CMS	1954 - 1962

Alverton was renamed *Thames* (1954-62) when attached to London Division RNR.

M1105

Amerton	1953	CMS	1954 - 1970
Mersey	1953	CMS	5.54 - 10.59
Clyde	1953	CMS	1960 - 1970

Amerton was renamed *Mersey* (5.54-10.59) when attached to Mersey Division RNR and *Clyde* (1960-70) when attached to Clyde Division RNR.

M1106

Appleton	1952	CMS	1954 - 1969

M1107

Beachampton	1953	CMS	1953 - 1971

M1108

Bevington	1953	CMS	1954 - 1955

M1109

Bickington	1953	CMS	1954 - 1986
Curzon	1953	CMS	1954 - 1960
Killiekrankie	1953	CMS	1962 - 1974

Bickington was renamed *Curzon* (1954-60) when attached to Sussex Division RNR and *Killiecrankie* (1962-74) when attached to Forth Division RNR.

M1110

Bildeston	1952	CMS	1953 - 1986

M1111

Edderton	1952	CMS	1954 - 1964

Between 1964-65 *Edderton* was converted to a Coastal Survey Vessel and recommissioned as *Myrmidon*.

M1112

Boulston	1952	CMS	1954 - 1969
Warsash	1952	CMS	1960 - 1961

Boulston was renamed *Warsash* (1960-61) when attached to Solent Division RNR.

M1113

Brereton	1953	CMS	1954 - 1991
St David	1953	CMS	1954 - 1961

Brereton was renamed *St David* (1954-61) when attached to South Wales Division RNR.

M1114

Brinton	1952	CMS	1954 - 1993

M1115

Bronington	1953	CMS	1954 - 1988
Humber	1953	CMS	1954 - 1958

Bronington was renamed *Humber* (1954-58) when attached to Humber Division RNR.

M1116

Burnaston	1952	CMS	1954 - 1969
Wilton	1972	CMS	1973 - 1994

M1117

Buttington	1953	CMS	1954 -1967
Venturer	1953	CMS	1955 - 1960
Thames	1953	CMS	1961 - 1966
Thames	1958	CMS	197x
(ex *Woolaston*)			

Buttington was renamed *Venturer* (1955-60) when attached to Severn Division RNR and *Thames* (1961-66) when attached to London Division RNR. At some point in the early 1970s *Thames* (ex-*Woolaston*) was displaying M1117 vice M1194. It is thought that some over eager official transferred not only the name, but also the pendant number when the ship was assigned to London Division RNR. I can find no official documents to support this, but a photograph of the ship taken in the early 1970s clearly shows the ship wearing the number, several years after *Buttington* had been decommissioned.

M1118

Calton	1953	CMS	1954 - 1966

M1119

Carhampton	1955	CMS	1956 - 1965

M1120

Caunton	1953	CMS	1954 - 1965

M1121

Chediston	1953	CMS	1954 - 1961
Montrose	1953	CMS	6.54 - 10.57

Chediston was renamed *Montrose* (6.54-10.57) when attached to Tay Division RNR.

M1122

Chilcompton	1953	CMS	1954 - 1969

M1123

Clarbeston	1954	CMS	1954 - 1969

M1124

Crichton	1953	CMS	1954 - 1985
Clyde	1953	CMS	1954 - 1960

St David	1953	CMS	1960 - 1976

Crichton was renamed *Clyde (*1954-60*)* when attached to Clyde Division RNR and *St David (*1960-76*)* when attached to South Wales Division RNR.

M1125

Cuxton	1953	CMS	1954 - 1991

M1126

Dalswinton	1953	CMS	1954 - 1972
Montrose	1953	CMS	1962 - 1971

Dalswinton was renamed *Montrose* (1962-71) when attached to Tay Division RNR.

M1127

Darlaston	1953	CMS	1954 - 1960

M1128

Derriton	1953	CMS	1954 - 1970
Killiekrankie	1953	CMS	1955 - 1960

Derriton was renamed *Killiekrankie* (1955-60) when attached to Forth Division RNR.

M1129

Oulston	1954	CMS	1956 - 1970

Oulston was placed in Reserve on completion. Transferred to Ireland where she commissioned in 1971 as *LE Grainne.*

M1130

Highburton	1954	CMS	1955 - 1976

M1131

Hickleton	1955	CMS	1955 - 1966

M1132

Blaxton	1955	CMS	1956 - 1957

M1133

Bossington	1955	CMS	1956 - 1987

M1134

Essington	1956	CMS	1955 - 1958

M1135

Fenton	1955	CMS	1955 - 1958

M1136

Fittleton	1954	CMS	1955 - 9.76
Curzon	1954	CMS	1961 - 1975

Fittleton was renamed *Curzon* (1961-75) when attached to Sussex Division RNR.

M1137

Flockton	1954	CMS	1955 - 1965

M1138

Floriston	1955	CMS	1955 - 1960

M1139

Somerleyton	1955	CMS	1956 - 1960

Somerleyton was placed in Reserve on completion. Transferred to RAN where she commissioned in 1962 as *HMAS Hawk*

M1140

Gavinton	1953	CMS	1954 - 1986

M1141

Glasserton	1953	CMS	1954 - 1981

M1142

Hazleton	1954	CMS	To SAN

M1143

Hexton	1954	CMS	1955 - 1956

M1144

Dunkerton	1954	CMS	To SAN

M1145

Dufton	1954	CMS	1955 - 1969

M1146

Hodgeston	1954	CMS	1954
Northumbria	1954	CMS	1954 - 1960
Venturer	1954	CMS	1962 - 1975

Hodgeston was renamed *Northumbria* (1954-60) when attached to Tyne Division RNR and *Venturer* (1962-75) when attached to Severn Division RNR between the dates shown.

M1147

Hubberston	1954	CMS	1955 - 1991

M1148

Ilmington	1954	CMS	1955 - 1957

M1149

Badminton	1954	CMS	1955 - 1965

M1150

Invermoriston	1954	CMS	1955 - 1966

M1151

Iveston	1954	CMS	1955 - 1992

M1152

Jackton	1955	CMS	1956 - 1961

Jackton was placed in Reserve on completion. Transferred to RAN where she commissioned in 1962 as *HMAS Teal.*

M1153

Kedleston	1953	CMS	1955 - 1991

M1154

Kellington	1954	CMS	1955 - 1992

M1155

Monkton	1955	CMS	1955 - 1972

M1156			
Kemerton	1953	CMS	1954 - 1966

M1157			
Kirkliston	1954	CMS	1954 - 1985
Kilmorey	1954	CMS	5.54 - 1960

Kirkliston was renamed *Kilmorey* (5.54-1960) when attached to Ulster Division RNR.

M1158			
Laleston	1954	CMS	1954 - 1982
M1159			
Lanton	1954	CMS	1955 - 1967
M1160			
Letterston	1954	CMS	1955 - 1969

M1161			
Leverton	1955	CMS	1955 - 1969
M1162			
Kildarton	1955	CMS	1955 - 1967
M1163			
Lullington	1955	CMS	1956 - 1965
M1164			
Maddiston	1956	CMS	1956 - 1969
M1165			
Maxton	1956	CMS	1957 - 1988

M1166			
Nurton	1956	CMS	1957 - 1993
Montrose	1956	CMS	1958 - 1961
Killiekrankie	1956	CMS	1972 - 1974

Nurton was renamed *Montrose* (1958-61) when attached to Tay Division RNR and *Killiekrankie* (1972-74) when attached to Forth Division RNR between the dates shown.

M1167			
Repton	1957	CMS	1957 - 1980
M1168			
Dilston	1954	CMS	1955 - 1963
M1169			
Penston	1955	CMS	1956 - 1967
M1170			
Picton	1955	CMS	1956 - 1966
M1171			
Aldington	1955	CMS	1956 - 1957
M1172			
Thankerton	1956	CMS	1957 - 1965
M1173			
Pollington	1957	CMS	1958 - 1985
M1174			
Puncheston	1956	CMS	1957 - 1971

M1175			
Quainton	1957	CMS	1959 - 1972
Northumbria	1957	CMS	4.60 - 1972

Quainton was renamed *Northumbria* (4.60-72) when attached to Tyne Division RNR.

M1176			
Rennington	1958	CMS	1958 - 1966
M1177			
Roddington	1955	CMS	1955 - 1962
M1178			
Santon	1955	CMS	1956 - 1966
M1179			
Sefton	1954	CMS	1955 - 1964
M1180			
Shavington	1955	CMS	1956 - 1985
M1181			
Sheraton	1955	CMS	1956 - 1993
M1182			
Shoulton	1954	CMS	1955 - 1978
M1183			
Singleton	1955	CMS	1956 - 1962

Singleton was placed in Reserve on completion. Transferred to RAN where she commissioned in 1962 as *HMAS Ibis*

M1184			
Sullington	1954	CMS	1955 - 1957

Between 1957-64 *Sullington* was converted to a Coastal Survey Vessel and recommissioned as *Mermaid*.

M1185			
Swanston	1954	CMS	1956 - 1959

Swanston was placed in Reserve on completion. Transferred to RAN where she commissioned in 1962 as *HMAS Gull*.

M1186			
Tarlton	1954	CMS	1955 - 1956
M1187			
Upton	1956	CMS	1956 - 1990
M1188			
Walkerton	1956	CMS	1958 - 1985
M1189			
Wasperton	1956	CMS	1957 - 1972
M1190			
Wennington	1955	CMS	To RIN
M1191			
Whitton	1956	CMS	To RIN
M1192			
Wilkieston	1956	CMS	1957 - 1969

M1193

Wolverton	1956	CMS	1958 - 1971

M1194

Woolaston	1958	CMS	1958 - 1975
Thames	1958	CMS	9.69 - 1975

Woolaston was renamed Thames (9.69-75) when attached to London Division RNR.

M1195

Wotton	1956	CMS	1957 - 1984

M1196

Yarnton	1956	CMS	1957 - 1971

M1197

Overton	1956	CMS	To RIN

M1198

Ashton	1956	CMS	1958 - 1974

M1199

Belton	1955	CMS	1957 - 1971

M1200

Soberton	1956	CMS	1957 - 1992

M1201

Durweston	1955	CMS	To RIN

M1202

Maryton	1958	CMS	1958 - 1968

M1203

Dartington	1956	CMS	1958 - 1969

M1204

Stubbington	1956	CMS	1956 - 1986

M1205

Wiston	1958	CMS	1960 - 1977

M1206

Fiskerton	1957	CMS	1957 - 1968

M1207

Castleton	1957	CMS	To SAN

M1208

Lewiston	1959	CMS	1960 - 1984

M1209

Chawton	1957	CMS	1958 - 1975

M1210

Stratton	1957	CMS	To SAN

M1211

Houghton	1957	CMS	1958 - 1969

M1212

Dumbleton	1957	CMS	To SAN

M1213

Oakington	1958	CMS	To SAN

M1214

Packington	1958	CMS	To SAN

M1215

Chilton	1957	CMS	To SAN

M1216

Crofton	1958	CMS	1958 - 1984

Warsash	1958	CMS	5.69 - 1975

Crofton was renamed Warsash (5.69-75) when attached to Solent Division RNR.

M2001

Dingley	1952	IMH	1954 - 1967

M2002

Aveley	1953	IMH	1954 - 1982

M2003

Brearley	1953	IMH	1955 - 1969
Waveney	1983	MCM	1983 - 1994

M2004

Brenchley	1954	IMH	1954 - 1965
Carron	1983	MCM	1983 - 1994

M2005

Brinkley	1954	IMH	1954 - 1965
Dovey	1983	MCM	1983 - 1994

M2006

Broadley	1953	IMH	1955 - 1959
Helford	1984	MCM	1984 - 1994

M2007

Broomley	1953	IMH	1954 - 1966
Watchful	1953	IMH	1.59 - 1966
Humber	1984	MCM	1984 - 1994

Broomley was renamed Watchful (no number displayed) when she operated with the Fishery Protection Squadron between 1.59 - 1966.

M2008

Burley	1954	IMH	1955 - 1968
Squirrel	1954	IMH	12.59 - 1968
Blackwater	1984	MCM	1984 - 1998

Burley was renamed Squirrel (no number displayed) when she operated with the Fishery Protection Squadron between 12.59 - 1968.

M2009

Chailey	1954	IMH	1955 - 1965
Itchen	1984	MCM	1984 - 1998

M2010

Cradley	1955	IMH	1955 - 1963
Isis	1955	IMH	1963 - 1981
Helmsdale	1985	MCM	1985 - 1994

Cradley allocated to London Division RNR in 1963 and renamed Isis

M2011
Cuffley	Canc	IMH	Canc
Orwell	1985	MCM	1985 - 2000

M2012
Downley	Canc	IMH	Canc
Ribble	1985	MCM	1985 - 1994

M2013
Edgeley	1955	IMH	See M2779
Spey	1985	MCM	1985 - 1994

M2014
Eversley	Canc	IMH	Canc
Arun	1985	MCM	1985 - 1998

M2015
Foxley	Canc	IMH	Canc

M2016
Hattersley	Canc	IMH	Canc

M2601
Inglesham	1952	IMS	1952 - 1966

M2602
Altham	1952	IMS	1952 - 1959

M2603
Arlingham	1953	IMS	1953 - 1978

M2604
Asheldham	1952	IMS	1952 - 1959

M2605
Bassingham	1952	IMS	1952 - 1961

M2606
Bedham	1953	IMS	1953 - 1958

M2607
Bisham	1954	IMS	1954 - 1956

M2608
Blunham	1952	IMS	1952 - 1967

M2609
Bodenham	1952	IMS	1952 - 1967

M2610
Boreham	1952	IMS	1952 - 1965

M2611
Bottisham	1953	IMS	1953 - 1965

M2612
Brantingham	1953	IMS	1953 - 1957

M2613
Brigham	1953	IMS	1953 - 1967

M2614
Bucklesham	1952	IMS	1952 - 1965

Bucklesham operated as a civilian-manned Torpedo Recovery Vessel from 1965-1978

M2615
Cardingham	1952	IMS	1952 - 1966

M2616
Chelsham	1952	IMS	1952 - 1971

Chelsham was transferred to the RAF at Plymouth where, between 1965 - 1971, she operated as *HMFA 5001*. She was returned to the RN in 1971.

M2617
Chillingham	1952	IMS	1952 - 1968

M2618
Cobham	1953	IMS	1953 - 1966

M2619
Darsham	1952	IMS	1952 - 1966

M2620
Davenham	1953	IMS	1953 - 1966

M2621
Dittisham	1953	IMS	1953 - 1982

M2622
Downham	1955	IMS	1955 - 1964

Downham operated as a civilian-manned Torpedo Recovery Vessel from 1964-1978

M2623
Edlingham	1955	IMS	1955 - 1956

M2624
Elsenham	1955	IMS	1955 - 1967

M2625
Etchingham	1957	IMS	1957 - 1966

M2626
Everingham	1954	IMS	1954 - 1964

Everingham operated as a civilian-manned Torpedo Recovery Vessel from 1964-1979

M2627
Felmersham	1953	IMS	1953 - 1966

M2628
Flintha	1955	IMS	1955 - 1982

M2629
Damerham	1953	IMS	1953 - 1966

M2630
Fritham	1953	IMS	1953 - 1964

Fritham operated as a civilian-manned Torpedo Recovery Vessel from 1964-1978

M2631
Glentham	1957	IMS	1957 - 1966

M2632
Greetham	1954	IMS	1954 - 1964

M2633
Halsham	1953	IMS	1953 - 1964

Halsham was transferred to the RAF in 1964 where she

operated as *HMFA 5002*. In 1974 she was further transferred to th Royal Corps of Transport and renamed *R.G. Masters VC.*

M2634

Harpham	1954	IMS	1954 - 1962

M2635

Haversham	1954	IMS	1954 - 1963

M2636

Lasham	1954	IMS	1954 - 1963

Both *Haversham* and *Lasham* operated as a civilian-manned Torpedo Recovery Vessels from 1964-1979.

M2637

Hovingham	1956	IMS	1956 - 1966

M2701

Cranham	1953	IMS	1953 - 1966

M2702

Frettenham	1954	IMS	To France

M2703

Isham	1954	IMS	To France

M2704

Kingham	1955	IMS	To France

M2705

Hildersham	1954	IMS	To RIN

M2706

Ledsham	1954	IMS	1954 - 1971

M2707

Littlesham	1954	IMS	To India

M2708

Ludham	1954	IMS	1954 - 1967

M2709

Mersham	1954	IMS	To France

M2710

Mickleham	1954	IMS	1954 - 1965

M2711

Mileham	1954	IMS	To FN

M2712

Neasham	1956	IMS	1956 - 1968

M2713

Nettleham	1956	IMS	1956 - 1966

M2714

Ockham	1959	IMS	1959 - 1966

M2715

Ottringham	1958	IMS	1958 - 1959

M2716

Pagham	1955	IMS	1955 - 1983

M2717

Fordham	1956	IMS	1956 - 1964

Fordham operated as a civilian-manned Degaussing Vessel from 1964-1979

M2718

Petersham	1955	IMS	To France

M2719

Pineham	1955	IMS	To France

M2720

Powderham	1958	IMS	1958 - 1964
Waterwitch	1958	Survey Vsl	1964 - 1986

Powderham was converted to an Inshore Survey Vessel in 1964 and renamed *Waterwitch.*

M2721

Pulham	1956	IMS	1956 - 1966
Isis	1956	IMS	1956 - 1963

Pulham was transferred to London Division RNR and renamed *Isis.*

M2722

Rackham	1956	IMS	1956 - 1966

M2723

Reedham	1958	IMS	1958 - 1966

M2724

Rendlesham	1954	IMS	To France

M2725

Ripplingham	1955	IMS	To France

M2726

Shipham	1955	IMS	1955 - 1983

M2727

Saxlingham	1955	IMS	1955 - 1966

M2728

Shrivenham	1956	IMS	1956 - 1966

M2729

Sidlesham	1955	IMS	1955 - 1964

M2730

Stedham	1955	IMS	To France

M2731

Sparham	1954	IMS	To France

M2732

Sulham	1955	IMS	To France

M2733

Thakenham	1957	IMS	1957 - 1979

M2734

Tibenham	1955	IMS	To France

M2735

Tongham	1955	IMS	1955 - 1979

M2736

Tresham	1954	IMS	1954 - 1964

M2737

Warmingham	1954	IMS	1954 - 1964

M2738

Wexham	1954	IMS	To France

M2739

Whippingham	1954	IMS	To France

M2777
Wintringham   1954 IMS   1954 - 1964
M2778
Woldingham   1955 IMS   1955 - 1966
M2779
Wrentham   1955 IMS   1955 - 1966
M2780
Yaxham   1958 IMS   1958 - 1963

Yaxham was converted to an Inshore Survey Vessel in 1963 and renamed Woodlark (A2780).

M2781
Portisham   1955 IMS   1955 - 1983
M2782
Popham   1955 IMS   1955 - 1966
M2783
Odiham   1955 IMS   1955 - 1979
M2784
Puttenham   1956 IMS   1956 - 1978
M2785
Birdham   1955 IMS   1955 - 1980

M2786
Rampisham   1957 IMS   1957 - 1966
Squirrel   1957 IMS   1958 - 1959

Rampisham was renamed Squirrel when operating with the Fishery Protection Squadron.

M2787
Abbotsham   1955 IMS   1955 - 1966
M2788
Georgeham   1957 IMS   1957 - 1968

M2789
Malham   1958 IMS   1958 - 1959

Malham was transferred to Ghana as GNS Yogada in 1959

M2790
Thatcham   1957 IMS   1957 - 1970

Thatcham operated as a civilian-manned Degaussing Vessel from 1970-1978

M2791
Sandringham   1957 IMS   1957 - 1966

Sandringham operated as a civilian-manned Personnel Ferry on the Clyde from 1972-1983.

M2792
Polsham   1958 IMS   1958 - 1966
M2793
Thornham   1957 IMS   1957 - 1984

M1A
Mersey   1913 Monitor   9.15 - 1.18
Roberts   1915 Monitor   1.18 - ....

M2A
Severn   1913 Monitor   9.15 - ....
M3A
Sir John Moore 1915 Monitor   1.18 - ....
M4A
Sir Thomas Picton 1915 Monitor 1.18 - ....
M5A
Terror   1916 Monitor   1.18 - ....

Flag 'M(I)' Superior

Armed Merchant Cruisers and Armed Boarding Steamers serving with the Royal Navy in WW1 were assigned flags superior from the International code, as opposed to the Naval code. International flag 'M' was a Blue square flag superimposed with a diagonal white cross. These numbers were assigned for visual signalling and were not applied to the hull.

M(I)00
Hazel	1907	ABS	9.15 - 1.18
Amsterdam	1894	ABS	1.18 - ....

M(I)01
Rowan	1909	ABS	4.15 - 1.18
Carron	1909	ABS	1.18 - ....

M(I)02
Woodnut	1906	ABS	4.15 - 1.18
City of Belfast	1893	ABS	1.18 - 6.18
Duchess of Devonshire	1897	ABS	6.18 - ....

M(I)03
Partridge	1906	ABS	4.15 - 1.18
Duchess of Devonshire	1897	ABS	1.18 - 6.18
Duke of Clarence	1892	ABS	6.18 - ....

M(I)04
Sarnia	1910	ABS	4.15 - 1.18
Duke of Clarence	1892	ABS	1.18 - 6.18

M(I)05
Heroic	1906	ABS	4.15 - 1.18
Duke of Cornwall	1898	ABS	1.18 - ....

M(I)06
Snaefell	1910	ABS	4.15 - 1.18
King Orry	1913	ABS	6.18 - 6.19

M(I)07
Louvain	1897	ABS	4.15 - 1.18
Fiona	1905	ABS	1.18 - Sunk
Peel Castle	1894	ABS	6.18 - 5.19

M(I)08
Amsterdam	1894	ABS	4.15 - 1.18
Grangemouth	1908	ABS	1.18 - 6.18
Rowan	1909	ABS	6.18 - ....

M(I)09
Duchess of Devonshire	1897	ABS	9.15 - 1.18
Grive	1905	ABS	1.18 - Sunk

M(I)10
Duke of Cornwall	1898	ABS	9.15 - 1.18
Hazel	1907	ABS	1.18 - 5.19

M(I)11
Duke of Albany	1907	ABS	9.15 - 8.16
Heroic	1906	ABS	1.18 - 6.18

M(I)12
Caeserea	1910	ABS	9.15 - 1.16
Dundee	1911	ABS	10.15 - 9.17
King Orry	1913	ABS	1.18 - 6.18

M(I)13
Peel Castle	1894	ABS	4.15 - 1.18

M(I)14
The Ramsey	1895	ABS	9.15 - Sunk
Duke of Clarence	1892	ABS	1.16 - 1.18
Louvain	1897	ABS	1.18 - Sunk

M(I)15
City of Belfast	1893	ABS	9.15 - 1.18
Partridge	1906	ABS	1.18 - ....

M(I)16
Royal Scot	1910	ABS	4.15 - 1.18
Peel Castle	1894	ABS	1.18 - 6.18

M(I)17
Fiona	1905	ABS	9.15 - 9.17
Perth	1915	ABS	1.18 - 6.18

M(I)18
King Orry	1913	ABS	4.15 - 1.18
Richard Welford	1908	ABS	1.18 - 8.19

M(I)19
Carron	1909	ABS	9.15 - 1.18

Rowan	1909	ABS	1.18 - 6.18
M(I)20			
York	1907	ABS	4.15 - 1.18
Royal Scot	1910	ABS	1.18 - 6.18
Bayano	1917	Convoy Esc	6.18 - ....
M(I)21			
Richard Welford	1908	ABS	4.15 - 1.18
Sarnia	1910	ABS	1.18 - 6.18
Camito	1915	Convoy Esc	6.18 - ....
M(I)22			
Grangemouth	1908	ABS	9.15 - 1.18
Snaefell	1910	ABS	1.18 - 6.18
Carrigan Head	1901	Convoy Esc	6.18 - ....
M(I)23			
Perth	1915	ABS	9.15 - 1.18
Stephen Furness	1910	ABS	1.18 - Sunk
Coronado	1915	Convoy Esc	6.18 - ....
M(I)24			
Grive	1905	ABS	2.16 - 12.17
Tithonus	1908	ABS	1.18 - 3.18
Naneric	1895	Convoy Esc	6.18 - ....
M(I)25			
Marcella	1887	Yacht	9.15 - 3.16
Woodnut	1906	ABS	1.18 - 3.18
Orvieto	1909	AMC	4.18 - ....
M(I)26			
Fauvette	1912	ABS	3.15 - 3.16
York	1907	ABS	1.18 - 3.18
Olympic	1911	AMC	4.18 - ....
M(I)27			
Stephen Furness	1910	ABS	3.16 - 12.17
Wyncote	1907	Convoy Esc	6.18 - ....
M(I)28			
Tithonus	1908	ABS	4.16 - 1.18
Almanzora	1908	AMC	6.18 - ....
M(I)29			
Alsation	1913	AMC	4.18 - 4.19
M(I)30			
Andes	1913	AMC	4.18 - 10.19
M(I)31			
Arlanza	1912	AMC	4.18 - 6.20
M(I)32			
Armadale Castle	1903	AMC	4.18 - 9.19
M(I)33			
Artois	1913	AMC	4.18 - 1.19

M(I)34			
Kildonan Castle	1899	AMC	4.18 - 1.19
M(I)35			
Changuinola	1912	AMC	4.18 - ....
M(I)36			
Columbella	1902	AMC	4.18 - 6.19
M(I)37			
Ebro	1915	AMC	4.18 - 10.19
M(I)38			
Gloucestershire	1910	AMC	4.18 - 7.19
M(I)39			
Hildebrand	1911	AMC	4.18 - 7.19
M(I)40			
Mantua	1908	AMC	4.18 - 12.19
M(I)41			
Marmora	1903	AMC	6.18 - 7.18
M(I)42			
City of London	1907	AMC	4.18 - 7.19
Moldavia	1903	AMC	4.18 - 5.18
M(I)43			
Morea	1908	AMC	4.18 - 10.19
M(I)44			
Motagua	1912	AMC	4.18 - 12.19
M(I)45			
Lepanto	1915	Convoy Esc	9.18 - 5.19
M(I)46			
Orcoma	1908	AMC	4.18 - 10.19
M(I)47			
Orotava	1889	AMC	4.18 - 1.19
M(I)48			
Narkunda	1918	AMC	4.18 - ....
Patia	1913	AMC	4.18 - 6.18
M(I)49			
Patuca	1913	AMC	4.18 - ....
M(I)50			
Almanzora	1908	AMC	1.18 - 6.18
Teutonic	1889	AMC	4.18 - ....
M(I)51			
Mantua	1908	AMC	9.15 - 1.18
Alsation	1913	AMC	1.18 - 4.18
Victorian	1904	AMC	4.18 - ....
M(I)52			
Teutonic	1889	AMC	9.15 - 1.18
Andes	1913	AMC	1.18 - 4.18
Virginian	1905	AMC	4.18 - ....
M(I)53			
Caronia	1905	AMC	9.15 - 9.16

Arlanza	1912	AMC	1.18 - 4.18
Discoverer	1913	Convoy Esc	6.18 - 3.19

M(I)54

Calgarian	1914	AMC	9.15 - 1.18
Armadale Castle	1903	AMC	1.18 - 4.18
Knight Templar	1905	Convoy Esc	6.18 - 2.19

M(I)55

Carmania	1905	AMC	9.15 - 7.16
Artois	1913	AMC	1.18 - 4.18
Edinburgh Castle	1910	AMC	4.18 - 7.19

M(I)56

Victorian	1904	AMC	4.15 - 1.18
Aquitania	1913	AMC	6.18 - ....

M(I)57

Princess	1905	AMC	1.16 - 1.18
Avoca	1907	AMC	1.18 - 4.18
Mauretania	1906	AMC	6.18 - 1919

M(I)58

Marmora	1903	AMC	9.15 - 1.18
Calgarian	1914	AMC	1.18 - 3.18
Naldera	1918	AMC	4.18 - 3.19

M(I)59

Macedonia	1904	AMC	9.15 - 1.18
Bostonian	1896	Convoy Esc	1.18 - 6.18
Orbita	1915	AMC	4.18 - 8.19

M(I)60

Otranto	1909	AMC	4.15 - 1.18
Carmania	1905	AMC	1.18 - ....

M(I)61

Orama	1911	AMC	9.15 - 10.17
Caronia	1905	AMC	1.18 - ....

M(I)62

Edinburgh Castle	1910	AMC	9.15 - 1.18

M(I)63

Armadale Castle	1903	AMC	9.15 - 1.18
Changuinola	1912	AMC	1.18 - 4.18

M(I)64

Kinfauns Castle	1899	AMC	9.15 - 1.16
Moldavia	1903	AMC	1.16 - 1.18
City of London	1907	AMC	1.18 - 4.18

M(I)69

Celtic	1901	AMC	9.15 - 1.16
City of London	1907	AMC	1.16 - 1.18

Columbella	1902	AMC	1.18 - 4.18

M(I)70

Laconia	1912	AMC	9.15 - 1.18
Ebro	1915	AMC	1.18 - 4.18

M(I)71

Laurentic	1908	AMC	9.15 - 1.17
Edinburgh Castle	1910	AMC	1.18 - 4.18

M(I)72

Virginian	1905	AMC	9.15 - 1.18
Gloucestershire	1910	AMC	1.18 - 1.14

M(I)73

Otway	1909	AMC	9.15 - 1.18
Hildebrand	1911	AMC	1.18 - 4.18

M(I)74

Cedric	1903	AMC	9.15 - 1.16
Kildonan Castle	1899	AMC	3.16 - 1.18

M(I)75

Avenger	1908	AMC	9.15 - 6.17
Laconia	1912	AMC	1.18 - Sunk

M(I)76

Patia	1913	AMC	9.15 - 1.18
Macedonia	1904	AMC	1.18 - 4.18

M(I)77

Patuca	1913	AMC	9.15 - 1.18
Mantua	1908	AMC	1.18 - 4.18

M(I)78

Ebro	1915	AMC	9.15 - 1.18
Marmora	1903	AMC	1.18 - 4.18

M(I)79

Avoca	1907	AMC	1.16 - 1.18
Moldavia	1903	AMC	1.18 - 4.18

M(I)80

Orotava	1889	AMC	9.15 - 1.18
Morea	1908	AMC	1.18 - 4.18

M(I)81

India	1896	AMC	4.15 - 8.15
Motagua	1912	AMC	1.18 - 4.18

M(I)82

Andes	1913	AMC	9.15 - 1.18
Ophir	1891	AMC	1.18 - 7.19

M(I)83

Digby	1913	AMC	9.15 - 1.18
(ren *Artois* 11.15)			

M(I)84

Motagua	1912	AMC	9.15 - 1.18
Orbita	1915	AMC	1.18 - 4.18

M(I)85

Changuinola	1912	AMC	9.15 - 1.18
Orcoma	1908	AMC	1.18 - 4.18

M(I)86

Orcoma	1908	AMC	9.15 - 1.18
Orotava	1889	AMC	1.18 - 4.18

M(I)87

Ambrose	1903	AMC	9.15 - 1.16
Gloucestershire	1910	AMC	1.16 - 1.18
Otranto	1909	AMC	1.18 - 4.18

M(I)88

Oropesa	1895	AMC	9.15 - 12.15
Champagne	1895	AMC	12.15 - 10.17
(ex *Oropesa*)			
Otway	1909	AMC	1.18 - Sunk

M(I)89

Columbella	1902	AMC	9.15 - 1.18
Patia	1913	AMC	1.18 - 4.18

M(I)90

Hilary	1908	AMC	9.15 - 5.17
Patuca	1913	AMC	1.18 - 4.18

M(I)91

Hildebrand	1911	AMC	9.15 - 1.18
Princess	1905	AMC	1.18 - ....

M(I)92

Ophir	1891	AMC	9.15 - 1.18
Sachem	1893	Convoy Esc	1.18 - ....

M(I)93

Arlanza	1912	AMC	9.15 - 1.18
Teutonic	1889	AMC	1.18 - 4.18

M(I)94

Victorian	1904	AMC	1.18 - 4.18

M(I)95

Virginian	1905	AMC	1.18 - 4.18

M(I)96

Discoverer	1913	Convoy Esc	1.18 - 6.18

M(I)97

Knight Templar	1905	Convoy Esc	1.18 - 6.18

M(I)98

Mechanician	1900	Convoy Esc	1.18 - 6.18

M(I)99

Quernmore	1898	Convoy Esc	1.18 - Sunk

M(I)A0

Almanzora	1908	AMC	9.15 - 1.18

M(I)A1

Orbita	1915	AMC	9.15 - 1.18

Flag 'N' Superior

Pre 1940:   Boarding Tugs, Cruisers, Coast Defence Ships, Destroyers, Minesweepers; Paddle Minesweepers, Minelayers, Seaplane Carriers, Survey Vessels; Torpedo Gunboats, Depot Ships and Fuel Ships.

1940-48:   Submarines

1948:   Minelayers

N01

Ettrick	1903	Destroyer	12.14 - 9.15
Alecto	1911	Depot Ship	1.18 - ....
Essex Queen	1897	Aux MS	1939 - 1940
Apollo	1943	Minelayer	1948 - 1962

N02

Moy	1904	Destroyer	12.14 - 9.15
Alouette	1894	ABS	1.18 - ....
Hazard	1937	MS	1937 - 1940

N03

Swale	1905	Destroyer	12.14 - 9.15
Glatton	1914	CDS	9.15 - 1.18
Andromache	1890	Minelayer	1.18 - 4.18
Achilles	1905	Cruiser	4.18 - 1921
Fitzroy	1919	MS	1939 - 1940
Whitethroat RCN	1944	Trawler	1948 - 1949

N04

Arun	1903	Destroyer	12.14 - 9.15
Crescent	1892	Pro. Cruiser	9.15 - 1.18
Angora	1911	Minelayer	1.18 - 11.19
Flinders	1919	MS	1939 - 1940

N05

Exe	1903	Destroyer	12.14 - 9.15
Edgar	1890	Cruiser	9.15 - 1.18
Apollo	1891	Minelayer	1.18 - ....
Kellet	1919	MS	1939 - 1940

N06

Itchen	1903	Destroyer	12.14 - 9.15
Forth	1886	Depot Ship	9.15 - 1.18
Aquarius	1900	Depot Ship	1.18 - 4.18
Active	1911	Cruiser	4.18 - 7.19
Salford	1919	MS	7.19 - 11.19
Alresford	1919	MS	1939 - 1940

N07

Liffey	1904	Destroyer	12.14 - 9.15
Onyx	1892	Depot Ship	9.15 - 1.18
Ark Royal	1914	Seaplane Car	1.18 - 4.18
Africa	1905	Battleship	4.18 - 1920

Beaumaris	1940	MS	1939 - 1940

N08

Stour	1905	Destroyer	1914 - 9.15
Pactolus	1896	Depot Ship	9.15 - 1.18
Arrogant	1896	Depot Ship	1.18 - ....
Argo	1900	Store Ship	1919 - 1921

N09

Cynthia	1898	Destroyer	12.14 - 9.15
Viscol	1916	Oiler	4.16 - 1.18
Bacchante	1901	Cruiser	1.18 - 1920
Cromarty	1941	MS	1939 - 1940
Thames Queen	1939	MS	.... - ....

N10

Garry	1905	Destroyer	12.14 - 9.15
Royal Arthur	1891	Cruiser	9.15 - 1.18
Biarritz	1915	Minelayer	1.18 - 4.18
Cochrane	1905	Cruiser	4.18 - 11.18
Alecto	1911	Depot Ship	1935 - 1940?

N11

Brazen	1896	Destroyer	12.14 - 9.15
Creosol	1916	Tanker	1.16 - 1.18
Bonaventure	1892	Depot Ship	1.18 - 4.20
Bramble	1938	MS	1938 - 1940
Miner I (ex M1)	1939	Minelayer	1948 - 1962
Minstrel (ex Miner I)	1939	Minelayer	1962 - 1967

N12

Ure	1904	Destroyer	12.14 - 9.15
Redoubtable	1892	Battleship	9.15 - 1.18
Bouncer	1886	Tender	1.18 - ....
Ravenswood	1941	MS	1939 - 1940
Miner II (ex M2)	1939	Minelayer	1948 - 1949
Gossamer (ex Miner II)	1939	Minelayer	1949 - 1970

N13

Aquarius	1900	Depot Ship	9.15 - 1.18
Argo	1900	Store Ship	.... - ....
Miner III (ex M3)	1939	Minelayer	1948 - 1972

N14			
Doon	1903	Destroyer	12.14 - 9.15
Theseus	1892	Cruiser	9.15 - 1.18
Brilliant	1891	Cruiser	1.18 - 4.18
Boston	1940	MS	1939 - 1940
Miner IV (ex M4)	1940	Minelayer	1948 - 1964

N15			
Humber	1913	Monitor	1914 - 4.15
Leander	1882	Depot Ship	9.15 - 1.18
Campania	1893	Seaplane Car	1.18 - 11.18
Blyth	1940	MS	1939 - 1940
Miner V (ex M5)	1942	Minelayer	1948 - 1960
Britannic (ex *Miner V*)	1942	Minelayer	1960 - 1970

N16			
Brilliant	1891	Cruiser	9.15 - 11.17
Canning	1896	Kite Balloon	1.18 - ....
Glen Gower	1922	MS	1939 - 1942
Miner VI (ex M6)	1942	Minelayer	1948 - 1966
Minor Eagle (ex *Miner VI*)	1942	Minelayer	1966 - 1976

N17			
Fervent	1895	Destroyer	12.14 - 9.15
Endymion	1891	Cruiser	9.15 - 1.18
Canopus	1897	Battleship	1.18 - 1920
Speedy	1938	MS	1938 - 1940
Miner VII (ex M7 ii)	1944	Minelayer	1948 - 1959
Steady (ex *Miner VII*)	1944	Minelayer	1959 - 1981

N18			
Jason	1892	Torpedo Gb	9.15 - 4.17
Carcass	1905	Tug	1.18 - 5.19
Selkirk	1918	MS	1939 - 1940
Miner VIII (ex M8)	1943	Minelayer	1948 - 1963
Mindful (ex *Miner VIII*)	1943	Minelayer	1963 - 1965

N19			
Porcupine	1895	Destroyer	12.14 - 9.15
Gibraltar	1892	Cruiser	9.15 - 1.18
Carmania II	1907	Trawler	1.18 - ....
Devonshire	1904	Cruiser	4.18 - 1921
Rothesay	1941	MS	1939 - 1940

N20			
Sirius	1890	Cruiser	9.15 - 1.18
Ceylon	1899	Tug	1.18 - 3.19
Folkestone	1930	MS	1939 - 1940
Sandown	1939	Survey Sp	.... - ....

N21			
Coquette	1897	Destroyer	12.14 - 9.15
Joanetta	1911	Tug	9.15 - 1.18
Charybdis	1893	Cruiser	1.18 - 4.18
Intrepid	1891	Minelayer	4.18 - Sunk
Abdiel	1967	Minelayer	1967 - 1988

N22			
Andromache	1890	Minelayer	9.15 - 1.18
Charm	1902	Tug	1.18 - 11.19
Britomart	1938	MS	1938 - 1940
Dabchick	1942	Minelayer	1948 - 1954

N23			
Lightning	1895	Destroyer	12.14 - 6.15
Grafton	1892	Cruiser	9.15 - 1.18
Chester III	1909	Tug	1.18 - 5.19
Abingdon	1918	MS	1939 - 1940
Adventure	1924	Minelayer	1948 - Sold

N24			
Patrol	1904	Cruiser	9.15 - 1.18
Chichester	1895	Tug	1.18 - 5.19
Hebe	1936	MS	1936 - 1940

N25			
Derwent	1903	Destroyer	12.14 - 9.15
Antelope	1893	Torpedo Gb	9.15 - 1.18
Chub	1909	Tug	1.18 - 6.18
Shannon	1906	Cruiser	6.18 - ....
Scarborough	1930	Sloop	1939 - 1940
Stonechat	1944	Trawler	1948 - 1967

N26			
Teviot	1903	Destroyer	12.14 - 9.15
Foresight	1904	Cruiser	9.15 - 1.18
Circe	1892	Torpedo Gb	1.18 - ....
Glen Usk	1914	Aux MS	.... - ....
Plover	1937	Minelayer	1948 - 1968

N27			
Iphigenia	1891	Minelayer	9.15 - 1.18
Codfish	1915	Tug	1.18 - 1.20
Blackpool	1940	MS	1939 - 1940

N28			
Carol	1913	Tanker	1914 - 9.15
Leda	1892	Torpedo Gb	9.15 - 1.18
Commonweal	1902	Tug	1.18 - 4.18
Donegal	1902	Cruiser	4.18 - 1920

N29			
Canopus	1897	Battleship	1914 - 1.18
Crescent	1892	Cruiser	1.18 - ....
Armentieres RCN	1917	Trawler	.... - 1940

N30

Intrepid	1891	Minelayer	1914 - 9.15
Cruden Bay	1899	Tug	1.18 - 1.20
Queen of Thanet	1916	Aux MS	1939 - 1940

N31

St George	1892	Depot Ship	1914 - 9.15
Daisy	1911	Trawler	1.18 - 3.20
Stornoway	1941	MS	1939 - 1940
Redshank (ex *Turbot*)	1942	Minelayer	1948 - 1957

N32

Rother	1904	Destroyer	12.14 - 9.15
Hermione	1893	Cruiser	9.15 - 1.18
Diadem	1896	Cruiser	1.18 - 1921
Tedworth	1917	MS	1939 - 1940

N33

Scotia	1902	ABS	9.15 - 1.18
Diamond	1904	Cruiser	1.18 - 4.18
Duke of Edinburgh	1904	Cruiser	6.18 - 1920
Stoke	1918	MS	1939 - 1940

N34

Test	1905	Destroyer	12.14 - 9.15
Princess Louise	1912	SSV	9.15 - 1.18
Diana	1895	Cruiser	1.18 - 4.18
Roxburgh	1904	Cruiser	4.18 - ....
Tenby	1941	MS	1939 - 1940

N35

Alecto	1911	Depot Ship	9.15 - 1.18
Doria	1909	Tug	1.18 - 1.19
Nootka RCN	1938	Trawler	1939 - 1940
Blackbird	1943	Minelayer	1948 - Sold

N36

Venerable	1899	Battleship	4.18 - 1920
Apollo	1891	Minelayer	1914 - 1.18
Doris	1896	Cruiser	1.18 - ....
Rhyl	1940	MS	1939 - 1940

N37

Juno	1895	Cruiser	9.15 - 1.18
Dragon	1893	Tug	1.18 - 1.19
Pangbourne	1918	MS	1939 - 1940

N38

Empress	1907	SplCar	9.15 - 1.18
Edgar	1890	Cruiser	1.18 - 4.18
Essex	1901	Cruiser	4.18 - ....
Skipjack	1934	MS	.... - 1940

N39

Bacchante	1901	Cruiser	1914 - 1.18

Empress	1907	SplCar	1.18 - 4.18
Albemarle	1901	Battleship	4.18 - 1919
Elgin	1919	MS	1939 - 1940
Abdiel	1940	Minelayer	.... - ....

N40

Cressy	1899	Cruiser	1914 - 9.14
Angora	1911	Minelayer	4.15 - 1.18
Endeavour	1912	Survey	1.18 - 4.18
Britannia	1904	Battleship	4.18 - 11.18
Fermoy	1919	MS	1939 - 1940

N41

Bonaventure	1892	Depot Ship	1914 - 9.15
Endymion	1891	Cruiser	1.18 - 4.18
London	1899	Battleship	4.18 - 1920
Albury	1918	MS	1939 - 1940

N42

Eden	1903	Destroyer	12.14 - 9.15
Tara	1900	ABS	9.15 - 1.16
Engadine	1911	SplCar	1.18 - 1919
Halcyon	1933	MS	1933 - 1940

N43

Thames	1885	Depot Ship	1914 - 9.15
Esther	1911	Trawler	1.18 - 9.19
Westward Ho!	1894	Aux MS	1939 - 1940

N44

Foyle	1903	Destroyer	12.14 - 9.15
Bullfrog	1881	BDV	1.16 - 1.18
Euryalus	1901	Cruiser	1.18 - 1920
Exmouth	1901	Battleship	4.18 - 1920
Lydd	1918	MS	1939 - 1940

N45

Kale	1904	Destroyer	12.14 - 9.15
Hearty	1885	Survey	9.15 - 1.18
Foremost	1913	Tug	1.18 - 11.19
Ross	1919	MS	1939 - 1940

N46

Prince of Wales	1902	Battleship	4.18 - 1920
Endeavour	1912	Survey	9.15 - 1.18
Foresight	1904	Cruiser	1.18 - 1920
Festubert RCN	1917	Trawler	.... - 1940

N47

Kestrel	1898	Destroyer	12.14 - 9.15
Foremost	1913	Tug	9.15 - 1.18
Forth	1886	Depot Ship	1.18 - 11.21
Sidmouth	1941	MS	1939 - 1940

N48			
Albion	1898	Battleship	9.15 - 1.18
Forward	1904	Cruiser	1.18 - 1921
Implacable	1899	Battleship	4.18 - 1921
Medway Queen	1924	Aux MS	1939 - 1940
N49			
Cygnet	1898	Destroyer	12.14 - 9.15
Latona	1890	Minelayer	9.15 - 1.18
Gibraltar	1892	Cruiser	1.18 - ....
Aberdare	1918	MS	1939 - 1940
N50			
Vulture	1898	Destroyer	12.14 - 9.15
Diadem	1896	Cruiser	9.15 - 1.18
Glatton	1914	CDS	1.18 - 9.18
Bridport	1940	MS	1939 - 1940
N51			
Euryalus	1901	Cruiser	9.15 - 1.18
Gorgon	1914	CDS	1.18 - ....
Waverley	1899	Aux MS	1939 - 1940
N52			
Hebe	1892	Depot Ship	1914 - 9.15
Gossamer	1890	Gunboat	1.18 - ....
Dunoon	1919	MS	1939 - 1940
N53			
Forward	1904	Cruiser	1914 - 9.15
Grafton	1892	Cruiser	1.18 - 4.18
Duncan	1901	Battleship	4.18 - 1920
Dunbar	1941	MS	1939 - 1940
N54			
Goliath	1898	Battleship	1914 - 5.15
Alouette	1894	ABS	7.15 - 1.18
Hannibal	1896	Battleship	1.18 - 1920
Moresby RAN	1918	MS	.... - ....
N55			
Electra	1896	Destroyer	12.14 - 5.15
Codfish	1915	Tug	9.15 - 1.18
Hearty	1885	Survey Ship	1.18 - 11.20
Widnes	1918	MS	1939 - 1940
N56			
Ocean	1898	Battleship	1914 - 9.15
Charm	1902	Tug	9.15 - 1.18
Hebe	1892	Depot Ship	1.18 - 10.19
Huntley	1919	MS	1939 - 1940
N57			
Vengeance	1899	Battleship	9.15 - 1.18
Hermione	1893	Cruiser	1.18 - ....

Bagshot	1918	MS	1939 - 1940
N58			
Erne	1903	Destroyer	12.14 - 2.15
Cruden Bay	1899	Tug	9.15 - 1.18
Highflyer	1898	Cruiser	1.18 - 4.18
Antrim	1903	Cruiser	4.18 - ....
Saltburn	1918	MS	1939 - 1940
N59			
Hogue	1900	Cruiser	1914 - 9.14
Paris	1913	Minelayer	1914 - 1.18
Intrepid	1891	Minelayer	1.18 - 4.18
Peterhead	1940	MS	1939 - 1940
N60			
Recruit	1896	Destroyer	12.14 - 5.15
Wave	1914	SSV	9.15 - 1..18
Iphigenia	1891	Minelayer	1.18 - 4.18
Dundalk	1919	MS	1939 - 1940
N61			
Diamond	1904	Cruiser	1914 - 9.15
Isis	1896	Cruiser	1.18 - 1920
Harrow	1918	MS	1939 - 1940
N62			
Carcass	1905	Tug	1914 - 9.15
Old Colony	1907	Minelayer	1.18 - ....
Saltash	1918	MS	1939 - 1940
N63			
Cerberus	1889	Tug	1914 - 1.16
Dragon	1893	Tug	1.16 - 1.18
Joanetta	1911	Tug	1.18 - 1919
Gossamer	1937	MS	1937 - 1940
N64			
Ceylon	1899	Tug	1914 - 1.18
Jupiter	1895	Battleship	1.18 - 2.18
Comox RCN	1938	Trawler	1939 - 1940
N65			
Chester	1909	Tug	1914 - 1.18
Juno	1895	Cruiser	1.18 - 1920
Sutlej	1899	Cruiser	4.18 - 1920
Bridlington	1940	MS	1939 - 1940
Ariadne	1943	Minelayer	1948 - 1962
Apollo	1943	Minelayer	.... - ....
N66			
Cambria	1897	ABS	8.14 - 9.15
Chichester	1895	Tug	9.15 - 1.18
King Emperor	1914	Trawler	1.18 - 4.18
Hibernia	1905	Battleship	4.18 - 1921

N67

Hindustan	1903	Battleship	4.18 - 1921
Chub	1909	Tug	1914 - 1.18
Latona	1890	Minelayer	1.18 - ....
Llandudno	1941	MS	1939 - 1940

N68

Boyne	1904	Destroyer	12.14 - 9.15
Gossamer	1890	Gunboat	9.15 - 1.18
Leander	182	Depot Ship	1.18 - 7.20
Sharpshooter	1936	MS	1936 - 1940

N69

Ouse	1905	Destroyer	12.14 - 9.15
Highflyer	1898	Cruiser	9.15 - 1.18
Leda	1892	Torpedo Gb	1.18 - ....
Sphinx	1939	MS	1939 - 1940
Linnet	1938	Minelayer	1948 - 1964

N70

Vulcan	1889	Depot Ship	9.15 - 1.18
Manxman	1904	Ac Carrier	1.18 - 6.18
Diamond	1904	Cruiser	6.18 - 1921
Ypres RCN	1917	Trawler	1938 - 1940
Manxman	1940	Minelayer	1948 - 1972

N71

Pandora	1902	Depot Ship	1914 - 1.18
Naiad	1890	Minelayer	1.18 - ....
Widgeon	1904	River Gb	11.19 - ....
Harrier	1934	MS	1934 - 1940

N72

Sapphire	1904	Cruiser	9.15 - 1.18
Nairana	1917	Seaplane Car	1.18 - ....
Teal	1901	River Gb	11.19 - ....

N73

Sentinel	1904	Cruiser	1914 - 1.18
Neptor	1915	Tug	1.18 - 6.18
Minotaur	1906	Cruiser	6.18 - 1920
Niger	1936	MS	1936 - 1940

N74

Sutlej	1899	Cruiser	9.15 - 1.18
Nettle	1902	Tender	1.18 - ....
Queen of Kent	1916	Accom Ship	1939 - 1940

N75

Triton	1907	Trawler	9.15 - 1.18
Onyx	1892	Depot Ship	1.18 - 4.20
Duchess of Cornwall	1896	Aux MS	NTU

N76

Tyne	1878	Depot Ship	9.15 - 1.18
Orvieto	1909	Minelayer	1.18 - 4.18
Rye	1940	MS	1939 - 1940

N77

Nith	1905	Destroyer	12.14 - 9.15
Neptor	1915	Tug	1.16 - 1.18
Pactolus	1896	Depot Ship	1.18 - ....
Rocksand	1918	MS	9.19 - ....
Romney	1940	MS	1939 - 1940

N78

Sapphire	1904	Cruiser	1914 - 9.15
Daisy	1911	Trawler	9.15 - 1.18
Pandora	1902	Depot Ship	1.18 - ....
Sutton	1918	MS	1939 - 1940

N79

Waveney	1903	Destroyer	12.14 - 9.15
Paris	1913	Minelayer	1.18 - ....
Cicero	1918	MS	9.19 - ....
Scott	1938	MS	1938 - 1940

N80

Ark Royal	1914	Seaplane Car	9.15 - 1.18
Patrol	1904	Cruiser	1.18 - 1920
Britannia	1896	Aux AA	1940 - 1942

N81

Ness	1905	Destroyer	12.14 - 9.15
Circe	1892	Torpedo Gb	9.15 - 1.18
Princess Louise	1912	SSV	1.18 - ....
Investigator RIN	1925	Survey Ship	1939 - ....

N82

Wallaroo	1890	Cruiser	9.15 - 1.18
Princess Margaret	1914	Minelayer	1.18 - ....
Hussar	1934	MS	1934 - 1940

N83

Esther	1911	Trawler	9.15 - 1.18
Ironsides	....	Yacht	9.18 - 3.20
Gleaner	1937	MS	1937 - 1940

N84

Redoubtable	1892	Battleship	1.18 - 1919
Proserpine	1896	Cruiser	1.18 - 11.19
Franklin	1937	MS	1937 - 1940

N85

Riviera	1911	Seaplane Car	9.15 - 9.18
Highflyer	1898	Cruiser	9.18 - 1921
Seagull	1937	MS	1937 - 1940

N86			
Zephyr	1895	Destroyer	12.14 - 9.15
Royal Arthur	1891	Cruiser	1.18 - ....
Salamander	1936	MS	1936 - 1940
N87			
Lyons	1885	Salvage Vsl	9.15 - 1.16
Ruthenia	1900	Water Carrier	1.16 - 1.18
Russell II	1906	Trawler	1.18 - ....
Speedwell	1935	MS	1935 - 1940
N88			
Ferol	1914	Oiler	1914 - 9.15
St George	1892	Depot Ship	1.18 - 6.18
Commonwealth	1903	Battleship	6.18 - 1921
Triad	1909	Yacht	1919 - ....
Fundy RCN	1938	Trawler	1938 - 1940
N89			
Servitor	1914	Oiler	1914 - 9.15
Sapphire	1904	Cruiser	1.18 - 6.18
Zealandia	1904	Battleship	6.18 - 1921
Fareham	1918	MS	1939 - 1940
N90			
Cherwell	1903	Destroyer	12.14 - 9.15
Reliance	1910	Store Carrier	9.15 - 1.16
Scotia	1902	ABS	1.18 - 4.18
Dominion	1903	Battleship	4.18 - 1921
Derby	1918	MS	1939 - 1940
N91			
Engadine	1911	SplCar	9.15 - 1.18
Scott	1913	Trawler	1.18 - ....
Swindon	1918	MS	7.19 - 11.19
Endeavour	1912	Survey	1939 - 1940
N92			
Mercedes	1902	Collier	1908 - 1920
Wear	1905	Destroyer	1914 - 9.15
Petroleum	1902	Oiler	9.15 - 1.16
Sentinel	1904	Cruiser	1.18 - ....
Aerolite	1880	Yacht	9.18 - ....
City of Rochester	1904	Aux AA	1939 - 1940
N93			
Trefoil	1913	Oiler	1914 - 9.15
Shackleton	1913	Trawler	1.18 - ....
Leda	1937	MS	1937 - 1940
N94			
Turmoil	1917	Oiler	9.15 - 4.17
Nairana	1917	Seaplane Car	4.17 - 1.18
Sirius	1890	Cruiser	1.18 - 4.18
Sigismund	1897	ABS	9.18 - 3.19

Gaspe RCN	1938	Trawler	1938 - 1940
N95			
Dee	1903	Destroyer	12.14 - 9.15
Maine II	1906	Hospital Ship	9.15 - 1.16
Skirmisher	1904	Cruiser	1.18 - 9.18
Rosita	1900	Yacht	9.18 - ....
Ilfracombe	1941	MS	1939 - 1940
N96			
Burma	1911	Oiler	1914 - 9.15
Argus	1917	Ac Carrier	1919 - 9.19
Research	1939	Survey Ship	1939 - ....
N97			
Attendant	1913	Oiler	1914 - 9.15
Thames	1885	Depot Ship	1.18 - 11.20
Polruan	1940	MS	1939 - 1940
N98			
Carol	1913	Oiler	1914 - 9.15
Theseus	1892	Cruiser	1.18 - ....
Pinner	1919	MS	6.19 - 11.19
Challenger	1931	Survey Sp	.... - ....
N99			
Commonweal	1902	Tug	2.15 - 1.18
Triton	1907	Trawler	1.18 - 1919
Jason	1937	MS	1937 - 1940
N0A			
Shackleton	1913	Trawler	9.15 - 1.18
Tyne	1878	Depot Ship	1.18 - 11.20
N1A			
Carmania II	1907	Trawler	9.15 - 1.18
Vengeance	1899	Battleship	1.18 - 1921
Isinglass	1919	MS	11.19 - ....
N2A			
Scott	1913	Trawler	9.15 - 10.15
Vienna	1894	ABS	1.18 - 8.19
N3A			
Russell II	1906	Trawler	9.15 - 1.18
Vindex	1905	Seaplane Car	1.18 - 1920
Marazion	1919	MS	6.19 - 11.19
Dunoon	1919	MS	11.19 - ....
N4A			
Welbeck	1915	Trawler	9.15 - 1.18
Vulcan	1889	Depot Ship	1.18 - ....
Marazion	1919	MS	11.19 - ....

N5A			
King Emperor	1914	Trawler	9.15 - 1.18
Wahine	1913	Minelayer	1.18 - ....
Swindon	1918	MS	11.19 - ....

N6A			
Wallaroo	1890	Cruiser	9.15 - 1.16
Steadfast	1906	Mooring Vsl	1.16 - 1.18
Wallaroo	1890	Cruiser	1.18 - ....
Moorhen	1901	River Gb	11.19 - ....

N7A			
Limpet	1912	Mooring Vsl	1.16 - 1.18
Wave	1914	Tender	1.18 - ....
Fermoy	1919	MS	7.19 - ....
Appledore	1919	MS	11.19 - 10.20

N8A			
Holdfast	1910	Mooring Vsl	1.16 - 1.18
Welbeck	1915	Trawler	1.18 - ....
Bradfield	1919	MS	11.19 - ....

N9A			
Fidget	1915	Mooring Vsl	1.16 - 1.18
Pegasus	1917	Seaplane Car	1.18 - ....
Alexander	1916	Icebreaker	11.19 - 1921

N0C			
Woodlark	1898	River Gb	11.19 - ....
N9C			
Abingdon	1918	MS	11.19 - ....

NA0			
Ormonde	1918	MS	8.19 - 11.19
Fermoy	1919	MS	11.19 - ....

NA1			
Sefton	1918	MS	8.19 - 11.19
Instow	1919	MS	11.19 - ....

NA2			
Longford	1919	MS	11.19 - ....

NA3			
Minoru	1919	MS	8.19 - 11.19
Monaghan	1919	MS	11.19 - ....

NA4			
Instow	1919	MS	8.19 - 11.19
Ross	1919	MS	11.19 - ....

NA5			
Salford	1919	MS	11.19 - ....
NA6			
Wem	1919	MS	11.19 - ....
NA7			
Wexford	1919	MS	11.19 - ....
NA8			
Sviatogor	1915	Icebreaker	11.19 - 11.21
NC0			
Banchory	1918	MS	11.19 - ....
NN3			
Alexander	1916	Icebreaker	10.19 - 11.19
NN4			
Sviatogor	1915	Icebreaker	10.19 - 11.19
NN5			
Snipe	1897	River Gb	11.19 - ....
NN8			
Nightingale	1897	River Gb	11.19 - ....

Flag 'P' Superior

Pre 1940: Cruisers, Coast Defence Ships, Destroyers, Boom Defence Vessels; Patrol Vessels. River Gunboats, Seaplane Carriers, Minelayers. (Various pendants superior and inferior were used to increase number range)

1940-48: Submarines; DCMB; CT Target Boats

1948: Coastal Forces

P00			
Amethyst	1903	Cruiser	9.15 - 1.18
Adamant	1911	Depot Ship	1.18 - ....
P01			
Greyhound	1900	Destroyer	12.14 - 9.15
Mars	1896	Battleship	9.15 - 1.18
Adventure	1904	Cruiser	1.18 - 1920
P02			
Kangaroo	1900	Destroyer	12.14 - 9.15
Caesar	1896	Battleship	9.15 - 1.18
Amethyst	1903	Cruiser	1.18 - 1920
P03			
Attentive	1904	Cruiser	1914 - 9.15
Aphis	1915	River Gb	1.18 - ....
P04			
Cornwall	1902	Cruiser	9.15 - 1.18
Argonaut	1898	Cruiser	1.18 - 1920
P05			
Dido	1896	Depot Ship	1914 - 9.15
Swiftsure	1903	Battleship	1.18 - 1920
Rosalind	1941	Trawler	1948 - 1962
P06			
Europa	1897	Cruiser	1914 - 9.15
Attentive	1904	Cruiser	1.18 - 1920
P07			
Star	1896	Destroyer	12.14 - 9.15
Challenger	1902	Cruiser	9.15 - 1.18
Bee	1915	River Gb	1.18 - ....
P08			
Glory	1899	Battleship	9.15 - 1.18
Berwick	1902	Cruiser	1.18 - 1920
P09			
Drake	1901	Cruiser	9.15 - 10.17

Blackcock	1886	Tug	1.18 - Sunk
P10			
King Alfred	1901	Cruiser	9.15 - 1.18
Caesar	1896	Battleship	1.18 - 1921
Signet	1939	BDV	1948 - 1958
P11			
P.11	1915	Patrol Boat	9.15 - 1921
Reigate	1918	BDV	1948 - 1958
P12			
P.12	1915	Patrol Boat	9.15 - 11.18
Lahore RIN	1941	Trawler	1948 - ....
P13			
Cheerful	1897	Destroyer	12.14 - 9.15
P.13	1916	Patrol Boat	9.15 - 8.17
(*P.13* renamed *P.75* in 1917)			
P14			
Albacore	1906	Destroyer	12.14 - 9.15
P.14	1916	Patrol Boat	9.15 - 1923
P15			
Racehorse	1900	Destroyer	12.14 - 9.15
P.15	1916	Patrol Boat	9.15 - 1921
P16			
Good Hope	1901	Cruiser	1914 - 11.14
P.16	1916	Patrol Boat	9.15 - 1921
Barcombe	1938	BDV	1948 - 1958
P17			
Hermione	1893	Cruiser	1914 - 9.15
P.17	1915	Patrol Boat	9.15 - 1921
Colne	1918	Trawler	1948 - ....
P18			
P.18	1916	Patrol Boat	9.15 - 1921

P19

P.19	1916	Patrol Boat	9.15 - 1923
Falconet	1938	BDV	1948 - 1958

P20

Diadem	1896	Cruiser	1914 - 9.15
P.20	1916	Patrol Boat	9.15 - 1923

P21

P.21	1916	Patrol Boat	9.15 - 1921

P22

P.22	1916	Patrol Boat	9.15 - 1923

P23

Gipsy	1897	Destroyer	12.14 - 9.15
P.23	1916	Patrol Boat	9.15 - 1923

P24

Conflict	1894	Destroyer	12.14 - 9.15
P.24	1915	Patrol Boat	9.15 - 1921
Medoc ORP	1930	Aux Pat Vsl	7.40 - 11.40

P25

Angler	1897	Destroyer	12.14 - 9.15
P.25	1916	Patrol Boat	9.15 - 1921
Pomerol ORP	1930	Aux Pat Vsl	1940 - 1941

P26

Crane	1896	Destroyer	12.14 - 9.15
P.26	1915	Patrol Boat	9.15 - 4.17
Sheldrake	1937	Sloop	1937 -1939
Lilac	1930	Trawler	1948 - ....

P27

Kent	1901	Cruiser	1914 - 9.15
P.27	1915	Patrol Boat	9.15 - 1923

P28

Leviathan	1901	Cruiser	1914 - 9.15
P.28	1916	Patrol Boat	9.15 - 1923
Locust	1939	River Gb	1948 - ....

P29

Topaze	1903	Cruiser	1914 - 9.15
P.29	1915	Patrol Boat	9.15 - 1923

P30

Surly	1894	Destroyer	12.14 - 9.15
P.30	1916	Patrol Boat	9.15 - 1923
Dipper	1943	Tug	1948

P31

Falcon	1899	Destroyer	12.14 - 9.15
P.31	1916	Patrol Boat	9.15 - 1926
Diver	1943	Tug	1948

P32

Minerva	1895	Cruiser	1914 - 9.15
P.32	1916	Patrol Boat	9.15 - 1921
Kittiwake	1936	Sloop	1936 - 1939

P33

Leven	1898	Destroyer	12.14 - 9.15
P.33	1916	Patrol Boat	9.15 - 1921
Tui RNZN	1941	Trawler	1948 - 1967

P34

Stag	1899	Destroyer	12.14 - 9.15
P.34	1916	Patrol Boat	9.15 - 1921
Mallard	1936	Sloop	1936 - 1939

P35

Mermaid	1898	Destroyer	12.14 - 9.15
P.35	1916	Patrol Boat	9.15 - 1923
Puffin	1936	Sloop	1936 - 1939

P36

Venus	1895	Cruiser	19.14 - 9.15
Kingfisher	1935	Sloop	1935 - 1939

P37

Adamant	1911	Depot Ship	9.15 - 1.18
Fumarole	1918	BDV	1948 - ....

P38

Hazard	1894	Depot Ship	1914 - 9.15

P39

Maidstone	1912	Depot Ship	9.15 - 1.18
Shearwater	1939	Sloop	Pre build
Halo	1918	BDV	.... - ....

P40

Fairy	1897	Destroyer	12.14 - 9.15
Illustrious	1896	Battleship	9.15 - 1.18
Bern	1942	WDV	1948 - 1956

P41

Sappho	1891	Cruiser	9.15 - 1.18
P.41	1917	Patrol Boat	1.18 - 1922
Tiree	1941	Trawler	1948 - 1955

P42

Arrogant	1896	Depot Ship	1914 - 9.15
PC.42	1917	Patrol Boat	1.18 - 1921

P43

Nettle	1902	Tender	9.15 - 1.18
PC.43	1917	Patrol Boat	1.18 - 1923
Fetlar	1941	Trawler	1948 - 1950

P44

Bouncer	1886	Tender	9.15 - 1.18
PC.44	1917	Patrol Boat	1.18 - 1923
Lindisfarne	1943	Trawler	1948 - ....

P45

Velox	1902	Destroyer	12.14 - 9.15
Hannibal	1896	Battleship	9.15 - 1.18
P.45	1917	Patrol Boat	1.18 - 1923
Damsay	1942	Trawler	1948 - 1956

P46

Princess Margaret	1914	Minelayer	9.15 - 1.18
P.46	1917	Patrol Boat	1.18 - 1925
Berberis	1928	Trawler	1948 - Sold

P47

Princess Irene	1914	Minelayer	1.15 - 5.15
Doris	1896	Cruiser	9.15 - 1.18
P.47	1917	Patrol Boat	1.18 - 1925
Sonnet	1939	BDV	1948 - 1959

P48

Biarritz	1915	Minelayer	3.15 - 1.18
P.48	1917	Patrol Boat	1.18 - 1923

P49

Ben-My-Chree	1908	Seaplane Car	9.15 - 1.17
P.49	1917	Patrol Boat	1.18 - 1923
Trondra	1941	Trawler	1948 - ....

P50

Desperate	1896	Destroyer	12.14 - 9.15
Jupiter	1895	Battleship	9.15 - 1.18
P.50	1916	Patrol Boat	1.18 - 1921
Planet	1938	BDV	1948 - 1958

P51

Latona	1890	Minelayer	1914 - 9.15
Polavon	1905	Distill Ship	9.15 - 1.18
PC.51	1916	Patrol Boat	1.18 - 1923

P52

Naiad	1890	Minelayer	1914 - 1.18
P.52	1916	Patrol Boat	1.18 - 1923

P53

Orvieto	1909	Minelayer	1.15 - 1.18
P.53	1917	Patrol Boat	1.18 - 1924

P54

Campania	1893	Seaplane Car	9.15 - 1.18
P.54	1917	Patrol Boat	1.18 - 1924

P55

Revenge	1892	Battleship	1914 - 9.15
Skirmisher	1904	Cruiser	9.15 - 1.18
PC.55	1917	Patrol Boat	1.18 - 1922
Steepholm	1943	Trawler	1948 - 1960

P56

Ostrich	1900	Destroyer	12.14 - 9.15
Charybdis	1893	Cruiser	9.15 - 1.18
PC.56	1917	Patrol Boat	1.18 - 1923

P57

Vienna	1894	ABS	4.15 - 1.18
P.57	1917	Patrol Boat	1.18 - 1920

P58

Diana	1895	Cruiser	9.15 - 1.18
P.58	1918	Patrol Boat	1.18 - 1921
Woodbridge Haven	1945	Depot Ship	1948 - 1965

P59

Gorgon	1914	CDS	9.15 - 1.18
P.59	1917	Patrol Boat	1.18 - 1938
Scarab	1915	River Gb	1948 - 1948

P60

Isis	1896	Cruiser	9.15 - 1.18
PC.60	1917	Patrol Boat	1.18 - 1924

P61

Talbot	1895	Cruiser	9.15 - 1.18
PC.61	1917	Patrol Boat	1.18 - 1923
Amritsar RIN	1941	Trawler	1948 - 1950

P62

Mersey	1913	Monitor	1914 - 9.15
Wyandra	1901	Decoy	9.15 - 1.18
PC.62	1917	Patrol Boat	1.18 - 1921
Widgeon	1938	Sloop	1938 - 1939

P63

Harrier	1893	Torpedo Gb	9.15 - 1.18
PC.63	1917	Patrol Boat	1.18 - 1923
Plantaganet	1939	BDV	1948 - 1959

P64

Adventure	1904	Cruiser	9.15 - 1.18
P.64	1917	Patrol Boat	1.18 - 1923

P65

Victorious	1895	Battleship	9.15 - 1.18
PC.65	1917	Patrol Boat	1.18 - 1923

P66

Bacchus	1915	Water Carrier	9.15 - 1.16

PC.66	1917	Patrol Boat	1.18 - 1923
P67			
Hungerford	1913	Distilling Sp	9.15 - 1.18
PC.67	1917	Patrol Boat	1.18 - 1921
P68			
Industry	1901	Stores Ship	9.15 - 1.18
PC.68	1917	Patrol Boat	1.18 - 1921
P69			
Ariadne	1898	Cruiser	9.15 - 1.18
PC.69	1917	Patrol Boat	1.18 - 1922
Koala RAN	1939	BDV	1948 - 1969
P70			
Terrible	1895	Cruiser	9.15 - 1.18
P71			
Farnborough	1904	Decoy Ship	1.16 - ....
Moorgate	1931	BDV	1948 - 1958
P72			
Syren	1900	Destroyer	12.14 - 9.15
Polshannon	1910	WTV	9.15 - 1.16
Cockchafer	1915	River Gb	1948 - 1949
P73			
Spiteful	1899	Destroyer	12.14 - 9.15
Leviathan	1901	Cruiser	9.15 - 1.18
P74			
Peterel	1899	Destroyer	12.14 - 9.15
Berwick	1902	Cruiser	9.15 - 1.18
P75			
Anglia	1900	ABS	8.14 - 4.15
Vindictive	1899	Cruiser	9.15 - 1.18
PC.75	1916	Patrol Boat	1.18 - 1923
P76			
Cambria	1897	ABS	8.14 - 8.15
Cumberland	1902	Cruiser	9.15 - 1.18
P77			
Diligence	1907	Depot Ship	1914 - 9.15
Hyderabad	1917	Decoy Ship	11.19 - ....
P78			
Argonaut	1898	Cruiser	1914 - 9.15
P79			
Zylpha	1894	Collier	1.16 - ....
P80			
Osprey	1897	Destroyer	12.14 - 9.15

Kent	1901	Cruiser	9.15 - 1.18
Carnarvon	1903	Cruiser	1.18 - ....
Hyderabad	1917	Decoy Ship	6.19 - 11.19
Kangaroo RAN	1940	BDV	1948 - 1966
P81			
Skipjack	1889	Torpedo Gb	9.15 - 1.18
Challenger	1902	Cruiser	1.18 - 1920
P82			
Cricket	1915	River Gb	1.16 - 1.18
Cicala	1915	River Gb	1.18 - ....
Nightingale	1931	Tender	1948 - ....
P83			
Myrmidon	1900	Destroyer	12.14 - 9.15
Magnificent	1894	Battleship	9.15 - 1.18
Cockchafer	1915	River Gb	1.18 - ....
Vesuvius	1932	Tender	1948 - ....
P84			
Olympia	1916	Oiler	1914 - 9.15
Cornwall	1902	Cruiser	1.18 - 1920
P85			
Thetis	1890	Minelayer	1914 - ....
Cricket	1915	River Gb	1.18 - ....
P86			
Flying Fish	1897	Destroyer	12.14 - 9.15
Prince George	1895	Battleship	9.15 - 1.18
Cumberland	1902	Cruiser	1.18 - ....
Indian Summer	1918	Drifter	1948 - Sold
P87			
Flirt	1897	Destroyer	12.14 - 9.15
Suffolk	1903	Cruiser	9.15 - 1.18
Dido	1896	Depot Ship	1.18 - ....
P88			
Research	1888	Depot Ship	9.15 - 1.18
Diligence	1907	Depot Ship	1.18 - ....
P89			
Speedwell	1889	Torpedo Gb	9.15 - 1.18
Guillemot	1939	Corvette	Pre build
P90			
Dryad	1893	Torpedo Gb	9.15 - 1.18
P91			
Waterwitch	1914	SSV	9.15 - 1.16
Europa	1897	Cruiser	1.18 - 1920
Whirlpool	1919	Drifter	1948 - ....

P92			
Mercedes	1902	Tanker	9.15 - 1.16
Glory	1899	Battleship	1.18 - 4.20

P93			
Isla	1903	Oiler	9.15 - 1.16
Glowworm	1916	River Gb	1.18 - ....
Birch	1939	Trawler	1948 - 1952

P94			
Fawn	1897	Destroyer	12.14 - 9.15
Glowworm	1916	River Gb	1.16 - 1.18
Gnat	1915	River Gb	1.18 - ....
Nettle	1933	Tender	1948 - ....

P95			
Kharki	1899	Oiler	9.15 - 1.16
Cockchafer	1915	River Gb	1.16 - 1.18
Harrier	1893	Torpedo Gb	1.18 - 2.20

P96			
Aphis	1915	River Gb	9.15 - 1.18
Hazard	1894	Depot Ship	1.18 - Sunk

P97			
Bat	1896	Destroyer	12.14 - 9.15
Gnat	1915	River Gb	9.15 - 1.18
Illustrious	1896	Battleship	1.18 - 4.19

P98			
Scarab	1915	River Gb	9.15 - 1.18
King Alfred	1901	Cruiser	1.18 - 1920

P99			
Bee	1915	River Gb	9.15 - 1.18
Kent	1901	Cruiser	1.18 - 1920

P100			
Blackthorn	1939	Trawler	1948 - Sold

P102			
Kiwi RNZN	1941	Trawler	1948 - 1949

P119			
Holly	1930	Trawler	1948 - Sold

P136			
Redwing	1933	Tender	1948 - 1957

P138			
Maple	1929	Trawler	1948 - Sold

P141			
Martinet	1938	BDV	1948 - 1958

P149			
Bahawalpur RPN	1942	Trawler	1948

P155			
Inchkeith RNZN	1941	Trawler	1948 - 1958

P160			
Sanda RNZN	1941	Trawler	1948 - 1958

P163			
Express	1988	PC	1994 -

P164			
Explorer	1986	PC	1994 -

P165			
Example	1985	PC	1994 -

P167			
Exploit	1988	PC	1994 -

P174			
Killegray RNZN	1941	Trawler	1948 - 1958

P175			
Scarba RNZN	1941	Trawler	1948 - 1958

P179			
Noontide	1918	Drifter	1948 - Sold

P190			
Laymoor	1959	BDV	1959 - 1984

P191			
Layburn	1960	BDV	1960 - 1978

P192			
Mandarin	1963	Mooring Vsl	1963 - 1992

P193			
Pintail	1963	Mooring Vsl	1963 - 1991

P194			
Garganey	1965	Mooring Vsl	1965 - 1995

P195			
Goldeneye	1966	Mooring Vsl	1966 - 1992

P196			
Goosander	1973	Mooring Vsl	1973 - 1995

P197			
Pochard	1973	Mooring Vsl	1973 - 1995

P200			
Barfoss	1942	BDV	1948 - 1968

P201			
Barbain	1940	BDV	1948 - 1971

P202			
Barfoot	1942	BDV	1948 - 1949

P203			
Barbrook	1938	BDV	1948 - 1958

P204			
Barhill	1942	BDV	1948 - 1970

P207			
Barcliff	1940	BDV	1948 - 1967

P209			
Barcastle	1938	BDV	1948 - 1962

P211			
Barholm	1942	BDV	1948 - 1962

P212			
Barcroft	1938	BDV	1948 - 1962

P214			
Barbecue	1944	BDV	1948 - 1970

P215			
Barndale	1939	BDV	1948 - 1970

P216

Barglow	1942	BDV	1948 - 1970

P217

Barilla	1943	BDV	1948 - 1958

P218

Barleycorn	1943	BDV	1948 - 1964

P219

Barmouth	1938	BDV	1948 - 1964

P222

Barbridge	1941	BDV	1948 - 1964
Forth	2016	OPV	2016 -

P223

Moorpout	1944	Mooring Vsl	1948 - ....
Medway	2017	OPV	2017 -

P224

Barspear	1943	BDV	1948 - 1962
Trent	2018	OPV	2018 -

P227

Barkis	1945	BDV	1948 - 1964

P232

Barmond	1942	BDV	1948 - 1974

P233

Burgonet	1939	BDV	1948 - 1958
Tamar	2018	OPV	2018 -

P234

Barova	1941	BDV	1948 - 1964
Spey	2019	OPV	2019 -

P235

Barthorpe	1940	BDV	1948 - 1963
BH7	1969	Hovercraft	1969 - 1985

P237

Barnaby	1943	BDV	1948 - 1964

P238

Barnehurst	1939	BDV	1948 - 1964

P239

Barlake	1940	BDV	1948 - 1963
Peacock	1982	OPV	1982 - 1997

P240

Barrhead	1940	BDV	1948 - 1964
Plover	1983	OPV	1983 - 1997

P241

Barnard	1942	BDV	1948 - 1970
Starling	1983	OPV	1983 - 1997

P242

Barbette II	1943	BDV	1948 - 1965
Swallow	1984	OPV	1984 - 1988

P243

Barbican	1938	BDV	1948 - 1968
Swift	1984	OPV	1984 - 1988

P244

Barfield	1938	BDV	1948 - 1970
Protector	1975	OPV	1983 - 1986

P245

Barneath	1942	BDV	1948 - 1958
Guardian	1975	OPV	1983 - 1986

P246

Barnwell	1940	BDV	1948 - 1958
Sentinel	1975	OPV	1984 - 1992

Sentinel (P246) was the fomer mercantile offshore supply vessel *Seaforth Warrior* purchased by the MoD in February 1983 for patrol duties around the Falkland Islands. She was subsequently commissioned as *Sentinel* on 14. 1.1984

P247

Baronia	1941	BDV	1948 - 1959

P248

Barlane	1938	BDV	1948 - 1958

P251

Baritone	1945	BDV	1948 - 1959

P252

Barcote	1940	BDV	1948 - 1963
Alert	1969	Tender	1975 - 1986
(ex *Loyal Governor*)			

Alert renamed *Lydford* (A251) in 1986.

P254

Barrage	1937	BDV	1948 - 1970
Vigilant	1970	Tender	1975 - 1986
(ex *Loyal Factor*)			

Vigilant renamed *Meavy* (A254) in 1986.

P256

Berar RIN	1942	Trawler	1948 - Sold
Cormorant	1976	PC	1985 - 1991

P257

Barberry	1943	BDV	1948 - 1958
Hart	1976	PC	1985 - 1991
Clyde	2006	OPV	2006 - 2020

Cormorant (P256) and *Hart* (P257) were former RAF RTTLs (*Sunderland* and *Stirling* respectively) based at Gibraltar. They were transferred to the Royal Navy, renamed and commissioned on 29.08.1985.

P258

Barwind	1942	BDV	1948 - 1964
Leeds Castle	1980	OPV	1980 - 2005

P259

Barrington	1940	BDV	1948 - 1969
Redpole	1967	PC	1985 - 1996

Redpole (P259) was the former RAF LRRSC *Sea Otter*. She was transferred to the RN in March 1985.

P260

Barlow	1938	BDV	1948 - 1958
Kingfisher	1974	PB	1974 - 1994

P261

Bartizan	1943	BDV	1948 - 1967
Cygnet	1975	PB	1975 - 1996

P262

Baron	1944	BDV	1948 - 1957
Peterel	1976	PB	1977 - 1990

P263

Sandpiper	1977	PB	1977 - 1991

P264

Archer	1985	PB	1985 -

P265

Barranca	1938	BDV	1948 - 1964
Dumbarton Castle	1981	OPV	1981 - 2008

P267

Barmill	1940	BDV	1948 - 1958

P269

Barbour	1941	BDV	1948 - 1952

P270

Barbourne	1942	BDV	1948 - 1964
Biter	1985	PC	1985 -

P271

Bardolf	1942	BDV	1948 - 1964
Scimitar	1969	FTB	1969 - 1981

P272

Islay	1941	Trawler	1948 - Sold
Smiter	1987	PC	1988 -

P273

Barbrake	1942	BDV	1948 - 1951
Pursuer	1988	PC	1988 -

P274

Barclose	1941	BDV	1948 - 1962
Cutlass	1970	FTB	1970 - 1981
Tracker	1997	PC	1997 -

P275

Barsing	1941	BDV	1948 - 1962
Sabre	1970	FTB	1970 - 1981
Raider	1998	PC	1998 -

P276

Barbastel	1945	BDV	1948 - 1965
Tenacity	1969	FPB	1969 - 1985

P277

Barcock	1941	BDV	1948 - 1962
Anglesey	1978	OPV	1979 - 2003

P278

Alderney	1979	OPV	1979 - 2002

P279

Blazer	1988	PC	1988 -

P280

Bownet	1939	BDV	1948 - 1958
Dasher	1988	PC	1988 -

P281

Barking	1941	BDV	1948 - 3.64
Attacker	1983	PC	1983 - 1992
Tyne	2002	OPV	2002 -

P282

Barfoam	1941	BDV	1948 - 1967
Chaser	1983	PC	1983 - 1992
Severn	2002	OPV	2002 -

P283

Dragonet	1939	BDV	1948 - 1961
Fencer	1983	PC	1983 - 1992
Mersey	2003	OPV	2003 -

P284

Moorsman	1944	BDV	1948 - ....
Hunter	1983	PC	1983 - 1991
Scimitar	1993	PC	2002 -

P285

Barcross	1941	BDV	1948 - 1951
Striker	1983	PC	1983 - 1992

Sabre   1993 PC   2002 -

Scimitar (P284) and *Sabre* (P285) were built in 1993 as *Grey Wolf* and *Grey Fox* respectively. They were operated covertly by British Forces on anti-gun running patrols in the waters off Northern Ireland until 2002 when they were renamed, commissioned and assigned to the Gibraltar PB Squadron.

P286
Karangi RAN   1941 BDV   1948 - 1965
P287
Barcarole   1945 BDV   1948 - 1967
P288
Gateshead   1942 Trawler   1948 - 1959
P289
Barsound   1941 BDV   1948 - 1964
P290
Barfount   1942 BDV   1948 - 1964
P291
Puncher   1988 PC   1988 -

P292
Barstoke   1941 BDV   1948 - 1960
Charger   1988 PC   1988 -

P293
Barrymore   1941 BDV   1948 - 1952
Ranger   1988 PC   1988 -

P294
Barfoil   1942 BDV   1948 - 1971
Trumpeter   1988 PC   1988 -

P295
Bardell   1942 BDV   1948 - 1950
Jersey   1976 OPV   1976 - 1993

P296
Barricade   1938 BDV   1948 - 1952
Jura   1973 OPV   1975 - 1977
Speedy   1979 Hydrofoil   1979 - 1982

P297
Barnstone   1939 BDV   1948 - 1969
Guernsey   1977 OPV   1977 - 2003

P298
Barrier   1938 BDV   1948 - 1963
Shetland   1976 OPV   1976 - 2002

P299
Barford   1941 BDV   1948 - 1958
Orkney   1976 OPV   1976 - 1999

P300
Lindisfarne   1977 OPV   1977 - 2003
P335
Ebbtide   1917 BDV   1948 - ....
P339
Calcutta RIN   1943 Trawler   1948 - 1949
P340
Hautapu RNZN   1942 Trawler   1948 - ....
P342
Foulness   1942 Trawler   1948 - 1957
P358
Nasik RIN   1944 Trawler   1948 - 1950
P387
Gorregan   1943 Trawler   1948 - 1957
P1007
Beachampton   1953 Patrol Boat   1971 - 1985
P1011
Brave Borderer   1958 MTB   1958 - 1970
P1012
Brave Swordsman   1958 MTB   1958 - 1972
P1041
Gay Archer   1952 FPB   1952 - 1963
P1042
Gay Bombadier   1952 FPB   1952 - 1963
P1043
Gay Bowman   1952 FPB   1952 - 1963
P1044
Gay Bruiser   1952 FPB   1952 - 1962
P1045
Gay Caribineer   1953 FPB   1953 - 1963
P1046
Gay Centurion   1952 FPB   1952 - 1962
P1047
Gay Charger   1953 FPB   1952 - 1967
P1048
Gay Charioteer   1953 FPB   1953 - 1971
P1049
Gay Cavalier   1953 FPB   1953 - 1963
P1050
Gay Dragoon   1953 FPB   1953 - 1962
P1051
Gay Fencer   1953 FPB   1953 - 1968
P1052
Gay Forester   1954 FPB   1954 - 1962
P1055
Monkton   1955 Patrol Boat   1972 - 1985
P1089
Wasperton   1956 Patrol Boat   1972 - 1985
P1093
Wolverton   1956 Patrol Boat   1971 - 1985
P1096
Yarnton   1956 Patrol Boat   1971 - 1985
P1101
Dark Adventurer   1954 FAC   1954 - 1964

P1102			
Dark Aggressor	1954	FAC	1954 - 1961
P1103			
Dark Antagonist	1954	FAC	1954 - 1966
P1104			
Dark Biter	1955	FAC	1955 - 1967
P1105			
Dark Avenger	1955	FAC	1955 - 1966
P1107			
Dark Rover	1954	FAC	1954 - 1966
P1108			
Dark Buccaneer	1954	FAC	1954 - 1966
P1109			
Dark Clipper	1955	FAC	1955 - 1967
P1110			
Dark Highwayman	1955	FAC	1955 - 1967
P1111			
Dark Killer	1956	FAC	1956 - 1966
P1112			
Dark Hussar	1957	FAC	1957 - 1966
P1113			
Dark Fighter	1955	FAC	1955 - 1967
P1114			
Dark Gladiator	1956	FAC	1956 - 1970
P1115			
Dark Hero	1957	FAC	1957 - 1968
P1116			
Dark Hunter	1954	FAC	1954 - 1962
P1118			
Dark Intruder	1955	FAC	1955 - 1966
P1119			
Dark Invader	1955	FAC	1955 - 1964
P1120			
Dark Scout	1958	FAC	1958 - 1961
P1505			
Proud Fusilier	1945	FAC	1948 - ....
P1506			
Proud Grenadier	1945	FAC	1948 - ....
P1507			
Proud Guardsman	1945	FAC	1948 - ....
P1508			
Proud Highlander	1945	FAC	1948 - ....
P1509			
Proud Knight	1945	FAC	1948 - ....
P1519			
Proud Lancer	1945	FAC	1948 - ....
P1522			
Proud Lagionary	1946	FAC	1948 - ....
P1596			
Proud Patriot	1944	FAC	1948 - ....
P1598			
Proud Patroller	1944	FAC	1948 - ....
P3101			
Shalford	1952	SDB	1952 - 1967
P3102			

Aberford	1952	SDB	1952 - 1964
P3103			
Axford	1954	SDB	1954 - 1966
P3104			
Beckford	1955	SDB	1955 - 1964
Dee (ex *Beckford*)	1955	SDB	1964 - 1982

Beckford was renamed *Dee* when she was assigned to the Mersey Division RNR as their seagoing Tender in 1964. In 1968 she was loaned to the Plessey Group for a period of radar trials and renamed *Robert Clive*. She rejoined the Mersey Division and reverted back to *Dee* the following year.

P3105			
Brayford	1954	SDB	1954 SAN
P3106			
Bryansford	1954	SDB	1954 - 1969
P3107			
Camberford	1953	SDB	1953 - 1962
P3108			
Desford	1954	SDB	1954 - 1955
P3109			
Greatford	1953	SDB	1953 - 1968
P3111			
Gifford	1954	SDB	1954 - 1968
P3113			
Droxford	1954	SDB	1954 - 1993
P3114			
Mayford	1954	SDB	1954 - ....
P3115			
Hinksford	1955	SDB	1955 - 1968
P3116			
Ickford	1954	SDB	1954 - 1967
P3117			
Kingsford	1955	SDB	1955 - 1971
P3119			
Dubford	1953	SDB	1953 - 1968
P3120			
Glassford	1955	SDB	1955 SAN
P3122			
Marlingford	1954	SDB	1954 - 1967
P3123			
Tilford	1956	SDB	1956 - 1967
P3124			
Montford	1957	SDB	1957 - 1966
P5701			
Bold Pioneer	1951	FAC	1951 - 1958
P5720			
Bold Pathfinder	1951	FAC	1951 - 1962
P0A			
Mantis	1915	River Gb	9.15 - 1.18
Ladybird	1916	River Gb	1.18 - ....

P1A			
Minerva	1895	Cruiser	9.15 - 1.18
Leviathan	1901	Cruiser	1.18 - 1920

P2A			
Topaze	1903	Cruiser	9.15 - 1.18
Lucia	1907	Depot Ship	1.18 - ....

P3A			
Carnarvon	1903	Cruiser	9.15 - 1.18
Magnificent	1894	Battleship	1.18 - 1921

P4A			
Cicala	1915	River Gb	9.15 - 1.18
Maidstone	1912	Depot Ship	1.18 - ....

P5A			
Ladybird	1916	River Gb	9.15 - 1.18
Mantis	1915	River Gb	1.18 - ....

P6A			
Tarantula	1915	River Gb	9.15 - 1.18
Mars	1896	Battleship	1.18 - 1920

P7A			
Moth	1915	River Gb	1.16 - 1.18
Minerva	1895	Cruiser	1.18 - 1920

P8A			
T.A. Jolliffe	1901	Tug	1.16 - 1.18
Moth	1915	River Gb	1.18 - ....

P9A			
Blackcock	1886	Tug	1.16 - 1.18
Prince George	1895	Battleship	1.18 - 1920

PA0			
Sachem	1893	Convoy Esc	7.17 - 1.18
Research	1888	Depot Ship	1.18 - ....

PA1			
Bostonian	1896	Convoy Esc	7.17 - 1.18
Sappho	1891	Cruiser	1.18 - 1921

PA2			
Knight Templar	1905	Convoy Esc	7.17 - 1.18
Scarab	1915	River Gb	1.18 - ....

PA3			
Discoverer	1913	Convoy Esc	7.17 - 1.18
Skipjack	1889	Torpedo Gb	1.18 - ....

PA4			
Quernmore	1898	Convoy Esc	7.17 - 1.18
Speedwell	1889	Torpedo Gb	1.18 - ....

PA5			
Mechanician	1900	Convoy Esc	7.17 - 1.18
Suffolk	1903	Cruiser	1.18 - 1920

PA6			
T.A. Jolliffe	1901	Tug	1.18 - ....

PA7			
Talbot	1895	Cruiser	1.18 - ....

PA8			
Tarantula	1915	River Gb	1.18 - ....

PA9			
Terrible	1895	Cruiser	1.18 - ....

P0C			
Thetis	1890	Minelayer	1.18 - ....

P1C			
Topaze	1903	Cruiser	1.18 - 1921

P2C			
Venus	1895	Cruiser	1.18 - ....

P3C			
Victorious	1895	Battleship	9.15 - 1922

P4C			
Vindictive	1899	Cruiser	1.18 - ....

P5C			
Wyandra	1901	Decoy	1.18 - ....

P6C			
Zylpha	1894	Collier	1.18 - ....

P7C			
Amphitrite	1898	Cruiser	1.18 - 1920

P8C			
Dwarf	1893	Gunboat	1.18 - ....

Flag 'R' Superior

Pre 1940: None

1940-48: Destroyers; Auxiliary AA Vessels; British Pacific Fleet

1948: Aircraft Carriers

R1
Formidable	1939	Ac Carrier	BPF 45/46

R2
Illustrious	1939	Ac Carrier	BPF 45/46

R5
Implacable	1939	Ac Carrier	BPF 45/46

R7
Indefatigable	1942	Ac Carrier	BPF 45/46

R8
Indomitable	1940	Ac Carrier	BPF 45/46

R00
Troubridge	1942	Destroyer	1942 - 1948

R01
Caprice	1943	Destroyer	1943 - 1948

R02
Zest	1943	Destroyer	1943 - 1948

R03
Kempenfelt	1943	Destroyer	1943 - 1948

R04
Cayuga RCN	1945	Destroyer	1945 - 1948

R05
Urania	1943	Destroyer	1943 - 1948
Eagle	1946	Ac Carrier	1949 - 1979
Invincible	1977	CVS	1977 - 2005

R06
Myngs	1943	Destroyer	1943 - 1948
Centaur	1945	Ac Carrier	1953 - 1965
Illustrious	1978	CVS	1978 - 2014

R07
Caesar	1944	Destroyer	1944 - 1948
Albion	1945	Ac Carrier	1954 - 1973
Ark Royal	1985	CVS	1981 - 2011

R08
Hardy (II)	1943	Destroyer	1943 - 1.44
Bulwark	1945	Ac Carrier	1954 - 1981
Queen Elizabeth	2017	Ac Carrier	2017 -

R09
Cadiz	1944	Destroyer	1944 - 1948
Ark Royal	1950	Ac Carrier	1950 - 1979

Prince of Wales	2019	Ac Carrier	2019 -

R10
Micmac RCN	1943	Destroyer	1945 - 1948
Indefatigable	1942	Ac Carrier	1948 - 1956

R11
Tumult	1942	Destroyer	1942 - 1948
Vikrant RIN (ex-*Hercules*)	1945	Ac Carrier	1961 - 1997

R12
Contest	1944	Destroyer	1944 - 1948
Hermes	1953	Ac Carrier	1953 - 1984

R14
Armada	1943	Destroyer	1943 - 1948

R15
Cavendish	1944	Destroyer	1944 - 1948
Vindex	1943	Esc Carrrier	1948 - Sold

R16
Crescent RCN	1944	Destroyer	1944 - 1948
Triumph	1944	Ac Carrier	1948 - 1956

R17
Valentine	1943	Destroyer	1943 - 1944
Algonquin RCN (ex *Valentine*)	1943	Destroyer	1944 - 1948

R18
St Kitts	1944	Destroyer	1944 - 1948

R19
Zephyr	1943	Destroyer	1943 - 1948

R20
Crusader RCN	1944	Destroyer	1944 - 1948

R21
Chivalrous	1945	Destroyer	1945 - 1948

R22
Ursa	1943	Destroyer	1943 - 1948
Viraat RIN (ex *Hermes*)	1953	Ac Carrier	1987 - 2017

R23

Teazer	1943	Destroyer	1943 - 1948
Victorious	1939	Ac Carrier	BPF 45/46

R24

Gravelines	1944	Destroyer	1944 - 1948

R25

Carysfort	1944	Destroyer	1944 - 1948

R26

Comet	1944	Destroyer	1944 - 1948

R27

Charger	1941	Esc Carrrier	US Navy
Croziers	1944	Destroyer	1944 - 1946

R28

Verulam	1943	Destroyer	1943 - 1948

R29

Charity	1944	Destroyer	1944 - 1948

R30

Carron	1944	Destroyer	1944 - 1948

R31

Vigo	1946	Destroyer	1945 - 1948
Warrior	1944	Ac Carrier	1948 - 1958

R32

Camperdown	1944	Destroyer	1944 - 1948

R33

Terpsichore	1943	Destroyer	1943 - 1948

R34

Cockade	1944	Destroyer	1944 - 1948

R35

Cromwell	1945	Destroyer	1945 - 1946

R36

Chieftain	1945	Destroyer	1945 - 1948
Magnificent	1944	Ac Carrier	1948

R37

Whelp	1943	Destroyer	1943 - 1948

R38

Crystal	1945	Destroyer	1945 - 1946
Hans Lody	1936	Destroyer	1946 - 1948
Victorious	1939	Ac Carrier	1948 - 1968

R39

Zealous	1944	Destroyer	1944 - 1948

R40

Nonsuch (ex *Z38*)	1941	Destroyer	1945 - 1948

R41

Volage	1943	Destroyer	1943 - 1948

R42

Undine	1943	Destroyer	1943 - 1948

R43

Comus	1945	Destroyer	1945 - 1948

R44

Lagos	1944	Destroyer	1944 - 1948

R45

Tenacious	1943	Destroyer	1943 - 1948

R46

Crown	1945	Destroyer	1945 - 1946

R47

Gabbard	1945	Destroyer	1945 - 1948

R48

Wrangler	1943	Destroyer	1943 - 1948

R49

Pique (ren *Cavalier*)	1944	Destroyer	1944
Hercules	1945	Ac Carrier	Incomplete

Construction of *Hercules* was suspended in May 1946, when 75 per cent complete, and was laid up in Gareloch off the Clyde. In January 1957, she was purchased by India and completed by Harland and Wolff. She was commissioned in 1961 as *Vikrant* (R11).

R50

Venus	1943	Destroyer	1943 - 1948

R51

Chevron	1944	Destroyer	1944 - 1948
Perseus	1944	Ac Carrier	1948 - 1952

R52

Chaplet	1944	Destroyer	1944 - 1948

R53

Undaunted	1943	Destroyer	1943 - 1948

R54

Zodiac	1944	Destroyer	1944 - 1948

R55

Finisterre	1944	Destroyer	1944 - 1948

R56

Tuscan	1942	Destroyer	1942 - 1948

R57

Cossack	1944	Destroyer	1944 - 1948

R58

Ranger (ren *Caesar*)	1944	Destroyer	1944

R59

Wakeful	1943	Destroyer	1943 - 1948

R60

Sluys	1945	Destroyer	1945 - 1948

R61

Chequers	1944	Destroyer	1944 - 1948
Colossus	1943	Ac Carrier	BPF 45/46

R62

Cassandra	1943	Destroyer	1943 - 1948

Glory	1943	Ac Carrier	BPF 45/46
Glory	1943	Ac Carrier	1949 - 1961

R63

Concord	1945	Destroyer	1945 - 1948
Venerable	1943	Ac Carrier	BPF 45/46

R64

Vixen	1943	Destroyer	1943 - 1944
Sioux RCN (ex *Vixen*)	1943	Destroyer	1944 - 1948
Theseus	1944	Ac Carrier	1948 - 1962

R65

St James	1945	Destroyer	1945 - 1948
Ocean	1944	Ac Carrier	BPF 45/46

R66

Zambesi	1943	Destroyer	1943 - 1948

R67

Tyrian	1942	Destroyer	1942 - 1948
Formidable	1939	Ac Carrier	1948 - 1953

R68

Crispin	1945	Destroyer	1945 - 1948
Ocean	1944	Ac Carrier	1948 - 1962

R69

Ulysses	1943	Destroyer	1943 - 1948

R70

Solebay	1944	Destroyer	1944 - 1948

R71

Constance	1944	Destroyer	1944 - 1948
Vengeance	1944	Ac Carrier	1948 - 1952

R72

Wizard	1943	Destroyer	1943 - 1948

R73

Cavalier	1944	Destroyer	1944 - 1948

R74

Hogue	1944	Destroyer	1944 - 1948

R75

Virago	1943	Destroyer	1943 - 1948

R76

Consort	1944	Destroyer	1944 - 1948
Pioneer	1944	Ac Carrier	1948 - 1953

R77

Trafalgar	1944	Destroyer	1944 - 1948
Majestic	1945	Ac Carrier	1948 - 1955

R78

Wessex	1943	Destroyer	1943 - 1948

R79

Athabaskan (II)	1946	Destroyer	1946 - 1948

R80

Barfleur	1943	Destroyer	1943 - 1948

R81

Zebra	1944	Destroyer	1944 - 1948

R82

Creole	1945	Destroyer	1944 - 1948

R83

Ulster	1942	Destroyer	1942 - 1948

R84

Saintes	1944	Destroyer	1944 - 1948

R85

Cambrian	1943	Destroyer	1943 - 1948

R86

Implacable	1939	Ac Carrier	1948 - 1954

R87

Whirlwind	1943	Destroyer	1943 - 1948
Illustrious	1939	Ac Carrier	1948 - 1955

R88

T28 (ex German)	1942	Destroyer	1945 - 1946

To RN as war prize. Transferred to France and renamed *Le Lorrain.*

R89

Termagant	1943	Destroyer	1943 - 1948

R90

Cheviot	1944	Destroyer	1944 - 1948

R91

Childers	1945	Destroyer	1945 - 1948

R92

Z 10 (ex German)	1936	Destroyer	1945 - 1946
Indomitable	1940	Ac Carrier	1948 - 1953

R93

Vigilant	1942	Destroyer	1942 - 1948
Terrible	1944	Ac Carrier	1948

Terrible was not completed before the end of WWII but was sold to Australia in 1948, completed, and commissioned into the RAN as HMAS *Sydney* in 1948.

R95

Zenith	1944	Destroyer	1944 - 1948
Powerful	1945	Ac Carrier	1948

Powerful was not completed before the end of WWII. Work recommenced in 1952 to a modified design for the RCN. She was completed, and commissioned into the RCN as HMCS *Bonaventure* in 1957.

R96			
Nootka RCN	1944	Destroyer	1944 - 1948
R97			
Grenville	1942	Destroyer	1942 - 1948
Leviathan	1945	Ac Carrier	Incomplete
R98			
Wager	1943	Destroyer	1943 - 1948
R99			
Urchin	1943	Destroyer	1943 - 1948
R108			
Unicorn	1941	Ac Carrier	BPF 45/46
R130			
Charger	Canc	Esc Carrrier	BPF 45/46

Charger was intended to be transferred to the RN but was retained by the US Navy and commissioned as USS *Charger*. However, NRPM 399, an update to DNC4 (A) dated 28.2.1946, assigned this BPF number to the vessel.

R200			
Aristocrat	1935	Ferry	1940 - 1945
R239			
Royal Eagle	1932	Aux AA	1939 - 1945
R301			
Activity	1942	Esc Carrrier	BPF 45/46
R302			
Ameer	1942	Esc Carrrier	BPF 45/46
R303			
Arbiter	1943	Esc Carrrier	BPF 45/46
R304			
Atheling	1942	Esc Carrrier	BPF 45/46
R305			
Begum	1942	Esc Carrrier	BPF 45/46
R306			
Chaser	1942	Esc Carrrier	BPF 45/46
R307			
Emperor	1942	Esc Carrrier	BPF 45/46
R308			
Fencer	1942	Esc Carrrier	BPF 45/46

R309			
Pursuer	1942	Esc Carrrier	BPF 45/46
R310			
Rajah	1943	Esc Carrrier	BPF 45/46
R311			
Ruler	1943	Esc Carrrier	BPF 45/46
R312			
Shah	1943	Esc Carrrier	BPF 45/46
R313			
Slinger	1942	Esc Carrrier	BPF 45/46
R314			
Speaker	1943	Esc Carrrier	BPF 45/46
R315			
Striker	1942	Esc Carrrier	BPF 45/46
R316			
Thane	1943	Esc Carrrier	BPF 45/46
R317			
Tracker	1942	Esc Carrrier	BPF 45/46
R318			
Trumpeter	1942	Esc Carrrier	BPF 45/46
R319			
Vindex	1943	Esc Carrrier	BPF 45/46
R320			
Queen	1943	Esc Carrrier	BPF 45/46
R321			
Smiter	1943	Esc Carrrier	BPF 45/46
R322			
Patroller	1943	Esc Carrrier	BPF 45/46
R323			
Ranee	1943	Esc Carrrier	BPF 45/46
R324			
Reaper	1943	Esc Carrrier	BPF 45/46
R373			
Laguna Belle	1896	Aux AA	1942 - 1944
R380			
Thames Queen	1898	Aux AA	1942 - 1945
R392			
Glen Avon	1912	Aux AA	1942 - 9.44
R399			
Queen Empress	1912	Aux AA	1942 - 1944

Flag 'R (Int)' Superior

US Navy minelayers serving with the Royal Navy in 1918 were assigned flags superior from the International code, as opposed to the Naval code. International flag 'R' was a red square flag superimposed by a yellow vertical cross. These numbers were assigned for visual signalling and were not applied to the hull.

R(I)00
Roanoke USN   1911 Minelayer   6.18 - ....
R(I)01
Baltimore USN   1888 Minelayer   6.18 - ....
R(I)02
San Francisco USN   1889 Minelayer   6.18 - ....
R(I)03
Cannonicus USN   1899 Minelayer   6.18 - ....
R(I)04
Canandiagua USN   1901 Minelayer   6.18 - ....
R(I)05
Quinnebaug USN   1898 Minelayer   6.18 - ....

R(I)06
Saranac USN   1899 Minelayer   6.18 - ....
R(I)07
Aroostock USN   1907 Minelayer   6.18 - ....
R(I)08
Shawmut USN   1908 Minelayer   6.18 - ....
R(I)09
Black Hawk USN   1913 Minelayer   6.18 - ....
R(I)10
Housatonic USN   1899 Minelayer   6.18 - ....

Flag 'S' Superior

Pre 1940: Auxiliary Patrol Vessels

1940–48: CMBs; MA/SBs; MGBs; SGBs

1948: Submarines (See Chapter 2).

S00
Acadia RCN   1913 Aux Pat Vsl 1914 - 1919
S14
Raccoon RCN   1931 Armed Yacht 1940 - 9.42
S301
SGB1   Canc SGB   c1941
S302
SGB2   Canc SGB   c1941

S303
SGB3   1941 SGB   1941 - 1943
Grey Seal (ex *SGB3*) 1941 SGB   1943 - 1949

S304
SGB4   1941 SGB   1941 - 1943
Grey Fox (ex *SGB4*) 1941 SGB   1943 - 1948

S305
SGB5   1941 SGB   1941 - 1943
Grey Owl (ex *SGB5*) 1941 SGB   1943 - 1949

S306
SGB6   1941 SGB   1941 - 1943
Grey Shark   1941 SGB   1943 - 1948
  (ex *SGB6*)

S307
SGB7   1941 SGB   1941 - 6.42

S308
SGB8   1941 SGB   1941 - 1943
Grey Wolf (ex *SGB8*) 1941 SGB   1943 - 1948

S309
SGB9   1942 SGB   1942 - 1943
Grey Goose   1942 SGB   1943 - 1953
  (ex *SGB9)*

Flag 'T' Superior

Pre 1940:   Torpedo Gunboats; Sloops; Netlayers; Minesweepers; Tenders; Patrol Tugs

1940-48:   Aux Patrol Vessels; Aux Minesweepers; River Gunboats; AS/ MS Trawlers and Whalers; Netlayers
and Tenders

1948:   None

T00

Acacia	1915	Sloop	9.15 - ....
Flying Fox	1918	MS	6.18 - ....
Beaufort	1919	Survey Vsl	11.19 - ....
Wakakura RNZN	1917	Trawler	1926 - 1945

T01

Anenome	1915	Sloop	9.15 - 1.18
Anchusa	1917	Sloop	1.18 - 7.18
Rugby	1918	MS	11.18 - 11.19
Collinson	1919	Survey Vsl	11.19 - ....
Cedar	1933	Trawler	1935 - 1946
Africana SAN	1930	Whaler	1939 - 1944

South African Navy vessels T01-T62 repeated numbers
in use by the Royal Navy. In 1944, to avoid confusion,
SAN vessel numbers were increased by adding either
500 (T01-21), 440 (T22-39) or 400 (T40-61).

T02

Aster	1915	Sloop	9.15 - 1.18
Amaryllis	1915	Sloop	1.18 - 6.18
Andromede FR	1917	Sloop	6.18 - 9.18
Eglinton	1916	Paddle MS	9.18 - ....
Crozier	1919	Survey	11.19 - ....
Acacia	1940	Trawler	1940 - 1947
Natalia SAN	1925	Whaler	1941 - 1944

T03

Bluebell	1915	Sloop	9.15 - 1.18
Anenome	1915	Sloop	1.18 - 6.18
Harebell	1918	Sloop	6.18 - 11.19
Fitzroy	1919	Survey Vsl	11.19 - ....
Cherwell	1918	Trawler	1920 - 1946
Goulding SAN	1921	Whaler	1940 - 1944

T04

Clacton	1904	Screw MS	9.15 - 8.16
Asphodel	1915	Sloop	1.18. - 11.19
Flinders	1919	Survey Vsl	11.19 - ....
Blackwater	1918	Trawler	1920 - 1946
Grimwood SAN	1924	Whaler	1940 - 1944

T05

Daffodil	1915	Sloop	9.15 - 1.18
Cowslip	1917	Sloop	1.18 - 4.18
Silvio	1918	MS	9.18 - ....
Kellett	1919	Survey Vsl	11.19 - ....
Fastnet	1919	Trawler	1933 - 1942
Larsen SAN	1924	Trawler	1940 - 1944
Ophelia	1940	Trawler	1940 - 1946

T06

Newmarket	1907	Screw MS	9.15 - 7.17
Aubretia	1916	Sloop	1.18 - ....
Alresford	1919	MS	11.19 - ....
Arran	1940	Trawler	1940 - 1946
Robinson SAN	1927	Whaler	1940 - 1944

T07

Folkestone	1903	Screw MS	9.15 - 1.18
Azalea	1915	Sloop	1.18 - 9.18
Cattistock	1917	MS	9.18 - ....
Caterham	1919	MS	11.19 - ....
Coral	1935	Trawler	1935 - 4.42
Whytock SAN	1924	Whaler	1940 - 1944

T08

Reindeer	1897	Screw MS	9.15 - 1.18
Southdown	1917	MS	9.18 - ....
Carstairs	1919	MS	11.19 - ....
Gannet	1927	Riv Gb	1940 - 1942
Oostewal SAN	1926	Whaler	1939 - 1944

T09

Whitby Abbey	1908	Screw MS	9.15 - 1.18
Berberis	1916	Sloop	1.18 - 9.18
Atherstone	1916	Paddle MS	9.18 - ....
Cypress	1930	Trawler	1935 - 1946
Swartberg SAN	1936	Whaler	1939 - 1944

T10

Hythe	1905	Screw MS	9.15 - 10.15
Gatwick	1916	Paddle MS	9.18 - ....
Mastiff	1938	Trawler	1938 - 11.39
Romeo	1941	Trawler	1941 - 1946
Arum SAN	1926	Whaler	1939 - 1944

T11

Dahlia	1915	Sloop	9.15 - 1.18
Gardenia	1917	Sloop	1.18 - 6.18
Harvester	1918	MS	6.18 - ....
Dragonfly	1938	Riv Gb	1940 - 2.41
Nerine SAN	1925	Trawer	1940 - 1944

T12

Daphne	1915	Sloop	9.15 - 1.18
Bluebell	1915	Sloop	1.18 - ....
Huntley	1919	MS	4.19 - 11.19
Amethyst	1934	Trawler	1935 - 11.40
Randfontein SAN	1926	Whaler	1941 - 1944
Rampur RIN	1941	Trawler	1943 - 1944

T13

Lynn	1889	Screw MS	9.15 - 1.18
David Haigh SAN	1918	Trawler	1943 - 1944

T14

Gazelle	1889	Screw MS	9.15 - 1.18
Buttercup	1915	Sloop	1.18 - ....
Jasper	1932	Trawler	1935 - 12.42
Almond	1940	Trawler	1940 - 2.41
Rondevlei SAN	1929	Whaler	1940 - 1944

T15

Foxglove	1915	Sloop	9.15 - 1.18
Camellia	1915	Sloop	1.18 - 9.18
Bagshot	1918	MS	4.19 - 11.19
Cornelian	1933	Trawler	1933 - 1946
Smalvlei SAN	1929	Whaler	1940 - 1944

T16

Hollyhock	1915	Sloop	9.15 - 1.18
Campanula	1915	Sloop	1.18 - 9.18
Ascot	1916	Paddle MS	9.18 - 11.18
Malvern	1919	MS	4.19 - 11.19
James Ludford	1919	Trawler	.... - 12.39
Mooivlei SAN	1935	Trawler	1939 - 1944
Hoxa	1941	Trawler	1941 - 1946

T17

Honeysuckle	1915	Sloop	9.15 - 1.18
Candytuft	1917	Sloop	1.18 - Sunk
Orby	1918	MS	1919 - ....
Colne	1918	Trawler	1920 - 1947
Blomvlei SAN	1935	Trawler	1939 - 1944

T18

Iris	1915	Sloop	9.15 - 1.18
Carnation	1915	Sloop	1.18 - ....
Nailsea	1918	MS	11.19 - ....
Vernon	1916	Trawler	1924 - 1938
Aristea SAN	1935	Trawler	1939 - 1944

Inchcolm	1941	Trawler	1941 - 1946

T19

Marigold	1915	Sloop	9.15 - 1.18
Ceanothus	1917	Sloop	1.18 - 9.18
Chepstow	1916	Paddle MS	9.18 - ....
Dorking	1918	MS	11.19 - ....
Crassula SAN	1935	Trawler	1939 - 1944
Holly	1930	Trawler	1935 - 1946

T20

Jonquil	1915	Sloop	9.15 - 1.18
Celandine	1916	Sloop	1.18 - 9.18
Croxton	1916	Paddle MS	9.18 - ....
Dee (ex *Battleaxe*)	1916	Trawler	1920 - 1946
Babiana SAN	1935	Trawler	1939 - 1944

T21

Laburnum	1915	Sloop	9.15 - 1.18
Ivy	1917	Sloop	1.18 - 9.18
Chelmsford	1916	Paddle MS	9.18 - ....
Petersfield	1919	MS	11.19 - ....
Peterel	1927	Riv Gb	1940 - 12.41
Bluff SAN	1935	Trawler	1939 - 1944

T22

Larkspur	1915	Sloop	9.15 - 1.18
Clematis	1915	Sloop	1.18 - 9.18
Goodwood	1916	Paddle MS	9.18 - ....
Pearl	1934	Trawler	1935 - 1946
Soetvlei SAN	1929	Whaler	1940 - 1944

T23

Lavender	1915	Sloop	9.15 - 1.18
Convovulus	1917	Sloop	1.18 - ....
Brakvlei SAN	1929	Whaler	1940 - 1944

T24

Lilac	1915	Sloop	9.15 - 1.18
Cornflower	1916	Sloop	1.18 - 9.18
Lingfield	1916	Paddle MS	9.18 - ....
Ruby	1933	Trawler	1935 - 1946
Hektor SAN	1929	Whaler	1940 - 1944

T25

Lily	1915	Sloop	9.15 - 1.18
Crocus	1915	Sloop	1.18 - ....
Elfin	1933	Tender	1933 - 1941
Odberg SAN	1936	Whaler	1941 - 1944

T26

Magnolia	1915	Sloop	9.15 - 1.18
Cyclamen	1916	Sloop	1.18 - 9.18
Newbury	1916	Paddle MS	9.18 - ....
Lilac	1930	Trawler	1939 - 1946

Southern Floe SAN	1936	Whaler	1940 - 2.41	**T35**			
				Clematis	1915	Sloop	9.15 - 1.18
T27				*Gazelle*	1889	Screw MS	1.18 - 9.18
Mallow	1915	Sloop	9.15 - 1.18	*Hexham*	1917	Paddle MS	9.18 - ....
Daffodil	1915	Sloop	1.18 -	*Kommetjie* SAN	1930	Whaler	1940 - 1944
Southern Maid	1936	Whaler	1940 - 1944	*Doon*	1917	Trawler	1920 - 1946
Sapphire	1935	Trawler	.... - 1946				
				T36			
T28				*Carnation*	1915	Sloop	9.15 - 1.18
Mimosa	1915	Sloop	9.15 - 1.18	*Gentian*	1915	Sloop	1.18 - 9.19
Dahlia	1915	Sloop	1.18 -	*Bradfield*	1919	MS	9.19 - 11.19
Locust	1939	Riv Gb	1940 - 1944	*Sherborne*	1918	MS	11.19 - ....
Southern Barrier	1936	Whaler	1940 - 1944	*Redwing*	1933	Tender	1933 - 1948
				Steenberg SAN	1929	Whaler	1940 - 1944
T29							
Primrose	1915	Sloop	9.15 - 1.18	**T37**			
Daphne	1915	Sloop	1.18 -	*Heliotrope*	1915	Sloop	9.15 - 1.18
Boyne	1918	Trawler	1920 - 1946	*Geranium*	1915	Sloop	1.18 - 9.18
Laurel	1930	Trawler	1940 - 1944	*Lanark*	1917	Paddle MS	9.18 - ....
Southern Isles SAN	1936	Whaler	1940 - 1944	*Pangbourne*	1918	MS	11.19 - ....
				Sycamore	1930	Trawler	1935 - 1946
T30				*Stellenberg* SAN	1929	Whaler	1940 - 1944
Sunflower	1915	Sloop	9.15 - 1.18				
Delphinium	1915	Sloop	1.18 -	**T38**			
Mazurka	1940	Trawler	1940 - 1946	*Myrtle*	1915	Sloop	9.15 - 1.18
Southern Sea SAN	1936	Whaler	1940 - 1944	*Gladiolus*	1915	Sloop	1.18 - ....
				Gretna	1918	MS	11.19 - ....
T31				*Maple*	1929	Trawler	1939 - 1946
Veronica	1915	Sloop	9.15 - 1.18	*Springs* SAN	1930	Whaler	1941 - 1944
Eglantine	1917	Sloop	1.18 -				
Cedarberg SAN	1936	Whaler	1941 - 1944	**T39**			
Magnolia	1930	Trawler	1935 - 1947	*Peony*	1915	Sloop	9.15 - 1.18
				Godetia	1916	Sloop	1.18 - ....
T32				*Elgin*	1919	MS	11.19 - ....
Azalea	1915	Sloop	9.15 - 1.18	*Ash*	1939	Trawler	1939 - 6.41
Folkestone	1903	Screw MS	1.18 -	*Pirouette*	1940	Trawler	1940 - 1946
Plumpton	1916	Paddle MS	9.18 - 10.18	*Sidney Smith* SAN	1929	Trawler	1940 - 1942
Dorking	1918	MS	12.18 - 11.19	*Parktown I* SAN	1929	Trawler	1942 - 6.42
Blaawberg SAN	1936	Whaler	1940 - 1944	(ex-*Sidney Smith*)			
Hawthorn	1930	Trawler	1935 - 1946				
				T40			
T33				*Snowdrop*	1915	Sloop	9.15 - 1.18
Begonia	1915	Sloop	9.15 - 8.17	*Heather*	1916	Sloop	1.18 - ....
Foxglove	1915	Sloop	1.18 -	*Forres*	1918	MS	11.19 - ....
Sydoslandet SAN	1935	Whaler	1941 - 4.42	*Topaze*	1935	Trawler	1935 - 4.41
Madras RIN	1919	Trawler	.... - 1942	*Nigel* SAN	1930	Whaler	1941 - 1944
Tanjore RIN	1919	Trawler	1942 - 6.42				
(ex-*Madras*)				**T41**			
				Narcissus	1915	Sloop	9.15 - 1.18
T34				*Heliotrope*	1915	Sloop	1.18 - ....
Camellia	1915	Sloop	9.15 - 1.18	*Wetherby*	1918	Paddle MS	9.18 - ....
Gaillardia	1917	Sloop	1.18 - 3.18	*Albury*	1918	MS	11.19 - ....
Banbury	1917	Paddle MS	9.18 -	*Sandpiper*	1933	Riv Gb	1940 - 1942
Beryl	1935	Trawler	1939 - 1946	*Albert Hulett* SAN	1929	Whaler	1939 - 1942
Florida SAN	1930	Whaler	1940 - 1944	*Langlaagte* SAN	1929	Whaler	1942 - 1946

T42

Zinnia	1915	Sloop	9.15 - 1.18
Hibiscus	1917	Sloop	1.18 - 12.18
Marlow	1918	MS	12.18 - 11.19
Stafford	1918	MS	11.19 - ....
Tourmaline	1935	Trawler	1935 - 2.41
Brakpan SAN	1936	Whaler	1941 - 1944
Star of Freedom	1917	Trawler	1939 - 1946

T43

Jessamine	1915	Sloop	9.15 - 1.18
Hollyhock	1915	Sloop	1.18 - 9.18
Gaddesdon	1917	MS	9.18 - 11.19
Caerleon	1918	MS	11.19 - ....
Seamew	1928	Riv Gb	1940 - 1941
Protea SAN	1936	Whaler	1941 - 1944

T44

Arabis	1915	Sloop	9.15 - 2.16
Honeysuckle	1915	Sloop	1.18 - ....
Irvine	1917	MS	1919 - 11.19
Lydd	1918	MS	11.19 - ....
Beech	1929	Trawler	1939 - 6.41
Sonneblom SAN	1936	Whaler	1941 - 1944

T45

Buttercup	1915	Sloop	9.15 - 1.18
Hydrangea	1916	Sloop	1.18 - ....
Kendal	1918	MS	9.18 - 11.19
Immortelle SAN	1936	Whaler	1941 - 1944
Turquoise	1935	Trawler	1935 - 1946

T46

Alyssum	1915	Sloop	9.15 - 1.18
Iris	1915	Sloop	1.18 - ....
Boksburg SAN	1926	Whaler	1941 - 1944
Berberis	1928	Trawler	1939 - 1946

T47

Poppy	1915	Sloop	9.15 - 3.17
Jessamine	1915	Sloop	1.18 - ....
Rugby	1918	MS	11.19 - ....
Germiston SAN	1923	Whaler	1941 - 1944
Excellent (ex *Nith*)	1918	Trawler	1922 - 1948

T48

Campanula	1915	Sloop	9.15 - 1.18
Jonquil	1915	Sloop	1.18 - ....
Shrewsbury	1918	MS	9.18 - 11.19
Krugersdorp SAN	1923	Whaler	1941 - 1944

T49

Gentian	1915	Sloop	9.15 - 1.18
Laburnum	1915	Sloop	1.18 - ....
Uppingham	1919	MS	1919 - 11.19

Eden	1918	Trawler	1941 - 1942
Bever SAN	1930	Whaler	1941 - 1944

T50

Gladiolus	1915	Sloop	9.15 - 1.18
Larkspur	1915	Sloop	1.18 - ....
Gribb SAN	1930	Whaler	1941 - 1944
Aberfoyle	1912	Tender	1920 - 1938
Balta	1940	Trawler	1940 - 1946

T51

Marguerite	1915	Sloop	9.15 - 1.18
Marjoram	1917	Sloop	1.18 - ....
Vulcan	1933	Trawler	1936 - 1947
Treern SAN	1929	Whaler	1942 - 1945

T52

Nigella	1915	Sloop	9.15 - 1.18
Lilac	1915	Sloop	1.18 - ....
Monarda	1919	Drifter	1939 - 11.41
Seksern SAN	1930	Whaler	1941 - 1944

T53

Pentstemon	1916	Sloop	9.15 - 1.18
Lily	1915	Sloop	1.18 - 9.18
Totnes	1916	Paddle MS	9.18 - ....
Imhoff SAN	1927	Whaler	1941 - 1944
Hornbeam	1929	Trawler	1939 - 1946

T54

Delphinium	1915	Sloop	9.15 - 1.18
Lobelia	1916	Sloop	1.18 - 9.18
Cheltenham	1916	Paddle MS	9.18 - ....
Benoni SAN	1925	Whaler	1942 - 1944
Oak	1928	Trawler	1939 - 1946

T55

Primula	1915	Sloop	9.15 - 3.16
Lupin	1916	Sloop	1.18 - ....
Syringa	1930	Trawler	1940 - 1946
Suderoy I SAN	1925	Whaler	1941 - 1942
Parktown II SAN	1925	Whaler	1942 - 1944
(ex-*Suderoy I*)			

T56

Geranium	1915	Sloop	1.16 - 1.18
Lychnis	1917	Sloop	1.18 - 9.18
Doncaster	1916	Paddle MS	9.18 - ....
Huntley	1919	MS	11.19 - ....
Jade	1933	Trawler	1939 - 4.42
Johannesburg SAN	1925	Whaler	1942 - 1944

T57

Godetia	1916	Sloop	9.15 - 1.18
Lynn	1889	Screw MS	1.18 - ....

Shirley	1916	Paddle MS	9.18 - ....
Dunoon	1919	MS	6.19 - 11.19
Bagshot	1918	MS	11.1 - ....
Aphis	1915	River Gb	1940 - 1947
Roodepoort san	1929	Whaler	1942 - 1944

T58

Rosemary	1915	Sloop	9.15 - 1.18
Magnolia	1915	Sloop	1.18 - 9.18
Harpenden	1918	Paddle MS	9.18 - ....
Malvern	1919	MS	11.19 - ....
Ladybird	1916	River Gb	1940 - 5.41
Tordonn san	1925	Trawler	1941 - 1944

T59

Crocus	1915	Sloop	9.15 - 1.18
Mallow	1915	Sloop	1.18 - 9.18
Epsom	1916	Paddle MS	9.18 - ....
Scarab	1915	River Gb	1940 - 1948
Pretoria san	1930	Whaler	1942 - 1944

T60

Berberis	1916	Sloop	9.15 - 1.18
Marguerite	1915	Sloop	1.18 - 9.18
Eridge	1916	Paddle MS	9.18 - ....
Cheam	1919	MS	11.19 - ....
Gnat	1915	River Gb	1940 - 10.41
Standerton san	1936	Whaler	1942 - 1944

T61

Pansy	1916	Sloop	9.15 - 1.18
Marigold	1915	Sloop	1.18 - ....
Longford	1919	MS	6.19 - 11.19
Bee	Canc	River Gb	Canc 3.40
Turffontein san	1936	Whaler	1942 - 1944

T62

Hydrangea	1916	Sloop	9.15 - 1.18
Mimosa	1915	Sloop	1.18 - 9.18
Haldon	1916	Paddle MS	9.18 - ....
Tarantula	1915	River Gb	1940 - 1941
Vereeniging san	1936	Whaler	1942 - 1944

T63

Genista	1916	Sloop	9.15 - 10.16
Montbretia	1917	Sloop	1.18 - ....
Garry (ex *Goldaxe*)	1916	Trawler	1920 - 1946

T64

Cornflower	1916	Sloop	9.15 - 1.18
Myosotis	1916	Sloop	1.18 - ....
Tern	1927	River Gb	1940 - 12.41

T65

Lupin	1916	Sloop	1.16 - 1.18
Myrtle	1915	Sloop	1.18 - ....
Repton	1919	MS	7.19 - ....
Robin	1934	River Gb	1940 - 12.41

T66

Petunia	1916	Sloop	1.16 - 1.18
Narcissus	1915	Sloop	1.18 - 9.18
Hurst	1916	Paddle MS	9.18 - ....
Willow	1930	Trawler	1935 - 1946

T67

Valerian	1916	Sloop	1.16 - 1.18
Silene	1918	Sloop	1.18 - ....
Gainsborough	1918	MS	11.19 - ....
Scorpion	1937	River Gb	1940 - 1942

T68

Myosotis	1916	Sloop	1.16 - 1.18
Nigella	1915	Sloop	1.18 - 9.18
Sandown	1916	Paddle MS	9.18 - ....
Burslem	1918	MS	11.19 - ....
Basset	1935	Trawler	1940 - 1948

T69

Amaryllis	1915	Sloop	9.15 - 1.18
Pansy	1916	Sloop	1.18 - ....
Mantis	1915	River Gb	1940 - 1.40

T70

Asphodel	1915	Sloop	9.15 - 1.18
Pentstemon	1916	Sloop	1.18 - ....
Moth	1915	River Gb	1940 - 12.41

T71

Snapdragon	1915	Sloop	1.16 - 1.18
Peony	1915	Sloop	1.18 - 9.18
Sligo	1918	MS	9.18 - 11.19
Cicala	1915	River Gb	1940 - 12.41

T72

Celandine	1916	Sloop	9.15 - 1.18
Petunia	1916	Sloop	1.18 - 9.18
Clonmel	1918	MS	9.18 - 11.19
Cockchafer	1915	River Gb	1940 - 1947

T73

Cyclamen	1916	Sloop	9.15 - 1.18
Polyanthus	1917	Sloop	1.18 - ....
Herald	1918	Survey	.... - 1942

T74

Lobelia	1916	Sloop	9.15 - 1.18
Poppy	1915	Sloop	1.18 - ....
Falcon	1931	River Gb	1931 - 1941

T75

Mignonette	1916	Sloop	9.15 - 3.17
Primrose	1915	Sloop	1.18 - ....
Cricket	1915	River Gb	1940 - 6.41

T76

Nasturtium	1915	Sloop	9.15 - 4.16
Reindeer	1897	Screw MS	1.18 - 9.18
Gainsborough	1918	MS	9.18 - 11.19
Lasso	1938	Cable Ship	1938 - 1940
Othello	1941	Trawler	1941 - 1946

T77

Verbena	1915	Sloop	9.15 - 1.18
Rosemary	1915	Sloop	1.18 - ....
Marlow	1918	MS	11.19 - ....
Bay	1939	Trawler	1939 - 1947

T78

Wallflower	1915	Sloop	9.15 - 1.18
Auricula	1917	Sloop	1.18 - ....
Gaddesdon	1917	MS	11.19 - ....
Kennet (ex *Iceaxe*)	1926	Trawler	1920 - 1945

T79

Wistaria	1915	Sloop	9.15 - 1.18
Snapdragon	1915	Sloop	1.18 - 9.18
Pangbourne	1918	MS	9.18 - 11.19
Irvine	1917	MS	11.19 - ....
Moy	1917	Trawler	1920 - 1946

T80

Snowdrop	1915	Sloop	1.18 - ....
Caterham	1919	MS	7.19 - 11.19
Kendal	1918	MS	11.19 - ....
Ouse	1917	Trawler	1920 - 2.41

T81

Spiraea	1917	Sloop	1.18 - 9.18
Shincliffe	1918	Paddle MS	9.18 - ....
Shrewsbury	1918	MS	11.19 - ....
Liffey (ex *Stoneaxe*)	1916	Trawler	1920 - 1947

T82

Sunflower	1915	Sloop	1.18 - ....
Nightingale	1931	Tender	.... - ....

T83

Sweetbriar	1917	Sloop	1.18 - 6.18
Syringa	1917	Sloop	6.18 - ....
Vernon (ex *Skylark*)	1932	Tender	.... - ....

T84

Tamarisk	1916	Sloop	1.18 - ....
Alder	1929	Trawler	1939 - 10.41

T85

Valerian	1916	Sloop	1.18 - 9.18
Lewes	1918	Paddle MS	9.18 - ....
Grasshopper	1939	River Gb	1940 - 2.42

T86

Verbena	1915	Sloop	1.18 - 9.18
Cupar	1918	MS	9.18 - 5.19
Wem	1919	MS	1919 - 11.19
Redwood	1928	Trawler	1939 - 1945

T87

Veronica	1915	Sloop	1.18 - ....
Truro	1919	MS	4.19 - 11.19
Agate	1935	Trawler	1940 - 8.41

T88

Viola	1916	Sloop	1.18 - ....
Amber	1934	Trawler	1939 - 1946

T89

Wallflower	1915	Sloop	1.18 - ....
Guardian	1932	Netlayer	1932 - 1948

T90

Whitby Abbey	1908	Screw MS	1.18 - ....
Burslem	1918	MS	6.18 - 11.19
Moonstone	1934	Trawler	1939 - 1946

T91

Wistaria	1915	Sloop	1.18 - 6.18
Penarth	1918	MS	6.18 - ....
Dundalk	1919	MS	4.19 - 11.19
Myrtle	1928	Trawler	1939 - 6.40
Coronation	1902	Aux AA	1940 - 1945

T92

Zinnia	1915	Sloop	1.18 - ....
Alresford	1919	MS	5.19 - 11.19
Dwarf	1936	Tender	1936 - 1948

T93

Coreopsis	1917	Sloop	1.18 - 6.18
Sir Bevis	1918	MS	6.18 - ....
Birch	1939	Trawler	1939 - 1948

T94

Arbutus	1917	Sloop	1.18 - 12.17
Melton	1916	Paddle MS	9.18 - ....
Mosquito	1939	River Gb	1940 - 6.40
Nettle (ex *Elfin*)	1933	Tender	1941 - 1958

T95

Rhododendron	1917	Sloop	1.18 - 5.18
Ard Patrick	1918	MS	9.18 - ....

Adastral	1916 Trawler	.... -	
T96			
Bryony	1917 Sloop	1.18 - 9.18	
Sherborne	1918 MS	9.18 - 11.19	
Larch	1928 Trawler	1939 - 1946	
T97			
Saxifrage	1918 Sloop	1.18 -	
Tamarisk	1925 MS	1939 - 8.40	
T98			
Chrysanthemum	1917 Sloop	1.18 - 9.18	
Munlochy	1918 MS	9.18 - 11.19	
Sligo	1918 MS	11.19 -	
Protector	1936 Netlayer	1936 - 1952	
T99			
Mistletoe	1917 Sloop	1.18 - 9.18	
Craigie	1918 MS	9.18 - 11.19	
Clonmel	1918 MS	11.19 -	
Ladas	1918 MS	1919 -	
Brora	1940 Trawler	1940 - 9.41	
T100			
Blackthorn	1939 Trawler	1940 - 1947	
T101			
Pine	1940 Trawler	1940 - 1.44	
T102			
Kiwi RNZN	1941 Trawler	1941 - 1946	
T103			
Walnut	1939 Trawler	1940 - 1948	
T104			
Cotillion	1940 Trawler	1940 - 1946	
T105			
Elm	1939 Trawler	1940 - 1946	
T106			
Coverley	1941 Trawler	1941 - 1947	
T107			
Fandango	1940 Trawler	1940 - 1946	
T108			
Hazel	1939 Trawler	1940 - 1946	
T109			
Foxtrot	1940 Trawler	1940 - 1946	
T110			
Chestnut	1940 Trawler	1940 - 11.40	
Mull	1941 Trawler	1941 - 1946	
T112			
Mangrove	1940 Trawler	1940 - 1943	
T113			
Wisteria	1939 Trawler	1940 - 1946	
T114			
Hoy	1941 Trawler	1941 - 1946	

T115			
Gavotte	1940 Trawler	1940 - 1946	
T116			
Hickory	1940 Trawler	1940 - 10.40	
T117			
Morris Dance	1940 Trawler	1940 - 1946	
T118			
Guava	1935 Trawler	1940 - 1946	
T119			
Rowan	1939 Trawler	1940 - 1946	
T120			
Hornpipe	1940 Trawler	1940 - 1946	
T121			
Pirouette	1940 Trawler	1940 - 1947	
T122			
Rumba	1940 Trawler	1940 - 1948	
T123			
Juniper	1939 Trawler	1940 - 6.40	
T124			
Deodar	1940 Trawler	1940 - 1946	
T125			
Sarabande	1940 Trawler	1941 - 1945	
Grimsby Town	1934 Trawler	1940 - 1945	
T126			
Olive	1940 Trawler	1940 - 1948	
T127			
Whitethorn	1939 Trawler	1940 - 1946	
T128			
Saltarello	1940 Trawler	1940 - 1946	
T129			
Fir	1940 Trawler	1940 - 1946	
T130			
Veleta	1941 Trawler	1941 - 1946	
T131			
Minuet	1941 Trawler	1941 - 1946	
T132			
Sword Dance	1940 Trawler	1940 - 7.42	
T133			
Quadrille	1941 Trawler	1941 - 1946	
T134			
Celia	1940 Trawler	1940 - 1946	
T135			
Rosalind	1941 Trawler	1941 - 1946	
T136			
Juliet	1940 Trawler	1940 - 1947	
T137			
Laertes	1940 Trawler	1940 - 7.42	
T138			
Macbeth	1940 Trawler	1940 - 1947	
T139			
Polka	1941 Trawler	1941 - 1946	
T140			
Coriolanus	1940 Trawler	1940 - 5.45	

T141					*Inchmarnock*	1941	Trawler	1941 - 1944
Pargo	1942	Trawler	To Brazil		**T167**			
					Hamlet	1940	Trawler	1940 - 1947
T142					**T168**			
Tarantella	1941	Trawler	1941 - 1943		*Bute*	1941	Trawler	1941 - 1946
Two-Step	1941	Trawler	1943 - 1946		**T169**			
(ex *Tarantella*)					*Jura*	1941	Trawler	1941 - 1.43
					T170			
T143					*Shiant*	1941	Trawler	1941 - 1944
Atalanta	1906	Netlayer	1940 - 1945		**T171**			
T144					*Flotta*	1941	Trawler	1941 - 11.41
Pladda	1941	Trawler	1941 - 1946		**T172**			
T145					*Islay*	1941	Trawler	1941 - 1946
Cava	1941	Trawler	1941 - 1947		**T173**			
T146					*Hildasay*	1941	Trawler	1941 - 6.45
Tango	1940	Trawler	1940 - 1946		**T174**			
T147					*Killegray* RNZN	1941	Trawler	1941 - 1946
Copinsay	1940	Trawler	1941 - 1946		**T175**			
T148					*Scarba* RNZN	1941	Trawler	1941 - 1946
Parati	1942	Trawler	To Brazil		**T176**			
T149					*Shapinsay*	1941	Trawler	1941 - 1946
Ronaldsay	1941	Trawler	1941 - 1946		**T177**			
T150					*Sluna*	1941	Trawler	1941 - 1946
Stroma	1941	Trawler	1941 - 1946		**T178**			
T151					*Stronsay*	1942	Trawler	1942 - 2.43
Valse	1941	Trawler	1941 - 1946		**T179**			
T152					*Switha*	1942	Trawler	1942 - 1946
Pampano	1942	Trawler	To Brazil		**T180**			
T153					*Tiree*	1941	Trawler	1941 - 1946
Horatio	1940	Trawler	1940 - 1.43		**T181**			
T154					*Trondra*	1941	Trawler	1941 - 1946
Cumbrae	1940	Trawler	1940 - 1946		**T182**			
T155					*Westray*	1941	Trawler	1941 - 1946
Inchkeith RNZN	1941	Trawler	1941 - 1946		**T183**			
T156					*Paru*	1945	Trawler	To Brazil
Papatera	1942	Trawler	To Brazil		**T184**			
T157					*Pelegrime*	1942	Trawler	To Brazil
Fluellen	1940	Trawler	1940 - 1947		**T185**			
T158					*Proctor*	1942	Trawler	1942 - 1946
Burra	1941	Trawler	1941 - 1946		**T186**			
T159					*Probe*	1942	Trawler	1942 - 1946
Staffa	1942	Trawler	1942 - 1946		**T187**			
T160					*Prodigal*	1941	Trawler	1942 - 1946
Sanda RNZN	1941	Trawler	1941 - 1946		**T188**			
T161					*Product*	1941	Trawler	1942 - 1946
Canna	1940	Trawler	1940 - 12.42		**T189**			
T162					*Professor*	1942	Trawler	1942 - 1946
Fara	1941	Trawler	1941 - 1946		**T190**			
T163					*Prong*	1942	Trawler	1942 - 1946
Skye	1942	Trawler	1942 - 1948		**T191**			
T164					*Proof*	1942	Trawler	1942 - 1946
Rysa	1941	Trawler	1941 - 12.43		**T192**			
T165					*Property*	1942	Trawler	1942 - 1946
Kintyre	1941	Trawler	1941 - 1946		**T193**			
T166					*Promise*	1941	Trawler	1942 - 1946

T194				**T221**				
Prophet	1942	Trawler	1942 - 1946	*Portsdown*	1941	Trawler	1941 - 1946
T195				**T222**				
Protest	1941	Trawler	1942 - 1946	*Yestor*	1941	Trawler	1941 - 1946
T196				**T223**				
Prowess (ex *Provost*)	1943	Trawler	1942 - 1946	*Bredon*	1941	Trawler	1941 - 2.43
T197				**T224**				
Brittany	1933	Netlayer	1940 - 1946	*Dunkery*	1941	Trawler	1941 - 1946
T198				**T225**				
Minster	1924	Netlayer	1924 - 1944	*Inkpen*	1941	Trawler	1941 - 1946
T199				**T226**				
Soemba RNLN	1925	Sloop	.... -	*Sir Galahad*	1941	Trawler	1941 - 1946
T200				**T227**				
Kerrera	1941	Trawler	1941 - 1944	*Sir Gareth*	1942	Trawler	1942 - 1946
T201				**T228**				
Eday	1941	Trawler	1941 - 1944	*Sir Lancelot*	1941	Trawler	1941 - 1946
T202				**T229**				
Fetlar	1941	Trawler	1941 - 1944	*Sir Tristram*	1942	Trawler	1942 - 1946
T203				**T230**				
Foula	1941	Trawler	1941 - 1946	*Sir Agravaine*	1942	Trawler	1942 - 1946
				T231				
T204				*Bonito*	1941	Trawler	1941 - 1946
Orfasy	1942	Trawler	1942 - 10.43	**T232**				
Ellesmere	1939	Whaler	1940 - 2.45	*Whiting*	1941	Trawler	1941 - 1946
				T233				
T205				*Moa* RNZN	1941	Trawler	1941 - 1943
Gruna	1941	Trawler	See T297	**T234**				
T207				*Tui* RNZN	1941	Trawler	1941 - 1946
Coll	1942	Trawler	1942 - 1946	**T235**				
T208				*St Cran*	(....)	....	.... - ....
Damsay	1942	Trawler	1942 - 1946	**T236**				
T209				*Bruray*	1942	Trawler	1942 - 1943
St Kilda	1942	Trawler	1942 - 1946	**T237**				
T210				*Scalpay*	1942	Trawler	1942 - 1946
Rousay	1941	Trawler	1941 - 1946	**T238**				
T211				*Fiaray*	1942	Trawler	1942 - 1946
Ruskholm	1942	Trawler	1942 - 1947	**T239**				
T212				*Gruinard*	1942	Trawler	1942 - 1943
Filla	1942	Trawler	1942 - 1946	**T240**				
T213				*Sir Geraint*	1942	Trawler	1942 - 1946
Unst	1942	Trawler	1942 - 1946	**T241**				
T214				*Sir Kay*	1942	Trawler	1942 - 1946
Bressay	1942	Trawler	1942 - 1946	**T242**				
T215				*Sir Lamorak*	1942	Trawler	1942 - 1946
Egilsay	1942	Trawler	1942 - 1946	**T243**				
T216				*Grayling*	1942	Trawler	1942 - 1946
Ensay	1942	Trawler	1942 - 1946	**T244**				
T217				*Mackerel*	1942	Trawler	1942 - 11.42
Eriskay	1942	Trawler	1942 - 1943	**T245**				
T218				*Ringwood*	1924	Netlayer	1941 - 1946
Birdlip	1941	Trawler	1941 - 6.44	**T246**				
T219				*Gweal*	1942	Trawler	1942 - 1946
Butser	1941	Trawler	1941 - 1946	**T247**				
T220				*Neave*	1942	Trawler	1942 - 1946
Duncton	1941	Trawler	1941 - 1946				

T248			
Ulva	1942	Trawler	1942 - 1946
T249			
Baroda RIN	1941	Trawler	1941 - 1947
T250			
Shillong RIN	1941	Trawler	1941 - 1947
T251			
Cuttack RIN	1941	Trawler	1941 - 1946
T252			
Ullswater	1939	Whaler	1939 - 1942
Dacca RIN	Canc	Trawler	Canc 1945
T253			
Lahore RIN	1941	Trawler	1941 - 1946
T254			
Agra RIN	1942	Trawler	1942 - 1946
T255			
Patna RIN	1942	Trawler	1942 - 1947
T256			
Berar RIN	1942	Trawler	1942 - 1947
T258			
Nasik RIN	1944	Trawler	1944 - 1948
T259			
Sholapore RIN	Canc	Trawler	Canc
T260			
Poona RIN	1942	Trawler	1940 - 1946
T261			
Amritsar RIN	1941	Trawler	1941 - 1948
T262			
Karachi RIN	1941	Trawler	1941 - 1947
T263			
Peshawar RIN	1942	Trawler	Canc 1945
T264			
Ahmedabad RIN	1943	Trawler	1943 - 1947
T265			
Chittagong RIN	Canc	Trawler	Canc 1945
T266			
Kolaba RIN	Canc	Trawler	Canc 1945
T267			
Lucknow RIN	1942	Trawler	1942 - 1946
T268			
Madura RIN	1942	Trawler	1942 - 1947
T269			
Rampur RIN	1944	Trawler	1944 - 1948
T270			
Barisal RIN	Canc	Trawler	Canc 1945
T271			
Hayling	1942	Trawler	1942 - 1943
T272			
Lundy	1942	Trawler	1942 - 1946
T273			
Bardsey	1943	Trawler	1943 - 1946
T274			
Anticosti RCN	1942	Trawler	1942 - 1945
T275			
Baffin RCN	1942	Trawler	1942 - 1947
T276			
Cailiff RCN	1942	Trawler	1942 - 1947
T277			
Miscou RCN	1942	Trawler	1942 - 1946
T278			
Campobello RCN	1942	Trawler	1942 - 3.43
T279			
Magdelen RCN	1942	Trawler	1942 - 1946
T280			
Manitoulin	1942	Trawler	1942 - 1946
T281			
Porcher	1942	Trawler	1942 - 1947
T282			
Prospect	1942	Trawler	1942 - 1946
T283			
Texada	1942	Trawler	1942 - 1946
T284			
Ironbound	1942	Trawler	1942 - 1946
T285			
Liscomb RCN	1942	Trawler	1942 - 1946
T286			
Dochet	1942	Trawler	1942 - 1946
T287			
Flint	1942	Trawler	1942 - 1946
T288			
Gateshead	1942	Trawler	1942 - 1948
T289			
Herschell	1942	Trawler	1942 - 1946
T290			
Gairsay	1942	Trawler	1942 - 8.44
T291			
Graemsay	1942	Trawler	1942 - 1946
T292			
Sheppey (ex *Raasay*)	1942	Trawler	1942 - 1946
T293			
Whalsay	1942	Trawler	1942 - 1943
T294			
Bern	1942	Trawler	1942 - 1946
T295			
Mousa	1942	Trawler	1942 - 1946
T296			
Oxna	1943	Trawler	1943 - 1946
T297			
Earraid (ex *Gruna*)	1941	Trawler	1941 - 1946
T298			
Hunda	1942	Trawler	1942 - 1946
T299			
Lal RIN	1931	Patrol Vsl	1941 - 1946
T300			
Moti RIN	1931	Patrol Vsl	1941 - 1946
T301			
Hira RIN	1931	Patrol Vsl	1941 - 1946

T302			
Nilam RIN	1931	Patrol Vsl	1941 - 1946
T303			
Zulfaquar RIN	(....)	APV	.... - ....
T304			
Bombadier	1943	Trawler	1943 - 1946
T305			
Fusilier	1942	Trawler	1942 - 1946
T306			
Bream	1942	Trawler	1942 - 1946
T307			
Herring	1942	Trawler	1942 - 4.43
T309			
Douwe Aukes RNLN	1922	Minelayer	1940 - 1945
T310			
Seica RIN	(....)	....	.... - ....
T311			
Mullet	1942	Trawler	1942 - 1946
T312			
Travancore RIN	1941	Trawler	1941 - 1947
T313			
Vizagapatam RIN	Canc	Trawler	Canc 1945
T314			
Trichinopoly RIN	Canc	Trawler	Canc 1945
T315			
Cochin RIN	1943	Trawler	1943 - 1950
T317			
Allahabad RIN	Canc	Trawler	Canc 1945
T318			
Benares RIN	Canc	Trawler	Canc 1945
T319			
Bareilly RIN	Canc	Trawler	Canc 1945
T320			
Ambala RIN	Canc	Trawler	Canc 1945
T321			
Sialkot RIN	Canc	Trawler	Canc 1945
T322			
Multan RIN	1944	Trawler	Canc 1945
T323			
Jubbalpore RIN	Canc	Trawler	Canc 1945
T324			
Pachmarhi RIN	Canc	Trawler	Canc 1945
T325			
Gaya RIN	Canc	Trawler	Canc 1945
T326			
Dinapore RIN	Canc	Trawler	Canc 1945
T327			
Monghyr RIN	Canc	Trawler	Canc 1945
T328			
Puri RIN	Canc	Trawler	Canc 1945
T329			
Sylhet RIN	Canc	Trawler	Canc 1945
T330			
Kiamari RIN	Canc	Trawler	Canc 1945
T331			

Bannu RIN	Canc	Trawler	Canc 1945
T332			
Quetta RIN	1944	Trawler	Canc 1945
T334			
Grenadier	1942	Trawler	1942 - 1946
T335			
Lancer	1942	Trawler	1942 - 1946
T336			
Sapper	1942	Trawler	1942 - 1946
T337			
Coldstreamer	1942	Trawler	1942 - 1946
T338			
Maimai RNZN	1943	Trawler	1943 - 1946
T339			
Calcutta RIN	1943	Trawler	1943 - 1948
T340			
Hautapu RNZN	1942	Trawler	1943 - 1945
T341			
Annet	1943	Trawler	1943 - 1946
T342			
Foulness	1942	Trawler	1942 - 1946
T343			
Waikato RNZN	1943	Trawler	1944 - 1946
T344			
Grassholm	1943	Trawler	1943 - 1946
T345			
Wallasea	1943	Trawler	1943 - 1.44
T346			
Cawnpore RIN	Canc	Trawler	Canc 1945
T347			
Pollock	1943	Trawler	1943 - 1946
T348			
Tawhai RNZN	1943	Trawler	1944 - 1946
T349			
Waima RNZN	1943	Trawler	1944 - 1946
T350			
Bryher	1943	Trawler	1943 - 1947
T351			
Pahau RNZN	1943	Trawler	1944 - 1945
T352			
St Agnes	1943	Trawler	1943 - 1946
T353			
Farne	1943	Trawler	1943 - 1946
T354			
Flatholm	1943	Trawler	1943 - 1946
T355			
Gillstone	1943	Trawler	1943 - 1946
T356			
Steepholm	1943	Trawler	1943 - 1946
T357			
Waipu RNZN	1943	Trawler	1944 - 1946
T359			
Caldy	1943	Trawler	1943 - 1946
T360			
Grain	1943	Trawler	1943 - 1946

T361			
Lindisfarne	1943	Trawler	1943 - 1946
T362			
Minalto	1943	Trawler	1943 - 1947
T363			
Rosevean	1943	Trawler	1943 - 1946
T364			
Waiau RNZN	Canc	Trawler	Canc 1943
T365			
Gulland	1943	Trawler	1943 - 1946
T366			
Longa	1943	Trawler	1943 - 1946
T367			
Ganilly	1943	Trawler	1943 - 7.44
T368			
Grilse	1943	Trawler	1943 - 1946
T370			
Gale RNZN	1935	MS	1940 - 1944
T371			
Breeze RNZN	1933	MS	1942 - 1944
T372			
Matai RNZN	1930	MS	1941 - 1945
T373			
Viti RAN	1940	MS	1941 - 1944
T374			
Mewstone	1943	Trawler	1943 - 1946
T375			
Oronsay	1943	Trawler	1943 - 1948
T376			
Skokholm	1943	Trawler	1943 - 1946
T377			
Ailsa Craig	1943	Trawler	1943 - 1946
T378			
Vatersay	1943	Trawler	1943 - 1946
T379			
Benbucula	1943	Trawler	1943 - 1946
T380			
Crowlin	1943	Trawler	1943 - 1946
T381			
Skomer	1943	Trawler	1943 - 1946
T382			
Kittern	1943	Trawler	1943 - 1946
T383			
Calvay	1943	Trawler	1943 - 1946
T384			
Colsay	1943	Trawler	1943 - 11.44
T385			
Fuday	1944	Trawler	1943 - 1946
T386			
Gilsay	1944	Trawler	1943 - 1944
Harris (ex *Gilsay*)	1944	Trawler	1944 - 1947
T387			
Gorregan	1943	Trawler	1943 - 1948

T388			
Mincarlo	1944	Trawler	1944
T389			
Hannaray	1944	Trawler	1944 - 1947
T390			
Hascosay	1944	Trawler	1944 - 1947
T391			
Hellisay	1944	Trawler	1944 - 1947
T392			
Hermetray	1944	Trawler	1944 - 1947
T393			
Guardsman	1944	Trawler	1944 - 1946
T394			
Home Guard	1944	Trawler	1944 - 1946
T395			
Royal Marine	1944	Trawler	1944 - 1946
T396			
Aroha RNZN	1942	Trawler	1943 - 1945
T397			
Awatere RNZN	1942	Trawler	1943 - 1945
T398			
Hawera RNZN	1912	MS	1941 - 1945
T399			
Hinau RNZN	1941	Trawler	1943 - 1945
T400			
Kapuni RNZN	1909	MS	1944 - 1945
T401			
Manuka RNZN	1941	Trawler	1942 - 1945
T402			
Rimu RNZN	1941	Trawler	1942 - 1945
T403			
Waiho RNZN	1944	Trawler	1944 - 1946
T404			
Biggal RNZN	1944	Trawler	1944 - 1946
T440			
Nigel SAN	1930	Whaler	1944 - 1946
T441			
Langlaagte SAN	1929	Whaler	1942 - 1946
T442			
Brakpan SAN	1936	Whaler	1944 - 1946
T443			
Protea SAN	1936	Whaler	1944 - 1946
T444			
Sonneblom SAN	1936	Whaler	1944 - 1946
T445			
Immortelle SAN	1936	Whaler	1944 - 1946
T446			
Boksburg SAN	1926	Whaler	1944 - 1946
T447			
Germiston SAN	1923	Whaler	1944 - 1946
T448			
Krugersdorp	1923	Whaler	1944 - 1946
T449			
Bever SAN	1930	Whaler	1944 - 1946

Pendant	Name	Year	Type	Dates
T450				
	Gribb SAN	1930	Whaler	1944 - 1946
T451				
	Treern SAN	1929	Whaler	1944 - 1946
T452				
	Seksern SAN	1930	Whaler	1944 - 1946
T453				
	Imhoff SAN	1927	Whaler	1944 - 1946
T454				
	Benoni SAN	1925	Whaler	1944 - 1946
T455				
	Parktown II SAN	1925	Whaler	1944 - 1946
T456				
	Johannesburg	1925	Whaler	1944 - 1946
T457				
	Roodepotort SAN	1929	Whaler	1944 - 1946
T458				
	Tordonn SAN	1925	Trawler	1944 - 1946
T459				
	Pretoria SAN	1930	Whaler	1944 - 1946
T460				
	Standerton SAN	1936	Whaler	1944 - 1946
T461				
	Turffontein SAN	1936	Whaler	1944 - 1946
T462				
	Soetvlei SAN	1929	Whaler	1944 - 1946
T463				
	Brakvlei SAN	1929	Whaler	1944 - 1946
T464				
	Hektor SAN	1929	Whaler	1944 - 1946
T465				
	Odburg SAN	1936	Whaler	1944 - 1946
T466				
	Southern Floe SAN	1936	Whaler	1944 - 1946
T467				
	Southern Maid SAN	1936	Whaler	1944 - 1946
T468				
	Southern Barrier SAN	1936	Whaler	1944 - 1946
T469				
	Southern Isles SAN	1936	Whaler	1944 - 1946
T470				
	Southern Sea SAN	1936	Whaler	1944 - 1946
T471				
	Cedarberg SAN	1936	Whaler	1944 - 1946
T472				
	Blaawberg SAN	1936	Whaler	1944 - 1946
T473				
	Sydostlandet SAN	1935	Whaler	1944 - 1946
T474				
	Florida SAN	1930	Whaler	1944 - 1946
T475				
	Kommetjie SAN	1930	Whaler	1944 - 1946
T476				
	Steenberg SAN	1929	Whaler	1944 - 1946
T477				
	Stellenburg SAN	1929	Whaler	1944 - 1946
T478				
	Springs SAN	1930	Whaler	1944 - 1946
T479				
	Parktown SAN	1925	Trawler	1944 - 1946
T501				
	Africana SAN	1930	Trawler	1944 - 1946
T502				
	Natalia SAN	1925	Trawler	4.40 - 6.46
T503				
	Goulding SAN	1921	Trawler	6.40 - 1946
T504				
	Grimwood SAN	1924	Trawler	5.40 - 3.46
T505				
	Larsen SAN	1924	Trawler	1.40 - 4.46
T506				
	Robinson SAN	1927	Trawler	6.40 - 4.46
T507				
	Whytock SAN	1924	Trawler	1941 - 6.46
T508				
	Oostewal SAN	1926	Trawler	1944 - 1946
T509				
	Swarteberg SAN	1923	Trawler	10.39 - 5.46
T510				
	Arum SAN	1926	Trawler	1.40 - 10.44
T511				
	Nerine SAN	1925	Trawler	12.39 - 10.44
T512				
	Randfontein SAN	1926	Trawler	1942 - 4.46
T513				
	David Haigh	1918	Trawler	9.39 - 6.46
T514				
	Rondevlei SAN	1929	Trawler	6.40 - 5.46
T515				
	Smalvlei SAN	1929	Trawler	6.40 - 5.46
T516				
	Mooivlei SAN	1935	Trawler	11.39 - 3.45
T517				
	Blomvlei SAN	1935	Trawler	3.40 - 3.45
T518				
	Aristea SAN	1935	Trawler	1.40 - 12.44
T519				
	Crassula SAN	1935	Trawler	6.40 - 12.46
T520				
	Babiana SAN	1935	Trawler	9.39 - 12.44
T521				
	Bluff SAN	1935	Trawler	9.39 - 12.44
T0A				
	Pelargonium	1918	Sloop	1.18 - ....
	Sonoma USN	1912	Tug	6.18 - ....
	Dundalk	1919	MS	11.19 - ....
T1A				
	Windflower	1918	Sloop	1.18 - ....

Ontario USN	1912	Tug	6.18 -		**TC2**			
					Blackmorevale	1917	MS	6.18 - ....
T2A					*Pontefract*	1916	Paddle MS	9.18 - ....
Tuberose	1917	Sloop	1.18 -					
Patuxent USN	1908	Tug	6.18 -		**TC3**			
					Cotswold	1916	MS	6.18 - ....
T3A					**TC4**			
Syringa	1917	Sloop	1.18 - 6.18		*Croome*	1917	MS	6.18 - ....
Patapsco USN	1908	Tug	6.18 -		**TC5**			
					Dartmoor	1917	MS	6.18 - ....
T4A					**TC6**			
Andromede Fr	1917	Sloop	1.18 - 6.18		*Garth*	1917	MS	6.18 - ....
Avocet USN	1918	Minesweeper	6.18 -		**TC7**			
					Hambledon	1917	MS	6.18 - ....
T5A								
Bobolink USN	1918	Minesweeper	6.18 -		**TC8**			
T6A					*Heythrop*	1917	MS	6.18 - ....
Cardinal USN	1918	Minesweeper	6.18 -		*Sutton*	1918	MS	11.19 - ....
T7A					**TC9**			
Finch USN	1918	Minesweeper	6.18 -		*Holderness*	1916	MS	6.18 - ....
Truro	1919	MS	11.19 -		*Fareham*	1918	MS	11.19 - ....
T8A					**TA0**			
Lapwing USN	1918	Minesweeper	6.18 -		*Tanager* USN	1918	MS	6.18 - ....
T9A					**TA1**			
Owl USN	1918	Minesweeper	6.18 -		*Widgeon* USN	1918	MS	6.18 - ....
					TA2			
T0C					*Teal* USN	1918	MS	6.18 - ....
Muskerry	1916	MS	6.18 -		**TA3**			
T1C					*Heron* USN	1918	MS	6.18 - ....
Oakley	1917	MS	6.18 -		**TA4**			
T2C					*Turkey* USN	1918	MS	6.18 - ....
Pytchley	1917	MS	6.18 -					
T3C					**TA5**			
Quorn	1917	MS	6.18 -		*Woodcock* USN	1918	MS	6.18 - ....
T4C					*Munlochy*	1918	MS	11.19 - ....
Tedworth	1917	MS	6.18 -					
T5C					**TA6**			
Zetland	1917	MS	6.18 -		*Yeovil*	1918	MS	1919 - 11.19
T6C					*Craigie*	1918	MS	11.19 - ....
Cottesmore	1917	MS	6.18 -					
T7C					**TA7**			
Meynell	1917	MS	6.18 -		*Nailsea*	1918	MS	1919 - 11.19
					Yeovil	1918	MS	11.19 - ....
T8C								
Gretna	1918	MS	9.18 - 11.19		**TA8**			
Bootle	1918	MS	11.19 -		*Northolt*	1918	MS	1919 - ....
					TA9			
T9C					*Tonbridge*	1918	MS	1919 - ....
Bootle	1918	MS	9.18 - 11.19					
TC0					**TN0**			
Belvoir	1917	MS	6.18 -		*Faversham*	1918	MS	10.18 - 11.19
TC1					*Derby*	1918	MS	11.19 - ....
Bicester	1917	MS	6.18 -					

TN1			
Badminton	1918	MS	10.18 - 11.19
Harrow	1918	MS	11.19 - ....

TN2			
Iroquois	1918	MS	10.18 - ....
Havant	1919	MS	11.19 - ....

TN3			
Tiverton	1918	MS	10.18 - 11.19
Stoke	1918	MS	11.19 - ....

TN4			
Derby	1918	MS	10.18 - 11.19

TN5			
Harrow	1918	MS	10.18 - 11.19
Blackburn	1918	MS	11.19 - ....

TN6			
Stoke	1918	MS	10.18 - 11.19
Leamington	1918	MS	11.19 - ....

TN7			
Spearmint	1918	MS	10.18 - ....
Ford	1918	MS	11.19 - ....

TN8			
Blackburn	1918	MS	10.18 - 11.19

TN9			
Mallaig	1918	MS	11.19 - ....
Bend Or	1918	MS	1919 - ....

T0N			
Sutton	1918	MS	1919 - 11.19
Morris Dance	1918	MS	6.19 - ....
Aberdare	1918	MS	11.19 - ....

T1N			
Fareham	1918	MS	1919 - ....
Step Dance	1918	MS	6.19 - ....
Widnes	1918	MS	11.19 - ....

T2N			
Sefton	1918	MS	8.18 - ....
Weybourne	1919	MS	5.19 - 6.19
Fandango	1917	MS	6.19 - 11.19
Prestatyn	1918	MS	11.19 - ....

T3N			
Cicero	1918	MS	8.18 - 5.19
Sir Hugo	1918	MS	5.19 - ....
Sword Dance	1918	MS	6.19 - ....

T4N			
Tring	1918	MS	8.18 - ....
Weybourne	1919	MS	11.19 - ....

T5N			
Kinross	1918	MS	8.18 - Sunk
Prestatyn	1918	MS	11.18 - 11.19
Newark	1918	MS	11.19 - ....

T6N			
Widnes	1918	MS	9.18 - ....
Sanfoin	1918	MS	11.18 - ....
Saltash	1918	MS	11.19 - ....

T7N			
Newark	1918	MS	1919 - 11.19
Faversham	1918	MS	11.19 - ....

T8N			
Merry Hampton	1918	MS	5.19 - ....
Badminton	1918	MS	11.19 - ....

T9N			
Saltash	1918	MS	10.18 - 11.19
Tiverton	1918	MS	11.19 - ....

T0/			
Ross	1919	MS	8.19 - 11.19
Tralee	1918	MS	11.19 - ....

T1/			
Leamington	1918	MS	12.18 - 11.19
Selkirk	1918	MS	11.19 - ....

T2/			
Ford	1918	MS	12.18 - 11.19

T3/			
Saltburn	1918	MS	12.18 - 11.19
Mistley	1918	MS	11.19 - ....

T4/			
Persimmon	1918	MS	4.19 - ....

T5/			
Mallaig	1918	MS	12.18 - 11.19
Saltburn	1918	MS	11.19 - ....

T6/			
Tralee	1918	MS	12.18 - 11.19
Forfar	1918	MS	11.19 - ....

T7/			
Stafford	1918	MS	7.19 - 11.19
Camberley	1918	MS	11.19 - ....

T8/				**T/5**			
Caerleon	1918	MS	1.19 - 11.19	Elgin	1919	MS	1919 - 11.19
T9/							
Albury	1918	MS	1.19 - 11.19	**T/6**			
T/0				Forfar	1918	MS	1919 - 11.19
Lydd	1918	MS	1.19 - 11.19	Donovan	1918	MS	11.19 - ....
T/1							
Forres	1918	MS	1919 - 11.19	**T/7**			
T/2				Camberley	1918	MS	1919 - 11.19
Selkirk	1918	MS	1919 - 11.19	**T/8**			
T/3				Petersfield	1919	MS	1919 - 11.19
Sir Visto	1918	MS	1919 -	**T/9**			
T/4				Havant	1919	MS	1919 - 11.19
Mistley	1918	MS	1919 - 11.19				

Flag 'U' Superior

Pre 1940:	None
1940–48:	Escort Vessels; Auxiliary Patrol Vessels, AS Trawlers
1948:	None

U01				**U20**			
Bridgewater	1928	Sloop	1940 - 1948	*Snipe*	1945	Sloop	1945 - 1948
U02				**U21**			
Arras FR	1917	Sloop	1940 - 1945	*Jumna* RIN	1940	Sloop	1940 - 1948
U03				**U22**			
Erne	1940	Sloop	1940 - 1948	*Folkestone*	1930	Sloop	1940 - 1948
U04				**U23**			
Vaillant FR	1921	Aux Pat Vsl	1940 - 1945	*Crane*	1942	Sloop	1942 - 1948
				U24			
U05				*Epinal* FR	1919	Sloop	1940 - 1945
Waterhen	Canc	Sloop	Canc 1945	**U25**			
Chanticleer	1942	Sloop	1942 - 11.43	*Scarborough*	1930	Sloop	1940 - 1948
				U26			
U06				*Foxglove*	1915	Sloop	1940 - 7.40
Pessac FR	1907	Aux Pat Vsl	1940 - 1941	**U27**			
				Hastings	1930	Sloop	1940 - 1946
U07							
Bittern	1937	Sloop	1940 - 4.40	**U28**			
Actaeon	1945	Sloop	1945 - 1948	*Penzance*	1930	Sloop	1940 - 8.40
				Wren	1942	Sloop	1942 - 1948
U08							
Woodpecker	1942	Sloop	1942 - 2.44	**U29**			
U09				*Whimbrel*	1942	Sloop	1942 - 1948
Cornwallis RIN	1917	Sloop	1940 - 1946	**U30**			
U10				*Mermaid*	1943	Sloop	1943 - 1948
Cauvery RIN	1943	Sloop	1943 - 1948				
U11				**U31**			
Lark	1943	Sloop	1943 - 2.45	*Wryneck*	Canc	Sloop	Canc 1945
U12				*Pomerol* FR	1930	Aux Pat Vsl	.... - ....
Sandwich	1928	Sloop	1940 - 1946				
U14				**U32**			
Rosemary	1915	Sloop	1940 - 1948	*Shoreham*	1930	Sloop	1940 - 1946
U15				**U33**			
Fowey	1930	Sloop	1940 - 1946	*Opossum*	1944	Sloop	1944 - 1948
				U34			
U16				*Falmouth*	1932	Sloop	1940 - 1948
Grimsby	1933	Sloop	1940 - 5.41	**U35**			
Amethyst	1943	Sloop	1943 - 1948	*Temeraire II* FR	1926	Aux Pat Vsl	.... - 1940
				U36			
U17				*Leith*	1933	Sloop	1940 - 1946
La Moqueuse FR	1940	MS	1940 - 1945	**U37**			
U18				*Partridge*	Canc	Sloop	Canc 1945
Flamingo	1939	Sloop	1940 - 1948	**U38**			
U19				*Cygnet*	1942	Sloop	1942 - 1948
Lupin	1916	Sloop	1940 - 1946				

U39			
Hind	1943	Sloop	1943 - 1948
U40			
Narbada RIN	1942	Sloop	1942 - 1948
U41			
Commandant Duboc FR	1939	MS	1940 - 1945
U42			
Modeste	1944	Sloop	1944 - 1948
U43			
Bideford	1931	Sloop	1940 - 1948
U44			
Parramatta RAN	1939	Sloop	1940 - 11.41
U45			
Wild Goose	1942	Sloop	1942 - 1948
U46			
Kistna RIN	1943	Sloop	1943 - 1948
U47			
Fleetwood	1936	Sloop	1940 - 1948
U49			
Pheasant	1942	Sloop	1942 - 1948
U50			
Rochester	1931	Sloop	1940 - 1948
U51			
Milford	1932	Sloop	1940 - 1948
U52			
Godavari RIN	1940	Sloop	1943 - 1948
U53			
Deptford	1935	Sloop	1940 - 1948
U54			
Moresby RAN	1918	Sloop	1940 - 1948
Nonsuch	Canc	Sloop	Canc 1945
U55			
Sauternes FR	1922	Aux Pat Vsl	1941 - 12.41
U56			
Enchantress	1934	Sloop	1940 - 1946
U57			
Black Swan	1939	Sloop	1940 - 1948
U58			
Hart	1943	Sloop	1943 - 1948
U59			
Lowestoft	1934	Sloop	1940 - 1946
U60			
Alacrity	1944	Sloop	1944 - 1948
U61			
Auckland	1938	Sloop	1940 - 6.41
U62			
Lapwing	1943	Sloop	1943 - 3.45
U63			
Belfort FR	1919	Depot Ship	1940 - 1945
U64			
Nereide	1944	Sloop	1944 - 1948

U65			
Wellington	1934	Sloop	1940 - 1945
U66			
Starling	1942	Sloop	1942 - 1948
U67			
Indus RIN	1934	Sloop	1940 - 4.42
U68			
Amiens FR	1919	Sloop	1940 - 1945
U69			
Redpole	1943	Sloop	1943 - 1948
U70			
Commandant Domine FR	1939	MS	1942 - 1945
U71			
Sparrow	1946	Sloop	1946 - 1948
U72			
Weston	1932	Sloop	1940 - 1948
U73			
Warrego RAN	1940	Sloop	1940 - 1948
U74			
Swan RAN	1936	Sloop	1940 - 1948
U75			
Egret	1938	Sloop	1940 - 8.43
U76			
Londonderry	1935	Sloop	1940 - 1948
U77			
Yarra RAN	1935	Sloop	1940 - 3.42
U78			
Vikings FR	1935	Trawler	1940 - 4.42
U79			
Clive RIN	1919	Sloop	1940 - 1948
U80			
Hindustan RIN	1930	Sloop	1940 - 1948
U81			
Stork	1936	Sloop	1940 - 1948
U82			
Magpie	1943	Sloop	1943 - 1948
U83			
Lawrence RIN	1919	Sloop	1940 - 1948
U84			
Dundee	1932	Sloop	1940 - 9.40
Nymphe	Canc	Sloop	Canc 1945
U86			
Pelican	1938	Sloop	1940 - 1948
U87			
Kite	1942	Sloop	1942 - 8.44
U89			
Chevreuil FR	1939	MS	1940 - 1945
U90			
Woodcock	1942	Sloop	1942 - 1948
U92			
La Capricieuse FR	1939	MS	1940 - 1945

U93
Coucy FR	1919	Gunboat	1940 - ....
Van Kinsbergen RNLN	1939	Artillery Ship	1940 - 1945

U94
Gazelle FR	1939	MS	1942 - 1945

U95
Sutlej RIN	1940	Sloop	1940 - 1948

U96
Peacock	1943	Sloop	1943 - 1948

U97
Annamite FR	1939	MS	1942 - 1945

U98
Leoville FR	1922	Aux Pat Vsl	.... - ....

U99
Ibis	1940	Sloop	1940 - 11.42

Flag 'W' Superior

Pre 1940:	Tugs, Salvage; Vessels and Lifting Craft
1940-48:	Tugs and Salvage Vessels
1948:	None

W00

Atalanta III	1907	Tug	1.18 - 1.20

W01

Autocrat	1915	Tug	9.18 - 2.20
Freebooter	1940	Tug	1940 - 1948

W02

St Abbs	1918	Tug	9.18 - 6.40
Hudson	1939	Tug	1940 - 1946

W03

Drage (ex *Dragon*)	1893	Tug	9.18 - ....
Pilot	1909	Tug	.... - 1948

W04

Bramley Moore	1916	Tug	1.18 - 9.18
St Genny	1919	Tug	9.18 - 1930
Toia RNZN	1919	Tug	1919 - 1945
Rockwing RCN	1945	Tug	1945 - 1948

W05

St Arvans	1919	Tug	9.18 - 1923
Emprise	1899	Tug	1919 - 1935
Prince Salvor	1943	Salvage Vsl	1943 - 1948

W06

St Clears	1919	Tug	1940 - 1948
Uplifter	1943	Salvage Vsl	1943 - 1948

W07

St Columb	1918	Tug	9.18 - 1.20
Stalwart	1939	Tug	1939 - 1941

W08

Genesee USN	1905	Tug	9.18 - ....
St Helier	1919	Tug	11.19 - 1920
Perseverance	1931	Tug	1936 - 1948

W09

Cartmel	1907	Tug	1.18 - ....
Caroline Moller	1919	Tug	1939 - 1942

W10

Central No1	1910	Tug	1.18 - ....

West Cocker	1919	Tug	.... - 4.42

W11

Central No2	1912	Tug	1.18 - ....
Frisky	1941	Tug	1941 - 19487

W12

Coringa	1914	Tug	1.18 - ....
Swarthy	1912	Tug	... - 1948

W14

Croft	1913	Tug	1.18 - ....
Integrity	1942	Tug	1942 - 1946

W15

Cynic	1916	Tug	1.18 - 1922
Firm	1910	Tug	.... - 1948
Rockcliffe	1945	Tug	1945 - 1946

W16

Conqueress	1913	Tug	1.18 - ....

W17

Criccieth	1905	Tug	1.18 - ....
Lariat	1942	Tug	1942 - 1946

W18

St Aubin	1918	Tug	9.18 - 1924
Tenacity	1940	Tug	1940 - 1948

W19

Director Gerling	1892	Tug	1.18 - ....
Cracker	1899	Tug	.... - 1948

W20

Dragon	1893	Tug	1.18 - 9.18
St Boniface	1919	Tug	11.19 - ....
Masterful	1942	Tug	1942 - 1948

W21

Dreadful	1912	Tug	1.18 - ....
Recovery	1908	Tug	1934 - 1948

W22

Epic	1909	Tug	1.18 - ....

St Finbarr	1919	Tug	11.19 - 1923		**W36**			
Wave	1939	Tug	1939 - 1945		*St Anne* RCN	1919	Tug	9.18 - 1922
					Danube V	1935	Tug	1935 - 1945
W23								
St Bees	1918	Tug	9.18 - 1922		**W37**			
Samsonia	1942	Tug	1942 - 1948		*George Dinsdale*	1913	Tug	1.18 - ....
W24					**W38**			
Advice	1899	Tug	.... - 1948		*George V*	1915	Tug	1.18 - ....
					Camel	1914	Tug	.... - 1948
W25					*Rockmount* RCN	1945	Tug	1945 - 1948
Flying Buzzard	1912	Tug	1.18 -					
St Issey	1918	Tug	11.19 - 12.42		**W39**			
					Guiana	1886	Tug	1.18 - ....
W26					*Restive*	1940	Tug	1940 - 1948
Flying Cormorant	1908	Tug	1.18 -					
St Sampson	1919	Tug	11.19 - 1942		**W40**			
Grappler	1908	Tug	.... - 1948		*St Athan*	1919	Tug	9.18 - ....
Rockglen RCN	1945	Tug	1945 - 1948		*St Olaves*	1918	Tug	1939 - 9.42
W27					**W41**			
Flying Falcon	1904	Tug	1.18 -		*Sonia*	1916	Tug	9.18 - ....
St Martin	1919	Tug	11.19 - 1946		*Atlas*	1909	Tug	.... - 1948
W28					**W42**			
Flying Foam	1917	Tug	1.18 -		*Heroine*	1909	Tug	1.18 - ....
Robust	1907	Tug	... - 1948		*Pert*	1916	Tug	.... - 1948
W29					**W43**			
Flying Spray	1917	Tug	1.18 -		*Hippopotamus*	1897	Lifting Craft	1.18 - ....
Trunnion	1938	Tug	1938 - 1948		*Salvonia*	1939	Tug	1939 - 1945
W30					**W44**			
Fortitude	1896	Tug	1.18 - 1923		*St Catherine*	1919	Tug	9.18 - ....
Jaunty	1941	Tug	1941 - 1948		*Seaman*	1924	Tug	1939 - 1945
W31					**W45**			
Francis Batey	1914	Tug	1.18 -		*Joseph Constantine*	1913	Tug	1.18 - ....
Flamer	1940	Tug	1940 - 1948		*Tyke*	1911	Tug	.... - 1948
W32					**W46**			
Furness	1898	Tug	1.18 -		*St Blazey*	1919	Tug	1919 - 1946
Industrious	1902	Tug	.... - 1948					
					W47			
W33					*St Cyrus*	1919	Tug	1919 - 1.41
Fylde	1904	Tug	1.18 -		*Kenia*	1927	Tug	1939 - 1945
Terrier	1913	Tug	... - 1948					
					W48			
W34					*Labour*	1916	Tug	1.18 - ....
St Botolph	1918	Tug	9.18 -		*Sandboy*	1912	Tug	.... - 1948
St Omar	1919	Tug	1919 - 1948					
Salvage Duke	1943	Salvage Vsl	1943 - 1948		**W49**			
					Lady Brassey	1913	Tug	1.18 - ....
W35					*Buccaneer*	1937	Tug	1937 - 1946
Champion	1939	Tug	1939 - 1945					

W50
Lady Crundall	1906	Tug	1.18 - ....
Allegiance	1943	Tug	1943 - 1948

W51
St Boswells	1919	Tug	9.18 - 1920
Alligator	1940	Tug	1940 - 1945

W52
Margaret Ham	1913	Tug	1.18 - ....
Gatling	1945	Arm. Stores	1945 - 1948
Rockport RCN	1945	Tug	1945 - 1948

W53
Marsden	1917	Tug	1.18 - ....
Sprite	1915	Tug	.... - 1948

W54
Merrimac	1918	Tug	1.18 - ....
Ancient	1915	Tug	.... - 1948

W55
Milewater	1888	Tug	1.18 - ....
St Day	1918	Tug	1918 - 1948

W56
Moonfleet	1917	Tug	1.18 - ....
St James	1919	Tug	1919 - ....
St Breock	1919	Tug	1919 - 2.42
(ex St James)			
Mammoth	1917	Tug	1943 - 1946

W57
Woonda	1915	Tug	9.18 - ....
Tampeon	1938	Tug	1938 - 1948

W58
Oceana	1889	Tug	1.18 - 10.18
(ex Cerberus)			
West Hyde	1919	Tug	.... - 1948

W59
Linnet	1880	Salvage Vsl	6.18 - 1919
Assurance	1940	Tug	1940 - Lost
C405	1931	Tug	.... - ....

W60
Sun VII	1918	Tug	9.18 - ....
Impetus	1940	Tug	1940 - 1948

W61
Paladin II	1913	Tug	1.18 - ....
Volatile	1899	Tug	.... - 1948

W62
Pilot	1909	Tug	1.18 - ....
Revue	1939	Tug	1939 - ....

W63
Blazer	1888	Tug	9.18 - ....
St Monance	1919	Tug	1919 - 1946

W64
Victor	1898	Tug	9.18 - ....
Rathven Burn	1919	Tug	.... - 1946

W65
Plunger	1900	Tug	9.18 - ....
Poet Chaucer	1919	Tug	.... - 1941

W66
Revenger	1905	Tug	9.18 - ....
St Dogmael	1918	Tug	1918 - 1950
Rockforest	1945	Tug	1945 - 1948

W67
Ranger	1880	Salvage Vsl	9.18 - 1919
Mary Tavy	1918	Tug	.... - 1948

W68
Rhinoceros	1897	Lifting Craft	1.18 - ....
Attentif FR	1939	Tug	1944 - 1945

W69
Joffre	1916	Tug	9.18 - ....
Bandit	1938	Tug	1938 - 1948
Briton (ex Bandit)	1938	Tug	1948 - 1948

W70
Mastodonte	1919	Tug	1939 - 1945

W71
Vulcain	1903	Tug	9.18 - ....
Energetic	1902	Tug	.... - 1948

W72
Seahorse	1880	Tug	1.18 - ....
Bustler	1941	Tug	1941 - 1948

W73
Stobo Castle	1917	Tug	1.18 - ....
Prudent	1940	Tug	1940 - 1948
Cautious	1940	Tug	1948 - 1948
(ex Prudent)			

W74
Stormbird	1885	Tug	1.18 - ....
St Fagan	1919	Tug	1919 - 6.40
Sabine	1917	Tug	1940 - 1950

W75			
Stormcock	1884	Tug	1.18 - ....
Confiance	1884	Tug	.... - ....
W76			
Sun II	1909	Tug	1.18 - ....
Washington	1881	Tug	9.18 - ....
Grinder	1943	Tug	Incomplete
W77			
Alliance	1910	Tug	9.18 - 12.41
W78			
Paladin	1913	Tug	1.18 - 9.18
Neptor	1915	Tug	9.18 - ....
West Bay	1918	Tug	.... - 1948
W79			
Stoic	1919	Tug	9.18 - 1920
Handmaid	1940	Tug	1940 - 1948
Rockland RCN	1945	Tug	1945 - 1948
W80			
Traveller	1885	Tug	1.18 - 1920
Rambler	1908	Tug	1940 - 1948
W81			
Rollcall	1918	Tug	9.18 - 6.21
St Mellons	1918	Tug	1918 - 1948
W82			
Hughli	1894	Salv	9.18 - 5.19
Richard Lee Barber	1940	Tug	1944 - 1945
W83			
Vanquisher II	1899	Tug	1.18 - 1919
Brigand	1937	Tug	1937 - 1948
W84			
Retort	1918	Tug	9.18 - ....
W85			
Resolve	1918	Tug	9.18 - 1948
W86			
Warrior	1895	Tug	1.18 - ....
Hellespont	1910	Tug	.... - 4.42
W87			
William Poulson	1917	Tug	1.18 - ....
Stormking	1942	Tug	1942 - 1948
Tryphon	1942	Tug	1948 - 1948
(ex *Stormking*)			
W88			

Wrestler	1915	Tug	1.18 - ....
Crocodile	1940	Tug	1940 - 1948
Rockpigeon RCN	1945	Tug	1945 - 1948
W89			
St Mellons	1918	Tug	9.18 - ....
Superman	1933	Tug	1939 - 1945
W90			
St Just	1918	Tug	1918 - 2.42
W91			
Zaree	1904	Tug	1.18 - ....
Roysterer	1919	Tug	.... - 1954
W92			
Respond	1918	Tug	9.18 - 1948
W93			
Dandy	1919	Tug	1919 - ....
Long Tow	1919	Tug	1939 - 1946
W94			
Gopher	1910	Tug	9.18 - ....
Abeille IV	1940	Tug	1940 - 1945
W95			
Rival (ex *Jason*)	1915	Tug	1937 - 1948
Rollicker	1918	Tug	1919 - 1948
W96			
St Giles	1919	Tug	9.18 - 1922
Prosperous	1942	Tug	1942 - 1948
W97			
Horsa (ex *Rescue*)	1942	Tug	1942 - 3.43
W98			
Marauder	1938	Tug	1938 - 1948
W99			
Cherbourgeois III	1913	Tug	1940 - 1945
W100			
Driver	1942	Tug	1942 - 1948
W101			
Energy	1942	Tug	1942 - 1948
W102			
Lantaka	(....)	Tug	Incomplete
W103			
Sprightly	1942	Tug	1942 - 1944
W104			
Tancred	1943	Tug	1943 - 1944
W105			
Growler	1942	Tug	1942 - 1948
W106			
Hesperia	1942	Tug	1942 - 2.45

W107

Cherbourgeous IV	1930	Tug	1940 - 1946
Adept	1941	Tug	1941 - 1942

W108

Adherent	1941	Tug	1941 - 1944

W109

Charon	1940	Tug	1940 - 1948
Alligator	1940	Tug	1948 - 1948
(ex *Charon*)			

W110

Hengist	1941	Tug	1941 - 1948
(ex *Decision*)			

W111

Dexterous	1942	Tug	1942 - 1948

W112

Griper	1942	Tug	1942 - 1946

W113

Aimwell	1942	Tug	1942 - 1948

W114

Bold	1942	Tug	1942 - 1948

W115

Destiny	1942	Tug	1942 - 1948

W116

Eminent	1942	Tug	1942 - 1946

W117

Oriana	1942	Tug	1942 - 1946

W118

Patroclus	1943	Tug	1943 - 1948

W119

Favourite	1942	Tug	1942 - 1946

W120

Weasel	1943	Tug	1943 - 1946

W121

Goliath	1921	Tug	1940 - 1945

W122

Gamtoos SAN	1936	Tug	1942 - 1946

W123

Nimble	1941	Tug	1941 - 1948

W124

Penfield	(....)	Tug	1940 - 1946

W125

Mediator	1944	Tug	1944 - 1948

W126

Forceful	1925	Tug	1941 - 1944

W127

Wato RAN	1904	Tug	1941 - 1946

W128

Waree RAN	1939	Tug	1942 - 1946

W129

Falcon	1892	Tug	1941 - 1945
Empire Josephine	1944	Tug	1944 - 1946

W131

Saucy	1942	Tug	1942 - 1948

W132

Neyroy	(....)	.....	.... - ....

W133

Advantage	1942	Tug	1942 - 1946

W134

Aspirant	1942	Tug	1942 - 1948

W135

Mindful	1943	Tug	1943 - 1946

W136

Vagrant	1943	Tug	1943 - 1948

W137

Director	1943	Tug	1943 - 1946

W138

Emulous	1943	Tug	1943 - 1946

W139

Freedom	1943	Tug	1943 - 1946

W140

Justice	1943	Tug	1943 - 1948

W141

Antic	1943	Tug	1943 - 1948

W142

Assiduous	1943	Tug	1943 - 1948

W143

Earner	1943	Tug	1943 - 1948

W144

Sesame	1943	Tug	1943 - 6.44

W145

Empire Griffin	1943	Tug	1943 - 1948

W146

Empire Samson	1943	Tug	1943 - 1948

W147

Empire Ned	1942	Tug	1942 - 1943
Empire Edward	1942	Tug	1943 - 1948
(ex *Empire Ned*)			

W148

Captive	1923	Tug	1942 - 2.46

W149

Reserve	1942	Tug	1942 - 1944

W150

Athlete	1943	Tug	1943 - 7.45

W151

Flare	1943	Tug	1943 - 1946

W152

Flaunt	1943	Tug	1943 - 1946

W153

Cheerly	1943	Tug	1943 - 1946

W154

Emphatic	1943	Tug	1943 - 1948

W155

Empire Fairy	1942	Tug	1942 - 1946

W156			
Schelde	1926	Tug	1940 - 1945

W157			
Empire Fred	1942	Tug	1942 - 1948

W158			
Cannon	1943	Tug	1943

W159			
Empire Sam	1942	Tug	1942 - 1948

W160			
Busy	1941	Tug	11.41 - 7.47

W161			
Confident	1941	Tug	12.41 - 7.47

W162			
Roode Zee	1938	Tug	1941 - 4.44

W163			
Zwarte Zee	1933	Tug	1940 - 1945

W164			
Reward	1944	Tug	1944 - 1948

W165			
Envoy	1944	Tug	1944 - 1948

W166			
Enticer	1944	Tug	1944 - 1946

W167			
Empire Maple	1941	Tug	1941 - 1948

W168			
Bannock	(....)	....	.... - ....

W169			
Turmoil	1944	Tug	1944 - 1948

W170			
Warden	1945	Tug	1945 - 1948

W171			
Capable	1945	Tug	1945 - 1948

W172			
Careful	1945	Tug	1945 - 1948

W173			
Expert	1945	Tug	1945 - 1948

W174			
Barwick	1919	Tug	1942 - 1944
Behest (ex *Barwick*)	1919	Tug	1944 - 1948

W175			
Enigma	1944	Tug	1944 - 1948

W176			
Salvestor	1942	Salv	1942 - 1948

W177			
Enforcer	1944	Tug	1944 - 1948

W178			
Enchanter	1944	Tug	1944 - 1948

W179			
Encore	1944	Tug	1944 - 1948

W180			
Empire Phyllis	1944	Tug	1944 - 1948

W181			
Empire Titania	1942	Tug	1942 - 1948

W182			
Bombshell	1945	Tug	1945 - 1948

W183			
Roundshot	1945	Tug	1945 - 1948

W184			
Grapeshot	1945	Tug	1945 - 1948

W185			
Chainshot	1946	Tug	1946 - 1948

W186			
Aywood	(....)	....	.... - ....

W187			
Empire Minnow	1942	Tug	1942 - 1948

W188			
Atoliu	(....)	....	.... - ....

W189			
Athelny	(....)	....	.... - ....

W190			
Salvictor	1944	Salvage Vsl	1944 - 1948

W191			
King Salvor	1942	Salvage Vsl	1942 - 1948

W192			
Valkyrian	(....)	....	.... - ....

W193			
Sea Giant	1920	Tug	1940 - 1946

189

Flag 'X' Superior

Pre 1940:	Coastguard and Fishery Protection vessels; Mooring Vessels and Fuel Ships
1940-48:	Miscellaneous Vessels; RFAs
1948:	Midget Submarines

X00

Oakol	1917	Tanker	11.45 - 1948

X01

Blackstone	1914	Oiler	1915 - 1.18
Anchorite	1916	Moor	1.18 - ....
Appleleaf	1916	Tanker	1939 - 1948

X02

Mixol	1916	Oiler	1916 - 1.18
Attendant	1913	Oiler	1.18 - ....
Prunella	1930	Decoy	1939 - 6.40

Prunella was a fictitious RFA identity assigned to Special Service freighter HMS *Cape Howe*. The name *Prunella* was used when the ship was in port so her true identity was not disclosed.

X03

Bullfrog	1915	Mooring Vsl	1.16 - 1.18
Bacchus	1936	Store Carrier	1939 - 1948

X04

Montcalm	1897	Decoy	1914 - 11.16
Barkol	1898	Tanker	1.18 - 1920
Robert Dundas	1938	Store Ship	1939 - 1948

Montcalm was taken up by the Admiralty and converted as the dummy battleship HMS *Audacious* a role in which she operated from 28.10.14 - 6.7.15 when the Dummy Battleship Squadron was disbanded.

X05

Perthshire	1893	Store Ship	1.16 - 1.18
Battersol	1898	Tanker	1.18 - 1920
Denbydale	1940	Tanker	.... - ....
C.625	1944	Lighter	1944 - 1963

Perthshire (X05) was hired by the Admiralty in 1914 for conversion to the dummy battleship *HMS Vanguard*, based at Loch Ewe. In November 1915, the Dummy Battleship Squadron was disbanded and *Perthshire* was purchased by the Admiralty for conversion to a stores Storeship. See also X48.

X06

Ruthenia	1900	Oiler	1.16 - 1.18
Belgol	1917	Oiler	1939 - 1948

X07

Ferol	1914	Oiler	1916 - 1.18
Birchol	1917	Oiler	1939 - 1948

X08

Servitor	1914	Oiler	1.16 - 1.18
Blackol	1906	Oiler	1.18 - 1920
Brambleleaf	1916	Tanker	1939 - 1944

X09

Reliance	1910	Store Carrier	1.16 - 1.18
Blackstone	1914	Oiler	1.18 - ....
Olwen	1917	Tanker	1939 - 1948

X10

Petroleum	1902	Oiler	1.16 - 1.18
Boxol	1917	Oiler	1.18 - ....

X11

Trefoil	1913	Oiler	1.16 - 1.18
Buffalo	1916	Mooring Vsl	1.18 - ....
Olynthus	1917	Tanker	1939 - 1948

X12

Turmoil	1917	Oiler	1.16 - 1.18
Bullfrog	1915	Mooring Vsl	1.18 - ....
Oligarch	1918	Tanker	1939 - 1946

X13

Maine II	1906	Hospital Ship	1.16 - 3.16

Was listed in Pendant Lists dated 2.1.16 and 2.4.16 as *Mediator.* Ship was renamed *Maine* on 14.7.1914 following the loss of the previous *Maine*.

X14

Burma	1911	Oiler	1.16 - ....
Derwentdale	1941	Tanker	1941 - 1948

X15

Attendant	1913	Oiler	1.16 - 1.18

Carol	1913	Oiler	1.18 - ....
Lambridge	1917	Decoy	1939 - 1941

Lambridge was a fictitious RFA identity assigned to Special Service freighter HMS *Botlea*. The name *Lambridge* was used when the ship was in port so her true identity was not disclosed.

X16

Carol	1913	Oiler	1916 - 1.18
Celerol	1917	Oiler	1939 - 1948

X17

Steadfast	1906	Mooring Vsl	1.16 - 1.18
City of Oxford	1882	Kite Balloon	1.18 - ....
Cherryleaf	1916	Tanker	1939 - 1948

X18

Limpet	1912	Mooring Vsl	1916 - 1.18
Creosol	1916	Oiler	1.18 - 2.18
Olcades	1918	Tanker	1939 - 1948

X19

Holdfast	1910	Mooring Vsl	1916 - 1.18
Dapper	1915	Mooring Vsl	1.18
Spabeck	1943	Water Carrier	1943 - 1948

X20

Fidget	1915	Mooring Vsl	1916 - ....
Distol	1916	Oiler	1939 - 1948

X21

Polavon	1905	Dist	1.16 - 1.18
Elderol	1917	Tanker	1939 - 1948
Northmark	1937	Tanker	1946 - 1948
Bulawayo	1937	Tanker	1948 - 1948

Northmark (X21) was the former German oiler *Nordmark*, captured by British Forces at Copenhagen on 9 May 1945. Due to a shortage of tankers the Admiralty directed that she be sailed to Rosyth. In January 1946 she was renamed *Northmark* and considered for service as a Royal Fleet Auxiliary. On completion of a refit in July 1948 she was renamed and commissioned as *HMS Bulawayo*.

X22

Bacchus	1915	Water Carrier	1.16 - 1.18
Ebonol	1917	Oiler	1.18 - 12.41

X23

Hungerford	1913	Dist	1.16 - 2.16
Elmol	1917	Oiler	1.18 - 1939
Larchol	1917	Tanker	1917 - 1948

X24

Industry	1901	Store Carrier	1.16 - 1.18
Ferol	1914	Oiler	1.18 - ....
Maine	1902	Hospital Ship	1920 - 1948

X25

Polshannon	1910	WTV	1.16 - 1.18
Fidget	1915	Mooring Vsl	1.18 - ....
Reliant	1922	Store Ship	1939 - 1948

X26

Olympia	1916	Oiler	1.16 - 2.16
Fortol	1917	Oiler	1939 - 1948

X27

Waterwitch	1914	SSV	1.16 - 1.18
Francol	1917	Oiler	1.18 - 3.42
Elderol	1917	Tanker	1939 - 1948

X28

Mercedes	1902	Oiler	1916 - 1.18
Greenol	1907	Oiler	1.18 - 1920
Growler	1890	Store Carrier	3.21 - 11.21
Maunder	1919	Decoy	1939 - 1943

Maunder was a fictitious RFA identity assigned to Special Service freighter HMS *King Gruffydd*. The name *Maunder* was used when the ship was in port so her true identity was not disclosed.

X29

Isla	1903	Oiler	1.16 - 1.18
Hickorol	1917	Oiler	1.18 - 1948

X30

Dapper	1915	Mooring Vsl	1916 - 1.18
Holdfast	1910	Mooring Vsl	1.18 - ....
Gold Ranger	1941	Tanker	1941 - 1948

X31

Kharki	1899	Oiler	1.16 - 1.18
Industry	1901	Store Carrier	1.18 - 1920
John Evelyn	1919	Arm Carrier	1939 - 1946

X32

Creosol	1916	Tanker	2.18 - Sunk
Califol	1916	Oiler	1.16 - 2.16
Roseleaf (ex *Califol*)	1916	Tanker	2.16 - ....
Innisshannon	1913	WTV	1.18 - 2.21
Abbeydale	1936	Tanker	1939 - 1948

X33

Texol	1916	Oiler	2.16 - 2.17
Appleleaf (ex *Texol*)	1916	Oiler	2.17 - 1.18
Isla	1903	Oiler	1.18 - ....

Arndale	1937	Tanker	1939 - 1948

X34

Mollusc (ex Trinculo)	1915	Mooring Vsl	1.16 - 1.18
Kharki	1899	Oiler	1.18 - ....
Aldersdale	1936	Tanker	1939 - 7.42

X35

Anchorite	1916	Mooring Vsl	1916 - 1.18
Kimmerol	1916	Oiler	1.18 - 1948

X36

Thrush	1889	Cg/FPV	1.16 - 4.17
Kurumba RAN	1916	Tanker	1.18 - ....
Cairndale	1938	Tanker	1939 - 5.41

X37

Melita (ex Ringdove)	1888	Salvage Vsl	4.16 - 1.18
Larchol	1917	Oiler	1.18 - 1948

X38

Volunteer	1916	Mooring Vsl	1.16 - 1.18
Limol	1917	Oiler	1.18 - ....
Activity	1942	Esc Carrier	1945 - 1946

X39

Steady	1916	Mooring Vsl	4.16 - 1.18
Limpet	1912	Mooring Vsl	1.18 - ....
Edgehill	1928	Decoy	1939 - 6.40

X40

Racia	1895	Tug	4.16 - ....
Melita (ex Ringdove)	1888	Salvage Vsl	1.18 - 1920
Orangeleaf	1916	Tanker	1939 - 1948

X41

Messenger	1916	Mooring Vsl	1.16 - 1.18
Robert Middleton	1938	Store Ship	1939 - 1948

X42

Lobster	1915	Tanker	1915 - 1920
Buffalo	1916	Mooring Vsl	4.16 - 1.18
Messenger	1916	Mooring Vsl	1.18 - ....
Green Ranger	1941	Tanker	1941 - 1948

X43

Philol	1916	Tanker	4.16 - 1.18
Mixol	1916	Oiler	1.18 - 1948

X44

City of Oxford	1882	Kite Balloon	4.16 - 1.18
Mollusc	1915	Mooring Vsl	1.18 - 1922
Cyprus	1936	Decoy	1939 - 1941
Dingledale	1941	Tanker	1941 - 1948

Cyprus was a fictitious RFA identity assigned to Special Service freighter HMS *Cape Sable*. The name *Cyprus* was used when the ship was in port so her true identity was not disclosed.

X45

Thermol	1916	Oiler	1916 - 1.18
Montenol	1917	Oiler	1.18 - 5.42

X46

Distol	1916	Oiler	4.16 - 1.18
Oakol	1917	Tanker	1.18 - 1.20
Oleander	1922	Tanker	1922 - 5.40

X47

Kimmerol	1916	Oiler	4.16 - 1.18
Palmol	1917	Tanker	1.18 - 1.20
Olna	1921	Tanker	1921 - 5.41
Freshtarn	1944	Water Carrier	1944 - 1948

X48

Cherryleaf (ex Persol)	1916	Oiler	2.16 - 1.18
Perthshire	1893	Tanker	1.18 - ....
Black Ranger	1940	Tanker	1941 - 1948

X49

Scotol	1916	Tanker	1916 - 1.18
Petrella	1918	Spirit Carrier	1.18 - 1946

X50

Brambleleaf (ex Rumol)	1916	Tanker	2.16 -
Slinger	1917	Catapult Ship	6.17 - 1.18
Petrobus	1917	Spirit Carrier	1.19 - 1948

X51

Petroleum	1902	Oiler	1.18 - 1936
Dewdale	1941	Tanker	1941 - 1948

X52

Petronel	1918	WTV	1.18 - 1948

X53

Philol	1916	Tanker	1.18 - 1948

X54

Polshannon	1910	WTV	1.18 - 7.21
Plumleaf	1916	Tanker	1939 - 4.42

X55

Kurumba	1916	Tanker	1918 - 1919
Prestol	1917	Tanker	1939 - 1948

X56

Thrush	1889	Cable	3.16 - ....

Purfol	1907	Oiler	1.18 - 1920
Pearleaf	1916	Tanker	1939 - 1946

X57

Gypol	1916	Oiler	2.16 - 3.17
Racer	1884	Salvage Vsl	1.18 - ....
Blue Ranger	1941	Tanker	1941 - 1948

X58

Fortol	1917	Tanker	1917 - 1939
Rapidol	1917	Tanker	1939 - 1948

X59

Reliance	1910	Store Carrier	1.18 - 12.19
Nasprite	1940	Spirit Carrier	1940 - 1948

X60

Prestol	1917	Tanker	1917 - 1.18
Ruthenia	1900	Oiler	1.18 - ....
Freshburn	1943	Water Carrier	1943 - 1948

X61

Scotol	1916	Oiler	1.18 - 1948

X62

Vitol	1917	Tanker	1917 - 3.18
Serbol	1917	Oiler	1.18 - 1948

X63

Trinol	1916	Oiler	2.16 - 1917
Servitor	1914	Oiler	1.18 - 1920
Looe	1924	Decoy	1939 - 1941
Freshford	1944	Water Carrier	1944 - 1948

Looe was a fictitious RFA identity assigned to Special Service freighter HMS *Beauly*. The name *Looe* was used when the ship was in port so her true identity was not disclosed.

X64

Kurumba ʀᴀɴ	1916	Tanker	1939 - 1948
Silverol	1907	Oiler	1.18 - 1920

X65

Slavol	1917	Oiler	1.18 - 3.42
Archer	1939	Esc Carrier	1944 - 1945
Wave Premier	1946	Tanker	1946 - 1948

X66

Montenol	1917	Tanker	1917 - 1.18
Slinger	1917	Catapult Ship	1.18 - 10.19
Bishopdale	1937	Tanker	1939 - 1948

X67

Francol	1917	Tanker	1917 - 1.18

Sprucol	1917	Oiler	1.18 - 1.20
Boardale	1937	Tanker	1939 - 4.40

X68

Steadfast	1906	Mooring Vsl	1.18 - ....
Broomdale	1937	Tanker	1939 - 1948

X69

Steady	1917	Mooring Vsl	1.18 - 7.40
Brown Ranger	1940	Tanker	1941 - 1948

X70

Teakol	1917	Oiler	1.18
Vineleaf (ex *Teakol*)	1917	Oiler	1.18 - 1.20
Echodale	1940	Tanker	1940 - 1948

Teakol allocated X70 in 1.18 but had been renamed *Vineleaf* in 1917.

X71

Crenella	1897	Tanker	1916 - 1919
Thermol	1916	Oiler	1939 - 1948

X72

Thrush	1889	Salvage Vsl	1.18 - Sunk
Antoine	1930	Decoy	1940 - 1941

Antoine was a fictitious RFA identity assigned to Special Service freighter HMS *Orchy*. The name *Antoine* was used when the ship was in port so her true identity was not disclosed.

X73

Trefoil	1913	Oiler	1.18 - 1935
Ennerdale	1941	Tanker	1941 - 1948

X74

Turmoil	1917	Oiler	1.18 - 1935
Biter	1940	Esc Carrier	1944 - 5.45

X75

Viscol	1916	Oiler	1.18 - 1948

X76

Vitol	1917	Tanker	1.18 - 3.18
Nimble	1906	Tender	1918 - ....
Freshpond	1945	Water Carrier	1945 - 1948

X77

Petrobus	1917	Spirit Carrier	7.17 - 1.18
Volunteer	1916	Mooring Vsl	1.18 - ....
Harlequin (ex *Strathmore*)	1897	MS	1939 - 1942

X78

Petrella	1918	Spirit Carrier	7.17 - 1.18
Waterwitch	1914	SSV	1.18 - 1921
Aberfoyle	1912	Tender	1939 - 1945

X79

Petronel	1918	WTV	7.17 - 1.18
Wave	1914	SSV	1.18 - 11.19
C.8	1941	Lighter	1941 - 1960

X80

Dredgol	1918	Tanker	1.18 - 1935
Cedardale	1939	Tanker	1939 - 1948

X81

British Light	1917	Oiler	1.18 - 6.18
Red Dragon	1912	Oiler	6.18 - ....
War Nizam	1918	Tanker	1939 - 1948

X82

War Nawab	1919	Tanker	1940 - 1944
Wave King	1944	Tanker	1944 - 1948

X83

Industry	1901	Store Ship	1920 - 1924
War Sepoy	1918	Tanker	1939 - 7.40

X84

War Pathan	1919	Tanker	1939 - 1948

X85

Chatsgrove	1918	Decoy	1939 - 1940

Chatsgrove was a fictitious RFA identity assigned to Special Service freighter HMS PC-74. The name Chatsgrove was used when the ship was in port so her true identity was not disclosed. Only operated in this role for a month.

X86

War Diwan	1919	Tanker	1939 - 12.44

X87

War Hindoo	1919	Tanker	1939 - 1948

X88

War Krishna	1919	Tanker	1939 - 1946

X89

War Bharata	1919	Tanker	1939 - 1948

X90

War Afridi	1919	Tanker	1939 - 1948
Bownet	1939	BDV	.... - ....

X91

War Brahmin	1919	Tanker	1939 - 1948

X92

Spa	1941	Water Carrier	1941 - 1948

X93

War Mehtar	1919	Tanker	1939 - 10.41

X94

War Pindari	1919	Tanker	1939 - 1948

X95

War Sudra	1920	Tanker	1939 - 1948

X96

Brutus	1920	Decoy	1939 - 1942

Brutus was a fictitious RFA identity assigned to Special Service freighter HMS City of Durban. The name Brutus was used when the ship was in port so her true identity was not disclosed.

X97

Magician	1939	Hospital Ship	1944

X98

C.112	(....)	....	.... - ....

X99

Freshpool	1943	Water Carrier	1943 - 1948

X100

Wave Emperor	1944	Tanker	1944 - 1948

X101

Mytilus	1916	Tanker	1941 - 1946
C.633	1945	Lighter	1945 - 1948

Mytilus was to have been renamed Empire Reserve but name was not taken up.

X102

Freshet	1940	Water Carrier	1940 - 1948

X103

Wave Governor	1944	Tanker	1944 - 1948

X104

Eaglesdale	1940	Tanker	1940 - 1948

X105

Easedale	1941	Tanker	1941 - 1948

X106

Dinsdale	1941	Tanker	1941 - 6.42

X107

Freshbrook	1941	Water Carrier	1941 - 1948

X108

Wave Monarch	1944	Tanker	1944 - 1948

X109

Freshener	1942	Water Carrier	1942 - 1948

X110

Wave Regent	1945	Tanker	1945 - 1948

X111

Wave Sovereign	1945	Tanker	1945 - 1948

X112

Ingeborg	1937	Tanker	1940 - 1945

X113

Freshspray	1946	Water Carrier	1946 - 1948

X114

C.614	1943	Lighter	1943 - 1948

X115
Airsprite 1942 Spirit Carrier 1942 - 1948
X116
Olna 1944 Tanker 1945 - 1948
X117
Freshmere 1942 Water Carrier 1942 - 1948
X118
Freshspring 1946 Water Carrier 1946 - 1948
X119
Wave Chief 1946 Tanker 1946 - 1948
X120
Freshlake 1942 Water Carrier 1942 - 1948
X121
Freshwell 1943 Water Carrier 1943 - 1948
X122
Spaburn 1946 Water Carrier 1946 - 1948
X123
Spalake 1946 Water Carrier 1946 - 1948
X124
Spapool 1946 Water Carrier 1946 - 1948

X125
Cyelse 1912 Trawler 5.45 - 1946
C. 641 1945 Lighter 1945 - 1956

X126
C. 642 1946 Lighter 1946 - 1948
X127
Spabrook 1944 Water Carrier 1944 - 1948
X128
Danmark 1931 Oil Hulk 1942 - 1948
X129
Wave Laird 1946 Tanker 1946 - 1948

X130
Wave Victor 1943 Tanker 1943 - 1948
(ex *Empire Bounty*)
X131
Wave Conqueror 1943 Tanker 1943 - 1948
(ex *Empire Law*)
X132
Wave Commander 1944 Tanker 1944 - 1948
(ex *Empire Paladin*)
X133
Wave Master 1944 Tanker 1944 - 1948
(ex *Empire Salisbury*)
X134
Wave Prince 1945 Tanker 1945 - 1948
(ex *Empire Herald*)
X135
Wave Ruler 1946 Tanker 1946 - 1948
(ex *Empire Evesham*)
X136
Wave Protector 1944 Tanker 1944 - 1948
X137
Wave Baron 1946 Tanker 1946 - 1948
X138
Wave Duke 1944 Tanker 1944 - 1948
X139
Wave Knight 1945 Tanker 1945 - 1948
X140
Wave Liberator 1944 Tanker 1944 - 1948
X141
Fort Duquesne 1944 Store Ship 1944 - 1948
X142
Fort Rosalie 1944 Store Ship 1944 - 1948

Flag 'Y' Superior

Pre 1940:   None

1940-48:   Ex-USCG Cutters; US Navy TF39; Store Carriers; Fuel and Water Carrying Vessels

1948:   Harbour Craft

Y00
Hartland   1928 Sloop   1941 - 11.42
Y01
Fossbeck   1930 Ac Trans   1939 - 1942
Y02
Hambleton USN   1941 Destroyer   TF39 1942

In 1942 US Navy Task Force 39 (TF39), comprising the battleship USS *Washington*, aircraft carrier USS *Wasp*, the cruisers USS *Wichita* and USS *Tuscaloosa*, together with eight destroyers, sailed across the Atlantic to reinforce the Royal Navy Home Fleet. During this period they were nominally assigned RN pendant numbers with a Y flag superior.

Y04
Walney   1930 Sloop   1941 - 11.42
Y10
Aberdovey   1963 Tender   1963 - 1995
Y11
Abinger   1964 Tender   1964 - 1995

Y12
Madison USN   1939 Destroyer   TF39 1942
Alness   1964 Tender   1964 - ....

Y13
Alnmouth   1964 Tender   1964 - 1991
Y14
Appleby   1965 Tender   1965 - 1999
Y15
Watercourse   1973 Water Carrier 1973 - 1998

Y16
Emmons USN   1941 Destroyer   TF39 1942
Ashcott   1965 Tender   1965 - ....
Waterfowl   1973 Water Carrier 1973 - ....

Y17
Waterfall   1966 Water Carrier 1966 - 1988
Y18
Watershed   1966 Water Carrier 1966 - 1992
Y19
Waterspout   1966 Water Carrier 1966 - 1996

Y20
Waterside   1967 Water Carrier 1967 - 1991

Y21
Sennen   1928 Sloop   1941 - 1946
Oilpress   1968 Tanker   1968 - ....

Y22
Oilstone   1968 Tanker   1968 - 1993
Y23
Oilwell   1969 Tanker   1969 - 1997
Y24
Oilfield   1968 Tanker   1968 - 1993

Y25
Plunkett USN   1940 Destroyer   TF39 1942
Oilbird   1968 Tanker   1968 - 1994

Y26
Oilman   1969 Tanker   1969 - ....
Y30
Watercourse   1973 Water Carrier 1973 - 1997
Y31
Waterfowl   1973 Water Carrier 1973 - 1991
Y32
Moorhen   1989 Moor   1989 - 2008
Y33
Moorfowl   1989 Moor   1989 - ....
Y34
Sterett USN   1938 Destroyer   TF39 1942
Y39
Chattenden   1943 Arm Carrier   1944 - 1967
Y43
Banff   1930 Sloop   1941 - 1946
Y50
Wichita USN   1937 Cruiser   TF39 1942
Y56
Landguard   1930 Sloop   1941 - 1946
Y59
Fishguard   1928 Sloop   1941 - 1946
Y60
Lulworth   1928 Sloop   1941 - 1946
Y64
Tuscaloosa USN   1933 Cruiser   TF39 1942

196

Y69			
Macomb USN	1941	Destroyer	TF39 1942
Y77			
Wasp USN	1939	Ac Carrier	TF39 1942
Y83			
Washington USN	1940	Battleship	TF39 1942
Y87			
Culver	1928	Sloop	1941 - 1.42
Y88			
Totland	1931	Sloop	1941 - 1946

Y91			
Rodman USN	1941	Destroyer	TF39 1942
Y92			
Gorleston	1929	Sloop	1941 - 1946
Y93			
Wilson USN	1939	Destroyer	TF39 1942
Y96			
MFV 96	1944	....	.... - ....
Y144			
Eroican	1914	Trawler	1940 - ....

Flag 'Z' Superior

Pre 1940:	None	
1940-48:	Cable Vessels; Gate, Mooring and Boom Defence Vessels; Netlaying Vessels; Naval Drifters.	
1948:	None	

Z00					**Z20**				
Acadia RCN	1913	APV	1940 - 1946		*Bloodhound*	1938	Target Vsl	1940 - 1943	
Z01					**Z21**				
Barbain	1940	BDV	1940 - 1948		*Jennet*	1926	Trawler	1939 - 1946	
Z03					**Z22**				
Barbrook	1938	BDV	1940 - 1948		*Barcroft*	1938	BDV	1940 - 1948	
Z04					**Z23**				
Punnet	1925	BDV	1940 - 1948		*Coldsnap*	1918	Drifter/BDV	1940 - 1946	
					Z24				
Z05					*Sandgate*	1917	BDV	1940 - 1948	
Suderoy V RCN	1930	Whaler	1941 - 1945		**Z25**				
Bayonet	1938	BDV	1940 - Sunk		*Southgate*	1917	BDV	1940 - 1946	
					Z26				
Z06					*Spinet*	1924	BDV	1939 - 1945	
Suderoy VI RCN	1929	Whaler	1941 - 1945		(ex *St Merryn*)				
Parkgate	1917	BDV	1940 - 1945		**Z27**				
					Magnet	1938	BDV	1940 - 1948	
Z07					**Z28**				
Polegate	1917	BDV	1940 - 1945		*Crescent Moon*	1918	Drifter/BDV	1940 - 1946	
Z08									
Cloud	1918	TRV	1941 - 1946		**Z29**				
Z09					*Queen of the Fleet*	1917	Exam Vsl	1940 - 1945	
Barcastle	1938	BDV	1940 - 1945		*Barbette (I)*	1937	BDV	1940 - 1941	
Z10									
Signet	1939	BDV	1940 - 1948		**Z30**				
Z11					*Coronet*	1917	BDV	1940 - 1948	
Reigate	1918	BDV	1940 - 1948		**Z31**				
Z12					*Barfair*	1938	BDV	1940 - 1946	
Rogate	1929	BDV	1940 - 1948		**Z32**				
Z14					*Barstoke*	1941	BDV	1941 - 1948	
Dunnet	1936	BDV	1940 - 1946		**Z33**				
Z15					*Burgonet*	1939	BDV	1940 - 1948	
Kookaburra	1940	BDV	1940 - 1948		**Z35**				
Z16					*Ebbtide*	1917	Drifter/BDV	1940 - 1946	
Barcombe	1938	BDV	1940 - 1948		**Z36**				
					Fumarole	1918	Drifter/BDV	.... -	
Z17					**Z37**				
Dowgate	1935	BDV	1940 - 2.42		*Barnstone*	1939	BDV	1940 - 1948	
Barilla	1943	BDV	1943 - 1948		**Z38**				
					Halo	1918	Drifter/BDV	.... - 1948	
Z18					**Z39**				
Barbarian	1937	BDV	1940 - 1946		*Barlake*	1940	BDV	1940 - 1948	
Z19					**Z40**				
Falconet	1938	BDV	1940 - 1948		*Barrhead*	1940	BDV	1940 - 1948	

Z41			
Martinet	1938	BDV	1940 - 1948
Z42			
Barfield	1938	BDV	1940 - 1948
Z43			
Barbican	1938	BDV	1940 - 1948
Z44			
Quannet	1926	BDV	1940 - 1946
Z45			
Ludgate	1917	BDV	1940 - 2.42
Sailor King	1914	MS	1943 - 1945
Z46			
Barnwell	1940	BDV	1940 - 1948
Z47			
Sonnet	1939	BDV	1940 - 1948
Z48			
Barlane	1938	BDV	1940 - 1948
Z49			
Eddy	1918	Drifter/BDV	1940 - 5.42
Z50			
Planet	1938	BDV	1940 - 1948
Z51			
Moonrise	1918	BGV	1943 - 1946
Z52			
Barcote	1940	BDV	1940 - 1948
Z53			
Horizon	1918	TRV	1941 - 1945
Z54			
Barrage	1937	BDV	1940 - 1948
Z55			
Mist	1918	Drifter/BDV	1940 - 1943
Z56			
Watergate	1917	BDV	1940 - 12.41
Z57			
Barlight	1938	BDV	1940 - 12.41
Mary Cam RAN	1918	Trawler/BDV	1942 - 1948
Z58			
Barwind	1942	BDV	1942 - 1948
Z59			
Barrington	1940	BDV	1940 - 1948
Z60			
Barlow	1938	BDV	1940 - 1948
Z61			
Seabreeze	1918	Drifter/BDV	1940 - 1946
Z62			
Lunar Bow	1918	Drifter/BDV	1940 - 1945
Z63			
Plantaganet	1939	BDV	1940 - 1948
Z64			
Sheen	1918	TRV	1941 - 1946
Z65			
Barranca	1938	BDV	1940 - 1948
Z66			
Bishopsgate	1932	BDV	1940 - 1948
Z67			
Barmill	1940	BDV	1940 - 1948
Z68			
Aldgate	1934	BDV	1940 - 12.41
Z69			
Koala RAN	1939	BDV	1940 - 1948
Z70			
Barcliff	1940	BDV	1940 - 1948
Z71			
Moorgate	1931	BDV	1940 - 1948
Z72			
Harmattan	1918	Drifter/BDV	1940 - 1945
Z73			
Barrymore	1941	BDV	1941 - 1948
Z74			
PC 74	1918	Sloop	1940 - 1948
Z75			
Barsing	1941	BDV	1941 - 1948
Z76			
Lasso	1938	Cable Ship	1940 - 1948
Z77			
Barmouth	1938	BDV	1940 - 1948
Z79			
Noontide	1918	Drifter/BDV	1940 - 1948
Z80			
Kangaroo RAN	1940	BDV	1940 - 1948
Z81			
Shower	1918	Drifter/BDV	1940 - 1946
Z82			
Dragonet	1939	BDV	1940 - 1948
Z83			
Tambar RAN	1912	BDV	1940 - 1945
Barricade	1938	BDV	1940 - 1948
Z84			
Barnehurst	1939	BDV	1940 - 1948
Z85			
Kilmun	1919	Cable Ship	1940 - 1948
Z86			
Indian Summer	1918	TRV	1942 - 1948
Z87			
Baronia	1941	BDV	1941 - 1948
Z88			
Westgate	1918	BDV	1940 - 1946
Z89			
Barsound	1941	BDV	1941 - 1948
Z90			
Bownet	1939	BDV	1940 - 1948
Z91			
Whirlpool	1919	Drifter/BDV	1940 - 1948

Z92			
Barndale	1939	BDV	1939 - 1948
Z93			
Leeward	1918	Drifter/BDV	1940 - 1948
Z94			
Barova	1941	BDV	1941 - 1948
Z95			
Barthorpe	1940	BDV	1940 - 1948
Z96			
Kinchela RAN	1914	BGV	1942 - 1946
Z97			
Landfall	1918	Drifter/BDV	1940 - 1946
Z98			
Barrier	1938	BDV	1940 - 1948
Z99			
Rennet	1928	BDV	1940 - 1946
Z100			
Barnet	1919	Trawler	1940 - 1946
Z101			
Fastnet	1919	BDV	1940 - 1942
Beryl II RAN	1914	Trawler	1944 - 1946
Z102			
Cambrian	1924	Trawler	1940 - 5.40
Z103			
Northlyn	1919	Trawler	1943 - 1948
Z104			
St Celestin	1925	BDV	1940 - 1946
Z105			
Star of the Realm	1917	BDV	1940 - 1946
Z106			
Basuto	1932	BDV	1940 - 1945
Z107			
Consbro	1930	BDV	1940 - 1945
Z108			
Stalberg	1929	BDV	1940 - 1945
Z109			
Count	1929	BDV	1940 - 1945
Z110			
James Barrie	1928	BDV	1940 - 1945
Z111			
Lord Gainford	1917	BDV	1940 - 1942
Z112			
Erna	1915	BDV	1940 - 1945
Z113			
Night Rider	1915	BDV	1940 - 1948
Z114			
Phyllisia	1918	BDV	1940 - 1946
Z115			
Sea Monarch	1915	Trawler	1940 - 1946
Z116			
Silanion	1930	BDV	1940 - 1945
Z117			
Florence Brierley	1918	BDV	1940 - 1946

Z118			
Vilda	1929	BDV	1940 - 1946
Z119			
Avon Water	1930	BDV	1940 - 1946
Z120			
Ben Rossal	1929	BDV	1940 - 1946
Z121			
Buckingham	1930	BDV	1940 - 1946
Z122			
Cadella	1913	BDV	1940 - 1946
Z123			
Loch Laggan	1914	Trawler	1940 - 1945
Z124			
Loch Shin	1930	Trawler	1940 - 5.40
Z125			
Milford Duke	1918	BDV	1940 - 1946
Z126			
Mount Ard	1931	BDV	1940 - 1946
Z127			
The Way	1931	BDV	1940 - 1946
Z128			
Tunisian	1930	BDV	1940 - 7.42
Z129			
William Hannam	1919	BDV	1940 - 1946
Z130			
Astros	1917	BBV	1940 - 1946
Z131			
Caliban	1919	BDV	1940 - 1946
Z132			
Clarinet	1911	BDV	1940 - 1946
Z133			
Doctor Lee	1914	BDV	1940 - 1946
Z134			
Gladys	1917	BDV	1934 - 1946
Z135			
Gwmaho	1917	BDV	1940 - 1946
Z136			
Imelda	1914	BDV	1940 - 1946
Z137			
Kuroki	1909	BDV	1940 - 1946
Z138			
Masona	1915	BDV	1940 - 1948
Z139			
Sarba	1913	BDV	1940 - 1946
Z140			
Settsu	1924	BDV	1940 - 1945
Z141			
Thomas Conolly	1918	BDV	1940 - 12.40
Z142			
William Caldwell	1918	BDV	1940 - 1946
Z143			
Ocean Eddy	1929	BDV	1940 - 1946
Z144			
Foss	1916	BDV	1940 - 1946

Z145			
Norina (ex Kunishi)	1917	Trawler	1940 - 1948
Z146			
Okino	1917	BDV	1940 - 1946
Z147			
Mary White	1935	BDV	1940 - 1946
Z148			
Dorileen	1917	BDV	1940 - 1946
Z149			
John Fitzgerald	1918	BDV	1940 - 1946
Z150			
Cuirass	1915	BDV	1940 - 1946
Z151			
Collena	1915	BDV	1940 - 1946
Z152			
Alida	1915	BDV	1940 - 1946
Z153			
Chorley	1914	BDV	1940 - 4.42
Z154			
Westlyn	1914	BDV	1940 - 1948
Z155			
Barbara Robb	1930	BDV	1940 - 1944
Z156			
Fort Ryan	1932	BDV	1940 - 1944
Z157			
Craig Island	1913	BDV	1940 - 1946
Z158			
Cramond Island	1910	Trawler	1940 - 4.41
Z159			
Ocean Brine	1914	Trawler/BDV	1940 - 1941
Z160			
River Annan	1919	BGV	1940 - 1945
Z161			
Strathspey	1906	BDV	1940 - 1942
Z162			
Norbreeze	1920	Drifter/BDV	1940 - 1946
Z163			
Ocean Swell	1920	Drifter/BDV	1940 - 1945
Z164			
Pecheur	1914	Netlayer	1940 - 1945
Z165			
Loch Long	1916	BDV	1940 - 1946
Z166			
Nancy Hague	1911	BDV	1940 - 1946
Z167			
Ethiopian	1936	Boom Car	1940 - 1946
Z168			
Devon City	1933	Boom Car	1940 - 1946
Z169			
Barbour	1941	BDV	1941 - 1948
Z170			
Barbourne	1942	BDV	1942 - 1948
Z171			
Bardolf	1942	BDV	1942 - 1948
Z172			
Prince de Leige BG	1926	BDV	1940 - 1945
Z173			
Barbrake	1942	BDV	1942 - 1948
Z174			
Barclose	1941	BDV	1941 - 1948
Z175			
Bernadette	1914	BDV	1940 - 1945
Z176			
Bullfinch	1940	Cable Ship	1940 - 1948
Z177			
Barcock	1941	BDV	1941 - 1948
Z178			
George Bligh	1917	BDV	1940 - 1945
Z179			
Girafe FR	(....)	BDV	1940 - 1945
Z180			
Nordland	1916	BDV	1940 - 1946
Z181			
Barking	1941	BDV	1941 - 1948
Z182			
Barfoam	1941	BDV	1941 - 1948
Z183			
Scomber	1914	BDV	1940 - 1948
Z184			
Barflake	1942	BDV	1942 - 11.43
Z185			
Barcross	1941	BDV	1941 - 1948
Z186			
Girard	1918	BDV	1940 - 1948
Z187			
Etruria	1930	BDV	1940 - 1946
Z188			
Digit	1902	Trawler	1940 - 1946
Z189			
Luminary	1919	Trawler	1940 - 1946
Z190			
Barfount	1942	BDV	1942 - 1948
Z191			
Roule FR	1933	Tug/BDV	1940 - 1945
Z192			
May	1927	Cable Ship	1940 - 1946
Z193			
Rocroi	1919	Trawler	1940 - 1940
Z194			
Barfoil	1942	BDV	1942 - 1948
Z195			
Bardell	1942	BDV	1942 - 1948
Z196			
Marignam	1919	BDV	1940 - 10.40
Z197			
Leonian	1936	BC	1940 - 1946
Z198			
Wyre	1911	BDV	1940 - 1945

Z199			
Kirriemore	1935	BC	1940 - 1946
Z200			
Barfoss	1942	BDV	1942 - 1948
Z201			
Fresne	(....)	.....	.... - ....
Z202			
Barfoot	1942	BDV	1942 - 1948
Z203			
Sunrise	1919	BDV	1940
Z204			
Coronatia	1902	BGV	1940 - 1946
Z205			
Barglow	1942	BDV	1942 - 1948
Z206			
Ristango	1913	Trawler/BGV	1940 - 11.40
Z207			
Collingwood	1902	BGV	1940 - 10.40
Fieldgate	1902	BGV	10.40 - 1945
(ex Collingwood)			
Z208			
Fernmoor	1936	Boom Car	1940 - 1946
Z209			
Barford	1941	BDV	1941 - 1948
Z210			
Buzzard	1898	BDV	1940 - 1941
Z211			
Barholm	1942	BDV	1942 - 1948
Z212			
Ben Tarbert	1912	BDV	1940 - 1941
Z213			
Marangi	(....)	....	.... - ....
Z214			
Barconia	Canc	BDV	Canc 1941
Z215			
Panorama	1919	BDV	1940 - 1946
(ex Rocroi)			
Z216			
Karangi RAN	1941	BDV	1942 - 1948
Z217			
Emile Baudot	1917	Cable Ship	1940 - 1945
Z218			
Trojan	1898	BGV	1940 - 1945
Z219			
Oranaise FR	1919	BDV	1940 - 1946
Z220			
Holdfast	1921	Cable Ship	1942 - 1946
Z221			
Kara Kara RAN	1926	BGV	1941 - 1948
Z222			
Barbridge	1941	BDV	1941 - 1948
Z223			
Aquila	1907	Cable Ship	1941 - 1946
Z224			
Barspear	1943	BDV	1943 - 1948
Z225			
Barhill	1942	BDV	1942 - 1948
Z226			
Lady Eleanor	1918	BDV	1940 - 1948
Z227			
Notre Dame de	1899	BGV	1940 - 1945
Mont Ligeon FR			
Z228			
Dunavon	1908	Cable Ship	1940 - 1945
Z229			
Teal	1919	BDV	10.40 - 1946
(ex Marignam)			
Z230			
Cecile Mapleson	1924	Cable Ship	1941 - 1944
Z231			
Jan de Waele BG	1925	Trawler	1940 - 1945
Z232			
Barmond	1942	BDV	1942 - 1948
Z233			
Maris Stella FR	1907	BGV	1940 - 1945
Z234			
Castlerock	1904	Trawler	1940 - 1945
Z235			
Ophir II	1906	Trawler	1939 - 1940
Z236			
Bullhead	1944	Cable Ship	1944 - 1948
Z237			
Barnaby	1943	BDV	1943 - 1948
Z238			
Marie Louise	1918	BDV	1940 - 1946
Z239			
Graaf Van	1925	Trawler	1940 - 1946
Vlaanderen			
Z240			
Laverock	1917	BDV	1940 - 1946
Z241			
Barnard	1942	BDV	1942 - 1948
Z242			
Barbette II	1943	BDV	1940 - 1948
Z243			
Laomedon	1912	Boom Car	1940 - 1946
Z244			
Natal II	1903	BDV	1940 - 1946
Z245			
Barneath	1942	BDV	1942 - 1948
Z246			
Arrest	1898	BDV	1941 - 1945
(ex Buzzard)			
Z247			
Beaulne Verneuil	1918	BGV	1940 - 1946
Z249			
George D Irvin	1911	BDV	1940 - 1941

Z250			
Barness	Canc	BDV	Canc 1941
Z251			
Easter Rose	1914	Drifter	1940 - 1945
Z252			
Bankville	1904	Cable Ship	1942 - 1946
Z253			
Lanakai RAN	1914	BGV	1942 - 1946
Z254			
Bulan	1924	Cable Ship	1941 - 1946
Z255			
Retriever	1909	Cable Ship	1942 - 1946
Z256			
Barleycorn	1943	BDV	1943 - 1948
Z257			
Barberry	1943	BDV	1943 - 1948
Z258			
Sprayville	1920	Cable Ship	1943 - 1946
Z259			
St Margarets	1943	Cable Ship	1943 - 1948
Z260			
Bullfrog	1944	Cable Ship	1944 - 1948
Z261			
Bartizan	1943	BDV	1943 - 1948
Z262			
Baron	1944	BDV	1944 - 1946
Z263			
Prefect (ex USN)	1944	BDV	1944 - 1945
Z264			
Protect	1944	BDV	1944
(Renamed Pretext - See Z284)			
Z265			
Preventer (ex USN)	1944	BDV	1944 - 1946
Z266			
Precept (ex USN)	1944	BDV	1944 - 1946
Z267			
Latimer	1941	Cable Ship	1943 - 1945
Z268			
Algerian	1924	Cable Ship	1943 - 1945
Z269			
Empire Baffin	1941	Cable Ship	1943
Sancroft	1941	Cable Ship	1943 - 1945
(ex Empire Baffin)			

Z270			
Gunbar RAN	1911	BDV	1943 - 1945
Z271			
Baritone	1945	BDV	1945 - 1948
Z272			
Companion	Canc	BDV	Canc 1945
Z273			
Compact	Canc	BDV	Canc 1945
Z274			
Compatriot	Canc	BDV	Canc 1944
Z275			
Competitor	Canc	BDV	Canc 1945
Z276			
Barbastel	1945	BDV	1945 - 1948
Z277			
Barkis	1945	BDV	1945 - 1948
Z278			
Complete	Canc	BDV	Canc 1945
Z279			
Complex	Canc	BDV	Canc 1944
Z280			
Compere	Canc	BDV	Canc 1944
Z281			
Competent	Canc	BDV	Canc 1944
Z282			
Compliment	Canc	BDV	Canc 1944
Z283			
Composure	Canc	BDV	Canc 1944
Z284			
Pretext (ex-USN)	1944	BDV	1944 - 1948
Z285			
Precise (ex-USN)	1944	BDV	1944 - 1946
Z286			
Barbecue	1944	BDV	1940 - 1948
Z287			
Barcarole	1945	BDV	1940 - 1948
Z303			
Ploughboy	1912	Drifter	1941 - 1947
Z304			
Girl Margaret	1914	Drifter/BDV	1940 - 1946

Flag 'DV' Superior

Pre 1940:   None

1940-48:   Isles class WDV

1948:   None

DVC1
| *Maria* | 1929 | Trawler | 1946 - 1950 |

Maria was the former Kriegsmarine weather ship *August Wriedt*. She was captured by HMS *Malvernian* on 29 May 1941. She served as a wreck dispersal vessel until 1950. (See pendant number 4.166)

DV2
| *Annet* | 1943 | Trawler | 1946 - 1948 |

DV3
| *Bardsey* | 1943 | Trawler | 1946 - 1948 |

DV4
| *Bern* | 1942 | Trawler | 1946 - 1948 |

DV5
| *Caldy* | 1943 | Trawler | 1946 - 1948 |

DV6
| *Coll* | 1942 | Trawler | 1946 - 1948 |

DV7
| *Earraid* | 1941 | Trawler | 1946 - 1948 |

DV8
| *Fetlar* | 1941 | Trawler | 1946 - 1948 |

DV9
| *Flatholm* | 1943 | Trawler | 1946 - 1948 |

DV10
| *Graemsay* | 1942 | Trawler | 1946 - 1948 |

DV11
| *Lindisfarne* | 1943 | Trawler | 1946 - 1948 |

DV12
| *Lundy* | 1942 | Trawler | 1946 - 1948 |

DV14
| *Neave* | 1942 | Trawler | 1946 - 1948 |

DV15
| *Scalpay* | 1942 | Trawler | 1946 - 1948 |

DV16
| *Skomer* | 1943 | Trawler | 1946 - 1948 |

DV17
| *Steepholm* | 1943 | Trawler | 1946 - 1948 |

DV18
| *Switha* | 1942 | Trawler | 1946 - 1948 |

DV19
| *Tiree* | 1941 | Trawler | 1946 - 1948 |

DV20
| *Trondra* | 1941 | Trawler | 1946 - 1948 |

'FY' Penn Superior

Pre 1940:   None

1940-48:   Armed Yachts, Aux Minesweepers, Auxiliary Patrol Vessels, Mine Destructors, Motor
                Minesweepers (MMS), Motor Fishing Vessels (MFV)

1948:   None

FY.001
Aarla   1903 Armed Yacht 1939 - 1945

FY.002
Campeador V   1938 Armed Yacht 1939 - 6.40
Alastor   1928 Armed Yacht 1940 - ....

FY.003
Alice   1930 Armed Yacht 1939 - 1948

FY.004
Anna Marie   1930 Armed Yacht 1939 - 1941
Torrent   1930 Armed Yacht 1941 - 4.41

FY.005
Coila   1922 Armed Yacht 1939 - 1948

FY.006
Conqueror   1911 Armed Yacht 1939 - 1945

FY.007
Carina   1899 Armed Yacht 1939 - 1945
Cutty Sark   1920 Armed Yacht 1939 - 1946

FY.008
Cynara Kalan   1913 Armed Yacht 1939 - 1940

FY.009
Evadne   1931 Armed Yacht 1939 - 1945

FY.010
Glen Strathallan   1928 Armed Yacht 1939 - 1945

FY.011
Hiniesta   1902 Armed Yacht 1939 - 1945

FY.012
Iolare   1902 Armed Yacht 1939 - 1945

FY.014
Lady Blanche   1907 Armed Yacht 1939 - 1945

FY.015
Lady Shahrazad   1904 Armed Yacht 1939 - 1945

FY.016
Lady Vagrant   1903 Armed Yacht 1939 - 1940

FY.017
Maid Marion   1938 Armed Yacht 1939 - 1945

FY.018
Medusa   1906 Armed Yacht 1939 - 11.39

Mollusc   1906 Armed Yacht 11.39 - 3.41
  (ex *Medusa*)

FY.019
Migrante   1929 Armed Yacht 1939 - 1945

FY.020
Oracle   1929 Armed Yacht 1939 - 1944

FY.021
Princess   1924 Armed Yacht 1939 - 1.40

FY.022
Radiant   1927 Armed Yacht 1939 - 1945

FY.023
Rhodora   1929 Armed Yacht 1939 - 9.40

FY.024
Rion   1928 Armed Yacht 1939 - 1944
Noir (ex *Rion*)   1928 Armed Yacht 1944 - 1945

FY.025
St Modwen   1911 Armed Yacht 1939 - 1945

FY.026
Shemara   1938 Armed Yacht 1939 - 1945

FY.027
Sona   1922 Armed Yacht 1939 - 1.42

FY.028
Valena   1908 Armed Yacht 1939 - 1945

FY.029
Altair   1905 Armed Yacht 1939 - 1945

FY.030
Viva II   1929 Armed Yacht 1939 - 5.41

FY.031
Virginia   1930 Armed Yacht 1939 - 1945

FY.032
Warrior II   1904 Armed Yacht 1939 - 7.40

FY.033
Zaza   1905 Armed Yacht 1939 - 1948

FY.034
Wigeon of Fearn   1936 Armed Yacht 1939 - 1945

FY.035
Kedah   1927 Armed Yacht 1939 - 1946

FY.036
Star of India   1888 Armed Yacht 1940 - 1945

FY.044
Tuscarora   1897 Armed Yacht 1940 - 1945

FY.045			
Aletes	1932	Armed Yacht	1940 - 1945
FY.046			
Black Bear	1930	Armed Yacht	1940 - 1945
FY.047			
Corsair	1930	Armed Yacht	1940 - 1948
FY.048			
Dorothy Duke	1918	Armed Yacht	1941 - 1945
FY.049			
Kenkora II	1930	Armed Yacht	1941 - 1946
FY.050			
Boy Pat	1915	Armed Yacht	1940 - 1945
FY.053			
Sargasso	1926	Armed Yacht	1939 - 6.43
FY.057			
Taransay	1930	Armed Yacht	1939 - 1945
FY.061			
Lexa	1936	Armed Yacht	1939 - 1945
FY.065			
Bhadravati RIN	1932	Aux PV	1939 - 1945
FY.073			
Satyavati RIN	1911	Aux PV	1939 - 1945
FY.075			
Rukmavati RIN	1904	Aux PV	1939 - 1946
FY.079			
Badora RIN	1914	Aux PV	1939 - 1944
FY.086			
Kutubtari RIN	1915	Aux PV	1939 - 1946
FY.090			
Laxmi RIN	1918	Aux PV	1939 - 1946
FY.092			
Nautilus RIN	1913	Trawler	1943 - 1946
FY00			
Tolga RAN	1925	Coaster	1944 - 1946
FY01			
Toorie RAN	1925	Coaster	1940 - 1945
FY03			
Cloud	1918	Drifter	1918 - 1946
FY04			
Coldsnap	1918	Drifter	1918 - 1945
FY05			
Crescent Moon	1918	Drifter	1918 - 1946
FY06			
Vigilant RAN	1938	Aux PV	1940 - 1944
FY07			
Narani RAN	1914	Coaster	1940 - 1946
FY08			
Coombar RAN	1912	Coaster	1941 - 1946
Kalan	1938	Armed Yacht	1939 - 1946
FY10			
Ebbtide	1917	Drifter	1924 - 1940
Paterson RAN	1920	Coaster	1940 - 1946

FY12			
Eddy	1918	Drifter	1918 - 5.42
Bombo RAN	1930	Coaster	1941 - 1948
FY15			
Birchgrove Park	1930	Collier	1941 - 1946
FY16			
Fumarole	1918	Drifter	1918 - ....
Warrawee RAN	1909	Coaster	1939 - 1946
FY18			
Allenwood RAN	1920	Coaster	1941 - 1946
FY19			
Kianga RAN	1922	Coaster	1941 - 1946
FY21			
Halo	1918	Drifter	1918 - ....
FY23			
Harmattan	1918	Drifter	1918 - 1946
FY24			
Horizon	1918	Drifter	1920 - 1945
FY28			
Indian Summer	1918	Drifter	1918 - 1942
FY30			
Landfall	1918	Drifter	1918 - 1946
FY31			
Leeward	1918	Drifter	1918 - 1948
FY32			
Lunar Bow	1918	Drifter	1918 - 1945
Medea RAN	1912	Coaster	1942 - 1946
FY33			
Uralba RAN	1942	Tender	1942 - 1945
FY34			
Mercedes RAN	1912	Coaster	1942 - 1946
FY38			
Gippsland RAN	1908	Tender	1942 - 1946
FY39			
Sulituan RAN	1912	Ketch	1942 - 1943
FY40			
Mist	1918	Drifter	1918 - 1943
FY45			
Noontide	1918	Drifter	1918 - ....
FY48			
Mary Cam RAN	1918	Trawler	1941 - 1948
FY50			
Seabreeze	1918	Drifter	1918 - 1946
FY51			
Sheen	1918	Drifter	1918 - 1946
FY52			
Shower	1918	Drifter	1918 - 1946
FY54			
Sunset	1918	Drifter	6.18 - 4.42

FY60
Whirlpool	1919	Drifter	10.19 - 1941

FY67
Arctic Prince	1915	Trawler	1939 - 1946

FY71
Beryl II RAN	1914	Trawler	1939 - 1944

FY74
Goorangai RAN	1919	Trawler	1939 - 11.40

FY75
Goolgwai RAN	1919	Trawler	1939 - 1948

FY76
Olive Cam RAN	1920	Trawler	1939 - 1946

FY78
Wongala RAN	1919	Trawler	1940 - 1948

FY79
Korawa RAN	1919	Trawler	1939 - 1946

FY80
Uki RAN	1923	Coaster	1939 - 1944

FY81
Bermagui RAN	1912	Coaster	1939 - 1945

FY82
Nambucca RAN	1936	Coaster	1939 - 1943

FY84
Coolebar RAN	1911	Coaster	1939 - 1946

FY85
Bonthorpe	1917	Trawler	1939 - 1941
Bonthorpe RAN	1917	Trawler	1941 - 1945

FY86
St Giles RAN	1919	Tug	1939 - 1946

FY87
Heros RAN	1919	Tug	1940 - 1946

FY88
Bingera RAN	1935	Coaster	1939 - 1946

FY89
Adele RAN	1915	Yacht	1939 - 5.43

FY90
Kybra RAN	1926	Coaster	1940 - 1946

FY91
Yandra RAN	1928	Coaster	1940 - 1946

FY92
Wyrallah RAN	1934	Coaster	1940 - 1948

Wyrallah (FY92) was renamed *Wilcannia* in February 1942.

FY93
Durraween RAN	1919	Trawler	1940 - 1946

FY94
Goonambee	1919	Trawler	1940 - 1944

FY95
Samuel Benbow	1918	Trawler	1940 - 1946

FY96
King Bay RAN	1938	Coaster	1940 - 1946

FY97
Alfie Cam RAN	1920	Trawler	1940 - 1944

FY98
Gunbar RAN	1911	Coaster	1940 - 1943

FY99
Terka RAN	1925	Coaster	1940 - 3.44

FY100
Lady Beryl	1935	Trawler	1939 - 1945

FY101
Alouette	1939	Trawler	1939 - 9.42

FY102
Hugh Walpole	1937	Trawler	1939 - 1945

FY103
Leyland	1936	Trawler	1939 - 11.42

FY104
Man o'War	1936	Trawler	1939 - 1945

FY105
Northern Pride	1936	Trawler	1939 - 1945

FY106
Thuringia	1933	Trawler	1939 - 5.40
Van Dyck BG	1926	Trawler	1941 - 1945

FY107
Stella Capella	1937	Trawler	1939 - 3.42
Sealyham	1936	Whaler	1941 - 1945

FY108
Pentland Firth	1934	Trawler	1939 - 9.42

FY109
Lord Hailsham	1934	Trawler	1939 - 2.43

FY110
York City	1933	Trawler	1939 - 1945

FY111
St Andronicus	1933	Trawler	8.39 - 10.39
Commander Holbrook	1915	Trawler	1940 - 1945

St Andronicus (FY111) was transferred to the French Navy as an APV, in October 1939, and renamed *L'Orientaise* (P134). She was scuttled by the French in 1940. Raised and repaired by the Germans she was commissioned into the Kriegsmarine as PA2.

FY112
Kelt	1937	Trawler	1939 - 1945

FY113
Warwickshire	1936	Trawler	1939 - 7.43
Commander Evans	1924	Trawler	1939 - 1945

FY114
Victorian	1935	Trawler	1939 - 1945

FY115			
Lord Snowden	1934	Trawler	1939 - 4.42
FY116			
Blackburn Rovers	1934	Trawler	1939 - 6.40
FY117			
Blackfly	1937	Trawler	1939 - 1946
FY118			
Brontes	1934	Trawler	1939 - 1946
FY119			
Cape Chelyuskin	1936	Trawler	1939 - 4.40
FY120			
Sindonis	1934	Trawler	1939 - 5.41
FY121			
Kingston Cornelian	1936	Trawler	1939 - 1.40
FY122			
Sedgefly	1939	Trawler	1939 - 12.39
FY123			
Daneman	1937	Trawler	1939 - 5.43
FY124			
Lady Elsa	1937	Trawler	1939 - 1942
FY125			
Grimsby Town	1934	Trawler	1939 - 1945
FY126			
Imperialist	1939	Trawler	1939 - 1945
FY127			
Loch Doon	1939	Trawler	1939 - 12.39
FY128			
Mildenhall	1936	Trawler	7.39 - 11.39
L'Ajaccienne FR	1936	Trawler	11.39 - 11.42
FY129			
Northern Spray	1936	Trawler	1939 - 1945
FY130			
Turcoman	1937	Trawler	1939 - 1945
FY131			
Stella Dorado	1935	Trawler	1939 - 6.40
FY132			
Pict	1936	Trawler	1939 - 1945
FY133			
Lord Hotham	1936	Trawler	1939 - 1945
FY134			
Reighton Wyke	1937	Trawler	1939 - 1945
FY135			
St Arcadius	1934	Trawler	1939
La Nantaise FR	1934	Trawler	1939
Loch Monteith	1936	Trawler	1939 - 1945

St Arcadius (FY135) was purchased by the RN in August 1939 and converted for A/S duties. She was shortly there-after transferred to the French Navy as an APV and re-named *La Nantaise* (P135). On 3 July 1940 she was siezed at Portsmouth in Operation Grab and reverted to her original name. See entry for FY360.

FY136			
Kingston Alalite	1933	Trawler	1939 - 11.40
FY137			
Wellard	1937	Trawler	1939 - 1945
FY138			
Visenda	1937	Trawler	1939 - 1946
FY139			
Lord Stamp	1935	Trawler	1939 - 1940
Hayburn Wyke	1917	Trawler	1940 - 1.45
FY140			
Arsenal	1933	Trawler	1939 - 11.40
FY141			
Bedfordshire	1935	Trawler	1939 - 5.42
FY142			
Cambridgeshire	1935	Trawler	1939 - 1945
FY143			
Cape Cormorin	1936	Trawler	1939 - 1946
FY144			
Spaniard	1937	Trawler	1939 - 12.42
FY145			
Kingston Galena	1934	Trawler	1939 - 7.40
FY146			
Northern Dawn	1936	Trawler	1939 - 1946
FY147			
Davy	1936	Trawler	1939 - 1946
FY148			
Lady Philomena	1936	Trawler	1939 - 1945
FY149			
Hammond	1936	Trawler	1939 - 4.40
FY150			
Istria	1936	Trawler	1939 - 1946
FY151			
Loch Melfort	1934	Trawler	1939 - 1946
FY152			
St Achilleus	1934	Trawler	1939 - 5.40
FY153			
Northern Wave	1936	Trawler	1939 - 1945
FY154			
Olinina	1934	Trawler	1939 - 1945
FY155			
Stella Pegasi	1935	Trawler	1939 - 1945
FY156			
Greenfly	1936	Trawler	1939 - 1945
FY157			
Lord Lloyd	1933	Trawler	1939 - 1945
FY158			
Wolves	1934	Trawler	1939 - 1945
FY159			
Saon	1933	Trawler	1939 - 1945
FY160			
Kingston Andalusite	1934	Trawler	1939 - 1945
FY161			
Westella	1934	Trawler	1939 - 6.40

FY162			
Arctic Explorer	1936	Trawler	1939 - 1942
FY163			
Lord Stanhope	1935	Trawler	1939 - 1945
FY164			
Arctic Pioneer	1937	Trawler	1939 - 5.40
FY165			
Bengali	1937	Trawler	1939 - 12.42
FY166			
Canadian Prince	1937	Trawler	8.39 - 11.39
La Bonoise	1937	Trawler	11.39 - 11.42
FY167			
Cape Warwick	1937	Trawler	1939 - 1946
FY168			
Spurs	1933	Trawler	1939 - 1945
FY169			
Jardine	1936	Trawler	1939 - 4.40
FY170			
Lord Wakefield	1933	Trawler	1939 - 7.44
FY171			
Derby County	1938	Trawler	1939 - 1946
FY172			
Larwood	1936	Trawler	1939 - 4.40
FY173			
Hampshire	1934	Trawler	9.39 - 11.39
Toulonnaise FR	1934	Trawler	11.39 - 11.42
FY174			
Kirkella	1936	Trawler	1939 - 1946
FY175			
Loch Oskaig	1937	Trawler	1939 - 1945
FY176			
St Amandus	1933	Trawler	7.39 - 10.39
La Cancalaise FR	1933	Trawler	10.39 - 4.40
Hertfordshire	1936	Trawler	1939 - 1942
Lady Estelle	1915	Trawler	1940 - 1946
FY177			
Lydiard	1935	Trawler	1939 - 1946
FY178			
Oriental Star	1934	Trawler	8.39 - 11.39
La Setoise FR	1934	Trawler	11.39 - 11.42
FY179			
Thornwick Bay	1936	Trawler	1939 - 1946
FY180			
Regal	1933	Trawler	1939 - 1945
FY181			
Lord Plender	1933	Trawler	1939 - 1946
FY182			

Warwick Deeping	1934	Trawler	1939 - 10.40
FY183			
St Attalus	1934	Trawler	7.39 - 9.39
Berkshire	1936	Trawler	1939 - 1945

St Attalus (FY183) was transferred to the French Navy as an APV and renamed *La Havraise* (P133). She was scuttled at Toulon on 27 November 1942. She was subsequently raised by the Germans and commissioned as *VJ 6078*. She was finally lost on 9 June 1944 having been torpedoed by the French submarine *Casabianca*.

FY184			
Kingston Chrysolite	1935	Trawler	1939 - 1945
FY185			
Vascama	1935	Trawler	1939 - 1943
FY186			
Arctic Ranger	1937	Trawler	1939 - 1946
FY187			
Lord Stonehaven	1934	Trawler	1939 - 1945
FY188			
Bandolero	1935	Trawler	1939 - 10.42
FY189			
Bradman	1937	Trawler	1939 - 4.40
Noble Nora	1912	Whaler	1940 - 1941
Noble Nora RNoN	1912	Whaler	1941 - 1943
FY190			
Cape Argona	1936	Trawler	1939 - 1946
FY191			
Cayton Wyke	1932	Trawler	1939 - 7.40
FY192			
Stafnes	1936	Trawler	1939 - 1945
FY193			
Kingston Olivine	1930	Trawler	1939 - 1945
FY194			
Northern Gem	1936	Trawler	1939 - 1945
FY195			
Drangey	1935	Trawler	1939 - 1946
FY196			
Leeds United	1933	Trawler	1939 - 1945
FY197			
Huddersfield Town	1933	Trawler	1939 - 1945
FY198			
Peridot	1933	Trawler	1939 - 3.40
FY199			
Loch Tulla	1934	Trawler	1939 - 1946
FY200			
Bernard Shaw	1929	Trawler	1939 - 1945
FY201			
Angle	1936	Trawler	1939 - 1945
FY202			
Arab	1936	Trawler	1939 - 1945

FY203

Kos V	1929	Whaler	1941
Risor RNoN (ex *Kos V*)	1929	Whaler	1941 - 1946

FY204

Ellesmere	1939	Whaler	1939 - 2.45

FY205

Buttermere	1939	Whaler	1939 - 1946

FY206

Thirlmere	1939	Whaler	1939 - 1946

FY207

Windermere	1939	Whaler	1939 - 1946

FY208

Indian Star	1936	Trawler	1939 - 1945

FY209

Melbourne	1936	Trawler	1939 - 5.40

FY211

Kingston Amber	1937	Trawler	1939 - 1946

FY212

Kingston Agate	1937	Trawler	1939 - 1946

FY213

Kingston Cairngorm	1935	Trawler	1939 - 10.40

FY214

Kingston Ceylonite	1935	Trawler	1939 - 1942

FY215

Kingston Coral	1936	Trawler	1939 - 1946

FY216

Kingston Crystal	1936	Trawler	1939 - 1946

FY217

Kingston Cyanite	1936	Trawler	1939 - 1946

FY218

Lord Essenden	1936	Trawler	1939 - 1945

FY219

Lord Middleton	1936	Trawler	1939 - 1946

FY220

Lord Austin	1937	Trawler	1939 - 6.44

FY221

Lord Nuffield	1937	Trawler	1939 - 1945

FY222

Lincolnshire	1936	Trawler	1939 - 1946

FY223

Leicester City	1934	Trawler	1939 - 1946

FY225

Ayrshire	1938	Trawler	1939 - 1945

FY229

Norwich City	1937	Trawler	1939 - 1942

FY230

Preston North End	1934	Trawler	1939 - 1945

FY232

Stoke City	1935	Trawler	1939 - 1946

FY233

Wolborough	1937	Trawler	1939 - 1946

FY234

St Cathan	1936	Trawler	1939 - 4.42

FY235

King Sol	1936	Trawler	1939 - 1945

FY236

Kingston Chrysoberyl	1935	Trawler	1939 - 1946

FY238

Viviana	1936	Trawler	1939 - 1946

FY239

Wastwater	1939	Whaler	1939 - 1946

FY240

St Elstan	1937	Trawler	1939 - 1945

FY241

Rutlandshire	1936	Trawler	1939 - 4.40

Rutlandshire (FY241) was lost during the Norwegian campaign. Salved and repaired by the Germans she was commissioned as *Ubier*. She was lost to a mine on 6 December 1942.

FY242

Paynter	1937	Trawler	1939 - 1945

FY243

Le Tiger	1937	Trawler	1939 - 1942

FY244

Victrix	1937	Trawler	1939 - 1945

FY245

Scottish	1937	Trawler	1939 - 1945

FY246

Cape Portland	1939	Trawler	1939 - 1945

FY247

Tekoura	1929	Trawler	1939 - 1945

FY248

Stella Canopus	1936	Trawler	1939 - 1945

FY249

Avanturine	1934	Trawler	1939 - 1940
Sphene	1934	Trawler	1940 - 1945

FY250

Notts County	1938	Trawler	1939 - 3.42

FY251

Egeland RNoN	1914	Whaler	1941 - 11.41

FY252

Viking Deeps	1916	Trawler	6.40 - 1944
Ullswater	1939	Whaler	1939 - 11.42

FY253

North Queen	1906	Trawler	2.40 - 6.45
Lady Rosemary	1937	Trawler	1939 - 1946

Lady Rosemary was temporarily loaned to the USN, complete with crew, from March to October 1942.

FY254

Brimnes	1933	Trawler	1939 - 1945

FY255			
Else Rykens	1935	Trawler	1939 - 1945
FY256			
Cape Palliser	1937	Trawler	1939 - 1945
FY257			
Paul Rykens	1935	Trawler	1939 - 1945
FY258			
Scalby Wyke	1935	Trawler	1939 - 1945
FY259			
Neil Mackay	1935	Trawler	1939 - 1945
FY260			
Peter Hendricks	1935	Trawler	1939 - 1946
FY261			
Aston Villa	1937	Trawler	1939 - 5.40
Retreiver	1930	Trawler	1941 - 1946
FY263			
Cape Siretoko	1939	Trawler	1939 - 4.40
FY264			
St Kenan	1936	Trawler	1939 - 1946
FY266			
Bretwalda	1925	Trawler	1940 - 1946
FY267			
Coventry City	1937	Trawler	1939 - 1942
FY270			
Cape Passaro	1938	Trawler	1939 - 5.40
FY271			
British Guiana	1936	Trawler	1939 - 1946
FY272			
British Honduras	1937	Trawler	1939 - 1946
FY273			
Eastern Dawn	1908	Drifter	1940 - 1943
FY276			
St Loman	1936	Trawler	1939 - 1946
FY278			
Young John	1914	Drifter	1940 - 1946
FY279			
Crannock	1911	Trawler	1939 - 1946
FY280			
St Zeno	1940	Trawler	1940 - 1946
FY282			
Fisher Lad	1919	Trawler	1939 - 1945
FY283			
Lady Madeleine	1939	Trawler	1940 - 1946
FY284			
Abiding Star	1917	Drifter	1941 - 1946
FY285			
The Provost	1908	Drifter	1939 - 1946
FY286			
Vizalma	1940	Trawler	1940 - 1945
FY287			
Craig Roy	1918	Drifter	1939 - 1945
FY288			
Invercairn	1916	Trawler	1939 - 1945

FY290			
Contrive	1911	Drifter	1940 - 1946
FY291			
Branch	1908	Drifter	1939 - 1946
FY292			
War Star	1914	Trawler	1940 - 1946
FY293			
Corcyra	1914	Trawler	1939 - 1945
FY294			
Svega	1929	Whaler	3.40 - 1942
FY295			
Carency	1916	Trawler	1939 - 1946
FY297			
Sumba	1927	Whaler	1940 - 1946
FY298			
Loyal Friend	1919	Trawler	1939 - 1945
FY300			
Sunnyside Girl	1919	Drifter	1939 - 1946
FY301			
Silja	1929	Whaler	1940 - 1948
FY302			
Fawn	1915	Drifter	1939 - 1946
FY303			
Stina	1928	Whaler	1940 - 1946
FY304			
Southern Chief	1926	Whaler	3.40 - 1946
FY305			
Transvaalia RNoN	1912	Whaler	1941 - 1943
FY306			
Haarlem	1938	Trawler	1940 - 1946
FY307			
Stora	1929	Whaler	6.40 - 1947
FY308			
John Williamson RNoN	1912	Whaler	8.41 - 1943
Alfeios RHN	1912	Whaler	1943 - ....
FY309			
Sposa	1926	Whaler	4.40 - 1945
FY310			
Ephretah	1918	Drifter	1940 - 1945
FY311			
Romsey	1930	Exam Vsl	1940 - 9.42
FY312			
Helier II	1936	Whaler	1940 - 1945
FY315			
Boarhound	1936	Whaler	1941 - 1945
FY316			
Gorse	1911	Drifter	1939 - 1945
FY317			
Quentin Roosevelt	1918	FPV	1940 - 1945
FY318			
Southern Breeze	1936	Whaler	3.40 - 1945

FY321					**FY351**			
Simbra	1937	Whaler	12.41 - 1946		*Trust*	1918	Drifter	1940 - 1946
FY323					**FY352**			
Southern Spray	1925	Whaler	3.40 - 1945		*Stella Carina*	1936	Trawler	1939 - 1945
FY324					**FY353**			
Sigfra	1937	Whaler	12.41 - 1945		*Chinthe*	1932	Aux MS	1942 - ....
FY325					**FY354**			
Southern Wave	1925	Whaler	3.40 - 1945		*Guiding Light*	1911	Drifter	12.39 - 1946
FY326					**FY355**			
Southern Shore	1928	Whaler	3.40 - 1946		*Castelnau* FR	1918	Trawler	1940 - 1946
FY327								
Senateur Duhamel	1927	Trawler	1940 - 5.42		**FY358**			
FY329					*Kos VI*	1929	Whaler	1941
Southern Star	1930	Whaler	3.40 - 1945		*Farsund* RNoN	1929	Whaler	1941 - 1946
FY330					(ex *Kos VI*)			
Van Oost BG	1926	Trawler	1940 - 1945					
FY331					**FY359**			
Sobkra	1937	Whaler	1941 - 1946		*Kos I*	1929	Whaler	1941
FY332					*Svolvaer* RNoN	1929	Whaler	1941 - 1946
Southern Flower	1928	Whaler	3.40 - 3.45		(ex *Kos I*)			
FY333								
Manor	1913	Trawler	1939 - 7.42		**FY360**			
FY334					*La Nantaise* FR	1934	Trawler	1940 - 7.45
Solvra	1937	Whaler	1941 - 1946		**FY362**			
FY335					*L'Atlantique* FR	1920	Trawler	1940 - 1946
Buchans II	1918	Trawler	1940 - 1946		**FY363**			
FY336					*Notre Dame de*	1931	Trawler	1940 - 1945
Ben Breac	1916	Trawler	1940 - 1944		*France* FR			
FY337					**FY370**			
Copious	1919	Drifter	1940 - 1945		*Asie*	1914	Trawler	1940 - 1946
FY338					**FY500**			
Northman	1911	Trawler	1940 - 1945		*Caswell*	1917	Trawler	1940 - 1946
FY339					**FY501**			
Setter (ex *Terje 4*)	1936	Whale	1941 - 1945		*Mary Herd*	1919	Drifter	1940 - 1945
FY340					**FY502**			
Cap d'Antifer FR	1920	Trawler	1941 - 1944		*Kings Grey*	1915	Trawler	1940 - 1946
FY341					**FY503**			
Duchesse de	1924	Trawler	1940 - 1945		*Bilsdean*	1917	Trawler	1940 - 1945
Brabant					**FY504**			
FY342					*Kos X* RNoN	1932	Whaler	11.40 - 9.41
Sorsra	1937	Whaler	12.41 - 1946					
FY343					**FY505**			
Reine des Flots	1923	Trawler	1940 - 1946		*Blighty*	1919	Trawler	1940 - 1943
FY345					*Podole* ORP	1919	Trawler	1943 - 1946
Sondra	1937	Whaler	12.41 - 10.45		(ex *Blighty*)			
FY346								
Ambrose Pare FR	1906	Trawler	1940 - 1946		**FY506**			
FY347					*British*	1930	Trawler	1939 - 1945
Lurcher	1928	Whaler	1941 - 1945		**FY507**			
FY348					*Brecon Castle*	1916	Trawler	1939 - 1945
Spaniel	1936	Whaler	1941 - 1946		**FY508**			
FY349					*Clyne Castle*	1929	Trawler	1939 - 1945
Bedlington	1936	Whaler	1941 - 1945		**FY509**			
FY350					*Conway Castle*	1916	Trawler	1939 - 1945
Mastiff (ex *Busen 9*)	1928	Whaler	1941 - 1945					

FY511				**FY536**			
Radnor Castle	1917	Trawler	1939 - 1947	John Cattling	1918	Trawler	1939 - 1945
FY512				**FY537**			
Cardiff Castle	1919	Trawler	1939 - 1946	Peter Carey	1919	Trawler	1939 - 1945
				FY538			
FY513				Harry Melling	1919	Trawler	1939 - 1945
Akranes	1929	Trawler	1939 - 7.41	**FY539**			
Soranus	1906	Trawler	1940 - 1945	Cranefly	1917	Trawler	1939 - 1946
				FY541			
FY514				Hildina	1918	Trawler	1939 - 1946
Dunedin	1910	Drifter	1940 - 1945	**FY542**			
FY515				Darnett Ness	1920	Trawler	1939 - 1945
Alexander Scott	1917	Trawler	1939 - 1945	**FY543**			
FY516				Contender	1930	Trawler	1940 - 1945
Commander Nasmith	1915	Trawler	1940 - 1945	**FY544**			
				Gwenllian	1911	Trawler	1939 - 1946
FY517				**FY545**			
Gadfly	1919	Trawler	1939 - 1945	Simpson	1917	Trawler	1942 - 1945
FY518				**FY546**			
Eroican	1914	Trawler	1940 - 1944	Grampian	1930	Trawler	1939 - 1946
FY519				**FY547**			
Lephreto	1917	Trawler	1939 - 1944	Lady Enid	1918	Trawler	1939 - 1945
FY520				**FY548**			
Thomas Leeds	1919	Trawler	1939 - 1945	Northcoates	1919	Trawler	1939 - 12.44
FY521				**FY550**			
Damito	1917	Trawler	1939 - 1945	Cotsmuir	1917	Trawler	1940 - 1945
FY522				**FY551**			
Their Merit	1918	Trawler	1939 - 1945	Fidget	1917	Drifter	1939 - 1946
FY523				**FY552**			
Colchester	1918	Trawler	7.41 - 1.46	Thomas Altoft	1919	Trawler	1939 - 1946
FY524				**FY553**			
Cerisio	1915	Trawler	1939 - 1945	Thomas Bartlett	1918	Trawler	1939 - 5.40
FY525				**FY554**			
Tehana	1929	Trawler	1939 - 1944	Dane	1911	Trawler	1940 - 1946
FY526				**FY555**			
Tewera	1930	Trawler	1939 - 1946	William Hallett	1917	Trawler	11.39 - 12.39
FY527				**FY556**			
Teroma	1919	Trawler	1939 - 1945	Glen Heather	1913	Drifter	1939 - 1945
FY528				**FY557**			
Rudilais	1920	Trawler	1939 - 1946	Hoverfly	1917	Trawler	1939 - 1945
FY529				**FY558**			
Neil Smith	1917	Trawler	1939 - 1945	Dorothy Lambert	1923	Trawler	1940 - 1946
FY530				**FY559**			
Richard Crofts	1918	Trawler	1939 - 1945	Andradite	1934	Trawler	1939 - 1946
FY531				**FY560**			
Daniel Clowden	1919	Trawler	1939 - 1945	Alexandrite	1933	Trawler	1939 - 1945
FY532				**FY561**			
T.R. Ferrans	1918	Trawler	1939 - 1945	Ohm	1915	Trawler	1939 - 1945
FY533				**FY562**			
Admiral Sir John Lawford	1930	Trawler	1939 - 1944	Rose of England	1909	Trawler	1939 - 1946
				FY564			
FY534				Milford Countess	1919	Trawler	1939 - 1946
Clotilde	1913	Trawler	1939 - 1945	**FY566**			
FY535				Arthur Cavanagh	1918	Trawler	1940 - 1945
William Cale	1917	Trawler	1939 - 1945				

213

FY567			
Michael Griffiths	1918	Trawler	1939 - 1945
FY568			
Gunner	1927	Trawler	1939 - 1946
FY569			
Erimo	1930	Trawler	1939 - 1945
FY570			
Dunraven Castle	1917	Trawler	1940 - 1945
FY571			
Eldorado	1902	Trawler	1940 - 1945
FY572			
Sargon	1913	Trawler	1939 - 1945
FY573			
Elena	1905	Trawler	1940 - 1945
FY574			
Windward Ho!	1920	Trawler	1939 - 1946
FY575			
Snakefly	1930	Trawler	1939 - 1945
FY576			
Egeria	1907	Drifter	1939 - 1945
FY578			
Erith	1917	Trawler	1940 - 1945
FY579			
Cape Barracouta	1930	Aux Pat Vsl	1940 - 1946
FY580			
Osako	1918	Trawler	1940 - 1945
FY581			
Wardour	1911	Trawler	1939 - 1946
FY582			
War Duke	1917	Trawler	1939 - 1946
FY583			
Carisbrooke	1928	Trawler	1939 - 1946
FY584			
Cambuslang	1942	MMS	1942 - 1943
Aegialia RHN	1942	MMS	1943 - ....
(ex *Cambuslang*)			
FY586			
Brabant	1918	Trawler	1939 - 1945
FY587			
Fezenta	1914	Trawler	1939 - 1945
FY588			
Lune	1930	Trawler	1939 - 1944
FY589			
Sandringham	1930	Trawler	1939 - 1946
FY591			
Green Pastures	1919	Drifter	1939 - 1945
FY592			
Courtier	1929	Trawler	1939 - 1945
FY593			
Tocsin	1912	Trawler	1940 - 1945
FY596			
Stonefly	1930	Trawler	1939 - 1945
FY597			
Charles Doran	1917	Trawler	1940 - 1945
FY598			
Arcady	1907	Drifter	1939 - 1945
FY599			
General Botha	1916	Trawler	1940 - 1945
FY600			
Flanders	1920	Trawler	1939 - 1945
FY601			
Solon	1931	Trawler	1939 - 1946
FY602			
Reboundo	1920	Trawler	1939 - 1945
FY604			
Righto	1920	Trawler	1939 - 1944
FY605			
Burke	1930	Trawler	1939 - 1946
FY608			
Lord Beaconsfield	1915	Trawler	1939 - 1945
FY610			
Akita	1939	Trawler	1939 - 1945
FY611			
Muroto	1930	Trawler	1939 - 1944
FY612			
Ijuin	1920	Trawler	1939 - 1946
FY613			
Milford Duchess	1919	Trawler	1939 - 1944
FY614			
Milford Prince	1920	Trawler	1939 - 1945
FY615			
Milford Queen	1917	Trawler	1939 - 1945
FY616			
Milford Princess	1924	Trawler	1939 - 1945
FY618			
Suma	1927	Trawler	1939 - 1946
FY619			
Cabuskenneth	1942	MMS	1942 - 1943
Monemvassia RHN	1942	MMS	1943 - ....
(ex *Cabuskenneth*)			
FY620			
Arley	1914	Trawler	1939 - 1945
FY621			
Brock	1914	Trawler	1939 - 1945
FY622			
Sir John Lister	1919	Trawler	1939 - 1945
FY623			
Dorinda	1917	Trawler	1939 - 1945
FY624			
Edward Walmsley	1919	Trawler	1939 - 1946
FY627			
George Cousins	1919	Trawler	1939 - 1945
FY628			
Picton Castle	1928	Trawler	1939 - 1945
FY629			
Sawfly	1928	Trawler	1939 - 1945

FY630			
Pointz Castle	1914	Trawler	1939 - 1945
FY631			
Raglan Castle	1919	Trawler	1939 - 1947
FY632			
Green Howard	1927	Trawler	1939 - 1946
FY633			
Comitatus	1919	Trawler	1939 - 1945
FY634			
Commodator	1918	Trawler	1939 - 1945
FY635			
Computator	1919	Trawler	1939 - 1945
FY636			
Commiles	1918	Trawler	1939 - 1945
FY637			
Concertator	1917	Trawler	1939 - 1946
FY639			
Kurd	1930	Trawler	1939 - 1945
FY642			
Loch Leven	1928	Trawler	1939 - 1946
FY643			
Tamora	1920	Trawler	1939 - 1946
FY645			
Almandine	1932	Trawler	1939 - 1945
FY649			
Goth	1925	Trawler	1939 - 1945
FY651			
Cape Melville	1929	Trawler	1939 - 1945
FY652			
Wellsbach	1930	Trawler	1939 - 1945
FY653			
Arkwright	1930	Trawler	1940 - 1945
FY654			
Nab Wyke	1930	Trawler	1939 - 1946
FY656			
Elbury	1925	Trawler	1939 - 1945
FY657			
Stella Rigel	1926	Trawler	1939 - 1945
FY659			
Nodzu	1929	Trawler	1939 - 1946
FY660			
Oku	1929	Trawler	1939 - 1945
FY661			
Honjo	1928	Trawler	1939 - 1.42
FY662			
Hatano	1925	Trawler	1939 - 1946
FY663			
Irvana	1917	Trawler	1939 - 1.42
FY665			
Maretta	1929	Trawler	1939 - 1945
FY666			
Fyldea	1930	Trawler	1939 - 1945
FY667			
James Lay	1918	Trawler	1939 - 1944
FY668			
Equerry	1929	Trawler	1939 - 1945
FY669			
Sicyon	1930	Trawler	1939 - 1946
FY670			
Cape Nyemetski	1936	Trawler	1939 - 1946
FY671			
Grosmont Castle	1917	Trawler	1940 - 1946
FY672			
Lord Melchett	1929	Trawler	1939 - 1946
FY673			
Calvi	1930	Trawler	1939 - 5.40
Firefly	1930	Trawler	1939 - 1945
FY674			
Curtana	1929	Trawler	1939 - 1945
FY675			
Cambusdoon	1942	MMS	1942 - 1943
Naphpaktia RHN	1942	MMS	1943 - ....
(ex *Cambusdoon*)			
FY676			
Darthema	1929	Trawler	1939 - 1945
FY677			
Monima	1929	Trawler	1939 - 1945
FY678			
Clevella	1930	Trawler	1939 - 1945
FY679			
Filey Bay	1931	Trawler	1939 - 1945
FY680			
Full Moon	1932	Whaler	5.41 - 1946
FY681			
Waterfly	1931	Trawler	1939 - 9.42
FY682			
Epine	1929	Trawler	1939 - 1946
FY683			
Star of Orkney	1936	Trawler	1939 - 1946
FY684			
Mount Keen	1936	Trawler	1939 - 1946
FY685			
George Robb	1930	Trawler	1939 - 1946
FY686			
Braconmoor	1917	Trawler	1939 - 1946
FY687			
Robert Stroud	1930	Trawler	1939 - 1946
FY688			
Loch Buie	1919	Trawler	1939 - 1946
FY690			
Ben Dearg	1920	Trawler	1939 - 1946
FY691			
Edwardian	1931	Trawler	1939 - 1946
FY692			
Kunishi	1927	Trawler	1939 - 1946
FY694			
Lord Ashfield	1929	Trawler	1939 - 1945

FY698			
Shepherd Lad	1925	Drifter	1939 - 1946
FY699			
Sandstorm	1925	Whaler	1942 - 1945
FY700			
Shooting Star	1925	Whaler	1942 - 1946
FY701			
Jeloy RNoN (ex *Pol II*)	1926	Whaler	4.41 - 1942
Levanter (ex *Jeloy*)	1926	Whaler	1942 - 1944
FY702			
Tromoy RNoN (ex *Pol IV*)	1926	Whaler	11.40 - 1944
Cloudburst (ex *Tromoy*)	1926	Whaler	1944 - 1946
FY703			
Wave Flower	1929	Trawler	1939 - 1.40
Sita RIN	1928	Drifter	1940 - 1943
FY704			
Loch Eribol	1929	Trawler	1939 - 1945
FY705			
Dorienta	1914	Drifter	1939 - 1946
FY706			
Stella Leonis	1928	Trawler	1939 - 1946
FY707			
Botanic	1928	Trawler	1939 - 2.42
FY708			
Golden Harvest	1914	Drifter	1939 - 1946
FY709			
Corena	1924	Trawler	1939 - 1946
FY710			
Gulfoss	1929	Trawler	1939 - 3.41
Cambuslie	1942	MMS	1942 - 1943
Amvrakia RHN (ex *Cambuslie*)	1942	MMS	1943 - ....
FY711			
Fort Royal	1931	Trawler	1939 - 2.40
FY712			
Lacennia	1930	Trawler	1939 - 1946
FY713			
Cordela	1930	Trawler	1939 - 1946
FY714			
Marsona	1918	Trawler	1939 - 8.40
FY715			
Alafoss	1929	Trawler	1939 - 1946
FY717			
Negro	1932	Trawler	1939 - 1945
FY718			
Gula	1936	Drifter	1940 - 1945
FY719			
Flicker	1932	Whaler	9.41 - 1945
FY720			
David Ogilvie	1917	Trawler	1939 - 1946
FY721			
Benvolio	1930	Trawler	1939 - 2.40
FY724			
General Birdwood	1919	Trawler	1939 - 1946
FY725			
St Minver	1919	Trawler	1939 - 1946
FY726			
Semnos	1934	Trawler	1939 - 1945
FY727			
Agnes Wickford	1909	Trawler	1939 - 1945
FY729			
Inverforth	1914	Trawler	1939 - 1945
FY730			
King Emperor	1914	Trawler	1940 - 1943
FY731			
Boy Philip	1930	Trawler	1939 - 1943
FY732			
Strymon RHN	1917	Trawler	1939 - 1941
FY733			
Silver Crest	1928	Drifter	1939 - 1946
FY734			
Abronia	1906	Trawler	1939 - 9.40
FY735			
Inchgower	1918	Trawler	1939 - 1946
FY736			
Justifier	1925	Drifter	1939 - 1946
FY737			
Osta	1915	Trawler	1939 - 1944
FY738			
Playmates	1925	Drifter	1939 - 1945
FY740			
Rose Hilda	1930	Drifter	1939 - 1946
FY741			
Harlech Castle	1916	Trawler	1940 - 1945
FY745			
Golden View	1918	Drifter	1939 - 1946
FY748			
Genius	1919	Drifter	1939 - 1945
FY749			
Benachie	1919	Drifter	1939 - 1946
FY750			
Runswick Bay	1929	Trawler	1939 - 1946
FY752			
June Rose	1918	Drifter	1939 - 1945
FY753			
St Melante	1927	Trawler	1939 - 1946
FY756			
Eveline RNLN	1912	Trawler	1940 - 1.42
FY757			
Athenian	1919	Trawler	1939 - 1944
FY758			
Borde	1921	Drifter	1939 - 1945

FY760			
New Comet	1915	Trawler	1939 - 1943
FY761			
Onetos	1913	Trawler	1939 - 1946
FY762			
Fort Robert	1918	Trawler	1939 - 1945
FY763			
Sunlight	1918	Trawler	1939 - 1944
FY765			
Ben Heilem	1919	Trawler	1939 - 1946
FY767			
Elizabeth Angela	1928	Trawler	1939 - 8.40
FY768			
Shamrock	1900	Trawler	1939 - 1945
FY770			
Witham	1919	Trawler	1939 - 1944
FY771			
Robert Hastie	1912	Trawler	1939 - 1946
FY774			
Berenga	1917	Trawler	1939 - 1945
FY775			
Claverton	1913	Trawler	1939 - 11.40
FY776			
Luda Lord	1913	Trawler	1939 - 1945
FY777			
Marano	1916	Trawler	1939 - 1945
FY778			
Revello	1908	Trawler	1939 - 12.43
FY779			
Loch Rannoch	1901	Trawler	1940 - 1944
FY780			
Lord Northcliffe	1916	Trawler	1939 - 1945
FY781			
Lois	1917	Trawler	1940 - 1944
FY782			
Lowther	1915	Trawler	1939 - 1946
Ormonde	1906	Trawler	1940 - 2.41
FY783			
Othello	1907	Trawler	1939 - 4.41
FY784			
Madden	1917	Trawler	1940 - 1946
FY785			
Raymont	1916	Trawler	1939 - 1946
FY786			
Recono	1916	Trawler	1939 - 1945
FY787			
Taipo	1916	Trawler	1939 - 1944
FY788			
Bandelero	1935	Trawler	1939 - 12.40
Tokyo II	1906	Trawler	1940 - 1944
FY789			
Atmosphere	1928	Drifter	1941 - 1945
FY791			
Cayrian	1911	Trawler	1939 - 1945
FY795			
Northward Ho	1919	Trawler	1939 - 1946
FY796			
Malacolite	1917	Trawler	1939 - 1945
FY798			
Liddoch	1919	Trawler	1940 - 1943
FY802			
Margaret Rose	1912	Trawler	1940 - 1946
FY803			
Ogano	1917	Trawler	1940 - 1944
FY804			
Georgette	1918	Trawler	1939 - 1946
FY806			
William Stephen	1917	Trawler	1939 - 10.43
FY807			
Ben Torc	1915	Trawler	1939 - 1946
Parkmore	1915	Trawler	1939 - 1946
FY808			
Ben Glas	1917	Trawler	1939 - 1944
FY810			
Ocean Breeze	1927	Drifter	1939 - 1943
FY813			
Imperia	1912	Trawler	1939 - 1945
FY814			
Valesca	1916	Trawler	1939 - 1945
FY815			
Venture	1905	Trawler	1939 - 1940
FY816			
Mewslade	1916	Trawler	1940 - 1946
FY818			
Lapwing	1904	Trawler	1939 - 1940
FY819			
Leonora	1904	Trawler	1939 - 1941
FY820			
Newhaven	1909	Trawler	1940 - 1945
FY821			
Resolvo	1913	Trawler	1939 - 10.40
FY822			
Resparko	1916	Trawler	1939 - 8.40
FY823			
Saturn	1916	Trawler	1939 - 1944
FY824			
Badinage	1916	Trawler	1941 - 1945
FY825			
Royallo	1916	Trawler	1939 - 9.40
FY826			
Dulcibelle	1918	Trawler	1939 - 1944
FY828			
Sasebo	1928	Trawler	BR 619(2)

217

FY829			
Yezo	1924	Trawler	1939 - 1946
FY830			
Refundo	1917	Trawler	1940 - 12.44
FY831			
Regardo	1915	Trawler	1939 - 1945
FY832			
Wallena	1914	Trawler	1939 - 1946
FY833			
Ingomar	1904	Trawler	1939 - 1940
FY834			
Restrivo	1914	Trawler	1939 - 1945
FY835			
Royallieu	1907	Trawler	1939 - 1945
FY836			
Billow (ex *Gos 3*)	1928	Whaler	1941 - 1945
FY838			
Retako	1914	Trawler	1939 - 1945
FY839			
Returno	1914	Trawler	1940 - 1944
FY840			
Rodino	1913	Trawler	1939 - 7.40
FY841			
Ronso	1915	Trawler	1940 - 1944
FY843			
Relonzo	1914	Trawler	1939 - 1.41
FY844			
Dalmatia	1928	Trawler	1939 - 1946
FY846			
Delphinus	1906	Trawler	1939 - 1945
FY847			
Bervie Braes	1917	Trawler	1939 - 1944
FY850			
Tumby	1918	Trawler	1939 - 1945
FY851			
Drummer Boy	1916	Trawler	1939 - 1945
FY852			
Earl Essex	1914	Trawler	1939 - 1946
FY853			
Emilion	1914	Trawler	1939 - 10.41
FY854			
Etruscan	1913	Trawler	1939 - 1944
FY855			
United Boys	1913	Drifter	1941 - 1945
FY857			
Kennymore	1914	Trawler	1939 - 11.40
FY859			
Leo	1904	Trawler	1939 - 1940
FY863			
Ocean View	1930	Trawler	1940 - 1945
FY865			
Garola	1912	Trawler	1939 - 1943
FY866			
Walwyns Castle	1913	Trawler	1940 - 1946

FY867			
Libra	1908	Trawler	1940 - 1945
FY868			
Fentonian	1912	Trawler	1939 - 1944
FY869			
Phase	1919	Drifter	1939 - 1946
FY871			
Viola	1905	Trawler	1939 - 1945
FY872			
Valmont	1916	Trawler	1939 - 1945
FY873			
Empyrian	1914	Trawler	1939 - 1945
FY874			
Powis Castle	1916	Trawler	1940 - 1945
FY875			
Remexo	1912	Trawler	1939 - 1945
FY876			
Princess Mary	1914	Trawler	1939 - 1945
FY877			
Lord Rodney	1928	Drifter	1939 - 1941
FY877			
Karmoy RNoN (ex *Globe V*)	1936	Whaler	4.41 - 1944
Fiery Cross (ex *Karmoy*)	1936	Whaler	1944 - 1946
FY878			
Exyahne	1914	Trawler	1939 - 1945
FY880			
Flying Wing	1915	Trawler	1939 - 1946
FY881			
Glatian	1913	Trawler	1939 - 1945
FY883			
Sethon	1916	Trawler	1940 - 1945
FY885			
Kingscourt	1917	Trawler	1939 - 1945
FY887			
Onward	1905	Trawler	1939 - 1944
FY889			
The Tower	1919	Trawler	1939 - 1945
FY891			
Feaco	1924	Drifter	1939 - 1945
FY892			
Norina	1927	Trawler	1939 - 1946
FY893			
Renzo	1913	Trawler	1939 - 1945
FY894			
Lucienne-Jeanne	1917	Trawler	1939 - 10.41
FY895			
Maria Elizabeth	1929	Drifter	1940 - 1945
FY896			
Loch Esk	1912	Trawler	1939 - 1943
FY896			
Isabel RNLN	1906	Trawler	1940 - 1945

FY898			
Clifton	1915	Trawler	1939 - 1946
FY899			
Christania T Purdy	1917	Trawler	1939 - 1946
FY900			
Red Gauntlet	1930	Trawler	1939 - 8.43
FY901			
Sanson	1907	Trawler	1939 - 1946
FY902			
Achievable	1927	Drifter	1939 - 1946
FY904			
Friarage	1930	Trawler	1940 - 1945
FY905			
Valdora	1916	Trawler	1939 - 1.40
FY906			
War Wing	1915	Trawler	1939 - 1946
FY907			
Oksoy RNoN	1935	Whaler	8.41 - 1944
(ex Pol VI)			
Cyclone (ex Oksoy)	1935	Whaler	1944 - 1945
Pinieos RHN	1935	Whaler	1945 - 10.45
(ex Cyclone)			
FY909			
Orvicto	1916	Trawler	1940 - 1945
FY911			
Ocean Cruiser	1913	Trawler	1939 - 1945
FY913			
Sunbeam II	1916	Drifter	1939 - 1945
FY914			
Achroite	1934	Trawler	1939 - 1945
FY915			
Tartan	1912	Trawler	1942 - 1946
FY918			
Three Kings	1912	Drifter	1939 - 1945
FY919			
Young Cliff	1925	Drifter	1939 - 1946
FY920			
Tranquil	1912	Trawler	1940 - 6.42
FY922			
Strive	1912	Drifter	1939 - 1945
FY923			
Jacketa	1926	Drifter	1939 - 1946
FY924			
John & Norah	1913	Drifter	1939 - 1945
FY926			
Olivae	1915	Drifter	1939 - 1946
FY927			
Swift Wing	1912	Drifter	1939 - 1946
FY928			
Feasible	1912	Drifter	1939 - 1945
FY929			
Lord Barham	1925	Drifter	1939 - 1946
FY930			
Lord Hood	1925	Drifter	1939 - 1946
FY931			
Aurilia	1914	Drifter	1940 - 1945
FY932			
Bergen RNoN	1907	Trawler	1940 - 1945
FY934			
Ross Ard	1911	Drifter	1939 - 1944
FY935			
Jeannie Leask	1909	Drifter	1939 - 1943
FY937			
Solstice	1918	Drifter	1939 - 1946
FY938			
Industry	1908	Drifter	1939 - 1945
FY939			
Tilly Duff	1919	Drifter	1939 - 1946
FY940			
Lichen	1911	Drifter	1939 - 1946
FY941			
Fairy Knowe	1913	Drifter	1939 - 1945
FY942			
Lovania	1912	Trawler	1940 - 1946
FY943			
M. H. Stephen	1918	Drifter	1939 - 1944
FY944			
Rose Bud	1907	Drifter	1939 - 1946
FY945			
Refraction	1919	Drifter	1939 - 1945
FY946			
Silver Seas	1931	Drifter	1939 - 1945
FY947			
Willing Boys	1930	Drifter	1939 - 1946
FY949			
Ascona	1930	Drifter	1939 - 1945
FY950			
Hosanna	1930	Drifter	1939 - 1945
FY951			
Ocean Vim	1930	Drifter	1939 - 1946
FY953			
Merbreeze	1931	Drifter	1939 - 1947
FY954			
Paramount	1911	Drifter	1939 - 1946
FY956			
Unicity	1917	Drifter	1939 - 1.42
FY957			
Liberty	1903	Drifter	1939 - 1945
FY958			
Jack Eve	1919	Drifter	1939 - 1945
FY960			
Alcor	1922	Drifter	1939 - 1945
FY961			
Exchequer	1914	Drifter	1940 - 1946
FY962			
Frons Olivae	1916	Drifter	1939 - 1945

FY963			
Gilt Edge	1916	Drifter	1939 - 1945
FY964			
Glow	1918	Drifter	1939 - 1945
FY965			
Guide On	1911	Drifter	1939 - 1946
FY967			
Rose Haugh	1918	Drifter	1939 - 1946
FY968			
Sarah Hyde	1921	Trawler	1939 - 1946
FY969			
Sea Holly	1918	Drifter	1939 - 1946
FY970			
Silver Spray	1907	Drifter	1939 - 1940
FY971			
Sweet Promise	1919	Drifter	1939 - 1943
FY972			
Lowther	1915	Trawler	1940 - 1946
FY973			
Tritonia	1930	Drifter	1939 - 1946
FY975			
Young Jacob	1914	Drifter	1939 - 1946
FY976			
Inverugie	1908	Drifter	1939 - 1945
FY977			
Internos	1908	Drifter	1939 - 1946
FY980			
Jenny Irvin	1919	Drifter	1939 - 1943
FY981			
Margaret Hide	1929	Drifter	1939 - 1945
FY983			
One Accord	1927	Drifter	1939 - 1946
FY984			
Overfall	1918	Drifter	1939 - 1945
FY985			
Betty Inglis	1895	Drifter	1939 - 1946
FY987			
Cloverdale	1907	Trawler	1939 - 1945
FY988			
Florio	1916	Trawler	1939 - 1945
FY990			
Eager	1912	Drifter	1939 - 1946
FY993			
Beaumaris Castle	1917	Trawler	1940 - 1945
FY996			
Cedric	1906	Trawler	1939 - 1944
FY997			
Ben Bhrachie	1916	Trawler	1940 - 1945
FY998			
Prince Leo	1913	Trawler	1939 - 1944
FY999			
Ben Earn	1916	Trawler	1940 - 1946
FY1500			
Advisable	1930	Drifter	1939 - 1945
FY1502			
Amalia	1917	Drifter	1939 - 1945
FY1503			
Ocean Lux	1930	Drifter	1939 - 1945
FY1504			
Ocean Lifebuoy	1929	Drifter	1939 - 1946
FY1505			
Fisher Boy	1914	Drifter	1939 - 1946
FY1506			
Lord Cavan	1915	Drifter	1939 - 6.40
FY1507			
Tweenways	1920	Drifter	1939 - 1946
FY1508			
Mare	1911	Drifter	1939 - 1945
FY1510			
Golden News	1914	Drifter	1939 - 1946
FY1511			
Ben and Lucy	1910	Drifter	1939 - 1946
FY1512			
Plumer	1919	Drifter	1939 - 1945
FY1514			
B.T.B.	1911	Drifter	1939 - 1946
FY1516			
Evening Primrose	1911	Drifter	1939 - 1945
FY1518			
John Alfred	1913	Trawler	1939 - 1945
FY1520			
Renascent	1926	Drifter	1939 - 1946
FY1521			
Welcome Home	1925	Drifter	1939 - 1946
FY1522			
Castle Bay	1918	Drifter	1939 - 1946
FY1523			
Thrifty	1916	Trawler	1939 - 1946
FY1524			
Kindred Star	1930	Drifter	1939 - 1946
FY1525			
Alcmaria	1916	Trawler	1939 - 1946
FY1526			
Violet Flower	1914	Trawler	1939 - 1945
FY1528			
Harvest Reaper	1925	Drifter	1939 - 1946
FY1529			
Avon Stream	1915	Trawler	1939 - 1945
FY1530			
The Roman	1909	Trawler	12.39 - 1944
FY1531			
Vireo	1912	Trawler	1939 - 1941
FY1534			
Golden Effort	1914	Drifter	1939 - 9.43
FY1536			
Troup Ahead	1913	Drifter	1939 - 1946
FY1538			
Prospects Ahead	1919	Drifter	1939 - 1946

FY1539			
Consolation	1917	Drifter	1939 - 1945
FY1540			
Rig	1911	Drifter	1939 - 1945
FY1541			
Thomsons	1907	Drifter	1939 - 1946
FY1542			
Rime	1919	Drifter	1939 - 1945
FY1543			
Eunice & Nellie	1918	Drifter	1939 - 1946
FY1544			
Gowan Craig	1915	Drifter	1939 - 1946
FY1547			
Lizzie Birrel	1913	Drifter	1939 - 1946
FY1550			
Concordia	1913	Drifter	1939 - 1946
FY1551			
Fairway	1918	Trawler	1941 - 1946
FY1552			
Coral Bank	1914	Drifter	1939 - 1946
FY1553			
Lydia Long	1918	Drifter	1939 - 1946
FY1554			
Red Sky	1918	Drifter	1939 - 1946
FY1555			
Capstone	1917	Trawler	1940 - 1945
FY1556			
Gloamin	1919	Drifter	1939 - 1945
FY1557			
Ben Roy	1929	Trawler	1939 - 1945
FY1558			
De la Pole	1919	Trawler	1939 - 1940
FY1559			
Donna Nook	1915	Trawler	1941 - 9.43
FY1560			
Franc Tireur	1916	Trawler	1941 - 9.43
FY1561			
Norland	1916	Trawler	1943 - 1945
FY1562			
Nairnside	1912	Drifter	1939 - 1945
FY1563			
Suthernes	1915	Trawler	1942 - 1945
FY1564			
Utilise	1918	Drifter	1939 - 1946
FY1565			
Yarta	1898	Armed Yt	1939 - 1945
FY1566			
Our Bairns	1917	Trawler	1939 - 1947
FY1567			
Maria Elena	1932	Drifter	1939 - 1945
FY1569			
Ben Urie	1916	Trawler	1939 - 1945
FY1572			
Stormwrack	1925	Whaler	1942 - 1945
FY1573			
Milford King	1917	Trawler	1939 - 1944
FY1577			
Rosette	1911	Trawler	1940 - 1945
FY1578			
Rose Valley	1918	Drifter	1939 - 12.43
FY1581			
Eloquent	1911	Drifter	1939 - 1945
FY1583			
Wigan	1916	Trawler	1942 - 1946
FY1584			
Willa	1935	Drifter	1942 - 1946
FY1585			
William Stephen	1917	Trawler	1939 - 10.43
FY1586			
Olympia	1917	Trawler	1939 - 1945
FY1587			
Shandwick	1912	Trawler	1940 - 1946
FY1588			
West Haven	1910	Drifter	1939 - 1945
FY1589			
Snap	(....)	Danlayer	1940 - 1945
FY1590			
Star of the Wave	1917	Trawler	1939 - 1945
FY1591			
Bengal	1905	Trawler	1939 - 11.39
Staunch (ex *Bengal*)	1905	Trawler	11.39 - ....
FY1592			
Stour	1917	Trawler	1939 - 1946
FY1593			
Lord Grey	1928	Trawler	1939 - 1946
FY1594			
Strathcoe	1916	Trawler	1942 - 1943
FY1595			
Sturton	1920	Trawler	1939 - 1944
FY1596			
Clythness	1920	Trawler	1939 - 1944
FY1597			
Majesty	1908	Drifter	1940 - 1946
FY1598			
Arcady	1907	Drifter	1939 - 1945
FY1599			
St. Olive	1914	Trawler	1940 - 1945
FY1600			
Banshee	1917	Drifter	1939 - 1946
FY1601			
Ebor Wyke	1929	Trawler	1939 - 5.45
FY1602			
Thalia	1904	Armed Yt	1940 - 10.42
FY1603			
Vernal	1919	Drifter	1939 - 1946
FY1607			
Burnhaven	1918	Drifter	1939 - 1945

FY1609			
Welbeck	1917	Trawler	1940 - 1946
FY1610			
Touchstone	1907	Trawler	1940 - 1941
FY1611			
Lord Inchcape	1924	Trawler	1939 - 10.40
FY1612			
Troubadour	1924	Arm Yt	1940 - 1942
FY1613			
Varanis	1910	Trawler	1939 - 1945
FY1614			
Arctic Hunter	1929	Trawler	1939 - 1945
FY1617			
Lord Irwin	1928	Trawler	1939 - 1946
FY1618			
Adam	1919	Trawler	1940 - 1945
FY1623			
Salpa	1918	Drifter	1939 - 1946
FY1624			
Perilia	1918	Drifter	1939 - 1946
FY1625			
Varanga	1929	Trawler	1939 - 1945
FY1626			
Rosa	1908	Drifter	1939 - 9.43
FY1627			
Scourge (ex *Lea Rig*)	1908	Drifter	11.39 - 1942
Skyrocket	1908	Drifter	1943 - ....
(ex *Scourge*)			
FY1628			
Norse	1930	Trawler	1939 - 1944
FY1629			
Silver Dawn	1925	Drifter	1939 - 1945
FY1630			
Starlight Rays	1918	Drifter	1939 - 1946
FY1632			
Strathgarry	1924	Trawler	1940 - 1945
FY1633			
Earl Kitchener	1915	Trawler	1939 - 1946
FY1634			
Jennifer	1927	Trawler	1940 - 1942
(ex *Braemar*)			
FY1635			
Jeannie Mackintosh	1915	Trawler	1940 - 1946
FY1636			
Euclase	1931	Trawler	1940 - 1946
FY1637			
Withernsea	1918	Trawler	1940 - 1946
FY1638			
Strathmaree	1914	Trawler	1939 - 1945
FY1639			
Clorinde	1931	Arm Yt	1940 - 1946
(ex *Braemar*)			

FY1640			
Sea Mist	1917	Trawler	1940 - 1945
FY1641			
Braemar	1929	Drifter	1940 - 1945
FY1642			
Mirabelle	1918	Trawler	1939 - 11.44
FY1643			
River Spey	1918	Trawler	1940 - 1944
FY1644			
Spindrift (ex *Polaris*)	1936	Whaler	4.40 - 1943
FY1645			
Everton	1915	Trawler	1939 - 1946
FY1646			
Else Rykens	1935	Trawler	1939 - 1945
FY1646			
Elsie Cam	1922	Trawler	1940 - 1946
FY1648			
Strathrannock	1919	Trawler	1940 - 1945
FY1649			
Morag	1929	Arm Yt	1940 - 1945
FY1650			
Hekla	1929	Trawler	5.40 - 10.40
Liberator (ex *Hekla*)	1929	Trawler	10.40 - 1945
FY1651			
Cadorna	1917	Trawler	1940 - 1945
FY1652			
Sevra	1929	Whaler	1940 - 11.40
FY1653			
True Reward	1913	Drifter	1940 - 1946
FY1654			
Ocean Pioneer	1915	Drifter	1940 - 1946
FY1655			
Girl Ethel	1914	Drifter	1940 - 1945
FY1657			
Shako	1913	Tug	1939 - 1945
FY1658			
Quintia	1914	Drifter	1940 - 1946
FY1659			
Mary J. Masson	1913	Drifter	1940 - 1947
FY1661			
Dick Whittington	1913	Drifter	1940 - 1945
FY1662			
John Stephen	1920	Trawler	1940 - 1945
FY1663			
Friesland RNLN	1921	Trawler	1940 - 1946
FY1664			
Shika	1929	Whaler	1940 - 1942
FY1665			
William Mannell	1917	Trawler	1940 - 1945
FY1668			
Star of Pentland	1915	Trawler	1940 - 1946
FY1669			
Craig Millar	1905	Trawler	1940 - 1945

FY1669			
Norbreck	1905	Trawler	1939 - 1945

FY1672			
Salvo	1918	MS Tug	1939 - 1945

FY1673			
Servitor	1918	MS Tug	1939 - 1945

FY1674			
Solitaire	1904	MS Tug	1939 - 6.44

FY1676			
Skudd VI	1930	Whaler	1940 - 1944
Sleet (ex *Skudd VI*)	1930	Whaler	1944 - 1945

FY1677			
Jean Edmunds	1916	Trawler	1940 - 1945

FY1678			
Star of Britain	1908	Trawler	1940 - 1944

FY1679			
Gaston Riviere FR	1918	Trawler	1940 - 1946

FY1680			
Ben Gulvain	1914	Trawler	1939 - 1946

FY1681			
Ben Bheulah	1917	Trawler	1939 - 1945

FY1683			
Trevo Terciero	1912	Trawler	1940 - 1942
Finesse	1912	Trawler	1942 - 1946

FY1686			
Bystander	1934	Yacht	1939 - 1947

FY1688			
Polar V RNoN	1931	Whaler	1940 - 1946

FY1691			
Polar VI	(....)	Whaler	1940 - 1945

FY1692			
Siesta	1924	Trawler	1942 - 1944
Adelphi	1924	Trawler	1944 - 1945

FY1693			
Bouvet I	1930	Whaler	1940 - 1946

FY1694			
Shila	1926	Trawler	1940 - 1946

FY1695			
Bouvet II	1930	Whaler	1940 - 1946

FY1696			
Shova	1912	Whaler	1940 - 1946

FY1697			
Kos XX	1936	Whaler	1941
Molde RNoN	1936	Whaler	1941 - 1946

FY1698			
Bouvet III	1930	Whaler	1940 - 1946

FY1700			
Sirra	1929	Whaler	1940 - 1946

FY1701			
Bouvet IV	1930	Whaler	1940 - 1946

FY1702			
Shusa	1929	Whaler	1940 - 1942

FY1703			
Typhoon (ex *Syrian*)	1919	Trawler	1939 - 1945

FY1704			
Roydur	1911	Whaler	1939 - 1944

FY1706			
Sternus	1925	Drifter	1939 - 1945

FY1707			
Svana	1930	Whaler	1940 - 4.42

FY1708			
Angele-Marie FR	1929	Trawler	1940 - 1946

FY1709			
Signa	1926	Whaler	1940 - 1945

FY1710			
Vierge de Lourdes FR	1917	Trawler	1940 - 1946

FY1711			
Vindelicia	1913	Trawler	1940 - 1943

FY1712			
Bjerk RNoN	1912	Whaler	1940 - 1945

FY1713			
Bruinvis RNLN	1929	Drifter	1940 - 1946

FY1714			
Perdrant FR	1919	Trawler	1940 - 1945

FY1715			
Flandre	1915	Trawler	1942 - 1945

FY1716			
Claesje RNLN	1933	Trawler	1940 - 1945

FY1717			
Spina	1926	Whaler	1940 - 1945

FY1718			
Roche Velen FR	1918	Trawler	1940 - 1945

FY1719			
Destinn	1914	Trawler	1940 - 1946

FY1720			
Uiver RNLN	1902	Trawler	1940 - 1945

FY1721			
Dew (ex *Kos VIII*)	1929	Whaler	11.40 - 1946

FY1722			
Nebb RNoN	1930	Whaler	1941 - 1945

FY1723			
Forde	1919	Trawler	1939 - 1940

FY1724			
Shera	1929	Whaler	1940 - 3.42

FY1725			
Kos 9	1930	Whaler	1940 - 1941
Firmament (ex *Kos 9*)	1930	Whaler	5.41 - 5.44

FY1725

Gos 9	1937	Whaler	1940 - 10.40
Narvik RNoN	1937	Whaler	10.40 - 1945
(ex Gos 9)			

Both *Firmament* (ex *Kos 9*) and *Narvik* (ex *Gos 9*) appear in various publications as FY1725. The only primary source for FY1725, located to date, is a 1944 copy of BR619(2) which assigns the number to *Narvik*. Details of *Firmament* have been included as it has not been possible to discount her at this time.

FY1726

Saurian	1916	Trawler	1940 - 1945

FY1727

William Bell	1918	Trawler	1940 - 1946

FY1728

Monique-Andre	1920	Trawler	1940 - 1946

FY1729

Caroline RNLN	1930	Trawler	1940 - 4.41

FY1730

Avola	1913	Trawler	1939 - 1946

FY1731

Hercules RNLN	1905	Trawler	1940 - 1946

FY1732

Syrian	1919	Trawler	1940 - 1946

FY1733

Ewald RNLN	1913	Trawler	1940 - 1945

FY1733

Tenby	1913	Trawler	1940 - 1945

FY1734

Satsa	1936	Whaler	1941 - 1945

FY1738

Sarka	1930	Whaler	1940 - 1946

FY1739

Amsterdam	1913	Trawler	1943 - 1946

FY1740

Tornado	1917	Trawler	1940 - 1943
Tornado II	1917	Trawler	1943 - 1946

FY1741

Manx Hero	1916	Trawler	1940 - 1943
Rotterdam	1916	Trawler	1943 - 1946

FY1742

Silva	1924	Whaler	1940 - 1946

FY1743

En Avant	1911	Trawler	1940 - 1945

FY1745

Dirkje RNLN	1934	Trawler	1940 - 1945

FY1746

Antioch II	1918	Trawler	1940 - 1945

FY1747

Alma RNLN	1915	Trawler	1940 - 1945

FY1748

Invertay	1916	Trawler	1940 - 1946

FY1749

Hatsuse	1927	Trawler	1939 - 1945

FY1750

Postboy	1941	Trawler	1940 - 1946

FY1752

Haug I RNoN	1924	Whaler	1940 - 1946

FY1753

Sarna	1930	Whaler	1940 - 2.41

FY1754

Ventose FR	1936	Trawler	1940 - 1944

FY1755

Soika	1925	Whaler	1940 - 1945

FY1757

Blue Haze	1919	Drifter	1940 - 1946

FY1759

Hav	1930	Whaler	1940 - 1942

FY1761

Dolfijn RNLN	1920	Trawler	1940 - 1942
Goeree RNLN	1920	Trawler	1942 - 1945

FY1763

Oderin	1941	MMS	1941 - 1946

FY1764

Domino	1930	Whaler	1941 - 1945

FY1765

Ligny	1918	Trawler	1940 - 1945

FY1766

Ben Idris	1931	Trawler	1941 - 1945

FY1767

Sukha	1929	Whaler	1940 - 1945

FY1768

Lucien Goucy FR	1935	Trawler	1940 - 2.45

FY1770

Craig Coilleach	1917	Trawler	1940 - 1946

FY1771

Eastcoates	1919	Trawler	1939 - 1945

FY1773

Sluga	1929	Whaler	1940 - 1946

FY1774

Lord Darling	1914	Trawler	1940 - 1944

FY1776

Quiet Waters	1931	Drifter	1939 - 1946

FY1777

Marjorie M Hastie	1930	Trawler	1940 - 1945

FY1778

Freres Coquelin	1934	Drifter	1940 - 1946

FY1779

Gerberdina Johanna	1912	Trawler	1940 - 1945

FY1780

Orpheus	1905	Trawler	1940 - 1946

FY1781

Viking Bank	1927	Trawler	1940 - 1945

FY1782			
Strenuous	1911	Drifter	1940 - 1946
FY1783			
Jacqueline Clasine	1906	Trawler	1940 - 1946
FY1784			
Myrland RNoN	1918	Trawler	1940 - 1944
FY1785			
Maria R Ommering	1914	Trawler	1940 - 1946
FY1787			
Bloemendahl	1917	Trawler	1940 - 1946
FY1788			
Sheraton	1907	Trawler	1940 - 1945
FY1789			
Noordvaarder	1898	Trawler	1940 - 1945
FY1790			
Southern Field	1929	Whaler	1940 - 1946
FY1791			
Pitsruan	1930	Trawler	1940 - 1944
FY1792			
Skudd IV	1929	Whaler	1940 - 1944
Spate	1929	Whaler	1944 - 1945
FY1793			
Chasse Marie FR	1920	Trawler	1940 - 1944
FY1794			
Rehearo	1917	Trawler	1940 - 1945
FY1795			
Hortensia	1907	Trawler	1940 - 1945
FY1796			
Southern Foam	1926	Whaler	1940 - 1946
FY1797			
Cap Ferrat FR	1938	Drifter	1940 - 1946
FY1798			
Andre et Louis FR	1907	Trawler	1940 - 1945
FY1799			
Tartarin FR	1931	Trawler	1940 - 1945
FY1800			
Libyan	1913	Trawler	1939 - 1944
FY1802			
Swona	1925	Whaler	1940 - 1944
FY1803			
Monique-Camille	1934	Trawler	1940 - 1946
FY1804			
Charles Vaillant	1916	Trawler	1940 - 1946
FY1805			
Pierre-Gustave	1932	Trawler	1940 - 1946
FY1806			
Skudd V	1929	Whaler	1940 - 1944
Surge (ex *Skudd V*)	1929	Whaler	1944 - 1945
FY1807			
Stormcentre	1919	Trawler	1942 - 1946
FY1809			

Armana	1930	Trawler	1940 - 1945
FY1810			
Strathderry	1911	Trawler	1940 - 1941
FY1812			
Bracondene	1916	Trawler	1939 - 1946
FY1813			
Strathdevon	1915	Trawler	1940 - 1942
FY1814			
Zareba	1921	Trawler	1940 - 1945
FY1815			
Nazareth FR	1918	Trawler	1940 - 1945
FY1817			
Swansea Castle	1912	Trawler	1940 - 1946
FY1818			
Ben Meidie	1917	Trawler	1940 - 1946
FY1819			
Moravia	1917	Trawler	1940 - 3.43
FY1820			
D.W. Fitzgerald	1916	Trawler	1940 - 1945
FY1821			
Peken	1908	Trawler	1940 - 1945
FY1822			
Rotherslade	1917	Trawler	1940 - 1945
FY1823			
Courser	1905	Trawler	9.40 - 1945
Cavalcade	1905	Trawler	1945 - 1946
(ex *Courser*)			
FY1825			
Kos XII	1932	Whaler	1940 - 1941
Hailstorm	1932	Whaler	9.41 - 1945
(ex *Kos XII*)			
FY1825			
Kos XIII	1932	Whaler	1940 - 1942
Brevik (ex *Kos XIII*)	1932	Whaler	1.42 - 1946

Both *Hailstorm* (ex *Kos XII*) and *Brevik* (ex *Kos XIII*) appear in various publications as FY1825. Details of both ships have been included as it has not been possible to discount either via primary sources.

FY1826			
Liberia	1906	Trawler	1940 - 1946
FY1827			
Chrysolite	1916	Trawler	1940 - 1946
FY1828			
Claribelle	1918	Trawler	1941 - 1946
FY1829			
Strephon	1913	Trawler	1940 - 1946
FY1830			
Junco	1917	Trawler	1940 - 1946
FY1831			
Rolls Royce	1906	Trawler	1940 - 1946

FY1832			
Eduard van	1925	Trawler	1940 - 1.41
Vlaenderen			
FY1834			
Sureaxe	1907	Trawler	1942 - 1945
FY1835			
Loch Park	1917	Trawler	1940 - 1945
FY1836			
Meror	1905	Trawler	1940 - 10.43
FY1837			
Kos XIV	1932	Whaler	1940 - 7.40
Mandal	1932	Whaler	7.40 - 1945
(ex *Kos XIV*)			
FY1841			
Aiglon	1907	Trawler	1940 - 1946
FY1842			
Busen 11	1931	Whaler	1941 - 12.41
Snowdrift	1931	Whaler	12.41 - 1943
(ex *Busen 11*)			
FY1844			
Rockall	1930	Drifter	1940 - 1945
FY1847			
Kos XVII	1932	Whaler	1940 - 7.40
Harstad	1932	Whaler	7.40 - 2.43
(ex *Kos XVII*)			
FY1849			
Saronta	1917	Trawler	1940 - 1945
FY1850			
Calvinia	1901	Trawler	1940 - 1945
FY1852			
Portia	1913	Trawler	1941 - 1946
FY1853			
Ceylonite	1918	Trawler	1940 - 1946
FY1854			
Busen 7	1926	Whaler	1941 - 9.41
Silhouette	1926	Whaler	9.41 - 1943
(ex *Busen 7*)			
FY1855			
Artegal	1918	Trawler	1940 - 1945
FY1857			
Chassiron	1913	Trawler	1939 - 1945
FY1858			
Night Hawk	1915	Trawler	1940 - 1946
FY1859			
Darwen	1916	Trawler	1939 - 1946
FY1860			
Biglieri	xxxx	Trawler	1942 - 1946
FY1862			
Wyoming	1915	Trawler	1939 - 5.44
FY1863			
Moonrise	1918	Trawler	1940 - 1946
FY1865			
Boy Scout	1913	Drifter	1939 - 1945
FY1866			
Heroine	1907	Trawler	1940 - 1944
FY1867			
Argo FR	1938	Drifter	1940 - 1946
FY1869			
Pointer	1906	Trawler	1940 - 1945
FY1870			
Byng	1920	Drifter	1939 - 1946
FY1871			
Polar VI	1925	Whaler	1940 - 1946
FY1872			
Citron	1911	Drifter	1940 - 1944
FY1873			
Ex Fortis	1914	Drifter	1939 - 1945
FY1874			
Sulla	1928	Whaler	1940 - 3.42
FY1875			
Gregory	1930	Trawler	1939 - 1945
FY1876			
Sunspot (ex *St Clair*)	1904	Trawler	9.40 - 1947
FY1877			
Kiddaw	1909	Drifter	1939 - 1945
FY1878			
Ratapiko	1912	Trawler	1940 - 1945
FY1879			
Comely Bank	1914	Drifter	1939 - 1944
FY1880			
Swan III	1902	Trawler	1940 - 1945
FY1882			
Nadine Fr	1919	Trawler	1940 - 1946
FY1883			
Our Kate	1910	Drifter	BR619(2)
FY1884			
Lord Keith	1930	Drifter	1939 - 1945
FY1886			
Avanturine	1930	Trawler	1940 - 12.43
FY1887			
Stefa	1929	Whaler	1940 - 1942
FY1888			
Rosemma	1912	Drifter	1940 - 1945
FY1889			
Busen 3	1924	Whaler	12.40 - 9.41
Icicle (ex *Busen 3*)	1924	Whaler	9.41 - 1946
FY1892			
Eadwine	1914	Drifter	1940 - 1946
FY1894			
Yashima	1929	Trawler	1940 - 1946

FY1895			
Balmoral	1916	Trawler	1939 - 1940
Avalanche	1916	Trawler	1940 - 1945
FY1897			
Orizaba	1908	Trawler	1940 - 1944
FY1900			
Restart	1912	Drifter	1940 - 1946
FY1903			
Sahra	1936	Whaler	1941 - 1944
FY1905			
Thorodd RNoN	1919	Whaler	1940 - 1945
FY1906			
Nordhav II	1913	Trawler	1940 - 3.45
FY1909			
Constant Hope	1913	Drifter	1940 - 1945
FY1910			
George & Albert	1916	Drifter	1939 - 1946
FY1912			
Young Alfred	1911	Drifter	1939 - 1946
FY1913			
Scarron	1913	Trawler	1939 - 1945
FY1914			
Elsie & Nellie	1916	Drifter	1940 - 1945
FY1915			
J.T. Hendry	1908	Drifter	1940 - 1945
FY1916			
Estrella do Mar	1914	Trawler	1940 - 1942
Dusk	1914	Trawler	1942 - 1946
FY1917			
Louise et Marie	1899	Trawler	1940 - 1946
FY1918			
Ocean Treasure	1913	Drifter	1940 - 1946
FY1919			
Congre FR	1918	Trawler	1940 - 1944
FY1920			
Busen 6	1928	Whaler	1941 - 9.41
Rainstorm	1928	Whaler	9.41 - 1946
FY1921			
Amsterdam	1913	Trawler	1940 - 1941
Andyk	1913	Trawler	1941 - 1946
(ex Amsterdam)			
FY1922			
Polo Norte POR	1917	Trawler	1941 - 1942
Moonshine	1917	Trawler	1942 - 1946
FY1923			
Springdale	1937	Trawler	1940 - 1947
FY1924			
Utvaer RNoN	1914	Trawler	1940 - 1942

FY1925			
Ocean Retriever	1912	Drifter	1940 - 9.43
FY1926			
George Adgell	1920	Trawler	1940 - 1946
FY1927			
Estrella d'Alva	1909	Trawler	1940 - 1942
Sunburst	1909	Trawler	1942 - 1946
FY1928			
Kos IV	1929	Whaler	1940 - 1941
Drobak	1929	Whaler	1941 - 1946
FY1930			
Kos XVIII	1913	Trawler	1940 - 1941
Vardo	1913	Trawler	7.40 - 1946
(ex Kos XVIII)			
FY1932			
Windsor Lad	(....)	MFV	1940 - 1945
FY1933			
Constant Friend	1912	Drifter	1940 - 1945
FY1934			
Northern Light	(....)	MFV	1940 - 1945
FY1935			
Mary A Hastie	1930	Trawler	1939 - 1945
FY1937			
Zwarte Zee	1899	Trawler	1940 - 1941
Ymuiden RNLN	1899	Trawler	1941 - 1946
(ex Zwarte Zee)			
FY1938			
Invercauld	1917	Trawler	1940 - 1945
FY1939			
Arnold Bennett	1930	Trawler	1939 - 1945
FY1940			
Girl Nancy	1910	Drifter	1940 - 1946
FY1941			
Strathugie	1914	Trawler	1940 - 1945
FY1942			
John Willment	1932	Drifter	1941 - 1946
FY1944			
Pierre Andre FR	1920	Drifter	1940 - 1946
FY1945			
Ann Melville	1909	Trawler	1940 - 1944
FY1946			
Olive Tree	1918	Drifter	1939 - 1945
FY1947			
Ocean Toiler	1915	Drifter	1941 - 1946
FY1948			
Coriolanus	1917	Trawler	8.40 - 12.40
Craftsman	1917	Trawler	12.40 - 1944

227

FY1949			
Hilda Cooper	1928	Drifter	1939 - 1945
FY1950			
Geordie	1911	Drifter	1939 - 1946
FY1951			
Corbrae	1935	Depot Ship	1940 - 1946
FY1952			
True Friend	1909	Drifter	1940 - 1946
FY1956			
Kos XV RNoN	1932	Whaler	7.40 - 1941
Grimstad	1932	Whaler	1941 - 1946
(ex *Kos XV*)			
FY1957			
Craig Alvah	1909	Drifter	1939 - 1945
FY1959			
Taeping	1937	MFV	1939 - 1946
FY1960			
Clan Mackay	1928	MFV	1940 - 1945
FY1961			
Boy John	1914	Drifter	1939 - 1945
FY1962			
Gowan	1907	Drifter	1939 - 1945
FY1963			
Thaw	1919	Drifter	1939 - 1946
FY1964			
Daisy Bank	1911	Drifter	1939 - 1944
FY1965			
Token	1914	Drifter	1939 - 12.41
FY1966			
Ugie Brae	1915	Drifter	1939 - 1946
FY1968			
Golden Sunbeam	1920	Drifter	1939 - 8.43
FY1969			
Ut Prosim	1925	Drifter	1939 - 3.43
FY1971			
Netsukis	1924	Drifter	1939 - 1946
FY1972			
Yorkshire Lass	1920	Drifter	1939 - 1946
FY1973			
Broadland	1913	Drifter	1940 - 6.45

FY1975			
Girl Ellen	1914	Drifter	1939 - 1946
FY1976			
Ocean Gain	1915	Drifter	1939 - 1946
FY1977			
Ocean Guide	1914	Drifter	1939 - 1946
FY1978			
Ocean Spray	1912	Drifter	1939 - 1946
FY1979			
Reids	1918	Drifter	1939 - 1945
FY1980			
Thermopylae	1913	Drifter	1939 - 1946
FY1982			
Hollydale	1919	Drifter	1940 - 1945
FY1984			
Rachel Flett	1914	Drifter	1939 - 1946
FY1985			
Darnaway	1918	Drifter	1939 - 1945
FY1986			
Santa	1936	Whaler	1941 - 11.53
FY1987			
Trophy	1911	Drifter	1939 - 1946
FY1988			
Brackendale	1916	Trawler	1939 - 1946
FY1989			
Silver Sky	1919	Drifter	1939 - 1946
FY1990			
Reverberation	1919	Drifter	1939 - 1945
FY1991			
Girl Gladys	1917	Drifter	1939 - 1946
FY1992			
Eileen Emma	1914	Drifter	1939 - 1946
FY1993			
Seddon	1916	Trawler	1941 - 1946
FY1994			
Golden Gift	1910	Drifter	1939 - 4.43
FY1995			
Romany Rose	1924	Drifter	1939 - 1945
FY1997			
Supporter	1914	Drifter	1939 - 11.44
FY1999			
Girl Winifred	1912	Drifter	1939 - 1945

Flag '4' Superior

Pre 1940:   None

1940-48:   Armed Yachts, Auxiliary AA Ships, Aux Minesweepers, Aux Patrol Vessels, Auxiliary Vessels, Convoy Escorts, Base and Accommodation Ships, Balloon Barrage, Torpedo Recovery, Wreck Dispersal, Wreck Locating, Examination Service and Armed Boarding Vessels.

1948:   None

4.00
Aquamarine	1927	ABV	1940 - 1944

4.01
Vigra	1899	Aux Pat Vsl	1940 - 1945

4.02
White Bear	1908	Armed Yacht	1939 - 1947

4.03
Kingston Beryl	1928	ABV	1939 - 12.43

4.04
Mitres	1917	Aux Pat Vsl	1940 - 1945

4.05
Sarpedon	1916	Aux Pat Vsl	1940 - 1975

4.06
Northern Princess	1936	ABV	1939 - 1942
Bruce (ex *Manxmaid*)	1910	Training Vsl	1941

4.07
Lacerta	1911	Aux Pat Vsl	1940 - 1946

4.08
Notre Dame D'etel FR	(....)	Aux Pat Vsl	1940 - 1945

4.09
Hektor Frans BG	1938	Aux Pat Vsl	1940 - 1945

4.11
Northern Duke	1936	ABV	1939 - 1942

4.12
Philante	1937	Armed Yacht	1940 - 1947

4.14
Gava	1920	Aux Pat Vsl	1939 - 1946

4.15
Sandown	1934	Aux AA	1942 - 1945

4.16
Arpha	1901	ABV	1939 - 1946

4.17
Carbineer II	1915	Aux Pat Vsl	1940 - 1946

4.18
Northern Sun	1936	ABV	1939 - 1945

4.21
Lairds Isle	1911	LSI(H)	1944 - 1945

4.22
Scawfell	1937	Aux AA	1941 - 1945

4.23
Fairway	1918	Aux Pat Vsl	1940 - 3.46

4.24
Elk	1902	Danlayer	1939 - 11.40

4.25
Northern Isles	1936	ABV	1939 - 1.45

4.26
Sagitta	1908	Armed Yacht	1940 - 1946

4.27
Millwater	1918	BBV	1940 - 1945

4.29
Jeannie Deans	1931	Aux AA	1941 - 1945

4.31
Kingston Topaz	1927	ABV	1939 - 1945

4.33
Vidonia	1907	Aux Pat Vsl	1940 - 10.44

4.34
Northern Chief	1936	ABV	1939 - 1942

4.35
Prins Albert	1937	LSI(S)	1941 - 1946

4.36
Goatfell	1934	Aux AA	1942 - 1946

4.37
Charles McIver	1936	Armed Yacht	1940 - 1945

4.38
Semla	1924	Aux Pat Vsl	1941 - 1946

4.39
Ryde	1937	Aux AA	1942 - 1945

4.40
Grey Mist	1920	Armed Yacht	1940 - 1947
Sprig o'Heather	1914	Aux Pat Vsl	1940 - 1942

4.41
Northern Sky	1936	Aux Pat Vsl	1939 - 1945

4.42
Duke of Argyll	1928	LSI(H)	1942 - 1945

4.43
St Tudno	1926	ABV	1939 - 1947

No.	Name	Year	Type	Service
4.44	Princess Beatrix	1939	LSI(M)	1940 - 1946
4.45	Kingston Jacinth	1929	ABV	1939 - 1.43
4.46	Flying Admiral	1917	Aux Pat Vsl	1940 - ....
4.47	Mona's Isle	1905	ABV	1939 - 1944
4.48	Ary	1904	WDV	1943 - 1946
4.49	Guelder Rose	....	Danlayer	1939 - 1945
4.50	Northern Gift	1936	ABV	1939 - 1945
4.51	River Leven	1918	Aux Pat Vsl	1939 - 1945
4.52	Alfredian	1913	Aux Pat Vsl	1940 - 1946
4.53	Hinba	1903	Armed Yacht	1940 - 1943
4.54	Kingston Onyx	1927	ABV	1939 - 9.44
4.55	Bunting	1896	Armed Yacht	1940 - 1944
4.56	St Katharine	1927	Armed Yacht	1940 - 1946
4.58	Northern Rover	1936	ABV	1939 - 11.39
4.59	St Dominica	1895	Armed Yacht	1940 - 1944
4.60	Hiniesta RIN	1902	RDF Cal Sp	1943 - 1946
4.62	Anglia	1913	Armed Yacht	1939 - 1946
4.63	Royal Ulsterman	1936	LSI(H)	1942 - 1946
4.63	St Adrian	1927	Armed Yacht	1939 - 1941
4.64	Ocean Rover	1919	Trawler	1940 - 1946
4.65	Lorna	1904	Armed Yacht	1940 - 1941
4.66	Ombra	1902	Armed Yacht	1940 - 1945
4.67	Malahne	1937	Armed Yacht	1940 - 1946
4.68	Goodwin	1917	ABV	1939 - 1942
4.69	Ulster Monarch	1929	LSI(H)	1940 - 1942
4.69	Kingston Periodot	1926	ABV	1939 - 1945
4.70	Franc Tireur	1916	Aux Pat Vsl	1940 - 9.43
4.71	Galvani	1929	Aux Pat Vsl	1940 - 1945
4.72	Sayonara	1911	Armed Yacht	1940 - 1946
4.73	Cacouna	1932	Armed Yacht	1940 - 1946
4.74	Iona	1920	Armed Yacht	1940 - 1946
4.75	Seaflower	1882	Armed Yacht	1940 - 1946
4.76	Northern Foam	1936	ABV	1936 - 1945
4.77	Glen Kidston	1930	Aux Pat Vsl	1939 - 7.45
4.79	Spitfire III	1938	Armed Yacht	1940 - 1944
4.80	Ocean's Gift BG	1907	Aux Pat Vsl	1940 - 1946
4.81	Kingston Sapphire	1929	ABV	1940 - 10.40
4.81	Bransfield RNoN	1918	Aux Pat Vsl	1943 - 1946
4.82	Rampant	1898	WDV	1940 - 1946
4.83	Tiercel	1913	Armed Yacht	1940 - 1945
4.84	Breda	1912	Armed Yacht	1939 - 2.44
4.85	Northern Reward	1936	ABV	1939 - 1942
4.86	Helvetia	1917	Aux Pat Vsl	1940 - 1946
4.87	Kings Grey	1915	Aux Pat Vsl	1939 - 1946
4.88	Prince Baudouin	1933	LSI(S)	1943 - 1945
4.89	Lady Hogarth	1937	Aux Pat Vsl	1939 - 1945
4.90	Sylvana	1907	Armed Yacht	1940 - 1945
4.91	Kingston Turquoise	1929	ABV	1939 - 1945
4.92	Azur	1929	Armed Yacht	1940 - 1946
4.93	Amazone	1936	Armed Yacht	1940 - 1945
4.94	Springtide	1937	MDV	1940 - 1947
4.95	Lady of Man	1930	LSI(H)	1942 - 1945
4.96	Biarritz	1915	LSI(H)	1942 - 1949
4.97	Loch Hope	1915	Aux Pat Vsl	1940 - 1945

4.99

Raymond BG	1930	BDV	1940 - 1945

4.100

North Ness	1917	Aux Pat Vsl	1940 - 1946

4.101

Oystermouth Castle	1913	Aux Pat Vsl	1939 - 1946

4.102

Patti	1929	Aux Pat Vsl	1940 - 1946

4.103

Pelagos	1918	Aux Pat Vsl	1940 - 1945

4.104

Namur	1917	Aux Pat Vsl	1940 - 1944

4.105

St Wistan	1937	Aux Pat Vsl	1940 - 1946

4.106

Northlyn	1919	Aux Pat Vsl	1939 - 1943

4.107

Canterbury	1929	LSI(H)	1942 - 1945

4.108

Victoria	1907	LSI(H)	1942 - 1945

4.109

Dipavati RIN	1936	Aux MS	1939 - 1946

4.110

Tervani	1911	Aux Pat Vsl	1940 - 2.43

4.111

Ramdas RIN	1936	Aux Pat Vsl	1939 - 1944

4.112

William Brady	1918	Aux Pat Vsl	1940 - 1946

4.114

Morgan Jones	1918	Aux Pat Vsl	1940 - 1945

4.115

Royal Scotsman	1936	LSI(H)	1942 - 1945

4.118

Alvis	1918	Aux Pat Vsl	1940 - 1945

4.119

Ampulla	1913	Aux Pat Vsl	1940 - 1946

4.120

Amroth Castle	1913	Aux Pat Vsl	1940 - 1945
Prince Charles	1930	LSI(S)	1941 - 1945

4.122

Cape Barracouta	1930	Aux Pat Vsl	1939 - 1940

4.123

Netravati RIN	1909	Aux Pat Vsl	1939 - 1945

4.124

Chalcedony	1928	Aux Pat Vsl	1939 - 1945

4.125

Chiltern	1917	Aux Pat Vsl	1940 - 1945

4.127

Mecklenburg	1922	LSI(H)	1942 - 1946

4.129

De La Pole	1919	Aux Pat Vsl	1941 - 1945

4.130

Bluebird	1911	Armed Yacht	1939 - 1946

4.131

Dhoon	1915	Aux Pat Vsl	1940 - 1941

4.132

Donna Nook	1915	Aux Pat Vsl	1940 - 9.43

4.134

Edwina	1915	Aux Pat Vsl	1941 - 1945

4.135

George R Purdy	1917	Aux Pat Vsl	1939 - 10.44

4.136

Evelyn Rose	1918	Aux Pat Vsl	1940 - 1945

4.138

Jacinta	1915	Aux Pat Vsl	1940 - 1944

4.139

St Nectan	1936	Aux Pat Vsl	1940 - 1946

4.140

Southcoates	1918	Aux Pat Vsl	1940 - 1945

4.141

Phrontis	1911	Aux Pat Vsl	1940 - 1946

4.142

Raetia	1912	Aux Pat Vsl	1939 - 1946

4.143

Sheldon	1912	Aux Pat Vsl	1940 - 1944

4.144

Eroican	1914	Trawler	1944 - 1945

4.146

Great Admiral	1908	Aux Pat Vsl	1940 - 1945

4.147

Astral	1930	WLV	1942 - 1945

4.148

Kastoria	1917	Aux Pat Vsl	1940 - 1946

4.149

St Anthony RIN	1936	Aux MS	1939 - 1945

4.151

Andanes	1916	BDV	1940 - 1946

4.153

Campina	1913	Aux Pat Vsl	1940 - 7.40

4.155

Caleta	1930	Armed Yacht	1940 - 1945

4.156

Dale Castle	1909	Aux Pat Vsl	1940 - 1946

4.157

Ebor Wyke	1911	Aux Pat Vsl	1940 - 1946

4.158

Kalavati RIN	1928	Aux MS	1939 - 1945

4.159

Electra II BG	1904	Aux Pat Vsl	1940 - 2.46

4.160

Sangarius	1915	Aux Pat Vsl	1940 - 1946

4.161

River Esk	1918	Aux Pat Vsl	1940 - 1945

4.162

Rugby	1900	Aux Pat Vsl	1940 - 1943

4.163

Caulonia	1912	Aux Pat Vsl	1940 - 3.43

4.166			
Seddon	1916	Aux Pat Vsl	1940 - 1946
4.167			
Maria	1929	WDV	1941 - 1946
(ex August Wriedt GER*)*			
4.169			
Lombard	1909	Aux MS	1940 - 1945
4.170			
Lorraine	1917	Aux Pat Vsl	1940 - 8.41
4.171			
Montano	1917	Aux Pat Vsl	1940 - 1944
4.172			
Cape Mariato	1936	Aux Pat Vsl	1940 - 1945
4.174			
Capstone	1917	Aux MS	1940 - 1940
Sutherness	1915	Aux Pat Vsl	1940 - 1945
4.177			
Avon	1907	Aux Pat Vsl	1940 - 12.41
4.179			
Parvati RIN	1927	Aux Pat Vsl	1940 - 4.41
4.180			
Queen Emma	1939	LSI(M)	1940 - 1946
4.185			
Umbriel	1939	Armed Yacht	1940 - 1945
4.186			
Irrawadi RIN	1913	Aux Pat Vsl	1940 - 1945
4.190			
Cape Trafalgar	1917	Aux Pat Vsl	1940 - 1947
4.191			
Heliopolis	1903	Armed Yacht	1940 - 1946
4.196			
Glengyle	1939	LSI(L)	1942 - 1946
4.197			
Tyrant	1930	Armed Yacht	1940 - 1943
4.198			
Ratnagiri RIN	1913	Aux Pat Vsl	1939 - 1945
4.199			
Strathella	1913	Aux Pat Vsl	1940 - 1945
4.200			
Aristocrat	1935	Ferry	1940 - 1945
4.201			
Tritelia	1916	Aux Pat Vsl	1939 - ....
4.203			
Loch Blair	1917	Aux Pat Vsl	1940 - 1946
4.204			
Foamcrest	1902	Aux Pat Vsl	1940 - 1946
4.206			
Sonavati RIN	1936	Aux Pat Vsl	1939 - 1945
4.207			
Louis Botha	1916	Aux Pat Vsl	1940 - 3.44
4.209			
Antwerp	1919	LSF	1941 - 1945

4.213			
Reflect	1908	Drifter	1941 - 1945
4.214			
Malines	1921	Convoy Esc	1940 - 1945
4.215			
Hiravati RIN	1930	Aux Pat Vsl	1939 - 1945
4.220			
Oscar Angele	1912	Aux MS	1940 - 1945
4.221			
Blenheim	1919	Depot Ship	1940 - 1948
4.222			
Dorothy Gray	1908	Aux Pat Vsl	1940 - 1944
4.223			
Andre-Marcel	1936	Drifter	1940 - 1945
4.224			
Atmah	1898	Armed Yacht	1940 - 1946
4.226			
Princes Astrid	1929	LSI(S)	1941 - 1945
4.228			
De Drie	1912	Hb Ser	1940 - 1945
Gezusters RNLN			
4.229			
Loch Moidart	1918	Aux MS	1940 - 1946
4.230			
Conquerante	1934	Aux MS	1940 - 1945
4.232			
President Herriot	(....)	Aux Pat Vsl	1940 - 1944
4.233			
Tranio	1917	Aux Pat Vsl	1940
Lady Stanley	1917	Aux Pat Vsl	1940 - 1945
(ex Tranio)			
4.235			
Dounie Braes	1918	Danlayer	1940 - 1945
4.236			
Golden Eagle	1909	Accom	1940 - 1945
4.237			
Emperor of India	1906	Aux AA	1940 - 1948
4.238			
Prinses	1930	LSI(S)	1940 - 1945
Josephine Charlotte			
4.239			
Royal Eagle	1932	Aux AA	1939 - 1945
4.241			
Balmoral	1900	Accom	1940 - 1943
4.242			
Kihna	1930	Armed Yacht	1942 - 1945
4.243			
Forfeit	1917	Aux Pat Vsl	1940 - 1946
4.244			
Delphin II ORP	1938	Aux Pat Vsl	1940 - 1946
4.245			
Isle of Guernsey	1929	LSI(H)	1944 - 1945

4.246			
River Lossie	1920	Aux Pat Vsl	1940 - 1945
4.247			
Queen Eagle	1940	Aux AA	1941 - 1943
4.248			
Maid of Orleans	1918	LSI(H)	1942 - 6.44
4.249			
Brigadier	1928	LSI(H)	1942 - 1946
4.250			
Glenearn	1938	LSI(L)	1942 - 1946
4.251			
Prince Leopold	1929	LSI(S)	1941 - 7.44
4.252			
Viking Deeps	1916	Aux Pat Vsl	1940 - 1944
4.254			
Sabina	1919	Aux Pat Vsl	1940 - 1944
4.255			
St Helier	1925	LSI(H)	1942 - 1945
4.256			
Glenroy	1938	LSI(L)	1942 - 1946
4.257			
Glacier	1909	Aux Pat Vsl	1940 - 6.44
4.258			
Stella Polaris	1936	Aux Pat Vsl	1940 - 1942
4.259			
Dranguet	1935	Aux MS	1940 - 1945
4.261			
Pozarica	1937	Aux AA	1940 - 2.43
4.262			
Isle of Thanet	1911	LSI(H)	1943 - 1945
4.263			
Tarana FR	1932	Aux Pat Vsl	1940 - 1945
4.265			
Anne-Gaston FR	1937	Drifter	1940 - 1945
4.266			
Couronne FR	1935	Aux Pat Vsl	1940 - 1947
4.267			
Charles Henri	1935	Drifter	1940 - 1945
4.268			
Beatrix Adriennes	(....)	Drifter	1940 - 1945
4.269			
Strijdt voor Christus BG	1938	Aux Pat Vsl	1940 - 4.42
4.270			
Bournemouth Queen	1908	Aux AA	1941 - 1943
4.271			
Kuvera	1919	Aux Pat Vsl	1940 - 1945
4.272			
Breeze	1934	Aux Pat Vsl	1941 - 1946
4.273			
Delila	1919	Aux Pat Vsl	1940 - 1946
4.274			
Agnes Nutten	1915	Aux Pat Vsl	1940 - 1946
4.275			
Fort Rose	1917	Aux Pat Vsl	1940 - 1945

4.277			
Honingsvaag RNoN	1940	Aux Pat Vsl	1940 - 1945
4.278			
Simmerson	1913	Aux Pat Vsl	1940 - 1946
4.279			
Agnes Wetherly	1917	Aux Pat Vsl	1940 - 1946
4.281			
Kernot	1930	Aux Pat Vsl	1940 - 1945
4.282			
Alastor	1928	Armed Yacht	1940 - 1945
4.283			
Invicta	1939	LSI(H)	1939 - 1945
4.284			
Monte Carlo	1931	Drifter	1942 - 1945
4.285			
Freelance	1908	Armed Yacht	1940 - 1945
4.286			
Anne	1925	Armed Yacht	1940 - 1946
4.291			
Minna	1939	Aux Pat Vsl	1940 - 1945
4.293			
Caduceus	1904	Training Vsl	1941 - 1945
4.294			
Tirade	1899	Aux Pat Vsl	1942 - 1946
4.295			
Ceto	1935	Armed Yacht	1940 - 1946
4.296			
Marion	1896	Armed Yacht	1940 - 1945
4.297			
Korab I ORP	1938	Aux Pat Vsl	1940 - 1946
4.300			
Gabrielle Denise	1910	Aux MS	1940 - 1945
4.301			
Skiddaw	1896	Aux AA	1942 - 1945
4.302			
Riskato	1915	Aux Pat Vsl	1940 - 1946
4.304			
Isle of May	1896	Armed Yacht	1940 - 1944
4.315			
Lapageria	1916	Aux Pat Vsl	1940 - 1942
4.318			
De Roza BG	1922	Aux Pat Vsl	1940 - 1945
4.322			
Horten RNoN	1929	Aux Pat Vsl	1940 - 1945
4.323			
Georges Le Verdier	1930	Aux Pat Vsl	1940 - 1945
4.325			
H.J. Bull	1935	Aux Pat Vsl	1940 - 1942
4.326			
Patrie FR	1920	Aux Pat Vsl	1940 - 1945
4.328			
Ravenswood	1891	Ferry	1941 - 1945
4.336			
Quercia	1912	Trawler	1942 - 1944

4.339			
Ythan Braes	1917	Trawler	1942 - 1944
4.340			
Dorade II	1906	Armed Yacht	1940 - 1945
4.364			
Ocean Brine	1914	Aux Pat Vsl	1941 - 1944
4.365			
Betty Bodie	1918	Drifter	1939 - 1946
4.368			
Glen More	1922	Aux AA	1942 - 1945
(ex *Glen Gower*)			
4.370			
Present Help	1911	Tender	1941 - 1945
4.371			
Pourquois Pas FR	1913	Aux MS	1940 - 1945
4.372			
Adoration	1912	Drifter	1940 - 1945
4.373			
Laguna Belle	1896	Aux AA	1942 - 1944
4.375			
Avalon	1915	Aux Pat Vsl	1940 - 1941
Adonis (ex Avalon)	1915	Aux Pat Vsl	1941 - 4.43
4.376			
Thalassa	1924	Armed Yacht	1942 - 1945
4.377			
Glen Usk	1914	Aux AA	1942 - 1945
4.379			
Strathelliot	1915	Danlayer	1940 - 1946
4.380			
Thames Queen	1898	Aux AA	1942 - 1945
4.381			
Titan	1935	Armed Yacht	1939 - 1943
4.382			
Bournemouth Queen	1908	Accom Ship	1943 - 1947
4.384			
Alisdair	1937	Armed Yacht	1939 - 1945
4.385			
Plinlimmon	1895	Aux AA	1942 - 1944
4.390			
Westward Ho	1894	Aux AA	1942 - 1944
4.392			
Glen Avon	1912	Aux AA	1942 - 9.44
4.394			
Creole	1927	Armed Yacht	1940 - 1946
4.395			
Moorfly	1942	Mooring Vsl	1942 - ....
4.396			
Moorcock	1942	Mooring Vsl	1942 - ....
4.399			
Queen Empress	1912	Aux AA	1942 - 1944
4.400			
Duke of Wellington	1935	LSI(H)	1942 - 1945

4.402			
Lorna Doone	1891	Aux AA	1942 - 1943
4.403			
Princess Elizabeth	1927	Aux AA	1942 - 1946
4.404			
Whippingham	1930	Aux AA	1942 - 1945
4.405			
Brenda	1906	Aux Pat Vsl	1940 - 1945
4.406			
Explorer	....	Aux Pat Vsl	1940 - 1945
4.407			
Freya	1917	Aux Pat Vsl	1940 - 1945
4.408			
Gillian	1919	Aux Pat Vsl	1939 - 8.45
4.409			
Norna	1909	Aux Pat Vsl	1940 - 1945
4.410			
Adriatic BG	1936	Aux Pat Vsl	1940 - 1945
4.411			
Brinmaric	1938	Armed Yacht	1940 - 1946
4.412			
Ben-My-Chree	1927	LSI(H)	1942 - 1946
4.413			
Amsterdam	1930	LSI(S)	1943 - 8.44
4.414			
Princess Maud	1934	LSI(H)	1942 - 1946
4.415			
Admiral Sir John Lawford	1930	WDV	1944 - 1946
4.416			
Lune	1930	WDV	1944 - 1946
4.417			
Laurel	1930	WDV	1944 - 1946
4.418			
Tehana	1929	WDV	1944 - 1947
4.419			
Princess Margaret	1931	LSI(S)	1943 - 1946
4.420			
Lamont	1939	LSI(L)	1942 - 1945
Ard Patrick	1939	LSI(L)	1945 - 1946
(ex *Lamont*)			
4.421			
Duke of Rothesay	1928	LSI(H)	1942 - 1945
4.422			
Pampas	1943	LSI(L)	1943 - 1944
Persimmon	1943	LSI(L)	1944 - 1946
(ex *Pampas*)			
4.423			
Viking	1905	LSI(H)	1943 - 1945
4.425			
Coryphene	1907	Esso	1944 - 1945

4.427			
Eridanus	1905	Esso	1944 - 11.44
4.428			
Choice	1899	Esso	1944 - 8.44
4.429			
Riano	1906	Aux Pat Vsl	1944 - 1944
4.430			
Ugie Bank	1913	Aux Pat Vsl	1939 - 1945
4.431			
Mikasa	1915	Aux Pat Vsl	1939 - 1944
4.432			
Avondee	1918	Trawler	1944 - 1944
4.433			
Braes O'Mar	1915	Trawler	1944 - 11.44
4.434			
Ambition	1902	Esso	1944 - 1945
4.435			
Crevette	1918	Esso	1944 - 10.44
4.436			
All Hallows	1914	Esso	1944 - 1944
4.437			
Strathmartin	1914	Esso	1944 - 1945
4.438			
East Coast	1907	Esso	1944 - 1945
4.439			
Shielburn	1911	Esso	1944 - 1944
4.440			
Dandolo	1910	Esso	1944 - 1945
4.441			
East Coast	1907	Esso	1944 - 1945
4.442			
Arabesque	1918	Aux Pat Vsl	1943 - 1944
4.443			
Barnsness	1907	BBV	1940 - 1944
4.444			
Benjamin Coleman	1918	Aux Pat Vsl	1940 - 1945
4.446			
Cloughstone	1907	BBV	1940 - 4.45
4.447			
Controller	1913	Esso	1940 - 1944
4.448			
Ibis II BG	1937	Esso	1943 - 1945
4.449			
Marie Jose Rosette	1936	Esso	1944 - ....
4.450			
Peggy Nutten	1907	Esso	1944 - 11.44
4.451			
Rigoletto	1906	Esso	1944 - 1945
4.452			
Bona	1906	Esso	1944 - 11.44
4.455			
Kerneval	1906	Esso	1944 - 11.44
4.456			
Roxano	1907	Esso	1939 - 1945
4.457			
Salvini	1916	BBV	1940 - 1945
4.458			
Strathalladale	1908	Esso	1944 - 10.44
4.459			
Strathfinella	1910	Esso	1944 - 10.44
4.460			
William Stroud	1914	Esso	1944 - 1945

Flag '5' Superior

Pre 1940:   None

1940-48:   Kil class Coastal Escorts

1948:   None

The Kil class were large submarine chasers of the PCE type acquired under lend-lease from the USA. Fifteen vessels were delivered to the Royal Navy, being variously classified as patrol sloops and, later, as corvettes. All have variously been recorded in published texts as being assigned numbers BEC1-15 and Z01-15. Although there is some photographic evidence of vessels carrying the BEC flag superior no evidence has yet been uncovered relating to Z flag superior.

5.01			
Kilbirnie	1943	PCE	1943 - 1946
5.02			
Kilbride	1943	PCE	1943 - 1946
5.03			
Kilchatten	1943	PCE	1943 - 1946
5.04			
Kilchrenan	1943	PCE	1943 - 1946
5.05			
Kildary	1943	PCE	1943 - 1946
5.06			
Kildwick	1943	PCE	1943 - 1946
5.07			
Kilham	1943	PCE	1943 - 1946
5.08			
Kilkenzie	1943	PCE	1943 - 1946
5.09			
Kilkhampton	1943	PCE	1943 - 1946
5.10			
Kilmalcolm	1943	PCE	1943 - 1946
5.11			
Kilmarnock	1943	PCE	1943 - 1946
5.12			
Kilmartin	1943	PCE	1943 - 1946
5.13			
Kilmelford	1943	PCE	1943 - 1946
5.14			
Kilmington	1943	PCE	1943 - 1946
5.15			
Kilmore	1943	PCE	1943 - 1946

Pendant Series 3800/4800

Ordered toward the end of WW1 these Patrol Gunboats (originally designated Fast Trawlers) were ordered from trawler-building firms. Many were cancelled but, those that reached service displayed the Fishery pendant superior to their Admiralty numbers as listed here.

3800					**4008**			
Kildary	1917	Patrol Gb	1917 - 1920		Kilbrittain	Canc	Patrol Gb	Canc 1918
3801					**4009**			
Kildorough	1917	Patrol Gb	1917 - 1920		Kilburn	1918	Patrol Gb	1918 - 1920
3802					**4010**			
Kilfenora	1917	Patrol Gb	1917 - 1920		Kilby	Canc	Patrol Gb	Canc 1918
3803					**4011**			
Kilgobnet	1918	Patrol Gb	1918 - 1920		Kilcar	Canc	Patrol Gb	Canc 1918
3804					**4012**			
Kilclare	1918	Patrol Gb	1918 - 1920		Kilcavan	Canc	Patrol Gb	Canc 1918
3805					**4013**			
Kilchrenan	1918	Patrol Gb	1918 - 1920		Kilchattan	1918	Patrol Gb	1918 - 1920
3806					**4014**			
Kildavin	1918	Patrol Gb	1918 - 1920		Kilchvan	1918	Patrol Gb	1918 - 1920
3807					**4015**			
Kildorrey	1918	Patrol Gb	1918 - 1920		Kilclief	1918	Patrol Gb	1918 - 1920
3808					**4016**			
Kilfullert	1918	Patrol Gb	1918 - 1920		Kilclogher	1918	Patrol Gb	1918 - 1920
3809					**4017**			
Kilkeel	1918	Patrol Gb	1918 - 1920		Kilcolgan	Canc	Patrol Gb	Canc 1918
3810					**4018**			
Kilcock	1918	Patrol Gb	1918 - 1920		Kilcommon	Canc	Patrol Gb	Canc 1918
3811					**4019**			
Kildimo	1918	Patrol Gb	1918 - 1920		Kilconnell	Canc	Patrol Gb	Canc 1918
3812					**4020**			
Kildysart	1918	Patrol Gb	1918 - 1920		Kilcoole	Canc	Patrol Gb	Canc 1918
3813					**4021**			
Kilgarven	1918	Patrol Gb	1918 - 1920		Kilcorney	Canc	Patrol Gb	Canc 1918
3814					**4022**			
Kilchreest	1918	Patrol Gb	1918 - 1920		Kilcot	Canc	Patrol Gb	Canc 1918
3815					**4023**			
Kilham	1918	Patrol Gb	1918 - 1920		Kilcreggan	Canc	Patrol Gb	Canc 1918
4000					**4024**			
Kilbane	Canc	Patrol Gb	Canc 1918		Kilcullen	Canc	Patrol Gb	Canc 1918
4001					**4025**			
Kilbarchan	Canc	Patrol Gb	Canc 1918		Kilcurrig	Canc	Patrol Gb	Canc 1918
4003					**4026**			
Kilberry	1918	Patrol Gb	1918 - 1920		Kildale	Canc	Patrol Gb	Canc 1918
4004					**4027**			
Kilbeggan	1918	Patrol Gb	1918 - 1920		Kildalkey	1918	Patrol Gb	1918 - 1920
4005					**4028**			
Kilbirnie	1919	Patrol Gb	1919 - 1920		Kildangan	1918	Patrol Gb	1918 - 1920
4006					**4029**			
Kilbrachan	Canc	Patrol Gb	Canc 1918		Kildare	1918	Patrol Gb	1918 - 1920
4007					**4030**			
Kilbride	1918	Patrol Gb	1918 - 1920		Kildonan	1918	Patrol Gb	1918 - 1919

4031				
Kildress	1918	Patrol Gb	1918 - 1919	
4032				
Kildwick	1918	Patrol Gb	1918 - 1919	
4033				
Kilfinny	1918	Patrol Gb	1918 - 1920	
4034				
Kilfree	1918	Patrol Gb	1918 - 1919	
4035				
Kilglass	Canc	Patrol Gb	Canc 1918	
4036				
Kilgowan	Canc	Patrol Gb	Canc 1918	
4037				
Kilkee	Canc	Patrol Gb	Canc 1918	
4038				
Kilkenny	Canc	Patrol Gb	Canc 1918	
4039				
Kilkenzie	Canc	Patrol Gb	Canc 1918	
4040				
Kilkerrin	Canc	Patrol Gb	Canc 1918	
4041				
Kilhampton	Canc	Patrol Gb	Canc 1918	
4042				
Killadoon	Canc	Patrol Gb	Canc 1918	
4043				
Killagon	Canc	Patrol Gb	Canc 1918	
4044				
Killaloo	Canc	Patrol Gb	Canc 1918	
4045				
Killane	Canc	Patrol Gb	Canc 1918	
4046				
Killarney	Canc	Patrol Gb	Canc 1918	
4047				
Killary	Canc	Patrol Gb	Canc 1918	
4048				
Killegar	Canc	Patrol Gb	Canc 1918	
4049				
Killena	1918	Patrol Gb	1918 - 1920	
4050				
Killerig	1918	Patrol Gb	1918 - 1920	
4051				
Killiney	1918	Patrol Gb	1918 - 1920	
4052				
Killour	1918	Patrol Gb	1918 - 1920	
4053				
Killowen	1918	Patrol Gb	1918 - 1920	
4054				
Killybegs	1918	Patrol Gb	1918 - 1920	
4055				
Killygordon	1918	Patrol Gb	1918 - 1920	
4056				
Kilmacolm	1918	Patrol Gb	1918 - 1920	
4057				
Kilmacrennan	1918	Patrol Gb	1918 - 1920	
4058				
Kilmaine	1918	Patrol Gb	1918 - 1920	
4059				
Kilmallock	1918	Patrol Gb	1918 - 1920	
4060				
Kilmanahan	1918	Patrol Gb	1918 - 1920	
4061				
Kilmarnock	1919	Patrol Gb	1919 - 1920	
4062				
Kilmartin	1919	Patrol Gb	1919 - 1920	
4063				
Kilmead	1919	Patrol Gb	1919 - 1920	
4064				
Kilmelford	1919	Patrol Gb	1919 - 1920	
4065				
Kilmersdon	1919	Patrol Gb	1919 - 1920	
4066				
Kilmington	1919	Patrol Gb	1919 - 1920	
4067				
Kilmore	1919	Patrol Gb	1919 - 1920	
4068				
Kilmuckridge	1919	Patrol Gb	1919 - 1920	
4069				
Kilmun	1919	Patrol Gb	1919 - 1920	

HMS *Hampshire* (50) was a Devonshire class armoured cruiser, launched in 1903. She is seen here wearing funnel bands - a system used to identify specific ships, prior to the introduction of pendant numbers. When pendant numbers were introduced, funnel bands were used as a means of identifying which flotilla or squadron specific vessels were assigned. *(Author's collection)*

SS *War Aconite* (Y3.2350) is typical of the thousands of merchant vessels chartered or managed by the Admiralty during WW1. All received 'Y' flag pendant numbers but, these were used as flag hoists and not painted on the hull. *(Allan C Green - Courtesy of the State Library of Victoria)*

HMS *Tartar* (D243/F43/G43/L43) was one of 16 Tribal class destroyers built for the Royal Navy just before the outbreak of WW2. Only four survived that conflict. *Tartar* was one, gaining 13 battle honours. The funnel band shows her as half leader of the 6th Flotilla. She is seen in company with sister ships *Matabele* (F26/G26/L26) and *Bedouin* (F67/G67/L67). *(Author's collection)*

HMS *Hotspur* (D101/H01) was an H class destroyer launched in 1936. In this image her pendant numbers are not displayed, perhaps removed by the wartime censor. She can still be identified as she is flying her pendant number, H01, from the port yardarm. *(Author's collection)*

HMS *Ellesmere* (FY204/T204) was the former Norwegian Whaler *Kos XIV*. Like most Trawlers, Drifters and Whalers requisitioned by the RN her pendant number is preceeded by the Fishery Pendant (seen here as the triangular yellow and blue quartered flag, superior to the numbers 204, flown from the starboard yardarm. The number would be represented as FY204.   (*Author's collection*)

HMS *Bombardier* (T304) was a Military class Admiralty trawler. This image is typical of the many oddities thrown up when studying pendant numbers. Taken on 23 May 1943, the vessel displays a number which bears no resemblance to its assigned number and, to date, no records have been uncovered which show F flag superior being assigned to trawlers.   (*Author's collection*)

HMS *Queen Empress* (J128/R399/4.399) was requisitioned during WW2 to serve as an auxiliary minesweeper. She was re-tasked to operate in the anti-aircraft role and was renumbered R399, as seen here. Not all auxiliary paddle steamers received new numbers upon being re-tasked.

(Author's collection)

HMS *Nubian* (D136/F36/G36/L36) was another destroyer of the Tribal class. She is seen here in 1942 when she was returning to the fleet after repairs to severe bomb damage. Her pendants show clearly on the glistening new paintwork. She survived the war and gained 13 battle honours.

(Author's collection)

HMS *Whitehall* (D94/GA7/I94) was a Modified W-class destroyer, seen here during service in WW2, following her 1943 conversion to a Long-Range Escort. Of note here is the application of her number, which includes a dash between the flag and numbers - although not common, flags and numbers were sometimes shown separated by a dash or a full stop. *(Author's collection)*

HMS *Mermaid* (B287/F30/U30) was a Modified Black Swan class sloop. Launched in November 1943, she served in Arctic waters. She was sold to the German Navy in 1959, being renamed *Scharnhorst*, and was broken up in 1990. *(Author's collection)*

HMS *Starling* (B295/F66/U66) was made famous by Captain Walker in anti U-boat operation. She was built in 1942 and broken up in 1965. These sturdy vessels, well armed with three twin 4-inch guns, proved good anti-submarine ships. Here she has her funnel painted with a black top showing her as a Leader and has her pendant number painted on her sides. *(Author's collection)*

HMS *Mounsey* (K569) was built in Boston, USA, being transferred to the Royal Navy under Lend Lease on 24 September 1943. She was returned to the US Navy in February 1946. In her short career in the RN she gained 3 battle honours (Normandy, Atlantic and Arctic, all in 1944). Her appearance, which showed she was of American design, called for clear identification when the two navies were operating together. *(Author's collection)*

HMAS *Bendigo* (A111/B237/J187/M187) was one of sixty Australian minesweepers (commonly known as corvettes) built during WW2 in Australian shipyards as part of the Commonwealth Government's wartime shipbuilding programme. She is seen here displaying her British Pacific Fleet number, assigned by the US Navy. (*Allan C Green - Courtesy of the State Library of Victoria*)

HMS *Enchantress* (B283/L56/U56) was Bittern-class sloop, intended for use as an Admiralty yacht. At the outbreak of WW2 she was re-armed and allocated to convoy escort duty. She is seen here, disarmed once more, prior to decommissioning for the last time in 1946.

(*Allan C Green - Courtesy of the State Library of Victoria*)

HMS *Atheling* (D51/R304) was a Ruler-class escort carrier, entering service in October 1943. In service the escort carriers were assigned pendant numbers with a 'D' flag superior but, only the numbers were displayed on the hull.   (*Allan C Green - Courtesy of the State Library of Victoria*)

HMS *Chaser* (D32/R306), an Attacker-class escort carrier, was one of many assigned to operations with the British Pacific Fleet. She is seen here, in Australia, with her US Navy assigned BPF number displayed.   (*Author's collection*)

One of the anomalies of the British Pacific Fleet campaign was the appearance of pendant numbers with an 'A' flag superior. HMS *Ruler* (A731/D73/R311), a Ruler-class escort carrier, is wearing one such vessel assigned a number, the origins of which remain a mystery.   (*Author's collection*)

The old County class cruiser *Cumberland* (57/C57/C177) of 1926 was modernised after the war and undertook trials of new equipment, as can be seen from her armament and radio arrays. She was broken up in 1959.   (*Author's collection*)

HMS/M *Spearhead* (P263/S42) was an S-class submarine built by Cammell Laird's Birkenhead shipyard and launched on 2 October 1944. The war-built S-class were numbered in the P200 series. She survived the war and was sold to the Portuguese in August 1948 and renamed NRP *Neptuno*.

(*Author's collection*)

HMS *Pioneer* (A198/B347/D76/R76) was a Colossus-class aircraft carrier built during WW2. She was modified, whilst under construction, to an aircraft maintenance carrier. She is seen here in Australian waters at the end of the war. Although she did not display her number, it can be made out from the flag hoist at the starboard yardarm.

(*Allan C Green - Courtesy of the State Library of Victoria*)

The Battle class destroyer *Armada* (D14/D73/R14) was one of a few of the class to operate with the British Pacific Fleet, though she reached the area after the cessation of hostilities. The funnel bands of one white over two black shows her as being assigned to the 19th Destroyer Flotilla.
(Allan C Green - Courtesy of the State Library of Victoria)

HMS *Tenacious* (D45/D46/F44/R45) paying off, in 1946, after service with the British Pacific Fleet. By this time she had reverted to her Royal Navy pendant number and flotilla funnel marking had given way to numerals, showing she was a member of the 24th Destroyer Flotilla. In 1951, she was selected for conversion to a Type 16 AS frigate at Rosyth and was assigned the pendant number F44. She was broken up in 1965. *(Allan C Green - Courtesy of the State Library of Victoria)*

The Algerine class minesweeper *Jewel* (J390/M390) is seen here post-war. Her funnel bands indicate she was the half leader and the torch on her funnel shows she was in the Dartmouth Training Squadron. Launched in 1944, she was broken up in 1967. *(Author's collection)*

The frigate *Torquay* (F43) is seen here leading ships of the Dartmouth Training Squadron, all wearing the school torch funnel badge. The *Torquay* is sporting her Leader's black funnel top.

(Author's collection)

HMS *Dieppe* (L108/L3016) has her pendant number on the bows, and also on the quarters. The lettering is certainly large enough to read. She was a Landing Ship Tank, built by Hawthorn, Leslie & Co Ltd, Hebburn Shipyard. Launched on 14 December 1944. she was named *Dieppe* in 1947. She was sold in 1980 and scrapped at Santander, Spain. (*Author's collection*)

The destroyer *Diamond* (D35/I81) was launched in June 1950. She had two funnels. The forward funnel was obscured by her lattice foremast so the after funnel carried the half leader's band. She was sold in November 1981. (*Author's collection*)

The cruiser *Blake* (99/C99) shows her flight deck marking clearly in this bird's eye view. She was originally a gun ship, but was later fitted with a flight deck aft. She was broken up in 1982.

(Author's collection)

The Battle class destroyer *Matapan* (D43/I43) was launched in 1945 and lay in reserve for many years before being converted to a sonar trials ship and equipped with a flight deck. Her two letter flight deck code is readily visible here, as is her flotilla marking on her forward funnel. She was in the 2nd Flotilla based at Portland. She wore pendant numbers on her sides and stern. It can be seen that following conversion she retained her 'D' superior pendant. She was sold in 1979.

(Author's collection)

The frigate *Ajax* (F114) shows her flight deck letters and side number. She was launched in 1962, and in mid-career had her twin 4.5-inch gun replaced by an Ikara AS missile launcher. She was broken up in 1988. *(Author's collection)*

The frigate *Apollo* (F70) returning to Devonport after operations off the Falklands in 1982. Note that the numbers have been painted over and everything else has been painted grey, including boats, life rafts, boot topping and funnel caps. The pendant numbers are showing through faintly as the Atlantic weather washed away the hastily applied grey paint. *(Author's collection)*

The Type 42 destroyer *Coventry* (D118) shows her pendant number on her side and her Flotilla number on her funnel, together with a half-leader band. She was lost on 26 May 1982 to attacks by Argentine aircraft in the Falklands operation. (*Author's collection*)

The Type 23 frigate *Monmouth* (F235) is one of 16 such frigates built for the Royal Navy. Named for Dukes, they all display the Ducal crown on their funnels together with emblems relating to individual vessels. Note the black flag flown at the top of the mainmast, the blacked out crown on the funnel and the black name on the starboard quarter - a reference to the dissolution of the title in the wake of the 1685 Monmouth rebellion against King James II of England. (*F.J. Patchett*)

Chapter 2

Submarine Fleet Pendant Numbers

In the early days of submarine development the British were, at most, lukewarm to this new naval weapon. Although the Admiralty had taken notice of such developments, the submarine was regarded as a weapon of weaker naval powers and policy was to steer clear of these new underwater vessels.

By 1901, the position had somewhat mellowed and an initial order for five vessels, to assist the Admiralty in assessing their potential, was placed. Early submarines were small craft, initially designed for harbour operations before larger coastal types and even later larger ocean classes were developed.

These early, un-named craft were identified by numbers being displayed on their bows. It was not until 1914 that a specific series of pendant numbers, with an 'I' flag superior, was issued to cover all submarines. These numbers were usually displayed on the conning tower, without the flag superior. The submarines also retained their names on the bows.

From late 1915 the pendants matched the boat names, with full names appearing on the conning tower. Although the pendants were standardised, the means of displaying them was not, with many different styles and colours of type being employed. Many vessels additionally displayed an abbreviated form of their number on the front of the conning tower.

During the inter-war period, numbers were reversed, with the flag superior becoming a flag inferior (e.g. H49 changed to 49H).

In 1925, it was deemed that submarines should be named, as some in the Admiralty considered that crews would find it difficult to form a bond of loyalty to a mere number. Subsequently, post-war submarines entered service with names rather than numbers but adhered to the flag inferior system (e.g. *Tarpon* = 17T).

Numbers were allocated in the range 00-99 (numbers 00,10, 13, 20, 30, 40, 50, 60 ,70 ,80 and 90 were not used) followed by a letter - usually that of the class. Thus, the P and O classes used flag 'P', while the R, S and T classes used flags 'R', 'S' and 'T' respectively. The River class used flag 'F', the Porpoise class flag 'M' and the U class flag 'C' (for coastal).

In 1936, during the Sino-Japanese war, submarines of the 4th Submarine Flotilla, based on the China Station, displayed on their conning tower, in lieu of their assigned numbers, two letter identification codes to reduce the risk of being targeted by Japanese pilots. These numbers were locally assigned and did not replace their assigned pennant numbers. (The codes were: *Odin* - OD; *Olympus* - OL; *Orpheus* - OR; *Osiris* - OS; *Oswald* - OW; *Otus* - OT; *Parthian* - PN; *Perseus* - PE; *Proteus* - PR; *Pandora* - PD; *Phoenix* - PX; *Rainbow* - RB; *Regulus* - RU).

Soon after the outbreak of WWII, the pendant system changed again with all flag inferiors being unified under the single letter 'N' - this system remained until 1940 when the 'N' flag inferior was changed to 'N' flag superior.

All new war construction received 'P' flag superior numbers as follows - the U/V classes received numbers in the P31 range, the S class P211, the T class P311 and the A class P411 up. P511 upwards was assigned to ex US Navy lend-lease submarines and P611 for foreign construction appropriated by the Admiralty. P711 upwards were assigned to captured enemy submarines. The final units of the V class, having exhausted numbers up to P99, backfilled spare numbers from P11.

By 1941, the subject of naming submarines was the subject of debate and the Hopwood Committee recommended a reversion to numbers in an effort to conceal the extent of submarine build programmes and the subsequent numbers entering service. Consequently, names were, once again, abandoned and all new boats were identified by numbers with flag 'P' superior.

The Submarine Service, it seems, disliked the lack of names and many adopted their previous names or created unofficial names relevant to their class.

This state of affairs continued until late 1942 when none other than Winston Churchill himself, resurrecting the 'loyalty to a number' argument directed that submarines should be named. In a memo to the First Lord of the Admiralty, dated 5 November 1942, Churchill asked to, "*see a list of the submarines that will come into service by December 31, 1943, in their classes, and also those at present in service with no names.*" He went on to state that, "*I have no doubt whatever that names should be given, and I will myself make some suggestions which may stimulate others.*" Still with the bit between his teeth, in a further memo to the First Sea Lord, dated 19 December 1942 he stated that, "*I am still grieved to see our submarines described as 'P.212', etc., in the daily returns. I thought you told me that you would give them names. It is in accordance with the tradition of the Service and with the feelings of the officers and men who risk their lives in these vessels. Not even to give them a name is derogatory to their devotion and sacrifice.*" Keeping up the pressure Churchill again wrote to the First Lord on 27 December 1942. He said, "*These names for submarines are certainly much better than the numbers. Please see my suggestions. I have no doubt a little more thought, prompted by the dictionary, would make other improvements possible. Now do please get on with it, and let them be given their names in the next fortnight.*"

This wasn't Churchill's only intervention on such matters - he was also concerned with the lack of names within the Coastal Forces fleet, although on this occasion his suggestions were more to do with group names. In 1943, he sent a memo to the First Lord, First Sea Lord and General Ismay with regard to MTB operations in the Mediterranean. He said, "*There is a question whether all the fast small craft should not have a name. I have thought of them as the 'Mosquito Fleet', but would it not be more dignified to call them the Hornet Fleet'? Or again, perhaps the 'Shark Fleet' - 'Sharks' for short.*" It is perhaps a measure of the man, that even with all of the pressures and demands of a global war, he was still able to keep his finger on the pulse of many of the lesser issues.

In 1943, names were once again assigned to submarines which, in some cases required a further change of pendant number - this resulted in some submarines having received two number identities and a name in the space of a few months.

The final number change came post-war when the 'S' flag superior was adopted. Generally, at this time, numbers were not displayed. In 1961, there was a slight adjustment to some numbers to allow post war Porpoise and Oberon class submarines to be numbered from S01 onwards. These numbers were displayed for a period but, due to the covert nature of submarine operations, such numbers are no longer displayed.

No Flag Superior

Although not officially pendant numbers, the early Holland class submarines were identified by their number which was displayed on the bow.

1
Holland No1   1901   Holland   1901 - 1913
2
Holland No2   1902   Holland   1901 - 1913
3
Holland No3   1903   Holland   1901 - 1913
4
Holland No4   1903   Holland   1901 - 9.12
5
Holland No5   1903   Holland   1901 - 1913

A Flag Superior

Initially the A class were assigned Roman numbers (I to XIII), displayed on the conning tower. From 1914 pendants with an 'I' flag superior were introduced, with numbers (less the flag superior) being displayed. For those boats remaining in service, from 1915, the submarines' own numbers were used as pendants, these being displayed on the conning tower.

A5
Submarine A5   1904   A Class   1915 - 1920
A6
Submarine A6   1904   A Class   1915 - 1920
A7
Submarine A7   1905   A Class   Sank 1.14
A8
Submarine A8   1905   A Class   1915 - 1920
A9
Submarine A9   1905   A Class   1915 - 1920
A10
Submarine A10   1905   A Class   1915 - 1919
A11
Submarine A11   1905   A Class   1915 - 1920
A12
Submarine A12   1905   A Class   1915 - 1920
A13
Submarine A13   1905   A Class   1915 - 1920

B Flag Superior

The B class submarines were initially assigned pendants with an 'I' flag superior, with numbers (less the flag superior) being displayed. From 1915 the submarines' own numbers were used as pendants, these being dis-

played on the conning tower.

B1
Submarine B1   1904   B Class   1915 - 1921
B2
Submarine B2   1905   B Class   Sunk 10.12
B3
Submarine B3   1905   B Class   1915 - 1919
B4
Submarine B4   1905   B Class   1915 - 1919
B5
Submarine B5   1905   B Class   1915 - 1921
B6
Submarine B6   1905   B Class   1915 - 1917
B7
Submarine B7   1905   B Class   1915 - 1917
B8
Submarine B8   1906   B Class   1915 - 1917
B9
Submarine B9   1906   B Class   1915 - 1917
B10
Submarine B10   1906   B Class   1915 - 8.16
B11
Submarine B11   1906   B Class   1915 - 1917

Submarines B6, B7, B8, B9 and B11 were converted to surface patrol craft at Malta in 1917. The electric motors were removed and the hull forward was rebuilt to accommodate a 12-pdr gun. The conning tower was replaced by a more conventional wheelhouse. The vessels were renamed S6, S7, S8, S9 and S11 respectively.

C Flag Superior

The C class submarines were initially assigned pendants with an 'I' flag superior, with numbers (less the flag superior) being displayed. From 1915 the submarines' own numbers were used as pendants, these being displayed on the conning tower.

C1
Submarine C1   1906   C I Class   1915 - 1921
C2
Submarine C2   1906   C I Class   1915 - 1920
C3
Submarine C3   1906   C I Class   1915 - 1918
C4
Submarine C4   1906   C I Class   1915 - 1922
C5
Submarine C5   1906   C I Class   1915 - 1919
C6
Submarine C6   1906   C I Class   1915 - 1919

C7
Submarine C7	1907	C I Class	1915 - 1919

C8
Submarine C8	1907	C I Class	1915 - 1920

C9
Submarine C9	1907	C I Class	1915 - 1922

C10
Submarine C10	1907	C I Class	1915 - 1922

C12
Submarine C12	1907	C I Class	1915 - 1920

C13
Submarine C13	1907	C I Class	1915 - 1920

C14
Submarine C14	1907	C I Class	1915 - 1921

C15
Submarine C15	1908	C I Class	1915 - 1922

C16
Submarine C16	1908	C I Class	1915 - 1922

C17
Submarine C17	1908	C I Class	1915 - 1919

C18
Submarine C18	1908	C I Class	1915 - 1921

C19
Submarine C19	1909	C II Class	1915 - 1920

C20
Submarine C20	1909	C II Class	1915 - 1921

C21
Submarine C21	1908	C II Class	1915 - 1921

C22
Submarine C22	1908	C II Class	1915 - 1920

C23
Submarine C23	1908	C II Class	1915 - 1921

C24
Submarine C24	1908	C II Class	1915 - 1921

C25
Submarine C25	1909	C II Class	1915 - 1921

C26
Submarine C26	1909	C II Class	1915 - 4.18

C27
Submarine C27	1909	C II Class	1915 - 4.18

C28
Submarine C28	1909	C II Class	1915 - 1921

C29
Submarine C29	1909	C II Class	1915 - 8.15

C30
Submarine C30	1909	C II Class	1915 - 1921

C31
Submarine C31	1909	C II Class	1915 - 1.15

C32
Submarine C32	1909	C II Class	1915 - 10.17

C33
Submarine C33	1910	C II Class	1915 - 8.15

C34
Submarine C34	1910	C II Class	1915 - 7.17

C35
Submarine C35	1909	C II Class	1915 - 4.18

C36
Submarine C36	1909	C II Class	1915 - 1919

C37
Submarine C37	1910	C II Class	1915 - 1919

C38
Submarine C38	1910	C II Class	1915 - 1919

Submarines *C26*, *C27* and *C35* (together with *C32*) operated in the Baltic, but were scuttled in 1918 to avoid capture following the Russian Revolution.

D Flag Superior

The D class submarines were initially assigned pendants with an 'I' flag superior, with numbers (less the flag superior) being displayed. From 1915 the submarines' own numbers were used as pendants, these being displayed on the conning tower.

D1
Submarine D1	1908	D Class	1915 - 1918

D2
Submarine D2	1910	D Class	Sunk 11.14

D3
Submarine D3	1910	D Class	1915 - 3.18

D4
Submarine D4	1911	D Class	1915 - 1921

D5
Submarine D5	1911	D Class	Sunk 11.14

D6
Submarine D6	1911	D Class	1915 - 6.18

D7
Submarine D7	1911	D Class	1915 - 1921

D8
Submarine D8	1911	D Class	1915 - 1921

D9
Submarine D9	1912	D Class	Ren *E1*

D10
Submarine D10	1912	D Class	Ren *E2*

E Flag Superior

The E class submarines were initially assigned pendants with an 'I' flag superior, with numbers (less the flag superior) being displayed. From 1915 the submarines' own numbers were used as pendants, these being displayed on the conning tower.

E1			
Submarine E1	1912	E Class	1915 - 4.18
E2			
Submarine E2	1912	E Class	1915 - 1921
E3			
Submarine E3	1912	E Class	1915 - 10.18
E4			
Submarine E4	1912	E Class	1915 - 1922
E5			
Submarine E5	1912	E Class	1915 - 3.16
E6			
Submarine E6	1912	E Class	1915 - 12.15
E7			
Submarine E7	1913	E Class	1915 - 9.15
E8			
Submarine E8	1913	E Class	1915 - 4.18
E9			
Submarine E9	1913	E Class	1915 - 4.18
E10			
Submarine E10	1913	E Class	1915 - 1.15
E11			
Submarine E11	1914	E Class	1915 - 1921
E12			
Submarine E12	1914	E Class	1915 - 1921
E13			
Submarine E13	1914	E Class	1915 - 8.15
E14			
Submarine E14	1914	E Class	1915 - 1.18
E15			
Submarine E15	1914	E Class	1915 - 4.15
E16			
Submarine E16	1914	E Class	1915 - 8.16
E17			
Submarine E17	1915	E Class	1915 - 1.16
E18			
Submarine E18	1915	E Class	1915 - 5.16
E19			
Submarine E19	1915	E Class	1915 - 4.18
E20			
Submarine E20	1915	E Class	1915 - 11.15
E21			
Submarine E21	1915	E Class	1915 - 1921
E22			
Submarine E22	1915	E Class	1915 - 4.16
E23			
Submarine E23	1915	E Class	1915 - 1922
E24			
Submarine E24	1915	E Class	1915 - 3.16
E25			
Submarine E25	1915	E Class	1915 - 1921
E26			
Submarine E26	1915	E Class	1915 - 7.16
E27			
Submarine E27	1917	E Class	1917 - 1922
E28			
Submarine E28	Canc	E Class	Canc 1915
E29			
Submarine E29	1915	E Class	1915 - 1922
E30			
Submarine E30	1915	E Class	1915 - 11.16
E31			
Submarine E31	1915	E Class	1915 - 1922
E32			
Submarine E32	1916	E Class	1916 - 1922
E33			
Submarine E33	1916	E Class	1916 - 1922
E34			
Submarine E34	1917	E Class	1917 - 7.18
E35			
Submarine E35	1916	E Class	1916 - 1922
E36			
Submarine E36	1916	E Class	1916 - 1.17
E37			
Submarine E37	1916	E Class	1915 - 12.16
E38			
Submarine E38	1916	E Class	1916 - 1922
E39			
Submarine E39	1916	E Class	1916 - 1921
E40			
Submarine E40	1916	E Class	1916 - 1921
E41			
Submarine E41	1915	E Class	1915 - 1922
E42			
Submarine E42	1915	E Class	1915 - 1922
E43			
Submarine E43	1915	E Class	1916 - 1921
E44			
Submarine E44	1916	E Class	1916 - 1921
E45			
Submarine E45	1916	E Class	1916 - 1922
E46			
Submarine E46	1916	E Class	1916 - 1922
E47			
Submarine E47	1916	E Class	1916 - 8.17
E48			
Submarine E48	1916	E Class	1916 - 1928
E49			
Submarine E49	1916	E Class	1916 - 3.17
E50			
Submarine E50	1916	E Class	1916 - 1.18
E51			
Submarine E51	1916	E Class	1916 - 1921
E52			
Submarine E52	1917	E Class	1917 - 1921

E53

Submarine E53	1916	E Class	1916 - 1922

E54

Submarine E54	1916	E Class	1916 - 1921

E55

Submarine E55	1916	E Class	1916 - 1922

E56

Submarine E56	1916	E Class	1916 - 1923

E57

Submarine E57	1917	E Class	Ren L1

E58

Submarine E58	1917	E Class	Ren L2

Submarines E1, E8, E9 and E19 were scuttled in the Baltic in 1918 to avoid capture following the Russian Revolution. E24, E34, E41, E45, E46 and E51 were all built as minelaying submarines.

F Flag Superior

The experimental F class were designed as small coastal submarines. In mid-1915 submarine pendant numbers replicated submarine names, which were displayed on the conning tower. A further five of the class were cancelled.

F1

Submarine F1	1915	F Class	1915 - 1920

F2

Submarine F2	1917	F Class	1917 - 1922

F3

Submarine F3	1916	F Class	1916 - 1920

G Flag Superior

The G class were designed as small coastal submarines. In mid-1915 the G class were assigned pendant numbers replicating their names, which were displayed on the conning tower.

G1

Submarine G1	1915	G Class	1915 - 1920

G2

Submarine G2	1915	G Class	1915 - 1920

G3

Submarine G3	1916	G Class	1916 - 1921

G4

Submarine G4	1915	G Class	1915 - 1928

G5

Submarine G5	1915	G Class	1915 - 1922

G6

Submarine G6	1915	G Class	1915 - 1921

G7

Submarine G7	1916	G Class	1916 - 11.18

G8

Submarine G8	1916	G Class	1916 - 1.18

G9

Submarine G9	1916	G Class	1916 - 9.17

G10

Submarine G10	1916	G Class	1916 - 1923

G11

Submarine G11	1916	G Class	1916 - 11.18

G12

Submarine G12	1916	G Class	1916 - 1920

G13

Submarine G13	1916	G Class	1916 - 1923

G14

Submarine G14	1917	G Class	1917 - 1921

H Flag Superior

Assigned to H class submarines from build to between the wars.

H1

Submarine H1	1915	H-1 Class	1915 - 1921

H2

Submarine H2	1915	H-1 Class	1915 - 1921

H3

Submarine H3	1915	H-1 Class	1915 - 7.16

H4

Submarine H4	1915	H-1 Class	1915 - 1921

H5

Submarine H5	1915	H-1 Class	1915 - 3.18

H6

Submarine H6	1915	H-1 Class	1915 - 1.16

H7

Submarine H7	1915	H-1 Class	1915 - 1921

H8

Submarine H8	1915	H-1 Class	1915 - 1921

H9

Submarine H9	1915	H-1 Class	1915 - 1921

H10

Submarine H10	1915	H-1 Class	1915 - 1.18

H11

Submarine H11	1915	H-1 Class	1915 - 1921

H12

Submarine H12	1915	H-1 Class	1915 - 1922

H13

Submarine H13	1915	H-1 Class	1915 - 1917

H14

Submarine H14	1915	H-1 Class	1915 - 1919

H15

Submarine H15	1915	H-1 Class	1915 - 1919

H16
Submarine H16   1915   H-1 Class   1915 - 1917
H17
Submarine H17   1915   H-1 Class   1915 - 1917
H18
Submarine H18   1915   H-1 Class   1915 - 1917
H19
Submarine H19   1915   H-1 Class   1915 - 1917
H20
Submarine H20   1915   H-1 Class   1915 - 1917

H6 was stranded on the Dutch coast 19.1.16. She was salvaged by the Dutch and purchased in February that year, being renamed *O8*. *H13, H16, H17, H18, H19* and *H20* were ceded to Chile 3.7.17 and renamed initially, *H1, H2, H3, H4, H5 and H6*. They were later named *Gualcolda, Tegualda, Rucumilla, Guale, Quidora* and *Fresia. H14* and *H15* were presented to the Royal Canadian Navy in February 1919 and renamed *CH14* and *CH15* respectively.

H21
Submarine H21   1917   H21 Class   1917 - 1926
H22
Submarine H22   1917   H21 Class   1917 - 1929
H23
Submarine H23   1918   H21 Class   1918 - 1934
H24
Submarine H24   1917   H21 Class   1917 - 1934
H25
Submarine H25   1918   H21 Class   1917 - 1929
H26
Submarine H26   1917   H21 Class   1918 - 1928
H27
Submarine H27   1918   H21 Class   1918 - 1935
H28
Submarine H28   1918   H21 Class   1918 - ....
H29
Submarine H29   1918   H21 Class   1918 - 8.26
H30
Submarine H30   1918   H21 Class   1918 - 1935
H31
Submarine H31   1918   H21 Class   1918 - ....
H32
Submarine H32   1918   H21 Class   1918 - ....
H33
Submarine H33   1918   H21 Class   1918 - ....
H34
Submarine H34   1918   H21 Class   1918 - ....
H35
Submarine H35   Canc   H21 Class   Canc 1917
H36

H36 *continued*
Submarine H36   Canc   H21 Class   Canc 1917
H37
Submarine H37   Canc   H21 Class   Canc 1917
H38
Submarine H38   Canc   H21 Class   Canc 1917
H39
Submarine H39   Canc   H21 Class   Canc 1917
H40
Submarine H40   Canc   H21 Class   Canc 1917
H41
Submarine H41   1918   H21 Class   1918 - 1920
H42
Submarine H42   1918   H21 Class   1919 - 3.22
H43
Submarine H43   1919   H21 Class   1919 - ....
H44
Submarine H44   1919   H21 Class   1919 - ....
H45
Submarine H45   Canc   H21 Class   Canc 1917
H46
Submarine H46   Canc   H21 Class   Canc 1917
H47
Submarine H47   1918   H21 Class   1918 - 7.29
H48
Submarine H48   1919   H21 Class   1919 - 1935
H49
Submarine H49   1919   H21 Class   1919 - ....
H50
Submarine H50   1919   H21 Class   1919 - ....
H51
Submarine H51   1918   H21 Class   1918 - 1924
H52
Submarine H52   1919   H21 Class   1919 - 1927
H53
Submarine H53   Canc   H21 Class   Canc 1917
H54
Submarine H54   Canc   H21 Class   Canc 1917

H41 sank before completion and although subsequently salvaged she was sold in 1920 incomplete.

I Flag Superior

I Flag superior pendants were carried from 1914 - mid 1915. After that time submarine pendants matched the boat's names. F, G, V and W class boats were assigned numbers in the 'I' series, but this system was superceded prior to the vessels entering service. There is, however, evidence that some of these vessels displayed numbers in the I series during sea trials - *V1* for example displayed 2A on her conning tower.

IA0
Submarine F1	1915	F Class	At Build

IA1
| *Submarine F2* | 1917 | F Class | At Build |

IA2
| *Submarine F3* | 1916 | F Class | At Build |

IA3
| *Submarine G1* | 1915 | G Class | At Build |

IA4
| *Submarine G2* | 1915 | G Class | At Build |

IA5
| *Submarine G3* | 1916 | G Class | At Build |

IA6
| *Submarine G4* | 1915 | G Class | At Build |

IA7
| *Submarine G5* | 1915 | G Class | At Build |

IA8
| *Submarine G6* | 1915 | G Class | At Build |

IA9
| *Submarine G7* | 1916 | G Class | At Build |

IAC
| *Nautilus* | 1914 | Exp'ment | 1917 - 1918 |

An unsuccessful experimental design, *Nautilus* was renamed *N1* in 1918 and displayed a prominent letter N on her conning tower. She never became operational and was scrapped in 1922.

ICA
| *Swordfish* | 1916 | Exp'ment | 1916 |

Another unsuccessful experimental design, *Swordfish* was renamed *S1* in 1916. The Admiralty were so concerned about the submarine's seakeeping properties that she was immediately paid off into reserve. During 1917 she was converted to a surface patrol vessel, reverting to the name *Swordfish* on recommissioning in August 1917. Barely more successful as a patrol vessel she was sold in 1922.

I0A
| *Submarine S2* | 1915 | S Class | To Italy |

I1A
| *Submarine S3* | 1915 | S Class | To Italy |

I2A
| *Submarine V1* | 1914 | V Class | At Build |

I3A
| *Submarine V2* | 1915 | V Class | At Build |

I4A
| *Submarine V3* | 1915 | V Class | At Build |

I5A
| *Submarine V4* | 1915 | V Class | At Build |

I6A
| *Submarine W1* | 1914 | W Class | At Build |

I7A
| *Submarine W2* | 1915 | W Class | At Build |

I8A
| *Submarine W3* | 1915 | W Class | At Build |

I9A
| *Submarine W4* | 1915 | W Class | At Build |

I0C
| *Submarine G8* | 1916 | G Class | At Build |

I1C
| *Submarine G9* | 1916 | G Class | At Build |

I2C
| *Submarine G10* | 1916 | G Class | At Build |

I3C
| *Submarine G11* | 1916 | G Class | At Build |

I4C
| *Submarine G12* | 1916 | G Class | At Build |

I5C
| *Submarine G13* | 1916 | G Class | At Build |

I6C
| *Submarine G14* | 1917 | G Class | At Build |

The F, S, V and W class submarines were experimental in nature and not all of the designs were considered successful. The S-class proved unsuitable for operations in the North Sea and only *S1* (I04) saw any service with the Royal Navy. When Italy entered the war in 1915 the opportunity was taken to transfer all three S-class boats to the Italian Navy. Their career was short, the Italians also finding them unsatisfactory and they were withdrawn from service in 1919. The W class boats suffered a similar fate. Being based on a French design, they too were found unsuitable for Northern waters and, in 1916, were also transferred to Italy.

I00
| *Submarine B11* | 1906 | B Class | 1914 - 1915 |

I01
| *Submarine A11* | 1905 | A Class | 1914 - 1915 |

I02
| *Submarine A12* | 1905 | A Class | 1914 - 1915 |

I03
| *Submarine A13* | 1905 | A Class | 1914 - 1915 |

I04
| *Submarine S1* | 1914 | S Class | 1914 - 1915 |

I10
| *Submarine A10* | 1905 | A Class | 1914 - 1915 |

I15
| *Submarine A5* | 1904 | A Class | 1914 - 1915 |

I16			
Submarine A6	1904	A Class	1914 - 1915
I17			
Submarine A7	1905	A Class	Sank 16.1.14
I18			
Submarine A8	1905	A Class	1914 - 1915
I19			
Submarine A9	1905	A Class	1914 - 1915
I20			
Submarine B10	1906	B Class	1914 - 1915
I21			
Submarine B1	1904	B Class	1914 - 1915
I22			
Submarine B2	1905	B Class	Sunk 10.12
I23			
Submarine B3	1905	B Class	1914 - 1915
I24			
Submarine B4	1905	B Class	1914 - 1915
I25			
Submarine B5	1905	B Class	1914 - 1915
I26			
Submarine B6	1905	B Class	1914 - 1915
I27			
Submarine B7	1905	B Class	1914 - 1915
I28			
Submarine B8	1906	B Class	1914 - 1915
I29			
Submarine B9	1906	B Class	1914 - 1915
I30			
Submarine C10	1907	C I Class	1914 - 1915
I31			
Submarine C1	1906	C I Class	1914 - 1915
I32			
Submarine C2	1906	C I Class	1914 - 1915
I33			
Submarine C3	1906	C I Class	1914 - 1915
I34			
Submarine C4	1906	C I Class	1914 - 1915
I35			
Submarine C5	1906	C I Class	1914 - 1915
I36			
Submarine C6	1906	C I Class	1914 - 1915
I37			
Submarine C7	1907	C I Class	1914 - 1915
I38			
Submarine C8	1907	C I Class	1914 - 1915
I39			
Submarine C9	1907	C I Class	1914 - 1915
I42			
Submarine C12	1907	C I Class	1914 - 1915
I43			
Submarine C13	1907	C I Class	1914 - 1915
I44			
Submarine C14	1907	C I Class	1914 - 1915
I45			
Submarine C15	1908	C I Class	1914 - 1915
I46			
Submarine C16	1908	C I Class	1914 - 1915
I47			
Submarine C17	1908	C I Class	1914 - 1915
I48			
Submarine C18	1908	C I Class	1914 - 1915
I49			
Submarine C19	1909	C II Class	1914 - 1915
I50			
Submarine C20	1909	C II Class	1914 - 1915
I51			
Submarine C21	1908	C II Class	1914 - 1915
I52			
Submarine C22	1908	C II Class	1914 - 1915
I53			
Submarine C23	1908	C II Class	1914 - 1915
I54			
Submarine C24	1908	C II Class	1914 - 1915
I55			
Submarine C25	1909	C II Class	1914 - 1915
I56			
Submarine C26	1909	C II Class	1914 - 1915
I57			
Submarine C27	1909	C II Class	1914 - 1915
I58			
Submarine C28	1909	C II Class	1914 - 1915
I59			
Submarine C29	1909	C II Class	1914 - 1915
I60			
Submarine C30	1909	C II Class	1914 - 1915
I61			
Submarine C31	1909	C II Class	1914 - 1.15
I62			
Submarine C32	1909	C II Class	1914 - 1915
I63			
Submarine C33	1910	C II Class	1914 - 1915
I64			
Submarine C34	1910	C II Class	1914 - 1915
I65			
Submarine C35	1909	C II Class	1914 - 1915
I66			
Submarine C36	1909	C II Class	1914 - 1915
I67			
Submarine C37	1910	C II Class	1914 - 1915
I68			
Submarine C38	1910	C II Class	1914 - 1915
I69			
Submarine E20	1915	E Class	1915 - 1915

I70

Submarine E21	1915	E Class	1915 - 1915

I71

Submarine D1	1908	D Class	1914 - 1915

I72

Submarine D2	1910	D Class	1914 - 11.14

I73

Submarine D3	1910	D Class	1914 - 1915

I74

Submarine D4	1911	D Class	1914 - 1915

I75

Submarine D5	1911	D Class	1914 - 11.14

I76

Submarine D6	1911	D Class	1914 - 1915

I77

Submarine D7	1911	D Class	1914 - 1915

I78

Submarine D8	1911	D Class	1914 - 1915

I79

Submarine E22	1915	E Class	1915 - 1915

I81

Submarine E1	1912	E Class	1914 - 1915

I82

Submarine E2	1910	E Class	1914 - 1915

I83

Submarine E3	1912	E Class	Sunk 10.14

I84

Submarine E4	1912	E Class	1914 - 1915

I85

Submarine E5	1912	E Class	1914 - 1915

I86

Submarine E6	1912	E Class	1914 - 1915

I87

Submarine E7	1913	E Class	1914 - 1915

I88

Submarine E8	1913	E Class	1914 - 1915

I89

Submarine E9	1913	E Class	1914 - 1915

I90

Submarine E10	1913	E Class	1914 - 1.15

I91

Submarine E11	1914	E Class	1914 - 1915

I92

Submarine E12	1914	E Class	1914 - 1915

I93

Submarine E13	1914	E Class	1914 - 1915

I94

Submarine E14	1914	E Class	1914 - 1915

I95

Submarine E15	1914	E Class	1914 - 1915

I96

Submarine E16	1914	E Class	1914 - 1915

I97

Submarine E17	1915	E Class	1915 - 1915

I98

Submarine E18	1915	E Class	1915 - 1915

I99

Submarine E19	1915	E Class	1915 - 1915

J Flag Superior

Assigned to J class submarines and displayed in full on their conning towers.

J1

Submarine J1	1915	J Class	1915 - 1919

J2

Submarine J2	1915	J Class	1915 - 1919

J3

Submarine J3	Canc	J Class	Canc 1915
Submarine J3 (ex J7)	1915	J Class	1915 - 1919

J4

Submarine J4	Canc	J Class	Canc 1915
Submarine J4 (ex J8)	1916	J Class	1916 - 1919

J5

Submarine J5	1915	J Class	1915 - 1919

J6

Submarine J6	1915	J Class	1915 - 10.18

J7

Submarine J7 (ii)	1917	J Class	1917 - 1919

On 25.3.19 the surviving J class submarines were transferred to the Royal Australian Navy.

K Flag Superior

Assigned to K class submarines from build to between the wars.

K1

Submarine K1	1916	K Class	1916 - 11.17

K2

Submarine K2	1916	K Class	1916 - 1926

K3

Submarine K3	1916	K Class	1916 - 1921

K4

Submarine K4	1916	K Class	1916 - 1.18

K5

Submarine K5	1916	K Class	1916 - 1.21

K6

Submarine K6	1916	K Class	1916 - 1926

K7

| Submarine K7 | 1916 | K Class | 1916 - 1921 |

K8

| Submarine K8 | 1916 | K Class | 1916 - 1923 |

K9

| Submarine K9 | 1916 | K Class | 1916 - 1926 |

K10

| Submarine K10 | 1916 | K Class | 1916 - 1921 |

K11

| Submarine K11 | 1916 | K Class | 1916 - 1921 |

K12

| Submarine K12 | 1917 | K Class | 1917 - 1926 |

K13

| Submarine K13 | 1916 | K Class | 1916 - 1917 |

K14

| Submarine K14 | 1917 | K Class | 1917 - 1926 |

K15

| Submarine K15 | 1917 | K Class | 1917 - 1924 |

K16

| Submarine K16 | 1917 | K Class | 1917 - 1924 |

K17

| Submarine K17 | 1917 | K Class | 1917 - 1.18 |

K18

| Submarine K18 | Canc | K Class | See *M1* |

K19

| Submarine K19 | Canc | K Class | See *M2* |

K20

| Submarine K20 | Canc | K Class | See *M3* |

K21

| Submarine K21 | Canc | K Class | See *M4* |

K22

| Submarine K22 | 1916 | K Class | 1917 - 1926 |

K23

| Submarine K23 | Canc | Mod K | Canc 1918 |

K24

| Submarine K24 | Canc | Mod K | Canc 1918 |

K25

| Submarine K25 | Canc | Mod K | Canc 1918 |

K26

| Submarine K26 | 1919 | Mod K | 1919 - 1931 |

K27

| Submarine K27 | Canc | Mod K | Canc 1918 |

K28

| Submarine K28 | Canc | Mod K | Canc 1918 |

K13 sank during trials in the Gareloch, 29.1.1917. She was salvaged and returned to service later that year as *K22*.

L Flag Superior

Assigned to L class submarines from build to between the wars.

L1

| Submarine L1 | 1917 | L I Class | 1917 - 1930 |

L2

| Submarine L2 | 1917 | L I Class | 1917 - 1930 |

L3

| Submarine L3 | 1917 | L I Class | 1917 - 1931 |

L4

| Submarine L4 | 1917 | L I Class | 1917 - 1934 |

L5

| Submarine L5 | 1918 | L I Class | 1918 - 1930 |

L6

| Submarine L6 | 1918 | L I Class | 1918 - 1935 |

L7

| Submarine L7 | 1917 | L I Class | 1917 - 1930 |

L8

| Submarine L8 | 1917 | L I Class | 1917 - 1930 |

L9

| Submarine L9 | 1918 | L II Class | 1918 - 1927 |

L10

| Submarine L10 | 1918 | L II Class | 1918 - 10.18 |

L11

| Submarine L11 | 1918 | L II Class | 1918 - 1932 |

L12

| Submarine L12 | 1918 | L II Class | 1918 - 1932 |

L13

| Submarine L13 | Canc | L II Class | Canc 1918 |

L14

| Submarine L14 | 1918 | L II Class | 1918 - 1934 |

L15

| Submarine L15 | 1918 | L II Class | 1918 - 1932 |

L16

| Submarine L16 | 1918 | L II Class | 1918 - 1932 |

L17

| Submarine L17 | 1918 | L II Class | 1918 - 1934 |

L18

| Submarine L18 | 1918 | L II Class | 1918 - 1936 |

L19

| Submarine L19 | 1919 | L II Class | 1919 - 1937 |

L20

| Submarine L20 | 1918 | L II Class | 1918 - 1935 |

L21

| Submarine L21 | 1919 | L II Class | 1919 - 1939 |

L22

| Submarine L22 | 1919 | L II Class | 1919 - 1935 |

L23

| Submarine L23 | 1919 | L II Class | 1919 - .... |

L24

| Submarine L24 | 1919 | L II Class | 1919 - 1.24 |

L25

| Submarine L25 | 1919 | L II Class | 1919 - 1935 |

L26			
Submarine L26	1919	L II Class	1919 - ....
L27			
Submarine L27	1919	L II Class	1919 - ....
L28			
Submarine L28	Canc	L II Class	Canc 1918
L29			
Submarine L29	Canc	L II Class	Canc 1918
L30			
Submarine L30	Canc	L II Class	Canc 1918
L31			
Submarine L31	Canc	L II Class	Canc 1918
L32			
Submarine L32	1919	L II Class	Canc 1918
L33			
Submarine L33	1919	L II Class	1919 - 1932
L34			
Submarine L34	Canc	L II Class	Canc 1919
L35			
Submarine L35	Canc	L II Class	Canc 1919
L36			
Submarine L36	Canc	L II Class	Canc 1919
L37			
Submarine L37	Canc	L II Class	Canc 1919
L38			
Submarine L38	Canc	L II Class	Canc 1919
L39			
Submarine L39	Canc	L II Class	Canc 1919
L40			
Submarine L40	Canc	L II Class	Canc 1919
L41			
Submarine L41	Canc	L II Class	Canc 1919
L42			
Submarine L42	Canc	L II Class	Canc 1919
L43			
Submarine L43	Canc	L II Class	Canc 1919
L44			
Submarine L44	Canc	L II Class	Canc 1919
L45			
Submarine L45	Canc	L II Class	Canc 1919
L46			
Submarine L46	Canc	L II Class	Canc 1919
L47			
Submarine L47	Canc	L II Class	Canc 1919
L48			
Submarine L48	Canc	L II Class	Canc 1919
L49			
Submarine L49	Canc	L II Class	Canc 1919
L50			
Submarine L50	Canc	L III Class	Canc 1919
L51			
Submarine L51	Canc	L III Class	Canc 1919

L52			
Submarine L52	1918	L III Class	1918 - 1935
L53			
Submarine L53	1919	L III Class	1919 - 1938
L54			
Submarine L54	1919	L III Class	1919 - 1938
L55			
Submarine L55	1918	L III Class	1918 - 6.19
L56			
Submarine L56	1919	L III Class	1919 - 1938
L57			
Submarine L57	Canc	L III Class	Canc 1919
L58			
Submarine L58	Canc	L III Class	Canc 1919
L59			
Submarine L59	Canc	L III Class	Canc 1919
L60			
Submarine L60	Canc	L III Class	Canc 1919
L61			
Submarine L61	Canc	L III Class	Canc 1919
L62			
Submarine L62	Canc	L III Class	Canc 1919
L63			
Submarine L63	Canc	L III Class	Canc 1919
L64			
Submarine L64	Canc	L III Class	Canc 1919
L65			
Submarine L65	Canc	L III Class	Canc 1919
L66			
Submarine L66	Canc	L III Class	Canc 1919
L67			
Submarine L67	Canc	L III Class	Canc 1919
L68			
Submarine L68	Canc	L III Class	Canc 1919
L69			
Submarine L69	1918	L III Class	1918 - 1939
L70			
Submarine L70	Canc	L III Class	Canc 1919
L71			
Submarine L71	1919	L III Class	1919 - 1938
L72			
Submarine L72	Canc	L III Class	Canc 1919
L73			
Submarine L73	Canc	L III Class	Canc 1919
L74			
Submarine L74	Canc	L III Class	Canc 1919

With the end of WWI many of the contracts for new submarines were cancelled. The hull of *L32*, which had already been launched, was sold incomplete. *L14, L17* and *L24 - L27* were completed as minelaying submarines.

M Flag Superior

Assigned to M class submarines from build to between the wars.

M1
Submarine M1   1917   M Class   1917 - 11.25
M2
Submarine M2   1919   M Class   1917 - 1.32
M3
Submarine M3   1918   M Class   1917 - 1932
M4
Submarine M4   1919   M Class   1917 - 1921

Originally to have been members of the K Class (*K18 - K21*), these orders were substituted for the four M Class submarines, Fisher's 'Dreadnoughts', designed to carry a single 12-inch gun. Work on *M4* was suspended at the end of the war and cancelled in November 1918. The incomplete vessel was launched in 1919 to clear the slipways and was subsequently sold for scrap in 1921. *M2* was converted in 1928 to carry a seaplane while *M3* was converted, between 1927-28, to a minelaying submarine.

Flag Inferior to 1939

During the inter-war period submarine pendant numbers were reversed, forming a new number. These numbers were flag inferior with the flag indicating the class of submarine. In the case of a named boat the flags used were, 'C' for the U class; 'F' for the Thames class; 'M' for the Porpoise class; 'P' for the Odin and Parthian classes; 'R' for the Rainbow class; 'S' for the S class and 'T' for the T class.

11T
Thetis   1936   T I Class   1936 - 1939
12F
Clyde   1934   Thames   1934 - 1939
14M
Porpoise   1932   Porpoise   1932 - 1939
15T
Triton   1937   T I Class   1937 - 1939
16R
Rainbow   1930   Rainbow   1930 - 1939
17T
Tarpon   1939   T I Class   1939 - 1939
18T
Triumph   1938   T I Class   1938 - 1939
19S
Starfish   1933   S I Class   1933 - 1939

21P
Oberon   1926   Oberon   1926 - 1939
22S
Sterlet   1937   S II Class   1937 - 1939
23L
L23   1919   L II Class   1939 - 1940
24T
Thistle   1938   T I Class   1938 - 1939
26L
L26   1919   L II Class   .... - 1939
27L
L27   1919   L II Class   .... - 1939
28H
H28   1918   H21 Class   .... - 1939
29P
Proteus   1929   Parthian   1929 - 1939
31H
H31   1918   H21 Class   .... - 1939
32H
H32   1918   H21 Class   .... - 1939
33H
H33   1918   H21 Class   .... - 1939
34H
H34   1918   H21 Class   .... - 1939
35P
Olympus   1928   Odin   1928 - 1939
36P
Perseus   1929   Parthian   1929 - 1939
37M
Seal   1938   Grampus   1938 - 1939
38T
Taku   1939   T I Class   1939 - 1939
39S
Snapper   1934   S II Class   1934 - 1939
41R
Regent   1930   Rainbow   1930 - 1939
42P
Pandora   1929   Parthian   1929 - 1939
43H
H43   1919   H21 Class   .... - 1939
44H
H44   1919   H21 Class   .... - 1939
45M
Narwhal   1935   Grampus   1935 - 1939
46P
Orpheus   1929   Odin   1929 - 1939
47S
Seawolf   1935   S II Class   1935 - 1939
48C
Undine   1937   U Class   1937 - 1939
49H
H49   1919   H21 Class   .... - 1939

50H			
H50	1919	H21 Class	.... - 1939
51P			
Otway ʀᴀɴ	1936	Oxley	1936 - 1939
52T			
Trident	1938	T I Class	1938 - 1939
53T			
Triad	1939	T I Class	1939 - 1939
54S			
Shark	1934	S II Class	1934 - 1939
55P			
Oxley ʀᴀɴ	1926	Oxley	1926 - 1939
56M			
Grampus	1936	Grampus	1936 - 1939
57F			
Severn	1934	Thames	1934 - 1939
58P			
Oswald	1928	Odin	1928 - 1939
59C			
Ursula	1938	U Class	1938 - 1939
61S			
Swordfish	1931	S I Class	1931 - 1939
62R			
Rover	1930	Rainbow	1930 - 1939
63T			
Tigris	1939	T I Class	1939 - 1939
64A			
Wilk ᴏʀᴘ	1929	Wilk	1929 - 1939
65S			
Salmon	1934	S II Class	1934 - 1939
66C			
Unity	1938	U Class	1938 - 1939
67P			
Osiris	1928	Odin	1928 - 1939
68T			
Truant	1939	T I Class	1939 - 1939
69S			
Spearfish	1936	S II Class	1936 - 1939
71F			
Thames	1932	Thames	1932 - 1939
72S			
Sealion	1934	S II Class	1934 - 1939
73S			
Sturgeon	1932	S I Class	1932 - 1939
74M			
Rorqual	1936	Grampus	1936 - 1939
75P			
Parthian	1929	Parthian	1929 - 1939
76T			
Tribune	1938	T I Class	1938 - 1939
77T			
Tetrarch	1939	T I Class	1938 - 1939

78T			
Talisman	1940	T I Class	1940 - 1939
79T			
Torbay	1940	T I Class	1940 - 1939
81S			
Sunfish	1936	S II Class	1936 - 1939
83M			
Cachalot	1937	Grampus	1937 - 1939
84P			
Odin	1928	Odin	1928 - 1939
85A			
Orzel ᴏʀᴘ	1938	Orzel	1938 - 1939
88R			
Regulus	1930	Rainbow	1930 - 1939
92P			
Otus	1928	Odin	1928 - 1939
94T			
Tuna	1940	T I Class	1939 - 1939
96P			
Phoenix	1929	Parthian	1929 - 1939
98S			
Seahorse	1932	S I Class	1932 - 1939
99P			
Poseidon	1929	Parthian	1929 - 6.31

N Flag Inferior

In 1939, the various class inferior flags were standard-ised and all submarines were given an 'N' Flag Inferior number. The rapidly changing pace of losses experienced during the war years meant that on occasion submarines had already been lost before the changes could be displayed.

11N			
Thetis	1936	T I Class	1939 - 6.39
12N			
Clyde	1934	Thames	1939 - 1940
14N			
Porpoise	1932	Porpoise	1939 - 1940
15N			
Triton	1937	T I Class	1939 - 1940
16N			
Rainbow	1930	Rainbow	1939 - 1940
17N			
Tarpon	1939	T I Class	1939 - 1940
18N			
Triumph	1938	T I Class	1939 - 1940
19N			
Starfish	1933	S I Class	1939 - 1940
21N			
Oberon	1926	Oberon	1939 - 1940

22N			
Sterlet	1937	S II Class	1939 - 1940
23N			
L23	1919	L II Class	1939 - 1940
24N			
Thistle	1938	T I Class	1939 - 1940
26N			
L26	1919	L II Class	1939 - 1940
27N			
L27	1919	L II Class	1939 - 1940
28N			
H28	1918	H21 Class	1939 - 1940
29N			
Proteus	1929	Parthian	1939 - 1940
31N			
H31	1918	H21 Class	1939 - 1940
32N			
H32	1918	H21 Class	1939 - 1940
33N			
H33	1918	H21 Class	1939 - 1940
34N			
H34	1918	H21 Class	1939 - 1940
35N			
Olympus	1928	Odin	1939 - 1940
36N			
Perseus	1929	Parthian	1939 - 1940
37N			
Seal	1938	Grampus	1939 - 1940
38N			
Taku	1939	T I Class	1939 - 1940
39N			
Snapper	1934	S II Class	1939 - 1940
41N			
Regent	1930	Rainbow	1939 - 1940
42N			
Pandora	1929	Parthian	1939 - 1940
43N			
H43	1919	H21 Class	1939 - 1940
44N			
H44	1919	H21 Class	1939 - 1940
45N			
Narwhal	1935	Grampus	1939 - 1940
46N			
Orpheus	1929	Odin	1939 - 1940
47N			
Seawolf	1935	S II Class	1939 - 1940
48N			
Undine	1937	U Class	1939 - 1940
49N			
H49	1919	H21 Class	1939 - 1940
50N			
H50	1919	H21 Class	1939 - 1940

51N			
Otway RAN	1936	Oxley	1939 - 1940
52N			
Trident	1938	T I Class	1939 - 1940
53N			
Triad	1939	T I Class	1939 - 1940
54N			
Shark	1934	S II Class	1939 - 1940
55N			
Oxley RAN	1926	Oxley	1939 - 9.39
56N			
Grampus	1936	Grampus	1939 - 1940
57N			
Severn	1934	Thames	1939 - 1940
58N			
Oswald	1928	Odin	1939 - 1940
59N			
Ursula	1938	U Class	1939 - 1940
61N			
Swordfish	1931	S I Class	1939 - 1940
62N			
Rover	1930	Rainbow	1939 - 1940
63N			
Tigris	1939	T I Class	1939 - 1940
64N			
Wilk ORP	1929	Wilk	1939 - 1940
65N			
Salmon	1934	S II Class	1939 - 1940
66N			
Unity	1938	U Class	1939 - 1940
67N			
Osiris	1928	Odin	1939 - 1940
68N			
Truant	1939	T I Class	1939 - 1940
69N			
Spearfish	1936	S II Class	1939 - 1940
71N			
Thames	1932	Thames	1939 - 1940
72N			
Sealion	1934	S II Class	1939 - 1940
73N			
Sturgeon	1932	S I Class	1939 - 1940
74N			
Rorqual	1936	Grampus	1939 - 1940
75N			
Parthian	1929	Parthian	1939 - 1940
76N			
Tribune	1938	T I Class	1939 - 1940
77N			
Tetrarch	1939	T I Class	1939 - 1940
78N			
Talisman	1940	T I Class	1940 - 1940

79N

Torbay	1940	T I Class	1940 - 1940

81N

Sunfish	1936	S II Class	1939 - 1940

83N

Cachalot	1937	Grampus	1939 - 1940

84N

Odin	1928	Odin	1939 - 1940

85N

Orzel ORP	1938	Orzel	1939 - 1940

88N

Regulus	1930	Rainbow	1939 - 1940

92N

Otus	1928	Odin	1939 - 1940

94N

Tuna	1940	T I Class	1940 - 1940

96N

Phoenix	1929	Parthian	1939 - 1940

98N

Seahorse	1932	S I Class	1939 - 12.39

N Flag Superior

In 1940, the 'N' Flag Inferior was changed to 'N' Flag Superior.

N11

Thorn	1941	T II Class	1941 - 8.42

N12

Clyde	1934	Thames	1940 - 1946

N14

Porpoise	1932	Porpoise	1940 - 1.45

N15

Triton	1937	T I Class	1940 - 12.40
O-15 RNLN	1931	O12	1940 - 1946

N16

Rainbow	1930	Rainbow	1940 - 10.40
Katsonis RHN	1926	Katsonis	1941 - 9.43
N16 (ex *U-1105*)	1944	Type VIIC	1945 - 1948

German U-Boat *U-1105* surrendered at Loch Eriboll on 10.5.45. She was taken over by the Royal Navy as submarine *N16*. She later went to the US Navy where she was sunk, on 18.11.48 during explosive trials in Cheaspeake Bay.

N17

Tarpon	1939	T I Class	1940 - 4.40
Urge (ex *P40*)	1940	U I Class	1940 - 4.42

N18

Triumph	1938	T I Class	1940 - 1.40
Matrozos RHN	1936	Perla	1942

N19

Starfish	1933	S I Class	1940 - 1.40
Utmost (ex *P42*)	1940	U I Class	1940 - 11.42
N19 (ex *U-1171*)	1943	Type VIIC	1945 - 1949

German U-Boat *U-1171* surrendered at Stavanger, Norway, on 9.5.45, leaving on 29th for an assembly area in Britain. She was taken over by the Royal Navy and became submarine *N19*. She was broken up at Sunderland in April 1949.

N20

N20 (ex *U-2348*)	1944	Type XXIII	1945 - 1949

German U-Boat *U-2348* also surrendered at Stavanger, Norway, on 9.5.45, leaving on 29th for an assembly area in Britain. She was taken over by the Royal Navy and became submarine *N20*. She was broken up at Belfast in April 1949.

N21

Oberon	1926	Oberon	1940 - Sunk
N21 (ex *U-1057*)	1944	Type VIIC	5.45 - 11.45

German U-Boat *U-1057* surrendered at Bergen, Norway, on 10.5.45, leaving on 30th for an assembly area in Britain. Initially taken over by the Royal Navy as submarine *N21* she was transferred to the Soviet Navy in November 1945 where she became *S-81*.

N22

Sterlet	1937	S II Class	1940 - 4.40
K.XIV RNLN	1932	K.XIV	1940 - 1946
N22 (ex *U-1058*)	1944	Type VIIC	5.45 - 11.45

German U-Boat *U-1058* surrendered at Lough Foyle, on 10.5.45. In November 1945 she was handed over to the Soviet Navy where she was renamed *S-82*.

N23

L23	1919	L II Class	1940- 1945
N23 (ex *U-1064*)	1944	Type VIIC	1945 - 2.46

German U-Boat *U-1064* surrendered at Trondheim, Norway, on 9.5.45. In February 1946 was handed over to the Soviet Navy and renamed *S-83*.

N24

Thistle	1938	T I Class	1940 - 4.40
K.XV ʀɴʟɴ	1932	K.XIV	1940 - 1946
N24 (ex *U-1305*)	1944	Type VIIC	5.45 - 11.45

German U-Boat *U-1305* surrendered at Loch Eriboll, on 10.5.45. Nominally renamed N24 by the Royal Navy she was handed over to the Soviet Navy in November 1945 and renamed *S-84*.

N25

Thunderbolt (ex *Thetis*)	1936	T I Class	1940 - 3.43
N25 (ex *U-1407*)	1945	Type XVII	1945 - 1947
Meteorite	1945	Type XVII	1947 - 1949

German U-Boat *U-1407* was an experimental submarine which was scuttled at Cuxhaven on 5.5.45 as World War II drew to a close. The vessel was later salvaged and taken to England for trials. She was initially allocated the name *N25*, but in 1947 was renamed *Meteorite*.

N26

L26	1919	L II Class	1940 - 1945
N26 (ex *U-1231*)	1943	Type IXC	1945 - 1947

German U-Boat *U-1231* surrendered at Lough Foyle on 14.5.45. Initially allocated the name *N26* by the Royal Navy, she was transferred to the Soviet Navy in 1947 where she was renamed *N-25*.

N27

L27	1919	L II Class	1940 - 1945
N27 (ex *U-2529*)	1944	Type XXI	1945 - 1947

German U-Boat *U-2529* surrendered at Kristiansand, Norway, on 9.5.45. She was allocated the name *N27* by the Royal Navy. In 1947 she was transferred to the Soviet Navy.

N28

H28	1918	H21 Class	1940 - 1944
N28 (ex *U-3035*)	1945	Type XXI	1945 - 1947

German U-Boat *U-3035* surrendered at Stavanger, Norway, on 9.5.45, leaving there on 31st for an assembly area in Britain. She was taken over by the Royal Navy and was renamed *N28*. In 1947 she was transferred to the Soviet Navy.

N29

Proteus	1929	Parthian	1940 - 1945
N29 (ex *U-3041*)	1945	Type XXI	1945 - 1947

German U-Boat *U-3041* surrendered at Horten, Norway, on 9.5.45, leaving there on 29th for an assembly area in Britain. She was allocated the name *N29* by the Royal Navy. In 1947 she was transferred to the Soviet Navy.

N30

N30 (ex *U-3515*)	1944	Type XXI	1945 - 1946

German U-Boat *U-3515* surrendered at Horten, Norway, on 9.5.45. She was taken over by the Royal Navy and renamed *N30*. In 1946 she was handed over to the Soviet Navy.

N31

H31	1918	H21 Class	1940 - 12.41
Atropo ɪᴛ	1938	Foca	.... - ....
N31 (ex *U-2353*)	1944	Type XXIII	1945 - 1946

German U-Boat *U-2353* surrendered at Kristiansand, Norway, on 9.5.45. Nominally renamed N31 by the Royal Navy she was handed over to the Soviet Navy in February 1946 and renamed *M-51*.

N32

H32	1918	H21 Class	1940 - 1944

N33

H33	1918	H21 Class	1940 - 1944

N34

H34	1918	H21 Class	1940 - 1945

N35

Olympus	1928	Odin	1940 - 5.42
N35 (ex *U-2326*)	1944	Type XXIII	1945 - 1946

German U-Boat *U-2326* surrendered at Dundee on 14.5.45. She was used by the Royal Navy as submarine *N35* until 1946 when she was handed over to France, where she was lost in an accident off Toulon on 6.12.46.

N36

Perseus	1929	Parthian	1940 - 12.41
Cagni ɪᴛ	1940	Cagni	.... - ....

N37

Seal	1938	Grampus	1940 - 5.40
Thrasher	1940	T II Class	1940 - 1948

N38

Taku	1939	T I Class	1940 - 1946

N39

Snapper	1934	S II Class	1940 - 2.41
K.IX RNLN	1922	K.VIII	1942

N41

Regent	1930	Rainbow	1940 - 4.43
N41 (ex *U-3017*)	1944	Type XXI	1945 - 1949

German U-Boat *U-3017* surrendered at Horten, Norway, on 9.5.45 and left on 29th for an assembly area in Britain. She was taken over by the Royal Navy and renamed *N41*. She was scrapped in November 1949.

N42

Pandora	1929	Parthian	1940 - 4.42

N43

H43	1919	H21 Class	1940 - 1944

N44

H44	1919	H21 Class	1940 - 1945

N45

Narwhal	1935	Grampus	1940 - 7.40
Trusty	1941	T II Class	1941 - 1948

N46

Orpheus	1929	Odin	1940 - 6.40

N47

Seawolf	1935	S II Class	1940 - 1945

N48

Undine	1937	U Class	1940 - 1.40
Traveller	1941	T II Class	1941 - 12.42

N49

H49	1919	H21 Class	1940 - 10.40
Bragadin IT	1929	Bragadin	.... - ....

N50

H50	1919	H21 Class	1940 - 1945

N51

Otway	1936	Oxley	1940 - 4.43

N52

Trident	1938	T I Class	1940 - 1946

N53

Triad	1939	T I Class	1940 - 10.40
K.XI RNLN	1924	KXI	1940 - 1945

N54

Shark	1934	S II Class	1940 - 7.40
O-19 RNLN	1938	O19	1940 - 7.45

HMS *Shark* was scuttled on 6.7.1940. Although she had been assigned N54 in 1940 and 54N the previous year, she was still displaying 54S at the time of her loss.

N55

Oxley	1926	Oxley	1940 - 4.42
Undaunted (ex *P34*)	1940	U I Class	1940 - 5.41
Corridoni IT	1930	Bragadin	.... - ....

N56

Grampus	1936	Grampus	1940 - 6.40
Union	1940	U I Class	1940 - 7.41
Nereus RHN	1927	Proteus	1941 - 1945

N57

Severn	1934	Thames	1940 - 1946

N58

Oswald	1928	Odin	1940 - 8.40
Alagi IT	1936	Adua	1943 - 1944

N59

Ursula	1938	U Class	1940 - 1950

N61

Swordfish	1931	S I Class	1940 - 11.40
K.XII RNLN	1924	K.XI	1940 - 2.42
Nebojsa YUG	1927	Hrabri	1941 - 1945

N62

Rover	1930	Rainbow	1940 - 1946

N63

Tigris	1939	T I Class	1940 - 2.43

N64

Wilk ORP	1929	Wilk	1940 - 1942

Polish crewed 1939-42. Laid up and returned to Polish Navy in 1951.

N65

Salmon	1934	S II Class	1940 - 7.40
Usk (ex *P41*)	1940	U I Class	1940 - 4.41
N65 (ex *U-776*)	1944	Type VIIC	5.45 - 12.45

German U-Boat *U-776* surrendered at Weymouth on 16.5.45. From there she went to Lough Foyle and became *N65* for tests carried out by the Royal Navy. One of 116 boats disposed of by the Royal Navy in Operation Deadlight she foundered on 3.12.45 WNW of Loch Ryan.

N66

Unity	1938	U Class	1940 - 4.40
Menotti ɪᴛ	1929	Bandiera	.... - ....

N67

Osiris	1928	Odin	1940 - 1946

N68

Truant	1939	T I Class	1940 - 1945

N69

Spearfish	1936	S II Class	1940 - 8.40

N71

Thames	1932	Thames	1940 - 7.40
Galatea ɪᴛ	1933	Sirena	.... - ....

N72

Sealion	1934	S II Class	1940 - 1945

N73

Sturgeon	1932	S I Class	1940 - 1948
Zeehond ʀɴʟɴ	1932	S I Class	1943 - 1945

N74

Rorqual	1936	Grampus	1940 - 1945

N75

Parthian	1929	Parthian	1940 - 8.43

N76

Tribune	1938	T I Class	1940 - 1948

N77

Tetrarch	1939	T I Class	1940 - 10.41

N78

Talisman	1940	T I Class	1940 - 9.42

N79

Torbay	1940	T I Class	1940 - 1945

N81

Sunfish	1936	S II Class	1940 - 1944

N82

Umpire	1940	U I Class	1940 - 7.41
Zoea ɪᴛ	1937	Foca	.... - ....

N83

Cachalot	1937	Grampus	1940 - 7.41
N83 (ex *U-1023*)	1944	Type VIIC	1945 - 1.46

German U-Boat *U-1023* surrendered on 10.5.45 at Weymouth. As part of Operation Deadlight she was towed from Lisahally in January 1946, but foundered on 9.1.46 NW of Malin Head.

N84

Odin	1928	Odin	1940 - 6.40

N85

Orzel ᴏʀᴘ	1938	Orzel	1940 - 6.40

N86

Tempest	1941	T II Class	1940 - 2.42
N86 (ex *U-249*)	1943	Type VIIC	5.45 - 12.45

German U-Boat *U-249* surrendered on 8.5.45 and was escorted into Portland by the sloops *Amethyst* and *Magpie*. She was transferred to Loch Ryan as Research vessel *N86*. As part of Operation Deadlight she was towed out to sea and sunk on 13.12.45, NW of Tory Island, by the submarine *Tantivy*.

N87

Una (ex *P32*)	1941	U I Class	1941 - 1948

N88

Regulus	1930	Rainbow	1940 - 12.40
Giada ɪᴛ	1941	Acciaio	.... - ....

N89

Upright (ex *P38*)	1940	U I Class	1940 - 1946

N91

Trooper	1942	T II Class	1942 - 10.43

N92

Otus	1928	Odin	1940 - 1946

N93

Unbeaten (ex *P33*)	1940	U I Class	1940 - 11.42

N94

Tuna	1940	T I Class	1940 - 1946

N95

Unique	1940	U I Class	1940 - 10.42

N96

Phoenix	1929	Parthian	1940 - 7.40
Brin ɪᴛ	1938	Brin	.... - ....

N97

Urchin (ex *P39*)	1940	U I Class	1940 - 1941
Sokol ᴏʀᴘ	1940	U I Class	1941 - 1946

Before being completed *Urchin* was loaned to the Polish Navy on 19.1.41 and renamed *Sokol*. The submarine was returned to the Royal Navy on 27.8.46 and renamed *P97*.

N98

Seahorse	1932	S I Class	1940 - 1.40
Turbulent	1941	T I Class	1941 - 3.43

N99

Upholder	1940	U Class	1940 - 4.42

P Flag Superior

In early 1941, it was decided that all new build submarines would carry a number in place of a name. 'P' Flag Superior numbers were allocated to all submarines constructed during the war. Number blocks were assigned to specific classes as follows: U/V class - P31-99 (once P99 was reached the V class were accorded spares from P11 onwards); S class - P211 onwards; T class - P311 onwards; A class - P411 onwards; Ex-US Navy - P511 onwards; Foreign submarines under RN control - P611 onwards and Captured submarines - P711 onwards. Exceptions to the above numbers were combinations ending with the number 13 or those numbers divisible by ten. By 1943 submarines were once again given names.

P9

O-9 RNLN	1925	O-9	1940 - 1944

P10

O-10 RNLN	1925	O-9	1940 - 1944

P11

Unbridled	Canc	V Class	Canc 1.44

P12

B1 RNoN	1922	B Class	1940

P14

O-14 RNLN	1931	O-12	1940 - 1943

P15

Rubis FR	1931	Rubis	1940 - 1945

P16

Upward	Canc	V Class	Canc 1.44

P17

Surcouf FR	1929	Surcouf	1940 - 1942
Le Glorieux FR	1931	L'Espoire	1942 - 1945

P18

Vagabond	1944	V Class	1944 - 1950

P19

Junon FFN	1935	Minerve	1940 - 1945

P21

O-21 RNLN	1939	O-21	1940 - 1945

P22

O-22 RNLN	1939	O-21	1940 - Sunk

P23

O-23 RNLN	1939	O-21	1940 - 1945

P24

O-24 RNLN	1940	O-21	1940 - 1946

P25

Vehement	Canc	V Class	Canc 1.44

P26

Minerve FFN	1934	Minerve	1940 - 1945

P27

Venom	Canc	V Class	Canc 1.44

P28

Verve	Canc	V Class	Canc 1.44

P29

Votary	1944	V Class	1944 - 1946

In July 1946 *Votary* was transferred to the Royal Norwegian Navy and renamed *Uthaug*.

P31

Umpire	1940	U I Class	1940 - 7.41
P31	1940	U II Class	1940 - 1943
Uproar (ex *P31*)	1940	U II Class	1943 - 1946

P32

P32	1940	U II Class	1940 - 8.41
Una	1941	U I Class	1941 - 1948

P33

Unbeaten	1940	U I Class	1940 - 11.42
P33	1941	U II Class	1941 - 8.41
Ceres FR	1938	Minerve	xxxx

P34

Undaunted	1940	U I Class	1940 - 5.41
P34	1941	U II Class	1941 - 1.43
Ultimatum (ex *P34*)	1941	U II Class	1.43 - 1948

P35

Union	1940	U I Class	1940 - 7.41
P35	1941	U II Class	1941 - 1.43
Umbra (ex *P35*)	1941	U II Class	1.43 - 1946

P36

Unique	1940	U I Class	1940 - 10.42
P36	1941	U II Class	1941 - 4.42

P37

Upholder	1940	U I Class	1940 - 4.42
P37	1941	U II Class	1941 - 1.43
Unbending (ex *P37*)	1941	U II Class	1.43 - 1950

P38

Upright	1940	U I Class	1940 - 1946
P38	1941	U II Class	1941 - 2.42

P39

P39	1941	U II Class	1941 - 3.42

P40

Urge	1940	U I Class	1940 - 4.42

P41

Usk	1940	U I Class	1940 - 4.41
P41	1941	U II Class	To RNoN
Pallas FR	1938	Minerve	1942 - 1945

In December 1941, prior to completion, *P41* was transferred to the Royal Norwegian Navy where she was renamed *Uredd*. She was mined off Bodo and lost in February 1943.

P42

Utmost	1940	U I Class	1940 - 11.42
P42	1941	U II Class	1941 - 1.43
Unbroken (ex *P42*)	1941	U II Class	1.43 - 1944

From 1944 - 1949 *Unbroken* was loaned to the Soviet Navy where she was renamed *V2*.

P43

P43	1941	U II Class	1941 - 1.43
Unison (ex *P43*)	1941	U II Class	1.43 - 1944

From 1944 - 1949 *Unison* was loaned to the Soviet Navy where she was renamed *V3*.

P44

P44	1941	U II Class	1941 - 1.43
United (ex *P44*)	1941	U II Class	1.43 - 1946

P45

P45	1942	U II Class	1941 - 1.43
Unrivalled (ex *P45*)	1942	U II Class	1.43 - 1946

P46

P46	1941	U II Class	1941 - 1.43
Unruffled (ex *P46*)	1941	U II Class	1.43 - 1946

P47

P47	1942	U II Class	1942 - 11.42

In November 1942 *P47* was transferred to the Royal Netherlands Navy and renamed *Dolfijn*.

P48

P48	1942	U II Class	1942 - 12.42

P49

P49	1942	U II Class	1942 - 1.43

Unruly (ex *P49*)	1942	U II Class	1.43 - 1946

P51

P51	1942	U II Class	1942 - 1.43
Unseen (ex *P51*)	1942	U II Class	1.43 - 1948

P52

P52	1942	U II Class	1942 - 10.42

From 11.10.42 - 25.8.46 *P52* was loaned to the Polish Navy and renamed *Dzik*. She was scrapped in 1958.

P53

P53	1942	U II Class	1942 - 1.43
Ultor	1942	U II Class	1.43 - 1946

P54

P54	1942	U II Class	1942 - 1.43
Unshaken (ex *P54*)	1942	U II Class	1.43 - 1946

P55

P55	1942	U II Class	1942 - 1.43
Unsparing (ex *P55*)	1942	U II Class	1.43 - 1946

P56

P56	1942	U II Class	1942 - 2.43
Usurper (ex *P56*)	1942	U II Class	2.43 - 10.43
H1 IT	xxxx	xxxx	xxxx

P57

P57	1942	U II Class	1942 - 2.43
Universal (ex *P57*)	1942	U II Class	2.43 - 1946

P58

P58	1942	U II Class	1942 - 2.43
Untamed (ex *P58*)	1942	U II Class	2.43 - 7.43
Vitality (ex *Untamed*)	1942	U II Class	7.43 - 1946

On 30.5.43 *Untamed* foundered during an exercise off the west coast of Scotland. She was salvaged two months later, refitted and returned to service as *Vitality*.

P59

P59	1943	U II Class	1943 - 2.43
Untiring (ex *P59*)	1943	U II Class	2.43 - 1945

From 1945 - 1952 *Untiring* was loaned to the Royal Hellenic Navy where she was renamed *Xifias*.

P61

P61 (ren *P211*)	1941	S II Class	1941 - 7.41

P61   1943   U II Class   1943 - 2.43
Varangian (ex *P61*) 1943   U II Class   2.43 - 1948

P62
P62 (ren *P212*)   1942   S II Class   1941 - 7.41
P62   1943   U II Class   1943 - 2.43
Uther (ex *P62*)   1943   U II Class   2.43 - 1950

P63
P63 (ren *P213*)   1942   S II Class   1941 - 7.41
P63   1943   U II Class   1943 - 2.43
Unswerving   1943   U II Class   2.43 - 1948
  (ex *P63*)

P64
P64 (ren *P214*)   1942   S II Class   1941 - 7.41
P64   1942   U II Class   1942 - 2.43
Vandal (ex *P64*)   1942   U II Class   2.43 - 24.2.43

P65
P65 (ren *P215*)   1943   S II Class   1941 - 7.41
P65   1942   U II Class   1942 - 2.43
Upstart (ex *P65*)   1942   U II Class   2.43 - 1945

From 1945 - 1952 *Upstart* was loaned to the Hellenic Navy where she was renamed *Amfitriti.* She was returned to the Royal Navy and sunk as an A/S target off the Isle of Wight 29.7.57.

P66
P66 (ren *P216*)   1942   S II Class   1941 - 7.41
P66   1943   U II Class   1943 - 2.43
Varne (ex *P66*)   1943   U II Class   2.43

Varne was transferred to Norway shortly before completion and renamed *Ula.* She was scrapped in 1965.

P67
P67 (ren *P217*)   1942   S II Class   1941 - 7.41
P67   1943   U II Class   1943 - 2.43
Vox (I) (ex *P67*)   1943   U II Class   2.43 - 5.43

From 1.5.43 - 17.9.46 *Vox* was transferred on loan to the Free French Navy and renamed *Curie.* She was returned to the Royal Navy and scrapped in 1949.

P68
P68 (ren *P218*)   1943   S II Class   1941 - 7.41
P68   1943   V Class   1943 - 2.43
Venturer (ex *P68*)   1943   V Class   2.43 - 1946

In August 1946 *Venturer* was transferred to the Royal Norwegian Navy and renamed *Utstein.*

P69
P69 (ren *P219*)   1941   S II Class   1941 - 7.41
P69   1943   V Class   1943 - 2.43
Viking (ex *P69*)   1943   V Class   2.43 - 8.46

In August 1946 *Viking* was transferred to the Royal Norwegian Navy and renamed *Utvaer.*

P71
P71 (ren *P221*)   1941   S II Class   1941 - 7.41
P71   1943   V Class   1943 - 2.43
Veldt (ex *P71*)   1943   V Class   2.43

In 1943 *Veldt* was transferred on loan to the Royal Hellenic Navy as *Pipinos.* She was returned 10.12.57 and scrapped the following year.

P72
P72 (ren *P222*)   1941   S II Class   19.41 - 7.41
P72   1943   V Class   1943 - 2.43
Vampire (ex *P72*)   1943   V Class   2.43 - 1950

P73
P73 (ren *P223*)   1942   S II Class   1941 - 7.41
P73   1943   V Class   1943 - 4.43
Vox II (ex *P73*)   1943   V Class   4.43 - 1946

P74
P74 (ren *P224*)   1942   S II Class   1941 - 7.41
P74   1943   V Class   1943 - 4.43
Vigorous (ex *P74*)   1943   V Class   4.43 - 1948

P75
P75 (ren *P225*)   1942   S II Class   1941 - 7.41
P75   1943   V Class   1943 - 4.43
Virtue (ex *P75*)   1943   V Class   4.43 - 1946

P76
P76 (ren *P226*)   1943   S II Class   1941 - 7.41
P76   1943   V Class   1943 - 4.43
Visigoth (ex *P76*)   1943   V Class   4.43 - 1950

P77
P77 (ren *P227*)   1943   S II Class   1941 - 7.41
P77   1943   V Class   1943 - 4.43
Vivid (ex *P77*)   1943   V Class   4.43 - 1950

P78
P78 (ren *P228*)   1942   S II Class   1941 - 7.41

P78

P78	1943	V Class	1943 - 4.43
Voracious (ex *P78*)	1943	V Class	4.43 - 1946

P79

P79 (ren *P229*)	1942	S II Class	1941 - 7.41
P79	1943	V Class	1943 - 4.43
Vulpine (ex *P79*)	1943	V Class	4.43 - 1947

In September 1947 *Vulpine* was loaned to the Royal Danish Navy where she was initially known as *U2*, before she was further renamed *Storen* in 1948.

P81

P81	1944	V Class	1943 - 4.43
Varne II (ex *P81*)	1944	V Class	4.43 - 1958

P82

P82	1944	V Class	1943 - 4.43
Upshot (ex *P82*)	1944	V Class	4.43 - 1949

P83

P83	1944	V Class	1943 - 4.43
Urtica (ex *P83*)	1944	V Class	4.43 - 1950

P84

P84	1944	V Class	1943 - 4.43
Vineyard (ex *P84*)	1944	V Class	4.43 - 6.44

In June 1944 *Vineyard* was loaned to the Free French Navy and renamed *Doris*. She was scrapped in 1950.

P85

P85	1944	V Class	1943 - 4.43
Variance (ex *P85*)	1944	V Class	4.43 - 8.44

In August 1944 *Variance* was transferred to the Royal Norwegian Navy as *Utsira*.

P86

P86	1944	V Class	1943 - 4.43
Vengeful (ex *P86*)	1944	V Class	4.43 - 1945

In 1945 *Vengeful* was transferred on loan to the Royal Hellenic Navy as *Delfin*. She was returned in 1957 and scrapped in 1958.

P87

P87	1944	V Class	1943 - 4.43
Vortex (ex *P87*)	1944	V Class	4.43 - 11.44

Between 15.11.44 - 1.9.46 *Vortex* was transferred on loan to the Free French Navy as *Morse*. Having re-turned from France she was further loaned to the Royal Danish Navy where she was named *U3* (1947 - 48) and further renamed *Saelen* until scrapped in 1958.

P88

P88 (ren *P238*)	1942	S II Class	1941 - 7.41
P88	Canc	V Class	1943 - 4.43
Veto (ex *P88*)	Canc	V Class	Canc 1944

P89

P89 (ren *P239*)	1942	S II Class	1941 - 7.41
P89	Canc	V Class	1943 - 4.43
Virile (ex *P89*)	Canc	V Class	Canc 1944

P91

P91	Canc	V Class	1943 - 4.43
Visitant (ex *P91*)	Canc	V Class	Canc 1944
P91 (ren *P311*)	1942	T III Class	See P311

P92

P92	Canc	V Class	1943 - 4.43
Upas (ex *P92*)	Canc	V Class	Canc 1944

P93

P93	Canc	V Class	1943 - 4.43
Ulex (ex *P93*)	Canc	V Class	Canc 1944

P94

P94	Canc	V Class	1943 - 4.43
Utopia (ex *P94*)	Canc	V Class	Canc 1944

P95

P95 (ren *P315*)	1942	T III Class	See P315
P95	1944	V Class	1943 - 4.43
Virulent (ex *P95*)	1944	V Class	4.43 - 5.46

On 29.5.46 *Virulent* was transferred on loan to the Royal Hellenic Navy as *Argonaftis*. She was returned in 1958 and scrapped in 1961.

P96

P96 (ren *P316*)	1942	T III Class	See P316
P96	1944	V Class	1943 - 4.43
Volatile (ex *P96*)	1944	V Class	4.43 - 5.46

Between May 46 and October 1958 *Volatile* was on loan to the Royal Hellenic Navy as *Triaina*.

P97

P97 (ex *Urchin*)	1940	U I Class	1946 - 1949
Tally Ho (ren *P317*)	1942	T III Class	See P317

On 19.1.41 *Urchin* was turned over, prior to completion, to the Polish Navy and renamed *Sokol*. She was returned to the Royal Navy on 27.8.46 and renamed *P97* (See *N97*).

P98

P98 (ren *P318*)	1943	T III Class	See P318

P99

P99 (ren *P319*)	1943	T III Class	See P319

P211

P211 (ex *P61*)	1941	S III Class	7.41 - 1.43
Safari (ex *P211*)	1941	S III Class	1.43 - 1946

P212

P212 (ex *P62*)	1942	S III Class	7.41 - 1.43
Sahib (ex *P212*)	1942	S III Class	1.43 - 4.43

P213

P213 (ex *P63*)	1942	S III Class	7.41 - 1942

Superstition surrounding the number thirteen caused *P213* to be renamed *P247* in 1942.

P214

P214 (ex *P64*)	1942	S III Class	7.41 - 1.43
Satyr (ex *P214*)	1942	S III Class	1.43 - 1948

P215

P215 (ex *P65*)	1943	S III Class	7.41 - 2.43
Sceptre (ex *P215*)	1943	S III Class	2.43 - 1948

P216

P216 (ex *P66*)	1942	S III Class	7.41 - 1.43
Seadog (ex *P216*)	1942	S III Class	1.43 - 1948

P217

P217 (ex *P67*)	1942	S III Class	7.41 - 1.43
Sibyl (ex *P217*)	1942	S III Class	1.43 - 1948

P218

P218 (ex *P68*)	1943	S III Class	7.41 - 2.43
Sea Rover (ex *P218*)	1943	S III Class	2.43 - 1948

P219

P219 (ex *P69*)	1941	S III Class	7.41 - 1.43
Seraph (ex *P219*)	1941	S III Class	1.43 - 1948

P221

P221 (ex *P71*)	1941	S III Class	7.41 - 1.43
Shakespeare (ex *P221*)	1941	S III Class	1.43 - 1.45

P222

P222 (ex *P72*)	1941	S III Class	7.41 - 12.42

P223

P223 (ex *P73*)	1942	S III Class	7.41 - 1.43
Sea Nymph	1942	S III Class	1.43 - 1948

P224

P224 (ex *P74*)	1942	S III Class	1943 - 1.43
Sickle (ex *P224*)	1942	S III Class	1.43 - 6.44

P225

P225 (ex *P75*)	1942	S III Class	1943 - 1.43
Simoom (ex *P225*)	1942	S III Class	1.43 - 11.43

P226

P226 (ex *P76*)	1943	S III Class	1943 - 2.43
Sirdar (ex *P226*)	1943	S III Class	2.43 - 1948

P227

P227 (ex *P77*)	1943	S III Class	1943 - 2.43
Spiteful (ex *P227*)	1943	S III Class	2.43 - 1948

P228

P228 (ex *P78*)	1942	S III Class	1943 - 3.43
Splendid (ex *P228*)	1942	S III Class	3.43 - 4.43

P229

P229 (ex *P79*)	1942	S III Class	1943 - 3.43
Sportsman (ex *P229*)	1942	S III Class	3.43 - 1948

P231

P231	1943	S III Class	1943 - 2.43
Stoic (ex *P231*)	1943	S III Class	2.43 - 1950

P232

P232	1943	S III Class	1943 - 2.43
Stonehenge (ex *P232*)	1943	S III Class	2.43 - 3.44

P233

P233	1943	S III Class	1943 - 2.43
Storm (ex *P233*)	1943	S III Class	2.43 - 1949

P234

P234	1943	S III Class	1943 - 2.43
Stratagem (ex *P234*)	1943	S III Class	2.43 - 11.44

P235

P235	1943	S III Class	1943 - 2.43
Strongbow (ex *P235*)	1943	S III Class	2.43 - 1948

P236

P236	1943	S III Class	1943 - 4.43
Spark (ex *P236*)	1943	S III Class	4.43 - 1948

P237

P237	1944	S III Class	1943 - 2.43
Scythian (ex *P237*)	1944	S III Class	2.43 - 1948

P238

P238 (ex *P88*)	1942	S III Class	1943 - 2.43
Stubborn (ex *P238*)	1942	S III Class	2.43 - 1946

P239

P239 (ex *P89*)	1942	S III Class	1943 - 2.43
Surf (ex *P239*)	1942	S III Class	2.43 - 1948

P241

P241	1943	S III Class	1943 - 2.43
Syrtis (ex *P241*)	1943	S III Class	2.43 - 3.44

P242

P242	1943	S III Class	1943 - 4.43
Shalimar (ex *P242*)	1943	S III Class	4.43 - 1950

P243

P243	1944	S III Class	1943 - 4.43
Scotsman (ex *P243*)	1944	S III Class	4.43 - 1948

P244

P244	1945	S III Class	1943 - 4.43
Sea Devil (ex *P244*)	1945	S III Class	4.43 - 1948

P245

P245	1943	S III Class	1943 - 4.43
Spirit (ex *P245*)	1943	S III Class	4.43 - 1948

P246

P246	1943	S III Class	1943 - 4.43
Statesman (ex *P246*)	1943	S III Class	4.43 - 1948

P247

P247 (ex *P213*)	1942	S III Class	1942 - 1.43
Saracen (ex *P247*)	1942	S III Class	1.43 - 8.43

P248

P248	1943	S III Class	1943 - 4.43
Sturdy (ex *P248*)	1943	S III Class	4.43 - 1948

P249

P249	1943	S III Class	1943 - 4.43
Stygian (ex *P249*)	1943	S III Class	4.43 - 1948

P251

P251	1944	S III Class	1943 - 4.43
Subtle (ex *P251*)	1944	S III Class	4.43 - 1948

P252

P252	1944	S III Class	1943 - 4.43
Supreme (ex *P252*)	1944	S III Class	4.43 - 1948

P253

P253	1944	S III Class	1943 - 4.43
Sea Scout (ex *P253*)	1944	S III Class	4.43 - 1948

P254

P254	1944	S III Class	1943 - 4.43
Selene (ex *P254*)	1944	S III Class	4.43 - 1948

P255

P255	1945	S III Class	1943 - 4.43
Seneschal (ex *P255*)	1945	S III Class	4.43 - 1948

P256

P256	1945	S III Class	1943 - 4.43
Sentinel (ex *P256*)	1945	S III Class	4.43 - 1948

P257

Saga	1945	S III Class	1945 - 10.48

On 11.10.48 *Saga* was transferred to Portugal as *Nautillo*.

P258

Scorcher	1944	S III Class	1944 - 1948

P259

Sidon	1944	S III Class	1944 - 1948

P261

Sleuth	1944	S III Class	1944 - 1948

P262

Solent	1944	S III Class	1944 - 1948

P263

Spearhead	1944	S III Class	1944 - 8.48

In August 1948 *Spearhead* was transferred to Portugal and renamed *Neptuno*.

P264

Springer	1945	S III Class	1945 - 1948

P265

Spur	1944	S III Class	1944 - 11.48

In November 1948 *Spur* was transferred to Portugal and renamed *Narval*.

P266
Sanguine   1945   S III Class 1945 - 1948
P267
Sea Robin   Canc   S III Class Canc 1945
P268
Sprightly   Canc   S III Class Canc 1945
P269
Surface   Canc   S III Class Canc 1945
P271
Surge   Canc   S III Class Canc 1945

P311
P311 (ex *P91*)   1942   T III Class 7.41 - 1.43

P311 was to have received the name *Tutankhamen* but was lost before this was formally done.

P312
P312 (ex *P92*)   1942   T III Class 7.41 - 1.43
Trespasser (ex *P312*) 1942 T III Class 1.43 - 1948

P313
P313 (ex *P93*)   1942   T III Class 7.41 - 1942

P314
P314   1942   T III Class 1943 - 1.43
Tactician (ex *P314*) 1942 T III Class 1.43 - 1948

P315
P315 (ex *P95*)   1942   T III Class 7.41 - 1.43
Truculent (ex *P315*) 1942 T III Class 1.43 - 1.50

P316
P316 (ex *P96*)   1942   T III Class 7.41 - 2.43
Templar (ex *P316*) 1942   T III Class 2.43 - 1948

P317
P317 (ex *P97*)   1942   T III Class 7.41 - 2.43
Tally Ho (ex *P317*) 1942 T III Class 2.43 - 1948

P318
P318 (ex *P98*)   1943   T III Class 7.41 - 2.43
Tantalus (ex *P318*) 1943 T III Class 2.43 - 1950

P319
P319 (ex *P99*)   1943   T III Class 7.41 - 2.43
Tantivy (ex *P319*) 1943   T III Class 2.43 - 1948

P321
P321   1943   T III Class 7.41 - 2.43
Telemachus (ex *P321*)1943 T III Class 2.43 - 1961

P322
P322   1943   T III Class 7.41 - 3.43
Talent I (ex *P322*) 1943 T III Class 3.43 - 12.43

HMS Talent (P322) transferred to the RNLN on 6.12.43 and renamed *Zwaardvisch*.

P323
P323   1943   T III Class 1943 - 2.43
Terrapin (ex *P323*) 1943 T III Class 2.43 - 5.45

P324
P324   1943   T III Class 1943 - 2.43
Thorough (ex *P324*)1943 T III Class 2.43 - 1961

P325
P325   1942   T III Class 1943 - 2.43
Thule (ex *P325*)   1942   T III Class 2.43 - 1962

P326
P326   1942   T III Class 1943 - 2.43
Tudor (ex *P326*)   1942   T III Class 2.43 - 1963

P327
P327   1943   T III Class 1943 - 2.43
Tireless (ex *P327*) 1943 T III Class 2.43 - 1968

P328
P328   1943   T III Class 1943 - 2.43
Token (ex *P328*)   1943   T III Class 2.43 - 1948

P329
P329   1942   T III Class 1943 - 2.43
Tradewind (ex *P329*)1942 T III Class 2.43 - 1955

P331
P331   1943   T III Class 1943 - 2.43
Trenchant (ex *P331*)1943 T III Class 2.43 - 1963

P332
P332   1944   T III Class 1943 - 4.43
Tiptoe (ex *P332*) 1944   T III Class 4.43 - 1975

P333
P333   1944   T III Class 1943 - 4.43
Trump (ex *P333*)   1944   T III Class 4.43 - 1971

P334
P334   1944   T III Class 1943 - 4.43
Taciturn (ex *P334*) 1944 T III Class 14.43 - 1971

P335

P335	1944	T III Class	1943 - 4.43
Tapir (ex *P335*)	1944	T III Class	4.43 - 1948

Tapir (P335) was loaned to the RNLN from 18.6.48 - 16.7.53 and renamed *Zeehond*.

P336

P336	1944	T III Class	1943 - 4.43
Tarn (ex *P336*)	1944	T III Class	4.43 - 4.45
Tijgerhaai (ex *Tarn*)	1944	T III Class	4.45

On completion *HMS Tarn* (P336) transferred to the RNLN on 6.4.45 and renamed *Tijgerhaai*.

P337

P337	1945	T III Class	1943 - 4.43
Tasman (ex *P337*)	1945	T III Class	4.43 - 4.45
Talent (ex *Tasman*)	1945	T III Class	4.45 - 1970

P338

P338	1945	T III Class	1943 - 4.43
Teredo (ex *P338*)	1945	T III Class	4.43 - 1965

P339

P339 (ex *P313*)	1942	T III Class	1942 - 1.43
Taurus (ex *P339*)	1942	T III Class	1.43 - 1948

HMS Taurus (P339) was loaned to the RNLN from 4.6.48 - 8.12.53 and renamed *Dolfijn*.

P341

P341	Canc	T III Class	Ren 2.43
Theban (ex *P341*)	Canc	T III Class	Canc 1944

P342

P342	1945	T III Class	1943 - 5.43
Tabard (ex *P342*)	1945	T III Class	5.43 - 1948

P343

P343	Canc	T III Class	Ren 4.43
Talent (ex *P343*)	Canc	T III Class	Canc 1944

P344

P344	Canc	T III Class	Ren 5.43
Threat (ex *P344*)	Canc	T III Class	Canc 1944

P345

P345	Canc	T III Class	Canc 1944

P346

P346	Canc	T III Class	Canc 1944

P347

P347	Canc	T III Class	Canc 1944

P348

P348	Canc	T III Class	Canc 1944

P349

P349	1944	T III Class	Ren 4.43
Thor (ex *P349*)	1944	T III Class	Incomplete

P351

P351	1944	T III Class	Ren 4.43
Tiara (ex *P351*)	1944	T III Class	Incomplete

Both *Thor* and *Tiara* had been launched when cancelled. The incomplete hulls were sold for breaking up.

P352

P352	1943	T III Class	1943 - 4.43
Totem (ex *P352*)	1943	T III Class	4.43 - 1948

P353

P353	1944	T III Class	1943 - 4.43
Truncheon (ex *P353*)	1944	T III Class	4.43 - 1948

P354

P354	1944	T III Class	1943 - 4.43
Turpin (ex *P354*)	1944	T III Class	4.43 - 1967

On 19.5.67 *HMS Turpin* (P354) was transferred to Israel and renamed *Leviathan*.

P355

P355	1945	T III Class	1943 - 4.43
Thermopylae (ex *P355*)	1945	T III Class	4.43 - 1970

P411

Acheron	1947	A Class	1945 - 1948

P412

Adept	Canc	A Class	Canc 1945

P414

Ace	1945	A Class	Canc 1945

P415

Alcide	1945	A Class	1945 - 1948

P416

Alderney	1945	A Class	1945 - 1948

P417

Alliance	1945	A Class	1945 - 1948

P418

Ambush	1945	A Class	1945 - 1948

P419

Auriga	1945	A Class	1945 - 1978

P421

Affray	1945	A Class	1945 - 4.51

P422

Anchorite	1946	A Class	1945 - 1948
(ex *Amphion*)			

P423

Andrew	1946	A Class	1945 - 1948

P424

Andromache	Canc	A Class	Canc 1945

P425

Answer	Canc	A Class	Canc 1945

P426

Aurochs	1945	A Class	1945 - 1948

P427

Aeneas	1945	A Class	1945 - 1948

P428

Antagonist	Canc	A Class	Canc 1945

P429

Antaeus	Canc	A Class	Canc 1945

P431

Anzac	Canc	A Class	Canc 1945

P432

Aphrodite	Canc	A Class	Canc 1945

P433

Achates	1945	A Class	Canc 1945

P434

Admirable	Canc	A Class	Canc 1945

P435

Approach	Canc	A Class	Canc 1945

P436

Arcadian	Canc	A Class	Canc 1945

P437

Ardent	Canc	A Class	Canc 1945

P438

Argosy	Canc	A Class	Canc 1945

P439

Amphion	1944	A Class	1945 - 1948
(ex *Anchorite*)			

P441

Alaric	1946	A Class	1945 - 1948

P442

Atlantis	Canc	A Class	Canc 1945

P443

Agile	Canc	A Class	Canc 1945

P444

Asperity	Canc	A Class	Canc 1945

P445

Austere	Canc	A Class	Canc 1945

P446

Aggressor	Canc	A Class	Canc 1945

P447

Astute	1945	A Class	1945 - 1948

P448

Agate	Canc	A Class	Canc 1945

P449

Artemis	1946	A Class	1945 - 1948

P451

Abelard	Canc	A Class	Canc 1945

P452

Acasta	Canc	A Class	Canc 1945

P453

Alcestis	Canc	A Class	Canc 1945

P454

Aladdin	Canc	A Class	Canc 1945

P455

Aztec	Canc	A Class	Canc 1945

P456

Artful	1947	A Class	1945 - 1972

P457

Adversary	Canc	A Class	Canc 1945

P458

Asgard	Canc	A Class	Canc 1945

P459

Awake	Canc	A Class	Canc 1945

P461

Astarte	Canc	A Class	Canc 1945

P462

Assurance	Canc	A Class	Canc 1945

Both *Ace* and *Achates* were at an advanced stage of build when the cancellation order was made. The incomplete hulls of both were sold for breaking up.

P511

P511 (ex *R3* usn)	1919	R Class	11.41 - 12.44

P512

P512 (ex *R17* usn)	1917	R Class	3.42 - 9.44

P514

P514 (ex *R19* usn)	1918	R Class	3.42 - 6.42

P551

P551 (ex *S25* usn)	1922	S Class	11.41 - 12.41

Although transferred to the Royal Navy *P551* commissioned with a Polish crew as *Jastrzab*. On 2.5.42 she was depth charged in error while operating with convoy QP.11. The crew were taken off the vessel and it was subsequently sunk by gunfire.

P552

P552 (ex *S1* usn)	1918	S Class	4.42 - 10.44

P553

P553 (ex *S21* usn)	1920	S Class	9.42 - 7.44

P554

P554 (ex *S22* usn)	1920	S Class	6.42 - 7.44

P555

P555 (ex *S24* usn) 1922 S Class 8.42 - 12.44

P556

P556 (ex *S29* usn) 1922 S Class 6.42 - 1.45

P611

P611 1940 ex-Turkish 1940 - 1942

P612

P612 1940 ex-Turkish 1940 - 1942

P614

P614 1940 ex-Turkish 1940 - 1946

P615

P615 1940 ex-Turkish 1940 - 4.43

P611 - P615 were four Turkish submarines under construction in the UK and, at the outbreak of war, were requisitioned by the Royal Navy. *P611* (ex *Oruc Reis*) and *P612* (ex *Murat Reis*) were commissioned into the RN for passage to Turkey, after which they were returned to their owners. *P614* (ex *Burak Reis*) was returned to Turkey in 1946. *P615* (ex *Uluc Ali Reis*) was torpedoed and sunk off Freetown in 1943.

P711

X-2 1934 Archimede 1942
   (ex *Galileo Galilei*)
P711 (ex *X-2*) 1934 Archimede 1942 - 1946

The former Italian submarine *Galileo Galilei* was captured in the Red Sea by the trawler HMS *Moonstone* in June 1940, and escorted to Aden. Renamed X-2 she was transferred to Alexandria for trials and evaluation. She was renamed *P711* in 1942 and was employed as a training submarine.

P712

P712 (ex *Perla*) 1936 Perla 7.42 - 12.42

Former Italian submarine captured off Beirut by the corvette HMS *Hyacinth* in July 1942. She was commissioned into the RN as P712. In December of that year she was transferred to Greece and renamed *Matrozos* (see N18)

P714

P714 (ex *Bronzo*) 1941 Acciaio 7.43 - 1.44

Former Italian submarine captured in July 1943, off Syracuse, by HM Ships *Boston*, *Cromarty*, *Poole* and *Seaham*. After evaluation and trials by the RN she was transferred to France in January 1944 and renamed *Narval*.

P715

P715 (ex *U-570*) 1941 Type VIIC 1941
Graph (ex *P715*) 1941 Type VIIC 1943 - 1944

A former German Navy Type VIIC U-boat she was damaged by RAF aircraft off Iceland on 27 August 1941 and captured by the armed trawler HMS *Northern Chief* and the destroyer HMS *Burwell*. Commissioned into the RN as *P715*, she was initially used for trials and evaluation. She was renamed HMS *Graph* in January 1943 and conducted operational patrols in the Bay of Biscay and North Sea and also as close escort to Arctic convoys.

R Flag Superior

Assigned to R class submarines from build to between the wars.

R1
Submarine R1 1918 R Class 1918 - 1923
R2
Submarine R2 1918 R Class 1918 - 1923
R3
Submarine R3 1918 R Class 1918 - 1923
R4
Submarine R4 1918 R Class 1918 - 1934
R5
Submarine R5 Canc R Class Canc 1919
R6
Submarine R6 Canc R Class Canc 1919
R7
Submarine R7 1918 R Class 1918 - 1923
R8
Submarine R8 1918 R Class 1918 - 1923
R9
Submarine R9 1918 R Class 1918 - 1923
R10
Submarine R10 1918 R Class 1918 - 1929
R11
Submarine R11 1918 R Class 1918 - 1923
R12
Submarine R12 1918 R Class 1918 - 1923

S Flag Superior

Submarines of the British Pacific Fleet were the first Royal Navy vessels to be assigned 'S' Flag Superior pendant numbers. These were assigned by the US Navy and were a temporary measure. Post-war Royal Navy numbering standardised all submarines with 'S' Flag Superior numbers although, to maintain anonymity, it is no longer practice to display such identifying markings.

S1

Amazone FR	1931	Diane	BPF 1945/46

S2

Rorqual	1936	Porpoise	BPF 1945/46

S3

Terrapin	1943	T III Class	BPF 1945/46

S4

Thorough	1943	T III Class	BPF 1945/46

S5

Thule	1942	T III Class	BPF 1945/46

S6

Tiptoe	1944	T III Class	BPF 1945/46

S7

Trenchant	1943	T III Class	BPF 1945/46

S8

Trump	1944	T III Class	BPF 1945/46

S9

Porpoise	1932	Porpoise	BPF 1945/46

S01

Porpoise	1956	Porpoise	1956 - 1985

S02

Rorqual	1956	Porpoise	1956 - 1977

S03

Narwhal	1957	Porpoise	1957 - 1983

S04

Grampus	1957	Porpoise	1957 - 1979

S05

Finwhale	1959	Porpoise	1959 - 1987

S06

Cachalot	1957	Porpoise	1957 - 1979

S07

Spiteful	1943	S II Class	1948 - 1952
Sealion	1959	Porpoise	1959 - 1987

On 25.1.52 *Spiteful* was loaned to France for anti-submarine training. She was renamed *Sirene*.

S08

Walrus	1959	Porpoise	1959 - 1987

S09

Auriga	1945	A Class	1948 - 1961
Oberon	1959	Oberon	1959 - 1987

S10

Seadog	1942	S III Class	BPF 1945/46
Odin	1960	Oberon	1960 - 1991

S11

Sea Scout	1944	S III Class	BPF 1945/46
Acheron	1947	A Class	1948 - 1961
Orpheus	1959	Oberon	1959 - 1994

S12

Selene	1944	S III Class	BPF 1945/46
Trespasser	1942	T III Class	1948 - 1961
Olympus	1961	Oberon	1961 - 1989

S13

Shakespeare	1941	S III Class	BPF 1945/46
Osiris	1962	Oberon	1962 - 1992

S14

Supreme	1944	S III Class	BPF 1945/46
Tactician	1942	T III Class	1948 - 1961
Onslaught	1960	Oberon	1960 - 1991

S15

Thrasher	1940	T II Class	BPF 1945/46
Alcide	1945	A Class	1948 - 1974
Otter	1961	Oberon	1962 - 1991

S16

Trident	1938	T I Class	BPF 1945/46
Alderney	1945	A Class	1948 - 1961
Oracle	1961	Oberon	1961 - 1997

S17

Tudor	1942	T III Class	BPF 1945/46
Alliance	1945	A Class	1948 - 1961
Ocelot	1962	Oberon	1962 - 1991

S18

Virtue	1943	V Class	BPF 1945/46
Ambush	1945	A Class	1948 - 1961
Otus	1962	Oberon	1962 - 1992

S19

Voracious	1943	V Class	BPF 1945/46
Tantivy	1943	T III Class	1948 - 1951
Opossum	1963	Oberon	1963 - 1996

S20

Vox	1943	V Class	BPF 1945/46
Affray	1945	A Class	1948 - 1951
Opportune	1964	Oberon	1964 - 1993
Astute	2007	Astute	See S94

S21

Sirdar	1943	S III Class	BPF 1945/46
Telemachus	1943	T II Class	1948 - 1961

Onyx	1966	Oberon	1966 - 1990
Ambush	2011	Astute	*See S94*

S22

Spark	1943	S III Class	BPF 1945/46
Anchorite	1946	A Class	1948 - 1961
Resolution	1966	Resolution	1966 - 1994
Artful	2014	Astute	*See S94*

S23

Spirit	1943	S III Class	BPF 1945/46
Andrew	1946	A Class	1948 - 1961
Repulse	1967	Resolution	1967 - 1996

S24

Spiteful	1943	S III Class	BPF 1945/46
Thorough	1943	T III Class	1948 - 1961
Thule	1942	T III Class	1961 - 1962

S25

Storm	1943	S III Class	BPF 1945/46

S26

Sturdy	1943	S III Class	BPF 1945/46
Aurochs	1945	A Class	1948 - 1961
Renown	1967	Resolution	1967 - 1995

S27

Stygian	1943	S III Class	BPF 1945/46
Aeneas	1945	A Class	1948 - 1961
Revenge	1968	Resolution	1968 - 1995

S28

Tantalus	1943	T III Class	BPF 1945/46
Token	1943	T III Class	1948 - 1970
Vanguard	1992	Vanguard	1992 -

S29

Tantivy	1943	T III Class	BPF 1945/46
Tradewind	1942	T III Class	1948 - 1955
Victorious	1993	Vanguard	1993 -

S30

Telemachus	1943	T III Class	BPF 1945/46
Explorer	1954	Ex Class	1954 - 1965
Vigilant	1995	Vanguard	1995 -

S31

Tradewind	1942	T III Class	BPF 1945/46
Trenchant	1943	T III Class	1948 - 1963
Vengeance	1998	Vanguard	1998 -

S32

Zwaardvisch	1943	T III Class	BPF 1945/46
Tiptoe	1944	T III Class	1944 - 1971

S33

O-19 RNLN	1938	O-19	BPF 1945/46
Trump	1944	T III Class	1944 - 1971

S34

Scythian	1944	S III Class	BPF 1945/46
Taciturn	1944	T III Class	1944 - 1971

S35

Sleuth	1944	S III Class	BPF 1945/46
Tapir	1944	T III Class	1944 - 1948

S36

Solent	1944	S III Class	BPF 1945/46
Untiring	1943	U II Class	1948

Untiring was loaned to Greece as *Xifias* 1945 - 1952

S37

Taciturn	1944	T III Class	BPF 1945/46
Talent	1945	T III Class	1948 - 1966

S38

Turpin	1943	T III Class	BPF 1945/46
Teredo	1945	T III Class	1948 - 1965

S39

Sidon	1944	S III Class	BPF 1945/46

S40

Sea Nymph	1942	S III Class	BPF 1945/46
Excalibur	1955	Ex Class	1955 - 1970
Upholder	1986	Upholder	1989 - 1994

S41

Stubborn	1942	S III Class	BPF 1945/46
Alaric	1946	A Class	1948 - 1971
Unseen	1989	Upholder	1989 - 1994

S42

Spearhead	1944	S III Class	BPF 1945/46
Tabard	1945	T III Class	1948 - 1974
Ursula	1991	Upholder	1991 - 1994

S43

Scorcher	1944	S III Class	BPF 1945/46
Amphion	1944	A Class	1948 - 1971
Unicorn	1992	Upholder	1992 - 1994

S44

Scotsman	1944	S III Class	BPF 1945/46
Sea Devil	1945	S II Class	1948 - 1966

S45

Tapir	1944	T III Class	BPF 1945/46
Spirit	1943	S II Class	1948 - 1950

S46

Taurus	1942	T III Class	BPF 1945/46
Statesman	1943	S II Class	1948 - 1952
Churchill	1968	Churchill	1968 - 1991

Statesman was loaned French as *Sultane* 1952-59.

S47

Totem	1943	T III Class	BPF 1945/46
Astute	1945	A Class	1948 - 1970

S48

O-21 RNLN	1939	O-21	BPF 1945/46
Sturdy	1943	S II Class	1948 - 1957
Conqueror	1969	Churchill	1969 - 1990

S49

O-23 RNLN	1939	O-21	BPF 1945/46
Artemis	1946	A Class	1948 - 1971

S50

O-24 RNLN	1940	O-21	BPF 1945/46
Courageous	1970	Churchill	1970 - 1992

S51

Visigoth	1943	V Class	BPF 1945/46
Subtle	1944	S II Class	1948 - 1959

S52

Totem	1943	T III Class	1948 - 1964

On 10.11.67 *Totem* (P352) was transferred to Israel an renamed *Dakar.* She was lost on her delivery voyage.

S53

Truncheon	1944	T III Class	1948 - 1968

S54

Turpin	1944	T III Class	1948 - 1965

S55

Thermopylae	1945	T III Class	1948 - 1970

S56

Sentinel	1945	S II Class	1948 - 1962

S57

Oxley RAN	1965	Oberon	1965 - 1992

S58

Scorcher	1944	S II Class	1948 - 1962

S59

Sidon	1944	S III Class	1948 - 1957
Otway RAN	1966	Oberon	1966 - 1994

S60

Onslow RAN	1968	Oberon	1967 - 1999

S61

Sleuth	1944	S II Class	1948 - 1958
Acheron	1947	A Class	1961 - 1972
Orion RAN	1974	Oberon	1974 - 1996

S62

Solent	1944	S II Class	1948 - 1961
Aurochs	1945	A Class	1961 - 1967
Otama RAN	1975	Oberon	1975 - 2000

S63

Andrew	1946	A Class	1961 - 1977

S64

Springer	1945	S II Class	1948 - 1958

On 9.10.58 *Springer* was transferred to Israel and renamed *Tanin.*

S64

Anchorite	1946	A Class	1961 - 1970

S65

Alcide	1945	A Class	1961 - 1974

S66

Sanguine	1945	S II Class	1948 - 10.58
Alderney	1945	A Class	1961 - 1972

In October 1958 *Sanguine* was transferred to Israel and renamed *Rahav.*

S67

Alliance	1945	A Class	1961 - 1981

S68

Ambush	1945	A Class	1961 - 1971

S69

Auriga	1945	A Class	1961 - 1975

S70

Ovens RAN	1967	Oberon	1967 - 1995

S72

Artemis	1946	A Class	1961 - 1972

S74

Tactician	1942	T III Class	1961 - 1963

S75

Seneschal	1945	S II Class	1948 - 1960

S76

Artful	1947	A Class	1948 - 1972
Sirdar	1943	S II Class	1948 - 1965

S77

Tireless	1943	T III Class	1948 - 1968

S84

Satyr	1942	S II Class	1948 - 1952

In February 1952 *Satyr* was one of four submarines loaded to the French Navy for anti-submarine training. She was renamed *Saphir* and returned to the Royal Navy in 1961. She was scrapped the following year.

S86

Templar	1942	T III Class	1948 - 1950

S87

Tally Ho!	1942	T III Class	1948 - 1967
Turbulent	1982	Trafalgar	1982 - 2012

S88

Tireless	1984	Trafalgar	1984 - 2014

S89

Seraph	1941	S II Class	1962 - 1965

S90

Torbay	1985	Trafalgar	1985 - 2017

S91

Trenchant	1986	Trafalgar	1986 -

S92

Talent	1988	Trafalgar	1988 -

S93

Triumph	1991	Trafalgar	1991 -

S94

Meteorite (ex *U1407*)	1945	Type XVII	Not Used
Astute	2007	Astute	2010 -

During their procurement and introduction into service several different series of pendant numbers have appeared in MoD publications and on official websites relating to the Astute class nuclear-powered submarines. Correspondence with the MoD has confirmed that actual numbers for the class are in the S94 - S100 range as detailed here. Previously published numbers have been included here for completeness.

S95

Artful	2014	Astute	2016 -

S96

Artful	1947	A Class	1948 - 1972
Ambush	2011	Astute	2013 -

S97

Audacious	2017	Astute	2020 -

S98

Anson	Bldg	Astute	Building

S99

Agamemnon	Bldg	Astute	Building

S100

Agincourt	Bldg	Astute	Building

S101

Dreadnought	1960	Dreadnought	1976 - 1982

S102

Valiant	1963	Valiant	1963 - 1994

S103

Warspite	1965	Valiant	1965 - 1991

S104

Sceptre	1976	Swiftsure	1976 - 2010

S105

Conqueror	1969	Churchill	*See S48*
Spartan	1978	Swiftsure	1978 - 2006

S106

Splendid	1979	Swiftsure	1979 - 2004

S107

Trafalgar	1981	Trafalgar	1981 - 2009

S108

Sovereign	1973	Swiftsure	1973 - 2006

S109

Superb	1974	Swiftsure	1974 - 2008

S110

Sceptre	1976	Swiftsure	*See S104*

S111

Spartan	1978	Swiftsure	*See S105*

S112

Splendid	1979	Swiftsure	*See S106*

S113

Trafalgar	1981	Trafalgar	*See S107*

S114

Turbulent	1982	Trafalgar	*See S87*

S115

Tireless	1984	Trafalgar	*See S77*

S116

Torbay	1985	Trafalgar	*See S90*

S117

Talent	1988	Trafalgar	*See S92*

S118

Tactician	Canc	Trafalgar	*Cancelled*

S119
Astute	2007	Astute	*See S94*

S120
Ambush	2011	Astute	*See S94*

S121
Artful	2014	Astute	*See S94*

S122
Audacious	2017	Astute	*See S94*

S123
Agamemnon	Bldg	Astute	*See S94*

S124
Anson	Bldg	Astute	*See S94*

S125
Agincourt	Bldg	Astute	*See S94*

S126
Tudor	1942	T III Class	1948 - 1963
Swiftsure	1971	Swiftsure	1971 - 1992

S129
Sportsman	1942	S II Class	1948 - 1951

In 1951 *Sportsman* was loaned to France for anti-submarine training and renamed *Sibylle*. She was lost without trace off Toulon 23.9.52.

S137
Scythian	1944	S II Class	1948 - 1960

S143
Scotsman	1944	S II Class	1948 - 1964

S153
Sea Scout	1944	S II Class	1948 - 1965

S154
Selene	1944	S II Class	1948 - 1961

V Flag Superior

V Class submarines were an experimental design from Vickers. From mid-1915 the submarine name was displayed as its pendant number.

V1
Submarine V1	1914	V Class	1914 - 1921

V2
Submarine V2	1915	V Class	1915 - 1921

V3
Submarine V3	1915	V Class	1915 - 1920

V4
Submarine V4	1915	V Class	1915 - 1920

W Flag Superior

W Class submarines were an experimental design from Armstrong Whitwworth. From mid-1915 the submarine name was displayed as its pendant number. Only W1 and W2 served with the Royal Navy. Being complete disasters, all four submarines were transferred to the Italian Navy, it being argued that they were better suited to the milder conditions of the Mediterranean.

W1
Submarine W1	1914	W Class	1914 - 1916

W2
Submarine W2	1915	W Class	1915 - 1916

X Flag Superior

With the exception of submarines *X1* and *Galileo Galilei*, the 'X' Flag Superior was used to identify the un-named midget submarines which began to enter service during WWII. 'XE' Flag Superior identified those vessels designed for operation in the Far East while 'XT' identified training boats. Due to the manner of their construction, being built and completed undercover, it has not been possible to identify specific launch or completion dates. With the exception of X51 to X54, those entries displaying a name were unofficial identities.

X1
X1	1923	X-1 Class	1925 - 1936

X2
Galileo Galilei	1934	Archimede	See P711

X3
X3 Piker	1942	X Class	1942 - 1945

X4
X4	(....)	X Class	.... - 1945

X5
X5 (Platypus)	1942	X Class	1942 - 9.43

X6
X6 (Piker II)	1943	X Class	1943 - 9.43

X7
X7 (Pdinichthys)	(....)	X Class	.... - 9.43

X8
X8 (Expectant)	(....)	X Class	.... - 9.43

X9
X9 (Pluto)	(....)	X Class	.... - 9.43

X10
X10	(....)	X Class	.... - 10.43

X20
X20 Exemplar	(....)	X Class	.... - 1945

X21

X21 Exultant	(....)	X Class	.... - 1945

X22

X22 Exploit	(....)	X Class	.... - 2.44

X23

X23 Xiphias	(....)	X Class	.... - 1945

X24

X24 Expeditious	(....)	X Class	.... - Pres

X25

X25 Xema	(....)	X Class	.... - 1945

X51

X51 (Stickleback)	1954	X51 Class	1954 - 1958

Stickleback transferred to Sweden 1958 and renamed *Spiggen*. Returned and placed on display at the Imperial War Museum, Duxford.

X52

X52	1954	X51 Class	Ren 12.54
Shrimp (ex *X52*)	1954	X51 Class	12.54 - 1965

X53

X53	1955	X51 Class	Ren 12.54
Sprat (ex *X53*)	1955	X51 Class	12.54 - 1966

X54

X54	1955	X51 Class	Ren 12.54
Minnow (ex *X54*)	1955	X51 Class	12.54 - 1966

XE1

XE1 (Executioner)	(....)	XE Class	.... - 1945

XE2

XE2 (Xerxes)	(....)	XE Class	.... - 1945

XE3

XE3 (Sigyn)	1944	XE Class	1944 - 1945

XE4

XE4 (Exciter)	(....)	XE Class	.... - 1945

XE5

XE5 (Perseus)	(....)	XE Class	.... - 1945

XE6

XE6 (Excalibur II)	(....)	XE Class	.... - 1945

XE7

XE7 (Exuberant)	1945	XE Class	1945 - 1953

XE8

XE8 (Expunger)	1945	XE Class	1945 - 1952

XE9

XE9 (Unexpected)	1945	XE Class	1945 - 1955

XE10

XE10	Canc	XE Class	Incomplete

XE11

XE11 (Lucifer)	(....)	XE Class	.... - 3.45

XE12

XE12 (Excitable)	1945	XE Class	1945 - 1952

XE14

XE14	Canc	XE Class	Canc 1944

XE15

XE15	Canc	XE Class	Canc 1944

XE16

XE16	Canc	XE Class	Canc 1944

XE17

XE17	Canc	XE Class	Canc 1944

XE18

XE18	Canc	XE Class	Canc 1944

XE19

XE19	Canc	XE Class	Canc 1944

XE20

XE20	(....)	XE Class	....

XE21

XE21	(....)	XE Class	....

XE22

XE22	(....)	XE Class	....

XE23

XE23	(....)	XE Class	....

XE24

XE24	(....)	XE Class	....

XE25

XE25	(....)	XE Class	....

XT1

XT1 Extant	1943	XT Class	Bu 1945

XT2

XT2 Sandra	1943	XT Class	Bu 1945

XT3

XT3 Herald	1943	XT Class	Bu 1945

XT4

XT4 Excelsior	1943	XT Class	Bu 1945

XT5

XT5 Extended	1943	XT Class	Bu 1945

XT6

XT6 Xantho	1943	XT Class	Bu 1945

XT7

XT7	Canc	XT Class	Canc 3.44

XT8

XT8	Canc	XT Class	Canc 3.44

XT9

XT9	Canc	XT Class	Canc 3.44

XT10

XT10	Canc	XT Class	Canc 3.44

XT11

XT11	Canc	XT Class	Canc 3.44

XT12

XT12	Canc	XT Class	Canc 3.44

XT14

XT14	Canc	XT Class	Canc 9.44

XT15				**XT18**			
XT15	Canc	XT Class	Canc 9.44	*XT18*	Canc	XT Class	Canc 9.44
XT16				**XT19**			
XT16	Canc	XT Class	Canc 9.44	*XT19*	Canc	XT Class	Canc 9.44
XT17							
XT17	Canc	XT Class	Canc 9.44				

Chapter 3

British Pacific Fleet Pendant Numbers

In 1941, after the losses of *Prince of Wales* and *Repulse* and the fall of Singapore, the Royal Navy had effectively withdrawn from the Pacific region, its subsequent operations in the area being limited to the Indian Ocean. British priorities were focussed on the war in Europe. Following the successful landings on the beaches of Normandy in June 1944, and the rapid land advances through the continent, the British leadership could see the looming end of the war in Europe. At the same time the United States were embroiled in their own battles against the Japanese in the Pacific theatre. The US Navy was beginning to recapture territory as it advanced across the Pacific and Winston Churchill, fearing that the UK would be squeezed out of the area, determined that UK territories in the region should be relieved by British Forces. With the demand on Royal Navy assets in the European theatre diminishing, the time seemed right for a return to the Pacific.

At the second Quebec conference in September 1944, President Franklin D Roosevelt accepted Churchill's suggestion that a British fleet be used in the main theatre of operations against Japan.

However, this decision was not universally liked, particularly by some within the US Navy, who regarded the Pacific as their war and were reluctant to accept a large British Fleet stumbling about in their backyard and more importantly - the British fleet would have to support itself. The US Navy logistics system was already under strain and would not be able to support a new fleet. Even in the UK ministers were wary of a vast British fleet becoming a bit part player and being subordinate to US fleet commanders.

The British Pacific Fleet was formed on 22 November 1944 under Admiral Sir Bruce Fraser. He quickly realised that both the Royal Navy and US Navy had very different operating doctrines - everything from tactics to fleet formations and communications. He quickly realised that for the RN to seamlessly operate within the Pacific that all fleets should be operate to the same doctrines and procedures and to Fraser it made sense that the Royal Navy should adopt US practices - after all they were by far the largest force and had been operating in the area for years.

Meetings between Fraser and Admiral Nimitz, C-in-C US Pacific Fleet, thrashed out various concepts of operations and, of particular interest, in the field of communications. To ensure timely and unrestricted communications between the two nations, the Royal Navy would adopt Pacific Ocean Area communications doctrines, procedures and cryptographic systems. This was to be utilised by embarking US Navy Communication Liaison Teams aboard some RN ships.

To ensure that all communications worked smoothly each ship was to be issued with a full outfit of USN signal publications. Amongst these books were the US Navy Radio Call Sign Book (DNC 3(A)), the US Navy Visual Call Sign Book (DNC 4(A)) and the US Naval Communication Instructions and Procedures (DNC 5).

Of these, DNC4(A) provided for a new series of pendant numbers to be assigned to Allied vessels operating with the US Navy. This is nothing new - in Chapter 1 it was noted that AS vessels lent to the US Navy in 1942 were also assigned numbers. What is of interest is that, until the turn of this century, although the existence of an area specific set of numbers was known about, very little information was available. The issuing authority for the US signal books was the Royal Australian Navy, publications being issued to BPF ships on their arrival in Australia. On departing from the BPF (or on the dissolution of the Allied command and the reversion of the BPF to totally national control, whichever was the earlier) the books were returned to the RAN. Presumably, on dissolution of Allied control, the RAN returned all stocks to the USN. Subsequent research seemed to support this - UK, US and Australian naval sources were contacted and, although both the US and Australian authorities were aware of the document, they were of the belief that all copies had been recalled and destroyed in accordance with USN instructions.

Early correspondence suggested that the Flag Superiors, seen on BPF ships, indicated the nationality of operators, for example British ships were identified by the letter 'B' and French ships with the letter 'F' etc. While this could have been plausible, it was difficult to confirm, one way or another, without access to the source document.

Initially, it was thought that these new numbers were assigned to Allied ships as US Navy lookouts were unfamiliar with the silhouettes of Allied vessels and such a system would prevent potential blue-on-blue engagements. This could be true but, in my opinion, unlikely. Firstly, it must be remembered that Allied ships already carried prominent numbers on their hulls. Secondly, photographs of the time show very few ships actually displaying these new numbers and, finally, at the time, US Navy ships were adopting various camouflage schemes. Central to all of these schemes was a reduction in size of their hull numbers to a mere three feet high - making them virtually invisible unless steaming in close company. Copies of DNC 4(A) have now been located and study of the US Navy entries reveal that many of the visual call signs differed from their hull numbers. It is more likely, therefore, that these numbers were intended to be used as visual identifiers when using flags or flashing light. The fact that they were applied to some hulls, and not all, is probably more a reflection of usual RN practice. Disproving earlier accounts of letters indicating nationality it can now be shown that each flag superior indicated role - for example, destroyers were prefixed 'D', submarines 'S' and cruisers 'C'.

The publication was updated by numbered NRPMs (Non-Registered Public Memoranda). At least twenty NRPMs were issued updating DNC 4(A). Most were minor changes of odd ships here and there. However, there was one major update - the introduction of the British Fleet Train saw a major update assigning a new series of numbers with a 'B' flag superior. It has long been suspected that NRPM 340 was the source of this update but a copy could not be found. Research has now located a copy within a US Archive but, Covid-19 restrictions mean that it has not been possible to access this record to confirm. As most pages that include 'B' pendants include the NRPM 340 notation it is probably a safe assumption.

Although listed in earlier chapters, the complete list of DNC 4(A) numbers is included below. It is to be noted that the list includes those ships that were allocated to the BPF and therefore some may not have made it into area before the end of the war.

DNC 4(A) US Navy Visual Call Sign Book (1944)
Section 5c: Ship Call Signs - Alphabetically by ships' names (Allied Ships)

A Flag Superior		A771	*Yunnan* RAN	B9	*Rodney*
		A772	*Bishopdale* RAN	B201	*Lothian*
A192	*Redpole*	A773	*Brajara* RAN	B206	*Empire Arquebus*
A422	*Queen Wilhelmena* RNLN	A774	*Kurumba* RAN	B207	*Empire Battleaxe*
A423	*King Haakon VII* RNoN	A775	*Reserve* RAN	B208	*Empire Mace*
A424	*Jan Van Brakel* RNLN	A776	*Sprightly* RAN	B209	*Empire Spearhead*
A425	*Van Kingsbergen* RNLN			B210	*Glen Earn*
A426	*Bearn* FR	*B Flag Superior*		B211	*Lamont*
A427	*Swan* RAN			B221	*Avon Vale*
A428	*Warrego* RAN	B1	*Anson*	B222	*Beaufort*
A430	*Cap des Palmes* FR	B2	*Duke of York*	B223	*Bicester*
A431	*La Grandiere* FR	B3	*Howe*	B224	*Melbreak*
A432	*Chasseur 6* FR	B4	*King George V*	B225	*Talybont*
A433	*Chasseur 5* FR	B5	*Nelson*	B226	*Bleasdale*
A434	*Dragueur 301* FR	B6	*Queen Elizabeth*	B227	*Brissenden*
A435	*Mameli* IT	B7	*Renown*	B228	*Cowdray*
A732	*Adamant*	B8	*Richelieu* FR	B229	*Easton*

B230	*Stevenstone*	B286	*Magpie*	B398	*SS Oxfordshire*
B231	*Haydon*	B287	*Mermaid*	B399	*SS Tjitjalengka*
B236	*Ballarat*	B288	*Hind*	B400	*SS Vasna*
B237	*Bendigo*	B289	*Aire*	B401	*City of Paris*
B238	*Burnie*	B290	*Widemouth Bay*	B402	*Lancashire*
B239	*Cairns*	B291	*Alacrity*	B403	*Southern Prince*
B240	*Cessnock*	B292	*Opossum*	B406	*Menestheus*
B241	*Gawler*	B293	*Peacock*	B411	*Leonian*
B242	*Geraldton*	B294	*Pelican*	B412	*Fernmoor*
B243	*Goulburn*	B295	*Starling*	B416	*Barbain*
B244	*Ipswich*	B296	*Helvig*	B417	*Barnwell*
B245	*Kalgoorlie*	B297	*Stork*	B418	*Barthorpe*
B246	*Launceston*	B301	*Artifex*	B419	*Bartizan*
B247	*Lismore*	B302	*Assistance*	B421	*SS Atlas*
B248	*Maryborough*	B303	*Diligence*	B422	*SS Empire Wolfe*
B249	*Pirie*	B304	*Resource*	B423	*SS Empire Boswell*
B250	*Tamworth*	B311	*Flamborough Head*	B424	*SS Edna*
B251	*Toowoomba*	B312	*Unicorn*	B426	*Springdale*
B252	*Whyalla*	B316	*Cuillin Sound*	B431	*SS Gurna*
B253	*Wollongong*	B317	*Deer Sound*	B432	*SS Prome*
B254	*Courier*	B319	*Holm Sound*	B433	*SS Empire Cheer*
B255	*Felicity*	B326	*Beauly Firth*	B436	*Guardian*
B256	*Hare*	B327	*Moray Firth*	B437	*Protector*
B257	*Liberty*	B328	*Solway Firth*	B441	*King Salvor*
B258	*Michael*	B332	*Empire Pitcairn*	B442	*Salvestor*
B259	*Minstrel*	B336	*Alaunia*	B443	*Salvictor*
B260	*Wave*	B337	*Ranpura*	B446	*Advantage*
B261	*Welcome*	B341	*Empire Penang*	B447	*Aimwell*
B262	*Coquette*	B342	*Mullion Cove*	B448	*Cheerly*
B263	*Mary Rose*	B343	*Dullisk Cove*	B449	*Destiny*
B264	*Moon*	B346	*Perseus*	B450	*Eminent*
B265	*Providence*	B347	*Pioneer*	B451	*Empire Josephine*
B266	*Avon*	B351	*Portland Bill*	B452	*Empire Sam*
B267	*Barle*	B352	*Selsey Bill*	B453	*Integrity*
B268	*Crane*	B356	*Beachy Head*	B454	*Lariat*
B269	*Derg*	B357	*Berry Head*	B455	*St Giles*
B270	*Findhorn*	B358	*Rattray Head*	B456	*Weasel*
B271	*Helford*	B359	*Rame Head*	B457	*Rockcliffe* RCN
B272	*Odzani*	B361	*Kelantan*	B458	*Rockglen* RCN
B273	*Parrett*	B366	*Mull of Kintyre*	B459	*Rockwing* RCN
B274	*Pheasant*	B371	*Bonaventure*	B460	*Rockforest* RCN
B275	*Plym*	B376	*Adamant*	B461	*Rockland* RCN
B276	*Redpole*	B377	*Aorangi*	B462	*Rockmount* RCN
B277	*Usk*	B381	*Montclare*	B463	*Rockpigeon* RCN
B278	*Whimbrel*	B382	*Tyne*	B464	*Rockport* RCN
B279	*Woodcock*	B386	*Maidstone*	B466	*HDML 1183*
B280	*Amethyst*	B391	*Gryfevale*	B467	*HDML 1184*
B281	*Arbutus*	B392	*Stag Pool*	B468	*HDML 1185*
B282	*Black Swan*	B394	*SS Empire Clyde*	B469	*HDML 1186*
B283	*Enchantress*	B395	*Gerusalemme*	B470	*HDML 1187*
B284	*Erne*	B396	*Maunganui* RNZN	B471	*HDML 1188*
B285	*Hart*	B397	*SS Ophir*	B472	*HDML 1189*

B473	*HDML 1190*	B542	*SS Kistna*	B616	*Strathadam* RCN
B474	*HDML 1191*	B543	*SS Kola*	B617	*Sussexvale* RCN
B475	*HDML 1192*	B544	*SS Pacheco*	B618	*Swansea* RCN
B476	*HDML 1193*	B545	*SS Prince De Liege*	B619	*Veryan Bay*
B477	*HDML 1194*	B546	*SS Prinses Maria*	B620	*Victoriaville* RCN
B478	*HDML 1400*	B547	*SS Robert Maersk*	B621	*Wentworth* RCN
B479	*HDML 1459*	B548	*Thyras*	B622	*Whitesand Bay*
B480	*HDML 1481*	B556	*Bacchus*	B623	*Antigonish* RCN
B481	*HDML 1482*	B557	*Bosphorus*	B624	*Beacon Hill* RCN
B482	*HDML 1483*	B558	*SS City of Dieppe*	B625	*Bentinck*
B483	*HDML 1489*	B559	*Fort Rosalie*	B626	*Cape Breton* RCN
B484	*HDML 1494*	B560	*Fort Sandusky*	B627	*Cap de la Madeleine* RCN
B496	*Lewes*	B561	*SS Fort Wayne*	B628	*Capilano* RCN
B501	*SS Carelia*	B562	*SS Jaarstroom*	B629	*Charlottetown* RCN
B502	*SS Darst Creek*	B563	*SS Marudu*	B630	*Cotton*
B503	*SS Empire Silver*	B564	*San Andres*	B631	*Dunver* RCN
B504	*SS Lomo Novio*	B565	*SS Slesvig*	B632	*Fitzroy*
B505	*SS Empire Crest*	B566	*Taluna*	B633	*Flamingo*
B506	*Aase Maersk*	B576	*SS Denbighshire*	B634	*Kirkland Lake* RCN
B507	*Arndale*	B577	*SS Fort Alabama*	B635	*La Hulloise* RCN
B508	*Broomdale*	B578	*Fort Constantine*	B636	*Levis* RCN
B509	*Brown Ranger*	B579	*Fort Dunvegan*	B637	*New Waterford* RCN
B510	*Cedardale*	B580	*SS Fort Edmondton*	B638	*Orkney* RCN
B511	*Dingledale*	B581	*SS Fort Kilmar*	B639	*Outremont* RCN
B512	*Eaglesdale*	B582	*SS Fort Providence*	B640	*Prince Rupert* RCN
B513	*Empire Herald*	B583	*SS Fort Wrangell*	B641	*Royal Mount* RCN
B514	*Empire Neptune*	B584	*SS Glenartney*	B642	*Springhill* RCN
B515	*Green Ranger*	B585	*SS Buffalo Park*	B643	*St Catherines* RCN
B516	*Olna*	B586	*Fort Beauharnois*	B644	*St John* RCN
B517	*Rapidol*	B587	*Fort Charlotte*	B645	*Stormont* RCN
B518	*San Adolfo*	B588	*Fort Duquesne*	B646	*St Stephen* RCN
B519	*San Amado*	B595	*Bentley*	B647	*Waskesiu* RCN
B520	*San Ambrosio*	B596	*Bigbury Bay*	B648	*Wild Goose*
B521	*Serbol*	B597	*Braithwaite*	B649	*Wren*
B522	*Wave Regent*	B598	*Buckingham* RCN	B650	*Cauvery*
B523	*Wave Emperor*	B599	*Cardigan Bay*	B651	*Godavari*
B524	*Wave Governor*	B600	*Carlplace* RCN	B652	*Hotham*
B525	*Wave King*	B601	*Carnarvon Bay*	B653	*Spragge*
B526	*Wave Monarch*	B602	*Cygnet*	B701	*Bulan*
B527	*SS Golden Meadow*	B603	*Fort Erie* RCN	B702	*St Margarets*
B528	*SS Iere*	B604	*Grou* RCN	B711	*Erin*
B529	*SS Seven Sisters*	B605	*Inch Arran* RCN	B712	*Eros*
B530	*Echodale*	B606	*Modeste*	B731	*Shillay*
B531	*SS Fort Colville*	B607	*Montreal* RCN	B732	*Trodday*
B532	*SS Fort Langley*	B608	*Port Colborne* RCN	B741	*Enticer*
B533	*Vacport*	B609	*Poundmaker* RCN	B742	*Envoy*
B536	*SS Corinda*	B610	*Prestonian* RCN	B743	*Growler*
B537	*SS Darvel*	B611	*Prince Robert* RCN	B744	*Mediator*
B538	*SS Gudrun Maersk*	B612	*Start Bay*	B745	*Reward*
B539	*SS Hermelin*	B613	*St Austell Bay*	B746	*Samson*
B540	*SS Heron*	B614	*St Brides Bay*	B801	*Rowena*
B541	*SS Kheti*	B615	*St Pierre* RCN	B802	*Seabear*

B803	*Thisbe*	**D12**	*Kempenfelt*	**D64**	*Cambrian*
		D13	*Napier* RAN	**D65**	*Caprice*
C Flag Superior		**D14**	*Nepal* RAN	**D67**	*Carron*
		D15	*Nizam* RAN	**D68**	*Carysfort*
C1	*Achilles* RNZN	**D16**	*Norman* RAN	**D69**	*Cavalier*
C2	*Leander* RNZN	**D17**	*Quadrant* RAN	**D70**	*Penn*
C3	*Hobart* RAN	**D18**	*Quality* RAN	**D71**	*Cassandra*
C30	*Australia* RAN	**D19**	*Queenborough* RAN	**D72**	*Cavendish*
C34	*Shropshire* RAN	**D20**	*Quiberon* RAN	**D73**	*Armada*
C39	*Tromp* RNLN	**D21**	*Quickmatch* RAN	**D75**	*Trafalgar*
C44	*Adelaide* RAN	**D22**	*Quilliam*	**D76**	*Alconquin* RCN
C59	*Heemskerck* RNLN	**D23**	*Ulster*	**D77**	*Haida* RCN
C61	*Westralia* RAN	**D24**	*Ulysses*	**D78**	*Huron* RCN
C76	*Kanimbla* RAN	**D25**	*Undaunted*	**D79**	*Iroquois* RCN
C77	*Manoora* RAN	**D26**	*Undine*	**D80**	*Micmac* RCN
C161	*Argonaut*	**D27**	*Urania*	**D81**	*Sioux* RCN
C162	*Belfast*	**D28**	*Urchin*	**D82**	*Hogue*
C163	*Bermuda*	**D29**	*Ursa*	**D84**	*Comet*
C164	*Black Prince* RNZN	**D30**	*Wager*	**D85**	*Comus*
C165	*Ceylon*	**D31**	*Wakeful*	**D86**	*Consort*
C166	*Cleopatra*	**D32**	*Wessex*	**D87**	*Constance*
C167	*Euryalus*	**D33**	*Whelp*	**D88**	*Contest*
C168	*Gambia*	**D34**	*Whirlwind*	**D89**	*Concord* (as *Corso*)
C169	*Glasgow*	**D35**	*Wizard*	**D90**	*Cossack*
C170	*Jamaica*	**D36**	*Wrangler*	**D91**	*Finisterre*
C171	*Liverpool*	**D37**	*Racehorse*	**D92**	*Gravelines*
C172	*Newfoundland*	**D38**	*Raider*	**D93**	*Lagos*
C173	*Phoebe*	**D39**	*Rapid*		
C174	*Sussex*	**D40**	*Redoubt*	***M Flag Superior***	
C175	*Uganda*	**D41**	*Relentless*		
C176	*Royalist*	**D42**	*Rocket*	**M1**	*Ariadne*
C177	*Cumberland*	**D43**	*Roebuck*	**M2**	*Apollo*
C178	*London*	**D44**	*Rotherham*	**M3**	*Manxman*
C179	*Newcastle*	**D45**	*Teazer*	**M150**	*Moresby* RAN
C180	*Nigeria*	**D46**	*Tenacious*		
C181	*Suffolk*	**D47**	*Termagant*	***R Flag Superior***	
C182	*Swiftsure*	**D48**	*Terpsichore*		
C183	*Mauritius*	**D49**	*Troubridge*	**R1**	*Formidable*
C184	*Ontario* RCN	**D50**	*Tumult*	**R2**	*Illustrious*
C185	*Superb*	**D51**	*Tuscan*	**R5**	*Implacable*
C186	*Devonshire*	**D52**	*Tyrian*	**R7**	*Indefatigable*
		D53	*Avondale*	**R8**	*Indomitable*
D Flag Superior		**D54**	*Blackmore*	**R23**	*Victorious*
		D55	*Brecon*	**R61**	*Colossus*
D4	*Stuart* RAN	**D56**	*Calpe*	**R62**	*Glory*
D5	*Arunta* RAN	**D57**	*Croome*	**R63**	*Venerable*
D6	*Vendetta* RAN	**D58**	*Eggesford*	**R64**	*Vengeance*
D7	*Van Galen* RAN	**D59**	*Farndale*	**R65**	*Ocean*
D8	*Tjerk Hiddes* RAN	**D60**	*Cockade*	**R108**	*Unicorn*
D9	*Bataan* RAN	**D61**	*Barfleur*	**R130**	*Charger*
D10	*Warramunga* RAN	**D62**	*Camperdown*	**R301**	*Activity*
D11	*Grenville*	**D63**	*Caesar*	**R302**	*Ameer*

R303	*Arbiter*	S3	*Terrapin*	S30	*Telemachus*
R304	*Atheling*	S4	*Thorough*	S31	*Tradewind*
R305	*Begum*	S5	*Thule*	S32	*Zwaardvisch* RNLN
R306	*Chaser*	S6	*Tiptoe*	S33	*O-19* RNLN
R307	*Emperor*	S7	*Trenchant*	S34	*Scythian*
R308	*Fencer*	S8	*Trump*	S35	*Sleuth*
R309	*Pursuer*	S9	*Porpoise*	S36	*Solent*
R310	*Rajah*	S10	*Seadog*	S37	*Taciturn*
R311	*Ruler*	S11	*Sea Scout*	S38	*Turpin*
R312	*Shah*	S12	*Selene*	S39	*Sidon*
R313	*Slinger*	S13	*Shakespeare*	S40	*Sea Nymph*
R314	*Speaker*	S14	*Supreme*	S41	*Stubborn*
R315	*Striker*	S15	*Thrasher*	S42	*Spearhead*
R316	*Thane*	S16	*Trident*	S43	*Scorcher*
R317	*Tracker*	S17	*Tudor*	S44	*Scotsman*
R318	*Trumpeter*	S18	*Virtue*	S45	*Tapir*
R319	*Vindex*	S19	*Voracious*	S46	*Taurus*
R320	*Queen*	S20	*Vox*	S47	*Totem*
R321	*Smiter*	S21	*Sirdar*	S48	*O-21* RNLN
R322	*Patroller*	S22	*Spark*	S49	*O-23* RNLN
R323	*Ranee*	S23	*Spirit*	S50	*O-24* RNLN
R324	*Reaper*	S24	*Spiteful*	S51	*Visigoth*
		S25	*Storm*		
S Flag Superior		S26	*Sturdy*		
		S27	*Stygian*		
S1	*Amazone* FR	S28	*Tantalus*		
S2	*Rorqual*	S29	*Tantivy*		

'A' Series Pendant Numbers

Having safely negotiated DNC4(A) and the BPF numbers we are now faced with the issue of 'A' flag superiors. Over the years there have been several images, of ships serving in the Pacific, displaying pendant numbers with an 'A' Flag Superior. These have included Escort Carriers, Sloops and Minesweepers but, to date no primary source for these has come to light.

DNC4(A) does have some entries for allied ships with an 'A' Flag Superior - these include Australian, Dutch Italian, Norwegian and French auxiliaries but, are unrelated to the following ships.

Royal Navy Escort Carriers were initially assigned, and displayed, pendant numbers with an 'R' Flag Superior (R301 - R319). Later on, several of the Escort Carriers were noted displaying 'A' series numbers (*Ruler* - A731; *Arbiter* - A387; *Slinger* - A452; *Striker* - A460; *Chaser* - A727). The Escort Carriers were employed as both ferry carriers (delivering crated aircraft to shore bases) and replenishment carriers (delivering replacement aircraft to the frontline carriers). Later on in the conflict, the ability to refuel the BPF had become so acute that some of the Escort Carriers, including *Atheling* and *Ruler*, were converted to Auxiliary Oilers. Could it be that this change of role precipitated a change of pendant? The changing requirements of the conflict and the fast pace of such redeployments could mean that such administrative changes, such as new numbers, could have been done locally, using numbers yet to be issued. The number assigned to *Arbiter* (A387) was assigned to IX211, but this was postwar. While this could account for the renumbering of the Escort Carriers, the following cannot.

RAN Bathurst class - 'A' series speculative table

B236	*Ballarat*	A110		B245	*Kalgoorlie*	A119
B237	*Bendigo*	A111		B246	*Launceston*	A120
B238	*Burnie*	A112		B247	*Lismore*	A121
B239	*Cairns*	A113		B248	*Maryborough*	A122
B240	*Cessnock*	A114		B249	*Pirie*	A123
B241	*Gawler*	A115		B250	*Tamworth*	A124
B242	*Geraldton*	A116		B251	*Toowoomba*	A125
B243	*Goulburn*	A117		B252	*Whyalla*	A126
B244	*Ipswich*	A118		B253	*Woollongong*	A127

Over the years, much correspondence has been received regarding a possible further series with 'A' Flag Superior applied to Royal Australian Navy Bathurst class minesweepers. Photographs of at least two ships have been seen (*Tamworth* - A124 and *Bendigo* - A111). There were eighteen ships deployed with the BPF, each being assigned 'B' Flag Superior numbers by DNC4(A). If these numbers are listed, in order, the 'A' numbers follow in a speculative sequence as below:

The above list shows a possible correlation between the two sequences but, other than two photographs there has been no further evidence to suggest the origin of the 'A' series numbers. Whereas the 'A' series relating to Escort Carriers could be attributed to a change of role, this doesn't seem to apply to the Bathurst class - most served as escorts during the fighting and reverted to minesweeping operations post-conflict. Although *Tamworth* operated in a training role towards the end of her career, the same cannot be said of *Bendigo*.

A scan of a further photograph was received which shows a Black Swan class sloop wearing pendant number A468. The image, we are told, shows an unidentified ship, as seen from HMS *Striker*.

What is certain is that there certainly was a separate series of numbers with an 'A' Flag Superior and, that it was widespread, having been noted on Escort Carriers, Sloops and Minesweepers. What has yet to be shown is the originator of these numbers. DNC 4(A) seems unlikely as copies are now available, as are subsequent updating documents in the form of Non-Registered Public Memoranda. Neither UK, nor Australian sources claim ownership. Neither have documents relating to such a number series been located in either nation's archives.

With no documentary evidence unearthed, other than a handful of photographs, and little chance of finding first hand accounts from those who were there, it may yet prove impossible to identify either the origins, or the extent of the elusive 'A' series. However, the RAN website, in its Ship History section, has recently listed four such numbers alongside Bathurst class ships (A111 - *Bendigo*; A116 - *Geraldton*; A117 *Goulburn* and A119 *Kalgoorlie*) - perhaps there is a chink of light at the end of the tunnel!

Chapter 4

Pendant Numbers by Ship Name

A

A5 (1904) A5, I15
A6 (1904) A6, I16
A7 (1905) A7, I17
A8 (1905) A8, I18
A9 (1905) A9, I19
A10 (1905) A10, I10
A11 (1905) A11, I01
A12 (1905) A12, I02
A13 (1905) A13, I03
Aachen (ex *4062*) (1945) L4062
Aachen (1986) L110
Aarla (1903) FY.001
Aase Maersk (1930) B506
Abadol (1899) Y7.172
Abbas (1911) Y3.224
Abbeville (ex *4041*) (1945) L4041
Abbeville (1984) L108
Abbeydale (1936) A109, X32
Abbotsham (1955) M2787
Abdiel (1915) F43, F49, F60, G07, H32
Abdiel (1940) I39, M38, M39, N39
Abdiel (1967) N21
Abeille IV (1940) W94
Abelard (Canc) P451
Abelia (1940) K184
Abercraig (1902) Y3.712, Y8.42
Abercrombie (1915) M00, M01
Abercrombie (1942) B98, F109
Aberdare (1918) J49, N49, T0N
Aberdeen (1936) L97
Aberdonian (1909) F74
Aberdovey (1963) Y10
Abereden (1917) Y3.2186
Aberford (1952) P3102
Aberfoyle (1912) T50, X78
Aberlour (1902) Y3.1200
Abiding Star (1917) FY284
Abingdon (1918) J23, N23, N9C

Abinger (1964) Y11
Aboukir (1900) N00
Aboukir (1906) Y2.190, Y3.1419
Abronia (1906) FY734
Abydos (1890) Y3.1009
Acacia (1915) M26, T00
Acacia (1940) T02
Acanthus (1941) K01
Acasta (1912) G40, H00, H59
Acasta (1929) H09
Acasta (Canc) P452
Accord (1957) A90
Ace (1945) P414
Achates (1912) H01, H02, H46
Achates (1929) H12
Achates (1945) P433
Acheron (1911) H00, H02, H05
Acheron (1930) H45
Acheron (1947) P411, S61, S11
Achievable (1927) FY902
Achilles (1905) 00, 24, N03
Achilles (1932) 70, C1, C70
Achilles (1968) F12
Achlibster (1906) Y3.1648
Achroite (1898) Y2.10, Y3.2218
Achroite (1934) FY914
Aconite (1941) K58
Acorn (1910) H02, H03, H64
Actaeon (1945) F07, U07
Active (1911) 01, A2, N06
Active (1929) H14
Active (1972) F171
Activity (1942) D94, R301, X38
Acute (1942) M106, J106
Ada (1906) Y3.1612
Adalia (1899) Y3.1596
Adam (1919) FY1618
Adamant (1911) P00, P37
Adamant (1940) A164, B376, F64, I64
Adamant (1992) A232
Adamton (1904) Y3.104

Adastral (1916) T95

Addington (1893) Y3.566

Adelaide ʀᴀɴ (1918) C44, I47

Adelaide ʀᴀɴ (1928) D47

Adele ʀᴀɴ (1915) FY89

Adelphi (1924) FY1692

Aden (1904) Y3.464

Adenwen (1912) Y2.186, Y3.1370

Adept (1941) W107

Adept (Canc) P412

Adept (1980) A224

Adherent (ex *Tenacity*) (1940) A256

Adherent (1941) W108

Admirable (Canc) P434

Admiral Cochrane (1917) Y3.1791

Admiral Cordington (1917) Y3.2158

Admiral Sir John Lawford (1930) FY533, 4.415

Adonis (1915) 4.375

Adoration (1912) 4.372

Adra (1916) Y3.1905

Adria ɪᴛ (1914) F141

Adrias ʀʜɴ (ex *Border*) (1942) L67

Adrias (ii) ʀʜɴ (ex *Tanatside*) (1942) L69

Adriatic (1904) Y3.526

Adriatic ʙɢ (1936) 4.410

Adur (1942) K296

Advantage (1942) B446, W133

Advent (1876) Y3.706

Adventure (1904) D10, P01, P64

Adventure (1924) M23, N23

Adversary (Canc) P457

Advice (1899) W24

Advice (1958) A89

Advisable (1930) FY1500

Aegialia ʀʜɴ (ex *Cambuslang*) (1942) FY584

Aeneas (1945) P427, S27

Aerolite (1880) N92

Aetos ʀʜɴ (1911) H89

Affleck (1943) K462

Affray (1945) P421, S20

Africa (1905) 02, 25, N07

Africa (Canc) D06

African Monarch (1898) Y3.771

African Prince (1903) Y3.1542

African Transport (1913) Y3.1003

Africana sᴀɴ (1930) T01, T501

Afridi (1907) D00, H40

Afridi (1937) F07, G07, L07

Agadir (1907) YA.13

Agamemnon (1906) 01, 03

Agamemnon (1929) M10

Agamemnon (Bldg) S99, S123

Agassiz ʀᴄɴ (1940) K129

Agate (1935) T87

Agate (Canc) P448

Agatha (1961) A116

Agberi (1905) Y2.57, Y2.133

Agedabia (ex *4085*) (1945) L4085

Agenoria (1901) Y3.1513

Aggressor (Canc) P446

Agheila (ex *4002*) (1945) L4002

Agheila (1987) L112

Agile (1958) A88

Agile (Canc) P443

Agincourt (1913) 04, 09, 53

Agincourt (1945) D86, I06

Agincourt (Bldg) S100, S125

Agnes (1903) Y3.1473

Agnes (1961) A121

Agnes Duncan (1912) Y3.1

Agnes Nutten (1915) 4.274

Agnes Wetherly (1917) 4.279

Agnes Wickford (1909) FY727

Agra ʀɪɴ (1942) T254

Ahmedabad ʀɪɴ (1943) T264

Aiglon (1907) FY1841

Aigwen (1910) Y2.199, Y3.9

Ailsa Craig (1906) Y3.2123

Ailsa Craig (1943) T377

Aimwell (1942) B447, W113

Aire (1886) Y3.584, Y8.16

Aire (1943) B289, K262

Airedale (1894) Y3.167

Airedale (1899) Y3.700

Airedale (1941) L07

Airedale (1961) A102

Airmyn (1903) Y3.51

Airsprite (1942) A115, X115

Aislaby (1891) Y3.636

Aisne (1945) D22, I22

Ajax (1912) 05, 40, 46

Ajax (1934) 22

Ajax (1962) F114

Akita (1939) FY610

Akranes (1929) FY513

Akyab (ex *Rampart*) (1945) L4037

Akyab (1984) L109

Alabama (1903) Y3.1064

Alacrity (1944) B291, F60, U60

Alacrity (1974) F174

Aladdin (Canc) P454

Alafoss (1929) FY715

Alagi ɪᴛ (1936) N58

Alamein (1945) D17, I17

Alaric (1946) P441, S41
Alarm (1910) H04, H05, H96
Alarm (1942) J140
Alaska (1918) Y3.2389
Alastor (1928) FY.002, 4.282
Alatrium (ex *Strathgyle*) (1907) Y3.716
Alaunia (1925) A117, B336, F17
Albacore (1906) D01, D76, P14
Albacore (1942) J101, M01
Albatross (1884) Y1.5, Y3.1696, Y6.9, Y9.29
Albatross (1898) D02, D32, D44
Albatross (1928) D22, I22
Albemarle (1901) 06, 07, N39
Alberni ʀᴄɴ (1940) K103
Albert Hulett sᴀɴ (1929) T41
Albiana (1905) Y3.1680
Albion (1898) N00, N48
Albion (1904) YA.9
Albion (1945) R07, D08
Albion (2001) L14
Albistan (1905) Y3.1146
Albrighton (1941) F112, L12
Albuera (1902) Y3.772
Albuera (Canc) I51
Albury (1918) J41, N41, T41, T9/
Alca (1927) M72
Alcantara (1914) M94
Alcantara (1939) F88
Alcaston (1953) M1102
Alcestis (Canc) P453
Alcide (1945) P415, S65, S15
Alcinous (1900) Y9.16
Alcmaria (1916) FY1525
Alconda (1906) Y3.1539
Alcor (1922) FY960
Aldenham (1941) L22
Alder (1909) Y3.569
Alder (1929) T84
Alder Lake ʀᴄɴ (1944) J480
Alderney (1945) P416, S16, S66
Alderney (1979) P278
Aldersdale (1936) X34
Aldgate (1934) Z68
Aldington (1955) M1171
Aldworth (1893) Y3.1188
Alecto (1911) J10, N01, N10, N35
Alert (1910) Y4.8
Alert (1945) F647, K647
Alert (1969) P252
Alesia (1897) Y3.1240
Aletes (1932) FY.045
Alexa (1872) Y3.1206

Alexander Wentzell (1899) Y3.1000
Alexander (1916) N9A, NN3
Alexander Scott (1917) FY515
Alexandra (1904) Y4.62
Alexandra (1906) Y3.1332
Alexandra (1907) YA.15
Alexandrite (1933) FY560
Alfalfa (1898) Y3.1223
Alfeios ʀʜɴ (1912) FY308
Alfie Cam ʀᴀɴ (1920) FY97
Alfredian (1913) 4.52
Alfriston (1953) M1103
Algerian (1924) Z268
Algeriana (1899) Y3.1373
Algerine (1941) J213
Algethi (1902) Y3.899
Algol (1916) Y3.1607
Algoma ʀᴄɴ (1940) K127
Algonquin ʀᴄɴ (1943) D76, D117, R17
Alice (1930) FY.003
Alice (1961) A113
Alice M. Craig (1900) Y3.34
Alicia (1903) Y3.1760
Alida (1915) Z152
Alisdair (1937) 4.384
Alisma (1940) K185
All Hallows (1914) 4.436
Allahabad ʀɪɴ (Canc) T317
Allanton (1901) Y3.1643
Allegiance (1943) A150, W50
Allen ᴜsɴ (1916) H(I)00, H(I)10
Allenwood ʀᴀɴ (1920) FY18
Alliance (1910) W77
Alliance (1945) P417, S17, S67
Allie (1919) Y3.922
Alligator (1940) W51
Alligator (ex *Charon*) (1940) A391, W109
Allington Castle (1944) F89, K689
Alma ʀɴʟɴ (1915) FY1747
Almandine (1932) FY645
Almanzora (1908) M(I)28, M(I)50, M(I)A0
Almerian (1897) Y3.1108
Almond (1940) T14
Almora (1899) Y3.1767
Alness (1964) Y12
Alnmouth (1964) Y13
Alnwick Castle (1944) F105, K405
Alouette (1894) N02, 54, Y4.5
Alouette (1939) FY101
Alresford (1919) J06, N06, T06, T92
Alsation (1913) M50, M(I)29, M(I)51
Alsation (1961) A106

Alsey (1932) M51

Alston (1903) Y3.1309

Alt (1911) Y3.2467

Altai (1902) Y3.264

Altair (1905) FY.029

Altham (1952) M2602

Alton (1896) Y3.1444

Alverton (1952) M1104

Alvis (1918) 4.118

Alynbank (1925) F84

Alysse ꜰʀ (ex *Alyssum*) (1941) K100

Alyssum (1915) T46

Alyssum (1941) K100

Amalia (1917) FY1502

Amatonga (1903) Y3.2185

Amaranthus (1940) K17

Amarapoora (1920) Y8.7

Amaryllis (1915) T02, T69

Amaryllis (Canc) K276

Amazon (1908) D01, D03, H37

Amazon (1926) D39, I39

Amazon (1971) F169

Amazone ꜰʀ (1931) S1

Amazone (1936) 4.93

Ambala ʀɪɴ (Canc) T320

Ambassador (1897) Y3.1959

Ambassador (1911) J109

Amber (1934) T88

Amberley Castle (1943) F286, K386

Amberton (1902) Y3.718

Ambient (1904) Y3.241

Ambition (1902) 4.434

Ambitious (1913) F169

Ambrose (1903) C1, M87, M(I)87

Ambrose Pare ꜰʀ (1906) FY346

Ambuscade (1913) H05, H54, H62

Ambuscade (1926) D38, I38

Ambuscade (1973) F172

Ambush (1945) P418, S18, S68

Ambush (2011) S21, S96, S120

Ameer (1942) D01, R302

American Transport (1911) Y3.1341

Amerton (1953) M1105

Amethyst (1903) P00, P02

Amethyst (1934) T12

Amethyst (1943) B280, F116, U16

Amherst (1935) A238

Amherst ʀᴄɴ (1940) K148

Amicus (1911) Y3.352

Amiens ꜰʀ (1919) U68

Ammen ᴜsɴ (1910) H(I)01, H(I)41

Amphion (1934) I29

Amphion (1944) P439, S43

Amphitrite (1898) D03, D52, P7C

Ampleforth (1914) Y3.479

Amplegarth (1910) Y3.1120

Ampulla (1913) 4.119

Amritsar ʀɪɴ (1941) P61, T261

Amroth Castle (1913) 4.120

Amsterdam (1894) M08, M(I)00, M(I)08

Amsterdam (1913) FY1739, FY1921

Amsterdam (1930) 4.413

Amvrakia ʀʜɴ (ex *Cambuslie*) (1942) FY710

Anchorite (1916) X01, X35

Anchorite (1946) P422, S22, S64

Anchusa (1917) T01

Anchusa (1941) K186

Ancient (1915) A374, W54

Andalnes (ex *4097*) (1945) L4097

Andalsnes (1981) L107

Andanes (1916) 4.151

Andelle (1922) F123

Andes (1913) M82, M(I)30, M(I)52, M(I)82

Andes (1939) F52

Andoni (1898) Y3.1015

Andradite (1934) FY559

Andrea Doria ɪᴛ (1916) B51

Andre et Louis ꜰʀ (1907) FY1798

Andre-Marce (1936) 4.223

Andree (1916) Y3.1929

Andrew (1946) P423, S23, S63

Andromache (1890) N03, N22

Andromache (Canc) P424

Andromeda (1967) F57

Andromede ꜰʀ (1917) T4A, T02

Andyk (ex *Amsterdam*) (1913) FY1921

Anenome (1915) M27, T01, T03

Anemone (1940) K48, M48

Angele-Marie ꜰʀ (1929) FY1708

Angle (1936) FY201

Angler (1897) D04, D36, P25

Anglesea (1914) Y3.1876

Anglesey (1978) P277

Anglia (1900) P75

Anglia (1913) 4.62

Anglier (1900) Y3.848

Anglo-Canadian (1901) Y3.1572

Anglo-Chilean (1916) Y3.1726

Anglo-Mexican (1908) Y3.2416

Anglo-Saxon (1902) Y3.2375

Angora (1911) D01, N04, N40

Anguilla (1943) K500

Ann Melville (1909) FY1945

Anna Marie (1930) FY.004

Annamite ꜰʀ (1939) U97	*Apollo* (1934) I63
Annan (1942) K297	*Apollo* (1943) M2, M01, N01, N65
Annan ʀᴄɴ (1943) K404	*Apollo* (1970) F70
Annapolis ʀᴄɴ (1918) I04	*Apostolis* ꜰʀ (ex *Hyacinth*) (1940) K84
Anna Sofie (1896) Y3.2049	*Appalachee* (1893) Y7.13
Anne (1911) Y3.1999	*Appenine* (1909) Y3.1553
Anne (1925) 4.286	*Appleby* (1965) A383, Y14
Anne-Gaston ꜰʀ (1937) 4.265	*Appledore* (1919) N7A
Annet (1943) A328, T341, DV2	*Appleleaf* (1916) A178, X01, X33, Y7.178
Annetta (1907) Y3.1632	*Appleleaf* (1955) A83
Anselma de Larringa (1898) Y3.1868	*Appleleaf* (1975) A79
Anson (1940) 79, B1, B79	*Appleton* (1952) M1106
Anson (Bldg) S98, S124	*Approach* (Canc) P435
Answer (Canc) P425	*Apsleyhall* (1911) Y3.548
Ant Cassar (1902) Y3.1459	*Apsleyhall* (ex *Newfield*) (1912) Y3.746
Antaeus (1906) Y3.568	*Aquamarine* (1927) 4.00
Antaeus (Canc) P429	*Aquarius* (1900) N06, N13
Antagonist (Canc) P428	*Aquila* (1907) Z223
Antar (1906) Y3.632	*Aquila* (1907) Y4.76
Antares (1942) J282	*Aquitania* (1913) F51, M(I)56
Antelope (1893) D25, N25	*Arab* (1901) D01, D05, D77, H08
Antelope (1929) H36	*Arab* (1936) FY202
Antelope (1972) F170	*Arabesque* (1918) 4.442
Antenor (1925) F21	*Arabier* (1911) Y3.902
Anthony (1929) H40	*Arabis* (1904) Y3.817
Antic (1943) A141, W141	*Arabis* (1916) Y3.1390
Anticosti ʀᴄɴ (1942) T274	*Arabis* (1915) T44
Antigone (1906) Y3.1822	*Arabis* (1940) K73
Antigonish ʀᴄɴ (1944) B623, F61, K661	*Arabis* ʀɴᴢɴ (1943) F85, K385
Antigua (1903) Y3.948	*Araby* (1904) Y3.1124
Antigua (1943) K501	*Aracari* (1908) Y7.2
Antinoe (1907) Y3.670	*Arachne* (1912) Y3.1504
Antinous (1907) Y3.1017	*Arakan* (1977) L4003
Antioch II (1918) FY1746	*Arakan* (ex *4164*) (1945) L4164
Antiope (ex *Cragside*) (1904) Y3.565	*Aral* (1891) Y7.190
Antoine (1930) X72	*Ararat* ʀᴀɴ (1943) K34, M34
Antonio (ex *Lundy*) (1910) Y3.1446	*Aras* (1893) Y7.28
Antrim (1903) 07, 09, N58	*Arawa* (1939) F12
Antrim (1967) D18	*Arbiter* (1943) D31, R303
Antwerp (1919) 4.209	*Arbutus* (1917) T94
Antwerp (ex *4074*) (1945) L4074	*Arbutus* (1940) K86, M86
Antwerp (1981) L106	*Arbutus* ʀɴᴢɴ (1944) B281, F103, K403
Anzac (1917) D07, F61, G50, G60, G70, H3A	*Arca* (1912) Y7.230
Anzac (Canc) P431	*Arcadian* (Canc) P436
Anzac ʀᴀɴ (1948) D59	*Arcady* (1907) FY598, FY1598
Anzio (1945) L101, L3003	*Archbank* (1905) Y3.1196
Aorangi (1924) B377, F41	*Archer* (1911) H06, H06, H10, H29
Aparima (1902) Y3.1907	*Archer* (1939) D78, X65
Aphis (1915) P03, P96, T57	*Archer* (1985) P264
Aphrodite (Canc) P432	*Arctic Explorer* (1936) A401, FY162
Apollo (1891) N05, N36	*Arctic Hunter* (1929) FY1614
Apollo (1906) Y3.812	*Arctic Pioneer* (1937) FY164

Arctic Prince (1915) FY67

Arctic Ranger (1937) FY186

Arcturus (1942) J283

Ard Patrick (1918) T95

Ard Patrick (ex *Lamont*) (1939) 4.420

Ardandearg (1895) Y3.238

Ardenhall (1912) Y3.254

Ardennes (ex 4073) (1945) L4073

Ardennes (1976) L4001

Ardent (1913) H78

Ardent (1929) H41

Ardent (1975) F184

Ardent (Canc) P437

Ardgair (1913) Y3.1891

Ardgarry (1914) Y3.721

Ardgartan (1918) Y3.2319

Ardgarth (1913) Y3.603, Y8.53

Ardgay (1918) Y3.2403

Ardgirvan (1918) Y3.2418

Ardgour (1914) Y3.717

Ardgowan (1918) Y3.2423

Ardgrange (1916) Y3.1521

Ardgroom (1918) Y3.2478

Ardgryfe (1909) Y3.1622

Ardoyne (1912) Y3.657

Ardrossan (1941) J131

Arendal RNoN (ex *Badsworth*) (1941) L03

Arethusa (1913) 3C

Arethusa (1934) 26, C26

Arethusa (1963) F38

Arethusa II (1906) Y4.52

Arezzo (1986) L111

Arezzo (ex 4128) (1945) L4128

Argo (1895) Y3.958

Argo (1900) N08, N13

Argo FR (1938) FY1867

Argon (ex Argus) (1904) C75

Argonaut (1898) P04, P78

Argonaut (1941) 61, C61, C161

Argonaut (1966) F56

Argosy (Canc) P438

Argus (1883) Y3.35

Argus (1904) Y3.2349

Argus (1904) C75

Argus (1917) 49, D49, I49, N96

Argus (1980) A135

Argyll (1892) Y3.1141

Argyll (1904) 80

Argyll (1989) F231

Ariadne (1898) P69

Ariadne (1943) M1, M65, N65

Ariadne (1971) F72

Ariadne Alexandra (1893) Y3.541

Ariadne Christine (1910) Y3.490, Y8.92

Ariel (1902) Y3.955

Ariel (1911) F92, H07, H11, H37

Aries (1942) J284

Ariguani (1926) F105

Aristea SAN (1935) T18, T518

Ariosto (1910) Y3.837

Aristocrat (1935) 4.200, R200

Ark Royal (1914) N07, N80

Ark Royal (1950) R09

Ark Royal (1985) R07

Arkansas USN (1911) 1A

Arkleside (1914) Y3.486

Arkwright (1930) FY653

Arlanza (1912) M93, M(I)31, M(I)53, M(I)93

Arleia (1915) Y3.2162, Y8.81

Arley (1914) FY620

Arlingham (1953) M2603

Armada (1943) D14, D73, R14

Armadale Castle (1903) M63, M(I)32, M(I)54, M(I)63

Armana (1930) FY1809

Armentieres RCN (1918) J29, N29

Armeria (1941) K187

Armidale RAN (1942) J240

Armourer (1888) Y8.76

Arndale (1937) A133, B507, X33

Arnewood (1916) Y3.1323

Arno (1894) Y2.42, Y6.8, Y8.67

Arno (1914) D06, D62, D6A

Arnold Bennett (1930) FY1939

Arnprior RCN (1944) K494, K398

Aro (1898) Y8.125, Y8.126

Aroha RNZN (1942) T396

Aroostock USN (1907) R(I)07

Arpha (1901) 4.16

Arran (1940) T06

Arranmore (1879) Y3.571

Arras FR (1917) U02

Arrest (ex *Buzzard*) (1898) Z246

Arrival (1904) Y2.14, Y8.37

Arrochar (1981) A382

Arrogant (1896) N08, P42

Arrogant (Canc) D14

Arromanches (ex *4086*) (1945) L4086

Arromanches (1981) L105

Arrow (1929) H42

Arrow (1974) F173

Arrowhead (1940) K145

Arsenal (1933) FY140

Artegal (1918) FY1855

Artemis (1946) P449, S49, S72
Artful (1947) P456, S76, S96
Artful (2014) S22, S95, S121
Arthur Cavanagh (1918) FY566
Artifex (1924) A118, B301, F28
Artificer (1907) Y3.1056
Artist (1909) Y3.1407
Artois (1913) M(I)33, M(I)55
Arum sᴀɴ (1926) T10, T510
Arun (1903) D07, D11, N04
Arun (1985) M2014
Arunta ʀᴄɴ (1940) D5, D130, I30
Arvida ʀᴄɴ (1940) K113
Arvonian (1905) Y3.538
Ary (1904) 4.48
Asbestos ʀᴄɴ (1943) K358
Ascania (1939) F68
Ascension (1943) K502
Ascona (1930) FY949
Ascot (1902) Y3.1517
Ascot (1916) T16
Asgard (Canc) P458
Ash (1939) T39
Ash Lake ʀᴄɴ (Canc) J481
Ashanti (1937) D151, F51, G51, L51
Ashanti (1959) F117
Ashcott (1965) Y16
Asheldham (1952) M2604
Ashleaf (1916) Y7.156
Ashtabula (1907) Y7.24
Ashton (1884) Y3.1855
Ashton (1901) Y3.1895
Ashton (1956) M1198
Ashtree (1909) Y3.148
Asie (1914) FY370
Aspenleaf (ex *Saxol*) (1899) Y7.170
Asperity (Canc) P444
Asphodel (1915) T04, T70
Asphodel (1940) K56, M56
Aspirant (1942) W134
Aspis ʀʜɴ (1907) L77
Assam ʀɪɴ (1943) F106, K306
Assam ʀɪɴ (Canc) J322
Assidious (1943) A142, W142
Assiniboine ʀᴄɴ (1931) I18, D18
Assistance (1900) 8C, C2
Assistance (1944) B302, F173
Assurance (1940) W59
Assurance (Canc) P462
Astarte (Canc) P461
Aster (1915) M28, T02
Aster (1941) K188

Asteria (1891) Y4.29
Aston Villa (1937) FY261
Astoria (1903) Y3.1140
Astral (1930) 4.147
Astraea (1898) Y3.564
Astrakhan (1892) Y7.29
Astros (1917) Z130
Asturian (1890) Y8.83
Asturias (1939) F71
Astute (1945) P447, S47
Astute (2007) S20, S94, S119
Asuncion de Larrinaga (1902) Y3.815
Atalanta (1906) T143
Atalanta III (1907) W00
Athabaskan ʀᴄɴ (1941) G07
Athabaskan (II) ʀᴄɴ (1946) R79
Atheling (1942) D51, R304
Athelny (....) W189
Athene (1940) D25
Athene (....) A427
Athenian (1919) FY757, Y7.1
Athenic (1906) Y3.522
Atherstone (1913) Y3.624
Atherstone (1916) T09
Atherstone (1939) F05, L05
Atherstone (1986) M38
Athlete (1943) W150
Atholl (1901) Y3.2407
Atholl ʀᴄɴ (1943) K15
Atlantic (1904) Y3.1778
Atlantic City (1912) Y3.516
Atlantis (Canc) P442
Atlas (1904) Y3.842
Atlas (1909) A278, B421, W41
Atmah (1898) 4.224
Atmosphere (1928) FY789
Atoliu (....) W188
Atreus (1911) M44
Atropo ɪᴛ (1938) N31
Attack (1911) H08, H14, H86
Attacker (1941) D02
Attacker (1944) L102, L3010
Attacker (1983) P281
Attendant (1913) N97, X02, X15, Y7.101
Attentif ꜰʀ (1939) W68
Attentive (1904) P03, P06, T06
Aubretia (1940) K96, M96
Auckland (1938) L61, U61
Auckland Castle (1883) Y3.957
Audacious (1912) 54
Audacious (1946) D29
Audacious (2017) S97, S112

Audacity (1939) D10

Audemer (1945) L4061

Audemer (1987) L113

Audrey (1961) A117

Auldmiur (1903) Y3.2308

Aurania (1924) F28

Aureole (1894) Y7.19

Auricula (1901) Y3.2157

Auricula (1917) T78

Auricula (1940) K12, M12

Auricula (1979) A285

Auriga (1945) P419, S09, S69

Aurilia (1914) FY931

Aurochs (1945) P426, S26, S62

Aurora (1913) 08, C1

Aurora (1936) 12, C12

Aurora (1962) F10

Ausonia (1921) A153, F53

Austere (Canc) P445

Australia ʀᴀɴ (1911) 09, 81, C6

Australia (1912) Y3.1014

Australia ʀᴀɴ (1927) C30, D84, I84

Australian Transport (1911) Y3.2240

Australier (1906) Y3.1457

Australford (ex *Strathavon*) (1907) Y3.200

Australplain (ex *Ardanmhor*) (1907) Y3.767

Australstream (ex *Daltonhall*) (1899) Y3.839

Austriana (1901) Y3.161

Author (ex *St Egbert*) (1914) Y3.1562

Autocrat (1915) W01

Avalanche (1916) FY1895

Avalon (1915) 4.375

Avanturine (1930) FY1886

Avanturine (1934) FY249

Aveley (1953) M2002

Avenger (1908) M75, M(I)75

Avenger (1940) D14

Avenger (1945) L103

Avenger (1975) F185

Aviator (1907) Y4.81

Aviemore (1902) Y3.1718

Avoca (1907) M(I)57, M(I)79

Avocet ᴜsɴ (1918) T4A

Avola (1913) FY1730

Avon (1896) D02, D08, D45

Avon (1907) 4.177

Avon (1943) B266, K97

Avon Stream (1915) FY1529

Avon Vale (1940) B221, D53, F206, L06

Avon Water (1930) Z119

Avondee (1918) 4.432

Avontown (1899) Y3.620

Awake (Canc) P459

Awatere ʀɴᴢɴ (1942) T397

Awe (1943) K526

Axford (1954) P3103

Axminster (1881) Y3.1215

Aylmer (1943) K463

Aylwin ᴜsɴ (1912) H(I)18

Ayr (1894) Y3.583

Ayrshire (1938) FY225

Aysgarth (1896) Y3.101

Aysgarth Force (1912) Y3.1886

Aywood (....) W186

Azalea (1915) T07, T32

Azalea (1940) K25, M25

Aztec (Canc) P455

Azur (1929) 4.92

B

B.T.B. (1911) FY1514

B1 (1904) B1, I21

B1 ʀɴᴏɴ (1922) P12

B2 (1905) B2, I22

B3 (1905) B3, I23

B4 (1905) B4, I24

B5 (1905) B5, I25

B6 (1905) B6, I26

B7 (1905) B7, I27

B8 (1906) B8, I28

B9 (1906) B9, I29

B10 (1906) B10, I20

B11 (1906) B11, I00

Babiana sᴀɴ (1935) T20, T520

Bacchante (1901) N09, N39

Bacchante (1968) F69

Bacchus (1915) P66, X22

Bacchus (1936) A103, B556, X03

Bacchus (1962) A404

Bachaquero (1937) F110

Baddeck ʀᴄɴ (1940) K147

Badger (1911) H09, H15, H52, H91

Badinage (1916) FY824

Badminton (1918) Y3.1170

Badminton (1918) TN1, T8N

Badminton (1954) M1149

Badora ʀɪɴ (1914) FY.079

Badsworth (1941) L03

Baffin ʀᴄɴ (1942) T275

Bagdale (1904) Y3.464

Bagshot (1918) J57, N57, T15, T57

Bahadur (1907) Y3.2336

Bahamas (1943) K503
Bahawalpur RPN (1942) P149
Bakara (1913) Y3.1429
Baku Standard (1893) Y7.33
Balakani (1899) Y7.44
Balboa (1891) Y3.778
Balch USN (1913) H(I)02
Baldersby (1913) Y3.701
Baldur (1937) F111
Balfour (1943) K464
Balgray (1903) Y3.986
Ballarat RAN (1940) B236, J184, M184
Ballinderry (1942) F155, K255
Ballogie (1879) Y3.1578
Balmain RAN (Canc) J467
Balmoral (1900) 4.241
Balmoral (1916) FY1895
Balsam (1942) K72
Balta (1940) T50
Baltavia (1924) PT1.5
Balteako (1920) Y5.6
Baltimore USN (1888) R(I)01
Baltonia (1925) Y5.1
Baluchistan RIN/RPN (1942) J182, M182
Balvenie (1911) Y3.353
Bamborough Castle (1944) F12, K412
Bampton (1910) Y3.455
Bamse (1875) Y3.1961
Banbury (1917) T34
Banchory (1914) Y3.473
Banchory (1918) NC0
Bandelero (1935) FY188, FY788
Bandit (1938) W69
Banff (1930) Y43
Bangarth (1906) Y3.60, Y8.46
Bangor (1940) J00, N00
Bangor (1999) M109
Bankdale (1907) Y3.2477
Bankville (1904) Z252
Bann (1942) K256
Bannock (....) W168
Bannu RIN (Canc) T331
Banshee (1917) FY1600
Baralong (1901) Y9.5
Barbados (1943) K504
Barbain (1940) B416, P201, Z01
Barbara (1897) Y3.740
Barbara (1963) A234
Barbara Robb (1930) Z155
Barbarian (1937) Z18
Barbary (1901) Y3.1361
Barbastel (1945) P276, Z276

Barbecue (1944) P214, Z286
Barberry (1943) P257, Z257
Barbette (i) (1937) Z29
Barbette (ii) (1943) P242, Z242
Barbican (1938) P243, Z43
Barbour (1941) P269, Z169
Barbourne (1942) P270, Z170
Barbrake (1942) P273, Z173
Barbridge (1941) P222, Z222
Barbrook (1938) P203, Z03
Barcarole (1945) P287, Z287
Barcastle (1938) P209, Z09
Barcliff (1940) P207, Z70
Barclose (1941) P274, Z174
Barcock (1941) P277, Z177
Barcombe (1938) P16, Z16
Barconia (Canc) Z214
Barcoo RAN (1943) F175, K375
Barcote (1940) P252, Z52
Barcroft (1938) P212, Z22
Barcross (1941) P285, Z185
Bardell (1942) P295, Z195
Bardolf (1942) P271, Z171
Bardsey (1943) A330, T273, DV3
Bareilly RIN (Canc) T319
Barfair (1938) Z31
Barfield (1938) P244, Z42
Barflake (1942) Z184
Barfleur (1943) D61, D80, R80
Barfoam (1941) P282, Z182
Barfoil (1942) P294, Z194
Barfoot (1942) P202, Z202
Barford (1941) P299, Z209
Barfoss (1942) P200, Z200
Barfount (1942) P290, Z190
Bargany (1911) Y3.38
Barglow (1942) P216, Z205
Barham (1914) 04, 10, 34, 97, I04
Barhill (1942) P204, Z225
Barholm (1942) P211, Z211
Barilla (1943) P217, Z17
Barisal RIN (Canc) T270
Baritone (1945) P251, Z271
Barking (1941) P281, Z181
Barkis (1945) P227, Z277
Barkol (1898) X04
Barlake (1940) P239, Z39
Barlane (1938) P248, Z48
Barlby (1895) Y3.804
Barle (1942) B267, K298
Barleycorn (1943) P218, Z256
Barlight (1938) Z57

Barlow (1938) P260, Z60

Barmill (1940) P267, Z67

Barmond (1942) P232, Z232

Barmoor (1909) Y3.164

Barmouth (1938) P219, Z77

Barnaby (1943) P237, Z237

Barnard (1942) P241, Z241

Barnard Castle (1944) K694

Barndale (1939) P215, Z92

Barneath (1942) P245, Z245

Barnehurst (1939) P238, Z84

Barness (Canc) Z250

Barnet (1919) Z100

Barnsness (1907) 4.443

Barnstone (1939) P297, Z37

Barnwell (1940) B417, P246, Z46

Baroda RIN (1941) T249

Baron (1944) P262, Z262

Baron Ailsa (1912) Y3.385

Baron Ardrossan (1905) Y3.1655 ,Y9.8

Baron Berwick (ex *Grelmay*) (1903) Y3.178

Baron Cathcart (1907) Y3.1801

Baron Cawdor (1905) Y3.1408

Baron Dalmeny (1900) Y3.1031

Baron Fairlie (1898) Y3.1413

Baron Garioch (1895) Y3.1068

Baron Herries (1907) Y1.8, Y3.105

Baron Inchcape (1917) Y3.2431

Baron Jedburgh (1912) Y3.1342

Baron Kelvin (1907) Y3.476

Baron Minto (1908) Y3.1402

Baron Napier (1909) Y3.2424

Baron Ogilvy (1909) Y3.1425

Baronia (1941) P247, Z87

Barova (1941) P234, Z94

Barq RIN (1942) M133

Barracuda RIN (1940) F164, F140

Barrage (1937) P254, Z54

Barranca (1938) P265, Z65

Barrhead (1940) P240, Z40

Barricade (1938) P296, Z83

Barrie RCN (1940) K138

Barrier (1938) P298, Z98

Barrington (1940) P259, Z59

Barrister (ex *St Hugo*) (1916) Y3.1153

Barrosa (1945) D68, I68

Barrowmore (1911) Y3.988

Barry (1907) Y4.28

Barrymore (194) P293, Z73

Barshaw (1910) Y3.1920

Barsing (1941) P275, Z75

Barsound (1941) P289, Z89

Barspear (1943) P224, Z224

Barstoke (1941) P292, Z32

Barthorpe (1940) B418, P235, Z95

Bartizan (1943) B419, P261, Z261

Barunga (1913) Y3.1428

Barwick (1919) W174

Barwind (1942) P258, Z58

Barwon RAN (1944) F406, K406

Basilisk (1910) D89, H33, H89, HC8

Basilisk (1930) H11

Bassano (1909) Y3.956

Basset (1935) T68

Basset (1963) A327

Bassingham (1952) M2605

Bastion (1945) L4040

Basuto (1932) Z106

Bat (1896) D09, D46, H87, P97

Bataan RAN (1944) D9, D191, I91

Bath (1918) I17

Bathurst RAN (1940) J158, M158

Batoum (1893) Y7.23

Batsford (1914) Y3.427

Battersol (1898) X05

Battleaxe (1945) D118, G18

Battleaxe (1977) F89

Battleford RCN (1941) K165

Battler (1942) D18

Battler (1945) L118, L3015

Bay (1939) T77

Bayano (1913) M78

Bayano (1917) M(I)20

Baycraig (ex *Craigina*) (1905) Y3.443

Bayfield (1941) J08, M108

Baykerran (ex *Kilkerran*) (1906) Y3.694

Bayleaf (1954) A79

Bayleaf (1981) A109

Bayleaf (1893) Y7.173

Bayntun (1942) K310

Bayol (1893) Y7.173

Bayonet (1938) Z05

Bazely (1942) K311

Beachampton (1953) M1107, P1007

Beachy Head (1944) B356, F02

Beacon Hill RCN (1943) B624, F407, K407

Beacon Light (1890) Y7.119

Beagle (1909) H24, HC5

Beagle (1930) H30

Beagle (1963) A327

Beagle (1967) A319, H319

Beale USN (1912) H(I)42

Bearn FR (1920) A426

Beas RIN (1958) F137

Beatrix Adriennes (....) 4.268
Beaufort (1919) T00
Beaufort (1941) B222, F14, L14
Beauharnois (1944) K540
Beaulieu (1963) A99
Beaulne Verneuil (1918) Z247
Beauly Firth (1944) B326, F187
Beaumaris (1940) J07, N07
Beaumaris Castle (1917) FY993
Beaver (1911) H07, H17, H20, H66, H77
Beaver (1982) F93
Bechuana (1894) Y3.2384
Beckford (1955) P3104
Beckenham (1901) Y3.2076
Bedale (1914) Y3.63
Bedale (1941) F126, L26
Beddgelert (1963) A100
Bedfordshire (1935) A402, FY141
Bedham (1953) M2606
Bedlington (1936) FY349
Bedouin (1937) F67, G67, L67
Bee (1915) P07, P99
Bee (1970) A216
Bee (Canc) T61
Beech (1929) T44
Beech Lake ʀᴄɴ (1945) J482
Beechleaf (1916) Y7.154
Beechtree (1912) Y3.207
Beechwood (1900) Y7.272
Beemah (1914) Y3.349
Begonia (1915) T33
Begonia (1918) Y3.2050
Begonia (1940) K66, M66
Begum (1942) D38, R305
Behest (1919) W174
Belfast (1938) 35, C35, C162
Belfast (Bldg) F90
Belford (1904) Y3.136
Belfort ꜰʀ (1919) U63
Belge (1914) Y3.664
Belgier (1914) Y3.925
Belgol (1917) A106, X06
Belgravian (1891) Y3.1312
Bellagio (1890) Y3.1548
Bellasco (1896) Y3.807
Bellbank (ex *Castle Bruce*) (1901) Y3.883
Bellechasse ʀᴄɴ (1941) J170
Belleisle (Canc) I88
Belle of England (1905) Y3.1587
Bellerby (1898) Y3.1136
Bellerophon (1907) 11, 63, 72
Bellerophon (1945) 20

Belleville ʀᴄɴ (1944) K332
Bellona (1909) 12, 87, 1C
Bellona (1942) 63, C63
Bellucia (1909) Y3.871
Bellview (1894) Y3.215
Bellwort (1941) K114
Belmont (1918) H46
Belton (1955) M1199
Belvoir (1917) TC0
Belvoir (1941) F132, L32
Bembridge (1964) A101
Ben and Lucy (1910) FY1511
Ben Bheulah (1917) FY1681
Ben Bhrachie (1916) FY997
Ben Breac (1916) FY336, Y7.3
Ben Dearg (1920) FY690
Ben Earn (1916) FY999
Ben Glas (1917) FY808
Ben Gulvain (1914) FY1680
Ben Heilem (1919) FY765
Ben Idris (1931) FY1766
Ben Lomond (1906) Y3.1333, Y3.1781
Ben Lomond (1945) L105, L3102
Ben Meidie (1917) FY1818
Ben Nevis (1905) Y2.228, Y3.1649, Y8.94
Ben Nevis (1945) L104, L3101
Ben Rossal (1929) Z120
Ben Roy (1929) FY1557
Ben Tarbert (1912) Z212
Ben Torc (1915) FY807
Ben Urie (1916) FY1569
Ben Venue (1877) Y3.1160
Ben Vrackie (1905) Y3.823
Ben-My-Chree (1908) P49
Ben-My-Chree (1927) 4.412
Benachie (1919) FY749
Benalla ʀᴀɴ (1942) J323, M323
Benares ʀɪɴ (Canc) T318
Benbow (1913) 14, 51, 75
Benbrook (1914) Y3.274
Benbucula (1943) T379
Bencleuch (1901) Y3.904
Bend Or (1918) TN9
Bendew (1909) Y3.42
Bendigo ʀᴀɴ (1940) B237, J187, M187
Bengal (1905) FY1591
Bengal ʀɪɴ (1942) J243, M243
Bengali (1937) FY165
Benguela (1897) Y3.1987
Benham ᴜsɴ (1913) H(I)03, H(I)31
Benheather (1913) Y3.761
Benito (ex *Falls of Nith*) (1907) Y3.1866

Benjamin Coleman (1918) 4.444
Benlarig (1904) Y3.617
Benlawers (1900) Y3.903
Benmohr (ex *Dalblair*) (1906) Y3.578
Benoni san (1925) T54, T454
Bentinck (1943) B625, K314
Bentley (1943) B595, K465
Benvolio (1930) FY721
Benwood (1910) Y3.2395
Berar rin (1942) J287, P256, T256
Berberis (1916) T09, T60
Berberis (1928) P46, T46
Berbice (1909) YA.18
Berenga (1917) FY774
Bergamot (1941) K189
Bergen rnon (1907) FY932
Berkeley (1940) L17
Berkeley (1986) M40
Berkeley Castle (1943) F387, K387
Berkshire (1936) FY183
Bermagui ran (1912) FY81
Bermuda (1941) 52, C52, C163
Bern (1942) A331, P40, T294, DV4
Bernadette (1914) Z175
Bernard (1900) Y3.1509
Bernard Shaw (1929) FY200
Bernicia (1912) Y8.36
Berry (1942) K312
Berry Head (1944) A191, B357, F18
Bervie Braes (1917) FY847
Berwen (ex *Beethoven*) (1903) Y3.1150
Berwick (1902) 36, P08, P74
Berwick (1926) 65
Berwick (1959) F115
Berwindvale (1911) Y3.1334
Beryl (1935) T34
Beryl II ran (1914) FY71, Z101
Bessarabia (1899) Y3.1652
Bestwood (1913) Y3.21
Betony (1943) K274
Betty (1962) A323
Betty Bodie (1918) 4.365
Betty Inglis (1895) FY985
Betwa (1917) Y3.2060
Betwa rin (1958) F139
Bever san (1930) T49, T449
Beverley (1919) H64
Bevington (1953) M1108
BH7 (1969) P235
Bhadravati rin (1932) F104, FY.065
Biarritz (1915) N10, P48, 4.96
Bibury (1964) A103

Bicester (1917) TC1
Bicester (1941) B223, F134, L34
Bicester (1983) M36
Bickerton (1943) K466
Bickington (1953) M1109
Bideford (1910) Y3.368
Bideford (1931) L43, U43
Bigbury Bay (1944) B596, F06, K606
Biggal rnzn (1944) T404
Biglieri (....) FY1860
Bihar rin (1942) J247, M247
Bilbster (1908) Y3.784
Bildeston (1952) M1110
Billow (1928) FY836
Bilsdean (1917) FY503
Bilswood (1915) Y3.1452
Bingera ran (193) FY88
Birch (1939) P93, T93
Birch Lake rcn (Canc) J483
Birchgrove Park (1930) FY15
Birchleaf (1916) Y7.155
Birchol (1917) X07, A127
Birchwood (1910) Y3.156
Birdham (1955) M2785
Birdlip (1941) T218
Birdoswald (1892) Y3.1322
Birkenhead (1915) 07, 15, 9A
Birkhall (1900) Y3.1637
Birmingham (1913) 16, 28, 45
Birmingham (1936) 20, C19
Birmingham (1973) D86
Birtley (1906) Y3.145
Biruta (1889) Y3.1411
Bisham (1954) M2607
Bishopdale ran (1937) A128, A772, X66
Bishopsgate (1932) Z66
Bison (1902) Y2.1
Biter (1940) D97, X74
Biter (1985) P270
Bittern (1897) D03, D10, D5A
Bittern (1937) L07, U07
Bittersweet rcn (1940) K182
Bjarmia (1894) Y3.1232
Bjerk rnon (1912) FY1712
Blaawberg san (1936) T32, T472
Black Bear (1930) FY.046
Black Hawk usn (1913) R(I)09
Black Prince (1904) 65, 81
Black Prince rnzn (1942) C81, C164
Black Ranger (1940) A163, X48
Black Rover (1973) A273
Black Swan (1939) B282, F57, L57, U57

Blackbird (1943) M15, N15

Blackburn (1918) TN5, TN8

Blackburn (1946) A251, F113

Blackburn Rovers (1934) FY116

Blackcock (1886) P09, P9A

Blackfly (1937) FY117

Blackheath (1911) Y3.704

Blackmore (1941) D54, F143, L43

Blackmorevale (1917) TC2

Blackol (1906) X08

Blackpool (1940) J27, N27

Blackpool (1957) F77

Blackstone (1914) X01, X09

Blackthorn (1939) P100, T100

Blackwater (1918) T04

Blackwater (1984) M2008

Blackwell (1907) Y3.1362

Blackwood (1942) K313

Blackwood (1955) F78

Blade RNLN (1915) H97

Blagdon (1893) Y3.549

Blairhall (1899) Y3.975

Blairmore (1901) Y3.2140

Blairmore RCN (1942) J314

Blake (1889) C3

Blake (1945) 99, C99

Blakemoor (1901) Y3.86

Blakeney (1964) A104

Blanche (1909) 17, 84, 6C

Blanche (1930) H47

Blankney (1940) F130, L30

Blaxton (1955) M1132

Blazer (1888) W63

Blazer (1988) P279

Bleamoor (1902) Y3.1841

Blean (1942) L47

Bleasdale (1941) B226, F150, L50

Blencathra (1940) F24, L24

Blenheim (1890) C2, C4

Blenheim (1919) F221, 4.221

Bligh (1943) K467

Blighty (1919) FY505

Blinjoe RNLN (1940) F165

Bloemendahl (1917) FY1787

Bloemfontein SAN (1944) M439

Blomvlei SAN (1935) T17, T517

Blonde (1910) 18, 64, C7

Bloodhound (1938) Z20

Bloomfield (1899) Y7.39

Bloomfield (1906) Y3.11

Blue Haze (1919) FY1757

Blue Ranger (1941) A157, X57

Blue Rover (1969) A270

Bluebell (1915) M29, T03, T12

Bluebell (1940) K80, M80

Bluebird (1911) 4.130

Bluff SAN (1935) T21, T521

Blunham (1952) M2608

Blyskawica ORP (1936) H34

Blyth (1940) J15, M15, N15

Blyth (2000) M111

Boadicea (1908) 11, 19, 4C

Boadicea (1930) H65

Boardale (1937) X67

Boarhound (1936) FY315

Bobolink USN (1918) T5A

Bodenham (1952) M2609

Bogam RAN (Canc) K09

Boksburg SAN (1926) T46, T446

Bold (1942) W114

Bold Pathfinder (1951) P5720

Bold Pioneer (1951) P5701

Boldwell (1901) Y3.158

Bolebroke (1941) L65

Boliviana (1900) Y3.1784

Bolton Castle (1914) Y3.1750

Boltonhall (1900) Y3.786

Bombadier (1943) T304

Bombay RIN (1941) J249, M249

Bombo RAN (1930) FY12

Bombshell (1945) W182

Bona (1906) 4.452

Bonaventure (1892) N11, N41

Bonaventure (1939) 31

Bonaventure (1942) A139, B371, F139

Bonawe (1904) Y3.1213

Bondicar (1910) Y3.88

Bonetta (1907) D11, D15, D78

Bonito (1941) T231

Bonthorpe RAN (1917) FY85

Bootle (1918) T8C, T9C

Bootle (1941) J143

Borage (1941) K120

Borde (1921) FY758

Border (1942) L67

Border Cities RCN (1944) J344

Border Knight (1899) Y3.1536

Borderer (1904) Y3.686

Boreas (1930) H77

Boreham (1952) M2610

Borodino (1911) Y4.6

Bortind RNoN (1912) J394

Boscastle (1912) Y3.43

Boscawen (1909) Y3.318

Bosphorus (1934) B557

Bossington (1955) M1133

Boston (1940) J14, N14

Bostonian (1896) M(I)59, PA1

Botanic (1928) FY707

Botha (1914) D80, F50, F61, G60, G77, H5C

Botlea (1917) F113

Bottisham (1953) M2611

Boulston (1952) M1112

Bouncer (1886) N12, P44

Bournemouth Queen (1908) 4.270, 4.382

Bouvet I (1930) FY1693

Bouvet II (1930) FY1695

Bouvet III (1930) FY1698

Bouvet IV (1930) FY1701

Boveric (1906) Y3.782

Bovisand (1997) A191

Bowen ᴿᴬᴺ (1942) J285, M285

Bowmanville ᴿᶜᴺ (1944) K446, K493

Bownet (1939) P280, X90, Z90

Boxer (1894) D16, H4C

Boxer (1942) A394, F121

Boxer (1962) A326

Boxer (1981) F92

Boxleaf (1916) Y7.159

Boxol (1917) A107, X10

Boy John (1914) FY1961

Boy Pat (1915) FY.050

Boy Philip (1930) FY731

Boy Scout (1913) FY1865

Boyne (1910) Y3.97

Boyne (1904) D12, H23, N68

Boyne (1918) T29

Boynton (1892) Y3.19

Brabandier (1906) Y3.994

Brabant (1918) FY586

Bracondale (1903) Y3.1456

Brackendale (1916) FY1988

Bracondene (1916) FY1812

Braconmoor (1917) FY686

Bradfield (1919) N8A, T36

Bradford (1918) H72

Bradford City (1910) Y3.500

Bradman (1937) FY189

Braemar (1929) FY1641

Braes O'Mar (1915) 4.433

Braeside (1909) Y3.863, Y8.38

Bragadin ɪᴛ (1929) N49

Braid (1943) K263

Braithwaite (1943) B597, K468

Brajara ᴿᴬᴺ (1934) A773

Brakpan ˢᴬᴺ (1936) T42, T442

Brakvlei ˢᴬᴺ (1929) T23, T463

Bramble (1938) J11, N11

Bramble (ii) (1945) J273, M11

Brambleleaf (1916) X08, X50, Y7.182

Brambleleaf (1953) A81

Brambleleaf (1976) A81

Bramham (1891) Y3.996

Bramham (1942) L51

Bramley Moore (1916) W04

Branch (1908) FY291

Brandenburg (1910) Y3.2038

Brandon ᴿᶜᴺ (1941) K149

Branksome Chine (1899) Y3.192

Bransfield ᴿᴺᵒᴺ (1918) 4.81

Brantford ᴿᶜᴺ (1941) K218

Brantingham (1897) Y3.963

Brantingham (1953) M2612

Brave (1943) J305, M305

Brave (1983) F94

Brave Borderer (1958) P1011

Brave Swordsman (1958) P1012

Brayford (1954) P3105

Brazen (1896) D14, D47, G46, N11

Brazen (1930) H80, F91

Bream (1942) T306

Brearley (1953) M2003

Brecon (1942) D55, F176, L76

Brecon (1978) M29

Brecon Castle (1916) FY507

Breconshire (1939) PT1.3

Breda (1912) 4.84

Bredon (1941) T223

Breeze (1934) 4.272

Breeze ᴿᴺᶻᴺ (1933) T371

Brenchley (1954) M2004

Brenda (1881) Y3.2190

Brenda (1906) 4.405

Brenda (1963) A325

Brendon (1911) Y3.315

Brentham (1910) Y3.166

Brereton (1953) M1113

Bressay (1942) T214

Bretagne (1903) Y3.2025

Bretwalda (1919) Y3.242

Bretwalda (1925) FY266

Brevik (1932) FY1825

Breynton (1909) Y3.383

Briarleaf (1916) Y7.151

Bridget (1963) A322

Bridgewater (1928) L01, U01

Bridlington (1940) J65, N65

Bridport (1940) J50, N50

Bridport (1992) M105
Brierton (1911) Y3.110
Brigadier (1928) 4.249
Brigand (1937) A383, W83
Brigham (1953) M2613
Brighton (1878) Y4.27
Brighton (1903) Y3.736
Brighton (1918) I08
Brighton (1959) F106
Brighton Belle (1900) J117
Brighton Queen (1905) J28
Brightside (....) Y3.1
Brigitta (1894) Y3.1901
Brika (1908) Y3.42
Brilliant (1891) D15, N14, N16
Brilliant (1903) Y3.1162
Brilliant (1930) H84
Brilliant (1978) F90
Brimnes (1933) FY254
Brin ɪᴛ (1938) N96
Brinkburn (1909) Y3.53
Brinkley (1954) M2005
Brinmaric (1938) 4.411
Brinton (1952) M1114
Brisbane River (1914) Y3.1392
Brisk (1910) H18, H22, H65, H70
Brissenden (1942) B227, F79, L79
Bristol (1910) 20, 99
Bristol (1969) D23
Britannia (1885) Y3.377
Britannia (1896) N80
Britannia (1904) 21, 27, N40
Britannia (1953) A00
Britannic (1942) N15
British (1930) FY506
British Admiral (1917) Y7.215
British Earl (1901) Y7.306
British Empress (1917) Y7.211
British Ensign (1917) Y7.236
British Guiana (1936) FY271
British Honduras (1937) FY272
British Isles (1917) Y7.237
British Knight (ex *Danubian*) (1909) Y7.35
British Light (1917) X81, Y7.242
British Major (1913) Y7.53
British Marquis (1908) Y7.30
British Marshal (1912) Y7.49
British Monarch (1913) Y3.1529
British Peer (1913) Y7.120
British Princess (1917) Y7.206
British Sovereign (1917) Y7.219
British Sun (1909) Y7.123

British Transport (1910) Y3.445
British Viscount (ex *Rocklight*) (1888) Y7.81
Britomart (1938) J22, N22
Briton (1938) A196, W69
Brittany (1933) T197
Brixham (1885) Y3.2008, Y8.58
Brixham (1940) J105, M105
Broadland (1913) FY1973
Broadley (1953) M2006
Broadmayne (1888) Y7.37
Broadsword (1946) D31, G31
Broadsword (1976) F88
Broadwater (1919) H81
Broadway (1920) H90
Brock (1914) FY621
Brocklesby (1912) Y4.60
Brocklesby (1940) F142, L42
Brocklesby (1982) M33
Brockville ʀᴄɴ (1941) J270
Brodick (1964) A105
Brodliffe (1898) Y3.1482
Brodness (1894) Y3.1486
Broke (1914) D10, G74, H23, H98
Broke (1920) F64, I83, D83
Bronington (1953) M1115
Brontes (1934) FY118
Bronwen (1913) Y3.300
Brook (1906) Y3.84, Y3.94, Y8.57
Brookby (1905) Y3.190
Brookwood (1904) Y3.1037
Broomdale (1937) A168, B508, X68
Broome ʀᴀɴ (1941) J191
Broomfield (1902) Y3.710
Broomhill (1909) Y3.319, Y8.51
Broomlands (....) Y3.9
Broomley (1953) M2007
Broompark (1910) Y3.1950
Brora (1940) T99
Brown Ranger (1940) A169, B509, X69
Bruce (1910) 4.06
Bruce (1918) D81, F40, F48
Bruinvis ʀɴʟɴ (1929) FY1713
Bruiser (1942) F127
Bruiser (1945) L127, L3025
Bruray (1942) T236
Bruse (1911) Y3.2067
Brutus (1920) X96
Bryansford (1954) P3106
Bryher (1943) T350
Brynawel (ex *Jedford*) (1893) Y3.1857
Bryntawe (1917) Y3.2264
Bryony (1917) T96

Bryony (1941) K192
Buccaneer (1890) Y2.152, Y3.1683, Y8.74, Y8.111
Buccaneer (1937) W49
Buchan Ness (1945) A315, F36, L106
Buchans II (1918) FY335
Buckie Burn (1919) A389
Buckingham (1930) Z121
Buckingham ᴿᶜᴺ (1944) B598, K685
Buckleigh (1917) Y3.1995
Bucklesham (1952) M2614
Buctouche ᴿᶜᴺ (1940) K179
Buddleia (1943) K275
Bude (1940) J116
Buffalo (1916) X11, X42
Buffalo Park (1944) B585
Buffs (1917) Y3.2242
Bugloss (1943) K306
Bulan (1924) B701, Z254
Bulawayo (1937) A121, X21
Bulgarian (1904) Y3.1075
Bulldog (1909) H25, HC4, HC7
Bulldog (1930) H91
Bulldog (1967) A317, H317
Bullen (1943) K469
Bullfinch (1898) D15, D17, D48, H04, H05
Bullfinch (1940) A176, Z176
Bullfrog (1881) N44
Bullfrog (1915) X03, X12
Bullfrog (1944) A160, Z260
Bullhead (1940) A136, Z236
Bullmouth (1893) Y7.72
Bulolo (1938) F82
Bulrush (1943) K307
Bulwark (1905) 95
Bulwark (1945) D34, R08
Bulwark (2001) L15
Bulysses (1900) Y7.47
Bunbury ᴿᴬᴺ (1942) J241, M241
Bundaberg ᴿᴬᴺ (1941) J231, M231
Bungaree ᴿᴬᴺ (1937) M29
Bunting (1896) 4.55
Burbridge (1912) Y3.190
Burdekin ᴿᴬᴺ (1943) F376, K376
Burdock (1940) K126
Buresk (1914) Y3.450
Burevestnik (1901) Y3.1207
Burges (1943) K347
Burghead Bay (1945) F622, K622
Burgonet (1939) P233, Z33
Burke (1930) FY605
Burley (1954) M2008
Burlington (1921) F130

Burlington ᴿᶜᴺ (1940) J250
Burma (1911) N96, X14
Burnaston (1952) M1116
Burnby (1905) Y3.289
Burnet (1943) K348
Burnham (1919) H82
Burnhaven (1918) FY1607
Burnhope (1907) Y3.116
Burnhope (1917) Y3.1849
Burnie ᴿᴬᴺ (1940) B238, J198
Burnstone (ex *Kilsyth*) (1903) Y3.596
Burra (1941) T158
Burriana (1906) Y3.675, Y8.56
Burrows ᵁˢᴺ (1910) H(I)04, H(I)23
Burrsfield (1902) Y3.680
Burslem (1918) T68, T90
Burton (1941) L08
Burwell (1918) H94
Burza ᴼᴿᴾ (1929) H73
Busen 11 (1931) FY1842
Busen 3 (1924) FY1889
Busen 6 (1928) FY1920
Busen 7 (1926) FY1854
Bushnell ᵁˢᴺ (1915) C4
Bushwood (1930) F119
Bustler (1941) A240, W72
Bustler (1980) A225
Busy (1941) W160
Bute (1941) T168
Butetown (1905) Y3.1751
Butetown (ex *Eda*) (1905) Y3.360
Butetown (1907) Y3.298
Butetown (ex *Karanja*) (1907) Y3.230
Butser (1941) T219
Buttercup (1915) T14, T45
Buttercup (1941) K193
Buttermere (1939) A403, FY205
Buttington (1953) M1117
Buttress (1945) L4099
Buxton (1918) H96
Buzzard (1898) Z210
Byard (1943) K315
Bylands (1899) Y3.623
Byng (1920) FY1870
Byron (1943) K508
Bystander (1934) FY1686
Bywell (1913) Y3.67

C

C1 (1906) C1, I31

C2 (1906) C2, I32	*Cachalot* (1937) 83M, 83N, N83
C3 (1906) C3, I33	*Cachalot* (1957) S06
C4 (1906) C4, I34	*Cacouna* (1932) 4.73
C5 (1906) C5, I35	*Cadella* (1913) Z122
C6 (1906) C6, I36	*Cadillac* (1909) Y7.262
C7 (1907) C7, I37	*Cadiz* (1944) D79, R09
C8 (1907) C8, I38	*Cadmus* (1911) Y3.1274
C8 (1941) X79	*Cadmus* (1942) J230, M230
C9 (1907) C9, I39	*Cadorna* (1917) FY1651
C10 (1907) C10, I30	*Caduceus* (1904) 4.293
C12 (1907) C12, I42	*Caerleon* (1918) T43, T8/
C13 (1907) C13, I43	*Caesar* (1896) D27, P02, P10
C14 (1907) C14, I44	*Caesar* (1944) D63, R07, D07
C15 (1908) C15, I45	*Caeserea* (1910) M12, M(I)12
C16 (1908) C16, I46	*Cagni* ɪᴛ (1940) N36
C17 (1908) C17, I47	*Caicos* (1943) K505
C18 (1908) C18, I48	*Cailiff* ʀᴄɴ (1942) T276
C19 (1909) C19, I49	*Caio Duilio* ɪᴛ (1913) B50
C20 (1909) C20, I50	*Cairn* (1965) A126
C21 (1908) C21, I51	*Cairnavon* (1905) Y3.175
C22 (1908) C22, I52	*Cairndale* (1938) X36
C23 (1908) C23, I53	*Cairndhu* (1911) Y3.273, Y7.273
C24 (1908) C24, I54	*Cairnross* (1912) Y3.436
C25 (1909) C25, I55	*Cairns* ʀᴀɴ (1941) B239, J183
C26 (1909) C26, I56	*Cairnvalona* (1918) Y3.2417
C27 (1909) C27, I57	*Cairo* (1919) 97, D87, I87
C28 (1909) C28, I58	*Caistor Castle* (1944) F690, K690
C29 (1909) C29, I59	*Caithness* (1897) Y3.969
C30 (1909) C30, I60	*Calcaria* (1910) Y3.2102
C31 (1909) C31, I61	*Calcutta* (1907) Y3.311
C32 (1909) C32, I62	*Calcutta* (1918) 74, D82, I82
C33 (1910) C33, I63	*Calcutta* ʀɪɴ (1943) P339, T339
C34 (1910) C34, I64	*Calder* (1887) Y3.646, Y8.17
C35 (1909) C35, I65	*Calder* (1943) K349
C36 (1909) C36, I66	*Caldergrove* (1909) Y3.1344
C37 (1910) C37, I67	*Caldwell* (1919) I20
C38 (1910) C38, I68	*Caldwell* ᴜsɴ (1917) H(I)05
C.64 (1915) Y4.48	*Caldy* (1943) A332, DV5, T359
C.65 (1915) Y4.49	*Caledon* (1916) 22, 65, 69, D53, I53
C85 (1940) A124	*Calendula* (1940) K28
C112 (....) A358, X98	*Caleta* (1930) 4.155
C405 (....) W59	*Calgarian* (1914) M54, M(I)54, M(I)58
C614 (1943) A113, X114	*Calgary* ʀᴄɴ (1941) K231
C625 (1944) X05	*Caliban* (1919) Z131
C633 (1945) A102, X101	*Califol* (1916) X32
C641 (1945) X125	*California* (1923) F55
C642 (1946) A201, X126	*Calliope* (1900) Y3.1076, Y3.1297
C648 (1946) A370	*Calliope* (1914) 23, 76, 78
C668 (1945) A356	*Caloric* (1914) Y7.48
C677 (....) A371	*Calpe* (1941) D56, F171, L71
C. A. Jaques (1909) Y3.1358	*Calton* (1953) M1118
Cabuskenneth (1942) FY619	*Calvay* (1943) T383

Calvi (1930) FY673
Calvinia (1901) FY1850
Calypso (1917) 24, 82, D61, I61
Calyx (1904) M86
Cam (1943) K264
Camberford (1953) P3107
Camberley (1918) T7/, T/7
Camberwell (1903) Y3.1013
Cambria (1897) N66, P76
Cambrian (1916) 25, 30, A3
Cambrian (1924) Z102
Cambrian (1943) D64, D85, R85
Cambrian King (1898) Y3.808
Cambridgeshire (1935) FY142
Cambusdoon (1942) FY675
Cambuslang (1942) FY584
Cambuslie (1942) FY710
Camden (1911) Y3.2105
Camel (1914) W38
Cameleon (1910) H21, H24, H66
Camellia (ex *Tynehome*) (1913) Y3.441
Camellia (1940) K31
Camellia (1915) T15, T34
Camerata (1910) Y3.326, Y4.326
Cameron (1905) Y3.1164
Cameron (1919) I05
Cameron (1991) A72
Camillo (1908) Y7.7
Camito (1915) F77, M(I)21
Camlake (1901) Y3.992
Campania (1893) N15, P54, D48
Campanula (1915) T16, T48
Campanula (1940) K18, M18
Campaspe RAN (Canc) K24
Campbell (1918) D60, G76, I60
Campbeltown (1919) I42
Campbeltown (1987) F86
Campeador V (1938) FY.002
Camperdown (1944) D32, D62, R32
Campfield (1895) Y3.1730
Campina (1913) 4.153
Campion (1941) K108
Campobello RCN (1942) T278
Campus (1905) Y3.1186
Camrose RCN (1940) K154
Canada (1913) 01, 26, 28
Canadian Prince (1937) FY166
Canadian Transport (1910) Y3.1599
Canadier (1906) Y3.1731
Canandiagua USN (1901) R(I)04
Canara (1905) Y3.1579
Canastota (1907) Y3.1656

Canberra RAN (1927) D33, I33, I85
Candytuft (1917) T17
Candytuft (1940) K09, M09
Candytuft (1943) K382
Canganian (1900) Y3.1253
Canna (1940) T161
Canning (1896) N16, Y4.46
Cannon (1943) W158
Cannonicus USN (1899) R(I)03
Canopus (1897) N17, N29
Canso RCN (1941) J21, M21
Canterbury (1915) 27, 59, 0A
Canterbury (1929) 4.107
Canterbury RNZN (1969) F421
Canton (1938) F97
Cap d'Antifer FR (1920) FY340
Cap de la Madeleine RCN (1944) B627, K663
Cap des Palmes FN (1935) A430, F136
Cap Ferrat FR (1938) FY1797
Capable (1945) A508, W171
Capable (1981) A226
Capac (1893) Y3.1350
Cape Antibes (1903) Y3.546
Cape Argona (1936) FY190
Cape Barracouta (1930) FY579, 4.122
Cape Breton RCN (1942) B626, K350
Cape Chelyuskin (1936) FY119
Cape Cormorin (1936) FY143
Cape Mariato (1936) 4.172
Cape Melville (1929) FY651
Cape Nyemetski (1936) FY670
Cape Ortegal (1911) Y3.864
Cape Palliser (1937) FY256
Cape Passaro (1938) FY270
Cape Portland (1939) FY246
Cape Sable (1936) F112
Cape Siretoko (1939) FY263
Cape Trafalgar (1917) 4.190
Cape Transport (1910) Y3.1719
Cape Warwick (1937) A404, FY167
Cape Wrath (1945) A202, F49
Capel (1943) K470
Capelcastle (1917) Y3.2291
Capelcourt (ex *Hermia*) (1903) Y3.562
Capelhall (1901) Y3.1812
Capelmead (ex *Armora*) (1911) Y3.49
Capelpark (ex *Rio Tinto*) (1888) Y3.1764
Capetown (1919) 88, D88, I88
Capilano RCN (1944) B628, K409
Caprice (1943) D01, D65, R01
Capstone (1917) FY1555, 4.174
Captive (1923) W148

Caradoc (1916) 28, 55, A0, D60, I60
Caraquet ʀᴄɴ (1941) J38
Carbineer II (1915) 4.17
Carcass (1905) N18, N62
Cardiff (1898) Y3.968
Cardiff (1917) 29, 39, D58, I58
Cardiff (1974) D108
Cardiff (Bldg) F89
Cardiff Castle (1919) FY512
Cardiff Hall (1912) Y3.750
Cardigan (1917) Y3.203
Cardigan Bay (1944) B599, F630, K630
Cardigan Bay (2005) L3009
Cardinal ᴜsɴ (1918) T6A
Cardingham (1952) M2615
Careful (1945) A293, W172
Careful (1982) A227
Carelia (1938) Y7.51
Carelia (1938) B501
Carency (1916) FY295
Carhampton (1955) M1119
Caribbean (1890) M79
Carina (1899) FY.007
Carisbrook (1902) Y3.1126
Carisbrooke (1928) FY583
Carisbrooke Castle (1943) F379, K379
Carlaston (1901) Y3.106, Y8.114
Carlisle (1918) 41, D67, I67
Carlow Castle (1917) Y3.1501
Carlplace ʀᴄɴ (1944) B600, K664
Carmania (1905) M55, M(I)55, M(I)60
Carmania II (1907) N19, N1A
Carmelite (1892) Y3.1619
Carnactic ʀɪɴ (1942) M199
Carnalea (1913) Y3.644, Y8.10
Carnarvon (1903) 30, P80, P3A
Carnarvon Bay (1945) B601, F636, K636
Carnarvon Castle (1926) F25
Carnatic ʀɪɴ (1942) J199
Carnation (1915) T18, T36
Carnation (1940) K00, M00
Carol (1913) N28, N98, X15, X16
Caroline (1914) 30, 44, 87
Caroline ʀɴʟɴ (1930) FY1729
Caroline Moller (1919) W09
Caronia (1905) M53, M(I)53, M(I)61
Carperby (1895) Y3.1180
Carrigan Head (1901) Y9.14
Carrigan Head (1901) M(I)22
Carron (1909) M19, M(I)01, M(I)19
Carron (1944) D30, D67, R30
Carron (1983) M2004

Carronade (Canc) G82
Carronpark (1912) Y3.356
Carrowdore (1914) Y3.2136
Carstairs (1919) T08
Carthage (1931) F99
Cartmel (1907) W09
Cartmel (1967) A350
Carventum (1907) Y3.2401
Carysfort (1914) 22, 31, 88
Carysfort (1944) D25, D68, R25
Cassandra (1916) 04, 32, 3C
Cassandra (1943) D10, D71, R62
Cassin ᴜsɴ (1913) H(I)06, H(I)25
Castelnau ꜰʀ (1918) FY355
Castle Bay (1918) FY1522
Castle Eden (1914) Y3.626
Castleford (1897) Y3.223
Castlemaine ʀᴀɴ (1941) J244, M244
Castlemoor (1906) Y3.2312
Castlerock (1904) Z234
Castleton (1891) Y3.722
Castleton (1919) I23
Castleton (1957) M1207
Castor (1915) 20, 33, C4
Caswell (1917) FY500
Caterham (1919) T07, T80
Caterino (1909) Y3.284
Cathay (1925) F05
Catherine (1942) J12
Cato (1914) Y8.32
Cato (1942) J16
Catterick (1941) L81
Cattistock (1917) T07
Cattistock (1940) F135, L35
Cattistock (1981) M31
Caucasian (1899) Y7.61
Caulonia (1912) 4.163
Caunton (1953) M1120
Cautious (1940) A385, W73
Cauvery ʀɪɴ (1943) B650, F110, U10
Cava (1941) T145
Cavalcade (1905) FY1823
Cavalier (1944) D69, D73, R73
Cavendish (1944) D15, D72, R15
Cavina (1924) F33
Cawnpore ʀɪɴ (Canc) T346
Cawsand (1968) A351
Cawsand (1997) A192
Cawsand Bay (1945) F644, K644
Cayman (1943) K506
Cayo Bonito (ex *Caledonier*) (1901) Y3.1307
Cayrian (1911) FY791

Cayton Wyke (1932) FY191
Cayuga rcn (1945) D104, R04
Ceanothus (1917) T19
Ceanothus (1943) K360
Cecile Mapleson (1924) Z230
Cedar (1933) T01
Cedar Branch (1910) Y3.889
Cedar Lake rcn (1945) J484
Cedarberg san (1936) T31, T471
Cedardale (1939) A380, B510, X80
Cedartree (1913) Y3.105
Cedric (1903) M74, M(I)74
Cedric (1906) FY996
Celandine (1916) T20, T72
Celandine (1940) K75, M75
Celerol (1917) A116, X16
Celia (1906) Y3.1554
Celia (1940) T134
Celia (1965) A206
Celtic (1901) M69, M(I)69
Celtic Pride (1910) Y4.35
Centaur (1916) 10, 34, 36
Centaur (1924) Y8.9
Centaur (1945) D39, R06
Cento (1911) Y3.292
Central No1 (1910) W10
Central No2 (1912) W11
Centurion (1911) 21, 35, 83, F50, I50
Cerberus (1889) N63
Cerera (1898) Y3.1228
Ceres (1917) 36, 58, 66, D59, I59
Ceres fr (1938) P33
Cerisio (1915) FY524
Cessnock ran (1941) B240, J175, M175
Ceto (1935) 4.295
Cevic (1908) Y7.16
Ceylon (1899) N20, N64
Ceylon (1942) 30, C30, C165
Ceylonite (1918) FY1853
Chailey (1954) M2009
Chainshot (1946) A313, W185
Chakrata (1913) Y3.1853
Chalcedony (1928) 4.124
Chalister (1913) Y3.1586
Chalkis (1878) Y8.59
Challenger (1902) D33, P07, P81
Challenger (1931) A301, J98, N98
Challenger (1981) K07
Chambly rcn (1940) K116
Chameleon (1944) J387, M387
Chamois (1942) J28
Champagne (1895) M(I)88

Champion (1915) 25, 37, C8
Champion (1939) W35
Champlain rcn (1919) H24
Chance (1942) J340
Changuinola (1912) M85, M(I)35, M(I)63, M(I)85
Chanticleer (1942) U05
Chaplet (1944) D52, R52, R27
Charger (1944) L107, L3026
Charger (1941) D27, R130
Charger (1988) P292
Charing Cross (1892) Y3.648
Charity (1944) D29, R29
Charles Doran (1917) FY597
Charles Goodanew (1911) Y8.71
Charles Henri (1935) 4.267
Charles McIver (1936) 4.37
Charles Mcleod (1944) L3021
Charles Vaillant (1916) FY1804
Charleston (1908) Y3.317
Charlestown (1918) I21
Charlock rcn (1943) K395
Charlotte (1966) A210
Charlottetown rcn (1941) B629, K244
Charm (1902) D19, N22, N56
Charon (1940) W109
Charterhouse (1895) Y3.763
Charybdis (1893) D56, N21, P56
Charybdis (1940) 88, C88
Charybdis (1968) F75
Chaser (1942) D32, R306
Chaser (1945) L132, L3029
Chaser (1983) P282
Chasse Marie fr (1920) FY1793, Y7.7
Chasseur 5 fr (1943) A433
Chasseur 6 fr (1943) A432
Chassiron (1913) FY1857
Chatham (1911) 18, 37, 38
Chatham (1988) F87
Chatsgrove (1918) X85
Chattenden (1943) Y39
Chaudiere rcn (1936) H99
Chawton (1957) M1209
Cheam (1919) T60
Chebogue rcn (1943) K317
Chedabucto (1941) J168
Chediston (1953) M1121
Cheerful (1897) D49, P13
Cheerful (1944) J388, M88
Cheerly (1943) B448, W153
Chelford (1906) Y3.1770
Chelmer (1943) F221, K221
Chelmsford (1916) T21

Chelsea (1919) I35
Chelsham (1952) M2616
Chelston (1904) Y3.814
Cheltenham (1916) T54
Cheltonian (1911) Y3.1330
Cheniston (1912) Y3.433
Chepstow (1916) T19
Chequers (1944) D61, R61
Cherbourgeois III (1913) W99
Cherbourgeous IV (1930) W107
Cherry Lake (Canc) J485
Cherryleaf (1916) X17, X48, Y7.181
Cherryleaf (1953) A82
Cherryleaf (1962) A82
Cherwell (1903) D13, D17, N90
Cherwell (1918) T03
Cheshire (1904) Y3.868
Cheshire (1927) F18
Chester (1909) N65
Chester (1915) 39, 50, C9
Chester III (1909) N23
Chesterfield (1913) Y4.64, Y8.20
Chesterfield (1920) I28
Chestnut (1940) T110
Chevington (1912) Y3.2045
Cheviot (1891) Y8.63
Cheviot (1944) D90, R90
Cheviot Range (1914) Y3.1374
Chevreuil FFN (1939) U89
Chevron (1944) D51, R51
Cheyenne (1908) Y7.196
Chichester (1895) N24, N66
Chichester (1955) F59
Chicoutimi RCN (1940) K156
Chiddingfold (1941) F131, L31
Chiddingfold (1983) M37
Chieftain (1945) D36, R36
Chignecto RCN (1940) J160
Chilcompton (1953) M1122
Childers (1945) D91, R91
Chillingham (1952) M2617
Chilliwack RCN (1940) K131
Chiltern (1917) 4.125
Chilton (1957) M1215
Chimu (1900) Y3.1755
China (1896) YA.6
Chingford (1889) Y3.896
Chinkoa (1913) Y9.3
Chinthe (1932) FY353
Chipana (1907) Y3.1818
Chiswick (1896) Y3.1561
Chitral (1925) F57

Chittagong RIN (Canc) T265
Chittagong RIN/ RPN (1942) J155, M155
Chivalrous (1945) D21, R21
Chiverstone (1897) Y3.1263
Choice (1899) 4.428
Cholmley (1880) Y3.2290
Chorley (1914) Z153
Christania T Purdy (1917) FY899
Christine (1967) A217
Christopher (1912) G58, H25, H51
Chrysanthemum (1917) L31, T98
Chrysanthemum (1941) K195
Chrysolite (1916) FY1827
Chub (1909) N25, N67
Chulmleigh (1899) Y3.1691
Churchill (1919) I45
Churchill (1968) S46
Cicala (1915) P82, P4A, T71
Cicala (1970) A263
Cicero (1918) N79, T3N
Cicero (1943) F170
Cilicia (1907) Y3.245
Cilicia (1938) F54
Cilurnum (1902) Y3.1485
Circassia (1937) F91, D81, N26
Circe (1892) N80
Circe (1942) J214, M214
Citadel (1945) L4038
Citron (1911) FY1872
City of Belfast (1893) M15, M(I)02, M(I)15
City of Dieppe (1929) B558, PT1.8
City of Durban (1920) F114
City of Dunkirk (1912) Y3.1547
City of London (1907) M(I)42, M(I)64, M(I)69
City of Lucknow (1917) Y3.1070
City of Madrid (1901) Y3.1753
City of Oxford (1882) X17, X44, Y4.50
City of Paris (1920) B401
City of Rochester (1904) Y4.13
City of Rochester (1904) J92, N92
City of Swansea (1882) Y3.929
Clacton (1904) M30, T04
Clacton (1941) J151
Claesje RNLN (1933) FY1716
Clam (1893) Y7.58
Clan Alpine (1899) Y3.1299
Clan Chattan (1902) Y3.1992
Clan Colquhoun (1899) Y3.1567
Clan Forbes (1903) Y3.1400
Clan Graham (1907) Y3.1757
Clan Keith (ex *Etonian*) (1914) Y3.1052
Clan Kennedy (ex *Ardgarroch*) (1907) Y3.1460

Clan Macaulay (1899) Y3.1677
Clan Macbeth (1913) Y3.1647
Clan Macbride (1912) Y3.1352
Clan MacDonald (1897) Y3.1783
Clan MacDougall (1904) Y3.1541
Clan Macfadyen (1899) Y3.1273
Clan Macintosh (1905) Y3.908
Clan Mackay (1928) FY1960
Clan MacKellar (1912) Y3.1904
Clan Maclachlan (1900) Y3.1663
Clan MacMaster (1917) Y3.1985
Clan Macnab (1904) Y3.1695
Clan Macnaughton (1911) M81
Clan MacNiel (1903) Y3.951
Clan Macpherson (1905) Y3.1448
Clan Macrae (1912) Y8.101
Clan Matheson (1917) Y3.1805
Clan Murray (1897) Y3.970
Clan Robertson (1897) Y3.1664
Clan Sinclair (1907) Y3.1605
Clan Urquhart (1899) Y3.1740
Clandeboye (1913) Y2.41, Y3.641, Y8.15
Clara (1898) Y3.157
Clarbeston (1954) M1123
Clare (1920) I14
Clare (1967) A218
Clareisland (1915) Y3.1713
Claremorris (1917) Y3.2093
Claribelle (1918) FY1828
Clarinet (1911) Z132
Clarkia (1940) A426, K88
Claro (1900) Y3.1795
Classic (ex Magic) (1893) YA.14
Claudius Aulagnon (1903) Y3.1208
Claveresk (1907) Y3.1585
Claverton (1913) FY775
Claymont (ex Porthcawl) (1915) Y3.331
Claymore (Canc) G34
Clayoquot RCN (1940) J174
Clearfield (1908) Y7.36
Clearpool (1907) Y3.1254
Clearway (1906) Y3.1139
Clematis (1915) Y3.1977
Clematis (1915) T22, T35
Clematis (1940) K36, M36
Cleopatra (1915) 40, 88, 1A
Cleopatra (1940) 33, C33, C166
Cleopatra (1964) F28
Clermiston (1895) Y3.68, Y8.73
Cleveland (1940) F146, L46
Clevella (1930) FY678
Clifford (1904) Y4.40

Clifftower (1917) Y3.1699
Clifton (1915) FY898
Clifton Grove (1883) Y3.2260, Y8.115
Cliftondale (1901) Y3.1261
Cliftonhall (1907) Y3.112
Cliftonian (1911) Y3.779
Clinton (1942) J286
Clintonia (1907) Y3.1815
Clive RIN (1919) L79, U79
Clivegrove (1906) Y3.800
Clodmoor (1902) Y3.1069
Clonlee (1898) Y3.2184
Clonmel (1918) T72, T99
Clorinde (1931) FY1639
Clotilde (1913) FY534
Cloud (1918) FY03, Z08
Cloudburst (1926) FY702
Cloughstone (1907) 4.446
Clovelly (1972) A389
Clover (1941) K134
Cloverdale (1907) FY987
Cluden (1896) Y3.1034
Clumberhall (1899) Y3.802
Clutha (1911) Y3.2066
Clyde (1934) 12F, 12N, N12
Clyde (1953) M1105, M1124
Clyde (2006) P257
Clydebank (1941) J200
Clydeburn (1902) Y8.12
Clydesdale (1905) Y3.967, Y8.102
Clyne Castle (1929) FY508
Clythness (1920) FY1596, Y7.4
Coaticook RCN (1943) K410
Cobalt RCN (1940) K124
Cobham (1953) M2618
Cobourg RCN (1943) K333
Cochin RIN (1943) T315
Cochrane (1903) F08
Cochrane (1905) 19, 41, I08, N10
Cockade (1944) D34, D60, R34
Cockatrice (1912) G57, H26, H73
Cockatrice (1942) J229, M29
Cockchafer (1915) P72, P83, P95, T72
Cockchafer (1973) A230
Codfish (1915) N27, N55
Codrington (1929) D65, I65
Coila (1911) Y3.887
Coila (1922) FY.005
Colac RAN (1941) J242, M05
Colchester (1918) FY523
Coldsnap (1918) FY04, Z23
Coldstreamer (1942) T337

Colin Stuart (1911) Y3.2243
Coll (1941) A333, DV6, T207
Collena (1915) Z151
Collie (1964) A328
Collingham (1889) Y3.423
Collingwood (1896) Y3.170
Collingwood (1902) Z207
Collingwood (1908) 02, 26, 42
Collingwood (1940) K180
Collinson (1919) T01
Colne (1918) P17, T17
Colombo (1918) 7A, D89, I89
Colonel Templer (1966) A229
Colossus (1910) 24, 43, 93
Colossus (1943) 15, R61
Colsay (1943) T384
Coltsfoot (1941) K140
Columba (1893) Y3.417
Columbella (1902) M89, M(I)36, M(I)69, M(I)89
Columbia ʀᴄɴ (1918) I49
Columbine (1940) K94, M94
Comanchee (1912) Y7.246
Combatant (1942) J341
Comely Bank (1914) FY1879
Comeric (1898) Y3.32
Comet (1882) Y3.2124
Comet (1910) H25
Comet (1931) H00
Comet (1944) D26, D84, R26
Comfrey (1942) K277
Comitatus (1919) FY633
Commandant d'Estienne d'Orves ꜰʀ (1942) K93
Commandant Detroyat (1941) K183
Commandant Domine ꜰʀ (1939) U70
Commandant Duboc ꜰʀ (1939) U41
Commandant Drogou (1941) K195
Commander Evans (1924) FY113
Commander Holbrook (1915) FY111
Commander Nasmith (1915) FY516
Commiles (1918) FY636
Commodator (1918) FY634
Commonweal (1902) N28, N99
Commonwealth (1902) Y3.138
Commonwealth (1903) 31, 44, N88
Comox ʀᴄɴ (1938) J64, N64
Compact (Canc) Z273
Companion (Canc) Z272
Compatriot (Canc) Z274
Compere (Canc) Z280
Competent (Canc) Z281
Competitor (1907) Y3.512
Competitor (Canc) Z275

Complete (Canc) Z278
Complex (Canc) Z279
Compliment (Canc) Z282
Composure (Canc) Z283
Computator (1919) FY635
Comus (1914) 02, 45, A7, 5C
Comus (1945) D20, D85, R43
Concertator (1917) FY637
Concord (1916) 15, 46, 2A
Concord (1945) D03, D89, R63
Concordia (1913) FY1550
Condamine ʀᴀɴ (1944) F698, K698
Condor (1903) Y3.1573
Confiance (1955) A289
Confiance (....) W75
Confident (1941) W161
Confident (1956) A290
Confield (1912) Y3.1395
Conflict (1894) D18, D96, P24
Congre ꜰʀ (1918) FY1919, Y7.6
Coniston (1952) M1101
Coniston Water (1908) Y3.1161
Conn (1943) K509
Conner ᴜꜱɴ (1917) H(I)60
Conquerante (1934) 4.230
Conqueress (1913) W16
Conqueror (1911) 06, 47, 95, F33
Conqueror (1911) FY.006
Conqueror (1969) S105
Conqueror (Canc) 45, I45
Conqueror (1969) S48
Conquest (1915) 37, 48, C0
Conrad ᴏʀᴘ (1918) D44
Consbro (1930) Z107
Consolation (1917) FY1539
Consort (1944) D76, D86, R76
Constance (1915) 49, 90, C5
Constance (1944) D71, D87, R71
Constant Friend (1912) FY1933
Constant Hope (1913) FY1909
Constantia (1890) Y3.1290
Constantine (1909) Y3.16
Contender (1930) FY543
Contest (1913) H28, H63
Contest (1944) D48, D88, R12
Contrive (1911) FY290
Controller (1913) 4.447
Convovulus (1917) T23
Convolvulus (1940) K45, M45
Conway Castle (1916) FY509
Conyngham ᴜꜱɴ (1915) H(I)07, H(I)33
Cook (1945) A307

Cooke (1943) K471
Coolebar ʀᴀɴ (1911) FY84
Coolebar ʀᴀɴ (1939) J25
Coombar ʀᴀɴ (1912) FY08
Cootamundra ʀᴀɴ (1942) J316, M186
Copenhagen (1907) Y3.1557
Copinsay (1940) T147
Copious (1919) FY337
Coppercliff ʀᴄɴ (1944) K495, K521
Copsewood (1908) Y3.885
Coquette (1897) D37, N21
Coquette (1943) B262, J350, M350
Coquitlam ʀᴄɴ (1944) J364
Coral (1935) T07
Coral Bank (1914) FY1552
Corbrae (1935) FY1951
Corby (1901) Y3.987
Corcyra (1914) FY293
Cordela (1930) FY713
Cordelia (1914) 50, 69, 78
Cordova (1905) Y3.766
Corena (1924) FY709
Coreopsis (1917) T93
Coreopsis (1940) K32, M32
Corfe Castle (Canc) K527
Corfu (1907) Y3.268
Corfu (1931) F86
Corgi (1964) A330
Coriander (ex Iris) (1941) K183
Corinda (1937) B536
Coringa (1914) W12
Corinth (1904) Y3.329
Corinthia (1901) Y3.259
Corinthian (1938) F103
Coriolanus (1917) FY1948
Coriolanus (1940) T140
Cormorant (1976) P256
Cormorin (1924) F49
Corncrake (1942) M55, M82
Cornel (1942) K278
Cornelian (1933) T15
Cornet Castle (Canc) K528
Cornflower (1916) T24, T64
Cornish Point (1914) Y3.1884
Cornishman (1891) Y8.113
Cornwall (1902) D31, P04, P84
Cornwall (1926) 56
Cornwall (1985) F99
Cornwallis (1901) 33
Cornwallis ʀɪɴ (1917) L09, U09
Cornwood (1911) Y3.23
Coronado (1915) M(I)23

Coronatia (1902) Z204
Coronation (1902) T91
Coronet (1917) Z30
Corridoni ɪᴛ (1930) N55
Corsair (1930) FY.047
Corso (1900) Y3.55, Y3.238
Cortes (1884) Y8.60
Corton (1913) Y3.1840
Corunna (1945) D97, I97
Coryphene (1907) 4.425
Cosby (1943) K559
Cossack (1907) D02, D19, H09
Cossack (1937) F03, G03, L03
Cossack (1944) D57, D90, R57
Cotillion (1940) T104
Cotovia (1911) Y3.1615
Cotsmuir (1917) FY550
Cotswold (1916) TC3
Cotswold (1940) F154, L54
Cottesmore (1917) T6C
Cottesmore (1940) F78, L78
Cottesmore (1982) M32
Cotton (1943) B630, K510
Coucy FFN (1919) U93
Count (1929) Z109
Counterguard (1945) L4043
Courageous (1916) 50, 51, 94
Courageous (1970) S50
Courbet ꜰʀ (1911) D11
Courier (1943) B254, J349, M49
Couronne ꜰʀ (1935) 4.266
Courser (1905) FY1823
Courtenay ʀᴄɴ (1941) J262
Courtier (1929) FY592
Cove (1912) Y6.4, Y8.117
Coventry (1917) 61, 4C, D43, I43
Coventry (1974) D118
Coventry (1986) F98
Coventry City (1937) A405, FY267
Coverley (1941) T106
Cowdray (1941) B228, F152, L52
Cowichan ʀᴄɴ (1940) J146
Cowra ʀᴀɴ (1943) J351, M351
Cowrie (1895) Y7.65
Cowslip (1917) T05
Cowslip (1941) F196, K196
Coya (1895) Y3.1353
Cracker (1899) A139, W19
Cradley (1955) M2010
Craftsman (1917) FY1948
Cragoswald (1899) Y3.790
Cragside (1892) Y3.556, Y8.35

Craig Alvah (1909) FY1957
Craig Coilleach (1917) FY1770
Craig Island (1913) Z157
Craig Millar (1905) FY1669
Craig Roy (1918) FY287
Craigendoran (1899) Y3.535
Craigie (1918) T99, TA6
Craigston (1911) Y3.306
Craigwen (ex *Orpheus*) (1912) Y3.199
Cramond Island (1910) Z158
Cranbrook RCN (1943) J372
Crane (1896) D20, D50, H72, P26
Crane (1942) B268, F123, U23
Cranefly (1917) FY539
Cranham (1953) M2701
Cranley (1903) Y3.1940
Crannock (1911) FY279
Cranstoun (1943) K511
Crassula SAN (1935) T19, T519
Crayford (1911) Y3.677
Crenella (1897) X71, Y7.143
Creole (1927) 4.394
Creole (1945) D82, R82
Creosol (1916) N11, X18, X32
Crescent (1892) A4, N04, N29
Crescent (1931) H48
Crescent RCN (1944) D16, R16
Crescent Moon (1918) FY05, Z28
Cresence (1936) D75
Cressington Court (1908) Y3.916
Cressy (1899) N40
Crevette (1918) 4.435
Criccieth (1905) W17
Criccieth (1970) A391
Crichton (1953) M1124
Cricket (1915) P82, P85, T75
Cricket (1973) A229
Cricklade (1970) A381
Crispin (1945) D168, R68
Crocodile (1940) A384, W88
Crocus (1915) T25, T59
Crocus (1940) K49, M49
Croft (1913) W14
Crofton (1958) M1216
Cromarty (1941) J09, N09
Cromarty (1970) A488
Cromer (1940) J128
Cromer (1990) M103
Cromwell (1945) R35
Cronstadt (1907) Y3.691
Croome (1917) TC4
Croome (1941) D57, F162, L62

Crosby Hall (1903) Y3.1549
Crossbow (1945) D96, G96
Crossby (1907) Y3.386
Crowlin (1943) T380
Crown (1945) R46
Crown of Arragon (1905) Y9.15
Crown of Castile (1905) Y9.4
Crown of Cordova (1901) Y3.781
Crown of Galicia (1906) Y9.6
Crown of Leon (1894) Y3.1005
Crown of Seville (1912) Y3.1443
Crown of Toledo (1912) Y3.1343
Croxdale (1906) Y3.2415
Croxteth (1918) Y3.2145
Croxton (1916) T20
Crozier (1919) T02
Croziers (1944) R27
Cruden Bay (1899) N30, N58
Crusader (1909) D03, D21, H66
Crusader (1931) H60
Crusader RCN (1944) D120, R20
Crystal (1945) R38
Cubitt (1943) K512
Cuckmere (1942) K299
Cuffley (Canc) M2011
Cuillin Sound (1944) B316, F188
Cuirass (1915) Z150
Cuirassier (1914) Y3.1707
Culgoa RAN (1944) F408, K408
Culver (1928) Y87
Culverin (Canc) G28
Cumberland (1902) D37, P76, P86
Cumberland (1926) 57, C57, C177
Cumberland (1986) F85
Cumbrae (1940) T154
Cumbrian (1907) Y3.2012
Cummings USN (1913) H(I)06, H(I)08
Cundall (1908) Y3.129
Cunene (1911) Y8.121
Cupar (1918) T86
Curacao (1917) D41, 62, A7, I41
Curlew (1917) 48, 80, 3C, D42, I42
Curran (1900) Y3.933, Y4.42
Curtana (1929) FY674
Curzon (1943) K513
Curzon (RNR) M1109, M1136
Cushing USN (1912) H(I)09
Cutlass (1970) P274
Cutlass (Canc) G74
Cuttack RIN (1941) T251
Cutty Sark (1920) FY.007
Cuxton (1953) M1125

Cuyahoga (1914) Y7.80
Cybele (1944) J399
Cyclamen (1916) T26, T73
Cyclamen (1940) K83, M83
Cycle (ex *Boveric*) (1906) Y3.2234
Cyclone (1935) FY907
Cyclone (1942) A111
Cyclops (1905) A1, C5, F31, I31
Cydonia (1910) Y3.344
Cyelse (1912) X125, Y7.8, Y7.16
Cyfarthfa (1904) Y3.205
Cygnet (1898) D22, D38, N49
Cygnet (1930) H83
Cygnet (1942) B602, F38, U38
Cygnet (1975) P261
Cymbeline (1902) Y7.17
Cymrian (1905) Y3.560
Cymric Prince (1901) Y3.1247
Cynara Kalan (1913) FY.008
Cynic (1916) W15
Cynthia (1898) D23, D39, N09
Cynthia (1943) J345
Cypress (1930) T09
Cyprus (1936) X44
Cyrus (1944) J421

D

D1 (1908) D1, I71
D2 (1910) D2, I72
D3 (1910) D3, I73
D4 (1911) D4, I74
D5 (1911) D5, I75
D6 (1911) D6, I76
D7 (1911) D7, I77
D8 (1911) D8, I78
D9 (1912) D9
D10 (1912) D10
D.W. Fitzgerald (1916) FY1820
Dabchick (1942) M22, N22
Dacca RIN (Canc) T252
Dacca RPN (1942) M245
Dacres (1943) K472
Daerwood RCN (1943) J357
Daffodil (1915) M31, T05, T27
Daffodil (1917) F101
Daffodil (1940) M07
Dagger (Canc) G23
Daghestan (1898) Y7.52
Daghestan (1900) Y3.202
Dago (1902) Y5.3

Dahlia (1915) M37, T11, T28
Dahlia (1940) K59, M59
Dailwen (ex *Mozart*) (1910) Y3.1318
Dainty (1932) H53
Dainty (1950) D108, I52
Daisy (1911) N31, N78
Daisy (1968) A145
Daisy Bank (1911) FY1964
Dakins (1943) K550
Daldorch (1907) Y2.235, Y3.104
Dale Castle (1909) 4.156
Daleby (1900) Y3.302
Dalecrest (1910) Y3.1277
Dalegarth (1899) Y3.729
Dalegarth Force (1913) Y3.1635
Daleham (1913) Y3.506
Dalemoor (1909) Y3.1001
Dalewood (1911) Y3.24
Dallington (1900) Y3.995
Dalmatia (1928) FY844
Dalmation (1965) A129
Dalrymple (1945) A302
Dalswinton (1953) M1126
Dalton (1887) Y3.930
Damerham (1953) M2629
Damito (1917) FY521, Y7.9
Dampier (1945) A303
Damsay (1942) A334, P45, T208
Danae (1918) 32, D44, I44
Danae (1965) F47
Danae (Canc) I05
Dandolo (1910) 4.440
Dandy (1919) W93
Dane (1911) FY554
Daneman (1937) FY123
Daniel Clowden (1919) FY531
Danmark (1931) X128
Danubian (1909) Y7.35
Danube V (1935) W36
Daphne (1915) M38, T12, T29
Daphne (1968) A156
Dapper (1915) X19, X30
Dara (1915) Y3.1435
Daring (1932) H16
Daring (1949) D05, I15
Daring (2006) D32
Dark Adventurer (1954) P1101
Dark Aggressor (1954) P1102
Dark Antagonist (1954) P1103
Dark Avenger (1955) P1105
Dark Biter (1955) P1104
Dark Buccaneer (1954) P1108

Dark Clipper (1955) P1109
Dark Fighter (1955) P1113
Dark Gladiator (1956) P1114
Dark Hero (1957) P1115
Dark Highwayman (1955) P1110
Dark Hunter (1954) P1116
Dark Hussar (1957) P1112
Dark Intruder (1955) P1118
Dark Invader (1955) P1119
Dark Killer (1956) P1111
Dark Rover (1954) P1107
Dark Scout (1958) P1120
Darlaston (1953) M1127
Darlington (1910) Y3.1816
Darnaway (1918) FY1985
Darnett Ness (1920) FY542
Darsham (1952) M2619
Darst Creek (1943) B502
Dart (1898) Y3.1046
Dart (1942) F21, K21
Darthema (1929) FY676
Dartington (1956) M1203
Dartmoor (1892) Y3.692
Dartmoor (1917) TC5
Dartmouth (1910) 52, A9
Darvel (1924) B537
Darwen (1916) FY1859
Dasher (1941) D37
Dasher (1988) P280
Datchet (1968) A357
Dauntless (1918) 71, D45, I45
Dauntless (2007) D33
Dauphin RCN (1940) K157
Davenham (1953) M2620
David Haigh SAN (1918) T13, T513
David Ogilvie (1917) FY720
Davis USN (1916) H(I)12, H(I)35
Davy (1936) FY147
Dawson RCN (1941) K104
Daybreak (1911) Y2.167, Y3.431
Dayton (1907) Y7.208
De Drie Gezusters RNLN (1912) 4.228
De Fontaine (1901) Y3.674
De la Pole (1919) FY1558, 4.129
De Roza BG (1922) 4.318
Dean Swift (ex *Dean*) (1911) Y1.7
Deane (1943) K551
Deccan RIN (1944) J129, M99
Decoy (1932) H75
Decoy (1949) D106, I56
Decoy (Canc) I40
Deddington (1903) Y3.530

Dee (1902) Y3.1631
Dee (1903) D14, D24, H31, N95
Dee (1916) T20
Dee (1955) P3104
Deepwater (1939) A156, J09
Deer Sound (1939) B317, F99
Deerhound (1966) A155
Defence (1907) 05
Defence (1944) 34
Defender (1911) H28, H29, H57
Defender (1932) H07
Defender (1950) D114, I47
Defender (2009) D36
Delaware (1893) Y7.2 8
Delaware USN (1909) 98
Delhi (1918) 6A, D74, I74
Delhi RIN (1932) C74
Delight (1932) H38
Delight (1950) D119, I08
Delight (Canc) I45
Delila (1919) 4.273
Delmira (1905) Y7.259
Deloraine RAN (1941) J232, M232
Delphic (1897) Y3.1514
Delphin II ORP (1938) 4.244
Delphinium (1915) T30, T54
Delphinium (1940) K77, M77
Delphinula (1907) Y7.188
Delphinus (1906) FY846
Delta (1907) YA.7
Demeterton (1914) Y3.770
Demetian (1900) Y2.49, Y3.1882
Demirhisar TK (1941) H80
Demon (Canc) I35
Denbigh Castle (1944) K696
Denbighshire (1938) B576
Denby Grange (1900) Y2.135
Denby Grange (1912) Y3.561
Denbigh Hall (1906) Y3.1924
Denbydale (1940) X05
Denmead (1969) A363
Dennis Rose (....) Y3.6
Denpark (1916) Y3.1856
Deodar (1940) T124
Deptford (1935) L53, U53
Derbent (1907) Y7.56
Derby (1918) J90, N90, TN0, TN4
Derby County (1938) FY171
Derby Haven (1944) A397, K438
Derbyshire (1935) F78
Derg (1943) B269, F257, K257
Derriton (1953) M1128

Dervish (Canc) I73
Derwent (1888) Y3.585, Y8.18
Derwent (1903) D15, N25
Derwent (1941) L83
Derwentdale (1941) A114, X14
Derwentdale (1964) A221
Derwent River (1915) Y3.1641
Desabla (1913) Y7.63
Desford (1954) P3108
Desire (Canc) I19
Despatch (1919) 30, D30, I30
Desperate (1896) D26, D40. P50
Desperate (Canc) I87
Destinn (1914) FY1719
Destiny (1942) B449, W115
Devaney (1906) Y4.74
Deveron (1942) K265
Devon City (1913) Y3.1942
Devon City (1933) Z168
Devon Coast (1909) Y2.37
Devonia (1905) J113
Devonshire (1904) 38, 53, N19
Devonshire (1927) 39, C39, C186
Devonshire (1960) D02
Devonshire (....) Y4.10
Dew (1929) FY1721
Dewa (1913) Y3.1242
Dewdale (1941) A151, X51
Dewdale (1965) A219
Dewsland (1883) Y3.86
Dexterous (1942) W111
Dexterous (1956) A93
Dexterous (1986) A231
Dhanush RIN (1942) K265
Dhoon (1915) 4.131
Diadem (1896) N32, N50, P20
Diadem (1906) Y3.266
Diadem (1942) 84, C84
Diamantina RAN (1944) F377, K377
Diamond (1904) 32, N33, N61, N70
Diamond (1932) H22
Diamond (1950) D35, I81
Diamond (2007) D34
Diana (1895) D18, N34, P58
Diana (1932) H49
Diana (1952) D126, I26
Diana (Canc) I77
Dianella (1940) K07
Dianthus (1940) K95, M95
Dick Whittington (1913) FY1661
Dido (1896) P05, P87, 37
Dido (1939) C37

Dido (1961) F104
Dieppe (1944) L108, L3016
Digby (1913) M83, M(I)83
Digby RCN (1942) J267
Digit (1902) Z188
Diligence (1907) P77, P88
Diligence (1944) B303, F174
Diligence (1980) A132
Dilston (1913) Y2.35
Dilston (1954) M1168
Dilwara (1935) Y4.2
Dinapore RIN (Canc) T326
Dingledale (1941) A144, B511, X44, Y7.44
Dingley (1952) M2001
Dinsdale (1941) X106
Diomede (1919) 92, D92, I92
Diomede (1969) F16
Dipavati RIN (1936) 4.109
Dipper (1943) P30
Director (1943) W137
Director (1956) A94
Director Gerling (1892) W19
Dirk (Canc) G02
Dirkje RNLN (1934) FY1745
Discoverer (1913) M(I)53, M(I)96, PA3
Disdain (1945) J442
Dispenser (1943) A262, A362
Distol (1916) X20, X46
Dittany (1942) K279
Dittisham (1953) M2621
Diver (1943) P31
Divis (1883) Y4.217
Dixie USN (1893) H(I)14
Djerissa (1910) Y3.231
Dochet (1942) T286
Dockleaf (1916) Y7.161
Doctor Lee (1914) Z133
Dodman Point (1945) A219, F19
Dolfijn RNLN (1920) FY1761
Dolphin (1902) I09
Dolwen (1976) A362
Domett (1943) K473
Domingo de Larringa (1899) Y3.658
Dominica (1943) K507
Dominion (1902) Y3.765
Dominion (1903) 41, 54, N90
Domino (1917) Y3.2171
Domino (1930) FY1764
Domira (1905) Y3.1044
Don (1892) Y3.561, Y8.4
Don Arturo (1906) Y3.1354
Don Benito (1906) Y3.1151

Don Cesar (1906) Y3.688
Don Diego (1906) Y3.1129
Don Emilio (1906) Y3.972
Donax (1913) Y7.124
Doncaster (1916) T56
Donegal (1902) 55, 9C, N28
Donna Nook (1915) FY1559, 4.132
Donovan (1918) T/6
Donovan (1943) F161
Doomba ʀᴀɴ (1919) J01
Doon (1903) D16, D27, H41, N14
Doon (1917) T35
Doonholm (1907) Y3.917
Dorade II (1906) 4.340
Doria (1909) N35
Dorie (1911) Y3.325
Dorienta (1914) FY705
Dorileen (1917) Z148
Dorinda (1917) FY623
Dorington Court (1908) Y3.1725
Doris (1896) D59, N36, P47
Doris (1968) A252
Dorisbrook (1915) Y3.669
Dorking (1918) T19, T32
Dornoch (1942) J173
Dornoch (1970) A490
Dorothy (1895) Y3.886
Dorothy (1902) Y2.110
Dorothy (1968) A173
Dorothy Duke (1918) FY.048
Dorothy Gray (1908) 4.222
Dorothy Lambert (1923) FY558
Dorsetshire (1927) 40
Douglas (1889) Y3.2078
Douglas (1918) D09, D90, F50, G00, I90
Dounie Braes (1918) 4.235
Douwe Aukes ʀɴʟɴ (1922) T309
Dove (1898) D28, D34, D51
Dovey (1943) F523, K523
Dovey (1983) M2005
Dowgate (1935) Z17
Dowlais (1904) Y3.1246
Downes ᴜsɴ (1913) H(I)11, H(I)21
Downham (1955) M2622
Downley (Canc) M2012
Drage (ex *Dragon*) (1893) W03
Dragon (1893) N37, N63, W20
Dragon (1917) 19, D46, I46
Dragon (2008) D35
Dragonet (1939) P283, Z82
Dragonfly (1938) T11
Dragueur 301 ꜰʀ (1943) A434

Drake (1901) P09
Drammenseren (1894) Y3.1902
Drangey (1935) FY195
Dranguet (1935) 4.259
Draug ʀɴᴏɴ (1908) H28
Drayton ᴜsɴ (1910) H(I)15, H(I)37
Dreadful (1912) W21
Dreadnought (1906) 00, 56,73
Dreadnought (1960) S101
Dredgol (1918) X80
Drina (1913) YA.3
Driver (1942) A199, W100
Drobak (1929) FY1928
Dromonby (1900) Y3.526
Dronning Maud (1917) Y3.1954
Droxford (1954) P3113
Druid (1911) H30, H33, H92
Druid (1952) I26
Drumheller ʀᴄɴ (1941) K167
Drummer Boy (1916) FY851
Drummondville ʀᴄɴ (1941) J253
Drury (1943) K316
Dryad (1893) P90
Dubbo ʀᴀɴ (1942) J251, M251
Dubford (1953) P3119
Dublin (1904) Y3.2159
Dublin (1912) 42, 57, 68
Duchess (1932) H64
Duchess (1951) I94
Duchess of Cornwall (1896) J75, N75
Duchess of Devonshire (1897) M09, M(I)02,
     M(I)03, M(I)09
Duchess of Fife (1903) J115
Duchess of Rothesay (1894) J107
Duchess ʀᴀɴ (1951) D154
Duchesse de Brabant (1924) FY341
Duckworth (1943) K351
Duff (1943) K352
Duffield (1906) Y3.1202
Dufton (1954) M1145
Duke of Albany (1907) M11, M(I)11
Duke of Argyll (1928) 4.42
Duke of Clarence (1892) M(I)03, M(I)04, M(I)14
Duke of Cornwall (1888) Y3.2120
Duke of Cornwall (1898) M10, M(I)05, M(I)10
Duke of Edinburgh (1904) 15, 58, N33
Duke of Rothesay (1928) 4.421
Duke of Wellington (1935) 4.400
Duke of York (1940) 17, B2, B17
Dulcibelle (1918) FY826
Dullisk Cove (1944) B343, F185
Dulverton (1941) L63

Dulverton (1982) M35
Dumbarton Castle (1943) F388, K388
Dumbarton Castle (1981) P265
Dumbleton (1957) M1212
Dunavon (1908) Z228
Dunbar (1941) J53, N53
Dunbarmoor (1903) Y3.743
Dunbridge (1917) Y3.2016
Duncan (1901) 43, 59, N53
Duncan (1932) D99, I99
Duncan (1957) F80
Duncan (2010) D37
Duncan usn (1913) H(I)11, H(I)16
Duncansby Head (1944) A158, F58
Dunclutha (1910) Y3.1335
Duncton (1941) T220
Dundalk (1919) J60, N60, T91, T0A
Dundas rcn (1941) K229
Dundas (1953) F48
Dundee (1911) M(I)12
Dundee (1932) L84, U84
Dundrennan (1912) Y3.1295
Dunedin (1910) FY514
Dunedin (1918) 96, D93, I93
Dunera (1937) Y4.1
Duneric (1896) Y3.757
Dungeness (1892) Y3.554
Dungeness (1945) F46
Dunkerton (1954) M1144
Dunkery (1941) T224
Dunkirk (1945) D09, I09
Dunnet (1936) Z14
Dunnet Head (1913) Y3.1858
Dunolly (1901) Y3.2369
Dunoon (1919) J52, N52, N3A, T57
Dunottar Castle (1936) F34
Dunraven (1910) Y3.283
Dunraven Castle (1917) FY570
Dunster (1902) Y3.457
Dunster (1969) A393
Dunvegan (1883) Y8.59
Dunvegan rcn (1940) K177
Dunver rcn (1942) B631, K03
Durban (1919) 99, D99, I99
Durham (1900) Y3.334
Durraween ran (1919) FY93
Durweston (1955) M1201
Dusk (1914) FY1916
Dutiful (1944) F176
Dwarf (1893) P8C
Dwarf (1936) A381, T92
Dykland (1914) Y3.463

E

E1 (1912) E1, I81
E2 (1910) E2, I82
E3 (1912) E3, I83
E4 (1912) E4, I84
E5 (1912) E5, I85
E6 (1912) E6, I86
E7 (1913) E7, I87
E8 (1913) E8, I88
E9 (1913) E9, I89
E10 (1913) E10, I90
E11 (1914) E11, I91
E12 (1914) E12, I92
E13 (1914) E13, I93
E14 (1914) E14, I94
E15 (1914) E15, I95
E16 (1914) E16, I96
E17 (1915) E17, I97
E18 (1915) E18, I98
E19 (1915) E19, I99
E20 (1915) E20, I69
E21 (1915) E21, I70
E22 (1915) E22, I79
E23 (1915) E23
E24 (1915) E24
E25 (1915) E25
E26 (1915) E26
E27 (1917) E27
E28 (Canc) E28
E29 (1915) E29
E30 (1915) E30
E31 (1915) E31
E32 (1916) E32
E33 (1916) E33
E34 (1917) E34
E35 (1916) E35
E36 (1916) E36
E37 (1916) E37
E38 (1916) E38
E39 (1916) E39
E40 (1916) E40
E41 (1915) E41
E42 (1915) E42
E43 (1915) E43
E44 (1916) E44
E45 (1916) E45
E46 (1916) E46
E47 (1916) E47
E48 (1916) E48
E49 (1916) E49
E50 (1916) E50

E51 (1916) E51
E52 (1917) E52
E53 (1916) E53
E54 (1916) E54
E55 (1916) E55
E56 (1916) E56
E57 (1917) E57
E58 (1917) E58
E.O. Saltmarsh (1903) Y3.132
Eadwine (1914) FY1892
Eager (1912) FY990
Eagle (1918) 94
Eagle (1946) R05, D29
Eaglesdale (1940) A104, B512, X104
Earl Essex (1914) FY852
Earl Kitchener (1915) FY1633
Earl of Durham (1905) Y3.495
Earl of Forfar (1910) Y2.136, Y3.752
Earl of Peterborough (1915) M01, M04, M09
Earlswood (1898) Y3.1749
Earner (1943) A209, W143
Earnest (1896) D05, D29, D79
Earnholm (1874) Y3.1972
Earraid (1941) A335, DV7, T297
Easedale (1941) A105, X105
Easingwold (1898) Y3.1148
East Coast (1907) 4.438, 4.441
East Wales (1915) Y3.1326
Eastbourne (1940) J127
Eastbourne (1955) F73
Eastcheap (1899) Y3.867
Eastcliffe (1917) Y3.1544
Eastcoates (1919) FY1771
Easter Rose (1914) Z251
Eastern City (1917) Y3.2392
Eastern Dawn (1908) FY273
Eastfield (1900) Y3.380
Eastgate (1915) Y3.450
Eastlands (1905) Y3.762
Easton (1942) B229, F09, L09
Eastview RCN (1943) K665
Eastville (1902) Y3.1397
Eastway (1943) F130
Eastwood (1904) Y3.379
Eaton Hall (1904) Y3.1636
Eavestone (1912) Y3.1286
Ebbtide (1917) FY10, P335, Z35
Eblana (1892) Y4.68
Ebonol (1917) X22
Ebor Wyke (1911) 4.157
Ebor Wyke (1929) FY1601
Ebro (1915) M78, M(I)37, M(I)70, M(I)78

Echo (1891) Y3.1709, Y8.33
Echo (1934) H23
Echo (1957) A70
Echo (2002) H87
Echodale (1940) A170, B530, X70
Echuca RAN/RNZN (1942) J252, M252
Echunga (1907) Y7.169
Eclipse (1894) D58
Eclipse (1934) H08
Eday (1941) T201
Edderton (1952) M1111
Eddy (1918) FY12, Z49
Eddybay (1951) A107
Eddybeach (1951) A132
Eddycliff (1952) A190
Eddycove (Canc) A205
Eddycreek (1953) A258
Eddyfirth (1953) A261
Eddymull (Canc) A287
Eddyness (1953) A295
Eddyreef (1952) A202
Eddyrock (1952) A198
Eden (1903) D17, N42
Eden (1918) T49
Edendale (1888) Y3.882
Edernian (1906) Y3.559
Edgar (1890) A5, N05, N38
Edgehill (1928) X39
Edgeley (1955) M2013
Edie (1903) Y3.65
Edinburgh (1938) 16, C16
Edinburgh (1982) D97
Edinburgh Castle (1910) F83, M62, M(I)55,
    M(I)62, M(I)71
Edith (1900) Y3.2235
Edith (1968) A177
Edith Cavell (1898) Y3.1834
Edlingham (1955) M2623
Edlington (1913) Y3.389
Edmundston RCN (1941) K106, M106
Edna (1905) Y3.1965
Edna (....) B424
Eduard van Vlaenderen (1925) FY1832
Edward L. Doheny (1913) Y7.203
Edward Walmsley (1919) FY624
Edwardian (1931) FY691
Edwina (1915) 4.134
Effingham (1921) 98, D98, I98
Effra (ex *Broompark*) (1910) Y3.2111
Egba (1914) Y8.77
Egeland RNoN (1914) FY251
Egeria (1907) FY576

Egeria (1958) A72

Egerton (1943) A208

Eggesford (1910) Y3.452

Eggesford (1942) D58, F15, L15

Egilsay (1942) T215

Eglantine (1917) T31

Eglantine RNoN (1941) K197

Eglinton (1916) T02

Eglinton (1939) F87, L87

Egret (1903) Y3.1788, Y9.28

Egret (1905) Y3.1209

Egret (1938) L75, U75

Egyptian Transport (1914) Y3.1911

Egyptiana (ex *Sandown*) (1905) Y3.1383

Eider (1900) Y3.1577

Eileen Emma (1914) FY1992

Ekins (1943) K552

El Hind (1938) F120

El Toro (1913) Y7.41

El Zorro (1914) Y7.38

Elax (1893) Y7.133

Elba (1899) Y3.2040

Elbury (1925) FY656

Elderol (1917) X21, X27, A154

Eldorado (1902) FY571

Eleanor (1888) Y6.1

Eleanor (1894) Y3.233

Electra (1896) D31, D52, N55

Electra (1934) H27

Electra II BG (1904) 4.159

Elena (1905) FY573

Elephant (1953) D61

Elfin (1933) T25

Elford (1915) Y3.751

Elfreda (1943) J402

Elgin (1906) Y3.1420

Elgin (1919) J39, N39, T39, T/5

Elizabeth Angela (1928) FY767

Elk (1902) 4.24

Elkhound (1966) A162

Elkstone (1970) A353

Ella Sayer (1898) Y3.519

Ellaston (1890) Y3.1926

Ellawood (1915) Y3.1479

Ellerdale (1913) Y3.328

Elleric (1897) Y3.1365

Ellerslie (1906) Y3.299

Ellesmere (1939) FY204, T204

Ellind (1896) Y3.1173

Elm (1939) T105

Elm Lake RCN (1945) J486

Elm Park (1917) Y3.1893

Elmleaf (1916) Y7.157

Elmmoor (1910) Y3.999

Elmol (1917) A123, X23

Elmsgarth (1896) Y3.1317

Elmgrove (ex *Treasury*) (1896) Y3.165

Elmtree (1916) Y3.1320

Eloquent (1911) FY1581

Elpenor (1917) Y3.1535

Elpiniki (1880) Y4.65

Else Rykens (1935) FY255, FY1646

Elsenham (1955) M2624

Elsie & Nellie (1916) FY1914

Elsie Cam (1922) FY1646

Elsing (1970) A277

Elsiston (1915) Y3.1768

Elswick Hall (1901) Y3.2480

Elswick House (1901) Y3.1621

Elswick Lodge (1900) Y3.1522

Elswick Manor (1901) Y3.1336

Elswick Tower (1901) Y3.1285

Elwick (1891) Y3.1809

Emerald (1904) Y2.9, Y3.653, Y8.72

Emerald (1920) 66, D66, I66

Emile Baudot (1917) Z217

Emile Bertin FR (1933) 45

Emilion (1914) FY853

Eminent (1942) B450, W116

Emmons USN (1941) Y16

Emperor (1942) D98, R307

Emperor of India (1906) J106, 4.237

Emperor of India (1913) 11, 16, 60

Emphatic (1943) A148, W154

Empire Anvil (1943) F184

Empire Arquebus (1943) B206, F170

Empire Baffin (1941) Z269

Empire Baltic (1945) L3519

Empire Battleaxe (1943) B207, F161

Empire Boswell (1942) B423

Empire Broadsword (1943) F163

Empire Cedric (1945) L3534

Empire Celtic (1945) L3512

Empire Cheer (1943) B433

Empire Chivalry (1937) F126

Empire Clyde (1924) B394

Empire Crest (1944) B505

Empire Crossbow (1943) F183

Empire Curlew (1945) L3042

Empire Cutlass (1943) F162

Empire Cymric (1944) L3010

Empire Demon (1942) A369

Empire Doric (1944) L3041

Empire Edward (1942) A147, W147

Empire Fairy (1942) W155
Empire Fred (1942) A372, W157
Empire Fulmar (1945) L3524
Empire Gaelic (1944) L3507
Empire Gannet (1944) L3006
Empire Grebe (1945) L3038
Empire Griffin (1943) W145
Empire Guillemot (1945) L3525
Empire Gull (1945) L3513
Empire Halberd (1943) F160
Empire Herald (1945) B513
Empire Imp (1942) A178
Empire Josephine (1944) B451, W129
Empire Kittiwake (1944) L3510
Empire Mace (1943) B208, F171
Empire Maple (1941) W167
Empire Minnow (1942) W187
Empire Ned (1942) W147
Empire Neptune (1945) B514
Empire Netta (1945) A382
Empire Nordic (1944) L3026
Empire Penang (1944) B341
Empire Petrel (1945) L3520
Empire Phyllis (1944) W180
Empire Plane (1941) A393
Empire Puffin (1945) L3015
Empire Rita (1945) A396
Empire Rosa (1945) A397
Empire Salvage (1940) A159
Empire Sam (1942) B452, W159
Empire Samson (1943) W146
Empire Shearwater (1945) L3033
Empire Silver (1940) B503
Empire Skua (1945) L3517
Empire Spearhead (1943) B209, F172
Empire Tern (1944) L3504
Empire Titania (1942) W181
Empire Wolfe (1941) B422
Empire Zona (1945) A309, A399
Empress (1889) Y3.1627
Empress (1907) N38, N39
Empress (1942) D42
Empress of Asia (1913) M65
Empress of Britain (1906) M57
Empress of Japan (1891) M66
Empress of Russia (1913) M68
Empress of Scotland (1930) F55
Emprise (1899) W05
Empyrean (1914) Y7.10, FY873
Emulous (1943) A174, W138
En Avant (1911) FY1743
Enard Bay (1944) F35

Enchanter (1944) W178
Enchantress (1934) B283, L56, U56
Encore (1944) A379, W179
Encounter (1934) H10
Endcliffe (1911) Y3.643, Y8.30
Endeavour (1912) J91, N40, N46, N91
Endeavour (1966) A213, A361
Endurance (1956) A171
Endurance (1990) A171
Endymion (1880) Y3.1399
Endymion (1891) A6, N17, N41
Energetic (1902) A171, W71
Energetic (1942) A147, W101
Enfield (1897) Y3.521
Enfield (1945) A395
Enforcer (1944) A177, W177
Engadine (1911) N42, N91
Engadine (1941) A428, D71
Engadine (1966) K08
England (1906) Y3.474
Enidwen (1899) Y3.503
Enigma (1944) A175, W175
Enosis (1906) Y3.913
Ennerdale (1941) A173, X73
Ennerdale (1962) A213
Ennisbrook (1914) Y3.382
Ennismore (1889) Y3.796
Ennistown (1908) Y3.2236
Ensay (1942) T216
Enterprise (1882) Y3.126
Enterprise (1919) 52, D52, I52
Enterprise (1958) A71
Enterprise (2002) H88
Enticer (1944) B741, W166
Envoy (1944) A165, B742, W165
Ephretah (1918) FY310
Epic (1909) W22
Epinal FR (1919) U24
Epine (1929) FY682
Epsom (1902) Y3.1835
Epsom (1916) T59
Eptalofos (1893) Y3.652
Eptapyrgion (ex *Essex Baron*) (1914) Y3.809
Epworth (1970) A355
Equerry (1929) FY668
Erebus (1916) F02, I02, M02
Eric Calvert (1889) Y3.1118
Erica (1940) K50
Ericsson USN (1914) H(I)17, H(I)39
Eridanus (1905) 4.427
Eridge (1916) T60
Eridge (1940) L68

Erika (1906) Y3.1062

Erimo (1930) FY569

Erin (1913) 56, 61, 76

Erin (1932) B711

Erinier (1898) Y3.1375

Eriskay (1942) T217

Erith (1917) FY578

Erivan (1893) Y7.54

Erlesburgh (1911) Y3.1339

Ermine (1912) Y7.25

Ermine (1912) Y4.25, Y7.25

Erna (1915) Z112

Ernard Bay (1944) K435

Erne (1903) N58

Erne (1940) B284, U03

Eroican (1914) FY518, Y144, 4.144

Eros (1900) Y8.52

Eros (1905) Y3.277

Eros (1936) B712

Errington Court (1909) Y3.339

Erroll (1905) Y3.950

Escapade (1934) H17

Escort (1934) H66

Escrick (1910) Y3.102

Esk (1934) H15

Eskdale ʀɴoɴ (1942) L36

Eskimo (1910) M75

Eskimo (1937) D275, F75, G75, L75

Eskimo (1961) F119

Eskmere (1916) Y3.1453

Eskwood (1911) Y3.222, Y8.66

Esneh (1908) Y3.966

Esperance Bay (1922) F67

Espiegle (1942) J216, M216

Esquimalt ʀcɴ (1941) J272

Essex (1901) 51, 62, N38

Essex Queen (1897) J101, N01

Essington (1943) K353

Essington (1956) M1134

Esther (1911) N43, N83

Estrella (1912) Y3.2019

Estrella d'Alva (1909) FY1927

Estrella do Mar (1914) FY1916

Esturia (1910) Y7.213

Etal Manor (1916) Y3.1237

Etchingham (1957) M2625

Ethelaida (1891) Y3.1714

Ethelaric (1917) Y3.1654

Ethel Duncan (1912) Y3.5

Ethel (1898) Y3.15

Ethelbryhta (1898) Y3.634

Ethelhilda (1897) Y3.708

Ethelinda (ex *Brooklet*) (1911) Y3.895

Ethelstan (1905) Y3.2239

Ethelwolf (1906) Y3.409

Ethelwynne (1904) Y3.1123

Ethiopian (1936) Z167

Etolia (1911) Y3.1096

Etruria (1930) Z187

Etruscan (1913) FY854

Etton (1905) Y3.1105

Ettrick (1903) D18, D32, N01

Ettrick ʀcɴ (1943) F254, K254

Ettrick (1970) A274

Ettrick (938) Y4.7

Euclase (1931) FY1636

Eunice & Nellie (1918) FY1543

Eupion (1914) Y7.69

Europa (1897) P06, P91

Euryalus (1901) D04, N44, N51

Euryalus (1939) 42, C42, C167

Euryalus (1963) F15

Eurydamas (1901) Y3.1491

Eurymedon (1902) Y3.2031

Eustace (1913) Y3.1537

Euston (1910) Y3.359

Euterpe (1901) Y3.491

Evadne (1931) FY.009

Evan Gibb (1945) L3037

Eveline ʀɴʟɴ (1912) FY756

Evelyn Rose (1918) 4.136

Evening Primrose (1911) FY1516

Evenlode (1942) K300

Everest (1907) Y3.90

Everingham (1954) M2626

Eversley (Canc) M2014

Everton (1915) FY1645

Ewald ʀɴʟɴ (1913) FY1733

Ex Fortis (1914) FY1873

Example (1985) A153, P165

Excalibur (1955) S40

Excellent (1907) Y3.125

Excellent (1918) T47

Exchequer (1914) FY961

Exe (1903) D19, D33, H70, N05

Exe (1942) F92, K92

Exeter (1929) 68

Exeter (1978) D89

Exford (1911) Y3.424

Exhorter (1937) A299

Exmoor (1912) Y3.364

Exmoor (i) (1940) L61

Exmoor (ii) (1941) F08, L08

Exmouth (1899) Y3.630

Exmouth (1901) 12, 63, N44
Exmouth (1934) H02
Exmouth (1955) F84
Expeller (1942) A183
Expert (1945) A172, W173
Exploit (1988) A167, P167
Explorer (....) 4.406
Explorer (1954) S30
Explorer (1986) A154, P164
Express (1897) D34, D80, D84
Express (1934) H61
Express (1988) A163, P163
Exyahne (1914) FY878
Eyebright RCN (1940) K150

F

F1 (1915) F1, IA0
F2 (1917) F2, IA1
F3 (1916) F3, IA2
F.A. Tamplin (1912) Y4.12, Y7.90
F. Matarazzo (1906) Y3.1172
Factor (1903) Y3.96
Fairfax (1921) F130
Fairhaven (1913) Y3.2428
Fairmuir (1915) Y3.1012
Fairway (1918) FY1551. 4.23
Fairy (1897) D35, D53, P40
Fairy (1902) Y3.1991, Y8.109
Fairy (1943) J403
Fairy Knowe (1913) FY941
Faithful (1944) F177
Faithful (1957) A85
Faithful (1985) A228
Fal (1942) K266
Falcon (1892) W129
Falcon (1899) D36, D54, P31
Falcon (1931) T74
Falconet (1938) P19, Z19
Falls City (1913) Y3.1488
Falmouth (1910) 90
Falmouth (1932) F34, L34, U34
Falmouth (1959) F113
Fame (1896) D37, D41
Fame (1934) D178, H78
Fancy (1943) J308, M308
Fandango (1917) T2N
Fandango (1940) T107
Fanning USN (1912) H(I)19, H(I)29
Fanny (1878) Y3.2029
Fantome (1942) J224

Fara (1941) T162
Fareham (1918) J89, N89, TC9, T1N
Farley (1916) Y3.1439
Farnborough (1904) Y3.859
Farnborough (1904) P71
Farndale (1940) D59, F70, L70
Farne (1943) T353
Farnham Castle (1944) F413, K413
Farraline (1903) Y8.31
Farringford (1904) Y3.951
Farsund RNoN (1929) FY358
Fastnet (1895) Y3.2103
Fastnet (1919) T05, Z101
Faulknor (1914) D16, G73, H31, H84
Faulknor (1934) H62
Fauvette (1912) M(I)26, Y8.44
Faversham (1918) TN0, T7N
Favonian (1894) Y3.961
Favourite (1942) W119
Favourite (1958) A87
Fawn (1897) D38, D55, H38, P94
Fawn (1915) FY302
Fawn (1968) A335
Faxfleet (1916) Y3.1191
Feaco (1924) FY891
Fearless (1912) 27, 46, 64
Fearless (1934) H67
Fearless (1963) L10, L3004
Feasible (1912) FY928
Felicity (1944) B255, J369
Felicity (1969) A112
Felixstowe (1941) J126
Fellside (1901) Y3.1685
Felmersham (1953) M2627
Felsted (1970) A348
Fenay Lodge (1903) Y3.429
Fencer (1942) D64, R308
Fencer (1983) P283
Fenchurch (1909) Y3.509
Fennel RCN (1940) K194
Fenton (1955) M1135
Fentonian (1912) FY868, Y7.11
Fergus RCN (1944) K686
Fermoy (1919) J40, N40, N7A, NA0
Fernandina (1908) Y3.2073
Ferndene (1899) Y3.1022
Fernfield (1895) Y3.1870
Ferngarth (1911) Y3.271
Fernhill (1908) Y3.2
Fernie (1940) F111, L11
Fernleaf (1916) Y7.162
Fernley (1901) Y3.768, Y8.95

Fernmoor (1936) B412, Z208

Ferol (1914) N88, X07, X24

Ferret (1911) F93, H32, H35, H93

Ferryhill (1909) Y3.819, Y8.13

Fervent (1895) D39, D97, N17

Festubert ʀᴄɴ (1917) N46, J46

Fetlar (1941) A336, DV8, P43, T202

Fezenta (1914) FY587

Fiaray (1942) T238

Fidelity (1920) D57

Fidget (1915) N9A, X20, X25

Fidget (1917) FY551

Fieldgate (1902) Z207

Fierce (1945) J453, M53

Fiery Cross (1936) FY877

Fife (1964) D20

Fife Ness (1945) F29

Fighter (1945) L109, L3038

Figuig ʀᴀɴ (ex *Grantala*) (1903) YA.8

Fiji (1939) 58

Filey Bay (1931) FY679

Filla (1942) T212

Finch ᴜsɴ (1918) T7A

Findhorn (1942) B270, K301

Finesse (1912) FY1683

Finisterre (1944) D55, R55, D91

Finland (1902) Y3.1878

Fintry (1970) A394

Finwhale (1959) S05

Fiona (1905) M17, M(I)07, M(I)17

Fiona (1973) A148

Fir (1940) T129

Fir Lake ʀᴄɴ (Canc) J487

Fireball (Canc) J464

Firedrake (1912) H33, H89, H97

Firedrake (1934) H79

Firefly (1930) FY673

Firfield (1915) Y3.944

Firm (1910) W15

Firmament (1930) FY1725

Firtree (1917) Y3.1973

Fiscus (1917) Y3.1890

Fisher Boy (1914) FY1505

Fisher Lad (1919) FY282

Fishguard (1928) Y59

Fishpool (1912) Y3.1292

Fiskerton (1957) M1206

Fittleton (1954) M1136

Fitzroy (1919) J03, N03, T03

Fitzroy (1943) B632, K553

Flamborough Head (1944) B311, F88

Flamer (1940) A131, W31

Flamingo (1939) B633, F18, L18, U18

Flanders (1920) FY600

Flandre (1915) FY1715

Flandrier (1905) Y3.1819

Flare (1943) W151

Flatholm (1943) A337, DV9, T354

Flaunt (1943) W152

Flax (1942) K284

Fleetwood (1936) L47, U47, F47

Fleswick (1900) Y3.2104

Fleur de Lys (1940) K122

Flicker (1932) FY719

Flinders (1919) J04, N04, T04

Flint (1942) T287

Flint Castle (1943) F383, K383

Flintha (1955) M2628

Flirt (1897) D56, P87

Flockton (1954) M1137

Florence (1980) A149

Florence Brierley (1918) Z117

Florentia (1912) Y3.2061

Florentino (1900) Y3.1694

Flores ʀɴʟɴ (1925   F66

Florida ᴜsɴ (1910) 99

Florida sᴀɴ (1930) T34, T474

Floridian (1913) Y9.11

Florio (1916) FY988

Floris (1912) Y4.79

Floriston (1955) M1138

Florizel (1943) J404

Flotta (1941) T171

Fluellen (1940) T157

Flusser ᴜsɴ (1909) H(I)49

Fly (1942) J306, M306

Flying Admiral (1917) 4.46

Flying Buzzard (1912) W25

Flying Cormorant (1908) W26

Flying Falcon (1904) W27

Flying Fish (1897) D40, D57, H69, P86

Flying Fish (1944) J370

Flying Foam (1917) W28

Flying Fox (1918) T00

Flying Spray (1917) W29

Flying Wing (1915) FY880

Foam (1943) J405

Foamcrest (1902) 4.204

Foley (1943) K474

Folkestone (1903) M33, T07, T32

Folkestone (1930) L22, N20, U22

Forceful (1925) W126

Forceful (1957) A86

Forceful (1985) A221

Ford (1918) TN7, T2/	*Fortitude* (1896) W30
Ford Castle (1911) Y3.189	*Fortol* (1917) A126, X26, X58
Forde (1919) FY1723	*Fortunatus* (1884) Y3.2056
Fordham (1956) M2717	*Fortune* (1913) H30
Foreland (1914) Y3.412	*Fortune* (1940) H70
Foremost (1913) N45, N47, D38	*Forward* (1904) N48, N53
Foreric (1898) Y3.1850	*Foss* (1916) Z144
Foresight (1904) N26, N46	*Fossbeck* (1930) Y01
Foresight (1934) H68	*Fotherby* (1969) A341
Forest Hill rcn (1943) K486, K360	*Foula* (1941) T203
Forester (1911) H34, H39, H58	*Foulness* (1942) P342, T342
Forester (1934) H74	*Fountains Abbey* (1879) Y3.2241
Forestmoor (1910) Y3.384	*Fowey* (1930) L15, U15
Forfar (1911) Y3.184	*Fox* (1967) A320
Forfar (1918) T6/, T/6	*Foxglove* (1915) L26, M41, T15, T33, U26
Forfar (1920) F30	*Foxhound* (1909) H16, H26, H58
Forfeit (1917) 4.243	*Foxhound* (1934) H69
Formidable (1898) 50	*Foxhound* (1962) A326
Formidable (1939) 67, R1, R67	*Foxley* (Canc) M2015
Fornebo (1906) Y7.148	*Foxtrot* (1940) T109
Forres (1918) T40, T/1	*Foyle* (1903) D20, N44
Fort Alabama (1944) B577	*Foyle* (1915) Y3.2211
Fort Austin (1978) A386	*Foylemore* (1911) Y3.1038
Fort Beauharnois (944) A285, B586	*Framlington Court* (1911) Y3.1205
Fort Charlotte (944) A236, B587	*Franc Tireur* (1916) FY1560, 4.70
Fort Colville (1943) B531, PT1.15	*Frances* (1979) A147
Fort Constantine (1944) A237, B578, PT1.20	*Frances Duncan* (1907) Y3.4
Fort Dunvegan (1944) A160, B579, PT1.19	*Francia* (1915) Y3.665
Fort Duquesne (1944) A229, B588, X141	*Francis Batey* (1914) W31
Fort Edmondton (1944) B580	*Francol* (1917) X27, X67
Fort Erie rcn (1944) B603, K670	*Frank Parish* (1900) Y3.1609
Fort Francis rcn (1943) F396, J396	*Frankenfels* (1913) Y3.836
Fort George (1991) A388	*Frankier* (1906) Y3.1204
Fort Grange (1976) A385	*Franklin* (1937) A304, J84, N84
Fort Kilmar (1944) B581	*Frankmere* (1911) Y3.2470
Fort Langley (1944) A230, B532	*Fraser* rcn (1931) H48
Fort Providence (1944) B582	*Fraser River* (1915) Y3.1045
Fort Robert (1918) FY762	*Fraserburgh* (1941) J124, M224
Fort Rosalie (1944) A186, B559, X142	*Fratton* (1925) B16
Fort Rosalie (1976) A385	*Frederick Clover* (1945) L3001
Fort Rose (1917) 4.275	*Fredericton* rcn (1941) K245
Fort Royal (1931) FY711	*Freebooter* (1940) A101, W01
Fort Ryan (1932) Z156	*Freedom* (1943) W139
Fort Sandusky (1944) A316, B560	*Freelance* (1908) 4.285
Fort Victoria (1990) A387	*Freesia* (1940) K43
Fort Wayne (1944) B561	*Fremantle* ran (1942) J246, M246
Fort William rcn (1941) J311, K236	*Freres Coquelin* (1934) FY1778
Fort Wrangell (1944) B583	*Freshbrook* (1941) A213, X107
Fort York (1941) J119	*Freshburn* (1943) X60
Forth (1886) D06, N06, N47	*Freshener* (1942) X109
Forth (1938) A187, F07, I07	*Freshet* (1940) X102
Forth (2016) P222	*Freshfield* (1896) Y3.2233

Freshford (1944) X63
Freshlake (1942) X120
Freshmere (1942) X117
Freshpond (1945) X76
Freshpool (1943) X99
Freshspray (1946) X113
Freshspring (1946) X118
Freshtarn (1944) X47
Freshwater (1940) A349
Freshwell (1943) X121
Fresne (....) Z201
Frettenham (1954) M2702
Freya (1917) 4.407
Friarage (1930) FY904
Friendship (1942) J398, K308
Friesland ʀɴʟɴ (1921) FY1663
Frinton (1903) Y3.878
Frisio ʀɴʟɴ (1940) K00
Frisky (1941) A111, W11
Frisky (1945) A396
Fritham (1953) M2630
Fritillary (1941) K199
Frixos (1907) Y3.1296
Frobisher (1916) G49
Frobisher (1920) 81, D81, F51, I81
Frolic (1943) J406
Frome (1943) K267
Frons Olivae (1916) FY962
Frontenac ʀᴄɴ (1943) K335
Froxfield (1970) A354
Fuday (1944) T385
Fulbeck (1969) A356
Fulgent (1910) Y3.151
Full Moon (1932) FY680
Fullerton (1912) Y3.287
Fumarole (1918) FY16, P37, Z36
Fundy ʀᴄɴ (1938) J88, N88
Furious (1916) 40, 47, 65
Furness (1898) W32
Fury (1911) H35, H42, H67, H76
Fusilier (1942) T305
Fylde (1904) W33
Fyldea (1930) FY666

G

G1 (1915) G1, IA3
G2 (1915) G2, IA4
G3 (1916) G3, IA5
G4 (1915) G4, IA6
G5 (1915) G5, IA7

G6 (1915) G6, IA8
G7 (1916) G7, IA9
G8 (1916) G8, I0C
G9 (1916) G9, I1C
G10 (1916) G10, I2C
G11 (1916) G11, I3C
G12 (1916 G12, I4C
G13 ʀɴʟɴ (1913) H35
G13 (1916) G13, I5C
G14 (1917) G14, I6C
G15 ʀɴʟɴ (1914) H66
G.R. Crowe (1907) Y7.184
Gabbard (1945) D47, R47
Gabriel (1915) F00, F67, F91, G21
Gabriel (Canc) J465
Gabrielle Denise (1910) 4.300
Gaddesdon (1917) T43, T78
Gadfly (1919) FY517
Gael (Canc) G07
Gafsa (ex *Dominion*) (1902) Y7.138
Gaillardia (1917) T34
Gainsborough (1918) T67, T76
Gairsay (1942) T290
Galatea (1914) 33, 66, 0C
Galatea ɪᴛ (1933) N71
Galatea (1934) 71, C71
Galatea (1963) F18
Gale ʀɴᴢɴ (1935) T370
Galileo Galilei ɪᴛ (1934) X2
Gallant (1935) H59
Gallant (Canc) G03
Gallier (1914) Y3.1738
Galt ʀᴄɴ (1940) K163
Galteemore (1943) F171
Galvani (1929) 4.71
Gambia (1940) 48, C48, C168
Gambia River (1915) Y3.1154
Gamtoos ꜱᴀɴ (1936) W122
Gananoque ʀᴄɴ (1941) J259
Ganges (1906) Y3.1668
Ganilly (1943) T367
Gannet (1927) T08
Gardenia (1901) Y3.357
Gardenia (1917) T11
Gardenia (1940) K99, M99
Gardiner (1943) K478
Garfield (1907) Y3.475
Garganey (1965) P194
Garland (1913) H32, H36, H55
Garland (1935) H37
Garlies (1943) K475
Garola (1912) FY865, Y7.14

Garron Head (1913) Y3.461
Garry (1905) D21, D41, H73, N10
Garry (1916) T63
Garryval (1907) Y3.1403
Garth (1917) TC6
Garth (1940) F120, L20
Garth Castle (1910) YA.2
Gartland (1892) Y3.921
Gasconia (1915) Y3.1268
Gascony (1908) Y3.1224
Gascoyne ran (1943) F354, K354
Gaspe rcn (1938) J94, N94
Gaston Riviere fr (1918) FY1679
Garthwaite (1917) Y3.1922
Gateshead (1942) P288, T288
Gatineau rcn (1934) H61
Gatling (1945) A376, W52
Gatwick (1916) T10
Gauntlet (Canc) G59
Gava (1920) 4.14
Gavinton (1953) M1140
Gavotte (1940) T115
Gawler ran (1941) B241, J188
Gay Archer (1952) P1041
Gay Bombadier (1952) P1042
Gay Bowman (1952) P1043
Gay Bruiser (1952) P1044
Gay Caribineer (1953) P1045
Gay Cavalier (1953) P1049
Gay Centurion (1952) P1046
Gay Charger (1953) P1047
Gay Charioteer (1953) P1048
Gay Dragoon (1953) P1050
Gay Fencer (1953) P1051
Gay Forester (1954) P1052
Gaya rin (Canc) T325
Gazelle (1889) M40, T14, T35
Gazelle fr (1939) U94
Gazelle (1943) J342
Geddington Court (1912) Y3.1861
Geelong ran (1941) J201
Gemini (1892) Y3.1717
Gena (1893) Y3.1502
General Birdwood (1919) FY724
General Botha (1916) FY599
General Church (1917) Y3.1923
General Craufurd (1915) M03, M05
General Gordon (1885) Y3.30
General Suworow (1888) Y3.1222
General Wolfe (1915) M04, M14
Genesee (1888) Y7.67
Genevieve (1980) A150

Genista (1916) T63
Genista (1941) K200
Genius (1919) FY748
Gentian (1915) T36, T49
Gentian (1940) K90
Geo (1915) Y3.140
Geordie (1911) FY1950
George & Albert (1916) FY1910
George Adgell (1920) FY1926
George Bligh (1917) Z178
George Cousins (1919) FY627
George D Irvin (1911) Z249
George Dinsdale (1913) W37
George Fisher (1877) Y3.1944
George R Purdy (1917) 4.135
George Robb (1930) FY685
George V (1915) W38
Georgeham (1957) M2788
Georges Le Verdier (1930) 4.323
Georges Leygues fr (1936) 90
Georgetown (1918) I40
Georgette (1918) FY804
Georgia (1891) Y7.239
Georgian rcn (1941) J144
Georgian Prince (1893) Y7.99
Georgina (1973) A152
Geraldton ran (1941) B242, J178
Geranium (1915) T37, T56
Geranium (1940) K16, M16
Gerberdina Johanna (1912) FY1779
Gerent (1888) Y3.978
Germanic (1905) Y3.849
Germiston san (1923) T47, T447
Gertie (1902) Y3.494, Y8.40
Gerusalemme (1919) B395
Ghazee (1904) Y3.954
Ghurka (1907) D04, H52
Giada it (1941) N88
Gibel Derif (1887) Y3.2028
Gibel Hamam (1895) Y3.2034
Gibraltar (1892) A7, N19, N49
Gibraltar (1914) Y3.647
Gibraltar (Canc) D68
Giffard rcn (1943) K402
Gifford (1954) P3111
Gift (Canc) G67
Gillian (1919) 4.408
Gillstone (1943) T355
Gilsay (1944) T386
Gilt Edge (1916) FY963
Giorgios Averoff rhn (1910) D54
Gippsland ran (1908) FY38

Gipsy (1897) D43, D58, P23

Gipsy (1935) H63

Girafe FR (....) Z179

Giralda (1887) Y3.7

Giralda (1894) Y3.627

Girard (1918) Z186

Girdle Ness (1945) A387, F04

Girdleness (ex *Grelisle*, ex *Rockabill*) (1905) Y3.1147

Girl Ellen (1914) FY1975

Girl Ethel (1914) FY1655

Girl Gladys (1917) FY1991

Girl Margaret (1914) Z304

Girl Nancy (....) FY1940

Girl Winifred (1912) FY1999

Gisella (1904) Y3.332

Glace Bay RCN (1944) K414

Glacier (1909) 4.257

Gladiator (1904) Y3.1892

Gladiolus (1915) T38, T50

Gladiolus (1940) K34, M34

Gladstone RAN (1942) J324, M324

Gladys (1917) Z134

Gladys Royle (1894) Y3.345

Glaisdale (1942) L44

Glamorgan (1902) Y3.309

Glamorgan (1964) D19

Glasgow (1936) 21, C21, C169

Glasgow (1976) D88

Glasgow (Bldg) F88

Glasserton (1953) M1141

Glassford (1955) P3120

Glatian (1913) FY881

Glatton (1914) N03, N50

Gleaner (1937) J83, N83

Gleaner (1983) A86, H86

Glen Avon (1912) J104, R392, 4.392

Glen Earn (1938) B210

Glen Gelder (1881) Y3.1933

Glen Gower (1922) J16, N16

Glen Heather (1913) FY556

Glen Kidston (1930) 4.77

Glen More (1922) J16, 4.368

Glen Park (1918) Y3.2296

Glen Strathallan (1928) FY.010

Glen Usk (1914) J26, N26, 4.377

Glenaffric (1905) Y3.1258

Glenarm (1943) K258

Glenartney (1939) B584

Glenbridge (1911) Y3.1331

Glenby (1900) Y3.590

Glencliffe (1917) Y3.487

Glencoe (1905) Y3.103

Glencoe (1971) A392

Glendene (1911) Y3.504

Glendevon 1907) Y3.1842

Glendhu (1905) Y3.56

Glenearn (1938) 4.250

Gleneden (1909) Y3.98

Glenelg (1904) Y3.879

Glenelg RAN (1942) J236, M236

Glenetive (1911) Y3.964

Glenfinlas (1906) Y3.945

Glenfoyle (1913) Y3.1235

Glenfruin (1904) Y3.499

Glengyle (1939) 4.196

Glenisla (1878) Y3.876

Glenloch (1896) Y3.1050

Glenmaroon (1917) Y3.2094

Glenmay (1905) Y3.511

Glenmorag (1906) Y3.1106

Glennevis (1917) Y3.1862

Glenorchy (1909) Y3.1592

Glenroy (1938) 4.256

Glenshiel (1909) Y3.1543

Glensloy (1911) Y3.1182

Glenspean (1912) Y3.1894

Glentaise (1905) Y3.2172

Glentham (1957) M2631

Glenturret (1896) Y3.340

Gloamin (1919) FY1556

Glocliffe (1915) Y3.1366

Glodale (1907) Y3.1039

Gloire FR (1933) 05

Gloria de Larrinaga (1908) Y3.1478

Gloriosa (Canc) K201

Glorious (1916) 56, 67, 77

Glory (1899) P08, P92

Glory (1943) 62, R62

Gloucester (1909) 58, 68

Gloucester (1937) 62, C62

Gloucester (1982) D96

Gloucester Coast (1913) Y2.77

Gloucestershire (1910) M(I)38, M(I)72, M(I)87

Glow (1918) FY964

Glowworm (1916) P93, P94

Glowworm (1935) H92

Glowworm (Canc) G45

Gloxinia (1940) K22

Glynn (1899) Y3.171

Gnat (1915) P94, P97, T60

Gnat (1969) A239

Goatfell (1934) J125, 4.36

Goathland (1942) L27

Godavari RIN (1940) B651, F52, U52

Goderich RCN (1941) J260
Godetia (1916) T39, T57
Godetia (i) (1940) K72, M72
Godetia (ii) (1941) K226
Goeree RNLN (1920) FY1761
Gold Ranger (1941) A130, X30
Gold Rover (1973) A271
Golden Eagle (1909) 4.236
Golden Effort (1914) FY1534
Golden Fleece (1944) J376, M376
Golden Gift (1910) FY1994
Golden Harvest (1914) FY708
Golden Meadow (1943) B527
Golden News (1914) FY1510
Golden Sunbeam (1920) FY1968
Golden View (1918) FY745
Goldeneye (1966) P195
Goldfinch (1910) H44
Goldmouth (1903) Y7.59
Goliath (1898) N54
Goliath (1921) W121
Gondwana RIN (Canc) J321
Gondwana RIN (1943) K348
Good Hope (1901) P16
Good Hope SAN (1944) F432, K432
Goodall (1943) K479
Goodson (1943) K480
Goodwin (1917) 4.68
Goodwood (1900) Y3.251
Goodwood (1916) T22
Goolgwai RAN (1919) FY75
Goonambee (1919) FY94
Goorangai RAN (1919) FY74
Goosander (1908) Y7.20
Goosander (1973) A164, P196
Gopher (1910) W94
Gordon Castle (1901) Y3.1442
Gore (1943) K481
Gorgon (1914) N51, P59
Gorgon (1943) J346
Gorleston (1929) Y92
Gorregan (1943) P387, T387
Gorse (1911) FY316
Gorsemore (1899) Y3.829
Gos 9 (1937) FY1725
Gosforth (1898) Y3.168, Y4.66, Y8.61
Goshawk (1911) H37, H45, H59
Gossamer (1890) D68, N52, N68
Gossamer (1937) J63, N63
Gossamer (1939) N12
Goth (1925) FY649
Gothic (1906) Y3.1829

Goulburn RAN (1940) B243, J167
Gould (1943) K476
Goulding SAN (1921) T03, T503
Gourko (1911) Y5.4
Gowan (1907) FY1962
Gowan Craig (1915) FY1544
Gozo (1943) J287
Graaf Van Vlaanderen (1925) Z239
Gracie Fields (1936) J100
Graemsay (1942) A338, DV10, T291
Graf Schuwalow (1889) Y3.1715
Graf Stroganoff (1903) Y3.1210
Grafton (1892) A8, N23, N53
Grafton (1935) H89
Grafton (1954) F51
Grafton (1994) F80, F88
Grafton (Canc) G76
Grain (1943) T360
Grainton (1911) Y3.508
Grampian (1930) FY546
Grampus (1910) H07, H31, H38, HA7
Grampus (1936) 56M, 56N, N56
Grampus (1957) S04
Granby RCN (1941) J264, M180
Grandmere RCN (1941) J258
Grangemouth (1908) M22, M(I)08, M(I)22
Grangetown (1917) Y3.1588
Gransha (1901) Y3.258, Y4.41
Grantley (1908) Y3.297
Grantleyhall (1902) Y3.816
Grapeshot (1945) A283, W184
Graph (1941) P715
Grappler (1908) W26
Grasmere (1970) A402
Grassholm (1943) T344
Grasshopper (1909) H17, H28, H60
Grasshopper (1939) T85
Gravelines (1944) D24, D92, R24
Grayling (1942) T243
Great Admiral (1908) 4.146
Great City (1914) Y3.1404
Greatford (1953) P3109
Greatham (1890) Y3.794
Greavesash (1917) Y3.1811
Grecian (1943) J352
Green Howard (1927) FY632
Green Pastures (1919) FY591
Green Ranger (1941) A152, B515, X42
Green Rover (1968) A268
Greenbank (1905) Y3.1381
Greenbatt (1908) Y3.290
Greenfly (1936) FY156

Greenhill (1901) Y3.177

Greenisland (1901) Y3.2366

Greenock (1942) J182

Greenol (1907) X28

Greenwich (1915) C6, CA, F10, I10

Greetham (1954) M2632

Gregory (1891) Y3.1527

Gregory (1930) FY1875

Gregynog (1899) Y3.673

Grelarlie (ex *Rachel*) (1910) Y3.719

Grelben (ex *Reliance*) (1906) Y3.997

Grelcaldy (ex *Caldy*) (1913) Y3.523

Greldale (1910) Y3.119

Greldon (1903) Y3.920

Grelgrant (ex *Hartland*) (1906) Y3.1267

Grelhame (ex *Tyninghame*) (1909) Y3.405

Grelhead (ex *Beachy Head*) (1915) Y3.1434

Grelrosa (ex *Arosa*) (1905) Y3.654

Grelstone (ex *Eddystone*) (1912) Y3.1143

Grelwen (1912) Y3.2113

Grenade (1935) H86

Grenade (Canc) G53

Grenadier (1942) T334

Grenville (1916) D90, F54, G61, G75, G85, G95, H27

Grenville (1935) H03

Grenville (1942) D11, D197, F197, R97

Gresham (1905) Y3.1826

Gretaston (1901) Y3.206

Gretna (1918) T38, T8C

Grey Fox (1941) S304

Grey Goose (1942) S309

Grey Mist (1920) 4.40

Grey Owl (1941) S305

Grey Rover (1969) A269

Grey Seal (1941) S303

Grey Shark (1941) S306

Grey Wolf (1941) S308

Greyhound (1900) D44, D59, H43, P01

Greyhound (1935) H05

Greyhound (Canc) G88

Greystoke Castle (1906) Y3.1490

Gribb sᴀɴ (1930) T50, T450

Griffin (1935) H31

Griffon (1896) D39, D45, D81

Grilse (1943) T368

Grimsby (1933) L16, U16

Grimsby (1998) M108

Grimsby Town (1934) FY125, T125

Grimstad (1932) FY1956

Grimwood sᴀɴ (1924) T04, T504

Grindall (1943) K477

Grinder (1943) W76

Grinder (1958) A92

Grindon Hall (1905) Y3.1220

Griper (1942) W112

Griper (1958) A91

Gripfast (1910) Y3.485

Grive (1905) M(I)09, M(I)24, Y1.3

Groeswen (1900) Y3.854

Grom ᴏʀᴘ (1936) H71

Groningen (1902) Y4.6

Grorud (1907) Y3.2318

Grosmont Castle (1917) FY671

Grou ʀᴄɴ (1943) B604, K518

Grove (1941) L77

Growler (1890) X28

Growler (1942) B743, W105

Gruinard (1942) T239

Gruna (1941) T205

Gruno ʀɴʟɴ (1912) F81

Gryfevale (1906) Y3.1555

Gryfevale (1929) B391

Guardian (1932) A145, B436, T89

Guardian (1975) P245

Guardsman (1944) T393

Guava (1935) T118

Gudrun Maersk (1936) B538

Guelder Rose (....) 4.49

Guelph ʀᴄɴ (1943) K687

Guernsey (Canc) G19

Guernsey (1977) P297

Guiana (1886) W39

Guide On (1911) FY965

Guiding Light (1911) FY354

Guildford Castle (1943) K378

Guillemot (1939) K89, L89, M89, P89

Guinevere (Canc) G40

Gula (1936) FY718

Gulfoss (1929) FY710

Gulland (1943) T365

Gulnare (1900) J134

Gunbar ʀᴀɴ (1911) FY98, Z270

Gunner (1927) FY568

Gurkha (1937) F20, G20, L20

Gurkha (1941) F63, G63

Gurkha (1960) F122

Gurna (1919) B431

Guysborough ʀᴄɴ (1941) J52

Gweal (1942) T246

Gwendoline (1973) A196

Gwenllian (1911) FY544

Gwmaho (1917) Z135

Gwynwood (1901) Y3.1777

Gymeric (1917) Y7.248
Gympie ʀᴀɴ (1942) J238, M238
Gypol (1916) X57

H

H1 (1915) H1
H1 ɪᴛ (....) P56
H2 (1915) H2
H3 (1915) H3
H4 (1915) H4
H5 (1915) H5
H6 (1915) H6
H7 (1915) H7
H8 (1915) H8
H9 (1915) H9
H10 (1915) H10
H11 (1915) H11
H12 (1915) H12
H13 (1915) H13
H14 (1915) H14
H15 (1915) H15
H16 (1915) H16
H17 (1915) H17
H18 (1915) H18
H19 (1915) H19
H20 (1915) H20
H21 (1917) H21
H22 (1917) H22
H23 (1918) H23
H24 (1917) H24
H25 (1918) H25
H26 (1917) H26
H27 (1918) H27
H28 (1918) 28H, 28N, H28, N28
H29 (1918) H29
H30 (1918) H30
H31 (1918) 31H, 31N, H31, N31
H32 (1918) 32H, 32N, H32, N32
H33 (1918) 33H, 33N, H33, N33
II34 (1918) 34H, 34N, H34, N34
H35 (Canc) H35
H36 (Canc) H36
H37 (Canc) H37
H38 (Canc) H38
H39 (Canc) H39
H40 (Canc) H40
H41 (1918) H41
H42 (1918) H42
H43 (1919) 43H, 43N, H43, N43
H44 (1919) 44H, 44N, H44, N44

H45 (Canc) H45
H46 (Canc) H46
H47 (1918) H47
H48 (1919) H48
H49 (1919) 49H, 49N, H49, N49
H50 (1919) 50H, 50N, H50, N50
H51 (1918) H51
H52 (1919) H52
H53 (Canc) H53
H54 (Canc) H54
H. C. Folger (1916) Y7.195
H. J. Bull (1935) 4.325
Haarlem (1938) FY306
Hadleigh Castle (1943) F355, K355
Hadley (1901) Y3.77
Haida ʀᴄɴ (1942) D63, D77, G63
Haigh Hall (1908) Y3.1244
Haileybury (1902) Y3.1469
Hailstorm (1932) FY1825
Haitan (1909) F133
Halberd (Canc) G99
Halcyon (1894) C76, C82
Halcyon (1933) J42, N42
Haldon (1916) T62
Haldon (1942) L19
Halifax ʀᴄɴ (1941) K237
Halladale (1944) F417, K417
Hallamshire (1907) Y3.744
Hallowell ʀᴄɴ (1944) K666
Halo (1918) FY21, P39, Z38
Halsham (1953) M2633
Halstead (1943) K556
Halton (1914) Y3.828
Halvard (1902) Y3.2353
Hambledon (1917) TC7
Hambledon (1939) F137, L37
Hambledon (1972) A1769
Hambleton ᴜsɴ (1941) Y02
Hamilton ʀᴄɴ (1918) I24
Hamlet (1940) T167
Hammond (1936) FY149
Hampshire (1903) 50
Hampshire (1908) Y3.2351, Y8.69
Hampshire (1934) FY173
Hampshire (1961) D06
Hampton (1919) F19, I19, M19
Handmaid (1940) W79
Hanley (1901) Y3.787
Hannah (1913) Y3.845
Hannaray (1944) T389
Hannibal (1896) D36, N54, P45
Hannington Court (1912) Y3.2175

Hans Lody (1936) R38

Hansa (1904) Y3.2524

Happy Return (Canc) J466

Hardanger (1905) Y3.1192

Harden (1912) Y6.3

Hardy (1912) H39, H67, H88

Hardy (1936) H87

Hardy (ii) (1943) R08

Hardy (1953) F54

Hare (1944) B256, J389, M389

Harebell (1918) T03

Harebell (Canc) K202

Harbury (1913) Y3.1484

Harflete (1912) Y3.496

Hargood (1943) K582

Harlech (1914) Y3.671

Harlech (1972) A1768

Harlech Castle (1916) FY741

Harlequin (1897) X77

Harlow (1915) Y3.672

Harlseywood (1907) Y3.394

Harmattan (1911) Y3.960

Harmattan (1918) FY23, Z72

Harmodious (1892) Y8.128

Harmonic (1905) Y3.240

Harpenden (1918) T58

Harperley (1906) Y8.119

Harpham (1954) M2634

Harpy (1909) D88, H19, H32, H71

Harrier (1893) P63, P95

Harrier (1934) J71, N71

Harris (1944) T386

Harrow (1918) J61, N61, TN1, TN5

Harry Melling (1919) FY538

Harstad (1932) FY1847

Hart (1943) B285, F58, U58

Hart (1976) P257

Hartburn (1900) Y3.531

Hartdale (1910) Y3.274

Hartfield (1915) Y3.1582

Hartland (1906) Y3.1267

Hartland Point (1944) A262, F25

Hartlepool (1903) Y3.107, Y7.150

Hartlepool (1942) J155

Hartley (1903) Y3.1575

Hartside (1909) Y3.235

Harvest Reaper (1925) FY1528

Harvester (1918) T11

Harvester (1939) H19

Harwich (1942) J190

Hascosay (1944) T390

Haslingden (1895) Y3.58

Hastings (1930) L27, U27

Hasty (1936) H24

Hatano (1925) FY662

Hatherleigh (1941) L53

Hatsuse (1927) FY1749

Hattersley (Canc) M2016

Hatumet (1905) Y3.1221

Haug I RNoN (1924) FY1752

Hautapu RNZN (1942) P340, T340

Hav (1930) FY1759

Havant (1919) TN2, T/7

Havant (1939) H32

Havelock (1915) M02, M05

Havelock (1939) H88

Haversham (1954) M2635

Havildar (1911) Y3.1934

Havock (1936) H43

Hawea RNZN (1944) F422

Hawera RNZN (1912) T398

Hawke (1891) A9

Hawke (Canc) 27

Hawkesbury RAN (1943) F363, K363

Hawkesbury RCN (1943) K415

Hawkins (1917) 8A, D86, I86

Hawthorn (1930) T32

Haworth (1912) Y3.803

Hawsker (1915) Y3.1614

Hayburn Wyke (1917) FY139

Haydon (1942) B231, F75, L75

Hayling (1942) T271

Hazard (1894) P38, P96

Hazard (1937) J02, N02

Hazel (1907) M00, M(I)00, M(I)10

Hazel (1939) T108

Hazel Branch (ex *Bellgrano*) (1906) Y3.1823

Hazelwood (1904) Y3.1629

Hazleton (1954) M1142

H.C. Henry (1909) Y7.32

HDML 1183 RNZN (1942) B466

HDML 1184 RNZN (1942) B467

HDML 1185 RNZN (1942) B468

HDML 1186 RNZN (1942) B469

HDML 1187 RNZN (1943) B470

HDML 1188 RNZN (1943) B471

HDML 1189 RNZN (1943) B472

HDML 1190 RNZN (1943) B473

HDML 1191 RNZN (1943) B474

HDML 1192 RNZN (1943) B475

HDML 1193 RNZN (1943) B476

HDML 1194 RNZN (1943) B477

HDML 1400 (1944) B478

HDML 1459 (1944) B479

HDML 1481 (Canc) B480
HDML 1482 (Canc) B481
HDML 1483 (1944) B482
HDML 1489 (1944) B483
HDML 1494 (Canc) B484
Headcliffe (1915) Y3.275
Headcorn (1971) A1766
Headley (1914) Y3.918
Heartsease (1940) K15
Hearty (1885) D45, N45, N55
Hearty (1939) H57
Heather (1916) T40
Heather (1940) K69
Heatherside (1909) Y3.407
Heathpark (1917) Y3.2267
Heathside (ex Neilrose) (1906) Y3.639
Hebble (1891) Y2.27, Y3.1594, Y8.3
Hebburn (1908) Y3.660, Y3.858
Hebe (1892) N52, N56
Hebe (1936) J24, N24
Hebe (1962) A406
Hecate (1965) A137
Hecla (1878) 7A, C7
Hecla (1940) F20, I20
Hecla (1944) F175
Hecla (1964) A133
Hector (1895) Y4.20, Y8.103
Hector (1906) Y3.2154
Hector (1924) F45
Hedingham Castle (1944) F386, K396, K529
Heighington (1891) Y3.107
Hekla (1929) FY1650
Hektor Frans BG (1938) 4.09
Hektor SAN (1929) T24, T464
Helen (1974) A198
Helford (1943) B271, F252, K252
Helford (1984) M2006
Helier II (1936) FY312
Heliopolis (1903) 4.191
Heliotrope (1915) T37, T41
Heliotrope (1940) K03, M03
Helga (1897) Y3.2266
Hellenes (1900) Y3.1231
Hellespont (1910) W86
Hellisay (1944) T391
Helmsdale (1907) Y3.1560
Helmsdale (1943) F253, K253
Helmsdale (1985) M2010
Helmsloch (1913) Y3.1698
Helmsman (1903) Y2.4, Y8.49
Helmsmuir (1913) Y3.599
Helredale (1906) Y3.1367

Helvellyn (1937) J120
Helvetia (1917) 4.86
Helvig (1937) B296, M49
Hematite (1903) Y3.2237
Hemlock (Canc) K203
Hendon (1899) Y3.186
Hengist (1941) A110, W110
Henley (1887) Y3.1657
Henry R. James (1909) Y3.753
Hepatica RCN (1940) K159
Herakles (1912) Y3.1386
Herald (1918) T73
Herald (1973) A138, H138
Hercules (1909) Y3.1952
Hercules (1910) 47, 54, 69
Hercules (1945) 49, R49
Hercules RNLN (1905) FY1731
Hereward (1936) H93
Hermelin (1940) B539
Hermes (1905) Y3.1454
Hermes (1919) 95, D95, I95
Hermes (1953) D61, R12
Hermetray (1944) T392
Hermione (1893) N32, N57, P17
Hermione (1908) Y7.1
Hermione (1939) 74, C74
Hermione (1967) F58
Hermiston (1901) Y3.471, Y8.97
Herne Bay (1945) K611
Hero (1936) H99
Heroic (1906) M05, M(I)05, M(I)11
Heroine (1907) FY1866
Heroine (1909) W42
Heron USN (1918) TA3
Heron (1937) B540
Heron Bridge (1918) Y3.2212
Heronspool (1903) Y3.1316
Heros RAN (1919) FY87
Herring (1942) T307
Herrington (1905) Y3.29
Herschel (1914) Y3.1639
Herschell (1942) T289
Hertfordshire (1936) A406, FY176
Hesleyside (1912) Y3.1761
Hespeler RCN (1943) K378, K489
Hesperia (1942) W106
Hesperus (1896) Y3.1530
Hesperus (1939) H57
Hever (1971) A1767
Hever Castle (1944) K521
Hexham (1917) T35
Hexton (1954) M1143

Heythrop (1917) TC8

Heythrop (1940) L85

Hibernia (1905) 60, 70, N66

Hibiscus (1917) T42

Hibiscus (1940) K24

Hickleton (1955) M1131

Hickorol (1917) A181, X29

Hickory (1940) T116

Hickory Lake (1944) J488

Hidalgo (1908) Y3.979

Highburton (1954) M1130

Highcliffe (1909) Y3.755

Highflyer (1898) D22, N58, N69, N85

Highgate (1899) Y3.162

Highlander (1939) H44

Highway (1943) F140

Hilary (1908) M90, M(I)90

Hilary (1931) F22

Hilda Cooper (1928) FY1949

Hildasay (1941) T173

Hildawell (1892) Y3.949

Hildebrand (1911) M91, M(I)39, M(I)73, M(I)91

Hildersham (1954) M2705

Hildina (1918) FY541

Hinau RNZN (1941) T399

Hinba (1903) 4.53

Hind (1911) H40, H47, H60

Hind (1943) B288, F39, U39

Hindustan (1903) 62, 71, N67

Hindustan (1917) Y3.1880

Hindustan RIN (1930) F80, L80, U80

Hiniesta RIN (1902) FY.011, 4.60

Hinksford (1955) P3115

Hinnoy RNoN (1935) J112

Hippopotamus (1897) W43

Hira RIN (1931) T301

Hiravati RIN (1930) 4.215

Hirondelle (1890) Y8.54, Y9.17

Hobart RAN (1934) C3, D63, I63

Hocking (1895) Y3.1109

Hockwold (1911) Y3.661

Hodder (1910) Y4.80, Y8.45

Hodgeston (1954) M1146

Hogue (1900) N59

Hogue (1944) D74, D82,R74

Holcombe (1942) L56

Holderness (1916) TC9

Holderness (1940) F148, L48

Holdfast (1910) N8A, X19, X30

Holdfast (1921) Z220

Holgate (1896) Y3.650

Holland No1 (1901) 1

Holland No2 (1902) 2

Holland No3 (1903) 3

Holland No4 (1903) 4

Holland No5 (1903) 5

Hollesley Bay (Canc) K614

Hollinside (1905) Y3.48

Hollinside (ex *Robert Coverdale*) (1911) Y3.246

Holly (1930) P119, T19

Holly Branch (1911) Y3.306

Hollydale (1919) FY1982

Hollyhock (1915) M42, T16, T43

Hollyhock (1940) K64, M64

Hollyleaf (1916) Y7.160

Holm Sound (1944) A189, B319, F189

Holmes (1943) K581

Holmpark (1914) Y3.322

Holm's Island (ex *Grelford*) (1898) Y3.1493

Holmside (1893) Y3.2180

Holmwood (1972) A1772

Holtby (1909) Y3.1860

Holywood (1907) Y3.22

Home Guard (1944) T394

Homer City (1915) Y3.198

Honesty (1942) K285

Honeysuckle (1915) M43, T17, T44

Honeysuckle (1940) K27, M27

Hong Siang (....) PT1.14

Honingsvaag RNoN (1940) 4.277

Honjo (1928) FY661

Honorius (1899) Y3.1540

Hood (1918) 51

Hope (1910) H41, H48, H68

Hopecrest (1918) Y3.2225

Hopelyn (1918) Y3.2026

Hopemoor (1911) Y3.1217

Horatio (1940) T153

Horden (1906) Y3.1226

Horizon (1918) FY24, Z53

Hornbeam (1929) T53

Horngarth (1911) Y3.1093

Hornby Castle (1899) Y3.1930

Hornet (1911) H08, H42, H49

Horning (1972) A1773

Hornpipe (1940) T120

Horsa (1894) Y3.1201

Horsa (1942) W97

Horsham RAN (1942) J235, M235

Horten RNoN (1929) 4.322

Hortensia (1907) FY1795

Hosanna (1930) FY950

Hoste (1916) G90

Hoste (1943) K566

Hostile (1936) H55
Hostilius (1900) Y3.1590
Hotham (1943) B652, F583, K583
Hotspur (1936) D101, H01
Houghton (1957) M1211
Hound (1942) J307, M307
Housatonic usn (1899) R(I)10
Hova (1910) Y3.1321, Y8.112
Hoverfly (1917) FY557
Hovingham (1956) M2637
Howe (1940) 32, B3, B32
Howitzer (Canc) G44
Howth Head (1906) Y3.1440
Hoxa (1941) T16
Hoy (1941) T114
Hubberston (1954) M1147
Huddersfield Town (1933) FY197
Hudson (1939) W02
Huelva (1915) Y3.1190
Hugh Walpole (1937) FY102
Hughli (1894) W82
Humber (1913) M00, M06, N15
Humber (1953) M1115
Humber (1984) M2007
Humberstone rcn (1944) K447, K497
Humphrey Gale (1944) L3509
Hunda (1942) T298
Hungerford (1913) P67, X23, Y3.1687, Y4.24
Hunsbridge (1912) Y3.1087
Hunsbrook (1909) Y3.1963
Hunsgate (1915) Y3.2442
Hunsgrove (1913) Y3.396
Hunsworth (1911) Y3.2255
Huntball (ex *Manica*) (1900) Y3.313, Y3.2173
Hunter (1936) H35
Hunter (1942) D80
Hunter (1945) L180, L3042
Hunter (1983) P284
Hunterfield (1903) Y3.2263
Huntley (1919) J56, N56, T12, T56
Huntscape (1911) Y3.2443
Huntsclyde (1904) Y3.1644, Y8.132
Huntscraft (1913) Y1.129
Huntsgulf (1892) Y3.1748, Y8.133
Huntshead (1916) Y3.1712
Huntstrick (1902) Y3.962
Huntsville rcn (1944) K461, K499
Huon ran (1914) H9A
Hurlford (1905) Y3.1159
Huron rcn (1942) D78, D224, G24
Hurricane (1939) H06
Hursley (1941) L84

Hurst (1910) Y3.793
Hurst (1916) T66
Hurst Castle (1944) K416
Hurstside (ex *Portreath*) (1907) Y3.335
Hurworth (1941) L28
Hurworth (1984) M39
Husky (1969) A178
Hussar (1934) J82, N82
Hval V rnon (1929) J393
Hyacinth (1940) K84
Hyacinthus (1902) Y3.1824
Hyanthes (1899) Y3.1349
Hyderabad (1917) P77, P80
Hyderabad rin (1941) K212
Hydra (1912) H43, H50, H94
Hydra (1942) J275, M275
Hydra (1965) A144
Hydrangea (1916) T45, T62
Hydrangea (1940) K39, M39
Hydrograaf rnln (1910) J392
Hylas (1899) Y3.1441
Hyltoni (1911) Y3.398
Hyndford (1905) Y3.928
Hyperion (1936) H97
Hyson (1899) Y3.2114
Hythe (1905) M36, T10
Hythe (1941) J194

I

Ibis (1888) Y3.2014
Ibis (1940) L99, U99
Ibis II bg (1937) 4.448
Icarus (1936) D03, I03
Icicle (1924) FY1889
Ickford (1954) P3116
Idaho (1907) Y3.2222
Iddesleigh (1904) Y3.448
Iddo (1901) Y3.2181
Idraet (1917) Y3.2127
Ierax rhn (1911) H29
Iere (1928) B528
Ijuin (1920) FY612
Ikala (1901) Y3.823
Ikalis (1900) Y3.1489
Ilchester (1974) A308
Ilderton (1903) Y3.844
Ile de France (1926) F78
Ilex (1937) D61, I61
Ilford (1901) Y3.1739
Ilfracombe (1941) J95, N95

Illustrious (1896) D40, P40, P97

Illustrious (1939) 87, R2, R87

Illustrious (1978) R06

Ilmington (1954) M1148

Ilvington Court (1911) Y3.1885

Ilwen (1904) Y3.279

Imelda (1914) Z136

Imersay (1944) J422, M422

Imhoff sᴀɴ (1927) T53, T453

Immingham (1906) Y8.50

Immortelle sᴀɴ (1936) T45, T445

Imogen (1936) D44, I44

Imperial (1902) Y3.539

Imperia (1912) FY813

Imperial (1936) D09, I09

Imperialist (1939) FY126

Impetus (1940) A112, W60

Impetus (1993) A345

Implacable (1899) 63, 72, N48

Implacable (1939) 86, R5, R86

Impoco (1913) Y7.22

Impudence (....) A297

Impulse (1993) A344

Impulsive (1937) D11, I11

Incemore (1898) Y3.735

Inch Arran ʀᴄɴ (1944) B605, K667

Inchcolm (1941) T18

Inchgower (1918) FY735

Inchkeith ʀɴᴢɴ (1941) P155, T155

Inchmoor (1900) Y3.594

Inchmarnock (1941) T166

Inconstant (1914) 73, 77, 5A

Inconstant (1941) H49

Indefatigable (1909) 13

Indefatigable (1942) 10, R7, R10

India (1896) M(I)81

Indian Star (1936) FY208

Indian Summer (1918) FY28, P86, Z86

Indian Transport (1910) Y3.467

Indiana (1902) Y3.375

Indomitable (1907) 05, 74, 77

Indomitable (1940) 92, R8, R92

Indrani (1888) Y9.7

Induna (1898) Y3.741

Indus ʀɪɴ (1934) L67, U67

Industrious (1902) A305, W32

Industry (1901) P68, X24, X31, X83

Industry (1908) FY938

Inflexible (1907) 47, 75, 83

Ingeborg (1937) X112

Ingersoll ʀᴄɴ (Canc) K336

Ingleby (1907) Y3.1613

Inglefield (1936) D02, I02

Inglesham (1952) M2601

Ingleside (1910) Y3.288

Inglis (1943) K570

Ingomar (1904) FY833

Ingonish ʀᴄɴ (1941) J69, M69

Inkpen (1941) T225

Inman (1943) K571

Innisshannon (1913) X32

Ino (1899) Y3.2064

Instow (1919) NA1, NA4

Instow (1974) A309

Instructor (ex *St Dunstan*) (1913) Y3.1078

Intaba (1910) Y1.4, Y9.30

Integrity (1942) A306, B453, W14

Intent (1911) Y3.69

Internos (1908) FY977

Intombi (1912) Y9.12

Intrepid (1891) N21, N30, N59

Intrepid (1936) D10, I10

Intrepid (1964) L11, L3005

Inver (1942) K302

Inveran (1906) Y3.1674

Inverawe (1914) Y3.1800

Inverbervie (1913) Y3.785

Invercairn (1916) FY288

Invercauld (1917) FY1938

Inverell ʀᴀɴ/ʀɴᴢɴ (1942) J233, M233

Inverforth (1914) FY729

Invergordon (1974) A311

Inveric (1901) Y3.460

Invermoriston (1954) M1150

Inverness (1902) Y3.1955

Inverness (1990) M102

Invertay (1916) FY1748

Inverugie (1908) FY976

Investigator ʀɪɴ (1925) J81, N80

Invicta (1905) Y4.10

Invicta (1939) 4.283

Invincible (1907) 85

Invincible (1977) R05

Iolanthe (1904) Y3.1534

Iolare (1902) FY.012

Iolo (1898) Y3.1157

Iona (1920) 4.74

Ionia ʀʜɴ (....) F178

Iperia (1899) Y3.1532

Iphigenia (1891) N27, N60

Ipswich ʀᴀɴ (1941) B244, J186

Irene (1972) A181

Iris (1915) M44, T18, T46

Irish Monarch (1908) Y3.738

Irismere (1906) Y3.1166
Iron Duke (1912) 14, 18, 76, 94
Iron Duke (1991) F234
Ironbound (1942) T284
Ironbridge (1974) A310
Ironsides (....) N83
Iroquois (1918) TN2
Iroquois RCN (1941) D79, D89, G89
Irrawadi RIN (1913) 4.186
Irresistible (1898) 64
Irthington (1897) Y3.373
Irtysh (1901) Y3.1464
Irtysh (1901) Y3.1464
Irvana (1917) FY663
Irvine (1917) T44, T79
Irwell (....) A282
Isaac Sweers RNLN (1940) G83
Isabel RNLN (1906) FY896
Isabel (1972) A183
Iser (1888) Y3.1134
Isham (1954) M2703
Isinglass (1919) N1A
Isis (1896) D60, N61, P60
Isis (1898) Y4.23
Isis (1936) D87, I87
Isis (1955) M2010
Isis (1956) M2721
Isla (1903) P93, X29, X33
Islanda (1900) Y3.1708
Islandmore (1909) Y3.1072
Islay (1941) P272, T172
Isle of Guernsey (1929) 4.245
Isle of Jersey (1929) Y9.3
Isle of Jura (1906) Y3.10
Isle of Lewis (1903) Y3.2069
Isle of May (1896) 4.304
Isle of Mull (1906) Y3.780
Isle of Thanet (1911) 4.262
Isleworth (ex *Eversley*) (1896) Y3.1155
Istria (1936) FY150
Italiana (1898) Y3.62
Itchen (1903) D22, N06
Itchen (1942) K227
Itchen (1984) M2009
Ithuriel (1916) D19, F88, G32, G50, G51, G63, H3A
Ithuriel (1941) H05
Itola (1900) Y3.1833
Itonus (1898) Y3.577
Iva (....) A298
Ivanhoe (1937) D16, I16
Iveston (1954) M1151

Ivy (1917) T21
Ivy (Canc) K204
Ivydene (1901) Y3.1863
Ixworth (1974) A318
Izaston (1898) Y3.1531

J

J1 (1915) J1
J2 (1915) J2
J3 (Canc) J3
J3 (ex *J7*) (1915) J3
J4 (Canc) J4
J4 (ex *J8*) (1916) J4
J5 (1915) J5
J6 (1915) J6
J7 (ii) (1917) J7
J. Duncan (1914) Y3.361
J. Oswald Boyd (1913) Y7.136
J.T. Hendry (1908) FY1915
J.Y. Short (1887) Y3.1011
Jaarstroom (1922) B562
Jabiru (1911) Y3.1671, Y9.24
Jacinta (1915) 4.138
Jack Eve (1919) FY958
Jackal (1911) H44, H55, H95
Jackal (1938) F22, G22
Jacketa (1926) FY923
Jackton (1955) M1152
Jacob Jones USN (1918) H(I)20
Jacob van Heemskerk RNLN (1939) C59, D20
Jacqueline Clasine (1906) FY1783
Jade (1933) T56
Jaffa (1897) Y5.2
Jaguar (1938) F34, G34
Jaguar (1957) F37
Jamaica (1940) 44, C44, C170
Jamaica Producer (1934) F124
James Barrie (1928) Z110
James Lay (1918) FY667
James Ludford (1919) T16
Jamuna RIN (1940) F21
Jan de Waele BG (1925) Z231
Jan van Brakel RNLN (1936) A424, M80
Jan van Gelder RNLN (1937) J60
Jane Radcliffe (1897) Y3.838
Janeta (1906) Y3.1104
Janus (1938) F53, G53
Jardine (1936) FY169
Jarvis USN (1912) H(I)15, H(I)21
Jaseur (1944) J428, M428

Jasmine (1941) K23, M23

Jason (1892) N18

Jason (1902) Y3.1919, Y3.2232

Jason (1937) J99, N99

Jasper (1932) T14

Jasper (1943) J407

Jaunty (1941) A140, W30

Javelin (1938) D261, F61, G61

Jawada (1945) L4063

Jean Bart FR (1939) B61

Jean Edmunds (1916) FY1677

Jeanie Deans (1931) J108, 4.29

Jeanne d'Arc FR (1930) 88

Jeannie Leask (1909) FY935

Jeannie Mackintosh (1915) FY1635

Jed (1942) F235, K235

Jedmoor (1914) Y3.576

Jeloy RNoN (1926) FY701

Jenkins USN (1912) H(I)19, H(I)22

Jennet (1926) Z21

Jennifer (1927) FY1634

Jenny Irvin (1919) FY980

Jersey (1938) F72, G72

Jersey (1976) P295

Jerseyman (1883) Y3.820

Jerseymoor (1915) Y3.1284

Jervis (1938) D100, F00, G00

Jervis Bay (1922) F40

Jessamine (1915) T43, T47

Jessie (1891) Y3.114

Jet (1914) Y3.953

Jewel (1944) J390, M390

Jhelum RPN (1942) F40

Joan (1972) A190

Joanetta (1911) D21, N21, N63

Joffre (1916) W69

Johan Maurits van Nassau RNLN (1943) K251

Johannesburg SAN (1925) T56, T456

John & Norah (1913) FY924

John H. Barry (1899) Y3.715

John O. Scott (1906) Y3.70, Y7.70

John Alfred (1913) FY1518

John Cattling (1918) FY536

John Evelyn (1919) X31

John Fitzgerald (1918) Z149

John Hardie (1906) Y3.648, Y7.648

John Sanderson (1889) Y3.1660 , Y6.5

John Shaw (1912) Y3.93

John Stephen (1920) FY1662

John Williamson RNoN (1912) FY308

John Willment (1932) FY1942

Johnstown (1904) Y3.115

Joliette RCN (1943) K418

Jonquiere RCN (1943) K318

Jonquil (1915) M46, T20, T48

Jonquil (1940) K68, M68

Joseph Cudahy (1917) Y7.223

Joseph Davis (1890) Y3.1119

Joyce (1972) A193

Jubbalpore RIN (Canc) T323

Julia (1897) C77, C80

Juliet (1940) T136

Juliston (1889) Y3.1059

Jumna (1929) Y3.792

Jumna RIN (1940) F11, F21, U21

Junco (1917) FY1830

June Rose (1918) FY752

Junee RAN (1943) J362, M362

Junin (1907) Y3.1313, Y8.108

Juniper (1939) T123

Juno (1895) N37, N65

Juno (1938) F46, G46

Juno (1965) F52

Junon FR (1935) P19

Jupiter (1895) D50, N64, P50

Jupiter (1938) F85, G85

Jupiter (1967) F60

Jura (1941) T169

Jura (1973) P296

Justice (1943) W140

Justifier (1925) FY736

Jutland (1946) D62, I62

K

K1 (1916) K1

K2 (1916) K2

K3 (1916) K3

K4 (1916) K4

K5 (1916) K5

K6 (1916) K6

K7 (1916) K7

K8 (1916) K8

K9 (1916) K9

K10 (1916) K10

K11 (1916) K11

K12 (1917) K12

K13 (1916) K13

K14 (1917) K14

K15 (1917) K15

K16 (1917) K16

K17 (1917) K17

K18 (Canc) K18

K19 (Canc) K19
K20 (Canc) K20
K21 (Canc) K21
K22 (1916) K22
K23 (Canc) K23
K24 (Canc) K24
K25 (Canc) K25
K26 (1919) K26
K27 (Canc) K27
K28 (Canc) K28
K.IX ʀɴʟɴ (1922) N39
K.XI ʀɴʟɴ (1924) N53
K.XII ʀɴʟɴ (1924) N61
K.XIV ʀɴʟɴ (1932) N22
K.XV ʀɴʟɴ (1932) N24
Kafue (1913) Y3.1670
Kaiping (1905) Y3.1745
Kalamalka ʀᴄɴ (1944) J395
Kalan (1938) FY08
Kalavati ʀɪɴ (1928) 4.158
Kale (1904) D23, D47, N45
Kale (1942) F241, K241
Kalgoorlie ʀᴀɴ (1941) B245, J192
Kalibia (1902) Y3.1710
Kalimba (1914) Y3.1545
Kamenetz Podolsk (1915) Y3.2302
Kamloops ʀᴄɴ (1940) K176, M82
Kamouraska (1911) Y3.699
Kamsack ʀᴄɴ (1941) K171
Kanaris ʀʜɴ (1941) L53
Kanawha (1893) Y7.197
Kandahar (1939) F28, G28
Kangaroo (1900) D48, D82, P02
Kangaroo ʀᴀɴ (1940) P80, Z80
Kaniere ʀɴᴢɴ (1944) F426
Kanimbla ʀᴀɴ (1935) C76, F23
Kapunda ʀᴀɴ (1942) J218, M218
Kapuni ʀɴᴢɴ (1909) T400
Kapuskasing ʀᴄɴ (1943) F326, J326
Kara Kara ʀᴀɴ (1926) Z221
Karachi ʀɪɴ (1941) T262
Karangi ʀᴀɴ (1941) F216, P282, P286, Z216
Karanja (1930) F128
Karapara (1915) YA.17
Kariba (1904) Y3.227
Karma (1902) Y3.373
Karmoy ʀɴₒɴ (1936) FY877
Karuma (1910) Y3.469
Karzad ʀᴘɴ (1930) F80
Kashmir (1939) F12, G12
Kassala (1897) Y2.125, Y3.542, Y8.88
Kassanga (1899) Y3.1098

Kastoria (1917) 4.148
Katanga (1901) Y3.884
Katharine Park (1903) Y3.1558
Katherine (1898) Y3.834
Kathiawar ʀɪɴ (1942) J155
Kathleen (1902) Y3.1121
Kathleen (1972) A166
Katie (1899) Y3.1789
Katoomba ʀᴀɴ (1941) J204, M204
Katsonis ʀʜɴ (1926) N16
Keats (1943) K482
Kedah (1927) FY.035
Kedleston (1953) M1153
Keith (1930) D06, I06
Kelantan (1921) B361, F166
Kellet (1919) N05, J05, T05
Kellington (1954) M1154
Kelly (1938) F01, G01
Kelowna ʀᴄɴ (1941) J261
Kelsomoor (1914) Y3.410
Kelt (1937) FY112
Kelvin (1939) D137, F37, G37
Kelvinbank (ex *Drumcliffe*) (1905) Y3.888
Kemerton (1953) M1156
Kempenfelt (1915) F87, G10, G12, G72, HA1
Kempenfelt (1931) D18
Kempenfelt (1943) D12, D103, R03
Kempthorne (1943) K483
Kendal (1918) T45, T80
Kendal Castle (1910) Y3.600
Kenia (1927) W47
Kenilworth (1895) Y3.703, Y3.2095
Kenilworth Castle (1943) F420, K420
Kenkora II (1930) FY.049
Kennet (1926) T78
Kennymore (1914) FY857
Kenogami ʀᴄɴ (1940) K125
Kenora (1907) Y3.1149
Kenora ʀᴄɴ (1941) J281
Kent (1901) P27, P80, P99
Kent (1926) 54
Kent (1961) D12
Kent (1998) F78
Kentville ʀᴄɴ (1942) J312
Kenya (1939) 14, C14
Keppel (1920) D84, F14, I84
Keppel (1954) F85
Kepwickhall (1916) Y3.1633
Keren (1930) F132, L110
Kerneval (1906) 4.455
Kernot (1930) 4.281
Kerrera (1941) T200

Kestrel (1898) D49, D60, N47
Keyingham (1908) Y3.587
Keynes (1915) Y3.2080
Kharki (1899) P95, X31, X34
Khartoum (1939) F45, G45
Khedive (1943) D62
Khephren (1905) Y3.1122
Kheti (1927) B541
Khukri ʀɪɴ (1956) F149
Khyber ʀɪɴ (1942) J190, M190
Kiama ʀᴀɴ/ ʀɴᴢɴ (1942) J353, M353
Kiamari ʀɪɴ (Canc) T330
Kianga ʀᴀɴ (1922) FY19
Kiddaw (1909) FY1877
Kihna (1930) 4.242
Kilbane (Canc) 4000
Kilbarchan (Canc) 4001
Kilbeggan (1918) 4004
Kilberry (1918) 4003
Kilbirnie (1919) 4005
Kilbirnie (1943) 5.01
Kilbrachan (Canc) 4006
Kilbride (1901) Y3.729
Kilbride (1918) 4007
Kilbride (1943) 5.02
Kilbrittain (Canc) 4008
Kilburn (1918) 4009
Kilby (Canc) 4010
Kilcar (Canc) 4011
Kilcavan (Canc) 4012
Kilchattan (1918) 4013
Kilchatten (1943) 5.03
Kilchreest (1918) 3814
Kilchrenan (1918) 3805
Kilchrenan (1943) 5.04
Kilchvan (1918) 4014
Kilclare (1918) 3804
Kilclief (1918) 4015
Kilclogher (1918) 4016
Kilcock (1918) 3810
Kilcolgan (Canc) 4017
Kilcommon (Canc) 4018
Kilconnell (Canc) 4019
Kilcoole (Canc) 4020
Kilcorney (Canc) 4021
Kilcot (Canc) 4022
Kilcreggan (Canc) 4023
Kilcullen (Canc) 4024
Kilcurrig (Canc) 4025
Kildale (Canc) 4026
Kildalkey (1918) 4027
Kildangan (1918) 4028

Kildare (1918) 4029
Kildarton (1955) M1162
Kildary (1917) 3800
Kildary (1943) 5.05
Kildavin (1918) 3806
Kildimo (1918) 3811
Kildin (1903) Y3.2065
Kildonan (1898) Y3.176
Kildonan (1918) 4030
Kildonan Castle (1899) M(I)34, M(I)74
Kildorough (1917) 3801
Kildorrey (1918) 3807
Kildress (1918) 4031
Kildwick (1918) 4032
Kildwick (1943) 5.06
Kildysart (1918) 3812
Kilfenora (1917) 3802
Kilfinny (1918) 4033
Kilfree (1918) 4034
Kilfullert (1918) 3808
Kilgarven (1918) 3813
Kilglass (Canc) 4035
Kilgobnet (1918) 3803
Kilgowan (Canc) 4036
Kilham (1918) 3815
Kilham (1943) 5.07
Kilhampton (Canc) 4041
Kilkee (Canc) 4037
Kilkeel (1918) 3809
Kilkenny (Canc) 4038
Kilkenzie (Canc) 4039
Kilkenzie (1943) 5.08
Kilkerrin (Canc) 4040
Kilkhampton (1943) 5.09
Killadoon (Canc) 4042
Killagon (Canc) 4043
Killaloo (Canc) 4044
Killane (Canc) 4045
Killarney (Canc) 4046
Killary (Canc) 4047
Killegar (Canc) 4048
Killegray ʀɴᴢɴ (1941) P174, T174
Killena (1918) 4049
Killerig (1918) 4050
Killiekrankie (RNR) M1109, M1128, M1166
Killiney (1918) 4051
Killingholme (1912) Y4.59
Killour (1918) 4052
Killowen (1918) 4053
Killybegs (1918) 4054
Killygordon (1918) 4055
Kilmacolm (1918) 4056

Kilmacrennan (1918) 4057
Kilmaho (1898) Y3.130
Kilmaine (1918) 4058
Kilmalcolm (1943) 5.10
Kilmallock (1918) 4059
Kilmanahan (1918) 4060
Kilmarnock (1919) 4061
Kilmarnock (1943) 5.11
Kilmartin (1919) 4062
Kilmartin (1943) 5.12
Kilmead (1919) 4063
Kilmelford (1919) 4064
Kilmelford (1943) 5.13
Kilmersdon (1919) 4065
Kilmington (1919) 4066
Kilmington (1943) 5.14
Kilmore (1919) 4067
Kilmore (1943) 5.15
Kilmorey (RNR) M1103, M1157
Kilmuckridge (1919) 4068
Kilmun (1919) Z85, 4069
Kilwinning (1898) Y3.1116
Kimberley (1939) D250, F50, G50
Kimberly usn (1917) H(I)57
Kimmerol (1916) X35, X47
Kinbrace (1944) A281
Kincardine (1906) Y3.201
Kincardine rcn (1944) K393, K490
Kinchela ran (1914) Z96
Kindred Star (1930) FY1524
Kinfauns Castle (1899) M64, M(I)64
King Alfred (1901) P10, P98
King Bay ran (1938) FY96
King Bleddyn (1905) Y3.501
King David (1906) Y3.468
King Edward VII (1903) 66
King Emperor (1914) FY730, N66, N5A, Y7.15
King George (1911) Y3.830
King George V (1911) 61, 70, 77
King George V (1939) 41, B4, B41
King Gruffyd (1919) F116
King Haakon VII RNoN (1942) A423
King Idwa (1906) Y3.1497
King John (1906) Y3.489
King Malcolm (1906) Y3.481
King Orry (1913) M18, M(I)06, M(I)12, M(I)18
King Salvor (1942) A291, B441, W191
King Sol (1936) FY235
King Solomon (....) T235
Kingarth (1944) A232
Kingcup (1940) K33
Kingfield (1902) Y3.1174

Kingfisher (1913) Y3.2217
Kingfisher (1935) K70, L70, M70, P36
Kingfisher (1942) A291
Kingfisher (1974) P260
Kingham (1955) M2704
Kings Grey (1915) FY502, 4.87
King's Lynn (1880) Y3.2082
Kingscourt (1917) FY885
Kingsdyk (1888) Y3.608
Kingsford (1955) P3117
Kingsley (1881) Y3.2356
Kingsmere (1906) Y3.1249
Kingsmill (1943) K484
Kingston (1939) F64, G64
Kingston Agate (1937) FY212
Kingston Alalite (1933) FY136
Kingston Amber (1937) FY211
Kingston Andalusite (1934) FY160
Kingston Beryl (1928) 4.03
Kingston Cairngorm (1935) FY213
Kingston Ceylonite (1935) A407, FY214
Kingston Chrysoberyl (1935) FY236
Kingston Chrysolite (1935) FY184
Kingston Coral (1936) FY215
Kingston Cornelian (1936) FY121
Kingston Crystal (1936) FY216
Kingston Cyanite (1936) FY217
Kingston Galena (1934) FY145
Kingston Jacinth (1929) 4.45
Kingston Olivine (1930) FY193, H209
Kingston Onyx (1927) 4.54
Kingston Periodot (1926) 4.69
Kingston Sapphire (1929) 4.81
Kingston Topaz (1927) 4.31
Kingston Turquoise (1929) 4.91
Kinloss (1945) A482
Kinross (1918) T5N
Kintail (1907) Y3.1216
Kinterbury (1980) A378
Kintuck (1891) Y3.1701
Kintyre (1941) T165
Kipling (1939) F91, G91
Kirkby (1891) Y3.545
Kirkdal (1910) Y3.1091
Kirkella (1936) FY174
Kirkholm (1917) Y3.1917
Kirkland Lake rcn (1944) B634, K337
Kirkliston (1954) M1157
Kirkwood (1911) Y3.25, Y3.413
Kirpan rin (1958) F144
Kirriemore (1935) Z199
Kistna (1923) B542

Kistna ʀɪɴ (1943) F46, U46
Kitchener ʀᴄɴ (1941) K225
Kite (1942) U87
Kittern (1943) T382
Kittiwake (1936) K30, L30, M30, P32
Kitty (1972) A170
Kiwi ʀɴᴢɴ (1941) P102, T102
Knaresborough Castle (1943) F389, K389
Knarsdale (1896) Y3.668
Knight Companion (1888) Y3.1389
Knight Templar (1905) M(I)54, M(I)97, PA2
Knightsgarth (1905) Y3.181
Knottingley (1907) Y3.33
Knowsley Hall (1903) Y3.1939
Knutsford (1903) Y3.122
Koala ʀᴀɴ (1939) P69, Z69
Kohistan (1908) Y3.1371
Kokanee ʀᴄɴ (1943) K419
Kola (1924) B543
Kolaba ʀɪɴ (Canc) T266
Kolpino (1906) Y5.5
Kommetjie ꜱᴀɴ (1930) T35, T475
Kondouriotis ʀʜɴ (1931) H07
Konkan ʀɪɴ (1942) J228, M228
Kookaburra (1940 Z15
Kootenay ʀᴄɴ (1932) H75
Kora (1906) Y3.2183
Korab I ᴏʀᴘ (1938) 4.297
Korawa ʀᴀɴ (1919) FY79
Kos I (1929) FY359
Kos IV (1929) FY1928
Kos V (1929) FY203
Kos VI (1929) FY358
Kos IX (1930) FY1725
Kos X ʀɴᴏɴ (1932) FY504
Kos XII (1932) FY1825
Kos XIII (1932) FY1825
Kos XIV (1932) FY1837
Kos XV ʀɴᴏɴ (1932) FY1956
Kos XVII (1932) FY1847
Kos XVIII (1913) FY1930
Kos XX (1936) FY1697
Koursk (1911) Y3.2269
Kowarra (1916) Y3.1009
Krakowiak ᴏʀᴘ (1940) L115
Kriezis ʀʜɴ (1940) K32
Kriti ʀʜɴ (1941) L84
Krugersdorp ꜱᴀɴ (1923) T48, T448
Kujawiak ᴏʀᴘ (1940) L72
Kukri ʀɪɴ (1942) F243, K243
Kumaon ʀɪɴ (1942) J164, M164
Kunishi (1927) FY692

Kura (1889) Y7.82
Kurd (1930) FY639
Kurdistan (1906) Y3.2096
Kurdistan (1914) Y3.1735
Kuroki (1909) Z137
Kurumba (1916) X55, X64
Kurumba ʀᴀɴ (1916) A774, X36
Kut (ex Harmodius) (1892) Y8.128
Kuthar ʀɪɴ (1958) F146
Kutubtari ʀɪɴ (1915) FY.086
Kuvera (1919) 4.271
Kybra ʀᴀɴ (1926) FY90
Kyleford (1905) Y3.403
Kylestrom (1905) Y3.556

L

L1 (1917) L1
L2 (1917) L2
L3 (1917) L3
L4 (1917) L4
L5 (1918) L5
L6 (1918) L6
L7 (1917) L7
L8 (1917) L8
L9 (1918) L9
L10 (1918) L10
L11 (1918) L11
L12 (1918) L12
L13 (Canc) L13
L14 (1918) L14
L15 (1918) L15
L16 (1918) L16
L17 (1918) L17
L18 (1918) L18
L19 (1919) L19
L20 (1918) L20
L21 (1919) L21
L22 (1919) L22
L23 (1919) 23L, 23N, L23, N23
L24 (1919) L24
L25 (1919) L25
L26 (1919) 26L, 26N, L26, N26
L27 (1919) 27L, 27N, L27, N27
L28 (Canc) L28
L29 (Canc) L29
L30 (Canc) L30
L31 (Canc) L31
L32 (1919) L32
L33 (1919) L33
L34 (Canc) L34

L35 (Canc) L35
L36 (Canc) L36
L37 (Canc) L37
L38 (Canc) L38
L39 (Canc) L39
L40 (Canc) L40
L41 (Canc) L41
L42 (Canc) L42
L43 (Canc) L43
L44 (Canc) L44
L45 (Canc) L45
L46 (Canc) L46
L47 (Canc) L47
L48 (Canc) L48
L49 (Canc) L49
L50 (Canc) L50
L51 (Canc) L51
L52 (1918) L52
L53 (1919) L53
L54 (1919) L54
L55 (1918) L55
L56 (1919) L56
L57 (Canc) L57
L58 (Canc) L58
L59 (Canc) L59
L60 (Canc) L60
L61 (Canc) L61
L62 (Canc) L62
L63 (Canc) L63
L64 (Canc) L64
L65 (Canc) L65
L66 (Canc) L66
L67 (Canc) L67
L68 (Canc) L68
L69 (1918) L69
L70 (Canc) L70
L71 (1919) L71
L72 (Canc) L72
L73 (Canc) L73
L74 (Canc) L74
L'Aconit FR (1941) K58
L'Ajaccienne FR (1936) FY128
L'Atlantique FR (1920) FY362
L'Incomprise FR (1937) H47
La Bonoise (1937) FY166
La Bouclier FR (1937) H20
La Cancalaise FR (1933) FY176
La Capricieuse FR (1939) U92
La Combattante FR (1942) L19
La Cordeliere FR (1937) H25
La Flore FR (1935) H63
La Grandiere FR (1939) A431

La Hulloise RCN (1943) B635, F668, K668
La Malbaie RCN (1941) K273
La Malouine (1940) K46
La Melpoméne FR (1935) H56
La Moqueuse FR (1940) U17
La Nantaise FR (1934) FY135, FY360
La Salle RCN (1943) K519
La Setoise FR (1934) FY178
La Vallee RCN (1943) J371
Labicum (ex *Strathblane*) (1907) Y3.734
Labour (1916) W48
Labrador (1966) A168
Labuan (1943) K584
Laburnum (1915) M47, T21, T49
Lacennia (1930) FY712
Lacerta (1911) 4.07
Lachine RCN (1941) J266
Lachlan RAN/RNZN (1944) F364, K364
Lachute RCN (1944) K440
Lackawanna (1894) Y7.247
Lackenby (1894) Y3.2482
Laconia (1912) M70, M(I)70, M(I)75
Laconia (1922) F42
Ladas (1918) T99
Ladoga (1914) Y3.2017
Lady Bertha (1877) Y3.601
Lady Beryl (1935) FY100
Lady Blanche (1907) FY.014
Lady Brassey (1913) W49
Lady Carrington (1908) Y3.857
Lady Charlotte (1905) Y3.256, Y3.2116
Lady Cory Wright (1906) Y6.7
Lady Crundall (1906) W50
Lady Eleanor (1918) Z226
Lady Elsa (1937) A408, FY124
Lady Enid (1918) FY547
Lady Estelle (1915) FY176
Lady Hogarth (1937) 4.89
Lady Iveagh (1892) Y3.698
Lady Madeleine (1939) FY283
Lady of Man (1930) 4.95
Lady Philomena (1936) FY148
Lady Plymouth (1915) Y3.2287
Lady Rosemary (1937) A409, FY253
Lady Shahrazad (1904) FY.015
Lady Somers (1929) F109
Lady Stanley (1917) 4.233
Lady Vagrant (1903) FY.016
Ladybird (1916) P0A, P5A, T58
Ladybird (1970) A253
Ladykirk (1904) Y3.355
Ladywood (1910) Y3.143

Laertes (1904) Y2.68
Laertes (1913) H45, H80, H94
Laertes (1940) T137
Laertes (1944) J433, M433
Laforey (1913) H03
Laforey (1941) F99, G99
Lagan (1942) K259
Lagos (1944) D44, D93, R44
Laguna Belle (1896) J112, R373, 4.373
Lahore ᴙɪɴ (1941) P12, T253
Lairds Isle (1911) 4.21
Lakeland (....) Y3.8
Lal ᴙɪɴ (1931) T299
Laleston (1954) M1158
Lambourne (1943) K268
Lambridge (1917) X15
Lamerton (1940) F88, L88
Lamington (1907) Y3.286
Lamlash (1973) A208
Lamont (1939) B211, 4.420
Lamson ᴜꜱɴ (1915) H(I)44
Lanakai ʀᴀɴ (1914) Z253
Lanark (1917) T37
Lanark ʀᴄɴ (1943) K669
Lancashire (1917) B402, Y4.3
Lancaster (1902) 71, 78
Lancaster (1918) G05
Lancaster (1990) F229, F232
Lancaster Castle (1944) F691, K691
Lance (1914) G96, H23, H46
Lance (1940) F87, G87
Lancer (1909) Y3.1865
Lancer (1942) T335
Landfall (1918) FY30, Z97
Landonia (1917) Y3.2138
Langoe (1904) Y3.298
Landguard (1930) Y56
Landrail (1914) H47, H54, H82
Langholm (1911) Y3.1279
Langlaagte ꜱᴀɴ (1929) T41, T441
Lantaka (....) W102
Lantan (1943) J208
Lanton (1954) M1159
Lanuvium (1906) Y3.2344
Laomedon (1912) Z243
Lapageria (1916) 4.315, Y7.46
Lapwing (1904) FY818
Lapwing (1911) H09, H48, H56
Lapwing ᴜꜱɴ (1918) T8A
Lapwing (1943) U62
Larch (1928) T96
Larch Lake ʀᴄɴ (1945) J489

Larchgrove (1894) Y3.615
Larchol (1917) A137, X23, X37
Larchwood (1910) Y3.211
Largo (1910) Y3.80
Largo Bay (1944) F423, K423
Largs (1938) F43
Largs Bay (2003) L3006
Lariat (1942) B454, W17
Laristan (1910) Y3.310
Lark (1913) H00, H34, H49
Lark (1943) U11
Larkspur (1915) M48, T22, T50
Larkspur (1940) K82, M82
Larne (1894) Y8.98
Larne (1910) H50, H57, H69
Larne (1940) F63
Larne (ii) (1943) J274
Larpool (1880) Y3.2006
Larsen ꜱᴀɴ (1924) T05, T505
Larwood (1936) FY172
Lasham (1954) M2636
Lasso (1938) A276, T76, Z76
Lassoo (1915) F41, G01
Latimer (1941) Z267
Latona (1890) N49, N67, P51
Latona (1940) I76, M76
Latrobe ʀᴀɴ (1942) J234, M234
Lauderdale (1941) L95
Launceston Castle (1943) F397, K397
Launceston ʀᴀɴ (1941) B246, J179
Laurel (1913) G98, H51, H91
Laurel (1930) T29, 4.417
Laurelleaf (1916) Y7.153
Laurentic (1908) M71, M(I)71
Laurentic (1927) F51
Lauzon ʀᴄɴ (1944) K671
Lavender (1915) M49, T23
Lavender (1940) K60, M60
Lavernock (1888) Y3.676
Laverock (1913) G93, H52, H53
Laverock (1917) Z240
Lawford (1913) G94, H06, H53
Lawford (1943) K514
Lawrence ʀɪɴ (1919) L83, U83
Lawson (1943) K516
Laxmi ʀɪɴ (1918) FY.090
Laxton (1905) Y3.696
Layburn (1960) P191
Laymoor (1959) P190
LCT(8) 4001 (1945) L4001
LCT(8) 4002 (1945) L4002
LCT(8) 4025 (1945) L4025

LCT(8) 4037 (1945) L4037
LCT(8) 4038 (1945) L4038
LCT(8) 4039 (1945) L4039
LCT(8) 4040 (1945) L4040
LCT(8) 4041 (1945) L4041
LCT(8) 4042 (1945) L4042
LCT(8) 4043 (1945) L4043
LCT(8) 4044 (1945) L4044
LCT(8) 4045 (1945) L4045
LCT(8) 4049 (1945) L4049
LCT(8) 4050 (1945) L4050
LCT(8) 4061 (1945) L4061
LCT(8) 4062 (1945) L4062
LCT(8) 4063 (1945) L4063
LCT(8) 4064 (1945) L4064
LCT(8) 4073 (1945) L4073
LCT(8) 4074 (1945) L4074
LCT(8) 4085 (1945) L4085
LCT(8) 4086 (1945) L4086
LCT(8) 4097 (1945) L4097
LCT(8) 4098 (1945) L4098
LCT(8) 4099 (1945) L4099
LCT(8) 4128 (1945) L4128
LCT(8) 4148 (1945) L4148
LCT(8) 4156 (1945) L4156
LCT(8) 4164 (1945) L4164
LCT(8) 4165 (1945) L4165
Le Fantasque ғʀ (1934) H52
Le Glorieux ғʀ (1931) P17
Le Malin ғʀ (1933) H22
Le Terrible ғʀ (1933) H27
Le Tiger (1937) FY243
Le Tigre (1937) A410
Le Triomphant ғʀ (1934) H02
Leafield (1905) Y3.406
Leamington (1918) G19, TN6, T1/
Leander (1882) D41, N15, N68
Leander (1904) Y3.363
Leander (1931) 75, C2, C75
Leander (1961) F109
Leaside ʀᴄɴ (1944) K460, K492
Lechlade (1972) A211
Leda (1892) N28, N69
Leda (1898) Y3.1433
Leda (1937) J93, N93
Ledbury (1912) Y3.1241
Ledbury (1941) F190, L90
Ledbury (1979) M30
Ledsham (1954) M2706
Leeds (1917) G27
Leeds Castle (1943) F384, K384
Leeds Castle (1980) P258

Leeds City (1908) Y3.1071
Leeds United (1933) FY196
Leeward (1918) FY31, Z93
Legion (1914) F94, G95, H54, H79
Legion (1940) F74, G74
Leicester (1891) Y8.23
Leicester City (1934) FY223
Leith (1933) L36, U36
Lemnos (1880) Y3.969
Lena (1902) Y3.432
Lena (1904) Y3.1019
Lennox (1914) H01, H55, H95
Lennox (ii) (1943) J276, M276
Leo (1904) FY859
Leonian (1936) B411, Z197
Leonidas (1913) H20, H51, H56
Leonora (1904) FY819
Leonatus (1915) Y3.1463
Leopard (1897) D50, D61, D75, H06
Leopard ғʀ (1924) H98
Leopard (1955) F14
Lephreto (1917) Y7.17
Leoville ғʀ (1922) U98
Lepanto (1915) M(I)45
Lephreto (1917) FY519, Y7.17
Lesley (1973) A172
Lethbridge ʀᴄɴ (1940) K160
Letitia (1925) F16, Y4.66
Letterston (1954) M1160
Leucadia (1910) Y3.1006
Levanter (1926) FY701
Leven (1898) D51, D62, P33
Levenpool (1911) Y3.713
Levenwood (1911) Y3.142
Leverton (1955) M1161
Leviathan (1901) P28, P73, P1A
Leviathan (1945) 97, R97
Levis (i) ʀᴄɴ (1940) K115
Levis (ii) ʀᴄɴ (1943) B636, K400
Levnet (1914) Y3.1461
Lewes (1918) B496, G68, T85
Lewiston (1959) M1208
Lexa (1936) FY.061
Lexie (1911) Y3.689
Leyland (1936) FY103
Liberator (1929) FY1650
Liberia (1906) FY1826
Liberty (1890) Y2.44, Y8.68
Liberty (1908) Y3.2303
Liberty (1903) FY957
Liberty (1908) YA.10
Liberty (1913) G99, H57, H81

Liberty (1944) B257, J391, M391

Libra (1908) FY867

Libyan (1913) FY1800, Y7.18

Lichen (1911) FY940

Liddesdale (1910) Y3.1813

Liddesdale (1940) F02, L100

Liddoch (1919) FY798

Liffey (1904) D24, D52, N07

Liffey (1916) T81

Lightfoot (1915) F78, G22, G76, H58, H76

Lightfoot (1942) J288

Lightning (1895) D98, N23

Lightning (1940) F55, G55

Ligny (1918) FY1765

Lilac (1915) M65, T24, T52

Lilac (1930) P26, T26

Lilah (1972) A174

Lily (1915) M66, T25, T53

Limbourne (1942) L57

Limeleaf (1916) Y7.158

Limol (1917) A120, X38

Limpet (1912) N7A, X18, X39

Linaria (1942) K282

Lincairn (1904) Y3.543

Lincoln (1918) G42

Lincoln (1959) F99

Lincolnshire (1936) FY222

Lindenhall (1900) Y3.159

Lindisfarne (1943) A339, DV11, P44, T361

Lindisfarne (1977) P300

Lindsay rcn (1943) K338

Ling (Canc) K205

Lingan (1911) Y3.1584

Lingay (1944) J423

Lingfield (1916) T24

Linhope (1894) Y3.2088

Linkmoor (1914) Y3.658

Linnet (1880) W59

Linnet (1913) H43, H53, H59

Linnet (1938) I68, M69, N69

Lion (1910) 22, 67, 79

Lion (1944) C34

Lion (Canc) 27, I27

Lioness (1944) J377, M377

Liscomb rcn (1942) T285

Lismore ran (1940) B247, J145

Listowel rcn (Canc) K439

Lithgow ran (1940) J206, M206

Little usn (1917) H(I)59

Littlesham (1954) M2707

Lively (1899) D53, D83, D91

Lively (1941) G40, F40

Liverpool (1909) 44, 80

Liverpool (1937) 11, C11, C171

Liverpool (1980) D92

Livingstonia (1906) Y3.1393

Lizard (1911) H58, H60, H62

Lizzie Birrel (1913) FY1547

Lizzie Westoll (1895) Y3.438

Llanberis (1890) Y3.1077

Llandaff (1955) F61

Llandovery (1973) A207

Llandrindod (1900) Y3.1175

Llandudno (1910) Y3.458

Llandudno (1941) J67, N67

Llangollen (1900) Y3.1080

Llangorse (1900) Y3.514

Llangorse (ex *Llanover*) (1904) Y3.1391

Llanstephan Castle (1914) F108

Llewellyn (1913) H61, H83, H99

Llewellyn rcn (1941) J278, M278

Lloyd George rcn (1943) J279, M279

Llwyngwair (1915) Y3.61

Lobelia (1916) T54, T74

Lobelia (1941) M05, K05

Lobster (1915) X42

Loch Achanalt (1944) K424

Loch Achray (1943) K426

Loch Affric (Canc) K601

Loch Alvie (1944) F428, K428

Loch Ard (1944) K602

Loch Arkaig (1945) F603, K603

Loch Assynt (1944) K438

Loch Blair (1917) 4.203

Loch Boisdale (1944) K432

Loch Buie (1919) FY688

Loch Clunie (Canc) K607

Loch Craggie (1944) F609, K609

Loch Cree (1944) K430

Loch Doon (1939) FY127

Loch Dunvegan (1944) F425, K425

Loch Eck (1944) K422

Loch Eribol (1929) FY704

Loch Ericht (Canc) K612

Loch Erisort (Canc) K613

Loch Esk (1912) FY896

Loch Fada (1943) F390, K390

Loch Fyne (1944) F429, K429

Loch Garve (Canc) K617

Loch Glashan (Canc) K618

Loch Glendhu (1944) F619, K619

Loch Gorm (1944) F620, K620

Loch Griam (Canc) K621

Loch Harray (Canc) K623

Loch Hope (1915) 4.97
Loch Insh (1944) F433, K433
Loch Katrine (1944) F625, K625
Loch Ken (Canc) K626
Loch Killin (1943) F391, K391
Loch Killisport (1944) F628, K628
Loch Kirbister (Canc) K629
Loch Laggan (1914) Z123
Loch Leven (1928) FY642
Loch Linfern (Canc) K631
Loch Linnhe (Canc) K632
Loch Lomond (1888) Y3.64
Loch Lomond (1944) F437, K437
Loch Long (1916) Z165
Loch Lyon (Canc) K635
Loch Melfort (1934) FY151
Loch Minnick (Canc) K637
Loch Moidart (1918) 4.229
Loch Monteith (1936) FY135
Loch More (1944) F639, K639
Loch Morlich (1944) K517
Loch Nell (Canc) K641
Loch Nevis (1934) M41
Loch Odairn (Canc) K642
Loch Oskaig (1937) FY175
Loch Ossain (Canc) K643
Loch Park (1917) FY1835
Loch Quoich (1944) F434, K434
Loch Rannoch (1901) FY779
Loch Ruthven (1944) F645, K645
Loch Ryan (Canc) K646
Loch Scavaig (1944) F648, K648
Loch Scridain (Canc) K649
Loch Shin (1930) Z124
Loch Shin (1944) K421
Loch Tanna (Canc) K652
Loch Tarbert (1944) F431, K431
Loch Tilt (Canc) K653
Loch Torridon (1945) K654
Loch Tralaig (1945) F655, K655
Loch Tulla (1934) FY199
Loch Urigill (Canc) K656
Loch Vennacher (Canc) K657
Loch Veyatie (1944) F658, K658
Loch Watten (Canc) K659
Lochee (1918) Y3.2129
Lochinvar (1915) F42, F52, G06, H49
Lochy (1943) F365, K365
Lockeport RCN (1941) J100, M100
Lockwood (1896) Y3.285
Lockwood (1899) Y3.27
Locust (1896) D29, D54, D84, H02

Locust (1939) P28, T28
Lodaner (1905) Y3.1524
Lodestone (1979) A115
Lofoten (1945) K07, L111, L3027
Logician (1894) Y3.2327
Lois (1917) FY781
Lombard (1909) 4.169
Lombok (1907) Y3.2321
Lomo Novio (1943) B504
Lompoc (1914) Y7.98
London (1899) 70, 81, D05, N41
London (1927) 69, C69, C178
London (1961) D16
London (1984) F95
Londonderry (1935) L76, U76
Londonderry (1958) F108
Long Branch RCN (1943) K487
Long Tow (1919) W93
Longa (1943) T366
Longbenton (1893) Y3.574
Longbow (Canc) G55
Longford (1919) NA2, T61
Longhirst (1904) Y3.931
Longscar (1903) Y3.1187
Longships (1917) Y3.2106
Longueuil RCN (1943) K672
Looe (1924) X63
Lookout (1914) G97, H24, H62
Lookout (1940) D232, F32, G32
Loosestrife (1941) K105
Lorca (1910) Y3.764
Lord Antrim (1902) Y3.748, Y8.107
Lord Ashfield (1929) FY694
Lord Austin (1937) FY220
Lord Barham (1925) FY929
Lord Beaconsfield (1915) FY608
Lord Cavan (1915) FY1506
Lord Charlemont (1886) Y3.1650
Lord Clive (1915) M03, M07, M08
Lord Darling (1914) FY1774
Lord Derby (1905) Y3.1667
Lord Dufferin (1898) Y3.756
Lord Erne (1900) Y3.1787
Lord Essenden (1936) FY218
Lord Gainford (1917) Z111
Lord Grey (1928) FY1593
Lord Hailsham (1934) FY109
Lord Hood (1925) FY930
Lord Hotham (1936) FY133
Lord Inchcape (1924) FY1611
Lord Irwin (1928) FY1617
Lord Keith (1930) FY1884

Lord Lloyd (1933) FY157
Lord Melchett (1929) FY672
Lord Middleton (1936) FY219
Lord Nelson (1906) 04, 82
Lord Northcliffe (1916) FY780
Lord Nuffield (1937) FY221
Lord Ormonde (1899) Y3.77
Lord Plender (1933) FY181
Lord Roberts (1900) Y3.984
Lord Rodney (1928) FY877
Lord Sefton (1907) Y3.1028
Lord Snowden (1934) FY115
Lord Stamp (1935) FY139
Lord Stanhope (1935) FY163
Lord Stewart (1905) Y3.609
Lord Stonehaven (1934) FY187
Lord Strathcona (1904) Y3.1686
Lord Wakefield (1933) FY170
Loraine (1916) Y5.8
Loring (1943) K565
Lorle (1896) Y3.655
Lorna (1904) 4.65
Lorna Doone (1891) J135, 4.402
Lorraine (1917) 4.170
Lossie (1896) Y8.39
Lossie (1943) K303
Lothian (1938) B201, F168
Lotus (i) (1942) K93
Lotus (ii) (1942) K130
Lotusmere (1908) Y3.698
Louis (1913) H07
Louis (1943) K515
Louis Botha (1916) 4.207
Louisburg (i) ʀᴄɴ (1941) K143
Louisburg (ii) ʀᴄɴ (1943) K401
Louise et Marie (1899) FY1917
Louvain (1897) M07, M(I)07, M(I)14
Lovania (1912) FY942
Lowdale (1893) Y3.122
Lowestoft (1913) 17, 83
Lowestoft (1934) L59, U59
Lowestoft (1960) F103
Lowmoor (1902) Y3.2309
Lowther (1915) FY782, FY972
Lowther Castle (1914) Y3.1623
Lowtyne (1892) Y3.1512
Loyal (1913) H50, H63, H80
Loyal (1941) F15, G15
Loyal Chancellor (1971) A1770
Loyal Factor (1970) A382
Loyal Friend (1919) FY298
Loyal Governor (1969) A510

Loyal Helper (1977) A157
Loyal Mediator (1978) A161
Loyal Moderator (1973) A220
Loyal Proctor (1972) A1771
Loyal Volunteer (1978) A160
Loyal Watcher (1978) A159
Loyalty (....) A358
Loyalty (1942) J217
LST(3) 3031 (1944) L3031
LST(3) 3033 (1945) L3033
Luce Bay (1945) K427
Lucellum (1913) Y7.5 8
Lucent (1879) Y3.1103, Y8.64
Lucerna (1892) Y7.66
Luchana (1904) Y3.821
Lucia (1907) F27, I27, P2A
Lucien Goucy ꜰʀ (1935) FY1768
Lucienne-Jeanne (1917) FY894
Lucifer (1913) H22, H52, H64
Lucigen (1907) Y7.3
Luciston (1910) Y3.1094
Lucknow ʀɪɴ (1942) T267
Luda Lord (1913) FY776, Y7.34
Ludgate (1905) Y3.327
Ludgate (1917) Z45
Ludham (1954) M2708
Ludlow (1917) G57
Ludworth (1907) Y3.82
Lugano (1917) Y3.1533
Lullington (1903) Y3.536
Lullington (1955) M1163
Lulworth (1928) Y60
Luminary (1919) Z189
Lunar Bow (1918) FY32, Z62
Lumen (1889) Y7.18
Lumina (1915) Y7.95
Lundy (1942) A336, A340, DV12, T272
Lundy Island (ex *Darleydale*) (1899) Y3.801
Lune (1930) FY588, 4.416
Lunenburg ʀᴄɴ (1941) K151
Lupin (1916) L19, T55, T65, U19
Lurcher (1912) H01, H65, H90
Lurcher (1928) FY347
Lutterworth (1891) Y8.24
Luxemburg (1910) Y3.732
Luxor (1918) Y3.2027
Lychnis (1917) T56
Lydd (1918) J44, N44, T44, T/0
Lydford (1969) A251
Lydia Long (1918) FY1553
Lydiard (1914) G48, H08, H66
Lydiard (1935) FY177

Lydie (1899) Y3.291
Lyemun (1942) J209
Lyme Bay (2005) L3007
Lyme Regis (i) (1941) J197
Lyme Regis (ii) (1942) J193
Lyness (1966) A339
Lynfield (1905) Y3.811
Lynn (1889) M39, T13, T57
Lynton Grange (1912) Y3.1380
Lynx (1913) H71
Lynx (1955) F27
Lyons (1885) N87
Lyra (1910) H60, H67, H97
Lysander (1913) H68, H81, H93
Lysander (1943) J379, M379

M

M1 (1917) M1
M1 (1939) M19
M2 (1919) M2
M2 (1939) M34
M3 (1918) M3
M3 (1939) M53
M4 (1919) M4
M4 (1940) M68
M5 (1940) M74
M6 (1942) M94
M7 (1944) M88
M8 (1943) M98
M15 (1915) M15
M16 (1915) M16
M17 (1915) M17
M18 (1915) M18
M19 (1915) M19
M20 (1915) M20
M21 (1915) M21
M22 (1915) M22
M23 (1915) M23
M24 (1915) M24
M25 (1915) M25
M26 (1915) M26
M27 (1915) M27
M28 (1915) M28
M29 (1915) M29
M30 (1915) M30
M31 (1915) M31
M32 (1915) M32
M33 (1915) M33
M. H. Stephen (1918) FY943
M. J. Hedley (1891) Y8.89

Maaloy RNoN (1935) J136
MAC 1 (*MTB 1*) (1936) J142
MAC 2 (*MTB 2*) (1936) J150
MAC 3 (*MTB 3*) (1936) J163
MAC 4 (*MTB 4*) (1936) J171
MAC 5 (*MTB 5*) (1937) J185
MAC 6 (*MTB 19*) (1936) J196
MAC 7 (*MTB 40*) (1937) J177
Maashaven (1906) Y3.2444
Mabel Baird (1901) Y3.947
Macbeth (1940) T138
Macdonough USN (1900) H(I)50
Macedonia (1904) M59, M(I)59, M(I)76
Mackay (1918) D70, FA6, I70
Mackerel (1942) T244
Mackworth (ex *Rugbeian*) (1904) Y3.739
Macclesfield (1914) Y8.55
Macomb USN (1941) Y69
Macquarie RAN (1945) F532, K532
Madame Alice (1904) Y3.1951
Madame Midas (1909) Y3.2011
Madden (1917) FY784
Maddiston (1956) M1164
Madeline (1894) Y3.534
Madison USN (1939) Y12
Madras RIN (1919) T33
Madras RIN (1942) J237, M237, T268
Madrono (1916) Y7.164
Madryn (1915) Y3.1086
Madura (1901) Y3.1706
Maenad (1915) G23, G26, G27, GA8, HA7
Maenad (1944) J435, M435
Magdeburg (1910) Y3.733
Magdala (1906) Y3.1090
Magdelen RCN (1942) T279
Magellan (1893) Y3.233, Y3.1679
Magic (1893) YA.14
Magic (1915) G01, G0A, GC0, H40, HC0
Magic (1943) J400
Magician (1939) X97
Magicienne (1944) J436, M436
Magnet (1938) Z27
Magnet (1979) A114
Magnificent (1894) D13, P83, P3A
Magnificent RCN (1944) 21, R36
Magnolia (1915) M67, T26, T58
Magnolia (1930) T31
Magog RCN (1943) K673
Magpie (1943) B286, F82, U82
Magpie (2018) H130
Mahone RCN (1940) J159
Mahratta (1942) G23

Mahratta ʀɪɴ (1943) K395
Maid Marion (1938) FY.017
Maid of Orleans (1918) 4.248
Maiden Castle (1944) K443
Maidan (1912) Y3.1128
Maidstone (1912) P39, P4A
Maidstone (1937) A185, B386, F44
Maimai ʀɴᴢɴ (1943) T338
Maindy Bridge (1899) Y3.605
Maindy Court (1917) Y3.2030
Maindy Dene (1918) Y3.2191
Maindy Manor (1917) Y3.2414
Maine (1902) X24
Maine (1906) D95, N95, X13
Maine (1924) A184
Majestic (1895) D04
Majestic (1904) Y3.797
Majestic (1945) 77, R77
Majesty (1908) FY1597
Majorca (1892) Y3.745
Malacolite (1917) FY796
Malahne (1937) 4.67
Malakuta (1914) Y3.989
Malaya (1915) 01, 06, 84, 3A, B01
Malcolm (1919) D19, I19
Malcolm (1955) F88
Maldenado (1919) Y3.2447
Malham (1958) M2789
Malines (1921) 4.214
Mallaig (1918) TN9, T5/
Mallard (1896) D26, D42, D55
Mallard (1936) K42, L42, M42, P34
Mallow (1915) M68, T27, T59
Mallow (1940) K81
Maloja (1923) F26
Malpeque ʀᴄɴ (1940) J148
Malplaquet (1946) I16
Malta (Canc) D93
Maltby (1906) Y3.843
Malvern (1919) T16, T58
Malvernian (1937) F102
Malwa ʀɪɴ (1944) J55
Mameli ɪᴛ (....) A435
Mameluke (1915) G02, G11, G22, G26, G27, GA2
Mameluke (1944) J437
Mammoth (1917) W56
Man o'War (1936) FY104
Manchester (1937) 15, C15
Manchester (1980) D95
Manchester City (1937) M17
Manchester Civilian (1913) Y3.414
Manchester Commerce (1906) Y3.1525

Manchester Engineer (ex *Nation*) (1905) Y3.877
Manchester Inventor (1907) Y3.663
Manchester Mariner (1904) Y3.855
Manchester Port (1904) Y3.893
Manchester Spinner (1903) Y3.459
Manchester Trader (1902) Y3.873
Manco (1908) Y9.25
Mandal (1932) FY1837
Mandarin (1963) P192
Mandate (1915) G02, H39, H9A, HA8
Mandate (1944) J438, M438
Mandrake (1942) K287
Manela (1920) F58
Mangrove (1940) T112
Manica (1900) Y4.17
Manica (1901) Y3.1305
Manistee (1920) F104
Manitoulin (1942) T280
Manly (1914) D20, G11, H69, H0A
Manly (1981) A92
Manly ᴜsɴ (1917) H(I)23, H(I)30
Manners (1915) G03, G84, HA9, HC1
Manners (1943) K568
Manoora ʀᴀɴ (1934) C77 ,F48
Manor (1913) FY333
Mansfield (1914) D37, G87, H70, H1A
Mansfield (1918) G76
Mansuri (1894) Y3.1325
Mantilla (1916) Y7.163
Mantis (1915) P0A, P5A, T69
Mantua (1908) M51, M(I)40, M(I)51, M(I)77
Manuka ʀɴᴢɴ (1941) T401
Manunda (1928) Y8.18
Manx Hero (1916) FY1741
Manxman (1891) Y3.2221
Manxman (1904) N70, I70
Manxman (1940) M3, M70, N70
Maori (1909) H16
Maori (1937) F24, G24, L24
Maple (1929) P138, T38
Maple Lake ʀᴄɴ (Canc) J490
Mapleleaf (1898) Y7.174
Maplewood (1915) Y3.1026
Maplin (1932) F107
Marangi (....) Z213
Marano (1916) FY777
Marauder (1938) A398, W98
Marazion (1919) N3A, N4A
Marcella (1887) M(I)25
Marchioness of Bute (1906) Y3.1528
Mare (1911) FY1508
Maresfield (1910) Y3.777

Maretta (1929) FY665
Margam Abbey (1907) Y3.515
Margaree RCN (1932) H49
Margaret Ham (1913) W52
Margaret Hide (1929) FY981
Margaret Rose (1912) FY802
Margarita (1900) Y3.582
Margit (1903) Y3.351
Marguerite (1915) T51, T60
Marguerite (1940) K54, M54
Maria (1929) 4.167
Maria de Larrinaga (1898) Y3.910
Maria Elena (1932) FY1567
Maria Elizabeth (1929) FY895
Maria R Ommering (1914) FY1785
Marie Elsie (1895) Y3.374
Marie Jose Rosette (1936) 4.449
Marie Louise (1918) Z238
Marie Rose (1901) Y3.261
Marie Suzanne (1898) Y3.265
Marignam (1919) Z196
Marigold (1915) HC0, M45, T19, T61
Marigold (1940) K87, M87
Mariner (1944) J380, M380
Marion (1896) 4.296
Maris Stella FR (1907) Z233
Marjoram (1917) T51
Marjoram (Canc) K206
Marjorie M Hastie (1930) FY1777
Marksman (1915) D18, F66, F85, G19, G23, G35,
    G62, H96, H4A
Marksman (1942) G23
Marlborough (1912) 66, 79, 85
Marlborough (1989) F233
Marlingford (1954) P3122
Marlow (1918) T42, T77
Marlwood (1906) Y3.26
Marmeluke (1944) M437
Marmion (1893) Y3.851
Marmion (1906) J114
Marmion (1915) G04, HC2
Marmion (1944) M381, J381
Marmora (1903) M58, M(I)41, M(I)58, M(I)78
Marne (1915) G05, H38, HA0, HA6
Marne (1940) D135, G35
Maron (1930) F87
Marrawa (1912) Y3.2285
Mars (1896) D42, P01, P6A
Mars (1909) Y3.244
Marsdale (1940) F100
Marsden (1901) Y3.219
Marsden (1917) W53

Marshal Ney (1915) M08, M12
Marshal Soult (1915) F01, I01, M09, M13
Marsona (1918) FY714
Marstonmoor (1906) Y3.1762
Marthara (1905) Y3.2325
Martial (1915) F77, G02, G06, HC3
Martin (1895) Y3.510
Martin (1910) H21, H65, H71
Martin (1942) G44
Martinet (1938) P141, Z41
Maruda (....) B563
Marvel (1915) G20, G21, G28, GA3
Marvel (1944) J443, M443
Marwarri (1900) Y3.1432
Mary (1973) A175
Mary A Hastie (1930) FY1935
Mary Cam RAN (1918) FY48, Z57
Mary Herd (1919) FY501
Mary J. Masson (1913) FY1659
Mary Rose (1915) G29, HC4
Mary Rose (1943) B263, J360, M360
Mary Tavy (1918) W67
Mary White (1935) Z147
Maryborough RAN (1940) B248, J195, M195
Marylyn (1930) Y4.8
Maryton (1958) M1202
Mashobra (1914) Y3.1394
Mashona (1937) F59, G59, L59
Maskinonge (1912) Y3.727
Masona (1915) Z138
Masterful (1942) A317, W20
Mastiff (1914) D66, G16, H72, H3A
Mastiff (1928) FY350
Mastiff (1938) T10
Mastiff (1966) A180
Mastodonte (1919) W70
Matabele (1937) F26, G26, L26
Matador (ex *St Veronica*) (1912) Y3.1758
Matai RNZN (1930) T372
Matane RCN (1943) K444
Matapan (1945) D43, I43
Matapedia RCN (1940) K112
Matchless (1914) D47, G90, H73, H4A
Matchless (1941) D252, G52
Matra (1905) Y3.2402
Matrozos RHN (1936) N18
Maude Larssen (1897) Y3.880
Maunder (1919) X28
Maunganui RNZN (1911) B396
Maureen (1904) Y3.613
Mauretania (1906) F65, M(I)57
Mauritius (1939) 80, C80, C183

Mavis (1925) Y4.67
Mavisbrook (1912) Y3.1168
Maxim (1945) A377
Maxton (1956) M1165
Maxwell Brander (1944) L3024
May (1927) Z192
Mayflower RCN (1940) K191
Mayford (1954) P3114
Maywood (1901) Y3.83
Mayu Burma (1942) K266, F205
Mazurka (1940) T30
McCall USN (1910) H(I)56
McDougal USN (1914) H(I)22, H(I)24
Meadowsweet (1942) K144
Meaford RCN (Canc) K445
Meavy (1970) A254
Mechanician (1900) M(I)98, PA5
Mecklenburg (1922) 4.127
Meda (1943) A352
Medea RAN (1912) FY32
Medea (1915) H44, H74, H9C
Mediator (1944) A125, B744, W125
Medicine Hat RCN (1941) J256
Medina (1916) D87, F70, G51, G52, G75
Medoc ORP (1930) P24
Medora (1916) G76
Medusa (1906) FY.018
Medusa (1915) H90, I06
Medusa (1919) F06
Medway (1916) F01, G00,G76, G2A
Medway (1928) 25, F25
Medway (2017) P223
Medway II (1918) J57
Medway Queen (1924) J48, N48
Megna (1916) Y3.1345
Melampus (1914) H43, H44, H75
Melbourne RAN (1912) 86, 93
Melbourne (1936) FY209
Melbreak (1942) B224, F173, L73
Meldon (1902) Y3.774
Meline (1917) Y7.168
Melita (1888) X37, X40
Melita (1942) J289, M289
Melpomene (1915) D50, G86, H09, H76, I04
Melrose Abbey (1898) Y3.1723
Melton (1912) Y3.108
Melton (1916) T94
Melton (1981) A83
Melville (1902) Y3.1754
Melville RCN (1941) J263
Melville USN (1915) H(I)16, H(I)25
Menace (1915) G30, G34, G6A, H7C

Menai (1981) A84
Menapier (1908) Y3.1743
Mendip (1940) L60
Menelaus (1895) Y3.2003
Mendocino (1917) Y7.166
Menelaus (1895) Y4.21, Y8.138
Menelaus (1915) F04
Menestheus (1929) B406, M93
Menotti IT (1929) N66
Mentor (1914) D54, H45, H77, H6A
Mentor (1981) A94
Meon RCN (1943) F269, K269, L369
Meon (1982) A87
Merbreeze (1931) FY953
Mercedes (1902) N92, P92, X28, Y3.1928
Mercedes RAN (1912) FY34
Mercedes de Larrinaga (1902) Y3.1606
Mercuria (1899) Y3.1314
Mercury (1934) J102
Mereddio (1897) Y3.123
Merida (1906) Y3.2206
Merioneth (1916) Y3.1506
Merionethshire (1913) Y3.1523
Mermaid (1898) D56, D63, H85, P35
Mermaid (1943) B287, F30, U30
Mermaid (1966) F76
Meror (1905) FY1836
Merrimac (1918) W54
Merrittonia (1944) K688
Merry Hampton (1918) T8N
Mersario (1906) Y3.1355
Mersey (1906) Y8.9
Mersey (1913) M10, M1A, P62
Mersey (1953) M1105
Mersey (2003) P283
Mersham (1954) M2709
Merton Hall (1889) Y3.1839
Mervyn (1908) Y3.209
Mesopotamia (ex *Ardgowan*) (1906) Y3.2311
Messenger (1916) X41, X42
Messina (1945) L112, L3043
Messina (1982) A107
Meteor (1914) D84, G45, H78, H7A
Meteor (1941) D273, G73
Meteorite (1945) N25, S94
Mewslade (1916) FY816
Mewstone (1943) T374
Mexican Prince (1893) Y7.132
Mexico City (1896) Y3.1329
Meynell (1917) T7C
Meynell (1940) F182, L82
MFV 96 (....) Y96

Miaoulis ʀʜɴ (1942) L91
Michael (1915) G07, H41, HA1, HC5
Michael (1944) B258, J444, M444
Michael Griffiths (1918) FY567
Mickleham (1954) M2710
Micmac ʀᴄɴ (1943) D80, D110, R10
Middleham Castle (1910) Y3.1185
Middlesbrough (1942) J164
Middlesex ʀᴄɴ (1943) J328
Middleton (1941) F174, L74, M34
Midge (1913) H03, H13, H40, H79
Midland ʀᴄɴ (1941) K220
Mignonette (1916) T75
Mignonette (1941) K38, M38
Migrante (1929) FY.019
Mikasa (1915) 4.431
Milbrook (1915) G08, G24, HA2, HC6
Milbrook (1981) A97
Mildenhall (1936) FY128
Mildura ʀᴀɴ (1941) J207, M207
Mileham (1954) M2711
Milewater (1888) W55
Milfoil (1942) K288
Milford (1932) L51, U51
Milford (1982) A91
Milford Countess (1919) FY564
Milford Duchess (1919) FY613
Milford Duke (1918) Z125
Milford King (1917) FY1573, Y7.36
Milford Prince (1920) FY614
Milford Princess (1924) FY616
Milford Queen (1917) FY615
Millicent Knight (1900) Y3.1099
Millpool (1906) Y3.567
Milltown ʀᴄɴ (1942) J317
Millwater (1918) 4.27
Milly (1904) Y3.434
Milne (1914) D12, G89, H80, H8A
Milne (1941) D58, G14
Milo (1903) Y3.1559
Milton (1874) Y3.150
Mimico ʀᴄɴ (1943) K485
Mimosa (1915) M95, T28, T62
Mimosa ꜰʀ (1941) K11, M11
Min (1897) Y3.1807
Minalto (1943) T362
Minas ʀᴄɴ (1941) J165
Mincarlo (1944) T388
Mindful (1915) F95, G04, G31, H91
Mindful (1943) W135
Mindful (1943) N18
Miner I (1939) M19, N11

Miner II (1939) M34, N12
Miner III (1939) M53, N13
Miner IV (1940) M68, N14
Miner V (1940) M74, N15
Miner VI (1942) M94, N16
Miner VII (1944) M88, N17
Miner VIII (1943) M98, N18
Mineric (1909) Y3.1618
Minerva (1895) P32, P1A, P7A
Minerva (1915) I00, F00
Minerva (1964) F45
Minerve ꜰʀ (1934) P26
Minieh (1876) Y3.1276
Minion (1915) F90, G09, G14, H82, HC7
Minna (1939) 4.291
Minnie de Larrinaga (1914) Y3.1445
Minnow (1955) X54
Minor Eagle (1942) N16
Minos (1914) G09, H81, H9A
Minotaur (1906) 71, 87, 91, N73
Minotaur (1943) 53
Minster (1924) T198
Minstrel (1911) H69, H72, H82
Minstrel (1939) N11
Minstrel (1944) B259, J445, M445
Minuet (1941) T131
Mira (1901) Y7.100
Mirabelle (1918) FY1642
Miramichi ʀᴄɴ (1941) J169
Miranda (1914) D24, G10, H83, HA0
Mirita (1916) Y7.125
Mirjam (1913) Y3.2153
Mirlo (1918) Y7.164
Mischief (1915) G10, G20, G32, GA4, H5A
Miscou ʀᴄɴ (1942) T277
Misoa (1937) F117
Mist (1918) FY40, Z55
Mistletoe (1917) T99
Mistley (1918) T3/, T/4
Mistral ꜰʀ (1925) H03
Mitres (1917) 4.04
Mixol (1916) A143, X02, X43
M.J. Craig (1898) Y3.2122
Moa ʀɴᴢɴ (1941) T233
Modbury (1942) L91
Modeste (1944) B606, F42, U42
Mogileff (1911) Y3.1935
Mohacsfield (1910) Y3.1167
Mohawk (1907) D05, D57, H19
Mohawk (1937) F31, G31, L31
Mohawk (1962) F125
Moidart (1878) Y3.2112

Mokta (1912) Y3.1138
Moldavia (1903) M(I)42, M(I)64, M(I)79
Molde RNoN (1936) FY1697
Molesey (ex *Rokeby*) (1899) Y3.570
Mollusc (1906) FY.018
Mollusc (1915) X34, X44
Mombassa (1905) Y3.1551
Monadnock (1902) Y3.1526
Mona's Isle (1905) 4.47
Monaghan (1919) NA3
Monaghan USN (1911) H(I)45
Monarch (1897) Y3.1450, Y3.2281
Monarch (1911) 55, 60, 88
Monarda (1919) T52
Moncton RCN (1941) K139
Monemvassia RHN (1942) FY619
Moneyspinner (1918) Y3.2090
Monghyr RIN (Canc) T327
Monima (1929) FY677
Monique-Andre (1920) FY1728
Monique-Camille (1934) FY1803
Monitoria (1909) Y3.265
Monksgarth (1907) Y3.182
Monkshaven (1911) Y3.1401
Monkshood (1941) K207
Monkstone (1909) Y3.262
Monkton (1955) M1155, P1055
Monmouth (1900) Y3.2400
Monmouth (1901) D28
Monmouth (Canc) D96
Monmouth (1991) F235
Monmouth Coast (1906) Y3.2168
Monnow RCN (1943) K441
Monowai RNZN (1924) F59
Mons (1915) G03, G10, G11, G1A, H89, H2A
Mons (Canc) I53
Montana (1917) Y7.167
Montano (1917) 4.171, Y7.19
Montbretia (1917) T63
Montbretia RNoN (1941) K208
Montcalm (1897) X04
Montcalm FR (1935) 56
Montclare (1921) A188, B381, F85
Monte Carlo (1931) 4.284
Montenegro (1900) Y3.1294
Montenol (1917) X45, X66
Montford (1957) P3124
Montgomery (1918) G95
Montreal RCN (1943) B607, K319
Montrose (1905) Y3.625
Montrose (1918) D01, F45, I01
Montrose (RNR) M1121, M1126, M1166

Montrose (1992) F236
Montserrat (1943) K586
Mooivlei SAN (1935) T16, T516
Mooltan (1923) F75
Moon (1915) F69, G11, G12, G16, H36, HC8
Moon (1943) B264, J329, M329
Moonfleet (1917) W56
Moonrise (1918) FY1863, Z51
Moonshine (1917) FY1922
Moonstone (1934) T90
Moorburn (1942) A267
Moorby (1896) Y3.662
Moorcock (1942) A269, 4.396
Mooress (1943) A271
Moorfire (1941) A272
Moorfly (1942) 4.395
Moorfowl (1919) A273
Moorfowl (1989) Y33
Moorgate (1907) Y3.668, Y8.100
Moorgate (1931) P71, Z71
Moorgrieve (1944) A274
Moorhen (1901) N6A
Moorhen (1989) Y32
Moorlands (1910) Y3.493
Moormyrtle (1945) A268
Moorpout (1944) P223
Moorside (1945) A270
Moorsman (1944) P284
Moorsom (1914) D27, H46, H84, HA2
Moorsom (1943) K567
Moose Jaw RCN (1941) K164
Morag (1929) FY1649
Moravia (1917) FY1819
Moray Firth (1904) Y3.404
Moray Firth (1944) B327, F62
Morden RCN (1941) K170
Mordenwood (1910) Y3.173
Morea (1908) M(I)43, M(I)80
Morecambe Bay (1944) F624, K624
Moresby (1915) F02, G85, H27, HC1
Moresby RAN (1918) J54, L54, M150, N54, U54
Moreton Bay (1921) F11
Morgan Jones (1918) 4.114
Morinier (1901) Y3.1214
Morlais (1911) Y3.2036
Morning Star (1915) G08, G12, G13, G18, H48, H6A, HC9
Morpeth Castle (1943) F693, K693
Morris (1914) D35, H47, H85, HA3
Morris Dance (1918) T0N, T117
Mosquito (1910) H29, HA3
Mosquito (1939) T94

Motagua (1912) M84, M(I)44, M(I)81, M(I)84
Moth (1915) P7A, P8A, T70
Moti RIN (1931) T300
Moto (1913) Y3.14
Mounsey (1915) G07, G14, G1A, H0C, HC0
Mounsey (1943) K569
Mount Ard (1931) Z126
Mount Berwyn (ex *War Puma*) (1918) Y3.2201
Mount Everest (ex *War Drake*) (1918) Y3.2485
Mount Keen (1936) FY684
Mountby (1898) Y3.1315
Mountcharles (1910) Y3.1642
Mountpark (1912) Y3.234
Mounts Bay (1945) F627, K627
Mounts Bay (2004) L3008
Mourino (1906) Y3.1921
Mourne (1942) K261
Mousa (1942) T295
Moy (1904) D25, D58, H76, N02
Moy (1917) T79
Moyle (1907) Y3.146
Moyola (1942) K260
Muirfield (1907) Y3.525
Mulgrave RCN (1942) J313
Mull (1941) T110
Mull of Galloway (1944) A226, F26
Mull of Kintyre (1945) A225, B366, F86
Mull of Oa (1945) F96
Mullet (1942) T311
Mullion Cove (1944) B342, F186
Multan RIN (1944) T322
Munardan (1917) Y3.1966
Muncaster Castle (1906) Y3.1611
Munificent (1892) Y3.993
Munlochy (1918) T98, TA5
Munster (1915) G33, G35, G7A, H7A, H8C
Murchison RAN (1944) F442, K442
Murcia (1913) Y3.1449
Murex (1892) Y7.111
Muriel (1898) Y3.12
Muristan (1913) Y3.154
Muritai (1910) Y9.9
Muroto (1930) FY611
Murray (1914) D33, H78, H86, HA4
Murray (1955) F91
Murrumbidgee RAN (Canc) K534
Musk (1942) K289
Muskerry (1916) T0C
Musket (Canc) G78
Musketeer (1915) G06, G15, G19, H42, H8A, H1C
Musketeer (1941) D186, G86

Mutine (1942) J227, M227
Myngs (1914) D41, G88, H87, HA5
Myngs (1943) D06, R06
Myosotis (1916) T64, T68
Myosotis (1941) K65, M65
Myrland RNoN (1918) FY1784
Myrmidon (1890) Y3.1492
Myrmidon (1900) D85, P93
Myrmidon (1942) G90
Myrmidon (1944) J454, M454
Myrtle (1915) T38, T65
Myrtle (1928) T91
Myrtle (1973) A199
Mystic (1915) G16, G3A, H42, H2C
Mystic (1944) J455, M455
Mytilus (1916) X101

N

N1 (1914) N1
N16 (ex *U-1105*) (1944) N16
N19 (ex *U-1171*) (1943) N19
N20 (ex *U-2348*) (1944) N20
N21 (ex *U-1057*) (1944) N21
N22 (ex *U-1058*) (1944) N22
N23 (ex *U-1064*) (1944) N23
N24 (ex *U-1305*) (1944) N24
N25 (ex *U-1407*) (1945) N25
N26 (ex *U-1231*) (1943) N26
N27 (ex *U-2529*) (1944) N27
N28 (ex *U-3035*) (1945) N28
N29 (ex *U-3041*) (1945) N29
N30 (ex *U-3515*) (1944) N30
N31 (ex *U-2353*) (1944) N31
N35 (ex *U-2326*) (1944) N35
N41 (ex *U-3017*) (1944) N41
N65 (ex *U-776*) (1944) N65
N83 (ex *U-1023*) (1944) N83
N86 (ex *U-249*) (1943) N86
Nab Wyke (1930) FY654
Nabob (1943) D77
Nada RYN (1940) K81
Nadder (1943) K392
Nadejda (1896) Y3.1744
Nadine FR (1919) FY1882
Nadur RCN (1942) K296
Naiad (1890) N71, P52
Naiad (1939) 93, C93
Naiad (1963) F39
Nailsea (1918) T18, TA7
Nairana (1917) N72, N94

Nairana (1943) D05

Nairn (1904) Y3.79

Nairnside (1912) FY1562

Naldera (1918) M(I)58

Nam Sang (1902) Y3.1851

Nambucca ʀᴀɴ (1936) FY82

Namur (1917) 4.104

Namur (1945) I58

Nanaimo ʀᴄɴ (1940) K101

Nancy (1973) A202

Nancy Hague (1911) Z166

Naneric (1895) M(I)24

Nanoose ʀᴄɴ (1938) J35

Nantwen (1912) Y3.430

Naomi ʀᴀɴ (Canc) K55

Napanee ʀᴄɴ (1940) K118

Naphpaktia ʀʜɴ (1942) FY675

Napier (1915) G18, G34, GA0

Napier ʀᴀɴ (1940) D13, D297, G97

Narani ʀᴀɴ (1914) FY07

Narbada ʀɪɴ (1942) F40, U40

Narborough (1916) F02, F11, G39

Narborough (1943) K578

Narcissus (1915) T41, T66

Narcissus (1941) K74, M74

Narkunda (1918) M(I)48

Narragansett (1903) Y4.38

Narvik ʀɴᴏɴ (1937) FY1725

Narvik ʀɴᴏɴ (1942) L44

Narvik (1945) L114, L3044

Narwhal (1915) F91, G35, G36, G47, H29

Narwhal (1935) 45M, 45N, N45

Narwhal (1957) S03

Nascent (1914) Y3.1427

Nascopie (1912) Y8.78

Nasik ʀɪɴ (1944) P358, T258

Nasprite (1940) A252, X59

Nasturtium (1915) T76

Nasturtium (1940) K107

Natal (1903) Z244

Natal (1905) 69

Natal ꜱᴀɴ (1944) A301, F10, F430, K430

Natal Transport (1910) Y3.264

Natalia ꜱᴀɴ (1925) T02, T502

Nautilus ʀɪɴ (1913) FY.092

Nautilus (1914) IAC

Nautilus ʀɴʟɴ (1929) M12

Navarino (1906) Y3.1291

Navarino (Canc) I82

Navarinon ʀʜɴ (1934) H23

Navarra (1909) Y3.365

Nawab (1914) Y3.1409

Nazareth ꜰʀ (1918) FY1815

Neasham (1956) M2712

Neave (1942) A342, DV14, T247

Nebb ʀɴᴏɴ (1930) FY1722

Nebojsa ʏᴜɢ (1927) N61

Nebula (1929) J104

Neebing (1903) Y3.2178

Needwood (1906) Y3.78

Negro (1916) G13

Negro (1932) FY717

Neil Mackay (1935) FY259

Neil Smith (1917) FY529

Nelson (1925) 28, B5, B28

Nemesis (1910) H72, H73, H88

Nene ʀᴄɴ (1942) F270, K270

Nepal (1941) D14, D125, G25

Nepean (1916) F03, G18, G83, H44, H9A, HA5

Nepean ʀᴀɴ (Canc) J468

Nepeta (1942) K290

Nephrite (1896) Y3.2151

Neptor (1915) N73, N77, W78

Neptune (1909) 02, 79, 89

Neptune (1933) 20

Nereide (1910) H70, H74, H89

Nereide (1944) F64, U64

Nereus (1916) F12, F33, F80, G19, H21, H37, HA0

Nereus ʀʜɴ (1927) N56

Nerine ꜱᴀɴ (1925) T11, T511

Nerissa (1916) F04, F05, G12, G35, H09, HA1

Nerissa (1940) G65

Nerissa (1944) J456, M456

Ness (1895) Y3.1194

Ness (1905) D26, D59, H77, N80

Ness (1942) F219, K219

Nessus (1915) F32, G00, G36, G37, G5A, G30

Nestor ʀᴀɴ (1940) G02

Netherby Hall (1905) Y9.10

Netley (2000) A282

Netravati ʀɪɴ (1909) 4.123

Netsukis (1924) FY1971

Nettle (1902) N74, P43

Nettle (1933) P94, T94

Nettle (1941) K212

Nettleham (1956) M2713

Nettleton (1891) Y3.902

Neuralia (1912) Y4.5

Neva (1909) Y3.2119

Nevada ᴜꜱɴ (1914) 2A

Nevasa 1913 Y4.6

Nevisbrook (1913) Y3.437

New Comet (1915) FY760, Y7.21

New Glasgow ʀᴄɴ (1943) K320
New Liskeard ʀᴄɴ (1944) F37, J397
New Waterford ʀᴄɴ (1943) B637, F321, K321
New Westminster ʀᴄɴ (1941) K228
New York ᴜsɴ (1912) 96
New Zealand (1911) 08, 53, 90
New Zealand (Canc) D43
New Zealand Transport (1913) Y3.1603
Newark (1918) G08, T5N, T7N
Newbigging (1892) Y3.1871
Newburn (1904) Y3.533
Newbury (1916) T26
Newby (1890) Y3.580
Newcastle (1936) 76, C76, C179
Newcastle (1975) D87
Newfoundland (1941) 59, C59, C172
Newglyn (1917) Y3.1810
Newhaven (1909) FY820
Newhaven (1942) J199
Newhaven (2000) A280
Newholm (1899) Y3.1115
Newlands (1902) Y3.1756
Newlyn (1913) Y3.324
Newmarket (1907) M32, T06
Newmarket (1918) G47
Newport (1917) G54
Newquay (1914) Y3.477
Newstead (1894) Y3.938
Newton (1888) Y3.2125
Newton (1975) A367
Newtownards (1912) Y3.610
Neyroy (....) W132
Neza ʀɪɴ (ex *Test*) (1942) K239
Niagara ʀᴄɴ (1918) I57
Nicator (1916) F05, G01, G55, HA4
Nicator (Canc) J457
Nicholson ᴜsɴ (1914) H(I)00, H(I)27
Nidd (1900) Y3.598, Y8.43
Nieuw Amsterdam (1937) F77
Nigaristan (1913) Y3.236
Nigel sᴀɴ (1930) T40, T440
Nigella (1915) T52, T68
Nigella (1940) K19
Niger (1936) N73, J73
Nigeria (1901) Y8.70
Nigeria (1939) 60, C60, C180
Night Hawk (1915) FY1858
Night Rider (1915) Z113
Nightingale (1897) NN8
Nightingale (1931) P82, T82
Niki ʀʜɴ (1906) L23
Nilam ʀɪɴ (1931) T302

Nimble (1906) X76
Nimble (1941) A223, W123
Nimble (1985) A222
Nimbus (1929) J133
Nimrod (1915) G71, H43, H90, H5A
Nipigon ʀᴄɴ (1940) J154
Nith (1905) D27, D60, H78, N77
Nith (1942) K215
Nitrogen (1912) Y7.145
Nizam (1916) F81, G28, G52, G53, HC6
Nizam ʀᴀɴ (1940) D15, D38, G38
Noble (1915) G09, G37, G38, G9A, H48
Noble (ex *Piorun*) (1940) G65
Noble (1941) D165, G84
Noble Nora ʀɴᴏɴ (1912) FY189
Nodzu (1929) FY659
Noelle (ex *Bronze Wings*) (1915) Y3.1437
Noir (1928) FY.24
Nolisement (1902) Y3.1836
Nomad (1916) G31
Nonpareil (1916) D0A, F71, G37, G53, G54
Nonpareil (1941) G16
Nonpariel (Canc) J459
Nonsuch (1915) G12, G19, G38, G39, GA5
Nonsuch (Canc) U54
Nonsuch (1941) D107, R40
Noontide (1918) FY45, P179, Z79
Noordvaarder (1898) FY1789
Nootka ʀᴄɴ (1938) J35, N35
Nootka ʀᴄɴ (1944) D196, R96
Nora (1907) Y3.1369
Norah (1973) A205
Noranda ʀᴄɴ (1941) J265
Norbreck (1905) FY1669
Norbreeze (1920) Z162
Norburn (1908) Y3.237
Nordenfelt (1945) A135
Nordhav II (1913) FY1906
Nordland (1916) Z180
Norfolk (1928) 78, C78
Norfolk (1967) D21
Norfolk (1987) F230
Norfolk Coast (1910) Y8.6
Norhilda (1910) Y3.579
Norina (1917) Z145
Norina (1927) FY892
Norland (1916) FY1561
Norma Pratt (ex *Silvercedar*) (1907) Y3.1368
Norman (1916) G14, G26, G54, G55, H0A
Norman ʀᴀɴ (1940) D16, D149, G49
Norman Bridge (1913) Y7.204
Normandiet (1902) Y3.1970

Normandy (1895) Y3.2163
Normanton (1912) Y3.191
Norna (1909) 4.409
Norse (1930) FY1628
Norseman (1916) F06, F13, F82, G51, G70, H22
Norseman (1941) G25
Norsyd ʀᴄɴ (1943) K520
North Bay ʀᴄɴ (1943) K339
North Britain (1907) Y3.304
North Ness (1917) 4.100
North Queen (1906) FY253
North Star (1916) F45, F53, G16
North Wales (1905) Y3.253
North Wales (1909) Y3.850, Y3.859
Northam Castle (1944) K447
Northcoates (1919) FY548
Northern Chief (1936) A411, 4.34
Northern Dawn (1936) A412, FY146
Northern Duke (1936) A413, 4.11
Northern Foam (1936) 4.76
Northern Gem (1936) FY194
Northern Gift (1936) 4.50
Northern Isles (1936) A414, 4.25
Northern Light (....) FY1934
North Pacific (1913) Y3.1630
North Point (1900) Y3.1610
Northern Pride (1936) FY105
Northern Princess (1936) 4.06
Northern Reward (1936) 4.85
Northern Rover (1936) 4.58
Northern Sky (1936) 4.41
Northern Spray (1936) FY129
Northern Sun (1936) 4.18
Northern Wave (1936) FY153
Northdene (1893) Y3.111
Northesk (1916) G15, G36, G83, H21
Northfield (1901) Y3.54
Northford (1895) Y3.1877
Northlyn (1919) Z103, 4.106
Northman (1911) FY338
Northmark (1937) X21
Northolt (1918) TA8
Northumberland (1992) F238
Northumbria (1894) Y3.827
Northumbria (RNR) M1146, M1175
Northville (1897) Y3.1113
Northwaite (1905) Y3.239
Northward Ho (1919) FY795
Northway (1943) F142
Norton (1907) Y3.488
Norwich City (1937) A415, FY229
Notre Dame D'etel ꜰʀ (....) 4.08

Notre Dame de France ꜰʀ (1931) FY363
Notre Dame de Mont Ligeon ꜰʀ (1899) Z227
Nottingham (1913) 35
Nottingham (1980) D91
Notts (1891) Y8.22
Notts County (1938) FY250
Novgorod (1913) Y3.2210
Novington (1912) Y3.152
Novorossia (1905) Y3.1430
Nox (Canc) J460
Nubian (1909) D06, D61, H70
Nubian (1937) D136, F36, G36, L36
Nubian (1960) F131
Nuceria (1914) Y3.1379
Nucula (1906)
Nucula (1906) Y7.73, Y7.220
Nugent (1917) D58, F46, F54, G17, G47
Nugget (1889) Y4.38
Nunima (1903) Y3.1088
Nunnery Castle (1944) K446
Nurton (1956) M1166
Nurtureton (1912) Y3.1346
Nutbourne (2000) A281
Nyanza (1897) Y3.1264
Nyasaland (1943) K587
Nyassa (1906) Y3.124
Nyland (1898) Y3.2081
Nymphe (1911) D25, H83, H98
Nymphe (Canc) U84

O

O-9 ʀɴʟɴ (1925) P9
O-10 ʀɴʟɴ (1925) P10
O-14 ʀɴʟɴ (1931) P14
O-15 ʀɴʟɴ (1931) N15
O-19 ʀɴʟɴ (1938) N54, S33
O-21 ʀɴʟɴ (1939) S48, P21
O-22 ʀɴʟɴ (1939) P22
O-23 ʀɴʟɴ (1939) P23, S49
O-24 ʀɴʟɴ (1940) P24, S50
O1 (ren *Oberon*) (1926) O1
OA1 ʀᴀɴ (ren *Otway*) (1926) OA1
OA2 ʀᴀɴ (ren *Oxley*) (1926) OA2
O'Brien ᴜꜱɴ (1915) H(I)28
Oak (1912) H12, H38, H56, H92
Oak (1928) T54
Oak Lake ʀᴄɴ (Canc) J491
Oakdale (1878) Y3.551
Oakfield (1912) Y3.1074
Oakham Castle (1944) F530, K530

Oakington (1958) M1213
Oakleaf (1899) Y7.172
Oakleaf (1981) A111
Oakley (1917) T1C
Oakley (i) (1940) L72
Oakley (ii) (1942) F198, L98
Oakmere (1910) Y3.875
Oakol (1917) X00, X46
Oakol (1946) A300
Oakville ʀᴄɴ (1941) K178
Oban (2000) A283
Obdurate (1916) F06, F07, F83, G26, H50, HA2
Obdurate (1942) D139, G39
Obedient (1915) G04, G25, G39, G40, H88, HA3
Obedient (1942) D248, G48
Oberon (1916) F27, F36, F84, G80, H35
Oberon (1926) 21P, 21N, N21
Oberon (1959) S09
Observer (1916) D79, F72, G41, G51, G55, G56
Ocean (1898) N56
Ocean (1944) 68, R65, R68
Ocean (1995) L12
Ocean Breeze (1927) FY810
Ocean Brine (1914) 4.364, Z159
Ocean Cruiser (1913) FY911
Ocean Eddy (1929) Z143
Ocean Gain (1915) FY1976
Ocean Guide (1914) FY1977
Ocean Lifebuoy (1929) FY1504
Ocean Lux (1930) FY1503
Ocean Monarch (1904) Y3.1570
Ocean Pioneer (1915) FY1654
Ocean Prince (1907) Y3.946
Ocean Retriever (1912) FY1925
Ocean Rover (1919) 4.64
Ocean Salvor (1943) A492
Ocean Spray (1912) FY1978
Ocean Swell (1920) Z163
Ocean Toiler (1915) FY1947
Ocean Transport (1913) Y2.73, Y3.759, Y8.120
Ocean Transport (1913) Y3.769
Ocean Treasure (1913) FY1918
Ocean View (1930) FY863
Ocean Vim (1930) FY951
Ocean's Gift ʙɢ (1907) 4.80
Oceana (1889) W58
Oceana (1906) Y3.1418
Oceano (1900) Y3.783
Oceanway (1943) F143
Ocelot (1962) S17
Ockenfels (1910) Y3.1962
Ockham (1959) M2714

Octavia (1916) F07, F09, G28, G51, G71
Octavia (1942) J290, M290
Odberg ꜱᴀɴ (1936) T25, T465
Oder (1874) Y3.1593
Oderin (1941) FY1763
Odessa (1896) Y3.1716
Odiham (1955) M2783
Odin (1928) 84P, 84N, N84
Odin (Canc) J461
Odin (1960) S10
Odzani (1943) B272, F356, K356
Offa (1916) D96, F73, G45, G56, G57
Offa (1941) D129, G29
Ogano (1917) FY803
Ohm (1915) FY561
Oilbird (1968) Y25
Oilfield (1896) Y3.31, Y7.31
Oilfield (1968) Y24
Oilman (1969) Y26
Oilpress (1968) Y21
Oilstone (1968) Y22
Oilwell (1969) Y23
Okement (1915) Y3.1421
Okino (1917) Z146
Oklahoma ᴜꜱɴ (1914) 4A
Oksoy ʀɴᴏɴ (1935) FY907
Oku (1929) FY660
Olcades (1918) X18, Y7.304
Old Colony (1907) N62
Oldenburg (1910) Y3.1763
Oleander (1922) X46
Oleander (1964) A124
Oligarch (1918) X12, Y7.286
Olinina (1934) FY154
Olivae (1915) FY926
Olive (1940) T126
Olive Branch (ex *Bellorado*) (1912) Y3.742
Olive Cam ʀᴀɴ (1920) FY76
Olive Tree (1918) FY1946
Olmeda (1964) A124
Olna (1921) X47
Olna (1944) A216, B516, X116
Olna (1965) A123
Olwen (1917) X09, Y7.242
Olwen (1964) A122
Olympia (1916) P84, X26, Y7.121
Olympia (1917) FY1586
Olympic (1911) M(I)26
Olympus (1928) 35P, 35N, N35
Olympus (1961) S12
Olynthus (1917) X11, Y7.264
Olynthus (1964) A122

Omagh (2000) A285

Ombra (1902) 4.66

Omdurman (Canc) I98

Onda (1895) Y3.1889

One Accord (1927) FY983

Onetos (1913) FY761

Onslaught (1915) G22, G32, G40, G41, G8A

Onslaught (1941) D04, D204, G04

Onslaught (1960) S14

Onslow (1916) F09, F34, F85, G29, H24

Onslow (1941) D49, G17

Onslow ʀᴀɴ (1968) S60

Ontario ᴜsɴ (1912) T1A

Ontario ʀᴄɴ (1943) C53, C184, 53

Onward (1905) FY887

Onyx (1892) D07, N07, N75

Onyx (1942) J221, M221

Onyx (1966) S21

Oola (1891) Y3.1303

Oostewal sᴀɴ (1926) T08, T508

Opal (1915) G02, G41, G42

Ophelia (1915) G03, G33, G57, G58, GA9

Ophelia (1940) T05

Ophir (1907) Y3.1949

Ophir (1891) M92, M(I)82, M(I)92

Ophir (1928) B397

Ophir II (1906) Z235

Opossum (1895) D12, D62, D99

Opossum (1944) B292, F33, U33

Opossum (1963) S19

Opportune (1915) G05, G27, G58, G59

Opportune (1942) D180, G80

Opportune (1964) S20

Opulent (1907) Y4.75

Oracle (1915) D46, F08, F76, G27

Oracle (1929) FY.020

Oracle (1961) S16

Orama (1911) M61, M(I)61

Oranaise ꜰʀ (1919) Z219

Orange River (1914) Y3.1846

Orangeleaf (1916) X40, Y7.173

Orangeleaf (1955) A80

Orangeleaf (1975) A110

Orangemoor (1911) Y3.365

Orangeville ʀᴄɴ (1944) K396, K491

Oransay (1904) Y3.1032

Orara ʀᴀɴ (1939) J130

Orator (ex *St Fillans*) (1912) Y3.1476

Orbita (1915) M(I)59, M(I)84, M(I)A1

Orby (1918) T17

Orcadia (1916) D30, G39, G53, G80

Orcadia (1944) J462, M462

Orchis (1940) K76

Orcoma (1908) M(I)46, M(I)85, M(I)86

Orestes (1916) D56, G33, G60, G61, H74

Orestes (1942) J277, M277

Orfasy (1942) T204

Orford (1916) D70, G38, G59, G61, H76

Orford Ness (1945) F67

Orfordness (ex *Blackfriar Gate*) (1906) Y3.941

Oriana (1916) F11, F14, F75, G69, H34

Oriana (1942) W117

Oribi (1941) G66

Oriental Star (1934) FY178

Orillia ʀᴄɴ (1940) K119

Oriole (1910) J110

Oriole (1916) D06, D1A, F16, F86, G44

Orion (1910) 52, 86, 91

Orion (1932) 85

Orion ʀᴀɴ (1974) S61

Orissa ʀɪɴ (1941) J200, M200

Orizaba (1908) FY1897, Y7.23

Orkan ᴏʀᴘ (1942) G90

Orkla (1888) Y3.5

Orkney ʀᴄɴ (1943) B638, K448

Orkney (1976) P299

Ormiston (1907) Y3.1806

Ormonde (1906) FY782

Ormonde (1918) NA0

Ormonde (1943) F172

Orna (1913) Y3.1825

Oronsay (1943) T375

Oronsay (2000) A284

Oropesa (1895) M88, M(I)88

Ortalan (1902) Y4.47

Orotava (1889) M80, M(I)47, M(I)80, M(I)86

Orpheus (1905) FY1780

Orpheus (1916) F17, F35, F87, G43, H28

Orpheus (1929) 46P, 46N, N46

Orpheus (1959) S11

Orsay (1945) J450, M450

Ortolan (1902) Y1.2

Orvicto (1916) FY909

Orvieto (1909) M(I)25, N76, P53

Orwell (1898) D49, D63, D86

Orwell (1942) D198, F98, G98

Orwell (1985) M2011

Orzel ᴏʀᴘ (1938) 85A, 85N, N85

Osako (1918) FY580

Oscar Angele (1912) 4.220

Oshawa ʀᴄɴ (1943) F330, J330

Osiris (1916) F26, F31, F88, G68, G72, H30

Osiris (1928) 67P, 67N, N67

Osiris (1962) S13

Osmanieh (1906) Y4.61, Y7.61
Osprey (1897) D64, P80
Ossory (1915) F93, G17, G23, HA4, HA5
Ossory (1944) J463, M463
Osta (1915) FY737
Ostrich (1900) D65, P56
Oswald (1928) 58P, 58N, N58
Otago RNZN (1958) F111
Otama RAN (1975) S62
Othello (1905) Y3.1029
Othello (1907) FY783
Othello (1941) T76
Otranto (1909) M60, M(I)60, M(I)87
Ottawa (1888) Y3.25, Y7.25
Ottawa (i) RCN (1931) H60
Ottawa (ii) RCN (1935) H31
Otter (1961) S15
Otto Trechmann (1911) Y3.544
Ottringham (1958) M2715
Otus (1928) 92P, 92N, N92
Otus (1962) S18
Otway (1909) M73, M(I)73, M(I)88
Otway (1936) N51, 51P, 51N
Otway RAN (1966) S59
Oudenarde (1945) I02
Oudh RIN (1942) J245
Oulston (1954) M1129
Our Bairns (1918) FY1566, Y7.24
Our Kate (1910) FY1883
Ouragan FR (1926) H16
Ouse (1905) D28, D66, H80, N69
Ouse (1917) T80
Outarde RCN (1941) J161
Outpost (ex *Vidette*) (1905) Y7.25
Outremont RCN (1943) B639, K322
Ovens RAN (1967) S70
Overdale (1903) Y3.919
Overfall (1918) FY984
Overton (1911) Y4.54
Overton (1956) M1197
Owen (1945) A311
Owen Sound RCN (1943) K340
Owl (1913) H31, H84, H93
Owl USN (1918) T9A
Oxford Castle (1943) F692, K692
Oxfordshire (1912) B398, Y8.6
Oxley (1926) N55
Oxley RAN (1926) 55P, 55N, S57
Oxlip (1941) K123
Oxna (1943) T296
Oxshott (1915) Y3.2084
Oyleric (ex *Barneson*) (1914) Y7.89

Oystermouth Castle (1913) 4.101

P

P.11 (1915) P11
P.12 (1915) P12
P.13 (1916) P13
P.14 (1916) P14
P.15 (1916) P15
P.16 (1916) P16
P.17 (1915) P17
P.18 (1916) P18
P.19 (1916) P19
P.20 (1916) P20
P.21 (1916) P21
P.22 (1916) P22
P.23 (1916) P23
P.24 (1915) P24
P.25 (1916) P25
P.26 (1915) P26
P.27 (1915) P27
P.28 (1916) P28
P.29 (1915) P29
P.30 (1916) P30
P.31 (1916) P31
P31 (1940) P31
P.32 (1916) P32
P32 (1940) P32
P.33 (1916) P33
P33 (1941) P33
P.34 (1916) P34
P34 (1941) P34
P.35 (1916) P35
P35 (1941) P35
P36 (1941) P36
P37 (1941) P37
P38 (1941) P38
P39 (1941) P39
P.41 (1917) P41
P41 (1941) P41
P42 (1941) P42
P43 (1941) P43
P44 (1941) P44
P.45 (1917) P45
P45 (1942) P45
P.46 (1917) P46
P46 (1941) P46
P.47 (1917) P47
P47 (1942) P47
P.48 (1917) P48
P48 (1942) P48

P.49 (1917) P49
P49 (1942) P49
P.50 (1916) P50
P51 (1942) P51
P.52 (1916) P52
P52 (1942) P52
P.53 (1917) P53
P53 (1942) P53
P.54 (1917) P54
P54 (1942) P54
P55 (1942) P55
P56 (1942) P56
P.57 (1917) P57
P57 (1942) P57
P.58 (1918) P58
P58 (1942) P58
P.59 (1917) P59
P59 (1943) P59
P61 (ren *P211*) (1941) P61
P61 (1943) P61
P62 (ren *P212*) (1942) P62
P62 (1943) P62
P63 (ren *P213*) (1942) P63
P63 (1943) P63
P.64 (1917) P64
P64 (1942) P64
P64 (ren *P214*) (1942) P64
P65 (1942) P65
P65 (ren *P215*) (1943) P65
P66 (ren *P216*) (1942) P66
P66 (1943) P66
P67 (ren *P217*) (1942) P67
P67 (1943) P67
P68 (ren *P218*) (1943) P68
P68 (1943) P68
P69 (ren *P219*) (1941) P69
P69 (1943) P69
P71 (ren *P221*) (1941) P71
P71 (1943) P71
P72 (ren *P222*) (1941) P72
P72 (1943) P72
P73 (ren *P223*) (1942) P73
P73 (1943) P73
P74 (ren *P224*) (1942) P74
P74 (1943) P74
P75 (ren *P225*) (1942) P75
P75 (1943) P75
P76 (ren *P226*) (1943) P76
P76 (1943) P76
P77 (ren *P227*) (1943) P77
P77 (1943) P77
P78 (ren *P228*) (1942) P78

P78 (1943) P78
P79 (ren *P229*) (1942) P79
P79 (1943) P79
P81 (1944) P81
P82 (1944) P82
P83 (1944) P83
P84 (1944) P84
P85 (1944) P85
P86 (1944) P86
P87 (1944) P87
P88 (Canc) P88
P88 (ren *P238*) (1942) P88
P89 (Canc) P89
P89 (ren *P239*) (1942) P89
P91 (Canc) P91
P91 (ren *P311*) (1942) P91
P92 (Canc) P92
P93 (Canc) P93
P94 (Canc) P94
P95 (ren *P315*) (1942) P95
P95 (1944) P95
P96 (1944) P96
P96 (ren *P316*) (1942) P96
P97 (ex *Urchin*) (1940) P97
P98 (ren *P318*) (1943) P98
P99 (ren *P319*) (1943) P99
P211 (ex *P61*) (1941) P211
P212 (ex *P62*) (1942) P212
P213 (ex *P63*) (1942) P213
P214 (ex *P64*) (1942) P214
P215 (ex *P65*) (1943) P215
P216 (ex *P66*) (1942) P216
P217 (ex *P67*) (1942) P217
P218 (ex *P68*) (1943) P218
P219 (ex *P69*) (1941) P219
P221 (ex *P71*) (1941) P221
P222 (ex *P72*) (1941) P222
P223 (ex *P73*) (1942) P223
P224 (ex *P74*) (1942) P224
P225 (ex *P75*) (1942) P225
P226 (ex *P76*) (1943) P226
P227 (ex *P77*) (1943) P227
P228 (ex *P78*) (1942) P228
P229 (ex *P79*) (1942) P229
P231 (1943) P231
P232 (1943) P232
P233 (1943) P233
P234 (1943) P234
P235 (1943) P235
P236 (1943) P236
P237 (1944) P237
P238 (ex *P88*) (1942) P238

P239 (ex *P89*) (1942) P239
P241 (1943) P241
P242 (1943) P242
P243 (1944) P243
P244 (1945) P244
P245 (1943) P245
P246 (1943) P246
P247 (ex *P213*) (1942) P247
P248 (1943) P248
P249 (1943) P249
P251 (1944) P251
P252 (1944) P252
P253 (1944) P253
P254 (1944) P254
P255 (1945) P255
P256 (1945) P256
P311 (ex *P91*) (1942) P311
P312 (ex *P92*) (1942) P312
P313 (ex *P93*) (1942) P313
P314 (1942) P314
P315 (ex *P95*) (1942) P315
P316 (ex *P96*) (1942) P316
P317 (ex *P97*) (1942) P317
P318 (ex *P98*) (1943) P318
P319 (ex *P99*) (1943) P319
P32 (1943) P321
P322 (1943) P322
P323 (1943) P323
P324 (1943) P324
P325 (1942) P325
P326 (1942) P326
P327 (1943) P327
P328 (1943) P328
P329 (1942) P329
P331 (1943) P331
P332 (1944) P332
P333 (1944) P333
P334 (1944) P334
P335 (1944) P335
P336 (1944) P336
P337 (1945) P337
P338 (1945) P338
P339 (ex *P313*) (1942) P339
P341 (Canc) P341
P342 (1945) P342
P343 (Canc) P343
P344 (Canc) P344
P345 (Canc) P345
P346 (Canc) P346
P347 (Canc) P347
P348 (Canc) P348
P349 (1944) P349

P351 (1944) P351
P352 (1943) P352
P353 (1944) P353
P354 (1944) P354
P355 (1945) P355
P511 (ex *R3* ᴜsɴ) (1919) P511
P512 (ex *R17* ᴜsɴ) (1917) P512
P514 (ex *R19* ᴜsɴ) (1918) P514
P551 (ex *S25* ᴜsɴ) (1922) P551
P552 (ex *S1* ᴜsɴ) (1918) P552
P553 (ex *S21* ᴜsɴ) (1920) P553
P554 (ex *S22* ᴜsɴ) (1920) P554
P555 (ex *S24* ᴜsɴ) (1922) P555
P556 (ex *S29* ᴜsɴ) (1922) P556
P611 (1940) P611
P612 (1940) P612
P614 (1940) P614
P615 (1940) P615
P711 (ex *X-2*) (1934) P711
P712 (ex *Perla*) (1936) P712
P714 (ex *Bronzo*) (1941) P714
P715 (ex *U-570*) (1941) P715
Pacheco (1927) B544
Pachmarhi ʀɪɴ (Canc) T324
Pacific (1914) Y3.847
Pacific Transport (1913) Y3.1693
Packice (1917) J80
Packington (1958) M1214
Pactolus (1896) D08, N08, N77
Padstow (1942) J180
Padstow (2000) A286
Padstow Bay (1945) F608, K608
Pagham (1955) M2716
Pahau ʀɴᴢɴ (1943) T351
Paignton (1911) Y3.117
Pakenham (1941) G06
Paladin (1913) W61, W78
Paladin (1916) D1A, F11, F14, F18, G30, G40,
   G73
Paladin (1941) D69, F169, G69
Palatine (1870) Y3.330
Palermo (1903) Y3.1197
Paliki (1889) Y3.1135
Pallas ꜰʀ (1938) P41
Palliser (1956) F94
Palm Branch (1897) Y3.1475, Y8.91
Palma (1903) Y9.2
Palmleaf (1916) Y7.152
Palmol (1917) X47
Palomares (1939) F98
Pampano (1942) T152
Pampas (1943) 4.422

Panama Transport (1913) Y3.1737

Panayiotis (ex *Essex Abbey*) (1911) Y3.1327

Pancras (1911) Y3.1569

Pandora (1902) N71, N78

Pandora (1929) 42P, 42N, N42

Pangbourne (1918) J37, N37, T37, T79

Pangim (1901) Y3.2118

Pangkor (1929) F167

Panorama (ex *Rocroi*) (1919) Z215

Pansy (1916) Y3.1565

Pansy (1916) T61, T69

Pansy (1940) K15

Panther (1897) D67, D69, D87

Panther (1941) G41

Panthir RHN (1911) H67

Papatera (1942) T156

Papua (1943) K588

Paragon (1889) Y3.825

Paragon (1913) H26

Paramount (1911) FY954

Parapet (1945) L4039

Parati (1942) T148

Pargo (1942) T141

Pargust (1907) Y3.540

Paris FR (1912) D00

Paris (1913) N59, N79

Parker USN (1913) H(I)30, H(I)38

Parker (1916) F10, G49, G71, G75, G75, G95, H71, HA5

Parkes RAN (1943) J361, M361

Parkgate (1906) Y3.592

Parkgate (1917) Z06

Parkmill (1909) Y3.193

Parkmore (1915) FY807

Parktown (i) SAN (1929) T39

Parktown (ii) SAN (1925) T55, T455, T479

Parramatta RAN (1910) HA0

Parramatta RAN (1939) L44, U44

Parret (1943) B273, K304

Parrsboro (1941) J117

Parry Sound RCN (1943) K341

Parthian (1916) G17, G52, G77, H91

Parthian (1929) 75P, 75N, N75

Partridge (1906) M03, M(I)03, M(I)15

Partridge (1916) G46, G62

Partridge (1941) G30

Partridge (Canc) U37

Paru (1945) T183

Parvati RIN (1927) 4.179

Pasley (1916) D42, F22, G05, G54

Pasley (1943) K564

Patagonier (1910) Y3.1498

Patapsco USN (1908) T3A

Patella (1909) Y7.86

Paterson RAN (1920) FY10

Pathan (1905) Y3.1505

Pathan RIN (1918) K26, L71

Pathfinder (1941) G10

Patia (1913) M76, M(I)48, M(I)76, M(I)89

Patna RIN (1942) T255

Patricia (1901) Y3.2160

Patrician (1916) F15, F23, F84, G14, G48, GA1, H86

Patria (1912) Y3.1233

Patrie FR (1920) 4.326

Patriot (1916) F85, G15, G56, G63, H87

Patroclus (1896) Y3.1780

Patroclus (1923) F22

Patroclus (1943) W118

Patrol (1904) N24, N80

Patroller (1943) D07, R322

Patterson USN (1911) H(I)20, H(I)31

Patti (1929) 4.102

Patuca (1913) M77, M(I)49, M(I)77, M(I)90

Patuxent USN (1908) T2A

Paul Rykens (1935) FY257

Paulding USN (1910) H(I)03, H(I)32

Pawnee (1907) Y3.2208

Paynter (1937) FY242

PC 74 (1918) Z74

PC.42 (1917) P42

PC.43 (1917) P43

PC.44 (1917) P44

PC.51 (1916) P51

PC.55 (1917) P55

PC.56 (1917) P56

PC.60 (1917) P60

PC.61 (1917) P61

PC.62 (1917) P62

PC.63 (1917) P63

PC.65 (1917) P65

PC.66 (1917) P66

PC.67 (1917) P67

PC.68 (1917) P68

PC.69 (1917) P69

PC.75 (1916) P75

Peacock (1943) B293, F96, U96

Peacock (1982) P239

Pearl (1934) T22

Pearleaf (1916) X56, Y7.180

Pearleaf (1959) A77

Pearlmoor (1905) Y3.1665

Pebble (1890) Y4.31

Pecheur (1914) Z164

Peebles (1911) Y3.840
Peel Castle (1894) M13, M(I)07, M(I)13, M(I)16
Pegasus (1917) D35, I35, N9A
Peggy Nutten (1907) 4.450
Pegwell Bay (1945) K638
Peken (1908) FY1821
Pelagos (1918) 4.103
Pelargonium (1918) T0A
Pelegrime (1942) T184
Pelham (1906) Y3.604
Pelican (1916) F10, F77, G58, HA8
Pelican (1938) B294, F86, L86, U86
Pellew (1916) G64, H75, H98
Pellew (1954) F62
Pelorus (1943) J291
Pembroke (1997) M107
Pembroke Castle (1944) K450
Penare (1900) Y3.160
Penarth (1918) T91
Pendarves (1892) Y3.229
Pendeen (1899) Y3.1779
Pendragon Castle (1908) Y3.1500
Penelope (1914) 17, 92, 8A
Penelope (1935) 97, C97
Penelope (1962) F127
Penetang rcn (1944) K676
Penfield (....) W124
Pengreep (1914) Y3.343
Penguin (1916) D56
Penhale (1911) Y3.346
Penhallow (1913) Y3.301
Penlee (1901) Y3.1503
Penmorvah (1913) Y3.307
Penmount (1900) Y3.2062
Penn (1916) F16, F19, G25, G50, G74
Penn (1941) D70, D177, G77
Pennywort (1941) K111
Pennyworth (ex *Gogovale*) (1916) Y3.1734
Penolver (1912) Y3.293
Penrose (1908) Y3.870
Pensacola (1914) Y3.212
Penshurst (1906) Y3.253
Pensilva (1913) Y3.399
Penston (1955) M1169
Pentland Firth (1934) A416, FY108
Pentland Range (ex *Kincraig*) (1901) Y3.1727
Pentstemon (1916) T53, T70
Pentstemon (1941) K61, M61
Pentwyn (1910) Y3.810
Pentyrch (1899) Y3.1956
Penvearn (1906) Y3.1040
Penylan (ex *Arlington Court*) (1905) Y3.338

Penylan (1906) Y3.983
Penylan (1942) L89
Penzance (1930) L28, U28
Penzance (1997) M106
Peony (1915) T39, T71
Peony (1940) K40
Pera (1903) Y3.1169
Perdita (1910) D06, Y4.44
Perdrant fr (1919) FY1714
Peregrine (1892) Y1.6
Peregrine (1916) G38, G60, G65, H94
Peridot (1933) FY198
Perilia (1918) FY1624
Perim (1877) Y3.1568
Perim (1943) K593
Periwinkle (1940) K55
Perkins usn (1910) H(I)26, H(I)33
Perla (1912) Y3.1131
Perseus (1929) 36P, 36N, N36
Perseus (1944) 51, A197, B346, R51
Perseverance (1931) A221, W08
Persian (1943) J347
Persier (1910) Y3.602
Persimmon (1918) T4/
Persimmon (1943) F181, 4.422
Pert (1916) A318, W42
Perth (1915) M(I)17, M(I)23
Perth ran (1934) D29, I29
Perthshire (1893) X05, X48
Perugia (1901) Y3.1049
Peshawar rin (1942) T263
Peshawar rin (1944) J55, M55
Peshawur (1905) Y9.1
Pessac fr (1907) U06
Petard (1916) F20, F32, G29, G31, G66, GA7
Petard (1941) D56, F26, G56
Peter Carey (1919) FY537
Peter Hendricks (1935) FY260
Peterborough rcn (1944) K342
Peterel (1899) D68, D88, H54, P74
Peterel (1927) T21
Peterel (1976) P262
Peterhead (1940) J59, N59
Petersfield (1919) T21, T/7
Petersham (ex *Clinton*) (1899) Y3.547
Petersham (1955) M2718
Petingaudet (1897) Y3.1832
Petone (1900) Y3.2343
Petrella (1918) X49, X78
Petrobus (1917) A250, X50, X77
Petrograd (1891) Y3.1986
Petrolea (1904) Y4.7, Y7.105

Petroleine (1908) Y7.301
Petroleum (1902) D99, N92, X10, X51
Petrolia RCN (1944) K453, K498
Petronel (1918) X52, X79
Petunia (1916) T66, T72
Petunia (1940) K79, M79
Pevensey Castle (1944) F449, K449
Peyton (1916) G66, G72, H77, H96
Phaeton (1914) 45, 93, 6A
Phaeton (1934) I48
Phase (1919) FY869
Pheasant (1916) G74, G89
Pheasant (1942) B274, F49, U49
Philante (1937) 4.12
Philoctetes (1922) F134
Philol (1916) A253, X43, X53
Philomel (1890) I38
Phlox (1942) K130
Phoebe (1894) Y3.1227
Phoebe (1916) D59, F53, F55, G37, G82, HA6
Phoebe (1939) 43, C43, C173
Phoebe (1964) F42
Phoenix (1911) H75, H94
Phoenix (1929) 96P, 96N, N96
Pholas (1908) Y7.146
Photinia (1913) Y3.520
Phrontis (1911) 4.141
Phyllisia (1918) Z114
Pickle (1943) J293, M293
Picotee (1940) K63
Pict (1936) FY132
Picton (1906) Y3.342
Picton (1955) M1170
Picton Castle (1928) FY628
Pictou RCN (1940) K146
Pierre Andre FR (1920) FY1944
Pierre-Gustave (1932) FY1805
Pietermaritzburg SAN (1943) M291
Pigeon (1916) F18, F21, F89, G59, H18, H67
Pikepool (1910) Y3.272
Pilot (1909) W03, W62
Pimpernel (1940) K71
Pincher (1910) D87, HC2
Pincher (1943) J294, M294
Pindos RHN (1941) L65
Pine (1940) T101
Pine Lake RCN (1944) J492
Pineham (1955) M2719
Pinemore (1898) Y3.1431
Pinewood (1914) Y3.87
Pinieos RHN (1935) FY907
Pink (1942) K137

Pink Rose (1892) Y3.1953
Pinner (1919) N98
Pintail (1939) K21, L21, M21
Pintail (1963) P193
Pioneer (1944) A198, B347, D76, R76
Piorun ORP (1940) G65
Pique (1942) J23
Pique (1944) R49
Pirie RAN (1941) B249, J189
Pirouette (1940) T39, T121
Pitcairn (1943) K589
Pitsruan (1930) FY1791
Pivoc (1899) Y3.1752
Pladda (1941) T144
Planet (1938) P50, Z50
Plantaganet (1939) P63, Z63
Planudes (1915) Y3.282
Plassy (1901) YA.4
Platypus RAN (1916) A314, C8, I56
Plawsworth (1917) Y3.2044
Playmates (1925) FY738
Plinlimmon (1895) J66, 4.385
Ploughboy (1912) Z303
Plover (1916) G29, G65, G67
Plover (1937) I26, M26, N26
Plover (1983) P240
Plucky (1916) D2A, F74, G67, G68, GA6
Plucky (1943) J295, M295
Plumer (1919) FY1512
Plumleaf (1916) X54, Y7.179
Plumleaf (1960) A78
Plumpton (1916) T32
Plunger (1900) W65
Plunkett USN (1940) Y25
Pluto (1944) J446, M46
Plutus (1910) Y3.666
Plym (1943) B275, F271, K271
Plymouth (1959) F126
Pochard (1973) A165, P197
Podole ORP (1919) FY505
Poet Chaucer (1919) W65
Poictiers (1946) I10
Pointer (1906) FY1869
Pointer (1967) A188
Pointz Castle (1914) FY630
Pola (1898) Y3.775
Polamhall (1901) Y3.1415
Polandia (1898) Y3.621
Polanna (1893) Y3.1238
Polar Circle (1990) A176
Polar Prince (1895) Y3.1417
Polar VI (....) FY1691

Polar V RNoN (1931) FY1688
Polar VI (1925) FY1871
Polaria (1893) Y3.1906
Polaris (1944) J447, M447
Polavon (1905) P51, X21, Y4.147
Polbrae (1896) Y3.1759
Poldennis (1910) Y3.618
Poldown (1904) Y3.1803
Polegate (1917) Z07
Poleric (1900) Y3.1301
Polesley (1905) Y3.832
Polgarth (1919) Y3.2223
Polglass Castle (1903) Y3.831
Polgowan (1900) Y3.1499, Y4.22
Policastria (1907) Y3.789
Politania (1910) Y3.633
Poljames (1872) Y3.2137
Polka (1941) T139
Polkerris (1889) Y3.860
Polladern (1911) Y3.1406
Pollcrea (1899) Y3.1184
Pollensa (1890) Y3.1625
Pollington (1957) M1173
Pollock (1943) T347
Polly Bridge (1916) Y4.77
Polmanter (1901) Y3.606
Polmina (1917) Y3.2085
Polmont (1912) Y3.1102
Polo Norte POR (1917) FY1922
Polpedn (1902) Y3.835
Polperro (1898) Y3.622
Polruan (1907) Y3.557
Polruan (1940) J97, M97, N97
Polsham (1958) M2792
Polshannon (1910) P72, X25, X54, Y7.284
Polstream (1906) Y3.2109
Poltava (1909) Y3.856
Poltolia (1905) Y3.2176
Polvarth (1909) Y3.1510
Polvena   (1904) Y3.1347
Polwell (1888) Y3.724
Polyanthus (1917) T73
Polyanthus (1940) K47, M47
Polymnia (1903) Y3.619
Polyphemus (Canc) D57
Polyxena (1896) Y3.599
Polzeath (1911) Y3.693
Pomaron (1907) Y3.296
Pomerol FR (1930) U31
Pomerol ORP (1930) P25
Poniard (Canc) G06
Pontefract (1916) TC2

Pontwen (1914) Y3.1601
Pontypridd (1883) Y3.575
Poole (1941) J147
Poona RIN (1942) T260
Popham (1955) M2782
Poplar Lake (1945) J493
Poppy (1915) T47, T74
Poppy (1941) K213
Porcher (1942) T281
Porchester Castle (1943) K362
Porcupine (1895) D69, D0A, N19
Porcupine (1941) G93
Porlock Bay (1945) F650, K650
Porpoise (1913) H27, H86, H95
Porpoise (1932) 14M, 14N, N14, S9
Porpoise (1956) S01
Port Arthur (1941) K233
Port Colborne RCN (1943) B608, K326
Port Curtis (1910) Y3.1396
Port Hope RCN (1941) J280
Port Macquarie (1912) Y3.1675
Port Quebec (1939) M59
Portage RCN (1942) F31, J331
Portchester Castle (1943) F362
Portcullis (1945) L4044
Porter USN (1915) H(I)14, H(I)34
Porthkerry (1911) Y3.163
Portia (1906) Y4.36
Portia (1913) FY1852
Portia (1916) F92, G73, G84, HA6
Portisham (1955) M2781
Portland (1999) F79
Portland Bill (1945) A205, B351, F05
Portrush (1916) Y3.1624
Portsdown (1941) T221
Portway (1944) F144
Portwood (1913) Y3.28
Poseidon (1929) 99P
Postboy (1941) FY1750
Postillion (1943) J296
Potentilla (1941) K214
Potomac (1893) Y3.959, Y7.20
Poundmaker RCN (1944) B609, K675
Pourquois Pas FR (1913) 4.371
Powderham (1958) M2720
Powerful (1945) 95, R95
Powerful (1985) A223
Powhatan (1898) Y7.97
Powis Castle (1916) FY874
Pozarica (1937) 4.261
Precept (ex-USN) (1944) Z266
Precise (ex-USN) (1944) Z285

Prefect (ex-USN) (1944) Z263
Premier (1943) D23
Prescott RCN (1941) K161
Present Help (1911) 4.370
President Herriot (....) 4.232
President Houduce FR (1930) K109
President Kruger SAN (1960) F150
President Pretorius SAN (1962) F145
President Steyn SAN (1961) F147
Prestatyn (1918) T2N, T5N
Presto (ex *Triumph*) (1893) Y3.2357
Prestol (1917) A155, X55, X60
Preston North End (1934) FY230
Preston USN (1909) H(I)47
Prestonian RCN (1944) B610, K662
Pretext (ex-USN) (1944) Z284
Pretoria (1900) Y3.1073
Pretoria SAN (1930) T59, T459
Pretoria Castle (1938) F61
Preventer (ex-USN) (1944) Z265
Priestfield (1901) Y3.316
Primo (1915) Y3.1794
Primrose (1910) Y3.2024
Primrose (1915) M96, T29, T75
Primrose (1940) K91, M91
Primula (1915) T55
Primula (1940) K14, M14
Prince (1916) F92, G42, G43, G77, H37
Prince Baudouin (1933) 4.88
Prince Charles (1930) 4.120
Prince Charles (1905) Y3.402
Prince David RCN (1930) F89
Prince de Leige BG (1926) B545, Z172
Prince Eugene (1915) M10, M11
Prince George (1895) D46, P86, P9A
Prince George (1910) YA.12
Prince Henry RCN (1930) F70
Prince Leo (1913) FY998
Prince Leopold (1905) Y3.401
Prince Leopold (1929) 4.251
Prince of Wales (1902) 81, 94, N46
Prince of Wales (1939) 53, I53
Prince of Wales (2019) R09
Prince Robert RCN (1930) B611, F56
Prince Rupert (1915) M07, M12
Prince Rupert RCN (1943) B640, K324
Prince Salvor (1943) A292, W05
Princes Astrid (1929) 4.226
Princess (1905) M(I)57, M(I)91
Princess (1924) FY.021
Princess Alberta (1905) Y4.58, Y7.58
Princess Beatrix (1939) 4.44

Princess Elizabeth (1927) J111, 4.403
Princess Ena (1906) Y4.57
Princess Irene (1914) P47
Princess Iris (1917) F90
Princess Louise (1912) N34, N80
Princess Margaret (1914) D00, N82, P46
Princess Margaret (1931) 4.419
Princess Mary (1914) FY876
Princess Maud (1902) Y4.63
Princess Maud (1934) 4.414
Princess of Wales (1896) Y4.30
Princess Royal (1911) 29, 68, 95
Princess Victoria (1912) Y4.9
Princess Victoria (1939) M03
Princetown (1905) Y3.1990
Prins Albert (1937) 4.35
Prinses Josephine Charlotte (1930) 4.238
Prinses Maria Pia (1938) B546
Privet (1942) K291
Probe (1942) T186
Proctor (1942) T185
Prodigal (1941) T187
Product (1941) T188
Professor (1942) T189
Prome (1937) B432
Prometheus (1896) Y7.275
Promise (1941) T193
Prompt (1943) A235
Prompt (1944) J378
Promus (1918) Y3.2046
Prong (1942) T190
Proof (1942) T191
Property (1942) T192
Prophet (1912) Y3.631
Prophet (1942) T194
Prosper (1917) Y3.2450
Proserpine (1896) N84
Prospect (1942) T282
Prospects Ahead (1919) FY1538
Prosperous (1942) A254, W96
Protea SAN (1936) T43, T443
Protea SAN (1941) A321
Protect (1944) Z264
Protector (1936) A146, B437, T98
Protector (1975) P244
Protector (2001) A173
Protest (1941) T195
Proteus (1929) 29P, 29N, N29
Proud Fusilier (1945) P1505
Proud Grenadier (1945) P1506
Proud Guardsman (1945) P1507
Proud Highlander (1945) P1508

Proud Knight (1945) P1509
Proud Lagionary (1946) P1522
Proud Lancer (1945) P1519
Proud Patriot (1944) P1596
Proud Patroller (1944) P1598
Providence (1943) B265, J325, M325
Prowess (ex *Provost*) (1943) T196
Prudent (1940) W73
Prudentia (1889) Y7.46
Prunella (1930) X02
Pruth (1916) Y3.2187
Puckeridge (1941) L108
Puffin (1936) K52, L52, M52, P35
Pukaki RNZN (1944) F424
Pulham (1956) M2721
Puma (1954) F34
Puncher (1943) D79
Puncher (1944) L115, L3036
Puncher (1988) P291
Puncheston (1956) M1174
Pundit (1902) Y3.2209
Punjab RIN (1941) J239, M239
Punjabi (1937) F21, G21
Punnet (1925) Z04
Purfol (1907) X56
Puri RIN (Canc) T328
Purley (1913) Y3.320
Pursuer (1942) D73, R309
Pursuer (1944) L116, L3504
Pursuer (1988) P273
Putney (ex *Lynton*) (1899) Y3.347
Puttenham (1956) M2784
Pylades (1916) F19, F28, F94, G62, G78, H96,
  H97
Pylades (1943) J401
Pyrrhus (1945) J448, M448
Pytchley (1917) T2C
Pytchley (1940) F192, L92

Q

Qu'appelle RCN (1934) H69
Quadrant RAN (1942) D11, D17, F01, G11
Quadrille (1941) T133
Quail (1895) D70, D85, D89, H32
Quail (1942) G45
Quainton (1957) M1175
Qualicum (1941) J138
Quality RAN (1942) D18, D262, G62
Quannet (1926) Z44
Quantock (1910) Y3.456

Quantock (1940) F158, L58
Quarrydene (1905) Y3.1617
Quatsino RCN (1941) J152
Quebec RCN (1941) 66
Queen (1884) Y3.709
Queen (1902) 82, 96
Queen (1943) D19, R320
Queen Adelaide (1911) Y3.728
Queen Alexandra (1914) Y3.604
Queen Amelie (1905) Y3.1027
Queen Eagle (1940) 4.247
Queen Elizabeth (1907) Y3.2288
Queen Elizabeth (1913) 00, 10, 97, B6, B10
Queen Elizabeth (1938) F50
Queen Elizabeth (2017) R08
Queen Emma (1939) 4.180
Queen Empress (1912) J128, R399, 4.399
Queen Helena (1904) Y3.1111
Queen Louise (1912) Y3.1340
Queen Margaret (1912) Y3.1571
Queen Mary (1912) 14
Queen Mary (1935) F35
Queen Maud (1909) Y3.1673
Queen of Bermuda (1932) F73
Queen of Kent (1916) J74, N74
Queen of Thanet (1916) J30, N30
Queen of the Fleet (1917) Z29
Queen Wilhelmina RNLN (1942) A422, F191
Queenborough RAN (1942) D19, D270, F02, F57,
  G70
Queenmoor (1903) Y3.507
Queensgarth (1908) Y3.180
Queensland (1894) Y3.267
Queensland Transport (1913) Y3.453
Queenswood (1897) Y3.1114
Quenast (1903) Y3.2451
Quentin (1941) G78
Quentin Roosevelt (1918) FY317
Quercia (1912) Y7.43, 4.336
Querida (1909) Y3.791
Quernmore (1898) M(I)99, PA4
Quesnel RCN (1940) K133
Quetta RIN (1944) T332
Quiberon RAN (1942) D20, D281, F03, G81
Quickmatch RAN (1941) D21, D292, F04, G92
Quickstep (1909) Y3.205
Quiet Waters (1931) FY1776
Quilliam RAN (1941) D22, G09
Quinnebaug USN (1898) R(I)05
Quinte RCN (1941) J166
Quintia (1914) FY1658
Quito (1900) Y3.1171

Quorn (1917) T3C
Quorn (1940) L66
Quorn (1988) M41

R

R1 (1918) R1
R2 (1918) R2
R3 (1918) R3
R4 (1918) R4
R5 (Canc) R5
R6 (Canc) R6
R7 (1918) R7
R8 (1918) R8
R9 (1918) R9
R10 (1918) R10
R11 (1918) R11
R12 (1918) R12
Raccoon RCN (1931) S14
Race Fisher (1892) Y2.36, Y3.586, Y4.33
Racehorse (1900) D66, D71, P15
Racehorse (1942) D37, D211, H11
Racer (1884) X57
Rachel Flett (1914) FY1984
Racia (1895) X40
Rackham (1956) M2722
Racoon (1910) HA7
Radiant (1916) D88, F56, F59, G65
Radiant (1927) FY.022
Radnor Castle (1917) FY511
Radstock (1916) D94, G76, G79, G81, H64
Raetia (1912) Y7.26, 4.142
Raglan (1915) M03, M09, M14
Raglan Castle (1919) FY631
Raider (1916) D95, G41, G81, G82, G86, H65
Raider (1942) D38, D115, H15
Raider (1998) P275
Rainbow (1930) 16R, 16N, N16
Rainstorm (1928) FY1920
Raithwaite (1899) Y3.550
Rajah (1943) D10, R310
Rajputana (1925) F35
Rajputana RIN (1941) J197, M197
Raleigh (1919) 96
Raloo (1898) Y3.174
Rambler (1908) W80
Ramdas RIN (1936) 4.111
Rame Head (1944) A134, B359, F34
Ramillies (1892) Y6.6
Ramillies (1916) 07, 21, 74, 98, B07
Rampant (1898) 4.82

Rampart (1945) L4037
Rampisham (1957) M2786
Rampur RIN (1941) T12
Rampur RIN (1944) T269
Ramsay (1902) Y3.720
Ramsey (1919) G60
Ramsey (1999) M110
Ramsgarth (1910) Y3.179
Ranchi (1925) F15
Randfontein SAN (1926) T12, T512
Ranee (1943) D03, R323
Ranella (1912) Y7.40
Ranger (1880) W67
Ranger (1895) D1A
Ranger (1988) P293
Ranger (ren *Caesar*) (1944) R58
Rangol (1893) Y7.174
Ranoncule FR (1941) K117
Ranpura (1924) A239, B337, F39
Ranunculus (1941) K117
Rapid (1916) G46, G63, G78, G83, H94
Rapid (1942) D39, D138, F138, H32
Rapidan (1907) Y3.1436
Rapidol (1917) A258, B517, X58
Ratapiko (1912) FY1878
Rathven Burn (1919) W64
Ratnagiri RIN (1913) 4.198
Rattler (1942) J217
Rattlesnake (1910) D94, F96, HC7
Rattlesnake (1943) J297, M297
Rattray Head (1945) B358, F73
Ravager (1942) D70
Ravager (1944) L117, L3505
Ravelston (1906) Y3.89
Ravenrock (1903) Y3.2195
Ravens Point (1918) Y3.2372
Ravenshoe (1919) Y3.470
Ravenstone (1905) Y3.440
Ravenswood (1891) 4.328
Ravenswood (1941) N12
Rawcliffe (1906) Y3.52
Rayford (1894) Y3.642, Y8.41
Rayleigh Castle (1944) K695
Raymond BG (1930) 4.99
Raymont (1916) FY785
Reading (1919) G71
Ready (1916) D97, G71, G84, G87, H74
Ready (1943) J223, M223
Reaper (1943) D82, R324
Reapwell (1899) Y3.428
Reboundo (1920) FY602
Reclaim (1948) A231

Reclaimer (1885) Y4.18
Recono (1916) FY786
Recovery (1908) A319, W21
Recruit (1896) N60
Recruit (1916) F63
Recruit (1943) J298, M298
Red Cap (1899) Y3.1364
Red Deer RCN (1941) J255
Red Dragon (1912) X81
Red Gauntlet (1930) FY900
Red Sky (1918) FY1554
Redbreast (1908) Y4.26
Redesmere (1911) Y3.92
Redgauntlet (1916) F16, F51, F58, F97, FA4, G78, H14
Redmill (1916) G75
Redmill (1943) K554
Redoubt (1916) D91, F56, F57, G67, H68
Redoubt (1942) D40, D141, H41
Redoubt (1945) L4001
Redoubtable (1892) N12, N84
Redpole (1910) H71, H77, H96
Redpole (1943) B276, F69, U69
Redpole (1967) P259
Redshank (1942) M31, N31
Redstart (1938) I62, M62
Redwing (1916) G76
Redwing (1933) P136, T36
Redwood (1928) T86
Reedham (1958) M2723
Reflect (1908) 4.213
Refraction (1919) FY945
Refugio (1905) Y3.1260
Refundo (1917) FY830
Regal (1933) FY180
Regardo (1907) Y7.33
Regardo (1915) FY831
Regent (1903) Y3.1975
Regent (1930) 41R, 41N, N41
Regent (1966) A486
Reggio (1944) L119, L3511
Regina RCN (1941) K234
Reginald Kerr (1944) L3009
Regis (1909) Y3.1030
Registan (1930) F106
Regulus (1930) 88R, 88N, N88
Regulus (1943) J327
Rehearo (1917) FY1794
Reid USN (1909) H(I)51
Reids (1918) FY1979
Reigate (1918) P11, Z11
Reighton Wyke (1937) FY133

Reindeer (1896) Y3.558
Reindeer (1897) M34, T08, T76
Reine des Flots (1923) FY343
Relentless (1902) Y3.194
Relentless (1916) F17, G57, G69, H49
Relentless (1942) D41, D185, F185, H85
Reliance (1906) Y3.997
Reliance (1910) D97, N90, X09, X59
Reliance (1944) F176
Reliant (1922) A238, X25
Reliant (1953) A84
Reliant (1976) A131
Relillio (1909) Y3.249
Relonzo (1914) FY843
Remembrance (1910) Y3.252
Remexo (1912) FY875
Remus (1908) Y3.685
Renard (1909) H27, H99
Renascent (1926) FY1520
Rendlesham (1954) M2724
Renfrew (ex *Galavale*) (1907) Y3.629
Renfrew RCN (Canc) K452
Rennet (1928) Z99
Rennington (1958) M1176
Renown (1916) 23, 64, 72, 99, B7, B72
Renown (1967) S26
Renvoyle (1910) Y3.1689
Renzo (1913) FY893
Repton (1894) Y3.71
Repton (1919) T65
Repton (1957) M1167
Repulse (1916) 26, 34, 54, 0A
Repulse (1967) S23
Reresby (1897) Y3.758
Research (1888) P88, PA0
Research (1939) J96, N96
Reserve (1942) A149, W149
Reserve RAN (1942) A775
Resolution (1915) 09, 57, 84, 1A, 8A, B09
Resolution (1966) S22
Resolve (1918) W85
Resolve (1945) A309, A399
Resolvo (1913) FY821
Resource (1928) A179, B304, F79, I79
Resource (1966) A480
Resparko (1916) FY822
Respond (1918) W92
Restart (1912) FY1900
Restigouche RCN (1931) H00
Restive (1940) A286, W39
Restless (1916) D85, F68, G85, G88, H82
Restormel (1900) Y3.215

Restrivo (1914) FY834
Resurgent (1950) A280
Retainer (1950) A329
Retako (1914) FY838
Retalick (1943) K555
Retort (1918) A320, W84
Retriever (1909) Z255
Retreiver (1917) F58, D89, F64, G66, H42
Retreiver (1930) FY261
Returno (1914) FY839, Y7.27
Reval (1898) Y3.697
Revello (1908) FY778
Revelstoke ʀᴄɴ (1943) J373, M373
Revenge (1892) P55
Revenge (1915) 06, 29, 98, 2A, B06
Revenge (1968) S27
Revenger (1905) W66
Reverberation (1919) FY1990
Revue (1939) W62
Rewa (1906) YA.5
Reward (1944) A264, B745, W164
Reynolds (1898) Y3.973
Rhinoceros (1897) W68
Rhio (1903) C Y3.372
Rhodanthe (1902) Y3.47
Rhodesian Transport (1914) Y3.1888
Rhododendron (1917) T95
Rhododendron (1940) K78
Rhodora (1929) FY.023
Rhydwen (1914) Y3.1293
Rhyl (1940) J36, M36, N36
Rhyl (1959) F129
Riano (1906) 4.429
Ribble (1943) F525, K251, K525
Ribble ʀᴄɴ (ex *Duddon*) (1943) K411
Ribble (1985) M2012
Ribbledale (1902) Y3.936
Ribera (1904) Y3.1165
Ribston (1894) Y3.1357
Ribston (1906) Y3.943
Ricardo A. Mestres (1914) Y7.114
Richard Crofts (1918) FY530
Richard de Larringa (1916) Y3.1462
Richard Lee Barber (1940) W82
Richard Welford (1908) M21, M(I)18, M(I)21
Richelieu ꜰʀ (1939) 58, B8, B62
Richmond (1917) G88
Richmond (1993) F239
Ridley (1913) Y3.388
Rievaulx Abbey (1908) Y2.56, Y8.47
Rifle (Canc) G21
Rifleman (1910) H82, H97, H99

Rifleman (1943) J299, M299
Rig (1911) FY1540
Righto (1920) FY604
Rigoletto (1906) 4.451
Rigorous (1916) D86, F69, G90, H83, G86
Rime (1919) FY1542
Rimouski ʀᴄɴ (1940) K121
Rimu ʀɴᴢɴ (1941) T402
Rinaldo (1943) J225, M225
Ring (1888) Y3.2135
Ringdove (1889) C78, C84
Ringdove (1938) I77, M77
Ringwood (1924) T245
Rio Blanco (1899) Y3.1925
Rio Claro (1904) Y3.833
Rio Lages (1900) Y3.881
Rio Pallaresa (1904) Y3.799
Rio Preto (1901) Y3.1477
Rio Tiete (1904) Y3.652
Rio Verde (1901) Y3.1724
Rion (1889) Y7.27
Rion (1928) FY.24
Riou (1943) K557
Ripley (1918) G79
Ripon (1945) A206, F106
Ripplingham (1955) M2725
Rising Castle (1944) K398
Riskato (1915) 4.302
Risor ʀɴᴏɴ (1929) FY203
Ristango (1913) Z206
Rival (1915) W95
Rival (1916) F18, F20, F24, G62, H34, H40, H97
River Annan (1919) Z160
River Araxes (1907) Y3.2194
River Crake (1877) Y3.1278
River Esk (1918) 4.161
River Fisher (1899) Y4.34
River Forth (1907) Y3.1438
River Leven (1918) 4.51
River Lossie (1920) 4.246
River Orontes (1912) Y3.1792
River Plate (Canc) I83
River Spey (1918) FY1643
Riverdale (1895) Y3.982
Riverside ʀᴄɴ (Canc) K451
Riverton (1899) Y3.1598
Riviera (1911) N85
Riviere du Loup ʀᴄɴ (1943) K357
RML 495 (1942) A495
RML 496 (1942) A496
RML 498 (1942) A498
RML 512 (1942) A512

RML 515 (1942) A515
RML 529 (1942) A529
Roanoke ᴜꜱɴ (1911) R(I)00
Rob Roy (1916) G41, G87, G92, H75, H0A, HA0
Robert Dundas (1938) A204, X04
Robert Hastie (1912) FY771
Robert Maersk (1937) B547
Robert Middleton (1938) A241, X41
Robert Stroud (1930) FY687
Roberts (1915) M04, M08, M1A
Roberts (1941) B99, F40
Robin (1934) T65
Robinson ꜱᴀɴ (1927) T06, T506
Robust (1907) A228, W28
Robust (1971) A366
Roc (1945) A122, F122
Rocio (1915) Y3.1474
Rochdale (1906) Y3.980
Roche Velen ꜰʀ (1918) FY1718
Rochester (1931) F50, L50, U50
Rock Light (1888) Y7.81
Rockall (1930) FY1844
Rockcliffe ʀᴄɴ (1943) J355
Rockcliffe (1945) A232, B457, W15
Rocket (1916) G43, G82, G88, H76
Rocket (1942) D42, D192, F193, H92
Rockforest (1945) A166, B460, W66
Rockglen ʀᴄɴ (1945) A296, B458, W26
Rockhampton ʀᴀɴ (1941) J203, M203
Rockingham (1919) G58
Rockland ʀᴄɴ (1945) A279, B461, W79
Rockmount ʀᴄɴ (1945) A138, B462, W38
Rockpigeon ʀᴄɴ (1945) A388, B463, W88
Rockpool (1912) Y3.1494
Rockport ʀᴄɴ (1945) B464, W52
Rockrose (1941) K51
Rocksand (1918) N77
Rocksand (1943) F184
Rockwing ʀᴄɴ (1945) A233, B459, W04
Rockwood (1942) L39
Rocro (1919) Z193
Roddam (1912) Y3.387
Roddington (1955) M1177
Rodino (1913) FY840
Rodman ᴜꜱɴ (1941) Y91
Rodney (1925) 29, B9, B29
Roe ᴜꜱɴ (1909) H(I)46
Roebuck (1901) D53, D67, D72
Roebuck (1942) D43, D195, F195, H95
Roebuck (1985) A130, H130
Roedean (1897) M35
Rogate (1929) Z12

Rohilkhand ʀɪɴ (1942) J180, M180
Roker (1898) Y3.31
Rollcall (1918) W81
Rollesby (1906) Y3.1203
Rollicker (1918) A200, W95
Rollicker (1971) A502
Rolls Royce (1906) FY1831
Roma (1889) Y3.492
Romanby (1908) Y3.1048
Romany (1902) Y7.34
Romany Rose (1924) FY1995
Romeo (1881) Y5.1
Romeo (1941) T10
Romera (1909) Y3.1388
Romford (1898) Y3.1047
Romney (1893) Y3.2020
Romney (1940) J77, N77
Romola (1916) G15, G18, G53, G83, H84
Romola (1944) J449, M449
Romsdalen (1895) Y3.518
Romsey (1930) FY311
Rona (1884) Y3.2205
Ronaldsay (1941) T149
Ronay (1945) J429, M429
Rondevlei ꜱᴀɴ (1929) T14, T514
Rondo (1914) Y3.74
Ronso (1915) FY841, Y7.29
Roode Zee (1938) W162
Roodepoort ꜱᴀɴ (1929) T57, T457
Rooke (1907) Y3.2197
Rorqual (1936) 74M, 74N, N74, S2
Rorqual (1956) S02
Rosa (1908) FY1626
Rosaleen (1908) Y4.39
Rosalie (1893) Y3.935
Rosalind (1913) Y7.9
Rosalind (1916) D87, G64, G89, G95, H77
Rosalind (1941) P05, T135
Rosamund (1944) J439
Rosario (1907) Y3.248
Rosario (1943) J219, M219
Rose Bud (1907) FY944
Rose Haugh (1918) FY967
Rose Hilda (1930) FY740
Rose of England (1909) FY562
Rose ʀɴᴏɴ (1941) K102
Rose Castle (1915) Y3.1604
Rose Marie (1902) Y3.1845
Rose Valley (1918) FY1578
Rosebank (1906) Y3.1156
Rosebay (1943) K286
Roseden (1918) Y3.2199

Rosehill (1911) Y3.952
Roselea (1902) Y3.892
Roseleaf (1916) Y7.171, X32
Roselys ꜰʀ (1941) K57
Rosemary (1915) L14, T58, T77, U14
Rosemma (1912) FY1888
Roseric (1910) Y3.2370
Rosette (1911) FY1577
Rosevean (1943) T363
Rosita (1900) N95
Ross (1919) J45, N45, NA4, T0/
Ross (1919) Y3.12, Y3.275
Ross Ard (1911) FY934
Rossano (1909) Y3.1597
Rossetti (1900) Y3.659
Rossia (1900) Y3.1212
Rossland ʀᴄɴ (1943) J358
Rosthern ʀᴄɴ (1940) K169
Rother (1904) D29, D73, N32
Rother (1914) Y3.2071
Rother (1941) F224, K224
Rotherham (1942) D44, D209, H09
Rotherhill (1910) Y3.6
Rotherslade (1917) FY1822
Rothesay (1941) J19, N19
Rothesay (1957) F107
Rothley (1911) Y3.1127
Rotoiti ʀɴᴢɴ (1944) F625
Rotterdam (1916) FY1741
Rouen (1912) Y3.44
Roule ꜰʀ (1933) Z191
Roumanian (1908) Y7.232
Roumanian Prince (1913) Y7.53
Roundshot (1945) W183
Rounton (1894) Y3.589
Rounton Grange (1913) Y3.1591
Rousay (1941) T210
Rover (1930) 62R, 62N, N62
Rowan (1909) M01, M(I)01, M(I)08, M(I)19
Rowan (1939) T119
Rowan ᴜsɴ (1916) H(I)36, H(I)61
Rowanol (1946) A284
Rowena (1899) Y3.695
Rowena (1916) D84, F45, G81, G90, H85
Rowena (1944) B801, J384, M384
Rowley (1943) K560
Roxano (1907) 4.456
Roxborough (1918) I07
Roxburgh (1904) 86, 3A, N34
Roxburgh (1908) Y3.1556
Royal Arthur (1891) A0, N10, N86
Royal Eagle (1932) 4.239, R239

Royal Marine (1944) T395
Royal Mount ʀᴄɴ (1944) B641, K677
Royal Oak (1914) 08, 38, 67, 4A, I08
Royal Sceptre (1906) Y3.1747
Royal Scot (1910) M16, M(I)16, M(I)20
Royal Scotsman (1936) F115, 4.115
Royal Sovereign (1915) 05, 59, 89, 5A, I05
Royal Transport (1913) Y3.350
Royal Ulsterman (1936) F63, 4.63
Royalist (1915) 75, 4A, 6A, 89
Royalist (1942) C89, C176
Royallieu (1907) FY835
Royallo (1916) FY825
Roydur (1911) FY1704
Roysterer (1919) W91
Roysterer (1972) A361
Rubio (1909) Y3.250
Rubis ꜰʀ (1931) P15
Ruby (1910) H22, H85, H98
Ruby (1933) T24
Rudilais (1920) FY528
Rudmore (1911) Y3.20
Ruel (1917) Y3.496, Y3.2198
Rugby (1900) 4.162
Rugby (1916) Y7.30
Rugby (1918) T01, T47
Rukmavati ʀɪɴ (1904) FY.075
Ruler (1943) A731, D72, R311
Rumba (1940) T122
Runnymede ʀᴄɴ (1943) K678
Runswick (1904) Y3.266
Runswick Bay (1929) FY750
Ruperra (1904) Y3.415
Rupert (1943) K561
Rushen Castle (1943) F372, K372
Rusken (1871) Y3.2134
Ruskholm (1942) T211
Russell (1901) 23
Russell (1954) F97
Russell II (1906) N87, N3A
Russian Prince (1912) Y7.53
Rustington (1909) Y3.635
Ruth (1907) Y3.1989
Ruthenia (1900) N87, X06, X60
Rutherford (1943) K558
Rutherglen (1906) Y2.108, Y3.1372
Rutlandshire (1936) FY241
Ryde (1937) J132, 4.39
Rye (1940) J76, N76
Ryhope (1907) Y3.46
Rysa (1941) T164
Rytonhall (ex *St Helena*) (1905) Y3.1081

S

S1 (1914) I04
S2 (1915) I0A
S3 (1915) I1A
Saba (1912) Y3.1563
Sabia (1903) Y3.1057
Sabina (1919) 4.254
Sabine (1917) W74
Sable (1916) G44, G91, H93
Sable (ex *Salmon*) (1916) H58
Sabre (1919) F41, G56, H18
Sabre (1970) P275
Sabre (1993) P285
Sabrina (1916) F15, G79, G92, H47
Sachem (1893) M(I)92, PA0
Sachtouris ʀʜɴ (1940) K40
Sackville ʀᴄɴ (1941) F181, K181
Safari (1941) P211
Safeguard (1914) C78, C80, C81
Saga (1907) Y3.1960
Saga (1945) P257
Sagama River (1914) Y3.2074
Sagenite (1904) Y3.1218
Sagitta (1908) 4.26
Sagittarius (1896) Y3.1900
Saguenay ʀᴄɴ (1930) D79, H01, I79
Sahara (1897) Y3.1896
Sahib (1942) P212
Sahra (1936) FY1903
Sailor King (1914) Z45
Sainfoin (1943) F183
St Abbs (1918) W02
St Achilleus (1934) FY152
St Adrian (1927) 4.63
St Agnes (1943) T352
St Albans (1918) I15
St Albans (2000) F83
St Amandus (1933) FY176
St Andrews (1906) Y3.247
St Andronicus (1933) FY111
St Ann ʀᴄɴ (....) J176
St Anne (1919) W36
St Anthony ʀɪɴ (1936) 4.149
St Arcadius (1934) FY135
St Arvans (1919) W05
St Attalus (1934) FY183
St Aubin (1918) W18
St Austell Bay (1944) B613, F634, K634
St Bees (1918) W23
St Blazey (1919) W46
St Boniface (1919) W20

St Boniface ʀᴄɴ (1942) J332
St Boswells (1919) W51
St Botolph (1918) W34
St Breock (1919) W56
St Brides Bay (1945) B614, F600, K600
St Cathan (1936) FY234
St Catherines ʀᴄɴ (1942) B643, K325
St Celestin (1925) Z104
St Clair ʀᴄɴ (1918) I65
St Clears (1919) A364, W06
St Columb (1918) W07
St Cran (....) T235
St Croix ʀᴄɴ (1919) I81
St Cyrus (1919) W47
St David (RNR) M1113, M1124
St David (1973) M07
St Day (1918) A255, W55
St Dimitrios (1901) Y3.543
St Dogmael (1918) W66
St Dominica (1895) 4.59
St Edmund (1904) Y3.133
St Elstan (1937) FY240
St Fagan (1919) W74
St Finbarr (1919) W22
St Francis ʀᴄɴ (1919) I93
St Genny (1919) W04
St George (1892) N31, N88
St George (1981) A382
St Giles ʀᴀɴ (1919) B455, FY86, W96
St Gothard (1903) Y3.1229
St Helena (1943) K590
St Helier (1919) W08
St Helier (1925) 4.255
St Issey (1918) W25
St James (1919) W56
St James (1945) D65, R65
St John ʀᴄɴ (1943) B644, K456
St Joseph ʀᴄɴ (1943) J359
St Just (1918) W90
St Katharine (1927) 4.56
St Kenan (1936) FY264
St Kilda (1942) T209
St Kitts (1944) D18, R18
St Lambert ʀᴄɴ (1943) K343
St Laurent ʀᴄɴ (1930) H83
St Leonards (1911) Y3.1873
St Loman (1936) A418, FY276
St Lucia (Canc) I42
St Margaret of Scotland (1909) YA.19
St Margarets (1943) A259, B702, Z259
St Martin (1919) W27
St Marys (1918) I12

St Melante (1927) FY753
St Mellons (1918) W81, W89
St Michael (1907) Y3.1508
St Minver (1919) FY725
St Mirren (1894) Y3.2457
St Modwen (1911) FY.025
St Monance (1919) W63
St Nazaire (1945) L125, L3517
St Nectan (1936) 4.139
St Ninian (1894) Y3.737
St Olaves (1918) W40
St Olive (1914) FY1599
St Omar (1919) W34
St Patrick (1906) Y3.1424
St Pierre RCN (1943) B615, K680
St Sampson (1919) W26
St Stephen (1911) Y3.795
St Stephen RCN (1944) B646, F454, K454
St Theodore (1913) Y3.890
St Thomas RCN (1943) K373, K488
St Tudno (1926) 4.43
St Vincent (1908) 16, 85, 7A
St Winifred (1913) Y3.852
St Wistan (1937) 4.105
St Zeno (1940) A419, FY280
Saintes (1944) D84, R84
Saladin (1919) F0A, H54, HA1
Salamander (1936) J86, N86
Salamis RHN (1930) H77
Saldanha (1911) Y3.1785
Salerno (1945) L121, L3513
Salford (1919) N06, NA5
Salisbury (1953) F32
Salisbury RCN (1919) I52
Sallyport (1945) L4064
Salmaid (1986) A187
Salmaster (1985) A186
Salmon (1916) F18, G93, G94, H36, H58, N65
Salmon (1934) 65S, 65N
Salmoor (1985) A185
Salopian (1926) F94
Salpa (1918) FY1623
Saltarello (1940) T128
Saltash (1918) J62, N62, T6N, T9N
Saltburn (1918) J58, N58, T3/, T5/
Saltmarshe (1907) Y3.76
Saluki (1969) A182
Salvage Duke (1943) A234, W34
Salvalour (1944) A494
Salveda (1943) A497
Salventure (1942) A384
Salvestor (1942) A499, B442, W176

Salvia (1940) K97, M97
Salvictor (1944) A500, B443, W190
Salvigil (1945) A501
Salvini (1916) 4.457
Salviola (1945) A502
Salvo (1918) FY1672
Salvonia (1939) W43
Samara (1906) Y3.563
Samnanger (1918) Y3.2411
Samoset (1908) Y7.104
Sampan (1898) Y3.109
Samphire (1941) K128
Sampson USN (1916) H(I)07, H(I)37
Samsonia (1942) A218, B746, W23
Samson (1953) A390
Samuel Benbow (1918) FY95
San Adolfo (1935) B518
San Amado (1934) B519
San Ambrosio (1935) B520
San Andres (1921) B564
San Domingo (Canc) I37
San Dunstano (1912) Y7.285
San Francisco USN (1889) R(I)02
San Fraterno (1913) Y7.137
San Gregorio (1913) Y7.68
San Jeronimo (1914) Y7.64
San Lorenzo (1914) Y7.16
San Melito (1914) Y7.130
San Nazario (1914) Y7.260
San Onofre (1914) Y7.176
San Patricio (1895) Y4.19, Y7.115
San Ricardo (1913) Y7.258
San Silvestre (1913) Y7.87
San Tirso (1913) Y7.42
San Valerio (1913) Y7.43
San Zeferino (1914) Y7.292
Sancroft (1941) Z269
Sanda RNZN (1941) P160, T160
Sandboy (1912) W48
Sandfly (1911) F95, H63, H87, H99
Sandgate (1917) Z24
Sandsend (1899) Y3.1251
Sandgate Castle (1943) K373
Sandhurst (1905) A4, C9, F92
Sandmartin (1926) M06
Sandown (1916) T68
Sandown (1934) J20, 4.15
Sandown (1939) N20
Sandown (1988) M101
Sandpiper (1933) T41
Sandpiper (1977) P263
Sandray (1944) J424, M424

Sandringham (1930) FY589
Sandringham (1957) M2791
Sandstorm (1925) FY699
Sandwich (1928) L12, U12
Sanfoin (1918) T6N
Sangarius (1915) 4.160
Sanguine (1945) P266, S66
Sanson (1907) FY901, Y7.31
Sansovino (1943) F162
Santa (1936) FY1986
Santa Isabel (1914) Y3.2075
Santa Theresa (1911) Y3.1874
Santaren (1912) Y3.1298
Santon (1955) M1178
Saon (1933) FY159
Sapper (1942) T336
Sapphire (1904) N72, N78, N89
Sapphire (1935) T27
Sappho (1891) P41, PA1
Sarabande (1940) T125
Saracen (1908) D07, D74, H38
Saracen (1942) P247
Sarah Hyde (1921) FY968
Sarah Radcliffe (1896) Y3.998
Saragossa (1916) Y3.1472
Saranac ᴜꜱɴ (1899) R(I)06
Sarawak (1943) K591
Sarba (1913) Z139
Sardonyx (1919) D95, F34, F53, H26
Sargasso (1908) Y3.927
Sargasso (1926) FY.053
Sargon (1913) FY572
Sarka (1930) FY1738
Sarna (1930) FY1753
Sarnia (1910) M04, M(I)04, M(I)21
Sarnia ʀᴄɴ (1942) J309
Saronta (1917) FY1849
Sarpedon (1894) Y3.2033
Sarpedon (1916) 4.05
Sarpedon (1916) F15, G14, G19, G21, G82, H69
Sasebo (1928) FY828
Saskatchewan ʀᴄɴ (1940) H70
Saskatoon ʀᴄɴ (1940) K158
Satellite (1943) M305
Satrap (1913) Y3.56
Satsa (1936) FY1734
Saturn (1916) FY823, Y7.37
Satyavati ʀɪɴ (1911) FY.073
Satyr (1916) F51, F59, G52, H78
Satyr (1942) P214, S84
Saucy (1942) A386, W131
Sault Sainte Marie ʀᴄɴ (1942) F34, J334

Saumarez (1916) H08, F00, G25, G45, G3A
Saumarez (1942) D12, G12
Saurian (1916) FY1726
Sauternes ꜰʀ (1922) U55
Savage (1910) D92, F97, HA9
Savage (1942) D27, G20, I16
Savoia ɪᴛ (1935) D04
Savorgnan de Brassa ꜰʀ (1937) K135
Sawfly (1928) FY629
Saxifrage (1918) T97
Saxifrage (1941) K04
Saxilby (1914) Y3.1269
Saxlingham (1955) M2727
Saxol (1899) Y7.170
Saxoleine (1899) Y7.297
Saxon (1881) Y3.285
Saxon (1895) Y4.73
Saxon Briton (1914) Y3.517
Saxon Monarch (1912) Y3.1466
Sayonara (1911) 4.72
Scalby Wyke (1935) FY258
Scaldie (1903) Y3.1195
Scalpay (1942) A343, DV15, T237
Scandinavia (1905) Y4.11
Scarab (1915) P59, P98, PA2, T59
Scarab (1971) A272
Scaravay (1944) J425
Scarba ʀɴᴢɴ (1941) P175, T175
Scarborough (1930) L25, N25, U25
Scarborough (1955) F63
Scarborough Castle (1944) K536
Scarlet Tower (ex *Nigretia*) (1910) Y3.13
Scarron (1913) FY1913
Scartho (1898) Y3.1980
Scatwell (ex *Maisie*) (1911) Y3.932
Scawby (1911) Y3.345
Scawfell (1937) J103, 4.22
Sceptre (1917) F17, F60, F79, H34, H79
Sceptre (1976) S104, S110
Sceptre (1943) P215
Schelde (1926) W156
Schieland (1909) Y3.2219
Scimitar (1918) F46, G41, H21
Scimitar (1969) P271
Scimitar (1993) P284
Scomber (1914) Z183
Scorcher (1944) P258, S43, S58
Scorpion (1910) D90, H30, HC3
Scorpion (1937) T67
Scorpion (1942) G72
Scorpion (1946) D64, G64
Scotia (1902) N33, N90

Scotol (1916) A161, X49, X61
Scotsman (1918) F56, G30, H52, H7A
Scotsman (1944) P243, S44, S143
Scott (1913) N91, N2A
Scott (1917) F98
Scott (1938) A308, J79, N79
Scott (1996) A131, H131
Scottier (ex *Kingsgate*) (1909) Y3.462
Scottish (1937) FY245
Scottish Monarch (1906) Y3.2330
Scottish Prince (1910) Y3.2188
Scourge (1908) FY1627
Scourge (1910) D96, F98, H8A
Scourge (1942) G01
Scout (1918) F55, G35, H51, H6A
Sculptor (1911) Y3.1451
Sculptor (ex *St Andrew*) (1912) Y3.451
Scylla (1940) 98, C98
Scylla (1968) F71
Scythe (1918) F47, G32, H22
Scythian (1944) P237, S34, S137
Sea Belle (1928) F60
Sea Centurion (1997) A98
Sea Chieftain (1998) A97
Sea Cliff RCN (1944) K344
Sea Crusader (1996) A96
Sea Devil (1945) P244, S44
Sea Giant (1920) W193
Sea Giant (1954) A288
Sea Holly (1918) FY969
Sea Mist (1917) FY1640
Sea Monarch (1915) Z115
Sea Nymph (1942) P223, S40
Sea Robin (Canc) P267
Sea Rover (1943) P218
Sea Salvor (1943) A503
Sea Scout (1944) P253, S11, S153
Sea Serpent (1898) Y8.29
Seabear (1918) F48, G29, H23
Seabear (1943) B802, J333, M333
Seabreeze (1918) FY50, Z61
Seadog (1942) P216, S10
Seafire (1918) F42, G68, H19
Seaflower (1882) 4.75
Seafox (1946) A214, F114
Seagull (1889) C81, C82, C85
Seagull (1899) Y3.2130
Seagull (1937) A309, J85, N85
Seaham (1941) J123
Seahorse (1880) W72
Seahorse (1932) 98S, 98N, N98
Seal (1897) D75, D77, D90

Seal (1938) 37M, 37N, N37
Sealion (1934) 72S, 72N, N72
Sealion (1959) S07
Sealyham (1936) FY107
Sealyham (1967) A197
Seamew (1928) T43
Seapool (1913) Y3.1626
Searcher (1919) F43, G72, H20
Searcher (1942) D40
Searcher (1944) L122, L3508
Seatonia (1898) Y3.1083
Seawolf (1918) D96, G47, H07
Seawolf (1935) 47S, 47N, N47
Sebastian (1914) Y7.60
Sebek (1909) Y3.911
Seddon (1916) FY1993, 4.166
Sedgefly (1939) FY122
Sedgepool (1918) Y3.2037
Sefton (1918) NA1, T2N
Sefton (1943) F123
Sefton (1954) M1179
Segontian (1901) Y3.1416
Seica RIN (....) T310
Seistan (1907) Y3.1666
Seksern SAN (1930) T52, T452
Selene (1944) P254, S12, S154
Selkirk (1918) J18, N18, T1/, T/2
Sellasia (1901) Y3.1377
Selsey Bill (1945) B352, F54
Semantha (1899) Y3.912
Semla (1924) 4.38
Semnos (1934) FY726
Senateur Duhamel (1927) FY327
Senator (1918) D02, D44, F35, G36
Seneschal (1945) P255, S75
Sennen (1928) Y21
Sentinel (1904) N73, N92
Sentinel (ren *Scorpion*) (1942) I43
Sentinel (1945) P256, S56
Sentinel (1975) P246
Sepoy (1918) D03, F49, G26
Sepoy (1943) J343
Seraph (1918) D04, F25, G60
Seraph (1941) P219, S89
Serapis (1918) D58, F21, F53, H2A
Serapis (1943) G94
Serbistan (1896) Y3.214
Serbol (1917) A162, B521, X62
Serene (1918) D97, F51, F7A, H25
Serene (1943) J354, M354
Servitor (1914) N89, X08, X63
Servitor (1918) FY1673

Sesame (1918) D98, F63, F5A, H35
Sesame (1943) W144
Sethon (1916) FY883
Setter (1916) F55, G98
Setter (1967) A189
Setter (1936) FY339
Settsu (1924) Z140
Seven Sisters (....) B529
Severn (1913) D70, M2A
Severn (1934) 57F, 57N, N57
Severn (2002) P282
Sevra (1929) FY1652
Seychelles (1943) K592
Seymour (1916) D09, F19, G00, G20, G70, H15
Seymour (1943) K563
SGB1 (Canc) S301
SGB2 (Canc) S302
SGB3 (1941) S303
SGB4 (1941) S304
SGB5 (1941) S305
SGB6 (1941) S306
SGB7 (1941) S307
SGB8 (1941) S308
SGB9 (1942) S309
Shackleton (1913) N93, N0A
Shackleton (1936) A310
Shadwell (1904) Y3.773
Shah (1943) D21, R312
Shakespear (1912) Y3.454
Shakespeare (1917) D50, F89
Shakespeare (1941) P221, S13
Shako (1913) FY1657
Shalford (1952) P3101
Shalimar (1943) P242
Shamrock (1900) FY768
Shamrock (1918) F50, H06, D94
Shamsher RIN/ RPN (1943) F392, K392
Shandwick (1912) FY1587
Shannon (1906) 74, 92, 8A, N25
Shapinsay (1941) T176
Shark (1912) D05, F36, FA1, H04
Shark (1934) 54S, 54N, N54
Shark (1943) G03
Sharpshooter (1917) F48, F61, G59, H91
Sharpshooter (1936) J68, N68
Shavington (1955) M1180
Shaw USN (1916) H(I)26, H(I)38
Shawinigan RCN (1941) K136
Shawmut USN (1908) R(I)08
Sheaf Arrow (1912) Y3.144
Sheaf Brook (ex *Coniston*) (1901) Y3.711
Sheaf Don (1917) Y3.1481

Sheaf Field (1906) Y3.225
Sheaf Lance (ex *War Haven*) (1918) Y3.2430
Shearwater (1939) K02, L39, M39, P39
Shediac RCN (1941) K110
Sheelah (1902) YA.11
Sheen (1918) FY51, Z64
Sheepdog (1969) A250
Sheffield (1936) 24, C24
Sheffield (1971) D80
Sheffield (1986) F96
Sheldon (1912) Y7.38, 4.143
Sheldrake (1911) F8A, H23, H88, H0A
Sheldrake (1937) K06, L06, M06, P26
Shemara (1938) FY.026
Shepherd Lad (1925) FY698
Shepparton RAN (1942) J248, M248
Shepperton (1935) M83
Sheppey (1942) T292
Shera (1929) FY1724
Sheraton (1907) FY1788
Sheraton (1955) M1181
Sherborne (1918) T36, T96
Sherborne Castle (1944) K453
Sherbrooke RCN (1940) K152
Sherwood (1904) Y3.678
Sherwood (1919) I80
Shetland (1976) P298
Shiant (1941) T170
Shiel (1943) K305
Shielburn (1911) 4.439
Shika (1929) FY1664
Shikari (1919) D85, I85
Shila (1926) FY1694
Shillay (1944) B731, J426, M426
Shillong RIN (1941) T250
Shincliffe (1918) T81
Shipham (1955) M2726
Shippigan RCN (1941) J212
Shirley (1916) T57
Shoalhaven RAN (1944) F535, K535
Sholapore RIN (Canc) T259
Shooting Star (1925) FY700
Shoreham (1930) L32, U32
Shoreham (2001) M112
Shoulton (1954) M1182
Shova (1912) FY1696
Shower (1918) FY52, Z81
Shrewsbury (1918) T48, T81
Shrewsbury Castle (1944) K374
Shrimp (ex *X52*) (1954) X52
Shrivenham (1956) M2728
Shropshire (1928) 73, C73, C34

Shuna (1915) Y3.1700

Shusa (1929) FY1702

Sialkot ʀɪɴ (Canc) T321

Siberian Prince (1915) Y3.1690

Sibir (1903) Y3.1968, Y8.135

Sibyl (1942) P217

Sicilia (1901) Y3.1262

Sicily (1914) Y3.1360

Sickle (1942) P224

Sicyon (1930) FY669

Sidlesham (1955) M2729

Sidmouth (1941) J47, N47

Sidney Smith sᴀɴ (1929) T39

Sidon (1944) P259, S39, S59

Siesta (1924) FY1692

Sigfra (1937) FY324

Sigismund (1897) N94

Signa (1926) FY1709

Signet (1939) P10, Z10

Sigourney usɴ (1917) H(I)58

Sigrid (1896) Y3.1219

Sikh (1903) Y3.2032

Sikh (1918) D06, D68, F34, H94

Sikh (1937) F82, G82, L82

Silanion (1930) Z116

Silene (1918) T67

Silhouette (1926) FY1854

Silja (1929) FY301

Silsden (1897) Y3.1376

Silva (1924) FY1742

Silver City (1901) Y3.1872

Silver Crest (1928) FY733

Silver Dawn (1925) FY1629

Silver Seas (1931) FY946

Silver Sky (1919) FY1989

Silver Spray (1907) FY970

Silverash (1904) Y3.416

Silverfield (1915) Y3.826, Y4.43

Silverlip (1913) Y7.75

Silverol (1907) X64

Silverton (1891) Y3.970

Silverton (1940) F55, L115

Silvia (1904) Y3.321

Silvio (1918) T05

Silvio (1943) F160

Simbra (1937) FY321

Simmerson (1913) 4.278

Simoom (1916) F57, G44, H8A

Simoom (1918) H53

Simoom (1942) P225

Simpson (1917) FY545

Sind ʀᴘɴ (1940) F52

Sind ʀɪɴ (1943) K274

Sind ʀɪɴ (Canc) J320

Sindonis (1934) FY120

Sineus (1892) Y3.1979

Singleton (1955) M1183

Singleton Abbey (1915) Y3.723

Sioux ʀᴄɴ (1943) D81, D164, R64

Sir Agravaine (1942) T230

Sir Bedivere (1966) L3004

Sir Bevis (1918) T93

Sir Caradoc (1972) L3522

Sir Francis (1910) Y3.208

Sir Galahad (1941) T226

Sir Galahad (1966) L3005

Sir Galahad (1986) L3005

Sir Gareth (1942) T227

Sir Geraint (1942) T240

Sir Geraint (1967) L3027

Sir Hugo (1918) T3N

Sir John Lister (1919) FY622

Sir John Moore (1915) M11, M3A

Sir Kay (1942) T241

Sir Lamorak (1942) T242

Sir Lamorak (1972) L3532

Sir Lancelot (1941) T228

Sir Lancelot (1963) L3029

Sir Percivale (1967) L3036

Sir Thomas Picton (1915) M06, M4A

Sir Tristram (1942) T229

Sir Tristram (1966) L3505

Sir Visto (1918) T/3

Sir Walter Raleigh (1908) D65

Sirdar (1918) D59, F51, G27, H1A

Sirdar (1943) P226, S21, S76

Sirius (1890) N20, N94

Sirius (1900) Y3.1538

Sirius (1940) 82, C82

Sirius (1964) F40

Sirra (1929) FY1700

Sita ʀɪɴ (1928) FY703

Sizergh Castle (1903) Y3.1797

Skaraas (1882) Y3.1947

Skate (1917) D16, F46, F62, G05, G42, H39

Skeena ʀᴄɴ (1930) D59, H43, I59

Skegness (ex *Polurrian*) (1900) Y3.1742

Skeldon (1903) Y3.1676

Skelwith Force (1908) Y4.56

Skerries (1906) Y3.702

Skiddaw (1896) J80, 4.301

Skilful (1917) F62, F78, G51, H41

Skinningrove (1895) Y3.2101

Skipjack (1889) P81, PA3

Skipjack (1934) J38, N38
Skipjack (1943) J300, M17
Skipper (1904) Y2.7, Y8.34
Skipton Castle (1907) Y3.1356
Skirmisher (1904) D55, N95, P55
Skokholm (1943) T376
Skomer (1943) A344, DV16, T381
Skua (ex *Walrus*) (1945) A217
Skudd IV (1929) FY1792
Skudd V (1929) FY1806
Skudd VI (1930) FY1676
Skye (1942) M163, T163
Skyrocket (1908) FY1627
Slav (1913) Y3.213
Slavol (1917) X65
Slavonic (1905) Y3.841
Slazak ORP (1941) L26
Slebech (1908) Y7.28
Sleet (1930) FY1676
Sleipner RNoN (1936) H48
Slemish (1909) Y3.147
Slesvig (1938) B565
Sleuth (1944) P261, S35, S61
Sligo (1918) T71, T98
Slinger (1917) X50, X66
Slinger (1942) A452, D26, R313
Slinger (1944) L123, L3510
Sluga (1929) FY1773
Sluna (1941) T177
Sluys (1945) D60, R60
Smalvlei SAN (1929) T15, T515
Smerdis (1917) Y3.2076
Smilax (1942) K280
Smiter (1943) D55, R321
Smiter (1944) L124
Smiter (1987) P272
Smith USN (1909) H(I)53
Smiths Falls RCN (1944) K345
SML 323 (1941) A323
SML 324 (1941) A234
SML 325 (1942) A325
SML 326 (1943) A326
SML 327 (1944) A327
SML322 (1941) A322
Snaefell (1907) J118
Snaefell (1910) M06, M(I)06, M(I)22
Snakefly (1930) FY575
Snap (....) FY1589
Snapdragon (1915) T71, T79
Snapdragon (1940) K10, K73, M10
Snapper (1934) 39S, 39N, N39
Sneaton (1915) Y3.858

Snider (1945) A375
Snipe (1897) NN5
Snipe (1945) F20, U20
Snowberry RCN (1940) K166
Snowdon (1896) Y3.1311
Snowden Smith (1944) L3028
Snowdonian (1907) Y3.1602
Snowdrift (1931) FY1842
Snowdrop (1915) T40, T80
Snowdrop (1941) K67, M67
Snowflake (1941) K211
Soberton (1956) M1200
Sobkra (1937) FY331
Soemba RNLN (1925) T199
Soetvlei SAN (1929) T22, T462
Soika (1925) FY1755
Sokol ORP (1940) N97
Solebay (1944) D70, R70
Solent (1910) Y3.155
Solent (1944) P262, S36, S62
Solfels (1913) Y8.134
Solitaire (1904) FY1674
Solo (1899) Y3.1867
Solon (1931) FY601
Solstice (1918) FY937
Solvra (1937) FY334
Solway Firth (1944) B328, F190
Somali (1910) YA.16
Somali (1937) F33, G33
Somaliland (1943) K594
Somerleyton (1955) M1139
Somersby (1913) Y3.465
Somerset (1994) F82
Somme (1918) D07, F44, G52
Somme (Canc) I31
Sommiena (ex *Tanagra*) (1899) Y3.1280
Sona (1922) FY.027
Sonavati RIN (1936) 4.206
Sondra (1937) FY345
Sonia (1916) W41
Sonneblom SAN (1936) T44, T444
Sonnet (1939) P47, Z47
Sonoma USN (1912) T0A
Soranus (1906) FY513
Sorata (1897) Y3.1518
Sorceress (1916) D92, G68, G93, G94, H66
Soroka (1906) Y3.1608
Sorrel RCN (1940) K153
Sorrento (1899) Y1.1
Sorrento (1912) Y3.1697
Sorsra (1937) FY342
Soudan (1901) YA.1

Southampton (1912) 35, 89, 9A
Southampton (1936) 83, C83
Southampton (1979) D90
Southcoates (1918) 4.140
Southdown (1917) T08
Southdown (1940) F25, L25
Southern Barrier ꜱᴀɴ (1936) T28, T468
Southern Breeze (1936) FY318
Southern Chief (1926) FY304
Southern Field (1929) FY1790
Southern Floe ꜱᴀɴ (1936) T26, T466
Southern Flower (1928) FY332
Southern Foam (1926) FY1796
Southern Gem (1937) K247
Southern Isles ꜱᴀɴ (1936) T29, T469
Southern Maid (1936) T27, T467
Southern Pride (1936) K249
Southern Prince (1929) B403, M47
Southern Sea ꜱᴀɴ (1936) T30, T470
Southern Shore (1928) FY326
Southern Spray (1925) FY323
Southern Star (1930) FY329
Southern Wave (1925) FY325
South Pacific (1913) Y3.942
Southgate (1899) Y3.729
Southgate (1917) Z25
Southina (1899) Y3.1308
Southland ʀɴᴢɴ (1961) F104
Southport (1900) Y3.1773
Southsea (1930) J113
Southville (1904) Y3.771
Southwaite (1904) Y3.2059
Southwold (1941) L10
Southwood (1880) Y3.2196
Sovereign (1973) S108
Soyo Maru (1906) Y7.73
Spa (1941) A192, X92
Spabeck (1943) A227, X19
Spabrook (1944) A224, X127
Spaburn (1946) A257, X122
Spalake (1946) A260, X123
Spaniard (1937) FY144
Spaniel (1936) FY348
Spaniel (1967) A201
Spanker (1889) C82, C83, C86
Spanker (1943) J226, M226
Spanker (1917) Y3.3
Spapool (1946) A222, X124
Sparham (1954) M2731
Spark (1943) P236, S22
Sparkler (1940) A504
Sparrow (1946) F71, U71

Sparrowhawk (1912) H61
Sparrowhawk (1918) D08, F29, F52, G53
Spartan (1942) 95, C95
Spartan (1978) S105, S111
Spate (1929) FY1792
Speaker (1943) D90, R314
Spear (1918) D09, F23, G55
Spear (Canc) G30
Spearfish (1936) 69S, 69N, N69
Spearhead (1944) P263, S42
Spearmint (1918) TN7
Speedwell (1889) P89, PA4
Speedwell (1935) J87, N87
Speedy (1918) D10, F27, G36
Speedy (1938) J17, N17
Speedy (1979) P296
Spen (1908) Y3.135
Spenser (1917) D40, F90, F0A
Spermina (1899) Y3.1137
Spetsai ʀʜɴ (1932) H38
Spey (1941) F246, K246
Spey (1985) M2013
Spey (2019) P234
Sphene (1934) FY249
Sphinx (1939) J69, N69
Spikenard ʀᴄɴ (1940) K198
Spilsby (1910) Y3.480
Spina (1926) FY1717
Spindrift (1918) G2, H57, HA7
Spindrift (1936) FY1644
Spinel (1893) Y3.257, Y4.55
Spinet (1924) Z26
Spiraea (1917) T81
Spiraea (1940) K08
Spirit (1943) P245, S23, S45
Spital (ex Daldorch) (1907) Y3.104
Spiteful (1899) D76, D91, P73
Spiteful (1943) P227, S07, S24
Spitfire (1912) H41, H85, H1A
Spitfire III (1938) 4.79
Spithead (1899) Y3.1467
Splendid (1918) D11, F24, F45, G57
Splendid (1942) P228
Splendid (1979) S106, S112
Spondilus (ex Berwindmoor) (1910) Y3.1036
Sportive (1918) D12, F21, G48
Sportsman (1914) Y8.79
Sportsman (1942) P229, S129
Sposa (1926) FY309
Spragge (1943) B653, K572
Sprat (1955) X53
Sprayville (1920) Z258

Sprig o'Heather (1914) 4.40
Sprightly (1900) D62, D77, D92
Sprightly RAN (1942) A203, A776, W103
Sprightly (Canc) P268
Springbank (1926) F50
Springbok (1917) F63, F65, G49, H40
Springdale (1937) B426, FY1923
Springer (1945) P264, S64
Springhill RCN (1943) B642, K323
Springs SAN (1930) T38, T478
Springtide (1937) 4.94
Sprite (1915) W53
Spruce Lake (1945) J494
Sprucol (1917) X67
Spur (1944) P265
Spurn Point (1945) F42
Spurs (1933) FY168
Squall (1935) J51
Squirrel (1904) C81, C83, C85
Squirrel (1944) J301
Squirrel (1954) M2008
Squirrel (1957) M2686
Staffa (1942) T159
Stafford (1918) T42, T7/
Stafnes (1936) FY192
Stag (1899) D43, D78, P34
Stag Pool (1930) B392
Stagpool (1905) Y3.749
Stalberg (1929) Z108
Stalker (1942) D91
Stalker (1944) L126, L3515
Stalwart (1918) D11, F4A
Stalwart RAN (1918) H4A, H14, H56
Stalwart (1939) W07
Stamfordham (1908) Y3.513, Y4.4
Standerton SAN (1936) T60, T460
Standish Hall (1912) Y3.528
Stanley (1919) I73
Stanley Hall (1894) Y3.2268
Star (1896) D68, D79, H07, P07
Star of Britain (1908) FY1678, Y7.39
Star of Freedom (1917) T42
Star of India (1888) FY.036
Star of Orkney (1936) FY683
Star of Pentland (1915) FY1668
Star of the Realm (1917) Z105
Star of the Wave (1917) FY1590
Starfish (1916) F60, F64, G50, H70
Starfish (1933) 19S, 19N, N19
Starlight Rays (1918) FY1630
Starling (1942) B295, F66, U66
Starling (1983) P241

Start Bay (1945) B612, F604, K604
Starwort (1941) K20
Statesman (1895) Y9.13
Statesman (1943) P246, S46
Statice (1943) K281
Staunch (ex *Bengal*) (1905) FY1591
Staunch (1910) H89, H2A
Staveley (1891) Y8.25
Stawell RAN/RNZN (1943) J348, M348
Stayner (1943) K573
Ste. Thérèse RCN (1943) K366
Steadfast (1906) N6A, X17, X68
Steadfast (1918) F24, F78, F99, H37
Steadfast (1943) J375
Steady (1916) X39, X69
Steady (1944) N17
Stedham (1955) M2730
Steelville (1915) Y3.1089
Steenberg SAN (1929) T36, T476
Steepholm (1943) DV17, P55, T356
Steersman (1909) Y2.2, Y8.48
Stefa (1929) FY1887
Stella Canopus (1936) FY248
Stella Capella (1937) FY107
Stella Carina (1936) FY352
Stella Dorado (1935) FY131
Stella Leonis (1928) FY706
Stella Pegasi (1935) FY155
Stella Polaris (1936) A417, 4.258
Stella Rigel (1926) FY657
Stellarton RCN (1944) K457
Stellenberg SAN (1929) T37, T477
Stellina (ex *Dawlish*) (1898) Y3.588
Step Dance (1918) T1N
Stephen (1910) Y8.82
Stephen Furness (1910) Y9.23
Stephen Furness (1910) M(I)23, M(I)27
Sterett USN (1910) H(I)12, H(I)39
Sterett USN (1938) Y34
Sterlet (1937) 22S, 22N, N22
Sterling (1918) D88, F56, FA3, H31
Sternus (1925) FY1706
Stettler RCN (1943) K681
Stevens USN (1918) H(I)62
Stevenstone (1942) B230, F16, L16
Stewart USN (1902) H(I)48
Stina (1928) FY303
Stobo Castle (1917) W73
Stockham (1943) K562
Stockton USN (1917) H(I)40
Stoic (1919) W79
Stoic (1943) P231

Stoke (1918) J33, N33, TN3, TN6
Stoke City (1935) FY232
Stokesley (1883) Y3.2057
Stone Town RCN (1944) K531
Stonechat RCN (1944) M25, N25
Stonecrop (1941) K142
Stonefly (1930) FY596
Stonehenge (1919) D93, F58, G99
Stonehenge (1943) P232
Stora (1929) FY307
Stord RNoN (1943) G26
Stork (1904) Y1.9
Stork (1916) F65, F66, G60, H90
Stork (1936) B297, F81, L81, U81
Storm (1943) P233, S25
Stormbird (1885) W74
Stormcentre (1919) FY1807
Stormcloud (1919) D89, H05
Stormcloud (1943) J367, M367
Stormcock (1884) W75
Stormking (1942) W87
Stormont RCN (1943) B645, K327
Stormwrack (1925) FY1572
Stornoway (1941) J31, N31
Stour (1905) D30, D79, D80, H83, N08
Stour (1917) FY1592
Strahan RAN (1943) J363, M363
Stratagem (1943) P234
Stratford RCN (1942) J310
Strathadam RCN (1944) B616, K682
Strathalladale (1908) 4.458
Strathbeg (1909) Y3.788
Strathcoe (1916) FY1594, Y7.22
Strathdee (1907) Y3.524
Strathderry (1911) FY1810
Strathdevon (1915) FY1813
Strathearn (1906) Y3.974
Strathella (1913) 4.199
Strathelliot (1915) 4.379
Strathesk (1909) Y3.1225
Strathfillan (1906) Y3.2397
Strathfinella (1910) 4.459
Strathgarry (1924) FY1632
Strathmaree (1914) FY1638
Strathmartin (1914) 4.437
Strathrannock (1919) FY1648
Strathroy RCN (1944) K455
Strathspey (1906) Z161
Strathugie (1914) FY1941
Stratton (1957) M1210
Strenuous (1905) D86
Strenuous (1911) FY1782

Strenuous (1918) G64, H03
Strenuous (1942) J338
Strephon (1913) FY1829
Strethendrick (1907) Y3.680
Strijdt voor Christus BG (1938) 4.269
Striker (1942) A460, D12, R315
Striker (1945) L128, L3516
Striker (1983) P285
Strive (1912) FY922
Stroma (1941) T150
Strombus (1899) Y7.4
Stromness (ex *Poldhu*) (1902) Y3.269
Stromness (1966) A344
Strongbow (1916) G44
Strongbow (1943) P235
Stronghold (1919) FA8, H50
Stronsay (1942) T178
Strule (1943) K258
Strymon RHN (1917) FY732
Stuart (1918) D200, G35, G46
Stuart Prince (1940) D17
Stuart RAN (1918) D4, D00, F20, I00
Stubbington (1956) M1204
Stubborn (1942) P238, S41
Student (1910) Y3.1692
Sturdy (1919) D87, F55, F96, H28
Sturdy (1943) P248, S26, S48
Sturgeon (1917) F47, F49, G17, G56, H2A
Sturgeon (1932) 73S, 73N, N73
Sturton (1912) Y3.1176
Sturton (1920) FY1595
Stygian (1943) P249, S27
Styx (Canc) J440
Subtle (1944) P251, S51
Success (1901) D24
Success (1918) D08, F1A
Success RAN (1918) H5A, H02
Success (1943) G26
Succour (1943) A505
Sudbury RCN (1941) K162
Suderoy I SAN (1925) T55
Suderoy V RCN (1930) Z05
Suderoy VI RCN (1929) Z06
Suffolk (1903) 20, P87, PA5
Suffolk (1926) 55, C55, C181
Suffolk Coast (1917) Y3.1765
Sui Sang (1895) Y3.1820
Sukha (1929) FY1767
Sulham (1955) M2732
Sulituan RAN (1912) FY39
Sulla (1928) FY1874
Sullington (1954) M1184

Sultan (1944) L3031
Sultan Venturer (1964) A103
Sultan Venturer (1970) A254
Sultanhisar ᴛᴋ (1940) H87
Suma (1927) FY618
Sumatra (1908) Y3.2295
Sumatra ʀɴʟɴ (1920) 40
Sumba (1929) FY297
Summerside ʀᴄɴ (1941) K141
Sun II (1909) W76
Sun VII (1918) W60
Sunbeam II (1916) FY913
Sunburst (1909) FY1927
Sundew (1941) K57
Sunfish (1895) D47, D8, D2A
Sunfish (1936) 81S, 81N, N81
Sunflower (1915) M97, T30, T82
Sunflower (1940) K41, K524, M41
Sunik (1915) Y4.16, Y7.57
Sunlight (1918) FY763
Sunningdale (1896) Y3.50
Sunniside (1905) Y3.645
Sunnyside Girl (1919) FY300
Sunray (1892) Y3.1875
Sunrise (1919) Z203
Sunset (1918) FY54
Sunspot (1904) FY1876
Superb (1907) 49, A0
Superb (1943) 25, C25, C185
Superb (1974) S109
Superman (1933) W89
Supporter (1914) FY1997
Supporter (1977) A158
Supreme (1944) P252, S14
Suram (1893) Y7.92
Surcouf ꜰʀ (1929) P17
Sureaxe (1907) FY1834
Surf (1896) Y3.2087
Surf (1942) P239
Surf Patrol (1951) A357
Surf Pilot (1938) A331
Surf Pioneer (1951) A365
Surface (Canc) P269
Surge (Canc) P271
Surge (1929) FY1806
Surly (1894) D82, D3A, P30
Surprise (1916) F66, F69, GA4
Surprise (1945) F436, K436
Sursay (1944) J427, M427
Susetta (1904) Y4.37
Susquehanna (1896) Y2.220, Y3.1564, Y8.93
Sussex (1928) 96, C96, C174

Sussexvale ʀᴄɴ (1944) B617, K683
Sutherland (1901) Y3.2436
Sutherland (1918) Y3.714
Sutherland (1996) F81
Suthernes (1915) FY1563, 4.174
Sutlej (1899) N65, N74
Sutlej (1908) Y3.1177
Sutlej ʀɪɴ (1940) F95, U95
Sutton (1918) J78, N78, TC8, T0N
Sutton Hall (1905) Y3.1741
Suvla (1945) L129, L3518
Suwanee (1888) Y7.14
Svana (1930) FY1707
Svega (1929) FY294
Svenner ʀɴᴏɴ (1943) G03
Sviatogor (1915) NA8, NN4
Svolvaer ʀɴᴏɴ (1929) FY359
Swainby (1917) Y3.1808
Swale (1905) D31, D83, N03
Swale (1942) F217, K217
Swallow (1918) D14, F22, F73
Swallow (1984) P242
Swan ʀᴀɴ (1915) HA1
Swan ʀᴀɴ (1936) A427, F74, L74, U74
Swan III (1902) FY1880
Swan River (1915) Y3.853
Swansea ʀᴄɴ (1942) B618, F328, K328
Swansea Castle (1912) FY1817
Swansea Vale (1909) Y3.172
Swanston (1954) M1185
Swartberg sᴀɴ (1936) T09, T509
Swarthy (1912) W12
Swashway (1944) F145
Swazi (1901) Y3.1804
Swedish Prince (1896) Y3.1079
Sweet Promise (1919) FY971
Sweetbriar (1917) T83
Sweetbriar (1941) K209
Sweethope (1905) Y3.1410
Swift (1907) D60, G75, H64, H3A
Swift (1943) G46
Swift (1984) P243
Swift Current ʀᴄɴ (1941) J254
Swift Wing (1912) FY927
Swift Wings (ex *Watermouth*) (1911) Y3.846
Swiftsure (1903) P05
Swiftsure (1943) 08, C182
Swiftsure (1971) S126
Swin (1944) A506
Swindon (1918) N91, N5A
Switha (1942) A346, DV18, T179
Swona (1925) FY1802

Sword (ex *Celt*) (Canc) G85
Sword Dance (1918) T3N
Sword Dance (1940) T132
Swordfish (1916) 30, D15
Swordfish (1931) 61S, 61N, N61
Swordsman (1918) D10, F3A, H8A
Sybille (1917) F16, F67, F77, H48
Sycamore (1930) T37
Sydney ʀᴀɴ (1912) 52, A1
Sydney ʀᴀɴ (1934) D48, I48
Sydoslandet sᴀɴ (1935) T33, T473
Sylhet ʀɪɴ (Canc) T329
Sylph (1916) D93, F54, F68, G69, H0A
Sylvana (1907) 4.90
Sylvia (1897) D23, D69, D84, H03
Sylvia (1944) J382, M382
Syndic (1910) Y3.472
Syren (1900) D85, D93, P72
*Syrian*V1919) FY1732
Syringa (1917) T83, T3A
Syringa (1930) T55
Syrtis (1943) P241

T

T. A. Jolliffe (1901) P8A, PA6
T. G. Hutton (1891) Y3.1060
T. R. Ferrans (1918) FY532
T28 (1942) R88
Tabarka (1913) Y3.336
Tabard (1945) S42, P342
Taciturn (1944) P334, S37, S34
Tacoma (1909) Y7.141
Tactician (1918) D74, G54, H99
Tactician (1942) P314, S74, S14
Tactician (Canc) S118
Tadoussac (1941) J220
Taeping (1937) FY1959
Taff (1943) F367, K367
Tafna (1911) Y3.1470
Tahay (1944) J452, M452
Tahchee (1914) Y7.109
Taipo (1916) FY787
Taitam (1943) J210
Taiyabi (1889) Y3.1483
Taku (1939) 38T, 38N, N38
Talavera (1945) I72
Talbot (1895) D61, P61, PA7
Talbot (1919) F06
Talent (ex P322) (1943) P322
Talent (ex *Tasman*) (1945) P337, S37

Talent (1988) S92, S117
Talent (Canc) P343
Talisman (1915) F44, F69, G08, G91, G4A
Talisman (1940) 78T, 78N, N78
Tally Ho! (1942) P97, P317, S87
Talune (1929) B566
Talwar ʀɪɴ (1958) F140
Talybont (1943) B225, F118, L18
Tamaha (1914) Y7.207
Tamar (2018) P233
Tamarac (1908) Y7.177
Tamarisk (1916) T84
Tamarisk (1925) T97
Tamarisk (1941) K216
Tambar ʀᴀɴ (1912) Z83
Tambar ʀᴀɴ (1939) J141
Tamora (1920) FY643
Tampeon (1938) A263, W57
Tamworth Castle (1944) K393
Tamworth ʀᴀɴ (1942) B250, J181
Tanafjord (1900) Y3.1981
Tanager ᴜsɴ (1918) TA0
Tanatside (1942) L69
Tancred (1902) Y7.55
Tancred (1917) F12, F85, G07, G08, G79, H67
Tancred (1943) W104
Tandil (1900) Y3.614
Tanganyika (1944) J383, M383
Tango (1940) T146
Tanjore ʀɪɴ (1919) T33
Tantallon (1898) Y3.591
Tantalus (1943) P318, S28
Tantivy (1943) P319, S19, S29
Tapir (1944) P335, S35, S45
Taplow (ex *Talevera*) (1905) Y3.1107
Tapton (1903) Y3.581
Tara (1900) N42
Tara (1918) D77, D93, G62, H92
Tarana ꜰʀ (1932) 4.263
Taranaki ʀɴᴢɴ (1959) F148
Taransay (1930) FY.057
Tarantella (1941) T142
Tarantia (1911) Y3.553
Tarantula (1915) P6A, PA8, T62
Tarbatness (1945) F84
Tarbatness (1967) A345
Tarlton (1954) M1186
Tarn (1944) P336
Tarpon (1917) F22, F65, F72, F79, H96
Tarpon (1939) 17T, 17N, N17
Tartan (1912) FY915
Tartar (1907) D08, D86, H29

Tartar (1937) D243, F43, G43, L43
Tartar (1960) F133
Tartarin FR (1931) FY1799
Tartary (1901) Y3.985
Tasajera (1938) F125
Tascalusa (1913) Y7.108
Tasman (1945) P337
Tasmania RAN (1918) D12, G97, H25, H7A
Tasmanian Transport (1913) Y3.1423
Tatarrax (1914) Y7.214
Tattoo RAN (1918) D09, F2A, H26, H6A
Tattoo (1943) J374
Taupo RNZN (1944) F421
Taurus (1917) D82, F39, F70, F71, H30
Taurus (1942) P339, S46
Tavy (1943) F272, K272
Tawhai RNZN (1943) T348
Tay (1942) F232, K232
Teakol (1917) X70
Teakol (1946) A167
Teakwood (1902) Y7.8
Teal (1901) N72
Teal USN (1918) TA2
Teal (1919) Z229
Teazer (1917) D83, F40, F71, F93, H17
Teazer (1943) D23, D45, F23, R23
Tecumseh (1908) Y7.71
Tedworth (1917) J32, N32, T4C
Tees (1911) Y8.14
Tees (1943) F293, K293
Teesbridge (1905) Y3.204
Teesdale (1904) Y3.2156
Teespool (1905) Y3.1252
Teessider (1909) Y8.62
Tehana (1929) FY525, 4.418
Tekoura (1929) FY247
Telemachus (1917) F23, F66, F81, F86, H36
Telemachus (1943) P321, S21, S30
Telemon (1904) Y8.87
Telena (1895) Y7.186
Tellus (1911) Y3.2220
Teme RCN (1943) K458
Temeraire (1907) 48, 92, A2
Temeraire (Canc) 36, I36
Temeraire (ii) FR (1926) U35
Tempest (1917) D81, F38, F72, F76, H71
Tempest (1941) N86
Templar (1942) P316, S86
Tempo (1911) Y3.75
Tempus (1904) Y3.1398
Tenacious (1917) F96, G02, G61, H1A
Tenacious (1943) D45, D46, F44, R45

Tenacity (1940) W18
Tenacity (1969) P276
Tenasserim (1905) Y3.1384
Tenby (1913) FY1733
Tenby (1941) J34, N34
Tenby (1955) F65
Tenedos (1918) D88, FA4, H04
Teredo (1945) P338, S38
Terek (1899) Y7.250
Terka RAN (1925) FY99
Termagant (1915) D36, D63, F47, F73, G24, H79
Termagant (1943) D47, D189, F189, R89
Tern (1927) T64
Teroma (1919) FY527
Terpsichore (1943) D33, D48, F19, R33
Terrapin (1943) P323, S3
Terrible (1895) P70, PA9
Terrible (1944) 93, R93
Terrier (1913) W33
Terror (1915) I03, F03, M5A
Terry USN (1909) H(I)43
Tervani (1911) 4.110
Test (1905) D32, D87, H84, N34
Test (1942) F56, K239
Tetcott (1941) F199, L99
Tetrarch (1917) F74, F87, G54, G55, H59
Tetrarch (1939) 77T, 77N, N77
Teutonic (1889) M52, M(I)50, M(I)52, M(I)93
Teviot (1903) D33, D88, N26
Teviot (1942) F222, K222
Teviotbank (1938) M04
Teviotdale (1898) Y3.120
Tewera (1930) FY526
Texada (1942) T283
Texas USN (1912) 0A
Texol (1916) X33
Thakenham (1957) M2733
Thalassa (1924) 4.376
Thalia (1904) FY1602
Thames (1885) N43, N97
Thames (1905) Y3.131
Thames (1932) 71F, 71N, N71
Thames (RNR) M1104, M1117, M1194
Thamesmede (ex *Transport)* (1907) Y3.362
Thames Queen (1898) J12, N09, R380, 4.380
Thane (1943) D83, R316
Thanet (1918) F57, G24, H29, D91
Thankerton (1956) M1172
Thatcham (1957) M2790
Thaw (1919) FY1963
The Countess (1902) Y3.2126
The Pas RCN (1941) K168

The Princess (1902) Y3.2092
The Provost (1908) FY285
The Ramsey (1895) M14, M(I)14
The Roman (1905) Y7.5
The Roman (1909) FY1530
The Sultan (1904) Y3.981
The Tower (1919) FY889
The Viceroy (1905) Y4.32
The Way (1931) Z127
Theban (Canc) P341
Their Merit (1918) FY522
Themistoklis rhn (1942) H50, L51
Thermidor (1901) Y7.139
Thermol (1916) X45, X71
Thermopylae (1913) FY1980
Thermopylae (1945) P355, S55
Theseus (1892) 2A, N14, N98
Theseus (1908) Y3.1746, Y8.65
Theseus (1944) 64, R64
Thespis (1901) Y8.104
Thessalia (1905) Y3.408
Thetford Mines rcn (1943) K459
Thetis (1890) P85, P0C
Thetis (1936) 11T, 11N
Thirlmere (1939) FY206
Thisbe (1917) F75, F82, G80, H72
Thisbe (1943) B803, J302, M302
Thistle (1938) 24T, 24N, N24
Thistleban (1910) Y3.937
Thistledhu (1901) Y3.381
Thomas Altoft (1919) FY552
Thomas Bartlett (1918) FY553
Thomas Conolly (1918) Z141
Thomas Leeds (1919) FY520
Thomsons (1907) FY1541
Thor (1944) P349
Thorlock rcn (1944) K394
Thorn (1900) D57, D70, D89
Thorn (1941) N11
Thornborough (1943) K574
Thornham (1957) M2793
Thornhill (1911) Y3.260
Thornley (1903) Y3.66
Thornol (1935) A261
Thornwick Bay (1936) FY179
Thorodd rnon (1919) FY1905
Thorough (1943) P324, S4, S24
Thorpwood (1912) Y3.331
Thracian (1920) D86, GA4, I86
Thrasher (1895) D79, D90, D94
Thrasher (1940) N37, S15
Threat (Canc) P344

Three Kings (1912) FY918
Thrifty (1916) FY1523
Throsk (1977) A379
Throstle (1912) Y3.263
Thrush (1889) C76, X36, X56, X72
Thruster (1917) F74, F76, G81, H73
Thruster (1942) F131, L131
Thruster (1945) L3520
Thule (1942) P325, S5, S24
Thunder rcn (1941) J156
Thunderbolt (1936) N25
Thunderer (1911) 32, 36, A3
Thunderer (Canc) 49, I49
Thuringia (1933) FY106
Thurland Castle (1914) Y3.1769
Thurso Bay (1945) K640
Thyme (1941) K210
Thyra S (1936) B548
Tiara (1944) P351
Tibenham (1955) M2734
Tiberia (1913) Y3.1495
Tickham (1942) L98
Tide Austral (1954) A99
Tideflow (1954) A97
Tideforce (2017) A139
Tidepool (1962) A76
Tiderace (1954) A97
Tiderange (1954) A98
Tiderace (2015) A137
Tidereach (1954) A96
Tidespring (1962) A75
Tidespring (2015) A136
Tidesurge (1954) A98
Tidesurge (2016) A138
Tiercel (1913) 4.83
Tiflis (1900) Y7.117
Tiger (1915) 42, 91, A4
Tiger (1945) 20, C20
Tiger (Canc) 50
Tigress (1911) H61, H92, H4A
Tigris (1939) 63T, 63N, N63
Tijgerhaai rnln (1944) P336
Tilbury (1918) F29, F79, FA0, G37, H38
Tilbury (1942) J228
Tilford (1956) P3123
Tillsonburg rcn (1944) K450, K496
Tilly Duff (1919) FY939
Timmins rcn (1941) K223
Tintagel (1918) D75, G51, H89
Tintagel Castle (1943) F399, K399
Tintern Abbey (1909) Y3.1983
Tintoretto (1902) Y3.1887

Tioga (1911) Y7.244
Tipperary (1915) H6C
Tippu Sultan RPN (1941) F249
Tiptoe (1944) P332, S6, S32
Tir RIN (1942) F256, K256
Tirade (1899) 4.294
Tirade (1917) F07, F81, G80, HA7
Tiree (1941) DV19, P41, T180
Tireless (1943) P327, S77
Tireless (1984) S88, S115
Titan (1935) 4.381
Titania (1915) 7C, AC, A132, F32, I32
Tithonus (1908) M(I)24, M(I)28
Tiverton (1918) Y3.537
Tiverton (1918) TN3, T9N
Tjerk Hiddes RNLN (1941) D8, G16
Tjitaroem (1910) Y3.2460
Tjitjalengka (1938) B399, Y4.9
Tobago (1918) F28, G61, HA8
Tobago (1943) K585
Tobruk RAN (1947) D37
Tocogay (1945) J451, M81
Tocsin (1912) FY593
Toia RNZN (1919) W04
Token (1914) FY1965
Token (1943) P328, S28
Tokyo (ii) (1906) FY788, Y7.40
Tolga RAN (1925) FY00
Tomahawk (1918) D79, F31, G34
Tompazis RHN (1941) K216
Tonawanda (1893) Y7.91
Tonbridge (1918) Y3.397
Tonbridge (1918) TA9
Tongham (1955) M2735
Tongkol RAN (1939) J137
Toorie RAN (1925) FY01
Toowoomba RAN (1941) B251, J157
Topaze (1903) P29, P2A, P1C
Topaze (1935) T40
Torbay (1919) D82, F35, F50, H24
Torbay (1940) 79T, 79N, N79
Torbay (1985) S90, S116
Torch (1918) D15, F37, G33
Torch (1979) A141
Tordonn SAN (1925) T58, T458
Toreador (1918) F6A, H55, HA3
Toreador (1980) A143
Tormentor (1917) F68, G06, G11, G54, H80
Tormentor (1979) A142
Tornado (1917) F78, F97
Tornado (ii) (1917) FY1740
Tornado (1979) A140

Toronto RCN (1943) K538
Torquay (1914) Y3.439
Torquay (1954) F43
Torrens RAN (1915) HA3
Torrent (1916) F67, F79
Torrent (1930) FY.004
Torrent (1971) A127
Torrid (1917) F75, F80, H35, H81
Torrid (1971) A128
Torridge (1912) Y3.308
Torridge (1943) K292
Torrington (1905) Y3.376
Torrington (1943) K577
Tortola (1943) K595
Tosto (1906) Y3.81
Totem (1943) P352, S47, S52
Totland (1931) Y88
Totnes (1916) T53
Touchstone (1907) FY1610
Toulonnaise FR (1934) FY173
Tourmaline (1898) Y3.1703
Tourmaline (1919) D10, D83, H00
Tourmaline (1935) T42
Tourmaline (1942) J339
Tower (1917) F08, F24, F98, H12
Towergate (1906) Y3.276
Towneley (1910) Y3.218
Townsville RAN (1941) J205, M205
Towy (1943) F294, K294
T.R. Thompson (1897) Y3.1035
Tracker (1942) D24, R317
Tracker (1945) L130, L3522
Tracker (1997) P274
Tradewind (1942) P329, S29, S31
Trafalgar (1911) Y3.2042
Trafalgar (1944) D75, D77, R77
Trafalgar (1981) S107, S113
Trafford Hall (1905) Y3.2041
Trail RCN (1940) K174
Trailer (1942) D80
Tralee (1918) T0/, T6/
Tranio (1917) 4.233
Tranquil (1912) FY920
Transcona RCN (1941) J271
Transporter (1911) Y3.17
Transvaal (1916) Y7.45
Transvaal SAN (1944) F602, K602
Transvaalia RNoN (1912) FY305
Transylvania (1925) F65
Travancore RIN (1941) T312
Traveller (1885) W80
Traveller (1941) N48

Trecarne (1915) Y3.1144
Trecarrell (1907) Y3.330
Tredegar Hall (1906) Y3.1067
Treern sᴀɴ (1929) T51, T451
Trefoil (1913) N93, X11, X73
Trefusis (1893) Y3.1181
Tregarth (1912) Y3.8
Tregarthen (1913) Y3.411
Tregothnan (1903) Y3.497
Tregurno (1911) Y3.367
Trehawke (1915) Y3.1447
Treinta-y-Tres (1906) Y3.2410
Trekieve (1898) Y3.1054
Trelawny (1907) Y3.278, Y8.96
Trelissick (1919) Y3.312
Trelyon (1898) Y3.1600
Tremadoc Bay (1945) F605, K605
Tremayne (1886) Y3.392
Tremeadow (1905) Y3.348
Tremorvah (1905) Y3.255
Trenchant (1916) F09, G78, G96, H60
Trenchant (1943) 331, S7, S31
Trenchant (1986) S91
Treneglos (1906) Y3.302, Y3.2028
Trent (1900) Y4.14
Trent (1942) K243
Trent (2018) P224
Trentham Hall (1897) Y3.1306
Trentonian ʀᴄɴ (1943) K368
Tresham (1954) M2736
Tresillian (1899) Y3.425
Trespasser (1942) P312, S12
Trevalgan (1911) Y3.502
Trevanion (1912) Y3.426
Treveal (1909) Y3.369
Trevean (1918) Y3.280
Trevelyan (1894) Y3.11
Trevethoe (1913) Y3.1465
Trevilley (1913) Y3.1634
Trevince (1907) Y3.270
Trevisa (1915) Y3.590
Trevose (1893) Y3.2207
Trevose (1896) Y3.1158
Trevo Terciero (1912) FY1683
Trevaylor (1912) Y3.419
Treverbyn (1910) Y3.914
Trevessa (1909) Y3.1239
Trewellard (1914) Y3.1142
Trewidden (1917) Y3.2376
Trewyn (1920) Y3.1025
Triad (1909) N88
Triad (1939) 53T, 53N, N53

Tribune (1918) D16, F33, F9A
Tribune (1938) 76T, 76N, N76
Trichinopoly ʀɪɴ (Canc) T314
Trident (1902) Y3.2213
Trident (1915) D38, F50, F81, G36, G92
Trident (1938) 52T, 52N, N52, S16
Trieste (1888) Y3.1183
Trillium ʀᴄɴ (1940) K172
Trincomalee (1945) I59
Trincomalee (Canc) I86
Trinculo (1908) Y3.102
Tring (1918) T4N
Tringa (1913) Y9.21
Trinidad (1884) Y3.1864
Trinidad (1918) D17, F54, G38, H4A
Trinidad (1940) 46, C46
Trinidadian (1892) Y7.224
Trinol (1916) X63
Trio (1875) Y3.1387
Trippe usɴ (1910) H(I)04, H(I)40
Trishul (1958) F143
Tristram (1917) F11, F25, F89
Tritelia (1916) 4.201
Triton (1907) N75, N99
Triton (1937) 15T, 15N, N15
Tritonia (1905) Y3.939
Tritonia (1930) FY973
Triumph (1938) 18T, 18N, N18
Triumph (1944) 16, A108, R16
Triumph (1991) S93
Trocas (1893) Y7.106
Trodday (1945) B732, J431, M431
Trois Rivieres ʀᴄɴ (1941) J269
Trojan (1896) Y3.726
Trojan (1898) Z218
Trojan (1918) D76, G66, H44
Trollope (1943) K575
Tromoy ʀɴoɴ (1926) FY702
Tromp ʀɴʟɴ (1937) C39, D28
Tromso (1944) L3006
Trondra (1941) A348, DV20, P49, T181
Trongate (1897) Y3.1405
Trooper (1942) N91
Trophy (1911) FY1987
Trostan (1883) Y2.31, Y3.95, Y8.1
Troubadour (1924) FY1612
Troubridge (1942) D40, D49, F09, R00
Trouncer (1943) D85
Trouncer (1945) L133, L3523
Troup Ahead (1913) FY1536
Troutpool (1903) Y3.1546
Trowbridge (1904) Y3.1152

Truant (1918) G23, H98, HA9
Truant (1939) 68T, 68N, N68
Truculent (1917) F12, F70, F82, H45
Truculent (1942) P315
True Friend (1909) FY1952
True Reward (1913) FY1653
Truelove (1943) J303, M303
Trump (1944) P333, S8, S33
Trumpeter (1942) D09, R318
Trumpeter (1945) L134, L3524
Trumpeter (1988) P294
Truncheon (1944) P353, S53
Trunnion (1938) W29
Truro (1919) T87, T7A
Truro RCN (1942) J268
Trust (1918) FY351
Trusty (1918) FA2, H56, HA5
Trusty (1941) N45
Truxtun USN (1902) H(I)52
Tryphon (1918) F32, F33, G42
Tryphon (1942) A243, W87
Tuberose (1917) T2A
Tucker USN (1915) H(I)36, H(I)41
Tudor (1942) P326, S17, S126
Tughril RPN (1941) F204
Tui RNZN (1941) P33, T234
Tulip (1940) K29, M29
Tumby (1918) FY850
Tumult (1918) D18, F26, G58
Tumult (1942) D50, D121, F121, R11
Tuna (1940) 94T, 94N, N94
Tung Shan (1899) Y3.1576
Tunisian (1930) Z128
Tunsberg Castle (1944) K374
Tunstall (1907) Y3.1130
Turbulent (1916) D92, F55, F62, G42, H34
Turbulent (1941) N98
Turbulent (1982) S87, S114
Turcoman (1937) FY130
Turffontein SAN (1936) T61, T461
Turino (1914) Y3.725
Turkey USN (1918) TA4
Turmoil (1917) N94, X12, X74
Turmoil (1944) W169
Turnbridge (1894) Y3.1914
Turpin (1943) P354, S38, S54
Turquoise (1893) Y4.30
Turquoise (1918) D85, G22, H02
Turquoise (1935) T45
Turritella (1906) Y7.147
Tuscaloosa USN (1933) Y64
Tuscan (1919) D80, FA5, GA1

Tuscan (1942) D51, D156, F156, R56
Tuscarora (1897) FY.044
Tuscarora (1908) Y7.191
Tusculum (ex *Strathdon*) (1907) Y3.731
Tuturi RNZN (1944) F517
Tweed (1907) Y3.197
Tweed (1942) K250
Tweeddale (1911) Y3.232
Tweenways (1920) FY1507
Twickenham (1912) Y3.1645
Twilight (1905) Y3.1199
Two-Step (1941) T142
Tycho (1904) Y3.1265
Tyke (1911) W45
Tyler (1943) K576
Tyne (1878) N76, N0A
Tyne (1900) Y3.1041
Tyne (1940) A194, B382, F24, I24
Tyne (2002) P281
Tynedale (1940) L96
Tynemouth (1909) Y3.79, Y3.1414
Tynwald (1936) D69
Typhoon (1919) FY1703
Typhoon (1958) A95
Tyrant (1917) F14, F90, G07, G49, G4A, H46
Tyrant (1930) 4.197
Tyrian (1919) D84, H01
Tyrian (1942) D52, D67, F67, R67

U

Uganda (1898) Y3.1669
Uganda (1905) Y3.1468
Uganda (1941) 66, C66, C175
Ugie Bank (1913) 4.430
Ugie Brae (1915) FY1966
Uiver RNLN (1902) FY1720
Ujina (1898) Y3.1766
Uki RAN (1923) FY80
Ulex (ex P93) (Canc) P93
Ulidia (1903) Y3.948
Ulleswater (1917) F83
Ullswater (1939) FY252, T252
Ulster (1917) F01, F17, F91, H09
Ulster (1942) D23, D83, F83, R83
Ulster Monarch (1929) 4.69, F69
Ulster Queen (1929) F118
Ultimatum (1941) P34
Ultor (1942) P53
Ulva (1942) T248
Ulysses (1917) F80, G77, G96

Ulysses (1943) D24, D169, F17, R69
Umba (1903) Y3.1455
Umbra (1941) P35
Umbriel (1939) 4.185
Umgeni (1898) Y2.107, Y9.26
Umona (1910) Y3.1385
Umpire (1917) F02, F26, F94, H10
Umpire (1940) N82, P31
Umtali (1896) Y2.106, Y3.1581, Y8.90, Y9.27
Una (1941) P32, N87
Unbeaten (1940) P33, N93
Unbending (1941) P37
Unbridled (Canc) P11
Unbroken (ex P42) 1941) P42
Uncas (1913) Y7.103
Undaunted (1914) 80, A5, 2C
Undaunted (1940) P34, N55
Undaunted (1943) D25, D53, F53, R53
Undine (1917) F03, G79, G97, H61
Undine (1937) 48C, 48N, N48
Undine (1943) D26, D142, F141, R42
Ungava RCN (1940) J149
Unicity (1917) FY956
Unicorn (1941) A195, B312, F72, I72, R108
Unicorn (1992) S43
Union (1940) N56, P35
Unique (1940) N95, P36
Unison (1941) P43
United (1941) P44
United Boys (1913) FY855
Unity (1913) H68, H87, H5A
Unity (1938) 66C, 66N, N66
Universal (1942) P57
Unrivalled (1942) P45
Unruffled (1941) P46
Unruly (1942) P49
Unseen (1942) P51
Unseen (1989) S41
Unshaken (1942) P54
Unsparing (1942) P55
Unst (1942) T213
Unswerving (1943) P63
Untamed (1942) P58
Untiring (1943) P59, S36
Upas (Canc) P92
Upcerne (1906) Y3.707
Upholder (1940) N99, P37
Upholder (1986) S40
Uplifter (1943) A507, W06
Upnor (1899) Y2.3
Uppingham (1919) T49
Upright (1940) P38, N89

Uproar (1940) P31
Upshot (1944) P82
Upstart (1942) P65
Upton (1956) M1187
Upward (Canc) P16
Uralba RAN (1942) FY33
Urania (1943) D27, D105, F08, R05
Urchin (1917) F04, F95, H62
Urchin (1940) N97
Urchin (1943) D28, D199, F196, R99
Ure (1904) D34, D91, N12
Urge (1940) P40, N17
Urpeth (1889) Y3.2179
Ursa (1902) Y3.2169
Ursa (1917) F05, F10, H63
Ursa (1943) D29, D222, F200, R22
Ursula (1917) F01, F06, F84, F88, H11
Ursula (1938) 59C, 59N, N59
Ursula (1991) S42
Urtica (1944) P83
Usher (1901) Y3.1275
Usk (1940) P41, N65
Usk (1943) B277, F295, K295
Uskmoor (1912) Y3.1519
Uskside (1913) Y3.216
Ussa (1911) Y3.1351
Usurper (ex P56) (1942) P56
Ut Prosim (1925) FY1969
Utah USN (1909) 3A
Uther (ex P62) (1943) P62
Utilise (1918) FY1564
Utmost (1940) P42, N19
Utopia (ex P94) (Canc) P94
Utvaer RNoN (1914) FY1924

V

V1 (1914) V1, I2A
V2 (1915) V2, I3A
V3 (1915) V3, I4A
V4 (1915) V4, I5A
Vaagso (1944) L3019
Vaceasay (1945) J432, M432
Vacport (1939) B533
Vagabond (1944) P18
Vagrant (1943) A266, W136
Vaillant FR (1921) U04
Vala (1894) Y3.446
Valdora (1916) FY905
Valegarth (1913) Y2.32, Y3.10ʳ
Valena (1908) FY.028

Valentia (1898) Y3.1008
Valentine (1917) D49, F30, F99, L69
Valentine (1943) R17
Valerian (1916) T67, T85
Valesca (1916) FY814
Valhalla (1917) D44, D68, F9A, G25, G45, G9A
Valiant (1914) 02, 34, 43, A6, B02
Valiant (1963) S102
Valkyrian (....) W192
Valkyrie (1917) D61, D67, F05, F58, F83, F86
Vallay (1944) M434, J434
Valleyfield RCN (1943) K329
Valmont (1916) FY872
Valorous (1917) D30, D82, F53, F92, G00, G20
Valse (1941) T151
Valverda (1918) Y3.2333
Vampire (1917) D70, F0A, G50, G70
Vampire RAN (1917) D68, I68
Vampire (1943) P72
Vampire RAN (1956) D11
Van Dyck BG (1926) FY106
Van Galen RNLN (1941) D7, G84
Van Kingbergen RNLN (1939) A425, U93
Van Meerlandt (1920) M36
Van Oost BG (1926) FY330
Vancouver (1905) Y3.416
Vancouver (1917) D33, F32, G04, H55
Vancouver RCN (1941) K240
Vandal (1942) P64
Vanellus (1912) Y9.19
Vanessa (1918) D29, G18, I29
Vanguard (1909) 39
Vanguard (1944) 23, B23
Vanguard (1992) S28
Vanity (1918) D28, L38, G19, G37
Vanoc (1917) F27, F61, F84, F1A, F8A, H33, H4A
Vanquisher (1917) D54, F08, F21, F62, F84, F85,
    F3A, H0A, I54
Vanquisher II (1899) W83
Vansittart (1919) D64, I64
Varanga (1929) FY1625
Varangian (1943) P61
Varanis (1910) FY1613
Vardo (1913) FY1930
Variance (1944) P85
Varne (1943) P66
Varne II (1944) P81
Vascama (1935) FY185
Vasilissa Olga RHN (1938) H86
Vasna (1917) B400, Y8.4
Vatersay (1943) T378
Vauxhall (1900) Y3.1092

Vectis (1913) Y2.23
Vectis (1917) D51, F06, F94, FA0
Vega (1917) D52, F09, F92, F4A, L41
Vegreville RCN (1941) J257
Vehement (1917) F12, F86, F1A, F5A, H2A
Vehement (Canc) P25
Veldt (1943) P71
Veleta (1941) T130
Velite IT (1941) H59
Vellore (1907) Y3.1471
Velox (1902) D71, P45
Velox (1917) D34, D40, F34, G65, H43, I34
Vendetta (1917) D69, F29, FA3
Vendetta RAN (1917) D6, D69, I69
Vendetta RAN (1954) D08
Venerable (1899) 96, A8, N36
Venerable (1943) 04, R63
Venetia (1897) Y3.555
Venetia (1905) Y4.1
Venetia (1917) D53, F14, F93, F9A, I53
Vengeance (1899) N57, N1A
Vengeance (1944) 71, R71
Vengeance (1998) S31
Vengeful (1944) P86
Venice (1914) Y3.128
Venom (Canc) P27
Venomous (1917) I75, D75, G98
Ventmoor (1900) Y3.593
Ventose FR (1936) FY1754
Venture (1905) FY815
Venture RCN (1925) D16
Venturer (RNR) M1117, M1146
Venturer (1972) M08
Venturer (ex *P68*) (1943) P68
Venturous (1917) D87, F21, F30, F51, F63, F87
Venus (1895) P36, P2C
Venus (1905) Y3.358
Venus (1943) D50, F50, R50
Venusia (ex *War Snake*) (1918) Y3.2331
Verbena (1915) T77, T86
Verbena (1940) K85, M85
Verdun (1914) Y3.1821
Verdun (1917) D71, D93, F16, F52, F91, F2A, L93
Vereeniging SAN (1936) T62
Verity (1919) D63, F36, I63
Vernal (1919) FY1603
Vernon (1916) T18
Vernon (1932) T83
Veronica (1915) M98, T31, T87
Veronica (1940) K37, M37
Versatile (1917) D32, D35, F29, F54, G10, I32
Verulam (1917) D54, F19, F96, FA2

Verulam (1943) D28, F29, R28
Vervain (1941) K190
Verve (Canc) P28
Veryan Bay (1944) B619, F651, K651
Vesper (1917) D55, F28, F39, I55
Vestal (1943) J215
Vestalia (1912) Y3.2456
Vestra (1897) Y3.447
Vesuvius (1932) P83
Vetch (1941) K132
Veteran (1919) D72, I72
Veto (Canc) P88
Veturia (1912) Y3.1848
Viceroy (1917) D27, D72, D91, F38, F99, L21
Vickerstown (ex *Turret Chief*) (1896) Y3.1324
Victor (1898) W64
Victor (1907) Y3.640, Y8.26
Victor (1913) H04, H36, H6A
Victoria (1907) 4.108
Victoria (1912) Y3.607
Victoria & Albert (1899) F14, I14
Victorian (1904) M56, M(I)51, M(I)56, M(I)94
Victorian (1935) FY114
Victoriaville RCN (1944) B620, K684
Victorious (1895) D48, P65, P3C
Victorious (1939) 38, R23, R38
Victorious (1993) S29
Victrix (1937) FY244
Vidal (1951) A200
Vidette (1918) D48, F07, I48
Vidonia (1907) Y7.12, 4.33
Vienna (1894) N2A, P57
Vienna (1929) F138
Vierge de Lourdes FR (1917) FY1710
Vigilant (1900) D43, D72, D92
Vigilant RAN (1938) FY06
Vigilant (1942) D93, F93, R93
Vigilant (1995) S30
Vigilant (1970) P254
Vigo (1905) Y3.1266
Vigo (1946) D231, R31
Vigorous (1943) P74
Vigra (1899) 4.01
Viking (1905) 4.423
Viking (1909) D09, D93, H90
Viking (1943) P69
Viking Bank (1927) FY1781
Viking Deeps (1916) FY252, 4.252
Vikings FR (1935) U78
Viknor (1888) M82
Vikrant RIN (1945) R11
Vilda (1929) Z118

Ville de Quebec RCN (1941) K242
Vimiera (1917) D23, D56, F28, H16, L29
Vimiera (Canc) G22
Vimy (1917) D33, I33
Vindelicia (1913) FY1711, Y7.5
Vindex (1905) N00, N3A
Vindex (1943) D15, R15, R319
Vindictive (1899) 7A, 7C, P75, P4C
Vindictive (1918) 31, 48, D36, I36
Vineleaf (1901) Y7.175
Vineleaf (1917) X70
Vineyard (1944) P84
Viola (1905) FY871
Viola (1916) T88
Violent (1917) D57, F31, F95, FA1
Violet (1897) D09, D73, D94
Violet (1940) K35
Violet Flower (1914) FY1526
Viraat RIN (1953) R22
Virago (1943) F76, D75, R75
Virent (1902) Y3.7
Vireo (1912) FY1531
Virgilia (1918) Y3.2409
Virginia (1930) FY.031
Virginian (1905) M72, M(I)52, M(I)72, M(I)95
Virile (Canc) P89
Virtue (1943) S18, P75
Virulent (1944) P95
Viscol (1916) A275, N09, X75
Viscount (1917) D32, D73, D92, F99, G24, I92
Visenda (1937) FY138
Visigoth (1906) Y3.805
Visigoth (1943) S51, P76
Visitant (Canc) P91
Vistula (1919) Y3.1580
Vitality (1942) P58
Viti RAN (1940) T373
Vitol (1917) X62, X76
Vitruvia (1913) Y4.15, Y7.79
Vittoria (1907) Y3.540
Vittoria (1917) F31, F64, F96, G05
Viva II (1929) FY.030
Vivacious (1917) D36, F32, G01, G71, I36
Viviana (1936) FY238
Vivid (1943) P77
Vivien (1918) D32, D73, G39, L33
Vixen (1900) D44, D74, D95
Vixen (1943) R64
Vizagapatam RIN (Canc) T313
Vizalma (1940) FY286
Volage (1943) D41, F41 ,R41
Volana (1913) Y8.8

Volatile (1899) W61
Volatile (1944) P96
Volga (1888) Y3.2320
Volhynia (1911) Y3.443, Y8.5
Volnay (1910) Y3.1053
Volo (1890) Y5.6
Vologda (1913) Y3.2270
Voltaire (1923) F47
Volturnus (1913) Y8.7
Volunteer (1916) X38, X77
Volunteer (1919) D71, F53, I71
Voracious (1943) S19, P78
Voronezh (1896) Y3.2274
Vortex (1944) P87
Vortigern (1917) D37, F35, G03, G21, I37
Votary (1944) P29
Vox (i) (1943) P67
Vox (ii) (1943) P73, S20
Voyager (1918) D31, G16, G36
Voyager ʀᴀɴ (1918) D31, I31
Voyager ʀᴀɴ (1952) D04
Vulcain (1903) W71
Vulcan (1889) N70, N4A
Vulcan (1933) T51
Vulpine (1943) P79
Vulture (1898) D75, N50

W

W1 (1914) W1, I6A
W2 (1915) W2, I7A
W3 (1915) I8A
W4 (1915) I9A
Wabana (1911) Y3.684
Waddon (1904) Y3.705
Wadsworth ᴜsɴ (1915) H(I)34 ,H(I)44
Wager (1943) D30, D298, R98
Wagga ʀᴀɴ (1942) J315, M183
Waglan (1943) J211
Wahine (1913) D02, N5A, Y4.51
Waiau ʀɴᴢɴ (Canc) T364
Waihemo (1904) Y3.1881
Waiho ʀɴᴢɴ (1944) T403
Waikato ʀɴᴢɴ (1943) T343
Waikato ʀɴᴢɴ (1964) F55
Waima ʀɴᴢɴ (1943) T349
Waimarino (1900) Y3.1941
Wainwright ᴜsɴ (1915) H(I)24, H(I)45
Waipu ʀɴᴢɴ (1943) T357
Waitemata (1908) Y3.2271
Wakakura ʀɴᴢɴ (1917) T00

Wakeful (1917) D65, F37, F59, H88, L91
Wakeful (1943) D31, D159, F159, R59
Wakeful (1965) A236
Walcheren (1945) L135, L3525
Waldegrave (1943) K579
Walke ᴜsɴ (1911) H(I)08, H(I)46
Walker (1917) D23, D27 ,F55 ,G08, G22, I27
Walkerton (1956) M1188
Wallace (1918) D20, D3A, L64
Wallaceburg ʀᴄɴ (1942) F336, J336
Wallaroo (1890) N82, N6A
Wallaroo ʀᴀɴ (1942) J222
Wallasea (1943) T345
Wallena (1914) FY832
Wallflower (1915) T78, T89
Wallflower (1940) K44, M44
Walmer Castle (1944) K460
Walney (1930) Y04
Walney (1991) M104
Walnut (1910) Y3.906
Walnut (1939) T103
Walpole (1918) D41, F15, I41
Walrus (1917) D24, G17
Walrus (1945) A217, F116
Walrus (1959) S08
Waltham (1906) Y3.1023
Walwyns Castle (1913) FY866
Wandby (1899) Y3.1288
Wanderer (1919) D74, I74
Waneta (1910) Y7.261
Wanganella (1929) Y8.12
Wanstead (1912) Y3.1348
Wapello (1912) Y7.70
War Aconite (1918) Y3.2350
War Admiral (1917) Y3.1897
War African (1918) Y7.266
War Afridi (1919) A290, X90, Y7.337
War Amazon (1918) Y3.2310
War Anchusa (1919) Y3.2472
War Anenome (1918) Y3.1971
War Angler (1918) Y7.263
War Anglian (1918) Y7.314
War Apricot (1918) Y3.2386
War Arabis (1918) Y3.1899
War Armour (1917) Y3.2251
War Arrow (1918) Y3.2379
War Aryan (1918) Y7.308
War Atlin (1918) Y3.2514
War Babine (1918) Y3.2489
War Bagpipe (1918) Y3.2277
War Bahadur (1918) Y7.319
War Balloon (1918) Y3.2253

War Baron (1917) Y3.1908
War Barrage (1918) Y3.2144
War Battery (1918) Y3.2245
War Beach (1918) Y3.2332
War Bee (1918) Y3.2445
War Beetle (1918) Y3.2352
War Begum (1919) Y7.329
War Bharata (1919) A289, X89, Y7.336
War Bison (1918) Y3.2228
War Bracken (1918) Y3.2399
War Brae (1918) Y3.2276
War Brahmin (1919) A288, X91, Y7.338
War Breaker (1918) Y3.2408
War Breeze (1919) Y3.2498
War Briton (1918) Y7.294
War Buckler (1918) Y3.2256
War Buffalo (1918) Y3.2247
War Burman (1919) Y7.316
War Camchin (1918) Y3.2515
War Camp (1918) Y3.2461
War Capitol (1919) Y3.2458
War Cariboo (1918) Y3.2516
War Casco (1918) Y3.2503
War Castle (1918) Y3.2377, Y8.124
War Cateran (1918) Y7.302
War Cayuse (1918) Y3.2487
War Celt (1919) Y3.2484
War Cherry (1919) Y3.2517
War Chief (1919) Y3.2499
War Chilkat (1918) Y3.2518
War Citadel (1918) Y3.2413
War Clarion (1918) Y3.2406
War Climax (1918) Y3.2361
War Clover (1917) Y3.1799
War Clyde (1918) Y3.2427
War Cobra (1917) Y3.2051
War Combe (1918) Y3.2393
War Coot (1918) Y3.2340
War Coppice (1918) Y3.2315
War Council (1917) Y3.1918
War Country (1918) Y3.2000
War Courage (1918) Y3.2388
War Cowslip (1918) Y3.2448
War Crag (1918) Y3.2328
War Crocus (1918) Y3.2280
War Cross (1917) Y3.1658
War Cuirass (1918) Y3.1997
War Cygnet (1918) Y3.2339
War Cypress (1917) Y3.1883, Y8.131
War Daffodil (1917) Y3.1843
War Dagger (1919) Y3.2486
War Dame (1917) Y3.2189

War Damson (1918) Y3.2432
War Dance (1917) Y3.2283
War Dart (1918) Y3.2466
War Deer (1918) Y3.2313
War Dirk (1918) Y3.2435
War Diwan (1919) X86, Y7.333
War Dog (1917) Y3.1903
War Dogra (1919) Y7.327
War Down (1918) Y3.2455, Y8.116
War Dream (1919) Y3.2462
War Drum (1918) Y3.2454
War Duchess (1918) Y3.2396
War Duke (1917) FY582
War Earl (1918) Y3.2433
War Edensaw (1918) Y3.2490
War Envoy (1918) Y7.295
War Ermine (1919) Y3.2463
War Expert (1918) Y7.254
War Faith (1918) Y3.2439
War Fantail (1918) Y3.2426
War Fiend (1919) Y3.2519
War Fife (1918) Y3.2306
War Fijian (1918) Y7.283
War Finch (1918) Y3.2387
War Firth (1918) Y3.2246
War Fish (1917) Y3.1948
War Flower (1917) Y3.1844
War Foam (1918) Y3.2231
War Forest (1918) Y3.2440
War Gascon (1919) Y8.122
War Gazelle (1918) Y3.2202
War Ghurka (1918) Y7.321
War Glen (1918) Y3.2203
War Gnat (1918) Y3.2404
War Grange (1917) Y3.1898, Y8.118
War Guava (1919) Y3.2502
War Hagara (1919) Y7.331
War Hamlet (1918) Y3.2329
War Hathor (1919) Y3.2446
War Hermit (1918) Y7.269
War Hero (1917) Y3.2004
War Highway (1918) Y3.2204
War Hind (1918) Y3.2381
War Hindoo (1919) A287, X87, Y7.334
War Hunter (1918) Y7.307
War Horus (1918) Y3.2505
War Hostage (1917) Y7.235
War Hound (1918) Y3.2412
War Huron (1918) Y3.2520
War Isis (1918) Y3.2284
War Island (1918) Y3.2337
War Jackdaw (1918) Y3.2252

War Jandoli (1919) Y7.324	*War Ontario* (1918) Y3.2476
War Jasmine (1919) Y3.2453	*War Osiris* (1918) Y3.2362
War Javelin (1918) Y3.2354	*War Ostrich* (1918) Y3.2323
War Jemadar (1918) Y7.299	*War Painter* (1918) Y7.270
War Joy (1918) Y3.2475	*War Palace* (1918) Y3.2474
War Karma (1918) Y3.2510	*War Panther* (1918) Y3.2238
War Kestrel (1918) Y3.2292	*War Parrot* (1918) Y8.125
War Khan (1919) Y7.323	*War Patriot* (1918) Y7.256
War Kinsman (1918) Y7.257	*War Pathan* (1919) X84, Y7.326
War Knight (1917) Y3.1728	*War Patrol* (1917) Y3.1659
War Kookri (1919) Y7.328	*War Penguin* (1918) Y3.2374
War Krishna (1919) X88, Y7.335	*War Persian* (1919) Y7.312
War Lance (1918) Y3.2347	*War Persian* (1919) Y3.2488
War Lark (1918) Y3.2483	*War Pibroch* (1918) Y3.2259
War Legate (1918) Y7.280	*War Pigeon* (1918) Y3.2338
War Lemur (1918) Y3.2254, Y8.99	*War Pike* (1918) Y3.2200
War Leopard (1918) Y3.2301	*War Pindari* (1919) A294, X94, Y7.341
War Lion (1917) Y3.2009	*War Pintail* (1918) Y3.2405
War Loch (1918) Y3.2249	*War Platoon* (1918) Y3.2469
War Magpie (1918) Y3.2335, Y8.137	*War Plum* (1919) Y3.2473
War Major (1917) Y3.1720	*War Pointer* (1918) Y3.2149
War Maker (1918) Y7.255	*War Power* (1918) Y3.2368
War Malayan (1918) Y7.267	*War Priam* (1918) Y3.2479
War Mallow (1919) Y3.2449	*War Prince* (1917) Y3.1838
War Mango (1918) Y3.2359, Y8.106	*War Prophet* (1918) Y7.268
War Manor (1918) Y3.2227	*War Puffin* (1918) Y3.2345
War Mansion (1918) Y3.2300	*War Pundit* (1918) Y7.315
War Master (1918) Y7.282	*War Python* (1918) Y3.2002
War Mastiff (1918) Y3.2342	*War Quail* (1918) Y3.2334
War Matron (1918) Y7.276	*War Quebec* (1918) Y3.2496
War Maxim (1918) Y3.2317	*War Queen* (1917) Y3.1721
War Mehtar (1919) X93, Y7.340	*War Rajah* (1918) Y7.317
War Melody (1918) Y3.2398	*War Rajput* (1918) Y7.287
War Merlin (1919) Y3.2459	*War Rambler* (1918) Y3.1996
War Mersey (1919) Y3.2465	*War Ranee* (1918) Y7.277
War Mogul (1919) Y7.332	*War Rapier* (1918) Y3.2434
War Mohawk (1918) Y3.2511	*War Redcap* (1918) Y3.2316
War Monarch (1917) Y3.1982	*War Rider* (1919) Y3.2452
War Monsoon (1918) Y3.2304	*War Roach* (1918) Y3.2299
War Mortar (1918) Y3.2324	*War Robin* (1918) Y3.2307
War Music (1918) Y3.2441, Y8.136	*War Roman* (1919) Y3.2494
War Musket (1918) Y3.2305	*War Roman* (1919) Y7.320
War Myrtle (1917) Y3.1969	*War Rose* (1917) Y3.1827
War Nanoose (1918) Y3.2492	*War Sailor* (1917) Y3.1909
War Nawab (1919) X82, Y7.330	*War Scot* (1918) Y7.305
War Nicola (1918) Y3.2491	*War Sepoy* (1918) X83, Y7.322
War Nipigon (1918) Y3.2508	*War Server* (1918) Y7.281
War Nizam (1918) X81, Y7.303	*War Setter* (1918) Y3.2229
War Noble (1919) Y3.2521	*War Shamrock* (1917) Y3.1722
War Nootka (1918) Y3.2522	*War Shark* (1919) Y3.2464
War Norman (1919) Y3.2493	*War Shell* (1918) Y3.2293
War Nymph (1918) Y3.2385	*War Shikari* (1919) Y7.325

War Sikh (1918) Y7.309
War Simoom (1918) Y3.2378
War Singer (1918) Y7.279
War Sioux (1918) Y3.2509
War Sirdar (1919) Y7.339
War Sirocco (1919) Y3.2481
War Sky (1918) Y3.2390
War Song (1917) Y3.1943
War Sorel (1918) Y3.2506
War Spaniel (1918) Y3.2294
War Sparrow (1918) Y3.2437
War Spartan (1918) Y7.289
War Spray (1918) Y3.2275
War Stag (1918) Y3.2248
War Star (1914) FY292
War Storm (1918) Y3.2501
War Subadar (1918) Y7.288
War Sudra (1920) A295, X95, Y7.342
War Sumas (1918) Y3.2513
War Summit (1919) Y3.2497
War Susquash (1918) Y3.2523
War Swallow (1918) Y3.2257
War Sword (1917) Y3.1910
War Tabard (1918) Y3.2273
War Tamar (1919) Y3.2504
War Tank (1918) Y3.2380
War Tanoo (1918) Y3.2507
War Tempest (1918) Y3.2346
War Thistle (1917) Y3.2286
War Tiger (1917) Y3.2005
War Torpedo (1918) Y3.2265
War Trefoil (1917) Y3.1854
War Tulip (1918) Y3.2373
War Tune (1917) Y3.1733
War Typhoon (1918) Y3.2360
War Tyee (1918) Y3.2512
War Valley (1918) Y3.2314
War Viceroy (1917) Y3.2272
War Viper (1918) Y3.2117
War Visor (1918) Y3.2230
War Vulture (1918) Y3.2261
War Wager (1918) Y7.265
War Wagtail (1918) Y3.2358
War Wasp (1917) Y3.1957
War Weapon (1918) Y3.2383
War Wing (1915) FY906
War Wizard (1918) Y3.2341
War Wolf (1917) Y3.2001, Y8.127
War Yukon (1918) Y3.2367
War Zephyr (1918) Y3.2382
Warburton RAN (Canc) K533
Warden (1945) A309, W170

Warden (1989) A368
Wardour (1911) FY581
Waree RAN (1939) W128
Warkworth (1917) Y3.1869
Warley Pickering (1912) Y3.990
Warmingham (1954) M2737
Warnow (1883) Y3.1002
Warramunga RAN (1942) D10, D123, I44
Warrawee RAN (1909) FY16
Warrego RAN (1911) HA2
Warrego RAN (1940) A312, A428, L73, U73
Warrington USN (1910) H(I)32, H(I)47
Warrior (1895) W86
Warrior (1905) Y3.924
Warrior (1905) 18
Warrior (1944) 31, R31
Warrior II (1904) FY.032
Warrnambool RAN (1941) J202
Warsash (RNR) M1112, M1103, M1216
Warspite (1913) 03, 12, 57, A9, I03
Warspite (1965) S103
Warwick (1917) D25, G96, H38, I25
Warwick Deeping (1934) FY182
Warwickshire (1936) FY113
Wasaga RCN (1941) J162
Washington (1907) Y3.370
Washington (1881) W76
Washington USN (1940) Y83
Waskesin RCN (1942) B647, K330
Wasp USN (1939) Y77
Wasperton (1956) M1189, P1089
Wastwater (1939) A420, FY239
Watchful (1911) C77, C84, C86
Watchful (1953) M2007
Watchman (1917) D26, G09, G23, I26
Watercourse (1973) Y15, Y30
Waterfall (1966) Y17
Waterfly (1931) FY681
Waterfowl (1973) Y31, Y16
Watergate (1917) Z56
Waterhen (1918) D22, G28, I22
Waterhen (Canc) U05
Waterland (1903) Y3.597, Y8.28
Waterloo (Canc) I07
Waterman (1977) A146
Watershed (1966) Y18
Waterside (1967) Y20
Waterspout (1966) Y19
Waterville (1891) Y3.1304
Waterway (1944) F146
Waterwitch (1914) P91, X27, X78
Waterwitch (1943) J304, M304

Waterwitch (1958) M2720
Wathfield (1905) Y3.687
Wato RAN (1904) W127
Wave (1914) N60, N7A, X79
Wave (1939) W22
Wave (1944) B260, J385, M385
Wave Baron (1946) A242, X137
Wave Chief (1946) A265, X119
Wave Commander (1944) A244, X132
Wave Conqueror (1943) A245, X131
Wave Duke (1944) A246, X138
Wave Emperor (1944) A100, B523, X100
Wave Flower (1929) FY703
Wave Governor (1944) A247, B524, X103
Wave King (1944) A182, B525, X82
Wave Knight (1945) A249, X139
Wave Knight (2000) A389
Wave Laird (1946) A119, X129
Wave Liberator (1944) A248, X140
Wave Master (1944) A193, X133
Wave Monarch (1944) A108, B526, ,X108
Wave Premier (1946) A129, X65
Wave Prince (1945) A207, X134
Wave Protector (1944) A215, X136
Wave Regent (1945) A210, B522, X110
Wave Ruler (1946) A212, X135
Wave Ruler (2001) A390
Wave Sovereign (1945) A211, X111
Wave Victor (1943) A220, X130
Wavelet (1905) Y3.915
Waveney (1903) D35, D96, H86, N79
Waveney (1942) F248, K248
Waveney (1983) M2003
Waverley (1899) J51, N51
Wayland (1921) F137
Wear (1905) Y3.153
Wear (1905) N92
Wear (1942) F230, K230
Wearbridge (1911) Y3.1255
Weardale (1903) Y3.1101
Wearpool (1913) Y3.1066
Wearside (1899) Y3.894
Wearsider (1912) Y8.110
Wearwood (1912) Y3.337
Weasel (1943) B456, W120
Webburn (1909) Y3.900
Wedgeport (1941) J139
Wedgwood (1910) Y3.100
Weehawken (1891) Y7.77
Welbeck (1915) N4A, N8A
Welbeck (1917) FY1609
Welbeck Hall (1914) Y3.1852

Welbury (1907) Y3.334
Welcome (1944) B261, J386, M386
Welcome Home (1925) FY1521
Welfare RCN (1943) J356 M356
Wellard (1937) A421, FY137
Wellington (1905) Y3.196
Wellington (1934) L65, U65
Wellington RNZN (1968) F69
Wellpark (1904) Y3.2216
Wells (1919) I95
Wellsbach (1930) FY652
Welshman (1891) Y8.123
Welshman (1940) M84
Wem (1919) NA6, T86
Wendy (1913) Y3.2091
Wenning (1887) Y2.39, Y8.19
Wennington (1955) M1190
Wensleydale (1942) L86
Wentworth RCN (1943) B621, K331
Wescott (1918) F03
Wessex (1918) D43, F32, I43
Wessex (1943) D32, D78, D278, R78
West Bay (1918) A373, W78
West Cocker (1919) A366, W10
West Haven (1910) FY1588
West Hyde (1919) W58
West Marsh (1896) Y3.1338
West Point (1912) Y3.2244
West Wales (1912) Y3.390
West York RCN (1944) K369
Westborough (1901) Y3.195, Y8.84
Westbury (1904) Y3.1271
Westcott (1918) D47, I47
Westella (1934) FY161
Westergate (1881) Y3.573
Western Coast (1916) Y3.1782
Western Isles (1902) F76
Westernland (1918) F87
Westfield (1901) Y3.498
Westgate (1899) Y3.1300
Westgate (1918) Z88
Westhope (1918) Y3.2226
Westlands (1905) Y3.1000
Westlyn (1914) Z154
Westminster (1918) D45, F02, L40
Westminster (1992) F237
Westmoor (1911) Y3.1302
Westmount RCN (1942) J318
Weston (1932) L72, U72
Westonby (1901) Y3.1245
Westphalia (1913) Y8.27
Westralia RAN (1929) C61, F95

Westray (1941) T182
Westville (1913) Y3.294
Westward Ho! (1894) J43, 4.390, N43
Westwood (1907) Y3.45
Wetaskiwin ʀᴄɴ (1940) K175
Wetherby (1918) T41
Wexford (1919) NA7
Wexford Coast (1915) Y4.53, Y8.80
Wexham (1954) M2738
Weybourne (1919) T2N, T4N
Weyburn ʀᴄɴ (1941) K173
Weymouth (1910) 03, 0C
Whaddon (1940) F145, L45
Whalsay (1942) T293
Wharfe (1890) Y3.2419, Y8.2
Whateley Hall (1904) Y3.1020
Wheatberry (1915) Y4.46
Wheatland (1941) F22, L122
Whelp (1943) D33, D237, R37
Whimbrel (1897) Y3.1681
Whimbrel (1907) Y9.20
Whimbrel (1942) B278, F29, U29, A179
Whinfield (1904) Y3.2022
Whinhill (1914) Y3.649, Y5.7, Y8.11
Whippingham (1930) J136, 4.404
Whippingham (1954) M2739
Whipple ᴜꜱɴ (1901) H(I)54
Whirlpool (1919) FY60, P91, Z91
Whirlwind (1917) D25, D27, D30, F56, G73, H41, I30
Whirlwind (1943) D34, D187, F187, R87
Whitby (1954) F36
Whitby Abbey (1908) M35, T09, T90
Whitby ʀᴄɴ (1943) K346
White Bear (1908) J30, 4.02
White Head (1880) Y8.1
White Rose (1911) Y3.2023
White Sea (1904) Y3.73
White Swan (1903) Y3.421, Y6.2
Whitehall (1892) Y3.1010
Whitehall (1919) D94, GA7, I94
Whitehaven (1941) J121
Whitehead (1880) Y8.1
Whitehead (1970) A364
Whitesand Bay (1944) B622, F633, K633
Whitethorn (1939) T127
Whitethroat ʀᴄɴ (1944) M03, N03
Whiting (1941) T232
Whitley (1918) D61, D97, F20, L23
Whitshed (1919) D77, FA7, I77
Whittaker (1943) K580
Whitton (1956) M1191

Whorlton (1907) Y3.220
Whyalla ʀᴀɴ (1941) B252, J153
Whytock ꜱᴀɴ (1924) T07, T507
W.I. Radcliffe (ex *Clarissa Radcliffe*) (1913) Y3.393
Wiay (1945) J441, M341
Wichita ᴜꜱɴ (1937) Y50
Widemouth Bay (1944) B290, F615, K615
Widgeon (1904) N71
Widgeon ᴜꜱɴ (1918) TA1
Widgeon (1938) K62, L62, M62, P62
Widnes (1918) J55, N55, T1N, T6N
Wigan (1916) FY1583
Wigeon of Fearn (1936) FY.034
Wight (ex *Vectis*) (1913) Y3.40
Wigtown Bay (1945) F616, K616
Wilberforce (1899) Y3.1595
Wild Goose (1942) B648, F45, U45
Wild Swan (1919) D62, I62
Wildrake (1908) Y9.18
Wileysike (1888) Y3.977
Wilk ᴏʀᴘ (1929) 64A, 64N, N64
Wilkes ᴜꜱɴ (1916) H(I)17, H(I)48
Wilkieston (1956) M1192
Willa (1935) FY1584
Willem van der Zaan ʀɴʟɴ (1938) M08
William Balls (1894) Y3.759
William Bell (1918) FY1727
William Brady (1918) 4.112
William Caldwell (1918) Z142
William Cale (1917) FY535
William Hallett (1917) FY555
William Hannam (1919) Z129
William Mannell (1917) FY1665
William O'Brien (1915) Y3.1993
William Poulson (1917) W87
William Scoresby (1925) J122
William Stephen (1917) FY806, FY1585
William Stroud (1914) 4.460
Williamstown (Canc) K66
Willing Boys (1930) FY947
Willow (1930) T66
Willow Branch (1892) Y3.1042
Willow Lake (1945) J495
Willowherb (1943) K283
Wilster (1903) Y3.1520
Wilson ᴜꜱɴ (1939) Y93
Wilston (1909) Y3.418
Wilston (1916) Y3.2279
Wilton (1916) Y3.1552
Wilton (1941) F128, L128
Wilton (1972) M1116
Wimbledon (1906) Y3.1684

Wimmera ʀᴀɴ (Canc) K86
Winamac (1913) Y7.96
Winchelsea (1917) D46, F40, I46, D66, F99
Winchester (1918) G43, H95, L55
Windermere (1939) FY207
Windflower (1918) T1A
Windflower ʀᴄɴ (1940) K155
Windrush (1943) K370
Windsor (1918) D42, F12, L94
Windsor Hall (1910) Y3.861
Windsor Lad (....) FY1932
Windward Ho! (1920) FY574
Winfield (1900) Y3.2394
Wingate (1913) Y3.354
Winlaton (1912) Y3.449
Winnie (1889) Y3.1704
Winnipeg ʀᴄɴ (1942) F337, J337
Winslow ᴜsɴ (1915) H(I)01, H(I)49
Wintringham (1954) M2777
Wirral (1890) Y8.85
Wirral (1911) Y3.865
Wisbech (1901) Y3.552
Wishart (1919) D67, I67
Wisley (1904) Y3.2326
Wistaria (1915) T79, T91
Wistaria (1939) T113
Wiston (1958) M1205
Witch (1919) D89, GA6, I89
Witham (1919) FY770
Witherington (1919) D76, I76
Withernsea (1918) FY1637
Wivern (1919) D66, I66
Wizard (1895) H7A, H3C
Wizard (1943) D35, D72, F72, R72
Wladimir Sawin (1898) Y3.1786
Wolborough (1937) FY233
Woldingham (1955) M2778
Wolf (1897) D97, D98, D95
Wolfe (1920) A190, F37
Wolfhound (1918) D44, D56, F18, F52, I56
Wollondilly ʀᴀɴ (Canc) K98
Wollongong ʀᴀɴ (1941) B253, J172
Wolsey (1918) D35, D64, D98, G40, L02
Wolverine (1910) H18,
Wolverine (1919) D78, I78
Wolverton (1956) M1193, P1093
Wolves (1934) FY158
Wolvesey Castle (1944) K461
Wongala ʀᴀɴ (1919) FY78
Woodbridge (1900) Y3.905
Woodbridge Haven (1945) K654, P58
Woodburn (1907) Y3.532

Woodcock ᴜsɴ (1918) TA5
Woodcock (1942) A468, B279, F90, U90
Woodfield (1905) Y3.1976
Woodlark (1898) N0C
Woodlark (1958) A2780
Woodnut (1906) M02, M(I)02, M(I)25
Woodpecker (1942) U08
Woodruff (1941) K53
Woodstock ʀᴄɴ (1941) F238, K238
Woodville (1892) Y3.572
Woolaston (1958) M1194
Woolston (1900) Y3.1082
Woolston (1918) D30, D63, D95, F08, L49
Woolwich (1912) AC, CA
Woolwich (1934) A180, F80, I80
Woonda (1915) W57
Worcester (1919) D96, GA8, I96
Worcestershire (1931) F29
Worden ᴜsɴ (1903) H(I)55
Wordsworth (1915) Y3.1189
Woron (1907) Y3.1007
Worthing (1941) J72
Wotton (1956) M1195
Wragby (1901) Y3.527
Wrangler (1907) Y7.42
Wrangler (1943) D36, D158, F157, R48
Wren (1919) D88, GA5, I88
Wren (1942) B649, F28, U28
Wrentham (1955) M2779
Wrestler (1915) W88
Wrestler (1918) D35, D62, F57, G31, I50, L10
Wrexham (1902) Y2.177
Wryneck (1918) D21, G05, L04
Wryneck (Canc) U31
Wuchang (1914) F30
Wyandra (1901) P62, P5C
Wychwood (1907) Y3.228
Wye (1943) F371, K371
Wyncote (1907) M(I)27
Wyoming ᴜsɴ (1911) 97
Wyoming (1915) FY1862
Wyrallah ʀᴀɴ (1934) FY92
Wyre (1911) Z198
Wyvisbrook (1912) Y3.812

X

X-2 (ex *Galileo Galilei*) (1934) P711
X1 (1923) X1
X3 Piker (1942) X3
X4 (....) X4

X5 (*Platypus*) (1942) X5
X6 (*Piker II*) (1943) X6
X7 (*Pdinichthys*) (....) X7
X8 (*Expectant*) (....) X8
X9 (*Pluto*) (....) X9
X10 (....) X10
X20 *Exemplar* (....) X20
X21 *Exultant* (....) X21
X22 *Exploit* (....) X22
X23 *Xiphias* (....) X23
X24 *Expeditious* (....) X24
X25 *Xema* (....) X25
X51 (*Stickleback*) (1954) X51
X52 (1954) X52
X53 (1955) X53
X54 (1955) X54
XE1 (*Executioner*) (....) XE1
XE2 (*Xerxes*) (....) XE2
XE3 (*Sigyn*) (1944) XE3
XE4 (*Exciter*) (....) XE4
XE5 (*Perseus*) (....) XE5
XE6 (*Excalibur II*) (....) XE6
XE7 (*Exuberant*) (1945) XE7
XE8 (*Expunger*) (1945) XE8
XE9 (*Unexpected*) (1945) XE9
XE10 (Canc) XE10
XE11 (*Lucifer*) (....) XE11
XE12 (*Excitable*) (1945) XE12
XE14 (Canc) XE14
XE15 (Canc) XE15
XE16 (Canc) XE16
XE17 (Canc) XE17
XE18 (Canc) XE18
XE19 (Canc) XE19
XE20 (....) XE20
XE21 (....) XE21
XE22 (....) XE22
XE23 (....) XE23
XE24 (....) XE24
XE25 (....) XE25
XT1 (*Extant*) (1943) XT1
XT2 (*Sandra*) (1943) XT2
XT3 (*Herald*) (1943) XT3
XT4 (*Excelsior*) (1943) XT4
XT5 (*Extended*) (1943) XT5
XT6 (*Xantho*) (1943) XT6
XT7 (Canc) XT7
XT8 (Canc) XT8
XT9 (Canc) XT9
XT10 (Canc) XT10
XT11 (Canc) XT11
XT12 (Canc) XT12

XT14 (Canc) XT14
XT15 (Canc) XT15
XT16 (Canc) XT16
XT17 (Canc) XT17
XT18 (Canc) XT18
XT19 (Canc) XT19

Y

Yandra ʀᴀɴ (1928) FY91
Yarborough (1900) Y3.1063, Y8.130
Yarmouth (1911) 72, 95, 1C
Yarmouth (1959) F101
Yarnton (1956) M1196, P1096
Yarra ʀᴀɴ (1910) HA4
Yarra ʀᴀɴ (1935) L77, U77
Yarta (1898) FY1565
Yashima (1929) FY1894
Yavuz ᴛᴜʀ (1911) B70
Yaxham (1958) M2780
Yearby (1896) Y3.1378
Yeovil (1918) TA6, TA7
Yestor (1941) T222
Yezo (1924) FY829
Ying Chow (1905) F102
Ymuiden ʀɴʟɴ (1899) FY1937
Yonne (1910) Y3.1243
York (1907) M20, M(I)20, M(I)26
York (1927) 90
York (1982) D98
York Castle (1901) Y3.1628
York Castle (1944) K537
York City (1933) FY110
Yorkmoor (1912) Y3.1480
Yorkshire Lass (1920) FY1972
Young Alfred (1911) FY1912
Young Cliff (1925) FY919
Young Jacob (1914) FY975
Young John (1914) FY278
Ypres ʀᴄɴ (1917) J70, N70
Ypres (Canc) G83
Yser (ex *Cayo Manzanillo*) (1904) Y3.841
Ythan Braes (1917) Y7.41, 4.339
Yukon (1912) Y3.444
Yunnan ʀᴀɴ (1934) A771

Z

Z 10 (1936) R92
Z6 ʀɴʟɴ (1915) H55

Z7 RNLN (1915) H93
Z8 RNLN (1915) H71
Zafra (1905) Y3.577
Zambesi (1900) Y3.1133
Zambesi (1943) D66, R66
Zamora (1905) Y3.378
Zanoni (1907) Y3.313
Zanzibar (1943) K596
Zareba (1921) FY1814
Zaree (1904) W91
Zaria (1904) Y9.22
Zaza (1905) FY.033
Zealandia (1904) 19, 73, 2C, N89
Zealous (1944) D39, R39
Zebra (1944) D81, R81
Zeebrugge (1945) L120, L3532
Zeehond RNLN (1932) N73
Zelo (1917) Y3.2107
Zena (1911) Y2.76, Y3.76
Zenith (1944) D95, R95
Zeno (1893) Y3.1145
Zephyr (1895) D98, D4A, N86
Zephyr (1943) D19, R19

Zest (1943) D02, F102, R02
Zetland (1917) T5C
Zetland (1942) F59, L59
Zillah (1900) Y3.1043
Zimorodok (1908) Y3.2174
Zinaida (1882) Y4.2
Zingara (1898) Y3.18
Zinnia (1915) T42, T92
Zinnia (1940) K98, M98
Zodiac (1944) D54, R54
Zoea IT (1937) N82
Zoroaster (1911) Y2.165, Y3.897
Zubian (1917) D20, D99
Zulfaquar RIN (....) T303
Zulfiquar RPN (1942) F265
Zulu (1909) D05, D10, D0A, H86
Zulu (1937) F18, G18, L18
Zulu (1962) F124
Zurichmoor (1910) Y3.2258
Zwaardvisch (1943) S32
Zwarte Zee (1899) FY1937
Zwarte Zee (1933) W163
Zylpha (1894) P79, P6C, Y3.139

Appendix 1

Mercantile Fleet Auxiliary

One of the probems with operating all over the World was the necessity to have a constant supply of fuel, stores and ammunition. Prior to WW1 the Royal Navy, with its huge fleet of steam-powered ships, was being supplied by an extensive network of bases, coaling stations and depots. To supplement and maintain these supplies the Admiralty chartered, or bought outright, Merchant Navy ships. In 1905 the Lords Commissioners of the Admiralty issued an instruction that heralded the formation of the Royal Fleet Auxiliary, to operate those support ships now owned by the Admiralty. Those ships on charter were to be known as the Mercantile Fleet Auxiliary. During WW1, as the need for fuel (both coal and, later, fuel oil), stores and ammunition increased, so did the demand for merchant ships to transport said stores. Hundreds of ships were chartered by the Admiralty - some on long term charter, some for single voyages. To aid visual identification, these ships were assigned pendant numbers with a Y flag and number pendant superior. These were not painted up on the hulls but used exclusively as flag hoists. Each letter/number combination indicated a different role, as below:

Y1	Flotilla Depots	Y6	Mine Carriers
Y2	Armament Carriers	Y7	Oilers and Water Carriers
Y3	Colliers	Y8	Store Carriers
Y4	Fleet Messengers	Y9	Squadron Supply Ships
Y5	Frozen Meat Ships	YA	Hospital Ships

A similar system was in operation in WW2 using the following flags.

Y1	Storeships, Carriers, Fleet Supply Ships	Y6	Mine Carriers
Y2	Armament Store Carriers & Issuing Ships	Y7	Tankers, Oil Fuel and Petrol Ships
Y3	Colliers	Y8	Hospital Ships
Y4	Transports	Y9	Hospital Carriers
Y5	Frozen Meat Ships	Y0	Miscellaneous Fleet Auxiliaries

There is still much research to be conducted in order to provide a full list of ship identification, number allocations and time periods but, with closed archives and no access to primary sources, the following will provide a baseline until the appropriate files can be studied. The section is listed with WW1 allocations first followed by WW2 assignments identified to date. Details are limited to number and ship name.

Y1. Flotilla Supply Ships (WW1)

Y1.1	Sorrento
Y1.2	Ortolan
Y1.3	Grive
Y1.4	Intaba
Y1.5	Albatross
Y1.6	Peregrine
Y1.7	Dean Swift (ex Swift)
Y1.8	Baron Herries
Y1.9	Stork

British Warships 1914-1918 (Dittmar & Colledge) suggest that pendants Y1.1 and Y1.5 - Y1.9 did not have a flag superior and were assigned only as 1 and 5-9.

Y2. Ammunition Carriers (WW1)

Y2.1	Bison
Y2.2	Steersman
Y2.3	Upnor

Y2.4	Helmsman
Y2.7	Skipper
Y2.9	Emerald
Y2.10	Achroite
Y2.14	Arrival
Y2.23	Vectis
Y2.27	Hebble
Y2.31	Trostan
Y2.32	Valegarth
Y2.35	Dilston
Y2.36	Race Fisher
Y2.37	Devon Coast
Y2.39	Wenning

Y2.41	Clandeboye	**Y3.22**	Holywood	**Y3.67**	Bywell
Y2.42	Arno	**Y3.23**	Cornwood	**Y3.68**	Clermiston
Y2.44	Liberty	**Y3.24**	Dalewood	**Y3.69**	Intent
Y2.49	Demetian			**Y3.70**	John O. Scott
Y2.56	Rievaulx Abbey	**Y3.25**	Ottawa	**Y3.71**	Repton
Y2.57	Agberi		Kirkwood	**Y3.72**	Riversdale
Y2.68	Laertes			**Y3.73**	White Sea
Y2.73	Ocean Transport	**Y3.26**	Marlwood	**Y3.74**	Rondo
Y2.76	Zena	**Y3.27**	Lockwood	**Y3.75**	Tempo
Y2.77	Gloucester Coast	**Y3.28**	Portwood		
Y2.106	Umtali	**Y3.29**	Herrington	**Y3.76**	Saltmarshe
Y2.107	Umgeni	**Y3.30**	General Gordon		Zena
Y2.108	Rutherglen				
Y2.110	Dorothy	**Y3.31**	Oilfield	**Y3.77**	Lord Ormonde
Y2.125	Kassala		Roker		Hadley
Y2.133	Agberi				
Y2.135	Denby Grange	**Y3.32**	Comeric	**Y3.78**	Needwood
Y2.136	Earl of Forfar	**Y3.33**	Knottingley		
Y2.152	Buccaneer	**Y3.34**	Alice M. Craig	**Y3.79**	Nairn
Y2.165	Zoroaster	**Y3.35**	Argus		Tynemouth
Y2.167	Daybreak	**Y3.36**	Boukadra		
Y2.177	Wrexham	**Y3.37**	Cimbrier	**Y3.80**	Largo
Y2.186	Adenwen	**Y3.38**	Bargany	**Y3.81**	Tosto
Y2.190	Aboukir	**Y3.39**	Chic	**Y3.82**	Ludworth
Y2.199	Aigwen	**Y3.40**	Wight (ex Vectis)	**Y3.83**	Maywood
Y2.220	Susquehanna	**Y3.41**	Alto (ex Tees)	**Y3.84**	Brook
Y2.228	Ben Nevis			**Y3.85**	Westgarth
Y2.233	Magellan	**Y3.42**	Brika		
Y2.235	Daldorch		Bendew	**Y3.86**	Dewsland
					Blakemoor
		Y3.43	Boscastle		
Y3. Colliers (WW1)		**Y3.44**	Rouen	**Y3.87**	Pinewood
		Y3.45	Westwood	**Y3.88**	Bondicar
Y3.1	Agnes Duncan	**Y3.46**	Ryhope	**Y3.89**	Ravelston
Y3.2	Fernhill	**Y3.47**	Rhodanthe	**Y3.90**	Everest
Y3.3	Hooton	**Y3.48**	Hollinside	**Y3.91**	Huntsfall
Y3.4	Frances Duncan	**Y3.49**	Capelmead (ex Armora)	**Y3.92**	Redesmere
Y3.5	Ethel Duncan	**Y3.50**	Sunningdale	**Y3.93**	John Shaw
Y3.6	Rotherhill	**Y3.51**	Airmyn		
Y3.7	Virent	**Y3.52**	Rawcliffe	**Y3.94**	Hindukoosh
Y3.8	Tregarth	**Y3.53**	Brinkburn		Brook
Y3.9	Aigwen	**Y3.54**	Northfield		
		Y3.55	Corso	**Y3.95**	Trostan
Y3.10	Isle of Jura			**Y3.96**	Factor
	Valegarth	**Y3.56**	Glendhu	**Y3.97**	Boyne
			Satrap	**Y3.98**	Gleneden
Y3.11	Trevelyan			**Y3.99**	Quaysider
Y3.12	Muriel	**Y3.57**	Hilda	**Y3.100**	Wedgwood
Y3.13	Scarlet Tower	**Y3.58**	Haslingden	**Y3.101**	Aysgarth
Y3.14	Moto	**Y3.59**	Streatham		
Y3.15	Ethel	**Y3.60**	Bangarth	**Y3.102**	Trinculo
Y3.16	Constantine	**Y3.61**	Llwyngwair		Escrick
Y3.17	Transporter	**Y3.62**	Italiana		
Y3.18	Zingara	**Y3.63**	Bedale	**Y3.103**	Glencoe
Y3.19	Boynton	**Y3.64**	Loch Lomond		
Y3.20	Rudmore	**Y3.65**	Edie	**Y3.104**	Adamton
Y3.21	Bestwood	**Y3.66**	Thornley		Spital (ex Daldorch)

Y3.105	Baron Herries	Y3.152	Novington	Y3.200	Australford		
	Cedartree	Y3.153	Wear		(ex Strathavon)		
		Y3.154	Muristan				
Y3.106	Carlston	Y3.155	Solent	Y3.201	Kincardine		
		Y3.156	Birchwood	Y3.202	Daghestan		
Y3.107	Heighington	Y3.157	Clara	Y3.203	Cardigan		
	Hartlepool	Y3.158	Boldwell	Y3.204	Teesbridge		
		Y3.159	Lindenhall				
Y3.108	Melton	Y3.160	Penare	Y3.205	Cyfarthfa		
Y3.109	Sampan	Y3.161	Austriana		Quickstep		
Y3.110	Brierton	Y3.162	Highgate				
Y3.111	Northdene	Y3.163	Porthkerry	Y3.206	Gretaston		
Y3.112	Cliftonhall	Y3.164	Barmoor	Y3.207	Beechtree		
Y3.113	Maston	Y3.165	Elmgrove (ex Treasury)	Y3.208	Sir Francis		
Y3.114	Jessie	Y3.166	Brentham	Y3.209	Mervyn		
Y3.115	Johnstown	Y3.167	Airedale	Y3.210	Gordonia		
Y3.116	Burnhope	Y3.168	Gosforth				
Y3.117	Paignton	Y3.169	Mostyn	Y3.211	Merranio		
Y3.118	Balham	Y3.170	Collingwood		Larchwood		
Y3.119	Greldale	Y3.171	Glynn				
Y3.120	Teviotdale	Y3.172	Swansea Vale	Y3.212	Pensacola		
Y3.121	Cairnnevis	Y3.173	Mordenwood	Y3.213	Slav		
		Y3.174	Raloo	Y3.214	Serbistan		
Y3.122	Lowdale	Y3.175	Cairnavon				
	Knutsford	Y3.176	Kildonan	Y3.215	Bellview		
		Y3.177	Greenhill		Restormel		
Y3.123	Mereddio						
Y3.124	Nyassa	Y3.178	Baron Berwick	Y3.216	Ukside		
Y3.125	Excellent		(ex Grelmay)	Y3.217	Divis		
Y3.126	Enterprise			Y3.218	Towneley		
Y3.127	Simoom	Y3.179	Ramsgarth	Y3.219	Marsden		
Y3.128	Venice	Y3.180	Queensgarth	Y3.220	Whorlton		
Y3.129	Cundall	Y3.181	Knightsgarth	Y3.221	Pelica		
Y3.130	Kilmaho	Y3.182	Monksgarth	Y3.222	Eskwood		
Y3.131	Thames	Y3.183	Goathland	Y3.223	Castleford		
Y3.132	E.O. Saltmarsh	Y3.184	Forfar	Y3.224	Abbas		
Y3.133	St Edmund	Y3.185	Sir Arthur	Y3.225	Sheaf Field		
Y3.134	Lizette	Y3.186	Hendon	Y3.226	Ovid		
Y3.135	Spen	Y3.187	Hornsea	Y3.227	Kariba		
Y3.136	Belford	Y3.188	Hitchen	Y3.228	Wychwood		
Y3.137	Burcombe	Y3.189	Ford Castle	Y3.229	Pendarves		
Y3.138	Commonwealth			Y3.230	Butetown (ex Karanja)		
Y3.139	Zylpha	Y3.190	Brookby	Y3.231	Djerissa		
Y3.140	Geo		Burbridge	Y3.232	Tweeddale		
Y3.141	Weltondale			Y3.233	Eleanor		
Y3.142	Levenwood	Y3.191	Normanton	Y3.234	Mountpark		
Y3.143	Ladywood			Y3.235	Hartsid		
Y3.144	Sheaf Arrow	Y3.192	Branksome Chine	Y3.236	Nigaristan		
Y3.145	Birtley		Silversand	Y3.237	Norburn		
Y3.146	Moyle						
Y3.147	Slemish	Y3.193	Parkmill	Y3.238	Ardandearg		
Y3.148	Ashtree	Y3.194	Relentless		Corso		
Y3.149	Shipcote	Y3.195	Westborough				
Y3.150	Milton	Y3.196	Wellington	Y3.239	Northwaite		
		Y3.197	Tweed	Y3.240	Harmonic		
Y3.151	Messidor	Y3.198	Homer City	Y3.241	Ambient		
	Fulgent	Y3.199	Craigwen (ex Orpheus)	Y3.242	Bretwalda		

Y3.243	Portsea	**Y3.282**	Planudes	**Y3.319**	Broomhill
Y3.244	Mars	**Y3.283**	Dunraven		
Y3.245	Cilicia	**Y3.284**	Caterino	**Y3.320**	Kingston
					Purley
Y3.246	Hollinside	**Y3.285**	Saxon		
	(ex Robert Coverdale)		Lockwood	**Y3.321**	Silvia
				Y3.322	Holmpark
Y3.247	St Andrews	**Y3.286**	Lamington	**Y3.323**	Onwen
Y3.248	Rosario	**Y3.287**	Fullerton	**Y3.324**	Newlyn
Y3.249	Relillio	**Y3.288**	Ingleside	**Y3.325**	Dorie
Y3.250	Rubio	**Y3.289**	Burnby	**Y3.326**	Camerata
Y3.251	Goodwood	**Y3.290**	Greenbatt	**Y3.327**	Ludgate
Y3.252	Remembrance	**Y3.291**	Lydie	**Y3.328**	Ellerdale
		Y3.292	Cento	**Y3.329**	Corinth
Y3.253	North Wales	**Y3.293**	Penolver		
	Penshurst	**Y3.294**	Westville	**Y3.330**	Palatine
		Y3.295	Molesey (ex Salamanca)		Trecarrell
Y3.254	Ardenhall	**Y3.296**	Pomaron		
Y3.255	Tremorvah	**Y3.297**	Grantley	**Y3.331**	Thorpwood
Y3.256	Lady Charlotte				Claymont (ex Porthcawl)
Y3.257	Spinel	**Y3.298**	Langoe		
Y3.258	Gransha		Butetown	**Y3.332**	Gisella
Y3.259	Corinthia			**Y3.333**	Melanie
Y3.260	Thornhill	**Y3.299**	Ellerslie		
Y3.261	Marie Rose	**Y3.300**	Bronwen	**Y3.334**	Durham
Y3.262	Monkstone	**Y3.301**	Penhallow		Welbury
Y3.263	Throstle				
		Y3.302	Daleby	**Y3.335**	Hurstside (ex Portreath)
Y3.264	Altai		Treneglos	**Y3.336**	Tabarka
	Natal Transport			**Y3.337**	Wearwood
		Y3.303	Fluent		
Y3.265	Marie Suzanne	**Y3.304**	North Britain	**Y3.338**	Penylan
	Monitoria				(ex Arlington Court)
		Y3.305	Carston		
Y3.266	Runswick		(ex Arthur Balfour)	**Y3.339**	Errington Court
	Diadem				
		Y3.306	Craigston	**Y3.340**	Cerbury
Y3.267	Queensland		Holly Branch		Glenturret
Y3.268	Corfu				
Y3.269	Stromness (ex Poldhu)	**Y3.307**	Penmorvah	**Y3.341**	Ellaline
Y3.270	Trevince	**Y3.308**	Torridge	**Y3.342**	Picton
Y3.271	Ferngarth	**Y3.309**	Glamorgan	**Y3.343**	Pengreep
Y3.272	Pikepool	**Y3.310**	Laristan	**Y3.344**	Cydonia
Y3.273	Cairndhu				
		Y3.311	North Cambria	**Y3.345**	Gladys Royle
Y3.274	Hartdale		(ex Calcutta)		Scawby
	Benbrook				
		Y3.312	Trelissick	**Y3.346**	Penhale
Y3.275	Headcliffe			**Y3.347**	Putney (ex Lynton)
	Ross	**Y3.313**	Huntball (ex Manica)	**Y3.348**	Tremeadow
			Zanoni	**Y3.349**	Beemah
Y3.276	Towergate			**Y3.350**	Royal Transport
Y3.277	Eros	**Y3.314**	Buranda	**Y3.351**	Margit
Y3.278	Trelawney	**Y3.315**	Brendon	**Y3.352**	Amicus
Y3.279	Ilwen	**Y3.316**	Priestfield	**Y3.353**	Balvenie
Y3.280	Trevean	**Y3.317**	Charleston	**Y3.354**	Wingate
Y3.281	Hillingdon	**Y3.318**	Boscawen	**Y3.355**	Ladykirk

Y3.356	Carronpark	**Y3.398**	Hyltonia	**Y3.444**	Yukon
Y3.357	Gardenia	**Y3.399**	Pensilva	**Y3.445**	British Transport
Y3.358	Venus	**Y3.400**	Diyatalawa	**Y3.446**	Vala
Y3.359	Euston	**Y3.401**	Prince Leopold	**Y3.447**	Vestra
Y3.360	Butetown (ex Eda)	**Y3.402**	Prince Charles	**Y3.448**	Iddesleigh
Y3.361	J. Duncan	**Y3.403**	Kyleford	**Y3.449**	Winlaton
		Y3.404	Moray Firth		
Y3.362	Thamesmede			**Y3.450**	Buresk
	(ex Transport)	**Y3.405**	Grelhame		Eastgate
			(ex Tyninghame)		
Y3.363	Sheaf Dart (ex Leander)			**Y3.451**	Sculptor (ex St Andrew)
Y3.364	Exmoor	**Y3.406**	Leafield	**Y3.452**	Eggesford
		Y3.407	Heatherside	**Y3.453**	Queensland Transport
Y3.365	Navarra	**Y3.408**	Thessalia	**Y3.454**	Shakespear
	Orangemoor	**Y3.409**	Ethelwolf	**Y3.455**	Bampton
		Y3.410	Kelsomoor	**Y3.456**	Quantock
Y3.366	Elswick Grange	**Y3.411**	Tregarthen	**Y3.457**	Dunster
Y3.367	Tregurno	**Y3.412**	Foreland	**Y3.458**	Llandudno
Y3.368	Bideford	**Y3.413**	Kirkwood		
Y3.369	Treveal	**Y3.414**	Manchester Civilian	**Y3.459**	Charston
Y3.370	Washington	**Y3.415**	Ruperra		Manchester Spinner
Y3.371	Gwladys				
Y3.372	Rhio	**Y3.416**	Silverash	**Y3.460**	Inveric
			Vancouver	**Y3.461**	Garron Head
Y3.373	Irthington			**Y3.462**	Scottier (ex Kingsgate)
	Karma	**Y3.417**	Columba	**Y3.463**	Dykland
		Y3.418	Wilston		
Y3.374	Marie Elsie	**Y3.419**	Trevaylor	**Y3.464**	Aden
Y3.375	Indiana	**Y3.420**	Rosemount		Bagdale
Y3.376	Torrington	**Y3.421**	White Swan		
Y3.377	Britannia	**Y3.422**	Darnholme	**Y3.465**	Somersby
Y3.378	Zamora	**Y3.423**	Collingham	**Y3.466**	Eskbridge
Y3.379	Eastwood	**Y3.424**	Exford	**Y3.467**	Indian Transport
Y3.380	Eastfield	**Y3.425**	Tresillian	**Y3.468**	King David
Y3.381	Thistledhu	**Y3.426**	Trevanion	**Y3.469**	Karuma
Y3.382	Ennisbrook	**Y3.427**	Batsford	**Y3.470**	Ravenshoe
Y3.383	Breynton	**Y3.428**	Reapwell	**Y3.471**	Hermiston
Y3.384	Forestmoor	**Y3.429**	Fenay Lodge	**Y3.472**	Syndic
Y3.385	Baron Ailsa	**Y3.430**	Nantwen	**Y3.473**	Banchory
Y3.386	Crossby	**Y3.431**	Daybreak	**Y3.474**	England
Y3.387	Roddam	**Y3.432**	Lena	**Y3.475**	Garfield
Y3.388	Ridley	**Y3.433**	Cheniston	**Y3.476**	Baron Kelvin
Y3.389	Edlington	**Y3.434**	Milly	**Y3.477**	Newquay
Y3.390	West Wales	**Y3.435**	Bretainer	**Y3.478**	Midland
		Y3.436	Cairnross	**Y3.479**	Ampleforth
Y3.391	Paddington	**Y3.437**	Nevisbrook	**Y3.480**	Spilsby
	(ex Swindon)	**Y3.438**	Lizzie Westoll	**Y3.481**	King Malcolm
				Y3.482	Emlyn
Y3.392	Tremayne	**Y3.439**	Torquay	**Y3.483**	Usworth
			Tyneford	**Y3.484**	Roath
Y3.393	W.I. Radcliffe			**Y3.485**	Gripfast
	(ex Clarissa Radcliffe)	**Y3.440**	Ravenstone	**Y3.486**	Arkleside
		Y3.441	Camellia (ex Tynehome)	**Y3.487**	Glencliffe
Y3.394	Harlseywood	**Y3.442**	Tiara	**Y3.488**	Norton
Y3.395	Boverton			**Y3.489**	King John
Y3.396	Hunsgrove	**Y3.443**	Baycraig (ex Craigina)	**Y3.490**	Ariadne Christine
Y3.397	Tonbridge		Volhynia	**Y3.491**	Euterpe

Y3.492	Roma	**Y3.540**	Vittoria	**Y3.578**	Benmohr (ex Dalblair)
Y3.493	Moorlands		Pargust	**Y3.579**	Norhilda
Y3.494	Gertie			**Y3.580**	Newby
		Y3.541	Ariadne Alexandra	**Y3.581**	Tapton
Y3.495	Tarpeia	**Y3.542**	Kassala	**Y3.582**	Margarita
	(ex Earl of Durham)			**Y3.583**	Ayr
		Y3.543	St Dimitrios	**Y3.584**	Aire
Y3.496	Harflete		Lincairn	**Y3.585**	Derwent
	Ruel			**Y3.586**	Race Fisher
		Y3.544	Otto Trechmann	**Y3.587**	Keyingham
Y3.497	Tregothnan			**Y3.588**	Stellina (ex Dawlish)
Y3.498	Westfield	**Y3.545**	Kirkby	**Y3.589**	Rounton
Y3.499	Glenfruin		Hillhouse		
Y3.500	Bradford City			**Y3.590**	Glenby
Y3.501	King Bleddyn	**Y3.546**	Cape Antibes		Trevisa
Y3.502	Trevalgan		Sydney Reid		
Y3.503	Enidwen			**Y3.591**	Datchet (ex Tantallon)
Y3.504	Glendene	**Y3.547**	Petersham (ex Clinton)	**Y3.592**	Parkgate
Y3.505	Gracefield	**Y3.548**	Apsleyhall	**Y3.593**	Ventmoor
Y3.506	Daleham	**Y3.549**	Blagdon	**Y3.594**	Inchmoor
Y3.507	Queenmoor	**Y3.550**	Raithwaite	**Y3.595**	Kinsale
Y3.508	Grainton	**Y3.551**	Oakdale	**Y3.596**	Burnstone (ex Kilsyth)
Y3.509	Fenchurch	**Y3.552**	Wisbech	**Y3.597**	Waterland
Y3.510	Martin	**Y3.553**	Tarantia (ex Kirkfield)	**Y3.598**	Nidd
Y3.511	Glenmay	**Y3.554**	Dungeness		
Y3.512	Competitor	**Y3.555**	Venetia	**Y3.599**	Polyxena
Y3.513	Stamfordham				Helmsmuir
Y3.514	Llangorse	**Y3.556**	Cragside		
Y3.515	Margam Abbey		Kylestrome	**Y3.600**	Kendal Castle
Y3.516	Atlantic City			**Y3.601**	Lady Bertha
Y3.517	Saxon Briton	**Y3.557**	Polruan	**Y3.602**	Persier
Y3.518	Romsdalen	**Y3.558**	Reindeer	**Y3.603**	Ardgarth
Y3.519	Ella Sayer	**Y3.559**	Edernian		
Y3.520	Photinia	**Y3.560**	Cymrian	**Y3. 604**	Pelham
Y3.521	Enfield				Queen Alexandra
Y3.522	Athenic	**Y3.561**	Don		
Y3.523	Grelcaldy (ex Caldy)		Denby Grange	**Y3.605**	Maindy Bridge
Y3.524	Strathdee			**Y3.606**	Polmanter
Y3.525	Muirfield	**Y3.562**	Capelcourt (ex Hermia)	**Y3.607**	Victoria
		Y3.563	Samara	**Y3.608**	Kingsdyke
Y3.526	Dromonby	**Y3.564**	Astraea	**Y3.609**	Lord Stewart
	Adriatic	**Y3.565**	Antiope (ex Cragside)	**Y3.610**	Newtownard
		Y3.566	Addington	**Y3.611**	Pearl
Y3.527	Wragby	**Y3.567**	Millpool	**Y3.612**	Dalrazan
Y3.528	Standish Hall	**Y3.568**	Antaeus	**Y3.613**	Maureen
Y3.529	Medomsley	**Y3.569**	Alder	**Y3.614**	Tandil
Y3.530	Deddington	**Y3.570**	Molesey (ex Rokeby)	**Y3.615**	Larchgrove
Y3.531	Hartburn	**Y3.571**	Arranmore	**Y3.616**	Zurbaran
Y3.532	Woodburn	**Y3.572**	Woodville	**Y3.617**	Benlarig
Y3.533	Newburn	**Y3.573**	Westergate	**Y3.618**	Poldennis
Y3.534	Madeline	**Y3.574**	Longbenton	**Y3.619**	Polymnia
Y3.535	Craigendoran	**Y3.575**	Pontypridd	**Y3.620**	Avontown
Y3.536	Lullington	**Y3.576**	Jedmoor	**Y3.621**	Polandia
Y3.537	Tiverton			**Y3.622**	Polperro
Y3.538	Arvonian	**Y3.577**	Itonus	**Y3.623**	Bylands
Y3.539	Imperial		Zafra	**Y3.624**	Atherstone
				Y3.625	Montrose

Y3.626	Castle Eden	**Y3.668**	Knarsdale	**Y3.712**	Abercraig
Y3.627	Giralda		Moorgate	**Y3.713**	Levenpool
Y3.628	Cromarty			**Y3.714**	Sutherland
Y3.629	Renfrew (ex Galavale)	**Y3.669**	Dorisbrook	**Y3.715**	John H. Barry
Y3.630	Exmouth	**Y3.670**	Antinoe	**Y3.716**	Alatrium (ex Strathgyle)
Y3.631	Prophet	**Y3.671**	Harlech	**Y3.717**	Ardgour
Y3.632	Antar	**Y3.672**	Harlow	**Y3.718**	Amberton
Y3.633	Politania	**Y3.673**	Gregynog	**Y3.719**	Grelarlie (ex Rachel)
Y3.634	Ethelbryhta	**Y3.674**	De Fontaine	**Y3.720**	Ramsay
Y3.635	Rustington	**Y3.675**	Burriana	**Y3.721**	Ardgarry
Y3.636	Aislaby	**Y3.676**	Lavernock	**Y3.722**	Castleton
Y3.637	Ivanhoe	**Y3.677**	Crayford	**Y3.723**	Singleton Abbey
		Y3.678	Sherwood	**Y3.724**	Polwell
Y3.638	Trader	**Y3.679**	Hampstead	**Y3.725**	Turino
	Elvaston			**Y3.726**	Trojan
		Y3.680	Burrsfield	**Y3.727**	Maskinonge
			Strethendrick	**Y3.728**	Queen Adelaide
Y3.639	Heathside (ex Neilrose)				
Y3.640	Aviator (ex Victor)	**Y3.681**	August Belmont	**Y3.729**	Dalegarth
Y3.641	Clandeboye		(ex Delphinula)		Southgate
Y3.642	Rayford				Kilbride
Y3.643	Endcliffe	**Y3.682**	Everilda		
Y3.644	Carnalea	**Y3.683**	Cornhill	**Y3.730**	Ernaston
Y3.645	Sunniside	**Y3.684**	Wabana	**Y3.731**	Tusculum (ex Strathdon)
Y3.646	Calder	**Y3.685**	Remus	**Y3.732**	Luxemburg
Y3.647	Gibraltar	**Y3.686**	Borderer	**Y3.733**	Magdeburg
		Y3.687	Wathfield	**Y3.734**	Labicum (ex Strathblane)
Y3.648	Charing Cross	**Y3.688**	Don Cesar	**Y3.735**	Incemore
	John Hardie	**Y3.689**	Lexie	**Y3.736**	Brighton
		Y3.690	Highland Monarch	**Y3.737**	St Ninian
Y3.649	Whinhill	**Y3.691**	Cronstadt	**Y3.738**	Irish Monarch
Y3.650	Holgate	**Y3.692**	Dartmoor		
Y3.651	Gileston	**Y3.693**	Polzeath	**Y3.739**	Mackworth
		Y3.694	Baykerran (ex Kilkerran)		(ex Rugbeian)
Y3.652	Eptalofos	**Y3.695**	Rowena		
	Rio Tiete	**Y3.696**	Laxton	**Y3.740**	Barbara
		Y3.697	Reval	**Y3.741**	Induna
Y3.653	Emerald				
Y3.654	Grelrosa (ex Arosa)	**Y3.698**	Lady Iveagh	**Y3.742**	Olive Branch
Y3.655	Lorle		Lotusmere		(ex Bellorado)
Y3.656	Basuta				
		Y3.699	Kamouraska	**Y3.743**	Dunbarmoor
Y3.657	Ardoyne	**Y3.700**	Airedale	**Y3.744**	Hallamshire
	Linkmoor	**Y3.701**	Baldersby	**Y3.745**	Majorca
		Y3.702	Skerries	**Y3.746**	Apsleyhall (ex Newfield)
Y3.658	Domingo de Larringa	**Y3.703**	Kenilworth	**Y3.747**	Llanthony Abbey
	Inglemoor	**Y3.704**	Blackheath	**Y3.748**	Lord Antrim
Y3.659	Rossetti	**Y3.705**	Waddon	**Y3.749**	Stagpool
Y3.660	Hebburn	**Y3.706**	Advent	**Y3.750**	Cardiff Hall
Y3.661	Hockwold	**Y3.707**	Upcerne	**Y3.751**	Elford
Y3.662	Moorby	**Y3.708**	Ethelhilda	**Y3.752**	Earl of Forfar
Y3.663	Manchester Inventor	**Y3.709**	Queen	**Y3.753**	Henry R. James
Y3.664	Belge	**Y3.710**	Broomfield	**Y3.754**	City
Y3.665	Francia			**Y3.755**	Highcliffe
Y3.666	Plutus	**Y3.711**	Sheaf Brook	**Y3.756**	Lord Dufferin
Y3.667	Winga		(ex Coniston)	**Y3.757**	Duneric
				Y3.758	Reresby

Y3.759	William Balls	**Y3.805**	Visigoth	**Y3.843**	Maltby
	Ocean Transport	**Y3.806**	Lynorra	**Y3.844**	Ilderton
		Y3.807	Bellasco	**Y3.845**	Hannah
Y3.760	Lunesdale	**Y3.808**	Cambrian King		
Y3.761	Benheather			**Y3.846**	Swift Wings
Y3.762	Eastlands	**Y3.809**	Eptapyrgion		(ex Watermouth)
Y3.763	Charterhouse		(ex Essex Baron)		
Y3.764	Lorca			**Y3.847**	Pacific
Y3.765	Dominion	**Y3.810**	Pentwyn	**Y3.848**	Anglier
Y3.766	Cordova	**Y3.811**	Lynfield	**Y3.849**	Germanic
				Y3.850	North Wales
Y3.767	Australplain	**Y3.812**	Apollo	**Y3.851**	Marmion
	(ex Ardanmhor)		Wyvisbrook	**Y3.852**	St Winifred
				Y3.853	Swan River
Y3.768	Fernley	**Y3.813**	Stream Fisher	**Y3.854**	Groeswen
Y3.769	Ocean Transport	**Y3.814**	Chelston	**Y3.855**	Manchester Mariner
Y3.770	Demeterton	**Y3.815**	Asuncion de Larrinaga	**Y3.856**	Poltava
Y3.771	African Monarch	**Y3.816**	Grantleyhall	**Y3.857**	Lady Carrington
	Southville		Farnborough		(ex Kilnsea)
Y3.772	Albuera	**Y3.817**	Arabis	**Y3.858**	Hebburn
Y3.773	Shadwell	**Y3.818**	Kyleakin		Sneaton
Y3.774	Meldon	**Y3.819**	Ferryhill		
Y3.775	Pola	**Y3.820**	Jerseyman	**Y3.859**	Farnborough
Y3.776	Hollington	**Y3.821**	Luchana		North Wales
Y3.777	Maresfield	**Y3.822**	Tarbetness		
Y3.778	Balboa			**Y3.860**	Polkerris
Y3.779	Cliftonian	**Y3.823**	Ikala	**Y3.861**	Windsor Hall
Y3.780	Isle of Mull		Ben Vrackie	**Y3.862**	Lowlands
Y3.781	Crown of Cordova			**Y3.863**	Braeside
Y3.782	Boveric	**Y3.824**	Tana	**Y3.864**	Cape Ortegal
Y3.783	Oceano	**Y3.825**	Paragon	**Y3.865**	Wirral
Y3.784	Bilbster	**Y3.826**	Silverfield	**Y3.866**	Imani
Y3.785	Inverbervie	**Y3.827**	Northumbria	**Y3.867**	Eastcheap
Y3.786	Boltonhall	**Y3.828**	Halton	**Y3.868**	Cheshire
Y3.787	Hanley	**Y3.829**	Gorsemore	**Y3.869**	Blush Rose
Y3.788	Strathbeg	**Y3.830**	King George	**Y3.870**	Penrose
Y3.789	Policastria	**Y3.831**	Polglass Castle	**Y3.871**	Bellucia
Y3.790	Cragoswald	**Y3.832**	Polesley	**Y3.872**	Netherlee
Y3.791	Querida	**Y3.833**	Rio Claro	**Y3.873**	Manchester Trader
Y3.792	Jumna	**Y3.834**	Katherine	**Y3.874**	Flixton
Y3.793	Hurst	**Y3.835**	Polpedn	**Y3.875**	Oakmere
Y3.794	Greatham	**Y3.836**	Frankenfels	**Y3.876**	Glenisla
Y3.795	St Stephen	**Y3.837**	Ariosto		
Y3.796	Ennismore	**Y3.838**	Jane Radcliffe	**Y3.877**	Manchester Engineer
Y3.797	Majestic				(ex Nation)
Y3.798	Hounslow (ex Barton)	**Y3.839**	Australstream		
Y3.799	Rio Pallaresa		(ex Daltonhall)	**Y3.878**	Frinton
Y3.800	Clivegrove			**Y3.879**	Glenelg
		Y3.840	Peebles	**Y3.880**	Maude Larssen
Y3.801	Lundy Island			**Y3.881**	Rio Lages
	(ex Darleydale)	**Y3.841**	Yser	**Y3.882**	Edendale
			(ex Cayo Manzanillo)		
Y3.802	Clumberhall		Slavonic	**Y3.883**	Bellbank
Y3.803	Haworth				(ex Castle Bruce)
Y3.804	Barlby	**Y3.842**	Atlas		

Y3.884	*Katanga*	**Y3.935**	*Rosalie*	**Y3.978**	*Gerent*
Y3.885	*Copsewood*	**Y3.936**	*Ribbledale*	**Y3.979**	*Hidalgo*
Y3.886	*Dorothy*	**Y3.937**	*Thistleban*	**Y3.980**	*Rochdale*
Y3.887	*Coila*	**Y3.938**	*Newstead*	**Y3.981**	*The Sultan*
		Y3.939	*Tritonia*	**Y3.982**	*Riverdale*
Y3.888	*Kelvinbank*	**Y3.940**	*City of Frankfort*	**Y3.983**	*Penylan*
	(ex *Drumcliffe*)			**Y3.984**	*Lord Roberts*
		Y3.941	*Orfordness*	**Y3.985**	*Tartary*
Y3.889	*Cedar Branch*		(ex *Blackfriar Gate*)	**Y3.986**	*Balgray*
Y3.890	*St Theodore*			**Y3.987**	*Corby*
Y3.891	*Polbain*	**Y3.942**	*South Pacific*	**Y3.988**	*Barrowmore*
Y3.892	*Roselea*	**Y3.943**	*Ribston*	**Y3.989**	*Malakuta*
Y3.893	*Manchester Port*	**Y3.944**	*Firfield*	**Y3.990**	*Warley Pickering*
Y3.894	*Wearside*	**Y3.945**	*Glenfinlas*	**Y3.991**	*Diligent*
Y3.895	*Ethelinda* (ex *Brooklet*)	**Y3.946**	*Ocean Prince*	**Y3.992**	*Camlake*
Y3.896	*Chingford*	**Y3.947**	*Mabel Baird*	**Y3.993**	*Munificent*
Y3.897	*Zoroaster*			**Y3.994**	*Brabandier*
Y3.898	*Dartmore*	**Y3.948**	*Antigua*	**Y3.995**	*Dallington*
Y3.899	*Algethi*		*Ulidia*	**Y3.996**	*Bramham*
Y3.900	*Webburn*			**Y3.997**	*Grelben* (ex *Reliance*)
Y3.901	*Huttonwood*	**Y3.949**	*Hildawell*	**Y3.998**	*Sarah Radcliffe*
		Y3.950	*Erroll*	**Y3.999**	*Elmmoor*
Y3.902	*Nettleton*				
	Arabier	**Y3.951**	*Clan MacNiel*	**Y3.1000**	*Alexander Wentzell*
			Farringford		*Westlands*
Y3.903	*Benlawers*				
Y3.904	*Bencleuch*	**Y3.952**	*Rosehill*	**Y3.1001**	*Dalemoor*
Y3.905	*Woodbridge*	**Y3.953**	*Jet* (ex *Aydon*)	**Y3.1002**	*Warnow*
Y3.906	*Walnut*	**Y3.954**	*Ghazee*	**Y3.1003**	*African Transport*
Y3.907	*Fairfield*	**Y3.955**	*Ariel*	**Y3.1004**	*Cape Finisterre*
Y3.908	*Clan Macintosh*	**Y3.956**	*Bassano*	**Y3.1005**	*Crown of Leon*
Y3.909	*Lingfield*	**Y3.957**	*Auckland Castle*	**Y3.1006**	*Leucadia*
Y3.910	*Maria de Larrinaga*	**Y3.958**	*Argo*	**Y3.1007**	*Woron*
Y3.911	*Sebek*	**Y3.959**	*Potomac*	**Y3.1008**	*Valentia*
Y3.912	*Semantha*	**Y3.960**	*Harmattan*		
Y3.913	*Enosis*	**Y3.961**	*Favonian*	**Y3.1009**	*Abydos*
Y3.914	*Treverbyn*	**Y3.962**	*Huntstrick*		*Kowarra*
Y3.915	*Wavelet*	**Y3.963**	*Brantingham*		
Y3.916	*Cressington Court*	**Y3.964**	*Glenetive*	**Y3.1010**	*Whitehall*
Y3.917	*Doonholm*	**Y3.965**	*Morazan*	**Y3.1011**	*J.Y. Short*
Y3.918	*Headley*	**Y3.966**	*Esneh*	**Y3.1012**	*Fairmuir*
Y3.919	*Overdale*	**Y3.967**	*Clydesdale*	**Y3.1013**	*Camberwell*
Y3.920	*Greldon*	**Y3.968**	*Cardiff*	**Y3.1014**	*Australia*
Y3.921	*Gartland*			**Y3.1015**	*Andoni*
Y3.922	*Allie*	**Y3.969**	*Lemnos*	**Y3.1016**	*Frederick Knight*
Y3.923	*Newtown*		*Caithness*	**Y3.1017**	*Antinous*
Y3.924	*Warrior*			**Y3.1018**	*Eveline*
Y3.925	*Belgier*	**Y3.970**	*Silverton*	**Y3.1019**	*Lena*
Y3.926	*Glentilt*		*Clan Murray*	**Y3.1020**	*Whateley Hall*
Y3.927	*Sargasso*			**Y3.1021**	*Avessac*
Y3.928	*Hyndford*	**Y3.971**	*Birchgrove*	**Y3.1022**	*Ferndene*
Y3.929	*City of Swansea*	**Y3.972**	*Don Emilio*	**Y3.1023**	*Waltham*
Y3.930	*Dalton*	**Y3.973**	*Chertsey* (ex *Reynolds*)	**Y3.1024**	*Buxton*
Y3.931	*Longhirst*	**Y3.974**	*Strathearn*	**Y3.1025**	*Trewyn*
Y3.932	*Scatwell* (ex *Maisie*)	**Y3.975**	*Blairhall*	**Y3.1026**	*Maplewood*
Y3.933	*Curran*	**Y3.976**	*Wallace*	**Y3.1027**	*Queen Amelie*
Y3.934	*Cyrene*	**Y3.977**	*Wileysike*	**Y3.1028**	*Lord Sefton*

Y3.1029 *Othello*	**Y3.1083** *Seatonia*	**Y3.1137** *Spermina*
Y3.1030 *Regis*	**Y3.1084** *Whitecourt*	**Y3.1138** *Mokta*
Y3.1031 *Baron Dalmeny*	**Y3.1085** *Norman Monarch*	**Y3.1139** *Clearway*
Y3.1032 *Oransay*	**Y3.1086** *Madryn*	**Y3.1140** *Astoria*
Y3.1033 *Southwark*	**Y3.1087** *Hunsbridge*	**Y3.1141** *Argyll*
Y3.1034 *Cluden*	**Y3.1088** *Nunima*	**Y3.1142** *Trewellard*
Y3.1035 *T.R. Thompson*	**Y3.1089** *Steelville*	**Y3.1143** *Grelstone* (ex *Eddystone*)
	Y3.1090 *Magdala*	**Y3.1144** *Trecarne*
Y3.1036 *Spondilus*	**Y3.1091** *Kirkdale*	**Y3.1145** *Zeno*
(ex *Berwindmoor*)	**Y3.1092** *Vauxhall*	**Y3.1146** *Albistan*
	Y3.1093 *Horngarth*	
Y3.1037 *Brookwood*	**Y3.1094** *Luciston*	**Y3.1147** *Girdleness*
Y3.1038 *Foylemore*	**Y3.1095** *Gyp*	(ex *Grelisle*, ex *Rockabill*)
Y3.1039 *Glodale*	**Y3.1096** *Etolia*	
Y3.1040 *Penvearn*	**Y3.1097** *Chertsey* (ex *Dunbar*)	**Y3.1148** *Easingwold*
Y3.1041 *Tyne*	**Y3.1098** *Kassanga*	**Y3.1149** *Kenora*
Y3.1042 *Willow Branch*	**Y3.1099** *Millicent Knight*	**Y3.1150** *Berwen* (ex *Beethoven*)
Y3.1043 *Zillah*	**Y3.1100** *Harewood*	**Y3.1151** *Don Benito*
Y3.1044 *Domira*	**Y3.1101** *Weardale*	**Y3.1152** *Trowbridge*
Y3.1045 *Fraser River*		**Y3.1153** *Barrister* (ex *St Hugo*)
Y3.1046 *Dart*	**Y3.1102** *Polish Monarch*	**Y3.1154** *Gambia River*
Y3.1047 *Romford*	*Polmont*	**Y3.1155** *Isleworth* (ex *Eversley*)
Y3.1048 *Romanby*		**Y3.1156** *Rosebank*
Y3.1049 *Perugia*	**Y3.1103** *Lucent*	**Y3.1157** *Iolo*
Y3.1050 *Glenlochy*	**Y3.1104** *Janeta*	**Y3.1158** *Trevose*
Y3.1051 *Baron Herries*	**Y3.1105** *Etton*	**Y3.1159** *Hurlford*
Y3.1052 *Clan Keith* (ex *Etonian*)	**Y3.1106** *Glenmorag*	**Y3.1160** *Ben Venue*
Y3.1053 *Volnay*	**Y3.1107** *Taplow* (ex *Talevera*)	**Y3.1161** *Coniston Water*
Y3.1054 *Trekieve*	**Y3.1108** *Almerian*	**Y3.1162** *Brilliant*
Y3.1055 *Haxby*	**Y3.1109** *Hocking*	**Y3.1163** *Waverley*
Y3.1056 *Artificer*	**Y3.1110** *Hamborn*	**Y3.1164** *Cameron*
Y3.1057 *Sabia*	**Y3.1111** *Queen Helena*	**Y3.1165** *Ribera*
Y3.1058 *Eltham*	**Y3.1112** *Killellan*	**Y3.1166** *Irismere*
Y3.1059 *Juliston*	**Y3.1113** *Northville*	**Y3.1167** *Mohacsfield*
Y3.1060 *T. G. Hutton*	**Y3.1114** *Queenswood*	**Y3.1168** *Mavisbrook*
Y3.1061 *Irina*	**Y3.1115** *Newholm*	**Y3.1169** *Pera*
Y3.1062 *Erika*	**Y3.1116** *Kilwinning*	**Y3.1170** *Badminton*
Y3.1063 *Yarborough*	**Y3.1117** *Normandier*	**Y3.1171** *Quito*
Y3.1064 *Alabama*	**Y3.1118** *Eric Calvert*	**Y3.1172** *F. Matarazzo*
Y3.1065 *Dauntless*	**Y3.1119** *Joseph Davis*	**Y3.1173** *Ellind*
Y3.1066 *Wearpool*	**Y3.1120** *Amplegarth*	**Y3.1174** *Kingfield*
Y3.1067 *Tredegar Hall*	**Y3.1121** *Kathleen*	**Y3.1175** *Llandrindod*
Y3.1068 *Baron Garioch*	**Y3.1122** *Khephren*	**Y3.1176** *Sturton*
Y3.1069 *Clodmoor*	**Y3.1123** *Ethelwynne*	**Y3.1177** *Sutlej*
Y3.1070 *City of Lucknow*	**Y3.1124** *Araby*	**Y3.1178** *Bedeburn*
Y3.1071 *Leeds City*	**Y3.1125** *Holmsbank*	**Y3.1179** *Sandhurst*
Y3.1072 *Islandmore*	**Y3.1126** *Carisbrook*	**Y3.1180** *Carperby*
Y3.1073 *Pretoria*	**Y3.1127** *Rothley*	**Y3.1181** *Trefusis*
Y3.1074 *Oakfield*	**Y3.1128** *Maidan*	**Y3.1182** *Glensloy*
Y3.1075 *Bulgarian*	**Y3.1129** *Don Diego*	**Y3.1183** *Trieste*
Y3.1076 *Calliope*	**Y3.1130** *Tunstall*	**Y3.1184** *Pollcrea*
Y3.1077 *Llanberis*	**Y3.1131** *Perla*	**Y3.1185** *Middleham Castle*
Y3.1078 *Instructor* (ex *St Dunstan*)	**Y3.1132** *Loos*	**Y3.1186** *Campus*
Y3.1079 *Swedish Prince*	**Y3.1133** *Zambesi*	**Y3.1187** *Longscar*
Y3.1080 *Llangollen*	**Y3.1134** *Iser*	**Y3.1188** *Aldworth*
Y3.1081 *Rytonhall* (ex *St Helena*)	**Y3.1135** *Paliki*	**Y3.1189** *Wordsworth*
Y3.1082 *Woolston*	**Y3.1136** *Bellerby*	**Y3.1190** *Huelva*

Y3.1191 *Faxfleet*	Y3.1248 *Bonvilston*	Y3.1303 *Oola*
Y3.1192 *Hardanger*	Y3.1249 *Kingsmere*	Y3.1304 *Waterville*
Y3.1193 *Chatton*	Y3.1250 *Seattle*	Y3.1305 *Manica*
Y3.1194 *Ness*	Y3.1251 *Sandsend*	Y3.1306 *Trentham Hall*
Y3.1195 *Scaldier*	Y3.1252 *Teespool*	
Y3.1196 *Archbank*	Y3.1253 *Canganian*	Y3.1307 *Cayo Bonito*
Y3.1197 *Palermo*	Y3.1254 *Clearpool*	(ex *Caledonier*)
Y3.1198 *Jutland*	Y3.1255 *Wearbridge*	
Y3.1199 *Twilight*	Y3.1256 *Treleigh*	Y3.1308 *Southina*
Y3.1200 *Aberlour*	Y3.1257 *Redbridge*	Y3.1309 *Alston*
Y3.1201 *Horsa*	Y3.1258 *Glenaffric*	Y3.1310 *Roselands*
Y3.1202 *Duffield*	Y3.1259 *Arum*	Y3.1311 *Snowdon*
Y3.1203 *Rollesby*	Y3.1260 *Refugio*	Y3.1312 *Belgravian*
Y3.1204 *Frankier*	Y3.1261 *Cliftondale*	Y3.1313 *Junin*
Y3.1205 *Framlington Court*	Y3.1262 *Sicilia*	Y3.1314 *Mercuria*
Y3.1206 *Alexa*	Y3.1263 *Chiverstone*	Y3.1315 *Mountby*
Y3.1207 *Burevestnik*	Y3.1264 *Nyanza*	Y3.1316 *Heronspool*
Y3.1208 *Claudius Aulagnon*	Y3.1265 *Tycho*	Y3.1317 *Elmsgarth*
Y3.1209 *Egret*	Y3.1266 *Vigo*	Y3.1318 *Dailwen* (ex *Mozart*)
Y3.1210 *Graf Stroganoff*	Y3.1267 *Grelgrant* (ex *Hartland*)	Y3.1319 *Port Colborne*
Y3.1211 *Hansley*	Y3.1268 *Gasconia*	Y3.1320 *Elmtree*
Y3.1212 *Rossia*	Y3.1269 *Saxilby*	Y3.1321 *Hova*
Y3.1213 *Bonawe*	Y3.1270 *Tammerfors*	Y3.1322 *Birdoswald*
Y3.1214 *Morinier*	Y3.1271 *Westbury*	Y3.1323 *Arnewood*
Y3.1215 *Axminster*	Y3.1272 *Rosefield*	
Y3.1216 *Kintail*	Y3.1273 *Clan Macfadyen*	Y3.1324 *Vickerstown*
Y3.1217 *Hopemoor*	Y3.1274 *Cadmus*	(ex *Turret Chief*)
Y3.1218 *Sagenite*	Y3.1275 *Usher*	
Y3.1219 *Sigrid*	Y3.1276 *Minieh*	Y3.1325 *Mansuri*
Y3.1220 *Grindon Hall*		Y3.1326 *East Wales*
Y3.1221 *Hatumet*	Y3.1277 *Mount Etna*	
Y3.1222 *General Suworow*	*Dalecrest*	Y3.1327 *Panayiotis*
Y3.1223 *Alfalfa*		(ex *Essex Abbey*)
Y3.1224 *Gascony*	Y3.1278 *River Crake*	
Y3.1225 *Strathesk*	Y3.1279 *Langholm*	Y3.1329 *Mexico City*
Y3.1226 *Horden*	Y3.1280 *Sommiena* (ex *Tanagra*)	Y3.1330 *Cheltonian*
Y3.1227 *Phoebe*	Y3.1281 *Tuskar*	Y3.1331 *Glenbridge*
Y3.1228 *Cerera*	Y3.1282 *Algiers*	Y3.1332 *Alexandra*
Y3.1229 *St Gothard*	Y3.1283 *Farnham*	Y3.1333 *Ben Lomond*
Y3.1230 *Export*	Y3.1284 *Jerseymoor*	Y3.1334 *Berwindvale*
Y3.1231 *Hellenes*	Y3.1285 *Elswick Tower*	Y3.1335 *Dunclutha*
Y3.1232 *Bjarmia*	Y3.1286 *Eavestone*	Y3.1336 *Elswick Manor*
Y3.1233 *Patria*	Y3.1287 *Breconian*	Y3.1337 *Wharfedale*
Y3.1338 *Newona*	Y3.1288 *Wandby*	Y3.1338 *West Marsh*
Y3.1235 *Glenfoyle*	Y3.1290 *Constantia*	Y3.1339 *Erlesburgh*
Y3.1236 *Burnholme*	Y3.1291 *Navarino*	Y3.1340 *Queen Louise*
Y3.1237 *Etal Manor*	Y3.1292 *Fishpool*	Y3.1341 *American Transport*
Y3.1238 *Polanna*	Y3.1293 *Rhydwen*	Y3.1342 *Baron Jedburgh*
Y3.1239 *Trevessa*	Y3.1294 *Montenegro*	Y3.1343 *Crown of Toledo*
Y3.1240 *Alesia*	Y3.1295 *Dundrennan*	Y3.1344 *Caldergrove*
Y3.1241 *Ledbury*	Y3.1296 *Frixos*	Y3.1345 *Megna*
Y3.1242 *Dewa*	Y3.1297 *Calliope*	Y3.1346 *Nurtureton*
Y3.1243 *Yonne*	Y3.1298 *Santaren*	Y3.1347 *Polvena*
Y3.1244 *Haigh Hall*	Y3.1299 *Clan Alpine*	Y3.1348 *Wanstead*
Y3.1245 *Westonby*	Y3.1300 *Westgate*	Y3.1349 *Hyanthes*
Y3.1246 *Dowlais*	Y3.1301 *Poleric*	Y3.1350 *Capac*
Y3.1247 *Cymric Prince*	Y3.1302 *Westmoor*	Y3.1351 *Ussa*

Y3.1352 *Clan Macbride*	**Y3.1406** *Polladern*	**Y3.1460** *Clan Kennedy*
Y3.1353 *Coya*	**Y3.1407** *Artist*	(ex *Ardgarroch*)
Y3.1354 *Don Arturo*	**Y3.1408** *Baron Cawdor*	
Y3.1355 *Mersario*	**Y3.1409** *Nawab*	**Y3.1461** *Levnet*
Y3.1356 *Skipton Castle*	**Y3.1410** *Sweethope*	**Y3.1462** *Richard de Larringa*
Y3.1357 *Ribston*	**Y3.1411** *Biruta*	**Y3.1463** *Leonatus*
Y3.1358 *C. A. Jaques*	**Y3.1412** *Doretta* (ex *Freshet*)	**Y3.1464** *Irtysh*
Y3.1359 *Warren*	**Y3.1413** *Baron Fairlie*	**Y3.1465** *Trevethoe*
Y3.1360 *Sicily*	**Y3.1414** *Tynemouth*	**Y3.1466** *Saxon Monarch*
Y3.1361 *Barbary*	**Y3.1415** *Polamhall*	**Y3.1467** *Spithead*
Y3.1362 *Blackwell*	**Y3.1416** *Segontian*	**Y3.1468** *Uganda*
Y3.1363 *Hackensack*	**Y3.1417** *Polar Prince*	**Y3.1469** *Haileybury*
Y3.1364 *Red Cap*	**Y3.1418** *Oceana*	**Y3.1470** *Tafna*
Y3.1365 *Elleric*	**Y3.1419** *Aboukir*	**Y3.1471** *Vellore*
Y3.1366 *Glocliffe*	**Y3.1420** *Elgin*	**Y3.1472** *Saragossa*
Y3.1367 *Helredale*	**Y3.1421** *Okement*	**Y3.1473** *Agnes*
	Y3.1422 *Southern*	**Y3.1474** *Rocio*
Y3.1368 *Norma Pratt*	**Y3.1423** *Tasmanian Transport*	**Y3.1475** *Palm Branch*
(ex *Silvercedar*)	**Y3.1424** *St Patrick*	**Y3.1476** *Orator* (ex *Fillans*)
	Y3.1425 *Baron Ogilvy*	**Y3.1477** *Rio Preto*
Y3.1369 *Nora*	**Y3.1426** *Gledhow*	**Y3.1478** *Gloria de Larrinaga*
Y3.1370 *Adenwen*	**Y3.1427** *Nascent*	**Y3.1479** *Ellawood*
Y3.1371 *Kohistan*	**Y3.1428** *Barunga*	**Y3.1480** *Yorkmoor*
Y3.1372 *Rutherglen*	**Y3.1429** *Bakara*	**Y3.1481** *Sheaf Don*
Y3.1373 *Algeriana*	**Y3.1430** *Novorossia*	**Y3.1482** *Brodliffe*
Y3.1374 *Cheviot Range*	**Y3.1431** *Pinemore*	**Y3.1483** *Taiyabi*
Y3.1375 *Erinier*	**Y3.1432** *Marwarri*	**Y3.1484** *Harbury*
Y3.1376 *Silsden*	**Y3.1433** *Leda*	**Y3.1485** *Cilurnum*
Y3.1377 *Sellasia*		**Y3.1486** *Brodness*
Y3.1378 *Yearby*	**Y3.1434** *Grelhead*	**Y3.1487** *Salient*
Y3.1379 *Nuceria*	(ex *Beachy Head*)	**Y3.1488** *Falls City*
Y3.1380 *Lynton Grange*		**Y3.1489** *Ikalis*
Y3.1381 *Greenbank*	**Y3.1435** *Dara*	**Y3.1490** *Greystoke Castle*
Y3.1382 *Bertrand*	**Y3.1436** *Rapidan*	**Y3.1491** *Eurydamas*
Y3.1383 *Egyptiana* (ex *Sandown*)	**Y3.1437** *Noelle* (ex *Bronze Wings*)	**Y3.1492** *Myrmidon*
Y3.1384 *Tenasserim*	**Y3.1438** *River Forth*	
Y3.1385 *Umona*	**Y3.1439** *Farley*	**Y3.1493** *Holm's Island*
Y3.1386 *Herakles*	**Y3.1440** *Howth Head*	(ex *Grelford*)
Y3.1387 *Trio*	**Y3.1441** *Hylas*	
Y3.1388 *Romera*	**Y3.1442** *Gordon Castle*	**Y3.1494** *Rockpool*
Y3.1389 *Knight Companion*	**Y3.1443** *Crown of Seville*	**Y3.1495** *Tiberia*
Y3.1390 *Arabis*	**Y3.1444** *Alton*	**Y3.1496** *Willaston*
Y3.1391 *Llangorse* (ex *Llanover*)	**Y3.1445** *Minnie de Larrinaga*	**Y3.1497** *King Idwal*
Y3.1392 *Brisbane River*	**Y3.1446** *Antonio* (ex *Lundy*)	**Y3.1498** *Patagonier*
Y3.1393 *Livingstonia*	**Y3.1447** *Trehawke*	**Y3.1499** *Polgowan*
Y3.1394 *Mashobra*	**Y3.1448** *Clan Macpherson*	**Y3.1500** *Pendragon Castle*
Y3.1395 *Confield*	**Y3.1449** *Murcia*	**Y3.1501** *Carlow Castle*
Y3.1396 *Port Curtis*	**Y3.1450** *Monarch*	**Y3.1502** *Gena*
Y3.1397 *Chatham* (ex *Eastville*)	**Y3.1451** *Sculptor*	**Y3.1503** *Penlee*
Y3.1398 *Tempus*	**Y3.1452** *Bilswood*	**Y3.1504** *Arachne*
Y3.1399 *Endymion*	**Y3.1453** *Eskmere*	**Y3.1505** *Pathan*
Y3.1400 *Clan Forbes*	**Y3.1454** *Hermes*	**Y3.1506** *Merioneth*
Y3.1401 *Monkshaven*	**Y3.1455** *Umba*	**Y3.1507** *Kildale*
Y3.1402 *Baron Minto*	**Y3.1456** *Bracondale*	**Y3.1508** *St Michael*
Y3.1403 *Garryvale*	**Y3.1457** *Australier*	**Y3.1509** *Bernard*
Y3.1404 *Great City*	**Y3.1458** *Silverdale*	**Y3.1510** *Polvarth*
Y3.1405 *Trongate*	**Y3.1459** *Ant Cassar*	**Y3.1511** *Luis*

Y3.1512 Lowtyne	Y3.1569 Pancras	Y3.1626 Seapool
Y3.1513 Agenoria	Y3.1570 Ocean Monarch	Y3.1627 Empress
Y3.1514 Delphic	Y3.1571 Queen Margaret	Y3.1628 York Castle
Y3.1515 Maylands	Y3.1572 Anglo-Canadian	Y3.1629 Hazelwood
Y3.1516 Largo Law	Y3.1573 Condor	Y3.1630 North Pacific
Y3.1517 Ascot	Y3.1574 Reading	Y3.1631 Dee
Y3.1518 Sorata	Y3.1575 Hartley	Y3.1632 Annetta
Y3.1519 Uskmoor	Y3.1576 Tung Shan	Y3.1633 Kepwickhall
Y3.1520 Wilster	Y3.1577 Eider	Y3.1634 Trevilley
Y3.1521 Ardgrange	Y3.1578 Ballogie	Y3.1635 Dalegarth Force
Y3.1522 Elswick Lodge	Y3.1579 Canara	Y3.1636 Eaton Hall
Y3.1523 Merionethshire	Y3.1580 Vistula	Y3.1637 Birkhall
Y3.1524 Lodaner	Y3.1581 Umtali	Y3.1638 Prairial
Y3.1525 Manchester Commerce	Y3.1582 Hartfield	Y3.1639 Herschel
Y3.1526 Monadnock	Y3.1583 Glenrazan	Y3.1640 Vimiera
Y3.1527 Gregory	Y3.1584 Lingan	Y3.1641 Derwent River
Y3.1528 Marchioness of Bute	Y3.1585 Claveresk	Y3.1642 Mountcharles
Y3.1529 British Monarch	Y3.1586 Chalister	Y3.1643 Allanton
Y3.1530 Hesperus	Y3.1587 Belle of England	Y3.1644 Huntsclyde
Y3.1531 Izaston	Y3.1588 Grangetown	Y3.1645 Twickenham
Y3.1532 Iperia	Y3.1589 Carmarthen	Y3.1646 Cloutsham
Y3.1533 Lugano	Y3.1590 Hostilius	Y3.1647 Clan Macbeth
Y3.1534 Iolanthe	Y3.1591 Rounton Grange	Y3.1648 Achlibster
Y3.1535 Elpenor	Y3.1592 Glenorchy	Y3.1649 Ben Nevis
Y3.1536 Border Knight	Y3.1593 Oder	Y3.1650 Lord Charlemont
Y3.1537 Eustace	Y3.1594 Hebble	Y3.1651 Reims
Y3.1538 Sirius	Y3.1595 Wilberforce	Y3.1652 Bessarabia
Y3.1539 Alconda	Y3.1596 Adalia	Y3.1653 Flawyi
Y3.1540 Honorius	Y3.1597 Rossano	Y3.1654 Ethelaric
Y3.1541 Clan MacDougall	Y3.1598 Riverton	Y3.1655 Baron Ardrossan
Y3.1542 African Prince	Y3.1599 Canadian Transport	Y3.1656 Canastota
Y3.1543 Glenshiel	Y3.1600 Trelyon	Y3.1657 Henley
Y3.1544 Eastcliffe	Y3.1601 Pontwen	Y3.1658 War Cross
Y3.1545 Kalimba	Y3.1602 Snowdonian	Y3.1659 War Patrol
Y3.1546 Troutpool	Y3.1603 New Zealand Transport	Y3.1660 John Sanderson
Y3.1547 City of Dunkirk	Y3.1604 Rose Castle	Y3.1661 Blake
Y3.1548 Bellagio	Y3.1605 Clan Sinclair	Y3.1662 Harlem
Y3.1549 Crosby Hall	Y3.1606 Mercedes de Larrinaga	Y3.1663 Clan Maclachlan
Y3.1550 Chatham (ex Clifton)	Y3.1607 Algol	Y3.1664 Clan Robertson
Y3.1551 Mombassa	Y3.1608 Soroka	Y3.1665 Pearlmoor
Y3.1552 Wilton	Y3.1609 Frank Parish	Y3.1666 Seistan
Y3.1553 Appenine	Y3.1610 North Point	Y3.1667 Lord Derby
Y3.1554 Celia	Y3.1611 Muncaster Castle	Y3.1668 Ganges
Y3.1555 Gryfevale	Y3.1612 Neotsfield (ex Ada)	Y3.1669 Uganda
Y3.1556 Roxburgh	Y3.1613 Ingleby	Y3.1670 Kafue
Y3.1557 Copenhagen	Y3.1614 Hawsker	Y3.1671 Jabiru
Y3.1558 Katharine Park	Y3.1615 Cotovia	Y3.1672 Foy
Y3.1559 Milo	Y3.1616 Islandia	Y3.1673 Queen Maud
Y3.1560 Helmsdale	Y3.1617 Quarrydene	Y3.1674 Inveran
Y3.1561 Chiswick	Y3.1618 Mineric	Y3.1675 Port Macquarie
Y3.1562 Author (ex St Egbert)	Y3.1619 Carmelite	Y3.1676 Skeldon
Y3.1563 Saba	Y3.1620 Afon Lliedi	Y3.1677 Clan Macaulay
Y3.1564 Susquehanna	Y3.1621 Elswick House	Y3.1678 Craonne
Y3.1565 Pansy	Y3.1622 Ardgryfe	Y3.1679 Magellan
Y3.1566 Betty	Y3.1623 Lowther Castle	Y3.1680 Albiana
Y3.1567 Clan Colquhoun	Y3.1624 Portrush	Y3.1681 Whimbrel
Y3.1568 Perim	Y3.1625 Pollensa	Y3.1683 Buccaneer

Y3.1684 Wimbledon	Y3.1736 Tynemede	Y3.1793 Uskmouth
Y3.1685 Fellside	Y3.1737 Panama Transport	Y3.1794 Primo
Y3.1686 Lord Strathcona	Y3.1738 Gallier	Y3.1795 Claro
Y3.1687 Hungerford	Y3.1739 Ilford	Y3.1796 North Sea
Y3.1688 Huntress	Y3.1740 Clan Urquhart	Y3.1797 Sizergh Castle
Y3.1689 Renvoyle	Y3.1741 Sutton Hall	Y3.1798 Daghild
Y3.1690 Siberian Prince	Y3.1742 Skegness (ex Polurrian)	Y3.1799 War Clover
Y3.1691 Chulmleigh	Y3.1743 Menapier	Y3.1800 Inverawe
Y3.1692 Student	Y3.1744 Nadejda	Y3.1801 Baron Cathcart
Y3.1693 Pacific Transport	Y3.1745 Kaiping	Y3.1802 Edenwood
Y3.1694 Florentino	Y3.1746 Theseus	Y3.1803 Poldown
Y3.1695 Clan Macnab	Y3.1747 Royal Sceptre	Y3.1804 Swazi
Y3.1696 Albatross	Y3.1748 Huntsgulf	Y3.1805 Clan Matheson
Y3.1697 Sorrento	Y3.1749 Earlswood	Y3.1806 Ormiston
Y3.1698 Helmsloch	Y3.1750 Bolton Castle	Y3.1807 Min
Y3.1699 Clifftower	Y3.1751 Butetown	Y3.1808 Swainby
Y3.1700 Shuna	Y3.1752 Pivoc	Y3.1809 Elwick
Y3.1701 Kintuck	Y3.1753 City of Madrid	Y3.1810 Newglyn
Y3.1702 Greleen	Y3.1754 Melville	Y3.1811 Greavesash
Y3.1703 Tourmaline	Y3.1755 Chimu	Y3.1812 Capelhall (ex Battenhall)
Y3.1704 Winnie	Y3.1756 Newlands	Y3.1813 Liddesdale
Y3.1706 Madura	Y3.1757 Clan Graham	Y3.1814 Polalp
Y3.1707 Cuirassier	Y3.1758 Matador (ex St Veronica)	Y3.1815 Clintonia
Y3.1708 Islanda	Y3.1759 Polbrae	Y3.1816 Darlington
Y3.1709 Echo	Y3.1760 Alicia	Y3.1817 Asiatic Prince
Y3.1710 Kalibia	Y3.1761 Hesleyside	Y3.1818 Chipana
Y3.1711 City of Cologne	Y3.1762 Marstonmoor	Y3.1819 Flandrier
Y3.1712 Huntshead	Y3.1763 Oldenburg	Y3.1820 Sui Sang
Y3.1713 Clareisland	Y3.1764 Capelpark (ex Rio Tinto)	Y3.1821 Verdun
Y3.1714 Ethelaida	Y3.1765 Suffolk Coast	Y3.1822 Antigone
Y3.1715 Graf Schuwalow	Y3.1766 Ujina	
Y3.1716 Odessa	Y3.1767 Almora	Y3.1823 Hazel Branch
Y3.1717 Gemini	Y3.1768 Elsiston	(ex Bellgrano)
Y3.1718 Aviemore	Y3.1769 Thurland Castle	
Y3.1719 Cape Transport	Y3.1770 Chelford	Y3.1824 Hyacinthus
Y3.1720 War Major	Y3.1771 Welsh Coast	Y3.1825 Orna
Y3.1721 War Queen	Y3.1772 Lancashire Coast	Y3.1826 Gresham
Y3.1722 War Shamrock	Y3.1773 Southport	Y3.1827 War Rose
Y3.1723 Melrose Abbey	Y3.1774 Westerham	Y3.1828 Rodskjaer
Y3.1724 Rio Verde	Y3.1775 Polcrest	Y3.1829 Gothic
Y3.1725 Dorington Court	Y3.1776 Fifetown (ex Blackburn)	Y3.1830 Franklin (ex Outpost)
Y3.1726 Anglo-Chilean	Y3.1777 Gwynwood	
	Y3.1778 Atlantic	Y3.1831 Frankburn
Y3.1727 Pentland Range	Y3.1779 Pendeen	(ex Robert Bruce)
(ex Kincraig)	Y3.1780 Patroclus	
	Y3.1781 Ben Lomond	Y3.1832 Petingaudet
Y3.1728 War Knight	Y3.1782 Western Coast	Y3.1833 Itola
Y3.1729 Branksome Hall	Y3.1783 Clan MacDonald	Y3.1834 Edith Cavell
Y3.1730 Campfield	Y3.1784 Boliviana	Y3.1835 Epsom
Y3.1731 Canadier	Y3.1785 Saldanha	Y3.1836 Nolisement
Y3.1732 Lord Byron	Y3.1786 Wladimir Sawin	Y3.1837 Tydeus
Y3.1733 War Tune	Y3.1787 Lord Erne	Y3.1838 War Prince
	Y3.1788 Egret	Y3.1839 Merton Hall
Y3.1734 Pennyworth	Y3.1789 Katie	Y3.1840 Corton
(ex Gogovale)	Y3.1790 Newhailes	Y3.1841 Bleamoor
	Y3.1791 Admiral Cochrane	Y3.1842 Glendevon
Y3.1735 Kurdistan	Y3.1792 River Orontes	Y3.1843 War Daffodil

Y3.1844 *War Flower*	**Y3.1901** *Brigitta*	**Y3.1958** *Biscaya*
Y3.1845 *Rose Marie*	**Y3.1902** *Drammenseren*	**Y3.1959** *Ambassador*
Y3.1846 *Orange River*	**Y3.1903** *War Dog*	**Y3.1960** *Saga*
Y3.1847 *Newminster Abbey*	**Y3.1904** *Clan MacKellar*	**Y3.1961** *Bamse*
Y3.1848 *Veturia*	**Y3.1905** *Adra*	**Y3.1962** *Ockenfels*
Y3.1849 *Burnhope*	**Y3.1906** *Polaria*	**Y3.1963** *Hunsbrook*
Y3.1850 *Foreric*	**Y3.1907** *Aparima*	**Y3.1964** *Princess Dagmar*
Y3.1851 *Nam Sang*	**Y3.1908** *War Baron*	**Y3.1965** *Edna*
Y3.1852 *Welbeck Hall*	**Y3.1909** *War Sailor*	**Y3.1966** *Munardan*
Y3.1853 *Chakrata*	**Y3.1910** *War Sword*	**Y3.1967** *P.L.M. 6*
Y3.1854 *War Trefoil*	**Y3.1911** *Egyptian Transport*	**Y3.1968** *Sibir*
Y3.1855 *Ashton*	**Y3.1912** *Ragni*	**Y3.1969** *War Myrtle*
Y3.1856 *Denpark*	**Y3.1913** *Anders*	**Y3.1970** *Normandiet*
Y3.1857 *Brynawel (ex Jedford)*	**Y3.1914** *Turnbridge*	**Y3.1971** *War Anenome*
Y3.1858 *Dunnet Head*	**Y3.1915** *Hamm*	**Y3.1972** *Earnholm*
Y3.1859 *Sarpen*	**Y3.1916** *Oreland*	**Y3.1973** *Firtree*
Y3.1860 *Holtby*	**Y3.1917** *Kirkholm*	**Y3.1974** *City of Liverpool*
Y3.1861 *Geddington Court*	**Y3.1918** *War Council*	**Y3.1975** *Regent*
Y3.1862 *Glennevis*	**Y3.1919** *Jason*	**Y3.1976** *Woodfield*
Y3.1863 *Ivydene*	**Y3.1920** *Barshaw*	**Y3.1977** *Clematis*
Y3.1864 *Trinidad*	**Y3.1921** *Mourino*	**Y3.1978** *Waheondah*
Y3.1865 *Lancer*	**Y3.1922** *Garthwaite*	**Y3.1979** *Sineus*
Y3.1866 *Benito (ex Falls of Nith)*	**Y3.1923** *General Church*	**Y3.1980** *Scartho*
Y3.1867 *Solo*	**Y3.1924** *Denbigh Hall*	**Y3.1981** *Tanafjord*
Y3.1868 *Anselma de Larringa*	**Y3.1925** *Rio Blanco*	**Y3.1982** *War Monarch*
Y3.1869 *Warkworth*	**Y3.1926** *Ellaston*	**Y3.1983** *Tintern Abbey*
Y3.1870 *Fernfield*	**Y3.1927** *Stend*	**Y3.1984** *Norriston*
Y3.1871 *Newbigging*	**Y3.1928** *Mercedes*	**Y3.1985** *Clan MacMaster*
Y3.1872 *Silver City*	**Y3.1929** *Andree*	**Y3.1986** *Petrograd*
Y3.1873 *St Leonards*	**Y3.1930** *Hornby Castle*	**Y3.1987** *Benguela*
Y3.1874 *Santa Theresa*	**Y3.1931** *Kathiamba*	**Y3.1988** *Krasnoiarsk*
Y3.1875 *Sunray*	**Y3.1932** *Norvo*	**Y3.1989** *Ruth*
Y3.1876 *Anglesea*	**Y3.1933** *Glen Gelder*	**Y3.1990** *Princetown*
Y3.1877 *Northford*	**Y3.1934** *Havildar*	**Y3.1991** *Fairy*
Y3.1878 *Finland*	**Y3.1935** *Mogileff*	**Y3.1992** *Clan Chattan*
Y3.1879 *Spanker*	**Y3.1936** *Fagertun*	**Y3.1993** *William O'Brien*
Y3.1880 *Hindustan*	**Y3.1937** *Lizzie*	**Y3.1994** *Austriafield*
Y3.1881 *Waihemo*	**Y3.1938** *Oliver*	**Y3.1995** *Buckleigh*
Y3.1882 *Demetian*	**Y3.1939** *Knowsley Hall*	**Y3.1996** *War Rambler*
Y3.1883 *War Cypress*	**Y3.1940** *Cranley*	**Y3.1997** *War Cuirass*
Y3.1884 *Cornish Point*	**Y3.1941** *Waimarino*	**Y3.1998** *Lorn Rhondda*
Y3.1885 *Ilvington Court*	**Y3.1942** *Devon City*	**Y3.1999** *Anne*
Y3.1886 *Aysgarth Force*	**Y3.1943** *War Song*	**Y3.2000** *War Country*
Y3.1887 *Tintoretto*	**Y3.1944** *George Fisher*	**Y3.2001** *War Wolf*
Y3.1888 *Rhodesian Transport*	**Y3.1945** *Finse*	**Y3.2002** *War Python*
Y3.1889 *Onda*	**Y3.1946** *Banne*	**Y3.2003** *Menelaus*
Y3.1890 *Fiscus*	**Y3.1947** *Skaraas*	**Y3.2004** *War Hero*
Y3.1891 *Ardgair*	**Y3.1948** *War Fish*	**Y3.2005** *War Tiger*
Y3.1892 *Gladiator*	**Y3.1949** *Ophir*	**Y3.2006** *Larpool*
Y3.1893 *Elm Park*	**Y3.1950** *Broompark*	**Y3.2007** *Verdanne*
Y3.1894 *Glenspean*	**Y3.1951** *Madame Alice*	**Y3.2008** *Brixham*
Y3.1895 *Ashton*	**Y3.1952** *Hercules*	**Y3.2009** *War Lion*
Y3.1896 *Sahara*	**Y3.1953** *Pink Rose*	**Y3.2010** *Wans Fell*
Y3.1897 *War Admiral*	**Y3.1954** *Dronning Maud*	**Y3.2011** *Madame Midas*
Y3.1898 *War Grange*	**Y3.1955** *Inverness*	**Y3.2012** *Cumbrian*
Y3.1899 *War Arabis*	**Y3.1956** *Pentyrch*	**Y3.2013** *Lochside*
Y3.1900 *Sagittarius*	**Y3.1957** *War Wasp*	**Y3.2014** *Ibis*

Y3.2015	Ardgancock	Y3.2067	Bruse	Y3.2123	Ailsa Craig
Y3.2016	Dunbridge	Y3.2068	Trader	Y3.2124	Comet
		Y3.2069	Isle of Lewis	Y3.2125	Newton
Y3.2017	Gibel-Derif	Y3.2070	Frankter	Y3.2126	The Countess
	Ladoga	Y3.2071	Rother	Y3.2127	Idraet
		Y3.2072	Lydia	Y3.2128	Luddick
Y3.2019	Estrella	Y3.2073	Fernandina	Y3.2129	Lochee
Y3.2020	Romney	Y3.2074	Sagama River	Y3.2130	Seagull
Y3.2021	Mount Snowdon	Y3.2075	Santa Isabel	Y3.2131	Hookroad
Y3.2022	Whinfield			Y3.2132	Hallgjerd
Y3.2023	White Rose	Y3.2076	Beckenham	Y3.2133	Orn
Y3.2024	Primrose		Smerdis	Y3.2134	Rusken
Y3.2025	Bretagne			Y3.2135	Ring
Y3.2026	Hopelyn	Y3.2078	Douglas	Y3.2136	Carrowdore
Y3.2027	Luxor	Y3.2079	Boldon	Y3.2137	Poljames
		Y3.2080	Keynes	Y3.2138	Landonia
Y3.2028	Gibel-Derif	Y3.2081	Nyland	Y3.2139	Phyllis
	Treneglos	Y3.2082	King's Lynn	Y3.2140	Blairmore
		Y3.2083	Capitol	Y3.2141	City of Brussels
Y3.2029	Fanny	Y3.2084	Oxshott	Y3.2142	Pandelis
Y3.2030	Maindy Court	Y3.2085	Polmina	Y3.2143	Polberg
Y3.2031	Eurymedon	Y3.2086	Beeswood	Y3.2144	War Barrage
Y3.2032	Sikh	Y3.2087	Surf	Y3.2145	Croxteth
Y3.2033	Sarpedon	Y3.2088	Linhope	Y3.2146	Enda
Y3.2034	Gibel-Hamam	Y3.2089	Albert Clement	Y3.2147	Erica
Y3.2035	Nosted I	Y3.2090	Moneyspinner	Y3.2148	Carol
Y3.2036	Morlais	Y3.2091	Wendy	Y3.2149	War Pointer
Y3.2037	Sedgepool	Y3.2092	The Princess	Y3.2150	Levensau
Y3.2038	Brandenburg	Y3.2093	Claremorris	Y3.2151	Nephrite
Y3.2039	City of Colombo	Y3.2094	Glenmaroon	Y3.2152	Clewbay
Y3.2040	Elba	Y3.2095	Kenilworth	Y3.2153	Mirjam
Y3.2041	Trafford Hall	Y3.2096	Kurdistan	Y3.2154	Hector
Y3.2042	Trafalgar	Y3.2097	Lightfoot	Y3.2155	Warlingham
Y3.2043	Albr. W. Selmer	Y3.2098	Stanja	Y3.2156	Teesdale
Y3.2044	Plawsworth	Y3.2099	Lucient	Y3.2157	Auricula
Y3.2045	Chevington	Y3.2101	Skinningrove	Y3.2158	Admiral Cordington
Y3.2046	Promus	Y3.2102	Calcaria	Y3.2159	Dublin
Y3.2047	Roishelm	Y3.2103	Fastnet	Y3.2160	Patricia
Y3.2048	Cresco	Y3.2104	Fleswick	Y3.2161	Hestmanden
Y3.2049	Anna Sofie	Y3.2105	Camden	Y3.2162	Arleia
Y3.2050	Begonia	Y3.2106	Longships	Y3.2163	Normandy
Y3.2051	War Cobra	Y3.2107	Zelo	Y3.2164	Volscian
Y3.2052	Notanda	Y3.2108	Fermia	Y3.2165	Denebola
Y3.2053	Freighter	Y3.2109	Polstream	Y3.2166	George Harper
Y3.2054	Vard	Y3.2110	Polleon	Y3.2168	Monmouth Coast
Y3.2055	Brand	Y3.2111	Effra (ex Broompark)	Y3.2169	Ursa
Y3.2056	Fortunatus	Y3.2112	Moidart	Y3.2170	Redruth
Y3.2057	Stokesley	Y3.2113	Grelwen	Y3.2171	Domino
Y3.2058	Kullaberg	Y3.2114	Hyson	Y3.2172	Glentaise
Y3.2059	Southwaite	Y3.2115	Huntscliff	Y3.2173	Huntball
Y3.2060	Betwa	Y3.2116	Lady Charlotte	Y3.2174	Zimorodok
Y3.2061	Florentia	Y3.2117	War Viper	Y3.2175	Hannington Court
Y3.2062	Penmount	Y3.2118	Pangim	Y3.2176	Poltolia
Y3.2063	Stryn	Y3.2119	Neva	Y3.2177	Luque
Y3.2064	Ino	Y3.2120	Duke of Cornwall	Y3.2178	Neebing
Y3.2065	Kildin	Y3.2121	Mile End	Y3.2179	Urpeth
Y3.2066	Clutha	Y3.2122	M.J. Craig	Y3.2180	Holmside

Y3.2181 *Iddo*	**Y3.2235** *Edith*	**Y3.2292** *War Kestrel*
Y3.2182 *Test*	**Y3.2236** *Ennistown*	**Y3.2293** *War Shell*
Y3.2183 *Kora*	**Y3.2237** *Hematite*	**Y3.2294** *War Spaniel*
Y3.2184 *Clonlee*	**Y3.2238** *War Panther*	**Y3.2295** *Sumatra*
Y3.2185 *Amatonga*	**Y3.2239** *Ethelstan*	**Y3.2296** *Glen Park*
Y3.2186 *Abereden*	**Y3.2240** *Australian Transport*	**Y3.2297** *Hartland Point*
Y3.2187 *Pruth*	**Y3.2241** *Fountains Abbey*	**Y3.2298** *Mary Aiston*
Y3.2188 *Scottish Prince*	**Y3.2242** *Buffs*	**Y3.2299** *War Roach*
Y3.2189 *War Dame*	**Y3.2243** *Colin Stuart*	**Y3.2300** *War Mansion*
Y3.2190 *Brenda*	**Y3.2244** *West Point*	**Y3.2301** *War Leopard*
Y3.2191 *Maindy Dene*	**Y3.2245** *War Battery*	**Y3.2302** *Kamenetz Podolsk*
Y3.2192 *War King*	**Y3.2246** *War Firth*	**Y3.2303** *Liberty*
Y3.2193 *Sunland*	**Y3.2247** *War Buffalo*	**Y3.2304** *War Monsoon*
Y3.2194 *River Araxes*	**Y3.2248** *War Stag*	**Y3.2305** *War Musket*
Y3.2195 *Ravenrock*	**Y3.2249** *War Loch*	**Y3.2306** *War Fife*
Y3.2196 *Southwood*	**Y3.2250** *Willingtonia*	**Y3.2307** *War Robin*
Y3.2197 *Rooke*	**Y3.2251** *War Armour*	**Y3.2308** *Auldmiur*
Y3.2198 *Ruel*	**Y3.2252** *War Jackdaw*	**Y3.2309** *Lowmoor*
Y3.2199 *Roseden*	**Y3.2253** *War Balloon*	**Y3.2310** *War Amazon*
Y3.2200 *War Pike*	**Y3.2254** *War Lemur*	
	Y3.2255 *Hunsworth*	**Y3.2311** *Mesopotamia*
Y3.2201 *Mount Berwyn*	**Y3.2256** *War Buckler*	(ex *Ardgowan*)
(ex *War Puma*)	**Y3.2257** *War Swallow*	
	Y3.2258 *Zurichmoor*	**Y3.2312** *Castlemoor*
Y3.2202 *War Gazelle*	**Y3.2259** *War Pibroch*	**Y3.2313** *War Deer*
Y3.2203 *War Glen*	**Y3.2260** *Clifton Grove*	**Y3.2314** *War Valley*
Y3.2204 *War Highway*	**Y3.2261** *War Vulture*	**Y3.2315** *War Coppice*
Y3.2205 *Rona*	**Y3.2262** *Aquarius*	**Y3.2316** *War Redcap*
Y3.2206 *Merida*	**Y3.2263** *Hunterfield*	**Y3.2317** *War Maxim*
Y3.2207 *Trevose*	**Y3.2264** *Bryntawe*	**Y3.2318** *Grorud*
Y3.2208 *Pawnee*	**Y3.2265** *War Torpedo*	**Y3.2319** *Ardgartan*
Y3.2209 *Pundit*	**Y3.2266** *Helga*	**Y3.2320** *Volga*
Y3.2210 *Novgorod*	**Y3.2267** *Heathpark*	**Y3.2321** *Lombok*
Y3.2211 *Foyle*	**Y3.2268** *Stanley Hall*	**Y3.2322** *Ryde*
Y3.2212 *Heron Bridge*	**Y3.2269** *Koursk*	**Y3.2323** *War Ostrich*
Y3.2213 *Trident*	**Y3.2270** *Vologda*	**Y3.2324** *War Mortar*
Y3.2214 *William Middleton*	**Y3.2271** *Waitemata*	**Y3.2325** *Marthara*
Y3.2215 *Mercurio*	**Y3.2272** *War Viceroy*	**Y3.2326** *Wisley*
Y3.2216 *Wellpark*	**Y3.2273** *War Tabard*	**Y3.2327** *Logician*
Y3.2217 *Kingfisher*	**Y3.2274** *Voronezh*	**Y3.2328** *War Crag*
Y3.2218 *Achroite*	**Y3.2275** *War Spray*	**Y3.2329** *War Hamlet*
Y3.2219 *Schieland*	**Y3.2276** *War Brae*	**Y3.2330** *Scottish Monarch*
Y3.2220 *Tellus*	**Y3.2277** *War Bagpipe*	**Y3.2331** *Venusia* (ex *War Snake*)
Y3.2221 *Manxman*	**Y3.2278** *Seabank*	**Y3.2332** *War Beach*
Y3.2222 *Idaho*	**Y3.2279** *Wilston*	**Y3.2333** *Valverda*
Y3.2223 *Polgarth*	**Y3.2280** *War Crocus*	**Y3.2334** *War Quail*
Y3.2224 *Blaamyra*	**Y3.2281** *Monarch*	**Y3.2335** *War Magpie*
Y3.2225 *Hopecrest*	**Y3.2282** *Dacapo*	**Y3.2336** *Bahadur*
Y3.2226 *Westhope*	**Y3.2283** *War Dance*	**Y3.2337** *War Island*
Y3.2227 *War Manor*	**Y3.2284** *War Isis*	**Y3.2338** *War Pigeon*
Y3.2228 *War Bison*	**Y3.2285** *Marrawa*	**Y3.2339** *War Cygnet*
Y3.2229 *War Setter*	**Y3.2286** *War Thistle*	**Y3.2340** *War Coot*
Y3.2230 *War Visor*	**Y3.2287** *Lady Plymouth*	**Y3.2341** *War Wizard*
Y3.2231 *War Foam*	**Y3.2288** *Queen Elizabeth*	**Y3.2342** *War Mastiff*
Y3.2232 *Jason*	**Y3.2289** *Southerndown*	**Y3.2343** *Petone*
Y3.2233 *Freshfield*	**Y3.2290** *Cholmley*	**Y3.2344** *Lanuvium*
Y3.2234 *Cycle* (ex *Boveric*)	**Y3.2291** *Capelcastle*	**Y3.2345** *War Puffin*

Y3.2346	*War Tempest*	**Y3.2403**	*Ardgay*	**Y3.2455**	*War Down*
Y3.2347	*War Lance*	**Y3.2404**	*War Gnat*	**Y3.2456**	*Vestalia*
Y3.2348	*Horn*	**Y3.2405**	*War Pintail*	**Y3.2457**	*St Mirren*
Y3.2349	*Argus*	**Y3.2406**	*War Clarion*	**Y3.2458**	*War Capitol*
Y3.2350	*War Aconite*	**Y3.2407**	*Atholl*	**Y3.2459**	*War Merlin*
Y3.2351	*Hampshire*	**Y3.2408**	*War Breaker*	**Y3.2460**	*Tjitaroem*
Y3.2352	*War Beetle*	**Y3.2409**	*Virgilia*	**Y3.2461**	*War Camp*
Y3.2353	*Halvard*	**Y3.2410**	*Treinta-y-Tres*	**Y3.2462**	*War Dream*
Y3.2354	*War Javelin*	**Y3.2411**	*Samnanger*	**Y3.2463**	*War Ermine*
Y3.2355	*Shoreham*	**Y3.2412**	*War Hound*	**Y3.2464**	*War Shark*
Y3.2356	*Kingsley*	**Y3.2413**	*War Citadel*	**Y3.2465**	*War Mersey*
Y3.2357	*Presto* (ex *Triumph*)	**Y3.2414**	*Maindy Manor*	**Y3.2466**	*War Dart*
Y3.2358	*War Wagtail*	**Y3.2415**	*Croxdale*	**Y3.2467**	*Alt*
Y3.2359	*War Mango*	**Y3.2416**	*Anglo-Mexican*	**Y3.2468**	*River Ribble*
Y3.2360	*War Typhoon*	**Y3.2417**	*Cairnvalona*	**Y3.2469**	*War Platoon*
Y3.2361	*War Climax*	**Y3.2418**	*Ardgirvan*	**Y3.2470**	*Frankmere*
Y3.2362	*War Osiris*	**Y3.2419**	*Wharfe*	**Y3.2471**	*Abus*
Y3.2363	*Loughbrow*	**Y3.2420**	*Orchid*	**Y3.2472**	*War Anchusa*
Y3.2364	*Grelfoyle*	**Y3.2421**	*Irwell*	**Y3.2473**	*War Plum*
Y3.2365	*Lady Rhondda*	**Y3.2422**	*Ardgell*	**Y3.2474**	*War Palace*
Y3.2366	*Greenisland*	**Y3.2423**	*Ardgowan*	**Y3.2475**	*War Joy*
Y3.2367	*War Yukon*	**Y3.2424**	*Baron Napier*	**Y3.2476**	*War Ontario*
Y3.2368	*War Power*	**Y3.2425**	*Hazelmead*	**Y3.2477**	*Bankdale*
Y3.2369	*Dunolly*	**Y3.2426**	*War Fantail*	**Y3.2478**	*Ardgroom*
Y3.2370	*Roseric*	**Y3.2427**	*War Clyde*	**Y3.2479**	*War Priam*
Y3.2371	*Rajput*	**Y3.2428**	*Fairhaven*	**Y3.2480**	*Elswick Hall*
Y3.2372	*Ravens Point*	**Y3.2429**	*Clapham*	**Y3.2481**	*War Sirocco*
Y3.2373	*War Tulip*			**Y3.2482**	*Lackenby*
Y3.2374	*War Penguin*	**Y3.2430**	*Sheaf Lance*	**Y3.2483**	*War Lark*
Y3.2375	*Anglo-Saxon*		(ex *War Haven*)	**Y3.2484**	*War Celt*
Y3.2376	*Trewidden*				
Y3.2377	*War Castle*	**Y3.2431**	*Baron Inchcape*	**Y3.2485**	*Mount Everest*
Y3.2378	*War Simoom*	**Y3.2432**	*War Damson*		(ex *War Drake*)
Y3.2379	*War Arrow*	**Y3.2433**	*War Earl*		
Y3.2380	*War Tank*	**Y3.2434**	*War Rapier*	**Y3.2486**	*War Dagger*
Y3.2381	*War Hind*	**Y3.2435**	*War Dirk*	**Y3.2487**	*War Cayuse*
Y3.2382	*War Zephyr*	**Y3.2436**	*Sutherland*	**Y3.2488**	*War Persian*
Y3.2383	*War Weapon*	**Y3.2437**	*War Sparrow*	**Y3.2489**	*War Babine*
Y3.2384	*Bechuana*	**Y3.2438**	*Oshogbe*	**Y3.2490**	*War Edensaw*
Y3.2385	*War Nymph*	**Y3.2439**	*War Faith*	**Y3.2491**	*War Nicola*
Y3.2386	*War Apricot*	**Y3.2440**	*War Forest*	**Y3.2492**	*War Nanoose*
Y3.2387	*War Finch*	**Y3.2441**	*War Music*	**Y3.2493**	*War Norman*
Y3.2388	*War Courage*	**Y3.2442**	*Hunsgate*	**Y3.2494**	*War Roman*
Y3.2389	*Alaska*	**Y3.2443**	*Huntscape*	**Y3.2495**	*Feldspar*
Y3.2390	*War Sky*	**Y3.2444**	*Maashaven*	**Y3.2496**	*War Quebec*
Y3.2391	*Courtown*	**Y3.2445**	*War Bee*	**Y3.2497**	*War Summit*
Y3.2392	*Eastern City*	**Y3.2446**	*War Hathor*	**Y3.2498**	*War Breeze*
Y3.2393	*War Combe*	**Y3.2447**	*Maldenado*	**Y3.2499**	*War Chief*
Y3.2394	*Winfield*	**Y3.2448**	*War Cowslip*	**Y3.2500**	*Pattersonian*
Y3.2395	*Benwood*	**Y3.2449**	*War Mallow*	**Y3.2501**	*War Storm*
Y3.2396	*War Duchess*	**Y3.2450**	*Prosper*	**Y3.2502**	*War Guava*
Y3.2397	*Strathfillan*	**Y3.2451**	*Quenast*	**Y3.2503**	*War Casco*
Y3.2398	*War Melody*	**Y3.2452**	*War Rider*	**Y3.2504**	*War Tamar*
Y3.2399	*War Bracken*	**Y3.2453**	*War Jasmine*	**Y3.2505**	*War Horus*
Y3.2400	*Monmouth*			**Y3.2506**	*War Sorel*
Y3.2401	*Carventum*	**Y3.2454**	*War Drum*	**Y3.2507**	*War Tanoo*
Y3.2402	*Matra*		*War Lemur*	**Y3.2508**	*War Nipigon*

Y3.2509	*War Sioux*	Y4.32	*The Viceroy*	**Y5.**	**Frozen Meat Ships**		
Y3.2510	*War Karma*	Y4.33	*Race Fisher*		**(WW1)**		
Y3.2511	*War Mohawk*	Y4.34	*River Fisher*				
Y3.2512	*War Tyee*	Y4.35	*Celtic Pride*	Y5.1	*Romeo*		
Y3.2513	*War Sumas*	Y4.36	*Portia*	Y5.2	*Jaffa*		
Y3.2514	*War Atlin*	Y4.37	*Susetta*	Y5.3	*Dago*		
Y3.2515	*War Camchin*			Y5.4	*Gourko*		
Y3.2516	*War Cariboo*	Y4.38	*Nugget*	Y5.5	*Kolpino*		
Y3.2517	*War Cherry*		*Narragansett*	Y5.6	*Volo*		
Y3.2518	*War Chilkat*			Y5.7	*Whinhill*		
Y3.2519	*War Fiend*	Y4.39	*Rosaleen*	Y5.8	*Loraine*		
Y3.2520	*War Huron*	Y4.40	*Clifford*				
Y3.2521	*War Noble*	Y4.41	*Gransha*				
Y3.2522	*War Nootka*	Y4.42	*Curran*	**Y6.**	**Mine Carrier (WW1)**		
Y3.2523	*War Susquash*	Y4.43	*Silverfield*				
Y3.2524	*Hansa*	Y4.44	*Perdita*	Y6.1	*Eleanor*		
		Y4.45	*Wheatberry*	Y6.2	*White Swan*		
		Y4.46	*Canning*	Y6.3	*Harden*		
Y4.	**Fleet Messengers (WW1)**	Y4.47	*Ortalan*	Y6.4	*Cove*		
		Y4.48	*C.64*	Y6.5	*John Sanderson*		
Y4.1	*Venetia*	Y4.49	*C.65*	Y6.6	*Ramillies*		
Y4.2	*Zinaida*	Y4.50	*City of Oxford*	Y6.7	*Lady Cory Wright*		
Y4.3	*Don Roderic*	Y4.51	*Wahine*	Y6.8	*Arno*		
Y4.4	*Stamfordham*	Y4.52	*Arethusa II*	Y6.9	*Albatross*		
Y4.5	*Alouette*	Y4.53	*Wexford Coast*				
		Y4.54	*Overton*				
Y4.6	*Groningen*	Y4.55	*Spinel*	**Y7.**	**Oiler (WW1)**		
	Borodino	Y4.56	*Skelwith Force*				
		Y4.57	*Princess Ena*	Y7.1	*Hermione*		
Y4.7	*Petrolea*	Y4.58	*Princess Alberta*	Y7.2	*Delaware*		
Y4.8	*Alert*	Y4.59	*Killingholme*	Y7.3	*Lucigen*		
Y4.9	*Princess Victoria*	Y4.60	*Brocklesby*	Y7.4	*Strombus*		
Y4.10	*Invicta*	Y4.61	*Osmanieh*				
Y4.11	*Scandinavia*	Y4.62	*Alexandra*	Y7.5	*Lucellum*		
Y4.12	*F.A. Tamplin*	Y4.63	*Princess Maud*		*The Roman*		
Y4.13	*City of Rochester*	Y4.64	*Chesterfield*				
Y4.14	*Trent*	Y4.65	*Elpiniki*	Y7.6	*Sylvia*		
Y4.15	*Vitruvia*			Y7.7	*Camillo*		
Y4.16	*Sunik*	Y4.66	*Gosforth*	Y7.8	*Teakwood*		
Y4.17	*Manica*		*Letitia*	Y7.9	*Rosalind*		
Y4.18	*Reclaimer*			Y7.10	*Hyrcania*		
Y4.19	*San Patricio*	Y4.67	*Mavis*	Y7.11	*Aragaz*		
Y4.20	*Hector*	Y4.68	*Eblana*	Y7.12	*Alchymist*		
Y4.21	*Menelaus*	Y4.73	*Saxon*	Y7.13	*Appalachee*		
Y4.22	*Polgowan*	Y4.74	*Devaney*	Y7.14	*Suwanee*		
Y4.23	*Isis*	Y4.75	*Opulent*	Y7.15	*Ialine*		
Y4.24	*Hungerford*	Y4.76	*Aquila*				
Y4.25	*Ermine*	Y4.77	*Polly Bridge*	Y7.16	*San Lorenzo*		
Y4.26	*Redbreast*	Y4.79	*Floris*		*Cyelse*		
Y4.27	*Brighton*	Y4.80	*Hodder*				
Y4.28	*Barry*	Y4.81	*Aviator* (ex *Victor*)	Y7.17	*Cymbeline*		
Y4.29	*Asteria*	Y4.147	*Polavon*	Y7.18	*Lumen*		
		Y4.217	*Divis*	Y7.19	*Aureole*		
Y4.30	*Turquoise*	Y4.326	*Camerata*	Y7.20	*Potomac*		
	Princess of Wales			Y7.21	*Osceola*		
				Y7.22	*Impoco*		
Y4.31	*Pebble*			Y7.23	*Batoum*		

Y7.24	Ashtabula	**Y7.58**	Clam	**Y7.101**	Satanta
			Princess Alberta	**Y7.102**	Trinculo
Y7.25	Ottawa			**Y7.103**	Uncas
	Ermine	**Y7.59**	Goldmouth	**Y7.104**	Samoset
		Y7.60	Sebastian	**Y7.105**	Petrolea
Y7.26	Luz Blanca			**Y7.106**	Trocas
Y7.27	Rion	**Y7.61**	Caucasian	**Y7.107**	Shabonee
Y7.28	Aras		Osmanieh	**Y7.108**	Tascalusa
Y7.29	Astrakhan			**Y7.109**	Tahchee
Y7.30	British Marquis	**Y7.62**	Oural	**Y7.110**	Winnebago
Y7.31	Oilfield	**Y7.63**	Desabla	**Y7.111**	Murex
Y7.32	H.C. Henry	**Y7.64**	San Jeronimo	**Y7.112**	Minhla
Y7.33	Baku Standard	**Y7.65**	Cowrie	**Y7.113**	Calcutta
Y7.34	Romany	**Y7.66**	Lucerna	**Y7.114**	Ricardo A. Mestres
		Y7.67	Genesee	**Y7.115**	San Patricio
Y7.35	British Knight	**Y7.68**	San Gregorio	**Y7.116**	Vennachar
	(ex Danubian)	**Y7.69**	Eupion	**Y7.117**	Tiflis
				Y7.118	Saxonian
Y7.36	Clearfield	**Y7.70**	Wapello	**Y7.119**	Beacon Light
Y7.37	Broadmayne		John O. Scott		
Y7.38	El Zorro			**Y7.120**	British Peer
Y7.39	Bloomfield	**Y7.71**	Tecumseh		(ex Carpathian)
Y7.40	Ranella	**Y7.72**	Bullmouth		
Y7.41	El Toro	**Y7.73**	Soyo Maru	**Y7.121**	Olympia
		Y7.74	Volute	**Y7.123**	British Sun
Y7.42	San Tirso	**Y7.75**	Silverlip	**Y7.124**	Donax
	Wrangler	**Y7.76**	Wabasha	**Y7.125**	Mirita
		Y7.77	Weehawken	**Y7.130**	San Melito
Y7.43	San Valerio	**Y7.78**	Unio	**Y7.131**	Silvertown
Y7.44	Balakani	**Y7.79**	Vitruvia	**Y7.132**	Mexican Prince
Y7.45	Massis	**Y7.80**	Cuyahoga	**Y7.133**	Elax
Y7.46	Prudentia			**Y7.134**	Argonauta (ex Oberon)
		Y7.81	British Viscount	**Y7.136**	J. Oswald Boyd
Y7.47	Bulysses		(ex Rocklight)	**Y7.137**	San Fraterno
Y7.48	Caloric			**Y7.138**	Gafsa (ex Dominion)
Y7.49	British Marshal	**Y7.82**	Kura	**Y7.139**	Thermidor
Y7.50	San Eduardo	**Y7.83**	Mina Brea	**Y7.140**	Sequoya
		Y7.84	Mascanomo	**Y7.141**	Tacoma
Y7.51	Paul Paix	**Y7.85**	Ponus	**Y7.142**	August Belmont
	Carelia	**Y7.86**	Patella	**Y7.143**	Crenella (ex Montcalm)
		Y7.87	San Silvestre	**Y7.144**	Berwindmoor
Y7.53	British Marshal	**Y7.88**	Massasoit	**Y7.145**	Nitrogen
	(ex Russian Prince)	**Y7.89**	Oyleric (ex Barneson)		
		Y7.90	F. A. Tamplin	**Y7.146**	Konakry
Y7.52	Daghestan	**Y7.91**	Tonawanda		Pholas
		Y7.92	Suram		
Y7.53	British Major	**Y7.93**	Khodoung	**Y7.147**	Turritella
	(ex Roumanian Prince)	**Y7.94**	Syriam	**Y7.148**	Fornebo
		Y7.95	Lumina	**Y7.149**	Berwindvale
Y7.54	Erivan	**Y7.96**	Winamac	**Y7.150**	Hartlepool
		Y7.97	Powhatan	**Y7.151**	Briarleaf
Y7.55	Kremlin	**Y7.98**	Lompoc	**Y7.152**	Palmleaf
	Tancred			**Y7.153**	Laurelleaf
		Y7.99	British General	**Y7.154**	Beechleaf
Y7.56	Derbent		(ex Georgian Prince)	**Y7.155**	Birchleaf
Y7.57	Sunik			**Y7.156**	Ashleaf
		Y7.100	Mira	**Y7.157**	Elmleaf

Y7.158	Limeleaf	**Y7.205**	Charles E. Harwood	**Y7.256**	War Patriot
Y7.159	Boxleaf	**Y7.206**	British Princess	**Y7.257**	War Kinsman
Y7.160	Hollyleaf	**Y7.207**	Tamaha	**Y7.258**	San Ricardo
Y7.161	Dockleaf	**Y7.208**	Dayton	**Y7.259**	Delmira
Y7.162	Fernleaf	**Y7.209**	Caloria	**Y7.260**	San Nazario
Y7.163	Mantilla	**Y7.210**	Motano	**Y7.261**	Waneta
Y7.164	Madrono	**Y7.211**	British Empress	**Y7.262**	Cadillac
Y7.164	Mirlo	**Y7.212**	Santa Rita	**Y7.263**	War Angler
Y7.166	Mendocino	**Y7.213**	Esturia		
Y7.167	Montana	**Y7.214**	Tatarrax	**Y7.264**	British Light
Y7.168	Meline	**Y7.215**	British Admiral		Olynthus (ex British Star)
Y7.169	Echunga	**Y7.216**	Mazout I		
		Y7.217	Cuyama	**Y7.265**	War Wager
Y7.170	Saxol	**Y7.218**	Col. E.L. Drake	**Y7.266**	War African
	Aspenleaf (ex Saxol)	**Y7.219**	British Sovereign	**Y7.267**	War Malayan
		Y7.220	Nucula (ex Soyo Maru)	**Y7.268**	War Prophet
Y7.171	Roseleaf	**Y7.221**	William Rockefeller	**Y7.269**	War Hermit
		Y7.222	Maumee	**Y7.270**	War Painter
Y7.172	Abadol	**Y7.223**	Joseph Cudahy	**Y7.271**	Paulsboro
	Oakleaf (ex Abadol)	**Y7.224**	Trinidadian	**Y7.272**	Beechwood
		Y7.225	Gold Shell		
Y7.173	Bayol	**Y7.226**	Topila	**Y7.273**	Broad Arrow
	Bayleaf (ex Bayol)	**Y7.227**	Los Angeles		Cairndhu
		Y7.228	Gargoyle		
Y7.174	Rangol	**Y7.229**	Standard Arrow	**Y7.274**	Saranac
	Mapleleaf (ex Rangol)	**Y7.230**	Arca	**Y7.275**	Prometheus
		Y7.231	Northwestern	**Y7.276**	War Matron
Y7.175	Vineleaf			**Y7.277**	War Ranee
Y7.176	San Onofre	**Y7.232**	British Baron	**Y7.278**	Sylvan Arrow
Y7.177	Tamarac		(ex Roumanian)	**Y7.279**	War Singer
Y7.178	Appleleaf			**Y7.280**	War Legate
Y7.179	Plumleaf	**Y7.233**	Bramell Point	**Y7.281**	War Server
Y7.180	Pearleaf	**Y7.234**	Winifred	**Y7.282**	War Master
Y7.181	Cherryleaf	**Y7.235**	War Hostage	**Y7.283**	War Fijian
Y7.182	Brambleleaf	**Y7.236**	British Ensign	**Y7.284**	Polshannon
Y7.183	Orangeleaf	**Y7.237**	British Isles	**Y7.285**	San Dunstano
Y7.184	G.R. Crowe	**Y7.238**	Wilhelm Jebsen		
Y7.185	Aungban	**Y7.239**	Georgia	**Y7.286**	British Lantern
Y7.186	Telena	**Y7.240**	William Ison		Oligarch
Y7.187	Escalona	**Y7.241**	J.M. Guffey		(ex British Lantern)
Y7.188	Delphinula				
Y7.189	Hotham Newton	**Y7.242**	British Light	**Y7.287**	War Rajput
Y7.190	Aral		Olwen (ex British Light)	**Y7.288**	War Subadar
Y7.191	Tuscarora			**Y7.289**	War Spartan
Y7.192	Cordelia	**Y7.243**	John D. Rockefeller	**Y7.290**	John M. Connelly
Y7.193	Manx Isles	**Y7.244**	Tioga	**Y7.291**	Herbert L. Pratt
Y7.194	Santa Maria	**Y7.245**	Hisko	**Y7.292**	San Zeferino
Y7.195	H.C. Folger	**Y7.246**	Comanchee	**Y7.293**	Lille
Y7.196	Cheyenne	**Y7.247**	Lackawanna	**Y7.294**	War Briton
Y7.197	Kanawha	**Y7.248**	Gymeric	**Y7.295**	War Envoy
Y7.198	Muskogee	**Y7.249**	Lumina	**Y7.296**	Le Coq
Y7.199	Albert Watts	**Y7.250**	British Duke (ex Terek)	**Y7.297**	Saxoleine
Y7.200	Charles Braley	**Y7.251**	William H. Telford	**Y7.298**	Lutetian
Y7.201	Herbert G. Wylie	**Y7.252**	Oneida	**Y7.299**	War Jemadar
Y7.202	Brabant	**Y7.253**	Frank H. Buck	**Y7.300**	Overbrook
Y7.203	Edward L. Doheny	**Y7.254**	War Expert	**Y7.301**	Petroleine
Y7.204	Norman Bridge	**Y7.255**	War Maker	**Y7.302**	War Cateran

Y7.303	*War Nizam*	**Y8.7**	*Volturnus*	**Y8.61**	*Gosforth*
		Y8.8	*Volana*	**Y8.62**	*Teessider*
Y7.304	*British Beacon*	**Y8.9**	*Mersey*	**Y8.63**	*Cheviot*
	Olcades	**Y8.10**	*Carnalea*	**Y8.64**	*Lucent*
	(ex *British Beacon*)	**Y8.11**	*Whinhill*	**Y8.65**	*Theseus*
		Y8.12	*Clydeburn*	**Y8.66**	*Eskwood*
Y7.305	*War Scot*	**Y8.13**	*Ferryhill*	**Y8.67**	*Arno*
Y7.306	*British Earl*	**Y8.14**	*Tees*	**Y8.68**	*Liberty*
Y7.307	*War Hunter*	**Y8.15**	*Clandeboye*	**Y8.69**	*Hampshire*
Y7.308	*War Aryan*	**Y8.16**	*Aire*	**Y8.70**	*Nigeria*
Y7.309	*War Sikh*	**Y8.17**	*Calder*	**Y8.71**	*Charles Goodanew*
Y7.310	*Luciline*	**Y8.18**	*Derwent*	**Y8.72**	*Emerald*
Y7.311	*W. L. Steed*	**Y8.19**	*Wenning*	**Y8.73**	*Clermiston*
Y7.312	*War Persian*	**Y8.20**	*Chesterfield*	**Y8.74**	*Buccaneer*
Y7.313	*Huntball*	**Y8.21**	*Woonas*	**Y8.76**	*Armourer*
Y7.314	*War Anglian*	**Y8.22**	*Notts*	**Y8.77**	*Egba*
Y7.315	*War Pundit*	**Y8.23**	*Leicester*	**Y8.78**	*Nascopie*
Y7.316	*War Burman*	**Y8.24**	*Lutterworth*	**Y8.79**	*Sportsman*
Y7.317	*War Rajah*	**Y8.25**	*Staveley*	**Y8.80**	*Wexford Coast*
Y7.318	*Vallejo*	**Y8.26**	*Victor*	**Y8.81**	*Arleia*
Y7.319	*War Bahadur*	**Y8.27**	*Westphalia*	**Y8.82**	*Stephen*
Y7.320	*War Roman*	**Y8.28**	*Waterland*	**Y8.83**	*Asturian*
Y7.321	*War Ghurka*	**Y8.29**	*Sea Serpent*	**Y8.84**	*Westborough*
Y7.322	*War Sepoy*	**Y8.30**	*Endcliffe*	**Y8.85**	*Wirral*
Y7.323	*War Khan*	**Y8.31**	*Farraline*	**Y8.87**	*Telemon*
Y7.324	*War Jandoli*	**Y8.32**	*Cato*	**Y8.88**	*Kassala*
Y7.325	*War Shikari*	**Y8.33**	*Echo*	**Y8.89**	*M.J. Hedley*
Y7.326	*War Pathan*	**Y8.34**	*Skipper*	**Y8.90**	*Umtali*
Y7.327	*War Dogra*	**Y8.35**	*Cragside*	**Y8.91**	*Palm Branch*
Y7.328	*War Kookri*	**Y8.36**	*Bernicia*	**Y8.92**	*Ariadne Christine*
Y7.329	*War Begum*	**Y8.37**	*Arrival*	**Y8.93**	*Susquehanna*
Y7.330	*War Nawab*	**Y8.38**	*Braeside*	**Y8.94**	*Ben Nevis*
Y7.331	*War Hagara*	**Y8.39**	*Lossie*	**Y8.95**	*Fernley*
Y7.332	*War Mogul*	**Y8.40**	*Gertie*	**Y8.96**	*Trelawny*
Y7.333	*War Diwan*	**Y8.41**	*Rayford*	**Y8.97**	*Hermiston*
Y7.334	*War Hindoo*	**Y8.42**	*Abercraig*	**Y8.98**	*Larne*
Y7.335	*War Krishna*	**Y8.43**	*Nidd*	**Y8.99**	*War Lemur*
Y7.336	*War Bharata*	**Y8.44**	*Fauvette*	**Y8.100**	*Moorgate*
Y7.337	*War Afridi*	**Y8.45**	*Hodder*	**Y8.101**	*Clan Macrae*
Y7.338	*War Brahmin*	**Y8.46**	*Bangarth*	**Y8.102**	*Clydesdale*
Y7.339	*War Sirdar*	**Y8.47**	*Rievaulx Abbey*	**Y8.103**	*Hector*
Y7.340	*War Mehtar*	**Y8.48**	*Steersman*	**Y8.104**	*Thespis*
Y7.341	*War Pindari*	**Y8.49**	*Helmsman*	**Y8.106**	*War Mango*
Y7.342	*War Sudra*	**Y8.50**	*Immingham*	**Y8.107**	*Lord Antrim*
Y7.648	*John Hardie*	**Y8.51**	*Broomhill*	**Y8.108**	*Junin*
		Y8.52	*Eros*	**Y8.109**	*Fairy*
		Y8.53	*Ardgarth*	**Y8.110**	*Wearsider*
Y8. Store Carriers (WW1)		**Y8.54**	*Hirondelle*	**Y8.111**	*Buccaneer*
		Y8.55	*Macclesfield*	**Y8.112**	*Hova*
Y8.1	*Whitehead*	**Y8.56**	*Burriana*	**Y8.113**	*Cornishman*
	Trostan	**Y8.57**	*Brook*	**Y8.114**	*Carlaston*
		Y8.58	*Brixham*	**Y8.115**	*Clifton Grove*
Y8.2	*Wharfe*			**Y8.116**	*War Down*
Y8.3	*Hebble*	**Y8.59**	*Dunvegan*	**Y8.117**	*Cove*
Y8.4	*Don*		*Chalkis*	**Y8.118**	*War Grange*
Y8.5	*Volhynia*			**Y8.119**	*Harperley*
Y8.6	*Norfolk Coast*	**Y8.60**	*Cortes*	**Y8.120**	*Ocean Transport*

Y8.121	*Cunene*
Y8.122	*War Gascon*
Y8.123	*Welshman*
Y8.124	*War Castle*
Y8.125	*War Parrot*
Y8.126	*Aro*
Y8.127	*War Wolf*
Y8.128	*Kut (ex Harmodius)*
Y8.129	*Huntscraft*
Y8.130	*Yarborough*
Y8.131	*War Cypress*
Y8.132	*Huntsclyde*
Y8.133	*Huntsgulf*
Y8.134	*Solfels*
Y8.135	*Sibir*
Y8.136	*War Music*
Y8.137	*War Magpie*
Y8.138	*Menelaus*

Y9. Squadron Supply Ships (WW1)

Y9.1	*Peshawur*
Y9.2	*Palma*
Y9.3	*Chinkoa*
Y9.4	*Crown of Castile*
Y9.5	*Baralong*
Y9.6	*Crown of Galicia*
Y9.7	*Indrani*
Y9.8	*Baron Ardrossan*
Y9.9	*Muritai*
Y9.10	*Netherby Hall*
Y9.11	*Floridian*
Y9.12	*Intombi*
Y9.13	*Statesman*
Y9.14	*Carrigan Head*
Y9.15	*Crown of Arragon*
Y9.16	*Alcinous*
Y9.17	*Hirondelle*
Y9.18	*Wildrake*
Y9.19	*Vanellus*
Y9.20	*Whimbrel*
Y9.21	*Tringa*
Y9.22	*Zaria*
Y9.23	*Stephen Furness*
Y9.24	*Jabiru*
Y9.25	*Manco*
Y9.26	*Umgeni*
Y9.27	*Umtali*
Y9.28	*Egret*
Y9.29	*Albatross*
Y9.30	*Intaba*

YA. Hospital Ships (WW1)

YA.1	*Soudan*
YA.2	*Garth Castle*
YA.3	*Drina*
YA.4	*Plassy*
YA.5	*Rewa*
YA.6	*China*
YA.7	*Delta*
YA.8	*Figuig* RAN *(ex Grantala)*
YA.9	*Albion*
YA.10	*Liberty*
YA.11	*Sheelah*
YA.12	*Prince George*
YA.13	*Agadir*
YA.14	*Magic*
	Classic (ex Magic)
YA.15	*Alexandra*
YA.16	*Somali*
YA.17	*Karapara*
YA.18	*Berbice*
YA.19	*St Margaret of Scotland*

Y1. Storeships and Carriers & Fleet Supply Ships (WW2)

Y1.1	*Anshun*
Y1.2	*Boniface*
Y1.3	*Breconshire*
Y1.4	*Hirondelle*
Y1.5	*Baltavia*
Y1.6	*Automedon*
Y1.7	*City of Tokio*
Y1.8	*City of Dieppe*
Y1.9	*Changteh*
Y1.10	*Rutland*
Y1.11	*Provider*
Y1.12	*Preserver*
Y1.14	*Hong Siang*
Y1.15	*Fort Colville*
Y1.16	*Angelo*
Y1.17	*Calderon*
Y1.18	*Tortuguero*
Y1.19	*Fort Dunvegan*
Y1.20	*Fort Constantine*
Y1.21	*Ledaal*
Y1.28	*Demodocus*
Y1.34	*Fort Kilmar*
Y1.44	*Drumlough*
Y1.47	*Fort Providence*
Y1.56	*Fort McDonnell*
Y1.61	*Fort Alabama*
Y1.75	*Fort Edmonton*

Y2. Armament Store Carriers & Armament Store Issuing Ships (WW2)

Y2.1	*Bison*
Y2.3	*Upnor*
Y2.4	*Ayrshire Coast*
Y2.5	*Kinterbury*
Y2.6	*C.I.D*
Y2.7	*Churruca*
Y2.8	*Ulster Coast*
Y2.9	*Bedenham*
Y2.11	*Pacheco*
Y2.12	*Carpio*
Y2.14	*Foreland*
Y2.17	*Imber*
Y2.19	*Errol*
Y2.20	*Colon*
Y2.21	*Adjutant*
Y2.22	*Heron*
Y2.23	*Procris*
Y2.25	*Sutherland*
Y2.27	*Brittany Coast*
Y2.28	*Fendris*
Y2.29	*Florence Cook*
Y2.30	*Fauvette*
Y2.36	*Kheti*
Y2.39	*Chattendaen*
Y2.41	*Little Orme*
Y2.42	*Ribblebank*
Y2.43	*Woodlark*
Y2.45	*Irwell*
Y2.46	*Bowstring*
Y2.47	*Tirydail*
Y2.49	*Switzerland*
Y2.51	*Mortar*
Y2.55	*Godig*
Y2.57	*Yarmouth Trader*
Y2.58	*Penstone*
Y2.59	*Ardgantock*
Y2.60	*Picardy*
Y2.61	*Ardchattan*
Y2.62	*Howitzer*
Y2.63	*Donaghmore*
Y2.64	*Isle Oransay*
Y2.65	*Empire Spinney*
Y2.67	*Scottish Co-Operator*
Y2.68	*Acrity*
Y2.69	*Carlo*
Y2.70	*Dunmore Head*
Y2.71	*Lucy Borchardt*
Y2.72	*Mourino*
Y2.73	*Stanland*
Y2.74	*Sardis*
Y2.75	*Calorie*
Y2.76	*Empire Gat*
Y2.77	*Palestinian Prince*

Y2.78	*Jacinth*	Y4.8	*Tjitjalengka*	Y7.30	*Rugby*
Y2.79	*Ngakoa*	Y4.9	*Marylyn*	Y7.31	*Sanson*
Y2.82	*Vanellus*	Y4.10	*Devonshire*	Y7.32	*Tillerman*
Y2.83	*Aire*			Y7.33	*Regardo*
Y2.84	*Alt*			Y7.34	*Luda Lord*
Y2.85	*Fred Everard*	**Y5. Frozen Meat Ships**		Y7.35	*The Roman*
Y2.86	*Throsk*	**(WW2)**		Y7.36	*Milford King*
Y2.87	*Tern*			Y7.37	*Saturn*
Y2.88	*Aldo*	Y5.1	*Baltonia*	Y7.38	*Sheldon*
Y2.89	*David M*	Y5.2	*Britanica*	Y7.39	*Star of Britain*
Y2.90	*Amal*	Y5.6	*Balteako*	Y7.40	*Tokyo II*
Y2.91	*Atid*	Y5.8	*Kaolack*	Y7.41	*Ythan Braes*
Y2.92	*Lateef*			Y7.42	*Triton*
Y2.93	*Bamora*			Y7.43	*Quercia*
Y2.94	*Philomel*	**Y6. Mine Carrier (WW2)**		Y7.44	*Dingledale*
Y2.95	*Hupeh*			Y7.45	*Transvaal*
Y2.96	*Shan Tung*	Y6.7	*Gurna*	Y7.46	*Lapageria*
Y2.97	*Hong Peng*	Y6.9	*Prome*	Y7.48	*San Amado*
Y2.98	*Haldis*			Y7.50	*Constance H*
Y2.99	*Tingsang*			Y7.72	*Bedale H*
Y2.100	*Darvel*			Y7.101	*Attendant*
Y2.101	*Corinda*	**Y7. Tankers, Oil Fuel &**		Y7.110	*Allegheny*
Y2.102	*Montague Douglas*	**Petrol Ships (WW2)**		Y7.115	*British Tommy*
Y2.103	*Bourbonnais*			Y7.121	*Athel Tarn*
Y2.104	*Hermelin*	Y7.1	*Athenian*	Y7.122	*San Casto*
Y2.105	*Prince de Liege*	Y7.2	*Aracari*	Y7.125	*San Claudio*
Y2.108	*Prinses Maria Pia*	Y7.3	*Ben Breac*		
Y2.109	*Gudrun-Maersk*	Y7.4	*Clythness*		
		Y7.5	*Vindelicia*	**Y8. Hospital Ships (WW2)**	
		Y7.6	*Congre*		
Y3. Colliers (WW2)		Y7.7	*Chasse Marie* FR	Y8.4	*Vasna*
		Y7.8	*Cyelse*	Y8.6	*Oxfordshire*
Y3.1	*Brightside*	Y7.9	*Damito*	Y8.7	*Amarapoora*
Y3.2	*J. Duncan*	Y7.10	*Empyrean*	Y8.9	*Centaur*
Y3.3	*Spanker*	Y7.11	*Fentonian*	Y8.12	*Wanganella*
Y3.5	*Orkla*	Y7.12	*Vidonia*	Y8.18	*Manunda*
Y3.6	*Dennis Rose*	Y7.14	*Garola*		
Y3.7	*Giralda*	Y7.15	*King Emperor*		
Y3.8	*Lakeland*	Y7.16	*Cevic*	**Y9. Hospital Carriers (WW2)**	
Y3.9	*Broomlands*	Y7.17	*Lephreto*		
Y3.11	*Bloomfield*	Y7.18	*Libyan*	Y9.3	*Isle of Jersey*
Y3.12	*Ross*	Y7.19	*Montano*	Y9.6	*Spes Helior*
		Y7.20	*Goosander*		
		Y7.21	*New Comet*		
Y4. Transports (WW2)		Y7.22	*Strathcoe*	**Y0. Miscellaneous Fleet**	
		Y7.23	*Orizaba*	**Auxiliaries (WW2)**	
Y4.1	*Dunera*	Y7.24	*Our Bairns*		
Y4.2	*Dilwara*	Y7.25	*Outpost (ex Vidette)*	Y0.1	*Fossbeck*
Y4.3	*Lancashire*	Y7.26	*Raetia*	Y0.3	*Otter Hound*
Y4.5	*Neuralia*	Y7.27	*Returno*	Y0.4	*Cranmere*
Y4.6	*Nevasa*	Y7.28	*Slebech*	Y0.11	*Gertruda*
Y4.7	*Ettrick*	Y7.29	*Ronso*		

Appendix 2

Royal Navy Deck Letters

With the advent of aviation at sea from around 1912, it became necessary to identify individual ships from the air. From the inter-war period Royal Navy battleships and cruisers embarked aircraft for spotter duties - these aircraft being launched from catapults and recovered by crane. While there are photographs of such vessels displaying two figure codes, usually painted on a turret roof, there seems to have been little formal structure for such identification markings. As the capital ships and cruisers dispensed with aircraft, in favour of heavier AA gun armament, such markings were removed.

It was not until towards the end of WW2 when, for the first time, Royal Navy carriers began to operate together, in large numbers, as part of the British Pacific Fleet. It became obvious that the need for some formalisation of deck markings was required. The US Navy system saw hull numbers being repeated, in large lettering, at the forward end of aircraft carrier flightdecks. The Royal Navy however, opted for a series of single letter codes which were randomly assigned at the start of a commission - so it was not unusual for an aircraft carrier to display more than one code throughout her career.

S.206/43 promulgated homing signal letters and distinguishing flags for aircraft carriers as follows:

(i) Fleet and Light Fleet Carriers: A single letter
(ii) Tracker Class, *Archer*, *Biter* and British Conversions: A single letter prefixed by the letter T
(iii) Smiter Class: A single letter prefixed by the letter R
(iv) Merchant Aircraft Carriers: A single letter prefixed by the letter M

While it appears that this document was related to homing signals and distinguishing flags, these letters did, in some cases, begin to appear as deck letters, either with or without the prefix. From a study of photographs it seems that Merchant Aircraft Carriers adopted the two letter system, whereas the remainder dropped the prefix. The escort carrier *Tracker* has been observed with the two character code 'TR' displayed on the flight deck. In the list that follows deck letters in brackets reflect those homing signal letters.

Promulgated on 19 April 1945, Confidential Admiralty Fleet Order (CAFO) 718/45 *Aircraft Carriers - Parent Ship Letters* directed that each aircraft carrier was to paint a distinguishing letter on the forward and after end of the flight deck to assist aircraft in distinguishing individual ships.

Letters were allocated by various shore authorities and on moving from one station to another, aircraft carriers were to remove the previous parent ship letter from the flight deck without further authority. Ships were to apply to the new issuing authority for a parent ship letter if this had not been provided.

Further changes to flight deck markings were promulgated in 1946 directing that letters were to be painted in white at each end of the flight deck in the following dimensions:

Height 24 ft; width 18 ft; thickness 4 ft. Each letter to be aligned on the centre line with its base aft at a distance of 20 ft from the bow and round-down respectively.

It wasn't until the 1950s that a rationalised system was adopted whereby the assigned code would align with the ships name. This could be the initial letter of the name but, in the case of the Illustrious and Implacable classes where many ships began with the same letter, other codes were adopted. The same code letter was also displayed on the tails of aircraft assigned to that ship.

The advent of the helicopter saw aircraft, once again, operating from vessels other than aircraft carriers. These ships carried a two letter identification marking assigned from build and, in most cases staying with the ship throughout her service life.

Letter	Name	Type	Class	Date
A	Attacker	Escort Carrier	Attacker	1943
A	Vengeance	Ac Carrier	Colossus	1945
A	Implacable	Ac Carrier	Illustrious	1946
A	Indomitable	Ac Carrier	Illustrious	1947
A	Albion	Ac Carrier	Centaur	1958
AB	Ambuscade	Frigate	Type 21	1975
AB	Albion	LPD	Albion	2003
AC	Achilles	Frigate	Leander	1970
AD	Ardent	Frigate	Type 21	1977
AE	Ariadne	Frigate	Leander	1973
AG	Avenger	Frigate	Type 21	1978
AJ	Ajax	Frigate	Leander	1964
AL	Alacrity	Frigate	Type 21	1977
AN	Antrim	Destroyer	County	1969
AN/AM	Andromeda	Frigate	Leander	1967
AO	Antelope	Frigate	Type 21	1975
AP	Apollo	Frigate	Leander	1972
AR	Arethusa	Frigate	Leander	1965
AS	Ashanti	Frigate	Type 81	1964
AS	Argus	RFA	Argus	1988
AT	Argonaut	Frigate	Leander	1967
AU	Aurora	Frigate	Leander	1964
AV	Active	Frigate	Type 21	1977
AW	Arrow	Frigate	Type 21	1976
AY	Argyll	Frigate	Type 23	1991
AZ	Amazon	Frigate	Type 21	1974
B	Battler	Escort Carrier	Attacker	1943
B	Venerable	Ac Carrier	Colossus	1943
B	Begum	Escort Carrier	Ruler	1945
B	Indefatigable	Ac Carrier	Illustrious	1946

B	*Bulwark*	Ac Carrier	Centaur	1954
BA	*Brave*	Frigate	Type 22	1986
BC	*Bacchante*	Frigate	Leander	1969
BD	*Sir Bedivere*	RFA	Sir	1967
BE	*Blue Rover*	RFA	Rover	1970
BF	*Belfast*	Frigate	Type 26	*Building*
BK	*Berwick*	Frigate	Type 12	1970
BK	*Bulwark*	LPD	Albion	2004
BL	*Blake*	Cruiser	Tiger	1970
BM	*Birmingham*	Destroyer	Type 42	1976
BR	*Brighton*	Frigate	Type 12	1971
BS	*Bristol*	Destroyer	Type 82	1973
BT	*Brilliant*	Frigate	Type 22	1981
BV	*Black Rover*	RFA	Rover	1974
BW	*Broadsword*	Frigate	Type 22	1979
BX	*Battleaxe*	Frigate	Type 22	1980
BZ	*Brazen*	Frigate	Type 22	1982
C	*Colossus*	Ac Carrier	Colossus	1945
C	*Indomitable*	Ac Carrier	Illustrious	1946
C	*Implacable*	Ac Carrier	Illustrious	1948
C	*Centaur*	Ac Carrier	Centaur	1954
CB	*Cardigan Bay*	RFA	Bay	2005
CD	*Clyde*	OPV	River	2007
CF	*Cardiff*	Destroyer	Type 42	1979
CH	*Challenger*	SOV	Challenger	1984
CL	*Cleopatra*	Frigate	Leander	1966
CL	*Cumberland*	Frigate	Type 22	1989
CM	*Chatham*	Frigate	Type 22	1990
CP	*Cleopatra*	Frigate	Leander	1974
CR	*Cardiff*	Frigate	Type 26	*Building*
CT	*Cutlass*	FTB	Sword	1970
CT	*Campbeltown*	Frigate	Type 22	1989
CV	*Coventry*	Destroyer	Type 42	1980
CV	*Coventry*	Frigate	Type 22	1988
CW	*Cornwall*	Frigate	Type 22	1988
CY	*Charybdis*	Frigate	Leander	1969
D	*Biter*	Escort Carrier	Archer	Unk

D	*Searcher*	Escort Carrier	Ruler	1945
D	*Colossus*	Ac Carrier	Colossus	1945
D	*Indefatigable*	Ac Carrier	Illustrious	1945
D	*Illustrious*	Ac Carrier	Illustrious	1946
DA	*Danae*	Frigate	Leander	1967
DA	*Daring*	Destroyer	Type 45	2009
DC	*Dumbarton Castle*	OPV	Castle	1982
DD	*RNAL 50*	RNAL	Dummy Deck	1972
DF	*Defender*	Destroyer	Type 45	2013
DI	*Dido*	Frigate	Leander	1963
DL	*Diligence*	RFA	Stena	1983
DM	*Diomede*	Frigate	Leander	1970
DM	*Diamond*	Destroyer	Type 45	2011
DN	*Danae*	Frigate	Leander	1976
DO	*Dido*	Frigate	Leander	1978
DR	*Dragon*	Destroyer	Type 45	2011
DT	*Dauntless*	Destroyer	Type 45	2010
DU	*Duncan*	Destroyer	Type 45	2013
DV	*Devonshire*	Destroyer	County	1965
E	*Emperor*	Escort Carrier	Ruler	1945
E	*Formidable*	Ac Carrier	Illustrious	1948
E	*Eagle*	Ac Carrier	Audacious	1957
EB	*Edinburgh*	Destroyer	Type 42	1984
ED	*Endurance*	Ice Patrol Ship	Endurance	1968
ED	*Endurance*	Ice Patrol Ship	Polar Circle	1992
EE	*Endurance*	Ice Patrol Ship	Polar Circle	1976
EE	*Endurance*	Ice Patrol Ship	Polar Circle	1994
EG	*Eagle*	Ac Carrier	Eagle	1930
EN	*Engadine*	RFA	Engadine	1967
ES	*Eskimo*	Frigate	Type 81	1963
EU	*Euryalus*	Frigate	Leander	1964
EX	*Exeter*	Destroyer	Type 42	1980
F	*Fencer*	Escort Carrier	Attacker	Unk
F	*Patroller*	Escort Carrier	Ruler	Unk
F	*Ranee*	Escort Carrier	Tracker	1945
F	*Formidable*	Ac Carrier	Illustrious	1948
FA	*Fort Austin*	RFA	Fort I	1979

FE	*Fort Rosalie*	RFA	Fort I	2000
FF	*Fife*	Destroyer	County	1969
FG	*Fort Grange*	RFA	Fort I	1978
FG	*Fort George*	RFA	Fort II	1992
FH	*Forth*	OPV	River II	2018
FM	*Falmouth*	Frigate	Type 12	1971
FS	*Fearless*	LPD	Fearless	1965
FV	*Fort Victoria*	RFA	Fort II	1992
G	*Smiter*	Escort Carrier	Ruler	1945
G	*Victorious*	Ac Carrier	Illustrious	1946
GA	*Galatea*	Frigate	Leander	1964
GC	*Gloucester*	Destroyer	Type 42	1984
GD	*Sir Galahad*	RFA	Sir	1970
GD	*Sir Galahad II*	RFA	Sir	1987
GL	*Glamorgan*	Destroyer	County	1966
GN	*Green Rover*	RFA	Rover	1969
GR	*Sir Geraint*	RFA	Sir	1967
GT	*Glasserton*	MCM	Ton	
GT	*Grafton*	Frigate	Type 23	1997
GU	*Gurkha*	Frigate	Type 81	1964
GV	*Gold Rover*	RFA	Rover	1974
GW	*Glasgow*	Destroyer	Type 42	1979
GW	*Glasgow*	Frigate	Type 26	*Building*
GY	*Grey Rover*	RFA	Rover	1970
H	*Hunter*	Escort Carrier	Attacker	1945
H	*Hermes*	Ac Carrier	Centaur	1958
HA	*Hampshire*	Destroyer	County	1963
HD	*Hydra*	Survey Ship	Hecla	1974
HE	*Hecla*	Survey Ship	Hecla	1965
HE	*Hermione*	Frigate	Leander	1967
HE	*Herald*	Survey Ship	Hecla	1978
HL	*Hecla*	Survey Ship	Hecla	1969
HM	*Hermione*	Frigate	Leander	1979
HR	*Hermes*	Ac Carrier	Hermes	1939
HR	*Herald*	Survey Ship	Hecla	1972
HR	*Herald*	Survey Ship	Hecla	1987
HT	*Hecate*	Survey Ship	Hecla	1965

HY	*Hydra*	Survey Ship	Hecla	1969
I	*Trouncer*	Escort Carrier	Ruler	1945
ID	*Intrepid*	LPD	Fearless	1967
IR	*Iron Duke*	Frigate	Type 23	1990
J	*Smiter*	Escort Carrier	Ruler	1945
J	*Trumpeter*	Escort Carrier	Ruler	1945
J	*Colossus*	Ac Carrier	Colossus	1946
J	*Eagle*	Ac Carrier	Audacious	1951
J	*Warrior*	Ac Carrier	Colossus	1953
JO	*Juno*	Frigate	Leander	1967
JP	*Jupiter*	Frigate	Leander	1969
K	*Khedive*	Escort Carrier	Ruler	1945
K	*Terrible*	Ac Carrier	Magnificent	1947
KE	*Kent*	Destroyer	County	1963
KT	*Kent*	Frigate	Type 23	2000
L	*Illustrious*	Ac Carrier	Illustrious	1943
L	*Glory*	Ac Carrier	Colossus	1945
L	*Centaur*	Ac Carrier	Centaur	1953
L	*Illustrious*	Ac Carrier	Invincible	1982
LA	*Lancaster*	Frigate	Type 23	1992
LB	*Largs Bay*	RFA	Bay	2004
LC	*Leeds Castle*	OPV	Castle	1981
LD	*Londonderry*	Frigate	Type 12	1969
LE	*Leander*	Frigate	Leander	1973
LN	*Sir Lancelot*	RFA	Sir	1964
LN	*London*	Destroyer	County	1966
LO	*London*	Destroyer	County	1963
LO	*London*	Frigate	Type 22	1987
LP	*Liverpool*	Destroyer	Type 42	1982
LT	*Lofoten*	LST	LST(3)	1967
LT	*Lowestoft*	Frigate	Type 12	1970
LY	*Lyness*	RFA	Ness	1966
M	*Implacable*	Ac Carrier	Illustrious	1943
M	*Empress*	Escort Carrier	Ruler	1945

(MA)	*Empire Macalpine*	MAC Ship	Grain Ship	1943
MA	*Acavus*	MAC Ship	Rapana	1943
MA	*Marlborough*	Frigate	Type 23	1991
(MB)	*Empire Maccabe*	MAC Ship	Tanker	1943
MB	*Empire MacColl*	MAC Ship	Tanker	1943
MB	*Mounts Bay*	RFA	Bay	2006
MC	*Manchester*	Destroyer	Type 42	1982
(MD)	*Amastra*	MAC Ship	Rapana	1943
(MD)	*Empire Macandrew*	MAC Ship	Grain Ship	1943
(MF)	*Empire Macrae*	MAC Ship	Grain Ship	1943
MF	*Ancylus*	MAC Ship	Rapana	1943
(MH)	*Empire Mackay*	MAC Ship	Tanker	1943
MH	*Empire Macalpine*	MAC Ship	Grain Ship	1943
(MJ)	*Rapana*	MAC Ship	Rapana	1943
MJ	*Empire Macmahon*	MAC Ship	Tanker	1943
(MK)	*Ancylus*	MAC Ship	Rapana	1943
MK	*Empire Macandrew*	MAC Ship	Grain Ship	1943
(ML)	*Acavus*	MAC Ship	Rapana	1943
ML	*Empire Maccabe*	MAC Ship	Tanker	1943
MM	*Empire Mackay*	MAC Ship	Tanker	1943
MM	*Mermaid*	Frigate	Yarrow	1973
MM	*Monmouth*	Frigate	Type 23	1992
(MN)	*Miralda*	MAC Ship	Rapana	1943
MN	*Empire Maccallum*	MAC Ship	Grain Ship	1944
(MO)	*Alexia*	MAC Ship	Rapana	1943
MO	*Empire Mackendrick*	MAC Ship	Grain Ship	1943
MO	*Mohawk*	Frigate	Type 81	1964
(MP)	*Adula*	MAC Ship	Rapana	1943
MP	*Alexia*	MAC Ship	Rapana	1943
MP	*Matapan*	Trials Ship	Battle	1975
(MQ)	*Empire Macmahon*	MAC Ship	Tanker	1943
MQ	*Adula*	MAC Ship	Rapana	1944
(MR)	*Empire Maccallum*	MAC Ship	Grain Ship	1943
MR	*Gadila*	MAC Ship	Rapana	1944
MR	*Montrose*	Frigate	Type 23	1993
(MS)	*Empire Maccoll*	MAC Ship	Tanker	1943
MS	*Empire Macdermott*	MAC Ship	Grain Ship	1944
(MU)	*Empire Mackenzie*	MAC Ship	Tanker	1943
MU	*Empire Macrae*	MAC Ship	Grain Ship	1943

(MV)	*Empire Macdermott*	MAC Ship	Grain Ship	1943
MV	*Rapana*	MAC Ship	Rapana	1944
MV	*Minerva*	Frigate	Leander	1968
MW	*Miralda*	MAC Ship	Rapana	1944
MW	*Medway*	OPV	River II	2019
MX	*Macoma*	MAC	Rapana	1944
N	*Puncher*	Escort Carrier	Ruler	1945
N	*Indomitable*	Ac Carrier	Illustrious	1943
N	*Implacable*	Ac Carrier	Illustrious	1945
N	*Venerable*	Ac Carrier	Colossus	1946
N	*Vengeance*	Ac Carrier	Colossus	1946
N	*Invincible*	Ac Carrier	Invincible	1980
NA	*Naiad*	Frigate	Leander	1965
NC	*Newcastle*	Destroyer	Type 42	1978
NF	*Norfolk*	Destroyer	County	1970
NF	*Norfolk*	Frigate	Type 23	1990
NL	*Northumberland*	Frigate	Type 23	1994
NM	*Nottingham*	Destroyer	Type 42	1983
NU	*Nubian*	Frigate	Type 81	1964
O	*Pretoria Castle*	Escort Carrier	Pretoria Castle	1945
O	*Trumpeter*	Escort Carrier	Ruler	1945
O	*Queen*	Escort Carrier	Ruler	1946
O	*Indomitable*	Ac Carrier	Illustrious	1945
O	*Ocean*	Ac Carrier	Colossus	1947
O	*Ark Royal*	Ac Carrier	Audacious	1955
O	*Ocean*	LPH	Ocean	1997
OA	*Olna*	RFA	Olwen	1966
OD	*Olmeda*	RFA	Olwen	1965
OW	*Olwen*	RFA	Olwen	1965
ON	*Olna*	RFA	Olwen	1975
P	*Premier*	Escort Carrier	Ruler	1945
P	*Pursuer*	Escort Carrier	Attacker	1945
P	*Victorious*	Ac Carrier	Illustrious	1945
P	*Triumph*	Ac Carrier	Colossus	1946
P	*Prince of Wales*	Ac Carrier	Queen Elizabeth	2020
PB	*Phoebe*	Frigate	Leander	1966

PC	*Protector*	Ice Patrol Ship	Guardian	1959
PC	*Polar Circle*	Ice Patrol Ship	Polar Circle	1991
PD	*Portland*	Frigate	Type 23	2000
PE	*Penelope*	Frigate	Leander	1963
PL	*Plymouth*	Frigate	Type 12	1961
PN	*Penelope*	Frigate	Leander	1982
PR	*Protector*	Ice Patrol Ship	Guardian	1966
PT	*Protector*	Ice Patrol Ship	Guardian	1968
*	*Protector*	Ice Patrol Ship	Polar Bjorn	2011

(* Protector is unique in that she retains commercial flight deck markings and is identified by her full name being displayed at the forward end)

PV	*Sir Percivale*	RFA	Sir	1968
Q	*Queen*	Escort Carrier	Ruler	1945
Q	*Illustrious*	Ac Carrier	Illustrious	1945
Q	*Vengeance*	Ac Carrier	Colossus	1947
Q	*Queen Elizabeth*	Ac Carrier	Queen Elizabeth	2018
(R)	*Argus*	Ac Carrier	Argus	1943
R	*Reaper*	Escort Carrier	Ruler	1945
R	*Ameer*	Escort Carrier	Ruler	1945
R	*Slinger*	Escort Carrier	Ruler	Unk
R	*Formidable*	Ac Carrier	Illustrious	1945
R	*Glory*	Ac Carrier	Colossus	1946
R	*Ark Royal*	Ac Carrier	Audacious	1958
R	*Ark Royal*	Ac carrier	Invincible	1985
(RA)	*Slinger*	Escort Carrier	Ruler	1943
(RB)	*Atheling*	Escort Carrier	Ruler	1943
(RD)	*Emperor*	Escort Carrier	Ruler	1943
RE	*Regent*	RFA	Regent	1969
(RF)	*Ameer*	Escort Carrier	Ruler	1943
RG	*Regent*	RFA	Regent	1970
(RH)	*Begum*	Escort Carrier	Ruler	1943
(RJ)	*Trumpeter*	Escort Carrier	Ruler	1943
(RK)	*Empress*	Escort Carrier	Ruler	1943
(RL)	*Khedive*	Escort Carrier	Ruler	1943
RL	*Rhyl*	Frigate	Type 12	1972
(RM)	*Speaker*	Escort Carrier	Ruler	1943

RM	*Richmond*	Frigate	Type 23	1996
(RN)	*Nabob*	Escort Carrier	Ruler	1943
(RO)	*Premier*	Escort Carrier	Ruler	1943
RO	*Rothesay*	Frigate	Type 12	1968
(RP)	*Shah*	Escort Carrier	Ruler	1943
(RQ)	*Patroller*	Escort Carrier	Ruler	1943
(RR)	*Rajah*	Escort Carrier	Ruler	1943
(RS)	*Ranee*	Escort Carrier	Tracker	1943
RS	*Resource*	RFA	Regent	1967
(RU)	*Trouncer*	Escort Carrier	Ruler	1943
(RV)	*Thane*	Escort Carrier	Ruler	1943
(RW)	*Queen*	Escort Carrier	Ruler	1943
(RX)	*Ruler*	Escort Carrier	Ruler	1943
(RY)	*Arbiter*	Escort Carrier	Ruler	1943
(RZ)	*Smiter*	Escort Carrier	Ruler	1943
S	*Searcher*	Escort Carrier	Attacker	1945
S	*Shah*	Escort Carrier	Ruler	1945
S	*Victorious*	Ac Carrier	Illustrious	1945
S	*Indefatigable*	Ac Carrier	Illustrious	1945
SA	*Sabre*	FTB	Sword	1971
SB	*St Albans*	Frigate	Type 23	2000
SC	*Scylla*	Frigate	Leander	1970
SC	*Scimitar*	FTB	Sword	1970
SD	*Sheffield*	Destroyer	Type 42	1975
SD	*Sheffield*	Frigate	Type 22	1988
SM	*Somerset*	Frigate	Type 23	1996
SN	*Southampton*	Destroyer	Type 42	1981
SP	*Spey*	OPV	River II	2021
SS	*Sirius*	Frigate	Leander	1966
ST	*Stromness*	RFA	Ness	1967
SU	*Sutherland*	Frigate	Type 23	1997
T	*Patroller*	Escort Carrier	Ruler	1945
T	*Stalker*	Escort Carrier	Attacker	1945
T	*Venerable*	Ac Carrier	Colossus	1946
T	*Theseus*	Ac Carrier	Colossus	1946
(TA)	*Attacker*	Escort Carrier	Attacker	1943
TA	*Tartar*	Frigate	Type 81	1964

(TB)	*Biter*	Escort Carrier	Archer	1943
TB	*Tarbatness*	RFA	Ness	1967
(TD)	*Ravager*	Escort Carrier	Attacker	1943
(TF)	*Fencer*	Escort Carrier	Attacker	1943
TF	*Tideforce*	RFA	Tide	2019
TG	*Tiger*	Cruiser	Tiger	1969
(TH)	*Hunter*	Escort Carrier	Attacker	1943
(TJ)	*Striker*	Escort Carrier	Attacker	1943
(TK)	*Stalker*	Escort Carrier	Attacker	1943
(TL)	*Battler*	Escort Carrier	Attacker	1943
TM	*Sir Tristram*	RFA	Sir	1967
TM	*Tamar*	OPV	River II	2020
(TO)	*Searcher*	Escort Carrier	Attacker	1943
(TP)	*Pursuer*	Escort Carrier	Attacker	1943
TP	*Tidepool*	RFA	Tide	1963
(TQ)	*Archer*	Escort Carrier	Archer	1943
TR	*Tracker*	Escort Carrier	Tracker	1943
TR	*Triumph*	Ac Carrier	Colossus	1965
TR	*Tiderace*	RFA	Tide	2018
(TS)	*Chaser*	Escort Carrier	Attacker	1943
TS	*Tidespring*	RFA	Tide	1963
TS	*Tidespring*	RFA	Tide	2016
TT	*Trent*	OPV	River II	2019
(TU)	*Pretoria Castle*	Escort Carrier	Pretoria Castle	1943
TU	*Tidesurge*	RFA	Tide	2019
(TV)	*Vindex*	Escort Carrier	Nairana	1943
(TW)	*Campania*	Escort Carrier	Campania	1943
(TX)	*Nairana*	Escort Carrier	Nairana	1943
(TY)	*Activity*	Escort Carrier	Activity	1943
TY	*Tenacity*	FTB	Vosper	1972
(U)	*Furious*	Ac Carrier	Furious	1943
U	*Pursuer*	Escort Carrier	Attacker	1943
U	*Unicorn*	Repair Carrier	Unicorn	1946
UD	*Undaunted*	Frigate	Type 15	1958
V	*Ravager*	Escort Carrier	Attacker	1945
V	*Vengeance*	Ac Carrier	Colossus	1945

V	Victorious	Ac Carrier	Illustrious	1945
V	Venerable	Ac Carrier	Colossus	1946
V	Victorious	Ac Carrier	Illustrious	1957
V	Vindex	Escort Carrier	Nairana	
VB	Beaver	Frigate	Type 22	1984
VI	Vidal	Survey Ship	Vidal	1954
W	Arbiter	Escort Carrier	Ruler	
W	Indomitable	Ac Carrier	Illustrious	1945
W	Warrior	Ac Carrier	Colossus	1946
WK	Wave Knight	RFA	Wave	2003
WL	Wave Ruler	RFA	Wave	2004
WM	Westminster	Frigate	Type 23	1994
X	Unicorn	Repair Carrier	Unicorn	1943
X	Vindex	Escort Carrier	Nairana	1945
X	Formidable	Ac Carrier	Illustrious	1945
X	Victorious	Ac Carrier	Illustrious	1945
X	Magnificent	Ac Carrier	Magnificent	1947
XB	Boxer	Frigate	Type 22	1984
Y	Nairana	Escort Carrier	Nairana	1945
Y	Victorious	Ac Carrier	Illustrious	
Y	Glory	Ac Carrier	Colossus	1945
Y	Venerable	Ac Carrier	Colossus	1946
Y	Unicorn	Repair Carrier	Unicorn	1947
Y	Illustrious	Ac Carrier	Illustrious	1953
YB	Lyme Bay	RFA	Bay	2007
YK	York	Destroyer	Type 42	1985
YM	Yarmouth	Frigate	Type 12	1968
Z	Campania	Escort Carrier	Campania	1945
Z	Colossus	Ac Carrier	Colossus	1945
Z	Albion	Ac Carrier	Centaur	1954
ZU	Zulu	Frigate	Type 81	1964